Freedom and the Court

Freedom and the Court

Civil Rights and Liberties in the United States

Eighth Edition

Henry J. Abraham
Barbara A. Perry

 University Press of Kansas

Published by the University Press of Kansas (Lawrence, Kansas 66049), which was
organized by the Kansas Board of Regents and is operated and funded by Emporia
State University, Fort Hays State University, Kansas State University, Pittsburg State
University, the University of Kansas, and Wichita State University.

Library of Congress Cataloging-in-Publication Data

Abraham, Henry Julian, 1921–
   Freedom and the court : civil rights and liberties in the United
States / Henry J. Abraham, Barbara A. Perry.—8th ed.
   p. cm.
Includes index.
   ISBN 0-7006-1261-0 (cloth : alk. paper)—ISBN 0-7006-1262-9 (paper :
alk. paper)
   1 Civil rights—United States. 2. United States. Supreme Court. I.
Perry, Barbara A. (Barbara Ann), 1956– . II. Title.
   KF4749.A73 2003
   342.73'085—dc21
            2003005819

British Library Cataloguing in Publication Data is available.

Printed in the United States of America

10 9 8 7 6 5 4 3 2 1

The paper used in this publication meets the minimum requirements of the American
National Standard for Permanence of Paper for Printed Library Materials Z39.48-1984.

To Our Parents

The memory of Liesel and Fred Abraham
and to
Lillian and Louis Perry

Contents

Preface to the Eighth Edition

Since *Freedom and the Court* was first published in 1967, it has sold over one hundred thousand copies—a fact that attests to its ongoing timeliness as a close study of the lines that must be drawn by a democratic society as it attempts to reconcile individual freedom with the rights and obligations of the community. As we embarked on the eighth edition, who could have known that our country would again face the essential questions of how to reconcile civil rights and liberties with national security in the aftermath of the September 11, 2001, terrorist attacks on the United States? Yet we already do know, based on its long history, that the Supreme Court of the United States will be called upon to act as the nation's constitutional conscience in deciding these wrenching disputes.

Like its seven predecessors, this edition, which thoroughly updates U.S. Supreme Court cases through 2002–3, focuses on the pivotal and fundamental issues of individual rights as they relate to freedom of religion and the attendant issue of the separation of church and state; freedom of expression; due process of law, particularly procedural safeguards in criminal law; and political, racial, and gender equality. The book continues to portray the intriguing human stories behind landmark constitutional law cases and theories, while delineating recent pathbreaking developments by the Rehnquist Court in civil rights and liberties. Holding fast, if narrowly, to some liberal precedents, for example, in the abortion realm, it has found majorities, again narrow ones, for more conservative results in religion cases and disputes over racial preferences. Moreover, this Court's state-centered jurisprudence has constricted the reach of some federal civil rights statutes. In addition to maintaining a history of the so-called double standard between civil liberties and economic rights (in which courts since 1937 had preferred the former), this edition of *Freedom and the Court* explains the recent remarkable return to certain pre–New Deal, pro-business commitments. For instance, at the end of the Court's 2000–2001 term, it granted new protections to landowners who maintain that certain environmental regulations diminish the value of their property. With its thorough analysis of how the U.S. Supreme Court applied most of the Bill of Rights to the states over a period of four decades in the twentieth century, primarily through the Fourteenth Amendment's due process clause, the book presents the major theories of "incorporation" and explains how current justices apply them, including the most recent capital punishment decisions. One of the more interesting recent developments in Fourteenth Amendment jurisprudence was the Court's 1999 partial resurrection of the amendment's privileges or immunities clause, which seven justices used to reject California's limitation on welfare benefits for new residents.

In our examination of the evolution of criminal rights in the United States, we analyze the war on crime in the 1990s, with its landmark legislation passed by Congress and interpreted by the Supreme Court, as well as its impact on Bill of Rights protections for criminals and those accused of crimes. Deciding disputes over the Fourth Amendment's search and seizure clause, the current Court has achieved split results on the complex tension between law enforcement and individual liberties. In the last few terms alone, the justices have upheld drug tests as a condition of obtaining a public school teaching job and of students participating in extracurricular activities, allowed police to detain a homeowner from entering his home while they waited for a warrant, and validated the arrest of a "soccer mom" for failure to wear her seat belt. At the same time, the Court has struck down drug officers' "patdowns" of bus passengers' overhead luggage, police use of external heat detectors to trace marijuana-growing ventures in private residences, tests for crack cocaine use among expectant mothers in public hospitals, and drug-sniffing canine searches of automobiles. These cases have produced unpredictable alliances among the justices, with the usually liberal-minded Justice David Souter writing the majority opinion upholding the arrest of the soccer mom, but with the more conservative Antonin Scalia penning the Court's opinion striking down the use of heat detectors in the marijuana case, while his liberal colleague, Justice John Paul Stevens, dissented. Then there was Chief Justice Rehnquist's dramatic upholding of the Warren-era controversial *Miranda* precedent!

Recent free-speech cases have run the gamut, from campaign finance to nude dancing and sexually explicit cable television programming and Internet sites. Recent Supreme Court decisions have upheld federal election law limits on how much political parties can spend in coordination with their congressional candidates and reaffirmed a state's power to impose limits on individual contributions to a candidate. Free expression arguments also failed to persuade a majority of the Court in a decision upholding local ordinances banning nude dancing, which adult clubs had asserted was a form of permissible expressive conduct. Yet a slim majority of the justices ruled that the federal Telecommunications Act, which required cable providers of sexually explicit material to "fully scramble" their signals or show such programming only when children are unlikely to be watching, violated the First Amendment's guarantees.

One of *Freedom and the Court*'s strengths in addressing religious liberty continues to be its comprehensive charts, which have been completely updated on free exercise of religion and establishment cases. The book also explains the ongoing impact of the Court's invalidation of the Religious Freedom Restoration Act of 1993, namely, that generally secular regulations, only incidentally touching on religious practices, pass constitutional muster. In the area of church-state separation, the Rehnquist Court has allowed accommodation of religion and government (in upholding public financing of educational materials and instruction for religious schools, as well as in approving the use of state-funded tuition vouchers for parents to send their children to religious schools) with the exception of a narrow group of school prayer cases, where a more liberal majority has successfully supported the separationist cause. A conservative majority, however, has allowed free expression to trump separation of church and state, with the Court's approval of religious activities on campuses ranging from elementary schools to universities.

In analyzing race and the equal protection of the laws, we trace the unresolved litigation surrounding utilization of race in state and federal affirmative action programs regarding university admissions, government set-asides for minority contractors, and so-called majority/minority voting districts. This edition of the book also explains the Court's use of equal protection analysis in its stunning *Bush v. Gore* decision, which, in effect, settled the deadlocked 2000 presidential election between Al Gore and George W. Bush.

Freedom and the Court concludes with an updated look at gender equality in both constitutional and statutory contexts. The bulk of recent gender cases have addressed sexual harassment issues, with the Supreme Court generally expanding protection of victims (including those of the same sex as their harassers) under federal statutes, though not without qualification (especially in school settings). The Court's 2000 invalidation of a portion of the 1994 Violence Against Women Act (VAWA), which allowed victims to sue their attackers for civil damages in federal courts, raised howls of protest from women's rights advocates. The slim majority of five justices argued that Congress had overstepped its interstate commerce power in creating that section of VAWA. The case exemplified how the more conservative justices may employ separation of powers and federalism rationales to limit expansion of gender claims. The Supreme Court has decided few abortion cases over the last five years, but it did strike down Nebraska's prohibition of so-called partial-birth abortions, arguing that the limitation would adversely affect even routine and widely used second-term procedures. Beyond gender, the justices have recently accepted a spate of handicap rights cases under the Americans with Disabilities Act (ADA). With the exception of ruling in favor of a professional golfer's right to use a cart in PGA tournaments, the Court has generally applied a narrow interpretation to the ADA. In order to delineate and clarify the issues and results of these landmark gender and disabilities cases, the book provides another comprehensive table.

In light of our respectively long associations with the Supreme Court and our many opportunities to observe it at firsthand (we even procured seats to the oral argument of the 2000 presidential election case, thanks to our friends and colleagues in the Clerk's Office!), undertaking this quadrennial review of civil rights and liberties cases is indeed a labor of love. We are delighted that this edition of *Freedom and the Court* is being published by the University Press of Kansas, whose work in our field of political science we particularly admire. Fred Woodward, director of the press, has been as supportive as he has been gentlemanly in encouraging us to continue with another rendition of this work. To him and to production editor Dorothea Anderson and assistant director and marketing manager Susan Schott we are most grateful. We are also indebted to Tia Trout, now a distinguished Truman Scholar and Sweet Briar College graduate, for her invaluable research assistance and computer expertise. The book's dedication speaks for itself.

Charlottesville, Virginia   H.J.A. and B.A.P.
April 2003

Preface to the First Edition

This is essentially a study of the lines that must be drawn by a democratic society as it attempts to reconcile individual freedom with the rights of the community. No single book could cope with the entire field of civil rights and liberties, and no attempt is made to do so here. Rather, it has been my aim to analyze and evaluate the basic problem of drawing lines between individual rights and community rights and to venture some conclusions or suggestions in those spheres that constitute the basic rights and liberties: freedom of religion and the attendant problem of separation of Church and State; freedom of expression; due process of law, particularly procedural safeguards in criminal law; and political and racial equality. The three introductory chapters, the third comprising a thorough analysis of the problem of Amendment Fourteen and "incorporation," are designed to focus the study and to stress my belief that it is essential to recognize and comprehend the significant role the judicial branch of the United States Government, with the Supreme Court as its apex, has played in defining and strengthening the basic rights and liberties that accrue to us from the principle of a government under constitutionalism, a government that is limited in its impact upon individual freedom.

As usual, I am indebted to many colleagues for stimulation, criticism, and encouragement. I am particularly grateful to Professor Alpheus T. Mason of Princeton, who read the entire manuscript; to Professors David Fellman of Wisconsin and Rocco J. Tresolini of Lehigh, who were generous discussants; and to my departmental colleague, Charles Jasper Cooper, who proved a valued "sounding board" down the hall. My research assistant, Judy F. Lang, was a delightful and industrious aid. Dr. Joan I. Gotwals of the Van Pelt Library kindly provided me with a "secret annex" in which I could work in quiet seclusion. Mrs. Dorothy E. Carpenter typed the manuscript cheerfully and conscientiously. Byron S. Hollingshead Jr., Helen M. Richardson, and Mary Ollmann of Oxford University

Press provided indispensable professional assistance. And my wife, Mildred, and our sons, Philip and Peter, to each of whom earlier books were happily dedicated, made it all worthwhile.

Wynnewood, Pennsylvania   H.J.A.
March 1967

1

Introduction

Although, as David Fellman points out, for more than two hundred years the American people, both in political theory and in public law, have been committed to the "primacy of civil liberties in the constellation of human interests,"[1] these civil liberties do not exist in a vacuum or even in an anarchic state but in a state of society. It is inevitable that the individual's civil rights and those of the community of which he or she is a part come into conflict and need adjudication.[2]

It is easy to state the need for a line between individual rights and the rights of the community, but how, where, and when this distinction is to be drawn are questions that will never be resolved to the satisfaction of the entire community. Consider John Stuart Mill's perceptive words in *On Liberty and the Subjugation of Women:* "But though the proposition is not likely to be contested in general terms, the practical question, where to place the limits—how to make the fitting adjustment between individual independence and social control—is a subject on which nearly everything remains to be done."[3] Liberty and order are difficult to reconcile, particularly in a democratic society such as ours. We must have both, but a happy balance is not easy to maintain. As a constitutional democracy, based upon a government of limited powers under a written constitution and a

---

1. *The Limits of Freedom* (New Brunswick, N.J.: Rutgers University Press, 1959), from the foreword (unpaginated).

2. Although some would object, the terms "rights" and "liberties" are used interchangeably in this book. They are to be distinguished from all the other rights and freedoms individuals may enjoy under law because they are especially protected, in one manner or another, against violations *by governments*. (In Canada the term "civil rights" refers exclusively to *private law*—the legal relationship between person and person in private life.) See J. A. Corry and Henry J. Abraham, *Elements of Democratic Government,* 4th ed. (New York: Oxford University Press, 1964), pp. 234–39.

3. (New York: Henry Holt, 1898), p. 16.

majoritarianism duly checked by carefully guarded minority rights, we must be generous to the dissenter. Again citing Mill, "[A]ll mankind has no right to silence one dissenter [for] all silencing of discussion is an assumption of infallibility." Even near unanimity under our system does not give society the right to deprive individuals of their constitutional rights. As Judge Jerome Frank observed, "The test of the moral quality of a civilization is its treatment of the weak and power-less."[4] Justice Hugo Black, dissenting from a Supreme Court reversal of some trespassing convictions, once wrote, "The worst citizen no less than the best is entitled to equal protection of the laws of his state and of his nation"[5]—and the citizen of whom he spoke was a defiant racist. Who or what he was is irrelevant, of course. Indeed, in Justice Frankfurter's oft-quoted words, "It is a fair summary of history to say that safeguards of liberty have been forged in controversies involving not very nice people."[6] The basic issue was memorably phrased by Justice Robert H. Jackson in the *West Virginia Flag Salute Case*,[7] in which the Supreme Court struck down a compulsory flag-salute resolution adopted by the West Virginia State Board of Education, arguing that it violated the guarantees of freedom of religion of the First and Fourteenth Amendments. As Justice Jackson put it, "[Those] who begin coercive elimination of dissent soon find themselves exterminating dissenters. Compulsory unification of opinion achieves only the unanimity of the graveyard." He elaborated in characteristically beautiful prose:

> If there is any fixed star in our constitutional constellation, it is that no official, high or petty, can prescribe what shall be orthodox in politics, nationalism, religion, or other matters of opinion or force citizens to confess by word or act their faith therein. . . . The very purpose of a Bill of Rights was to withdraw certain subjects from the vicissitudes of political controversy, to place them beyond the reach of majorities and officials and to establish them as legal principles to be applied by the courts. One's right to life, liberty, and property, to free speech, a free press, freedom of worship and assembly, and other fundamental rights may not be submitted to vote, [for] *they depend on the outcome of no elections.*[8]

In stating valid principles, these words unavoidably raise an equal number of questions; nevertheless, they point up the irreducible basis for our thinking about civil rights and liberties.

The framers of our Constitution chose a limited majority rule, but majority rule nonetheless; while tyranny by the majority is barred, so is tyranny by a mi-

---

4. *United States v. Murphy,* 222 F.2d 698 (1955) at 706.
5. *Bell v. Maryland,* 378 U.S. 226 (1964) at 328.
6. *United States v. Rabinowitz,* 339 U.S. 56 (1950) at 69.
7. *West Virginia State Board of Education v. Barnette,* 319 U.S. 624 (1943). See *infra* chapter 5.
8. Ibid. at 638, 642; italics supplied.

nority. And the law must be obeyed—until such time as it is validly altered by legislative, judicial, or executive action, or by constitutional amendment. Notwithstanding the numerous philosophical arguments to the contrary, disobedience of the law is barred, no matter which valid governmental agency has pronounced it or what small margin has enacted it. *It must be barred.* Liberty is achieved only by a rule of law—which serves as the cement of society.[9] Government cannot long endure when any group or class of persons—no matter how just the cause may be or how necessary remedial action may seem to be—is permitted to decide which law it shall obey and which it shall flout. As Justice Abe Fortas observed during the student uprisings of the late 1960s, "Dissent and dissenters have no monopoly on freedom. They must tolerate opposition. They must accept dissent from their dissent."[10] Civil disobedience has often been invoked—and will indubitably continue to be invoked—but those who invoke it must be willing to face the consequences. James F. Childress, an expert in the philosophy of civil disobedience and a professor of religious studies, aptly defined it as "a public nonviolent *submissive* violation of law as a form of protest."[11] Moreover, in Professor J. A. Corry's words, civil disobedience must be *civil,* not uncivil, disobedience, with the basic aim of persuasion, not violence.[12] No one knew this and practiced it with more conviction than the late Dr. Martin Luther King Jr., who once noted tellingly: "I believe in the beauty and majesty of the law so much that when I think a law is wrong, I am willing to go to jail and stay there."[13] And so he did, on numerous occasions.

Under our system of government, of course, some agency must serve as the arbiter of what is and what is not legal or constitutional. The Founding Fathers did recognize and call for the creation of an arbiter, not only between the states and the national government but also between any level of government and the individual. There was no unanimity as to who might arbitrate; and the records of the debates at the Constitutional Convention now available to us demonstrate that nearly every segment of the incipient governmental framework received at least some consideration for the role of arbiter: the states themselves, Congress, the executive, the judiciary, and several combinations of these. But it was fairly clear that the role would fall to the judiciary and that it should include the power

9. See Sydney H. Schanberg, "The Rules Are All We've Got," *New York Times,* July 7, 1981, p. A23.

10. The phrase also appears in his definitive book on the subject, *Concerning Dissent and Civil Disobedience* (New York: New American Library, 1968), p. 126. (Fortas resigned from the U.S. Supreme Court in mid-1969.)

11. *Civil Disobedience and Political Obligation: A Study in Christian Social Ethics* (New Haven, Conn.: Yale University Press, 1973); italics supplied.

12. See his 1971 CBC Massey Lectures, *The Power of the Law* (Toronto: CBC Learning Systems, 1971), p. 41. The looting during the July 1977 New York City "blackout" is an obvious example of such a totally "uncivil" response.

13. As quoted in the *New York Times,* October 16, 1966, p. E8.

of *judicial review,* which authorizes the Supreme Court to hold unconstitutional, and hence unenforceable, any law or official action based upon a law, and any other action by a public official that it deems—upon careful reflection and in line with the inherited tradition of the law and judicial restraint—to be in conflict with the Constitution.[14]

Scholars continue to argue over the authenticity of the power of judicial review. That so many doubts and challenges are raised is due primarily to the failure of the Founding Fathers to spell it out in the Constitution *in so many words.* Yet the records of the Philadelphia Constitutional Convention of 1787 indicate that the idea or principle of judicial review was a matter of distinct concern to the framers, who, after all, had little use for unrestrained popular majoritarian government; that judicial review was indeed known to the colonists because the British Privy Council had established it over acts passed by colonial legislatures; that at least eight[15] of the ratifying state conventions had expressly discussed *and* accepted the judicial power to pronounce legislative acts void; and that prior to 1789 some eight instances of *state* court judicial review against state legislatures had taken place. The language of both Article 3 and the famed "supremacy clause" of Article 6 clearly implies the necessary but controversial weapon. Research by constitutional historians such as Charles A. Beard, Edward S. Corwin, and Alpheus T. Mason indicates that between twenty-five and thirty-two of the forty delegates at Philadelphia generally favored the adoption of judicial review.[16] Although it remained for Chief Justice John Marshall to state it definitively in 1803 in *Marbury v. Madison,*[17] the issue has been decisively settled by history; the debate over the legitimacy of judicial review is now an academic exercise.

Since the enactment of the "Judges' Bill" in 1925, the Supreme Court has been all but a complete master of its docket. The bill gave to the Court absolute discretionary power to choose those cases it would hear on a writ of certiorari, a discretionary writ granted only if four justices agree to do so. Well over seven thousand "cert." petitions reach the Court annually, but a mere 2 percent are granted. In theory certain classes of cases do reach the Court as a matter of "right," namely, those that come to it on writs of *appeal;* but even here ultimate review is not automatic, since the tribunal itself must decide whether the question presented is of a "*substantial* federal nature," and Congress reduced the

---

14. See Henry J. Abraham, "Judicial Review: I—The Supreme Power," in his *Judicial Process: An Introductory Analysis of the Courts of the United States, England, and France,* 7th ed. (New York: Oxford University Press, 1998), pp. 299–345.

15. Virginia, Rhode Island, New York, Connecticut, Massachusetts, New Jersey, North Carolina, and South Carolina.

16. See, in particular, Beard's article "The Supreme Court—Usurper or Grantee?" 27 *Political Science Quarterly* 1 (1912).

17. 1 Cranch 137.

availability of these writs dramatically in 1988–89. The Court's original jurisdiction docket is so small as to be ignored for the purpose of this discussion.[18]

Since 1937 the overwhelming majority of judicial vetoes imposed upon the several states and almost *all* of those against the national government have been invoked because they infringed personal liberties, other than those of "property," safeguarded under the Constitution. This preoccupation with the "basic human freedoms"[19] is amply illustrated by the statistics of the docket of the Supreme Court and the application of its power of judicial review.[20] Well over half of all cases decided by the Court now fall into this category of "basic human freedoms." Thus, whereas in the 1935–36 term only 2 of 160 signed written opinions had done so, in the 1979–80 term the ratio had increased to 80 out of 149—a trend that has continued unabated.[21]

18. See Abraham, op. cit., pp. 169–83, for an overview of matters of jurisdiction.

19. See *infra* chapter 2. As seen in these pages, they comprise the five enumerated by the First Amendment; the guarantees of procedural due process in the pursuit of criminal justice; and racial, political, ethnic, and sexual equality. (They are also known as the "cultural freedoms.") The trend of public attitudes in the latter 1960s and the 1970s seemed to give fresh emphasis to the concept of privacy, personified by such Supreme Court decisions as those dealing with birth control and abortions. (See especially *Griswold v. Connecticut,* 381 U.S. 479 [1965]; *Roe v. Wade,* 410 U.S. 113 [1973]; *Doe v. Bolton,* 410 U.S. 179 [1973]; and their progeny, including the latter two cases' decisive reaffirmation and extension in a trio of 1983 decisions written by Justice Powell: *Akron v. Akron Center for Reproductive Health,* 462 U.S. 416; *Planned Parenthood Association of Kansas City, Mo. v. Ashcroft,* 462 U.S. 476; and *Simopoulos v. Virginia,* 462 U.S. 506. Another, less sweeping, reaffirmation came in 1986 in *Thornburgh v. American College of Obstetricians and Gynecologists,* 476 U.S. 747. For updates see *infra* chapter 3.)

20. In 1976 a total of 5,320 civil rights suits were brought in federal courts against employers alone—a 1,500 percent increase since 1970! In the fall of 1977, during a discrimination case in his Alexandria, Virginia, courtroom, seventy-five-year-old U.S. District Court Judge Oren R. Lewis commented: "I am old enough to know. When I first came on the bench [in 1960] I never had a discrimination case. Now that is almost all you have" (*Washington Post,* November 15, 1977, p. A1). The number of federal civil rights suits filed by state-prison inmates alone soared from 5,000 in 1973 to 27,889 in 1988. Another indicator: between its enactment in 1871 and 1920, only 21 cases were brought under the previous year's Civil Rights Act, which authorizes suits against "every person" who "under color of law" violates the civil rights of another. In 1976 a total of 17,543 such suits were filed—a figure that has continued to increase steadily (see A. E. Dick Howard, *I'll See You in Court: The States and the Supreme Court* [Washington, D.C.: National Governors' Association Center for Policy Research, 1980]).

21. Some additional representative statistics: 1965, 39 of 120; 1966, 55 of 132; 1967, 77 of 156; 1968, 70 of 116; 1969, 51 of 105; 1970, 77 of 141; 1971, 82 of 132; 1972, 86 of 164; 1973, 85 of 156; 1974, 63 of 137; 1975, 76 of 144; 1976, 87 of 160; 1977, 84 of 142; 1978, 88 of 138; 1980–81, 71 of 123; 1981–82, 81 of 150; 1982–83, 72 of 162; 1983–84, 85 of 151; 1984–85, 71 of 142; 1985–86, 75 of 147; 1986–87, 91 of 152; 1987–88, 78 of 142; 1988–89, 73 of 134; 1989–90, 66 of 129; 1990–91, 59 of 112; 1991–92, 55 of 107; 1992–93, 47 of 116; 1993–94, 38 of 90; 1994–95, 49 of 94; and 1995–96, 48 of 90.

It is undeniable that the contemporary scene has witnessed an unprecedented concern with the identification and strengthening of our basic civil rights and liberties—significantly due to their articulation by the federal judiciary beginning with the late 1920s but not reaching full stride until the FDR era of the 1930s—but this fact does not gainsay the continuing need for the recognition and evaluation of the appropriate parameters of that ubiquitous line between individual rights and privileges, on the one hand, and societal obligations and responsibilities, on the other. There are no simple answers, and all too often those answers are subject to the Al Smith aphorism that "it all depends whose ox is being gored." Thus, almost by definition, liberty and equality, *both* of which are cherished constitutional guarantees, find themselves at war, an indication of the delicate and difficult response to where and how to draw the line between personal rights and societal constraints.

There are a number of such troublesome current issues:

- the personal right to obtain an abortion versus a state's right to regulate—even interdict—it
- a racial group's claim to an entitlement for "affirmative action" versus another's cry of "reverse discrimination"
- the right to freedom of association versus that of being judged on the basis of individual merit rather than by characteristics of birth
- freedom of the press versus a reporter's obligation as a citizen to aid in the pursuit of criminal justice
- the alleged right of insisting on prayer in the public schools as a constitutionally provided element of the free exercise of religion versus the counterinsistence that such a practice violates that same First Amendment's strictures against the establishment of religion and in favor of the separation of church and state
- an accused's alleged Fourth Amendment right to have illegally obtained evidence barred versus society's outcry over whether the "culprit shall go free just because the constable blundered" (a famed Justice Benjamin N. Cardozo question)
- the presumed First Amendment right to satisfy one's personal—even erotic—tastes in the arts and literature versus society's insistence that this right is limited by its right to guard against obscenity (and just how does one define this term?)
- the seemingly logical right of adult individuals to engage in private, consensual sexual behavior of their choice as an element of privacy versus society's age-old rejection and punishment of sodomy (no matter by whom it is practiced).

All these fascinatingly dichotomous, wrenching issues point to the need to find an acceptable line under our commitment to "Equal Justice Under Law," that hallowed creed inscribed above the portals of the Supreme Court of the United

States. It is a creed that emphasizes the need for justice as well as for law; its clarion call is for "equal justice" under "law" and not, as some would have it, "equal justice at any cost."

It is that fundamental dilemma—a line drawing of acute complexity, that search for a viable accommodation between our cherished rights and obligations under our governmental system, as ultimately pronounced by the highest tribunal of the land—which this book will address.

2
The "Double Standard"

The Court's willingness—indeed, eagerness as of some seven decades ago—to strike a much bolder blow for basic freedoms and against governmental encroachment in the "cultural" or "noneconomic" realm than in the "economic-proprietarian" one points to a judicial fait accompli: the embrace of a judicial "double standard" that accords a closer, higher level of scrutiny to cases in the cultural/noneconomic/civil rights/civil libertarian category than in the economic-proprietarian one. It is a judicially created and carefully drawn distinction—first developed in the 1920s and 1930s, continuously refined since, and decidedly in use today—designed to balance individual freedoms and community needs. That such a double standard now exists is thus a matter of record—but so is the collaterally complicating development of an extremely difficult double standard within a double standard, under which the higher or privileged category side of the basic double standard is further divided into various subcategories that are judicially accorded separate recognitions of review entitlement. These categories or classifications range from the topmost one of "suspect" legislation or executive action to the bottommost one of legislation or executive action reviewed by the judiciary on the basis of mere standards or perceptions of "reasonableness." In the following pages we shall endeavor to explain the concept of the double standard, trace its evolution and application, and analyze its justification.

THE EVOLUTION OF THE DOUBLE STANDARD

The earliest lines, drawn by the Marshall Court (1801–35), defined and strengthened the young nation, guarding the federal government against the state governments and furthering its growth and ability to function. They were also drawn to protect the property interests of individuals. From 1836 to 1864 Chief Justice

Roger B. Taney's Court sought in a variety of ways to redress the imbalance in part, as it saw it, in favor of the states, while continuing to defend the ownership of land and slaves. The disastrous *Dred Scott*[1] decision bears lasting witness to that posture. The rulings of the next two, arguably rather undistinguished, eras of Chief Justices Salmon P. Chase (1864–74) and Morrison R. Waite (1874–88) were predominantly concerned with confirming state authority over individuals and federal authority over interstate commerce. In general they heralded the broadly proprietarian notions of the next five decades under Chief Justices Melvin W. Fuller (1888–1910), Edward D. White (1910–21), and William Howard Taft (1921–30). The chief concern of this long era was to guard the sanctity of property. Socioeconomic experimentation by the legislatures, such as minimum-wage, maximum-hour, and child-labor regulations, was regarded with almost[2] unshakable disapproval by a solid majority of the Court. Again and again the justices struck down, as unconstitutional violations of *substantive* due process of law, legislation that large majorities on both the national and state levels deemed wise and necessary. They reasoned that because of the *substance* (i.e., the nature of the content) of the legislation involved—what the law was all about—such statutory experimentations deprived "persons" (i.e., property owners, chiefly businessmen) of their liberty and property without due process of law. The "deprivation" of substantive due process was then judicially regarded as proscribed by the wording and command of Amendments Five and Fourteen of the Constitution. "The Justices," as economist John R. Commons wrote in 1924, "spoke as the first authoritative faculty of political economy in the world's history."[3] Admittedly, an occasional enactment would survive—such as maximum hours in hazardous occupations (an eight-hour Utah law for copper miners and smelters in 1896);[4] for women in most industrial establishments (a ten-hour Oregon law in 1908);[5] and even one for both men and women (another ten-hour Oregon mill and factory

---

1. *Dred Scott v. Sandford,* 19 Howard 393 (1857). Ironically, Taney had emancipated the slaves he had inherited. Also of interest is that while Taney, Wayne, and Catron had voted to free the African captives in the famed case of *United States v. The Schooner Armistad,* 40 U.S. 518 (1841), they voted against Dred Scott sixteen years later. Justice Story wrote the majority opinion in *Amistad;* Justice Baldwin dissented. See Keith E. Whittington, "The Road Not Taken: *Dred Scott,* Judicial Authority, and Political Questions," 63 *Journal of Politics* 365 (May 2001).

2. "Almost," but not quite; cf. notes. 4–6. For a different judgment, see John E. Semonche, *Charting the Future: The Supreme Court Responds to a Changing Society, 1890–1920* (Westport, Conn.: Greenwood Press, 1978). Semonche's thesis is that the Court's "obstacles [placed] in the path of the popular will . . . were relatively . . . few" (at p. 432).

3. As quoted by Arthur S. Miller in "The Court Turns Back the Clock," *Progressive,* October 1976, p. 22.

4. *Holden v. Hardy,* 169 U.S. 366.

5. *Muller v. Oregon,* 208 U.S. 412. Generally credited to the first use of the "Brandeis Brief."

statute, this one in 1917).[6] But until the advent of the "Roosevelt Court" in 1937, the Supreme Court under Chief Justice Charles Evans Hughes (1930–41) continued the substantive due process veto and struck down between 1934 and 1936 a total of sixteen New Deal laws that had been enacted chiefly under the taxing and interstate commerce powers of Congress.[7] Although President Roosevelt lost his battle to "pack" the Court in February 1937, he was able, within a matter of three months, to win the war with two favorable decisions by the Hughes Court, a political victory often styled as "the switch in time that saved nine."

Here the chief justice and Associate Justice Owen J. Roberts—deferring to the legislature and recognizing the political facts of life—joined their colleagues Louis D. Brandeis, Benjamin N. Cardozo, and Harlan F. Stone in upholding a Washington State *minimum-wage law* for women and children—the first time that such a statute was upheld by the Court.[8] (It would be another four years before the Court would have the opportunity to uphold,[9] again for the first time, a *federal child-labor law,* a segment of the Fair Labor Standards Act of 1938, which also provided for minimum wages and maximum hours for all workers in interstate commerce. It had been declared beyond the power of Congress by a lower federal court.) In the other great early spring 1937 "switch-in-time" case, the new 5:4 majority upheld the National Labor Relations Act of 1935 against the challenge that it, too, exceeded the powers of Congress.[10] When Justice Willis van Devanter retired in May 1937, after having served twenty-six years on the Court, and Democratic Senator Hugo LaFayette Black of Alabama replaced him, the day of resorting to declarations of unconstitutionality on grounds of alleged infringement of economic "substantive due process" had, in effect, passed beyond recall—while in the future loomed a new and different kind of substantive due process interest. The post-1937 Court was radically different from that of the first four decades of the twentieth century—faced as it was with an agenda of increasingly complex economic, political, and social pressures and problems, both domestic and international.

Gradually the Court thus embarked upon a policy of paying close attention to any legislative and executive attempt to curb basic rights and liberties in the "noneconomic" sphere. During the remaining years of the Hughes Court and continuing through the Stone Court (1941–46), the Vinson Court (1946–53), and particularly the Warren Court (1953–69), the chief concern was to find a balance between the basic civil rights and liberties of the individual and those of the com-

---

6. *Bunting v. Oregon,* 243 U.S. 426.

7. For explanatory and statistical matter through the fall of 1997, see Henry J. Abraham, *The Judicial Process: An Introductory Analysis of the Courts of the United States, England, and France,* 7th ed. (New York: Oxford University Press, 1998), pp. 299–320.

8. *West Coast Hotel Co. v. Parrish,* 300 U.S. 379 (1937).

9. *United States v. Darby Lumber Co.,* 312 U.S. 100 (1941).

10. *National Labor Relations Board v. Jones and Laughlin Steel Corporation,* 301 U.S. 1 (1937).

munity of which he or she is a part. That concern continued under the Burger Court (1969–86), which, with the exception of the criminal justice sector, did not reveal any clearly demonstrable tendency to chip away at the legacy of the Warren Court, and indeed charted sundry new rights, among them those of privacy (including abortion, gender equality, and "affirmative action"). The Rehnquist Court (1986–) has displayed a more cautious approach toward broadening individual rights (as when it refused in 1997 to create a federal constitutional right of physician-assisted suicide based on either the equal protection or the due process clause). An increasingly firm majority of the justices as of the 1990s also departed from more liberal precedents on abortion, race preferences (e.g., affirmative action and majority/minority voting districts), church-state, and criminal rights issues. The Rehnquist Court has even demonstrated a more favorable outlook toward property rights.[11] Nevertheless, the post-1937 change in judicial attitude continues to reflect a conviction that certain fundamental freedoms ipso facto require closer judicial scrutiny lest they be irretrievably lost. A properly lodged complaint with the Court that legislative or executive action, be it state or national, had violated the complainant's due process of law, be it substantive or procedural—and/or the equal protection of the law (applicable to the state level only)—would be assured at least of judicial interest and probably of close scrutiny. That this concern has in effect thereby created a "double standard" of judicial attitude, whereby governmental economic experimentation is accorded close to carte blanche by the courts, but alleged violations of individual civil rights and liberties are given meticulous judicial attention, is an issue that will be carefully examined.[12] Historically, the jurisprudential postures of certain justices have aided in the creation of a double standard.[13]

Despite his close adherence to a philosophy of judicial self-restraint, characterized by deference to the legislature, Justice Oliver Wendell Holmes Jr. spent much of his thirty-year career (1902–32) on the highest bench—which fell in its substantive *economic* due process era—in dissent from judicial vetoes of economic legislation. He did so not because he particularly liked the legislation but because he was convinced that democracy meant that people had the right to be foolish and unwise. In his own words, he was willing to go so far as "to help my country go to hell if that's what it wants." Yet he nevertheless drew the line and called a firm halt to legislative experimentation when it came to basic "*non*eco-

11. For an interesting commentary, as of early 1971, contending that once judicially pronounced there has never been any major policy reversal in the realm of civil rights and liberties on the part of the Court, see an article by former Associate Justice of the Supreme Court Arthur J. Goldberg for the *New York Times,* April 12 and 13, 1971, pp. 37c and 37m, respectively. By and large, that contention remains true to this day.

12. See especially *infra* this chapter.

13. For contentions as to the latter-day development of a double standard, or even double standards, within the original double standard, consult the Gunther, Wilkinson, Abraham, and Funston articles cited below.

nomic" rights. Prior to Holmes, Justice John Marshall Harlan had been the sole consistent dissenter in the economic substantive due process era. Harlan, grand-father of President Eisenhower's appointee of the same name, served from 1877 until his death in 1911. Though a onetime Kentucky slaveholder, he, as well as Holmes, deserves the title of "great dissenter,"[14] for he believed in a full measure of judicial self-restraint regarding legislative economic-proprietarian enact-ments. This stance was dramatically illustrated by his solitary dissent in the 1895 case of *United States v. E. C. Knight Co.,*[15] when his eight colleagues on the Court virtually wiped out the hoped-for weapons of the fledgling Sherman Anti-Trust Act of 1890 by ruling that "commerce succeeds to manufacture and is not a part of it."[16] On the other hand, Harlan's resolute attachment to the role of the Court as the guardian of both the letter and the spirit of the basic constitutional guarantees of civil rights and liberties is well demonstrated in his lone dissenting opinion in *Plessy v. Ferguson.*[17] In this 1896 decision the Court, with Justice Henry B. Brown—a native of Massachusetts, a graduate of Harvard and Yale, and a resident of Michigan—delivering the majority opinion of seven, upheld the "separate but equal" doctrine in racial segregation:

> We consider the underlying fallacy of the plaintiff's [Homer Plessy, a Louisianan, seven-eighths white, who had refused to give up his seat in a railroad car reserved for white passengers under an 1890 Louisiana statute] argument to consist in the assumption that the enforced separation of the two races stamped the colored race with a badge of inferiority. If this be so, it is not by reason of anything found in the act, but *solely because the col-ored race chooses to put that construction on it.*[18]

Thundered Harlan, one of only two southerners then on the Court:

> Our Constitution is color-blind, and neither knows nor tolerates classes among citizens. In respect of civil rights, all citizens are equal before the law. The humblest is the peer of the most powerful. The law regards man as man and takes no account of his surroundings or of his color when his civil rights as guaranteed by the supreme law of the land are involved.[19]

14. See Henry J. Abraham, "John Marshall Harlan: A Justice Neglected," 41 *Virginia Law Review* 871 (November 1955). The title of *the* great dissenter will presumably always be the property of Justice Douglas, who in his almost thirty-seven (!) years on the Court (1939–75) dissented no fewer than 795 times. Holmes's dissents numbered 172, placing him fifteenth; Harlan penned 376, third on the list. (Dissents may be written or unwritten.)
15. 156 U.S. 1.
16. Ibid., majority opinion by Chief Justice Fuller at 9. Its impact was not effectively reversed until the Court's 1937 decision in *National Labor Relations Board v. Jones and Laughlin Steel Corporation,* 301 U.S. 1.
17. 163 U.S. 537.
18. Ibid. at 551; italics supplied. Justice David Brewer did not participate in the case.
19. Ibid. at 559.

As we shall see, Harlan was the first Supreme Court jurist to advocate—unsuccessfully during his time of service—the *total* applicability of the federal Bill of Rights to the several states.[20] That he and Holmes were not particularly close personally did not alter their jurisprudential kinship.

In this respect, however, Harlan was even closer to Louis Dembitz Brandeis, Woodrow Wilson's close ideological ally whom the president nominated to the highest bench in 1916, five years after Harlan's death and fourteen years after Holmes's appointment to the Court. A pioneering lawyer and crusading supporter of social welfare legislation, a bitter opponent of trusts and monopolies, and the first Jew to be nominated to the Court, Brandeis won a furious and bitter four-month confirmation battle, which was the longest in Court history. He was finally confirmed by a vote of 47:22, all but one[21] of the negative votes being cast by Brandeis's fellow Republicans![22] Justice Brandeis disappointed neither his nominator nor his "public." He and Holmes, while of widely divergent backgrounds and temperaments, not only became warm friends but were usually on the same side of the Court's decisions, particularly in the interpretation of substantive due process and the double standard. That their reasons for agreement were often quite different affected neither the basic fact of agreement nor the close relationship between them.[23] Holmes did not live to see his position vindicated; he died at age ninety-three in 1935, three years after retiring from his beloved bench. He knew, however, that his successor, Cardozo, would follow in his footsteps, and there were ample signs that if the jurisprudential era begun by the Fuller Court had not yet run its course, it was becoming increasingly beleaguered. Brandeis did see the new era dawn. After twenty-three years on the Court, he retired in 1939 at the age of eighty-three, secure in the knowledge that his philosophy would be followed by the post-1937 Court. FDR awarded his seat to a longtime Brandeis admirer, William O. Douglas—who, during his record-setting thirty-six and a half years

20. E.g., *Hurtado v. California,* 110 U.S. 516 (1884); *Maxwell v. Dow,* 176 U.S. 581 (1900); and *Twining v. New Jersey,* 211 U.S. 78 (1908)—to name just three cases. His lone success was the quasi-"incorporation" of the economic-proprietarian concept of eminent domain in *Chicago, Burlington and Quincy Railroad v. Chicago,* 166 U.S. 226 (1897), an 8:1 opinion written by him (see later discussion), obviously joined by all on the Court except Justice Brewer, because the constitutional protection here conferred dealt with *property* rights as a constituent element of due process of law, although the railroad lost the case on the merits.

21. Democrat Francis G. Newlands of Nevada.

22. Quite a number either did not vote or were paired, however. See A. L. Todd, *Justice on Trial: The Case of Louis D. Brandeis* (New York: McGraw-Hill, 1964), for a fascinating account of the confirmation battle. Brandeis was a registered Republican, but he probably voted the Democratic ticket more frequently.

23. See the fine analysis of the two great justices in Samuel J. Konefsky's *Legacy of Holmes and Brandeis: A Study in the Influence of Ideas* (New York: Macmillan, 1956; pap. ed. New York: Collier Books, 1961).

on the Court,[24] would go far beyond his idol in the furthering of libertarian activism.

THE EXPRESSION AND JUSTIFICATION OF THE DOUBLE STANDARD

In creating the double standard, the *post*-1937 Court came to *assume* as constitutional all legislation in the economic-proprietarian sector *unless* proved to the contrary by a complainant,[25] but to view with a suspicious eye legislative and executive experimentation with other basic human freedoms generally regarded as the "cultural freedoms" guaranteed by the Bill of Rights—among them speech, press, worship, assembly, petition, due process of law in criminal justice, a fair trial. In short, without denying its ultimate responsibility, the Court came to accept legislative action in the economic realm but kept and, of course, continues to keep a very close watch over legislative activities described as "basic" or "cultural." What we have, then, is a judicially recognized area of "preferred freedoms." Any quest for an obvious, clear line between "property rights" and "basic human rights" is, of course, doomed to fail, because by definition and implication *both are guaranteed freedoms* under our national and state constitutions. Property, too, is a "human right," and there is a fundamental interdependence "between the personal right to liberty and the personal right in property," as Justice Stewart wrote in a 1972 opinion for the Court.[26] Committed to that philosophy, the distinguished jurist Learned Hand never failed to reject, and challenge, any advocacy of the double standard. A policy urging that the courts, "when concerned with interests other than property . . . should have a wider latitude for enforcing their own predilections than when they were concerned with property itself" was to him a dereliction of the judicial function if not of the oath of office of the Constitution; "just why property itself was not a 'personal right,'" Hand observed, "nobody took the time to ex-

24. He served until late 1975, when debilitating illness dictated his retirement, and died in 1980.

25. A major contemporary example is the Court's 8:0 upholding in 1984 of Hawaii's Land Reform Act of 1967, under which the state used its power of eminent domain to break up large estates and transfer land ownership to the estates' tenants (*Hawaii Housing Authority v. Midkiff*, 467 U.S. 229). Speaking for the Court, Justice O'Connor found an appropriate "public use" taking rather than a violation of the nonimpairment of the obligation of contract safeguard of Article 1, Section 10.

26. *Lynch v. Household Finance Corp.*, 405 U.S. 538 (1972) at 552. Thus to Stewart property rights and nonproperty rights can *both* be fundamental, and, further, they can be interdependent and symbiotic. At least one student of the problem has attempted to distinguish between "personal" or "individual" and "corporate" or "institutional" property—the former being entitled to double standard inclusion, the latter not. (See Richard H. Rosswurn, "The Double Standard Under Constitution and Supreme Court: An Alternate Model" [paper presented at the annual meeting of the Southern Political Science Association, Gatlinburg, Tenn., November 1–3, 1979].)

plain."[27] And as Paul Freund, noted scholar of constitutional law and Hand's admirer, has reminded us, it is indeed difficult to "compare the ultimate values of property with those of [for example] free inquiry and expression, or to compare the legislative compromises in the two realms; for laws dealing with libel or sedition or sound tracks or non-political civil service are as truly adjustments and accommodations as are laws fixing prices or making grants of monopolies."[28] However, the values of property are not ignored by the judiciary when, in fact, illegal legislative action takes place[29]—or when basic property rights of individuals or groups are adjudged violated beyond the legal or constitutional pale.[30]

Recently the Court has modified the more traditional double standard to give "strict judicial scrutiny" to certain types of equal protection *and* due process cases, especially the former. Depending on the type of legislative statutory classification, the Court now habitually places or views the case before it in different categories or levels, accordingly affecting its treatment of the issue at hand. Thus, for the economic-proprietarian cases (which were discussed earlier in this chapter) the Court still uses the "traditional" equal protection (and due process) test of examining whether the legislature had a "reasonable" or "rational" or "relevant" basis for making its statutory classification.[31] Despite the fact that, ever since the 1937 "switch in time that saved nine," basic civil rights and liberties issues have led to closer scrutiny by the Court, the demonstration of a classification in a law which either affects so-styled "fundamental interests" (e.g., voting rights,[32] the right to interstate travel)[33] or touches what has become a "suspect

27. "Chief Justice Stone's Conception of the Judicial Function," 46 *Columbia Law Review* 698 (1946).

28. *The Supreme Court of the United States* (Cleveland: World, 1961), p. 35.

29. For example, in 1952 the Supreme Court by an 8:1 vote—Justice Burton dissenting—declared as a violation of substantive due process a provision of the Pure Food and Drug Act which provided for federal powers of factory inspection. The Court ruled this provision to be an unconstitutionally vague deprivation of liberty and property safeguarded by the Fifth Amendment (*United States v. Cardiff*, 344 U.S. 174).

30. E.g., *Lloyd v. Tanner*, 407 U.S. 551 (1972), where the Court "balanced" the property rights of a private shopping center with the right of freedom of expression (distribution of leaflets) and found on behalf of the former by a 5:4 vote. In the words of Justice Powell's majority opinion: "Although accommodations between [speech and property values] are sometimes necessary, and the courts properly have shown a solicitude for the [First Amendment], this Court has never held that a trespasser or an uninvited guest may exercise general rights of free speech on private property used non-discriminatorily for private purposes only" (at 567–68).

31. But also for borderline cases, such as *Central State University v. AAUP*, 67 LW 3577, in which the Court upheld 8:1 an Ohio law exempting public university professors from the regular collective bargaining process, here a controversial policy compelling more teaching and thus, by implication, less research.

32. E.g., *Harper v. Virginia Board of Elections*, 383 U.S. 663 (1966).

33. E.g., *Shapiro v. Thompson*, 394 U.S. 618 (1968)—at least when it involves, as it did here, "a basic necessity of life." See also *Cedar Rapids Community School District v. Garrett F.*, 526 U.S. 66 (1999).

category" of legislation (e.g., race,[34] national origin or alienage, "the first cousin of race,"[35] and, as of 1968 but apparently no longer after mid-1976, illegitimacy)[36] has now received an even higher level of Court scrutiny. In some cases the category, while not "suspect," is nonetheless accorded especially close attention—sex, for example, which is second only to race in contemporary equal protection of the laws litigation.[37] Once an issue has accordingly been placed on that special level of scrutiny, the Court in effect shifts the burden of proof of its constitutionality *to the legislature and/or the executive* and requires that *it* demonstrate a *"compelling* state interest" for its legislative classification—as it succeeded in doing, for example, in the *Japanese Exclusion Case* of 1944.[38] Once the "fundamental interest" or "suspect"[39] category classification is demonstrated in a case, the "strict judicial scrutiny" that thereby results leads to considerably greater judicial protection of these rights. In essence, as was suggested earlier, we see the Court using a complicated double standard within a double standard, under which various subcategories are judicially accorded separate recognition of review-entitlement to accomplish this contemporary

---

34. E.g., *Loving v. Virginia,* 388 U.S. 1 (1967). Ironically, the first reference to it was by Justice Black in the *Japanese Exclusion Case, Korematsu v. United States,* 323 U.S. 214 (1944): [All] legal restrictions which curtail the civil rights of a single racial group are immediately suspect. This is not to say that all such restrictions are unconstitutional. It is to say that courts must subject them to the most rigid scrutiny. Pressing public necessity may sometimes justify the existence of such restrictions [as a 6:3 Court majority here found]; racial antagonism never can" (at 216; italics supplied).

35. E.g., *Graham v. Richardson,* 403 U.S. 365 (1971). The quoted passage comes from *Trimble v. Gordon,* 430 U.S. 762 (1977) at 777. See *Plyler v. Doe,* 462 U.S. 725 (1983); and *Bernal v. Fainter,* 467 U.S. 216 (1984). Cf. *Mathews v. Diaz,* 426 U.S. 67 (1976); *Hampton v. Mow Sun Wong,* 426 U.S. 88 (1976); *Ambach v. Norwick,* 441 U.S. 68 (1979); and *Cabell v. Chavez-Salido,* 454 U.S. 432 (1982).

36. E.g., *Levy v. Louisiana,* 391 U.S. 68 (1968); *Labine v. Vincent,* 401 U.S. 532 (1971); *Weber v. Aetna Casualty Insurance Company,* 406 U.S. 164 (1972). For the "removal decision," see *Norton v. Mathews* and *Mathews v. Lucas,* 427 U.S. 495 (1976).

37. E.g., *Reed v. Reed,* 404 U.S. 71 (1971); *Frontiero v. Richardson,* 411 U.S. 677 (1973); and *Helgemoe v. Meloon,* 436 U.S. 950 (1978). But compare and contrast those with, e.g., *Kahn v. Shevin,* 416 U.S. 351 (1974); *Schlesinger v. Ballard,* 419 U.S. 498 (1975); and *General Electric Co. v. Gilbert,* 429 U.S. 125 (1976). See *infra* Table 8.1, for an updated account.

38. See *supra* note 34.

39. The "traditional indices of suspectness," viewed by Justice Stone in his *Carolene* footnote as "discrete and insular minorities," were characterized as follows in Justice Powell's majority opinion in *San Antonio School District v. Rodriguez,* 411 U.S. 1 (1973): "The class [is] saddled with such disabilities, or subjected to such a history of purposeful unequal treatment, or relegated to such a history of purposeful unequal treatment, or relegated to such a position of political powerlessness as to command extraordinary protection from the majoritarian political process." See also his concurring opinion, as well as Justice Brennan's, for the majority in *Plyler v. Doe,* 462 U.S. 725 (1982).

task[40]—triggering widespread accusations of judicial arrogation of legislative authority (in addition to compounding doctrinal confusion that renders both lay and professional analysis inordinately complex).

Of Preferred Freedoms

Although he did not personally use the words until four years later,[41] the articulation of the concept of "preferred freedoms" is appropriately credited to a footnote appended to an opinion for the Court by then Associate Justice Stone in the 1938 case of *United States v. Carolene Products Company.*[42] Stone's Footnote Four, which would become a "widely honored cornerstone of constitutional law,"[43] and in fact signaled the Court's altered definition of its role in reviewing the constitutionality of various types of legislation, probably evolved from the celebrated Cardozo opinion delivered a few months earlier in *Palko v. Connecticut.*[44] In his last personally delivered opinion prior to his fatal illness in 1938, Justice Cardozo established two major categories of rights: those that *are* and those that *are not* "implicit in the concept of ordered liberty." Cardozo justified this distinction, later referred to as the "Honor Roll of Superior Rights," by explaining that "we reach a different plane of social and moral values when we pass to . . . freedom of thought and speech [which] is the matrix, the indispensable condition, of nearly every other form of freedom."[45] Stone wrote his opinion in the *Carolene* case with Cardozo's distinction in mind. And, in a very real sense, he took it one step further: he explicitly enunciated the activist doctrine of the "double standard."[46] *Carolene* dealt with an ordinary federal interstate commerce statute, the Filled Milk Act of 1923, which regulated adulterated ("filled") milk, and it would normally have passed into the annals of what the New Deal–deferential Court regarded as routine exercise of valid congressional legislative power over interstate commerce.[47] However, addressing himself to the inherent con-

40. For two excellent treatments of this vexing and complicated issue, see Gerald Gunther, "The Supreme Court: 1971 Term; In Search of Evolving Doctrine on a Changing Court: A Model for a Newer Equal Protection," 86 *Harvard Law Review* 1 (1972); and J. Harvie Wilkinson III, "The Supreme Court, the Equal Protection Clause and the Three Faces of Constitutional Equality," 61 *Virginia Law Review* 945 (1975). Also see *supra* this chapter.

41. In *Jones v. Opelika*, 316 U.S. 584 (1942) at 608.

42. 304 U.S. 144. Justice McReynolds was the lone dissenter in the 6:1 holding. Justices Cardozo and Reed did not participate.

43. See Geoffrey P. Miller, "The True Story of *Carolene Products,*" 1987 *Supreme Court Review* 397, at 398.

44. 302 U.S. 319 (1937). The case will be discussed more fully *infra* in chapter 3.

45. Ibid. at 326–27.

46. See Robert M. Cover, "The Origins of Judicial Activism in the Protection of Minorities," 91 *Yale Law Journal* 1287 (1982).

47. The statute prohibited the interstate shipment of "skimmed milk compounded with any fat or oil other than milk fat, so as to resemble milk or cream" (504 U.S. 144 at 146).

gressional regulatory power, Stone was moved to comment in the body of the opinion that

> the existence of facts supporting the legislative judgment is to be presumed, for regulatory legislation affecting ordinary commercial transactions is not to be pronounced unconstitutional unless, in the light of the facts made known or generally assumed, it is of such a character as to preclude the assumption that it rests upon some rational basis within the knowledge and experience of legislators.[48]

This expression of the double standard, from one who had come to the Court from one of the largest New York corporate law offices, is a reminder that Marxian forecasts and interpretations of the attitude of justices on the highest bench are not always accurate!

Having said what he did, Stone then appended his now famous Footnote Four[49]—viewed as "mythologized, created as a symbol," in an intriguing contemporary analysis by University of Chicago professors Rosenberg and Rohrbacher[50]— from which we will examine the following three paragraphs:

1. There may be narrower scope for operation of the presumption of constitutionality when legislation appears on its face to be *within a specific prohibition of the Constitution,* such as those of the first ten amendments which are deemed equally specific when held to be embraced within the Fourteenth.
2. It is unnecessary to consider now whether legislation which restricts *those political processes* which can ordinarily be expected to bring about repeal of undesirable legislation, is to be subjected to more exacting judicial scrutiny

---

48. 304 U.S. 144 at 152.

49. It is now generally accepted that most of the famed footnote was in fact authored by Stone's brilliant law clerk, Louis Lusky, and that Hughes in effect wrote its first paragraph. Hughes was eager to present a formal connection with constitutional text. Stone's concern was with the context of fundamental rights. For the footnote's popularization much credit is due to Professor Alpheus Thomas Mason, longtime McCormick Professor of Jurisprudence at Princeton University. See Lusky's *By What Right?* (Charlottesville, Va.: The Michie Co., 1975), for a full discussion of Footnote Four. Some forty years later, Lusky provided an intriguing, significant, never heretofore publicized, additional explanation and fascinating facsimilied documentation of the footnote's genesis and adoption in his book *Our Nine Tribunes: The Supreme Court in Modern America* (Westport, Conn.: Praeger Publishers, 1993). See especially chapter 7, "The *Carolene Products* Footnote," and the appendix, pp. 177–90.

50. Gerald N. Rosenberg and Christopher M. Rohrbacher, "The Changing Meanings of Supreme Court Decisions: *Carolene Products* Footnote 4 as a Political Symbol" (paper presented at the annual meeting of the American Political Science Association, Boston, September 3–6, 1998).

under the general prohibitions of the Fourteenth Amendment than are most other types of legislation. . . .

3. Nor need we enquire whether similar considerations enter into review of statutes directed at particular religious . . . or national . . . or racial minorities . . . ; *whether prejudice against discrete and insular minorities* may be a special condition, which tends seriously to curtail the operation of *those political processes* ordinarily to be relied upon to protect minorities, and which may call for a correspondingly more searching judicial inquiry. . . .[51]

At first glance the language in paragraph 1 may suggest to some—as it did to Justice Frankfurter[52]—that *any* legislation which on its face appears to abridge the constitutional guarantees of the Bill of Rights would have to fall *automatically.* However, as soon became evident, Stone had reference primarily to the five guarantees of the First Amendment (religion, speech, press, assembly, and petition) and secondarily to the proposition that such legislation should simply be *inspected* more critically by the judiciary than where exclusively economic rights are at issue.[53] Stone's colleagues Black, Douglas, Murphy, and Rutledge[54] embraced his position readily—although not necessarily for the same reasons—and their opinion frequently prevailed during their joint tenure on the Court between 1943 and 1949, sometimes gaining Jackson's vote, occasionally even Frankfurter's or Reed's. Thus, at least five votes to carry the day were often available, and a series of memorable decisions was made in behalf of the new concept.[55] And, contrary to some reporting, justices did in fact use

51. Italics supplied.

52. See, e.g., his concurring opinion in *Kovacs v. Cooper,* 336 U.S. 77 (1949).

53. For an interesting analysis of the genesis and application of the "preferred freedom" concept, see Robert B. McKay, "The Preference for Freedom," 34 *New York University Law Review* 1184 (November 1959). He is very critical of the Frankfurter position on both factual and logical grounds.

54. Actually it was Rutledge, not Stone, who stated the "preferred freedom" doctrine most clearly, most expressly, and most extremely, in what was the heyday of the avowed utilization of the doctrine, in the 5:4 *Union Organization Case* of 1945—in which the now Chief Justice Stone dissented, together with Roberts, Reed, and Frankfurter (*Thomas v. Collins,* 323 U.S. 516 [1945] at 529–30, 540). Rutledge referred to "the preferred place given in our scheme to the great, the indispensable democratic freedoms secured by the First Amendment." He carried his colleagues Black, Douglas, and Murphy, and Jackson concurred to make the majority of five. (Black, uncomfortable with the "preferred" concept, would later "substitute" that of "absolute," which he avowedly adapted, based upon his literalist reading of the Constitution, in 1951, in *Dennis v. United States,* 341 U.S. 494, although he did not formally employ the term "absolute" itself until a few months later in *Carlson v. Landon,* 342 U.S. 524 at 555.)

55. E.g., *Hague v. CIO,* 307 U.S. 496 (1939); *Bridges v. California,* 314 U.S. 252 (1941); *Jones v. Opelika,* 319 U.S. 103 (1943); *West Virginia State Board of Education v. Barnette,* 319 U.S. 624 (1943); *Thomas v. Collins,* loc. cit.; *Saia v. New York,* 334 U.S. 558 (1948); *Kovacs v. Cooper,* loc. cit.; and *Terminiello v. Chicago,* 337 U.S. 1 (1949).

the term "preferred position" in majority and minority opinions[56]—and they not only continued to do so but occasionally still do—notwithstanding Frankfurter's angry characterization of it as "a mischievous phrase."[57] However, when Justices Murphy and Rutledge both died in the summer of 1949, their replacements, Tom C. Clark and Sherman Minton, together with Chief Justice Fred M. Vinson (Stone had died on the bench in 1946), consigned the "preferred freedom" doctrine to relative limbo. It remained there until Earl Warren succeeded Vinson on the latter's death in 1953 and the Court renewed its continuing emphasis on civil rights and liberties, with the Warren Court—or, arguably, the Brennan Court—utilizing the *Carolene Products* Footnote Four as an inspirational tool.

Paragraph 2 calls for a special judicial scrutiny of assaults on "those political processes" which in a very real sense make all other rights in our democratic society possible: equal access to the voting booth, for both nomination and election, and the ability to seek redress of political grievances, whether by striving for public office or by "getting at the rascals" in office. It was this basic requirement of a representative democracy that precipitated the momentous Supreme Court decisions in the *Suffrage Cases* of 1941 and 1944. In the first, *United States v. Classic,*[58] the Court overruled precedent[59] and held that the language of the Constitution equated "primaries" with "elections" in races for federal office, and that the former would henceforth be subject to congressional regulation to the same extent and in the same manner as the latter. The second case, *Smith v. Allwright,*[60] logically resulted from the first. Here the Court, again overruling precedent,[61] outlawed, as an unconstitutional violation of the Fifteenth Amendment, the so-called white primary, a device to bar blacks from the effective exercise of the ballot in several states of the Deep South. Rejecting the contention that the Democratic Party of Texas was "a voluntary association" and thus free to discriminate in its membership, the 8:1 majority held that the party acted as an agent of the state of Texas because of the character of its duties—such as providing election machinery and candidates. Of equal, if not greater, importance in the judicial assault on legislation restricting basic political processes is the matter of equitable representation. In March 1962 the Supreme Court finally found sufficient votes to declare that the age-old practice of deliberate mal-, mis-, or nonapportionment of representative legislative districts in the several states was a controversy that it had the power, the right, and the duty to adjudicate.

56. E.g., Stone in *Jones v. Opelika,* 316 U.S. 584 (1942) at 608; Douglas in *Murdock v. Pennsylvania,* 319 U.S. 105 (1943) at 115; Rutledge in *Thomas v. Collins,* op. cit. at 530; and Reed in *Kovacs v. Cooper,* op. cit. at 88. See also *Prince v. Massachusetts,* 321 U.S. 158 (1944); *Follett v. McCormick,* 321 U.S. 573 (1944); *Marsh v. Alabama,* 326 U.S. 501 (1946) at 509; and *Saia v. New York,* op. cit. at 562.

57. *Kovacs v. Cooper,* op. cit. at 90. For example, Black did in his dissenting opinion in *Morey v. Doud,* 354 U.S. 457 (1957) at 471.

58. 313 U.S. 299 (1941).

59. *Newberry v. United States,* 256 U.S. 232 (1921).

60. 321 U.S. 649 (1944). Justice Roberts was the sole dissenter here.

61. *Grovey v. Townsend,* 295 U.S. 45 (1935).

This decision in the case of *Baker v. Carr*[62]—which Chief Justice Warren[63] regarded as "the most important case we decided in my time"[64]—sharply departed from the erstwhile Court practice of regarding this kind of controversy as a "political question"[65] to be "handled" by the political rather than the judiciary branch. Baker broke with that precedent. Justice Frankfurter—"the Emily Post of the Supreme Court," in Fred Rodell's nastily memorable phrase—joined by his disciple on the bench, John Marshall Harlan II, wrote an impassioned sixty-eight-page dissenting opinion reiterating his lifelong judicial philosophy that the courts must stay out of what he termed the "political thicket." Warning that the Court would find itself immersed in a "mathematical quagmire," he admonished the majority of six: "There is not under our Constitution a judicial remedy for every political mischief. In a democratic society like ours, relief must come through an aroused popular conscience that sears the conscience of the people's representatives."[66] But the majority of the general public had seen one attempt after another to "sear the conscience" frustrated for generations. Indeed, in many of the transgressing states the very imbalance of representative districts rendered "an aroused public conscience" impossible. The Court, prodded by a swelling chorus of citizens who were discriminated against, notably the urban masses, had had enough, and the commands of Article 1 and Amendment Fourteen provided the necessary interpretative authority to bring about the "more exacting judicial scrutiny" called for in the second paragraph of Justice Stone's Footnote Four.[67]

62. 369 U.S. 186 (1962).

63. Ironically, fifteen years earlier, as governor of California, he had successfully opposed reapportionment. It matters what post one holds.

64. Interview with author, Washington, D.C., May 24, 1969. Warren's view of the case's significance—whether or not one accepts his ranking—was amply vindicated, and quickly so: after but eight years following the extensions of *Baker*-opened principles-cum-yardsticks to congressional districts, the Bureau of the Census reported that the average deviation from the ideal district size in the Ninety-third (January 1973) Congress was but half of 1 percent, as contrasted with 17 percent in the Eighty-eighth (January 1965)!

65. E.g., *Colegrove v. Green,* 328 U.S. 549 (1946); and *South v. Peters,* 339 U.S. 276 (1950).

66. 369 U.S. 186, dissenting opinion at 270. For almost three decades after *Baker* the Court managed to avoid the ancient political hanky-panky of the gerrymander. When it finally "handled" it in 1986, it did so in a disturbingly split 4:3:2 holding in *Davis v. Bandemer,* 478 U.S. 109. In effect, the holding seemed to say that gerrymandering *may* be illegal or unconstitutional as a violation of the equal protection clause. *But* it will be very hard to prove it—and here it was not proved. What we are seeing, of course, is additional judicial involvement. When the Court was confronted with an opportunity to rule on California's grotesque gerrymander that gave the Democrats control of the state's congressional delegation in 1982, it meekly affirmed the lower court holdings, sanctioning them in a one-sentence ruling (6:3) in 1989 (*Badham v. Eu,* 488 U.S. 1024).

67. In 1999 the Court, in a highly charged political issue, ruled 5:4 that in apportionment cases the decennial census must be by actual count rather than, as suggested by the Democratic Party, by at least partial sampling. *Department of Commerce v. U.S. House of Representatives,* 525 U.S. 326.

The decision in *Baker v. Carr*[68] that the federal courts do have jurisdiction in cases involving state legislative apportionment became a vehicle for logical substantive extensions. In the 1963 *Georgia County Unit Case,*[69] the Court agreed with the lower federal district court that the notorious "county unit" scheme[70] violated the equal protection of the laws clause of the Fourteenth Amendment, enunciating the principle of "one person, one vote"[71] — the equality of every voter with every other voter in the state when he or she casts a vote in a statewide election. One year later the Court extended the principle to *congressional* districts.[72] Perhaps most dramatically, in a group of six cases in June 1964 it required that representation for *both* houses of state legislatures must be apportioned to reflect "approximate equality" (a decision not only extended subsequently to reach local elections of varied character[73] but one that would ultimately result in the further extension to a Court call for "absolute equality"!).[74] Wrote Chief Justice Warren for a majority of six: "Legislatures represent people, not trees or acres. Legislators are elected by voters, not farms or cities or economic interests. . . . To the extent that a citizen's right to vote is debased, he is that much less a citizen. The

---

68. The vote was 6:2. Justice Charles E. Whittaker did not participate.

69. *Gray v. Sanders,* 372 U.S. 368.

70. Under it each of Georgia's counties received a minimum of two and a maximum of six electoral votes (for the eight most populous counties), with each county's vote going to the candidate receiving the largest popular vote therein—resulting in rank discrimination that saw the small counties receiving from 11 to 120 times as much representative weight as the largest.

71. Justice Douglas spoke for the 8:1 Court here.

72. *Wesberry v. Sanders,* 376 U.S. 1 (1964).

73. E.g., *Avery v. Midland County,* 390 U.S. 474 (1968); and *Hadley v. Junior College Dist. of Metro. Kansas City, Mo.,* 397 U.S. 50 (1970).

74. *Kirkpatrick v. Preisler,* 394 U.S. 526 (1969); and *Wells v. Rockefeller,* 394 U.S. 542 (1969). But in 1973 the Court refused (6:3) to extend the principle to *elected judges* (*Wells v. Edwards,* 409 U.S. 1095) and to such special-purpose governing agencies as a board of directors of a water district (*Salyer Land Co. v. Tulare Lake Basic Water Storage District,* 410 U.S. 719). And during the same term of Court it permitted (5:3) a Virginia deviation of 16.4 percent, holding (via Justice Rehnquist) that its "one person, one vote" doctrine, which it did emphatically reaffirm here, need not be applied so strictly to *state* as to *congressional* apportionment. Rehnquist reasoned that a state legislative apportionment plan could therefore include "a certain amount of arithmetical discrepancy if it was deliberately drawn to conform to the boundaries of political subdivisions" (*Mahan v. Howell,* 410 U.S. 315). The rationale of the latter decision was subsequently confirmed in a series of cases involving 7.8 and 9.9 percent variances in other states (*Gaffney v. Cummings,* 412 U.S. 735; and *White v. Regester,* 412 U.S. 755), both in 1973, too. On the other hand, the latter case sustained, for the first time, an attack on multimember districts as tending "unconstitutionally to minimize the voting strength of racial groups." But a mere 4.4 percent deviation in congressional districting was vetoed by the Court at the same time (*White v. Weiser,* 413 U.S. 783), and an attempt by North Dakota to deviate by 20 percent was unanimously declared unconstitutional in 1975 (*Chapman v. Meier,* 420 U.S. 1). See also *Ball*

weight of a citizen's right to vote cannot be made to depend on where he lives."[75] Stone would have been pleased; Frankfurter was not.

In paragraph 3 Stone so explicitly spells out the double standard as to be appropriately credited with its parenthood. It is self-evident that the special judicial protection he suggests for frequently unpopular racial, religious, and political minorities and other often helpless and small groups is preeminently designed for and directed to their political-cultural activities. Underlying his call for special scrutiny is the fact that these groups demonstrably needed or need special aid and protection to attain and maintain their full measure of constitutionally guaranteed citizenship. The current struggle of political, religious, gender, and particularly racial minority groups bears witness to the case for the "preferred freedom" doctrine, suggested by Stone on that Opinion Monday in 1938 and widely cited and adopted as an important protector of minority rights as of the late 1960s and early 1970s.[76]

But is the implicit double standard justifiable at all? Do particular justices of the Supreme Court of the United States have a moral as well as a constitutional mandate to create and apply such a standard, to guard against what has been called the "mistaken self-abnegation" that would allow the basic freedoms to be "eroded to the point where their restoration becomes impossible"?[77] The at least distinct possibility of a judicial enhancement of economic-proprietarian protective claims came in a 1992 case, closely watched by property rights advocates and the environmental community, *Lucas v. South Carolina Coastal Council.*[78] The 6:3 ruling by Justice Scalia held that South Carolina might have to compensate a person who was prevented from developing beachfront property because of environmental regulations approved by the South Carolina state legislature. Lucas had purchased the property with the reasonable expectation that it could be developed under existing state law; that, absent the state's ability to justify its actions under its laws in force at the time of Lucas's purchase in 1986, its action

---

v. James, 451 U.S. 355 (1981), which upheld (5:4) voting for directors of a public water district *restricted* to property owners. The dichotomy in the Court's now rigid "one person, one vote" approach between federal and state redistricting/reapportionment was reemphasized in two controversial 1983 holdings, both 5:4, but in opposite divisions, due to Justice O'Connor's posture: *Karcher v. Daggett,* 462 U.5. 725, where the population differential in a congressional district was *less* than seven-tenths of 1 percent from "OK" ones, and *Brown v. Thomson,* 462 U.S. 835, where the state legislative district differential was a major 89 percent (one seat to Wyoming's least populous county). But compare the Court's 9:0 ruling in 1989, declaring New York City's government, as then constituted, to violate the "one person, one vote" principle (*Board of Estimate of City of New York v. Morris,* 489 U.S. 688).

75. *Reynolds v. Sims,* 377 U.S. 533 at 562. Five other cases were decided simultaneously, all based on the same general principle, with the votes ranging from 8:1 to 6:3 (see pp. 633–713 of the opinion).

76. See Rosenberg and Rohrbacher, op. cit., *supra.*

77. Loren P. Beth, "The Case for Judicial Protection of Civil Liberties," 17 *Journal of Politics* 112 (February 1955).

78. 505 U.S. 1003.

might constitute the kind of compensable "taking" protected under the Fifth Amendment of the U.S. Constitution. Property owners were guardedly optimistic that the Lucas decision would constitute a significant step toward greater protection for them—and a chipping away at the double standard. They were encouraged further by the Court's 5:4 ruling in 1994, written by Chief Justice Rehnquist in *Dolan v. City of Tigard,*[79] overturning an Oregon Supreme Court decision that the city could condition the approval of its building permit to Ms. Dolan on the dedication of a portion of her property for flood control and traffic improvements. Seeing a "taking" protected by the Fifth Amendment to the U.S. Constitution, the chief justice, in a lengthy opinion, asserted significantly: "[W]e see no reason why the Takings Clause of the Fifth Amendment, as much a part of the Bill of Rights as the First Amendment or Fourth Amendment, should be relegated to the status of a poor relation in these comparable circumstances."[80] Businesses were further heartened by the Supreme Court's 1996 ruling in *BMW v. Gore,* where Justice Stevens, writing for a five-person majority, declared that a car owner's $2 million judgment against the Bavarian Motor Works for a flawed paint job was "grossly excessive" and violated the Constitution. Moreover, by unanimous vote in 1999 the Court ruled that landowners who sue local governments over their land-use regulations can be entitled to a jury trial.[81] And in 2001 a $5\frac{1}{2}{:}3\frac{1}{2}$ majority, albeit in a splintered decision, granted new protections to landowners who maintain that environmental regulations diminish the value of their property, ruling that government can be required to compensate them for interfering with their ability to develop their land.[82] On the other hand, a 6:3 majority rejected in 2002 the argument of a group of California property owners that governmental *freezes* on development are ipso facto tantamount to official seizures, that is, "takings." Led by Justice Stevens, the prevailing justices held that such claims must be considered case by case, balanced against other factors.[83] But the final verdict is still out on the degree of protection that the Court will afford property interests. Obviously, there is considerable room for disagreement, both in legal contemplation and in political philosophy,[84] some of which is outlined later in this chapter.

79. 512 U.S. 687.
80. Ibid.
81. *Cleveland v. Policy Management Systems Corporation,* 526 U.S. 795.
82. *Palazzolo v. Rhode Island,* 533 U.S. 606.
83. *Tahoe-Sierra Preservation Council v. Tahoe Regional Planning Agency,* 535 U.S.
___.

84. See, for example, the divergent points of view presented by Richard Funston and Henry J. Abraham in 90 *Political Science Quarterly* 2 (summer 1975), entitled, respectively, "The Double Standard of Constitutional Protection in the Era of the Welfare State" and "'Human' Rights vs. 'Property' Rights: A Comment on the 'Double Standard.'" See also the profoundly thoughtful analytical essay by Robert G. McCloskey, "Economic Due Process and the Supreme Court: An Exhumation and Reburial," in Philip B. Kurland, ed., *Supreme Court Review* (Chicago: University of Chicago Press, 1962). Also noteworthy is

A Trio of Suggested Justifications for the Double Standard

Of the numerous reasons which have been advanced in support of the double standard, three in particular have commanded potent, although not unanimous, backing.

The Crucial Nature of Basic Freedoms. As Justices Holmes, Brandeis, Cardozo, and Stone, among others, so ably demonstrated, those freedoms which can be considered basic are those upon which all other freedoms in democratic society rest. For example, when the principles of freedom of speech and press are contingent upon prior censorship, they become a mockery. When the right to worship depends upon majoritarian whims or police ordinances, it becomes meaningless. When the rights to register and vote are dependent upon the race of the applicant or the amount of his property, they become travesties of the democratic political process. To paraphrase Justice Jackson in the *West Virginia Flag Salute Case*,[85] the very purpose of the Bill of Rights was to withdraw those freedoms which can be considered basic from the "vicissitudes" of political controversy, from the grasps of majorities and public officials, and to hold them aloft as legal principles to be applied by the judiciary. Thus, such fundamental rights as freedom of expression and religion simply are not delegatable to the majority will; such economic-proprietarian problems as the rate of income tax assuredly

the clarion call for a restoration of the erstwhile judicial protection of economic-proprietarian liberties by Bernard H. Siegan in his *Economic Liberties and the Constitution* (Chicago: University of Chicago Press, 1980). He fully supports the erstwhile *Lochner* doctrine and decision on property/liberty grounds. So does Howard Gillman, but on a different rationale, in his 1994 prize-winning *The Constitution Besieged: The Rise and Demise of* Lochner *Era Police Powers Jurisprudence* (Durham, N.C.: Duke University Press). See also Leonard W. Levy's case for a judicial return to "the same constitutional respect" for property rights as is now given "to other civil or human rights so essential to the pursuit of happiness," in his "Property as a Human Right," 5 *Constitutional Commentary* 1 (winter 1988) at 184. Note, too, John Brigham's contention for the existence of a "new" proprietarian double standard in his essay "Constitutional Property: The Standard and Beyond," in Michael W. McCann and Gerald L. Houseman, eds., *Judging the Constitution: Critical Essays on Judicial Lawmaking* (Glenview, Ill.: Scott, Foresman, 1989).

And for what may arguably be viewed as amounting to a call for an "on its head" double standard, see Chief Justice Rehnquist's opinion for the Court in *Payne v. Tennessee*, 501 U.S. 808 (1991). There, joined by four other justices, he provided a blueprint for a new approach in cases involving economic doctrine in terms of the application of stare decisis: in them, he wrote, the obligation to adhere to precedent should be at its "acme" because people need stability to plan their business affairs involving, for example, "property and contract rights," whereas the same test should not govern in criminal cases involving "procedural and evidentiary rules." For an excellent overview, entitled "The Rehnquist Court and Economic Rights: A Revival of Economic Due Process," see Tinsley E. Yarbrough's paper presented at the annual meeting of the Southern Political Science Association, Tampa, Fla., November 2–4, 1995.

85. *West Virginia State Board of Education v. Barnette,* 319 U.S. 624 (1943).

are. As Justice Stone put it in a memorable dissenting opinion less than three years following his Footnote Four in *Carolene:*

> The very fact that we have constitutional guarantees of civil liberties and the specificity of their command where freedom of speech and religion are concerned require some accommodation of the powers which government normally exercises, when no question of civil liberty is involved, to the constitutional demand that these liberties be protected against the action of government itself. . . . The Constitution expresses more than the conviction of the people that democratic processes must be preserved at all costs. It also is an expression of faith and a command that freedom of mind and spirit must be preserved, which government must obey, if it is to adhere to that justice and moderation without which no free government can exist.[86]

Thus embracing a demonstrable change in its own scale of jurisprudential values, it fell to the post-1937 Court to recognize and attempt to preserve those freedoms which are deemed basic or crucial to the democratic process. And to achieve this, the Court has moved to apply the double standard to them when the other branches of government have either consciously or unconsciously failed to heed or comprehend the essence of Stone's admonition—as perceived by a majority of its membership.

A sophisticated, complex, and original defense-cum-contribution for the partial justification under this first rubric of *a,* but not necessarily *the,* double standard assessed herein is John Hart Ely's influential *Democracy and Distrust: A Theory of Judicial Review.*[87] Seminal to his theory is his exhortation for a *process*-oriented jurisprudence (which he saw in much of what the Warren Court did, e.g., in the legislative apportionment "one person, one vote" cases) but against a value-imposing one, such as that manifested by an earlier Court in *Lochner v. New York*[88] and by the Burger Court in the contentious abortion cases of *Roe v. Wade* and *Doe v. Bolton.*[89] He sternly rejects judicial intervention for both. Thus, while applauding as the essence of judicial review the Warren Court's safeguarding of the basic processes of democracy and its preservation of minority rights as part of that process, he is critical of what he perceived as the Court's, as well as others', notion that its justices had a better understanding of or handle on attitudes commonly held by the body politic.

The Explicit Language of the Bill of Rights. An excellent case can be made for the viability of the double standard simply based upon the very language of the

---

86. *Minersville School District v. Gobitis,* 310 U.S. 586 (1940) at 602–3, 606–7.
87. (Cambridge, Mass.: Harvard University Press, 1980).
88. 418 U.S. 445 (1905).
89. 410 U.S. 113 and 410 U.S. 179 (1973), respectively.

Bill of Rights (most of which, as we shall see,[90] has been made applicable to the several states by way of the "due process of law" clause of the Fourteenth Amendment). The economic-proprietarian safeguards of the Bill of Rights are couched in the most general of terms: the command of the Fifth and Fourteenth Amendments that no person "be deprived of life, liberty, or *property, without due process of law*" raises more questions than it settles. Certainly the Founding Fathers did not specify what they meant by "property" except that one should not be "deprived" of it without "due process of law." As already noted, during the fifty years prior to 1937 the Court interpreted the clause so stringently that legislative efforts in the economic-proprietarian sphere were all but futile. To do so the Court had to read into the language of the "due process" clauses concepts that *may* have been implicit but were certainly not explicit. On the other hand, the language governing what we commonly regard as our basic human freedoms is not only explicit, it is categorical. Madison's terminology for the First Amendment is precise:

> Congress shall make no law respecting an establishment of religion, or prohibiting the free exercise thereof; or abridging the freedom of speech, or of the press; or the right of the people peaceably to assemble, and to petition the government for redress of grievances.

Succeeding amendments in the Bill of Rights, such as those embodied in Amendments Four, Five, and Six, refer specifically to a host of other basic rights as well, be they substantive or procedural. That their interpretation has proved difficult and troublesome over the years does not, however, invalidate their explicitness, and it is their explicitness that makes a strong case for invocation of the double standard.[91]

Yet an acceptance of the double standard does not necessarily mean embracing the "literalism" of Justice Black, whose support of the doctrine was grounded on the Constitution's *verbiage*. If he found it spelled out, it became an *absolute,* which, by definition, places him in the camp of those who see a double standard, although he steadfastly refused to accept the slogan. To him it was the explicitness of the language, its categoricalness, that is decisive. Thus, his firm contention, re-

---

90. See *infra* chapter 3.

91. In Justice Black's always eminently quotable exhortation, "I think that state regulations [of economic affairs] should be viewed quite differently than where it [*sic*] touches or involves freedom of speech, press, religion, assembly, *or other specific safeguards of the Bill of Rights.* It is the duty of this Court to be alert to see that these *constitutionally preferred rights* are not abridged" (dissenting opinion in *Morey v. Doud,* 354 U.S. 457 [1957] at 471; italics supplied). See Archibald Cox, *The Role of the Supreme Court in American Government* (New York: Oxford University Press, 1976), p. 51, for another illustration for support of the dichotomy.

iterated throughout his long career on the high bench,[92] that when the First Amendment says "Congress *shall make no law . . . abridging* the freedom of speech, or of the press," it means just that: no law! It most emphatically does not mean, for example, "no law except such as may be necessary to prevent the viewing of obscene movies," or "no law except what may be needed to curb seditious utterances," or "no law except one to punish libel and slander." As he put it in a famous article:

> Some people regard the prohibitions of the Constitution, even its most unequivocal commands, as mere admonitions which Congress [and, by implication, the states] need not always observe . . . formulations [that] rest, at least in part, on the premise that there are no "absolute" prohibitions in the Constitution, and that all constitutional problems are questions of reasonableness, proximity, and degree. . . .
>
> I cannot accept this approach to the Bill of Rights. It is my belief that there *are* "absolutes" in our Bill of Rights, and they were put there on purpose by men who knew what words meant, and meant their prohibitions to be "absolutes." . . . I am primarily discussing here whether liberties *admittedly* covered by the Bill of Rights can nevertheless be abridged on the ground that a superior public interest justifies the abridgement. I think the Bill of Rights made its safeguard superior.[93]

And later, discussing the First Amendment, which was to him "the heart of our Bill of Rights, our Constitution, and our nation," Black wrote: "The phrase 'Congress shall make no law' is composed of plain words, easily understood. . . . Neither as offered nor as adopted is the language of this Amendment anything less than absolute. . . ."[94] Whether or not one agrees with Black's "absolutist" thesis—and a good many observers, of course, do not[95]—it nonetheless lends strong support to the argument for the existence of a hierarchy of values and the prior-

92. Hugo L. Black, "The Bill of Rights," 35 *New York University Law Review* 866 (April 1960). See also his "follow-up" article in 37 *New York University Law Review* 569 two years later; his March 1968 Carpentier Lee Lectures; his famed TV interview with reporters Eric Sevareid and Martin Agronsky in December 1968; and his definitive book, based on the Carpentier Lee Lectures, *A Constitutional Faith* (New York: Knopf, 1968). "Thus it is *language and history,*" he wrote in the latter, "that are the crucial factors that influence me in the interpretation of the Constitution—not reasonableness or desirability as determined by the Justices of the Supreme Court" (at p. 8; italics supplied). He died on September 25, 1971, having served more than thirty-four years.

93. "The Bill of Rights," op. cit., at 866–67.

94. See especially his *A Constitutional Faith,* op. cit., particularly chapter 3, "The First Amendment," pp. 43ff. See also "The Bill of Rights," op. cit., at 874. For a superb study of Black's absolutism, see James J. Magee, *Mr. Justice Black: Absolutist on the Court* (Charlottesville: University Press of Virginia, 1980).

95. E.g., Leonard W. Levy, *Freedom of Speech and Press in Early American History: Legacy of Suppression* (New York: Harper and Row, 1963), p. xxi; Harry M. Clor, *Ob-*

ity within that hierarchy of those liberties specifically listed in the Bill of Rights. Even Justice Frankfurter, who rejected absolutism as well as any formula such as the double standard, declared in a significant opinion that matters like press censorship and separation of church and state are different from economic policy matters because "history, through the Constitution, speaks so decisively as to forbid legislative experimentation" with them.[96]

The Appropriate Expertise of the Judiciary. If one accepts the first two reasons in support of the double standard, a third follows quite logically: no other agency or institution of the United States government has proved itself either so capable of performing, or so willing to undertake, the necessary role of guardian of our basic rights as the judicial branch. Since the legislative and executive branches, for reasons inherent in our political system, have failed to fulfill this role adequately, it has fallen to the judiciary. And it is a role procedurally enhanced by the Supreme Court's all but absolute prerogative of determining the kind of cases that will reach its docket—which thus enables it to concentrate on articulating the libertarian realm. As Robert H. Jackson, who came to the Supreme Court from prominent service in the executive branch, observed: "The people have seemed to feel that the Supreme Court, whatever its defects, is still the most detached, dispassionate, and trustworthy custodian that our system affords for the translation of abstract into concrete constitutional commands."[97] With these words he echoed James Madison, who, in presenting the original Bill of Rights to Congress in 1789, remarked:

> If they are incorporated into the Constitution, independent tribunals of justice will consider themselves in a peculiar manner the guardians of those rights; they will be an impenetrable bulwark against every assumption of power in the legislative or executive; they will be naturally led to resist every encroachment upon rights expressly stipulated for in the Constitution by the declaration of rights.[98]

scenity and Public Morality: Censorship in a Liberal Society (Chicago: University of Chicago Press, 1969), p. 89; and Walter F. Berns, The First Amendment and the Future of American Democracy (New York: Basic Books, 1977).

96. American Federation of Labor v. American Sash and Door Co., 335 U.S. 538 (1949) at 550. For a fine, perceptive, evaluative biographical essay on Felix Frankfurter, see Joseph P. Lash, From the Diaries of Felix Frankfurter (New York: Norton, 1975). See also Michael E. Parrish, Felix Frankfurter and His Times (New York: Free Press, 1982).

97. The Supreme Court in the American System of Government (Cambridge, Mass.: Harvard University Press, 1955), p. 23. Designed as the Godkin Lectures at Harvard University, the book was edited and published with the aid of Jackson's son after his father's death of a heart attack shortly before he was to deliver the lectures—a task then assumed by the son.

98. Annals of Congress, 1st Cong., 1st sess., June 8, 1789 (Washington, D.C., 1834), vol. 1, p. 457.

Yet if the Supreme Court is indeed the appropriate governmental agency to buttress and safeguard our fundamental rights, few would seriously contend that, in equal measure, its province is to rule on the validity of economic legislation and administration. Because of its insufficient expertise and its crowded docket, the Court is not prepared to make the kind of economic judgments that would veto legislative actions and intent. It is the people's representatives who are best qualified to give expression to the requirements of economic life, to the experimentation and resolution that go into public planning. "We refuse to sit as a 'superlegislature,'" as Justice Black once noted, "to weigh the wisdom of legislation. . . . Whether the legislature takes for its textbook Adam Smith, Herbert Spencer, Lord Keynes, or some other is no concern of ours."[99] Or, in the words of then Associate Justice Abe Fortas: "The courts may be the principal guardians of the liberties of our people. They are not the chief administrators of its economic destiny."[100] Or, as Justice Stewart suggested in a later case, in which the Court refused to extend the "strict scrutiny" of the "new" equal protection concepts to state welfare programs, "the intractable economic, social, and even philosophical problems presented by public welfare assistance programs are not the business of this Court."[101]

Here, then, judicial self-restraint and the assumption of legislative know-how and representativeness are in philosophical accord—and it is here that the double standard thus finds perhaps its clearest justification. Few have stated this distinction as well as Justice Oliver Wendell Holmes Jr., who was no personal friend of legislative "fooling around" with "economic do-gooding." But he was a jurist who believed resolutely—although he was often alone and practically never carried the Court with him on that issue—that under a democratic government the people have every right to experiment legislatively with their economic fate, even if he personally were to consider their action ignorant. As he said to his colleague Stone, after more than a half century on the Supreme Courts of Massachusetts and the United States, and at the age of ninety:

> Young man [Stone was then sixty], about seventy-five years ago I learned that I was not God. And so, when the people want to do something [in the realm of economic legislation] I can't find anything in the Constitution expressly forbidding them to do, I say, whether I like it or not, "Goddamit, let 'em do it."[102]

Holmes expressed the same judicial posture more specifically to John W. Davis, the unsuccessful Democratic nominee for the presidency in 1924, sometime U.S.

---

99. *Ferguson v. Skrupa,* 372 U.S. 726 (1963) at 730.
100. *Baltimore and Ohio Railroad Co. v. United States,* 386 U.S. 372 (1967) at 471.
101. Opinion for the Court in *Dandridge v. Williams,* 397 U.S. 471 (1970) at 487.
102. As quoted by Charles P. Curtis in *Lions Under the Throne* (Boston: Houghton Mifflin, 1947), p. 281.

solicitor general, and famed corporate attorney: "Of course, I know, and every other sensible man knows, that the Sherman Law [Anti-Trust Act of 1890] is damned nonsense, but if my country wants to go to hell, I am here to help it."[103] Yet, for the First Amendment liberties, Holmes rejected this "pure democracy" approach. He was convinced that the Constitution neither provided nor intended the luxury of such risk in that sphere. Whereas property, to him, was "social" in origin, civil liberties were "human." In full concord with such post-1916 allies as Justices John H. Clarke, Brandeis, Stone, and, on occasion, Hughes,[104] he simply did not consider the average American citizen "very enlightened"—to employ Justice Jackson's phrase—on the subject of civil rights and liberties. Hence Holmes suggested that judges "should not be too rigidly bound to the tenets of judicial self-restraint in cases involving civil liberties."[105] Or, as New York State Supreme Court Justice Samuel Hofstadter put the general issue, "If a judge loses his capacity for indignation in the presence of injustice, he may not be less of a judge, but he is less of a man."[106]

The above-suggested trio[107] of justifications, considered separately and together, suggests a prima facie case for the existence of the judicial double stan-

103. As related by Francis Biddle in *Justice Holmes, Natural Law, and the Supreme Court* (New York: Macmillan, 1961), p. 9.

104. Holmes served on the Court from 1902 to 1932; Clarke, from 1916 to 1922; Brandeis, from 1916 to 1939; Stone, from 1925 to 1946 (the last five years as chief justice); and Hughes, from 1910 to 1916 (associate justice) and again from 1930 to 1941 (as chief justice). See Appendix A.

105. As asserted by Chief Justice Stone in a letter to Clinton Rossiter, April 12, 1941, and noted by Alpheus T. Mason in his *Harlan Fiske Stone: Pillar of Law* (New York: Viking, 1956), p. 516.

106. Obituary, *New York Times,* July 12, 1970, p. 65L.

107. Several earlier editions of this book (1967, 1972, 1977, and 1982) all argued—albeit in terms of decreasing conviction—for the existence of a *fourth* justification for the application by the judiciary of the described double standard, namely, the discrepancy in readily available and effective access to the judicial process, especially to the appellate levels, between economic-proprietarian and civil rights—civil liberties interests, be they on an individual or group level. If, as is patently demonstrable, that was indeed the case throughout the history of our judicial process, it is assuredly no longer the case. The post–World War II receptiveness by the judiciary to the docketing of allegations of denial of civil rights and liberties—which began to see its day in court under the chief justiceship of Fred M. Vinson (1946–53), came into full bloom during that of Earl Warren (1953–69) and has become a widely presumed quasi entitlement—is proof positive of the now well-established ability of once-encumbered individuals and groups to be heard at the bar of the courts. This does not, of course, mean that a du Pont firm might not have more financial and personnel clout in fielding legal talent facilely than, say, a member of the Jehovah's Witnesses. But if help is needed, it is now clearly available: the plethora of libertarian activist interest groups; public interest attorneys; public defenders; congressionally funded legal aid; and a generally more sympathetic and receptive judiciary have all combined to render unrealistic, indeed inaccurate, a continuing claim for the existence of that fourth factor—although it may command resuscitation.

dard. In purely academic terms, the double standard may be neither morally nor logically convincing, and it raises very serious, indeed fundamental, questions about the nature of judicial power and that of the judicial process under the American system. Thus veteran constitutional law expert Gerald Gunther wisely asks, can the different standards of review really "be justified because of an inherent difference in the 'fundamentalness' of economic right, and other personal rights?" Furthermore, "are the 'social' and even 'philosophical' problems truly less intractable in the modern areas of intervention?" Is it really true that "protection of property and economic interest have less textual and historical basis than protection of other interests?"[108] Alexander M. Bickel pondered the issue in his book *The Supreme Court and the Idea of Progress:* Holmes believed that Brandeis was convinced that the best defense "for leaving fundamental responsibilities to this Court" was that constitutional restrictions enabled minorities to get an untroubled night's sleep. And the best defense for not leaving fundamental responsibilities to the Court is that the political process should rule.[109] Yet, *pace* these fundamental and haunting doubts, the double standard, as it is now in place, does stand as a practical recognition of one of that system's crucial and realistic facets of government and politics under law. Within often ill-defined limits, the case for the special protection of civil rights and liberties is strong.

Granting the strength of the case, however, by no means vitiates the presence of some troubling questions, among which the following are both typical and sensitive:

1. Given the Court's recent modifications of the double standard,[110] how will additional lines be drawn?
2. What are the factors that influence further line drawing, and what issues will be considered likely targets?
3. What compels line drawing in each instance? Is it judicial philosophy, the quest for justice, the democratic ethos, personality, political or social pressures?
4. Has the Court favored certain civil liberties more than others, and why, thereby further defining or confusing the double standard as it draws new lines? What determines how finely these lines will be drawn?
5. What are the current motivations behind contemporary line drawing, and have they changed since the double standard was created?

The chapters that follow deal with some of these fundamental, haunting questions.

---

108. *Cases and Materials on Individual Rights in Constitutional Law*, 3d ed. (Mineola, N.Y.: Foundation Press, 1981), pp. 161–62.

109. (New York: Harper and Row, 1970), p. 37.

110. For an insightful critique of the ramifications of returning to pre-1937 jurisprudence, see Tinsley E. Yarbrough's *The Rehnquist Court and the Constitution* (New York: Oxford University Press, 2000), chapter 4, "The Double Standard."

3

The Bill of Rights and Its Applicability to the States

HISTORICAL BACKGROUND

The applicability of the Bill of Rights to the several states is an intriguing question laced with some fascinating constitutional and political history. The English common law, colonial charters, legislative enactments, and a variety of events in the thirteen colonies were the chief elements contributing to the basic rationale for a Bill of Rights. But to create the latter was far from the presumably facile task viewed by some rather naively as all but unanimously preordained. Much opposition abounded, largely based on the belief by a good many that a Bill of Rights was simply unnecessary, that the states, after all, had their own bills of rights, and that the body of the Constitution, as it finally surfaced at the September 17, 1787, conclusion of the Constitutional Convention's deliberations, contained ample safeguards against national (federal) mischief. Yet, ultimately persuaded by that trio of noble Virginians, Messrs. Jefferson, Madison, and Mason—the first two named had first to convince themselves of its wisdom while Mason never had any doubt of its need—what we know today as our 462-word Bill of Rights, comprising the first eight articles of amendment to the basic document (or ten, to some who prefer to include Amendments Nine and Ten), was born and submitted to the First Congress for its approval in April 1789, with the young but politically savvy Madison as its floor manager.[1] Congress eventually sent twelve amendments to the states for ratification as the Bill of Rights, but two failed to be adopted (one calling for apportionment of legislators, the other dealing with the pay of members of Congress).

---

1. See the vivid study by Robert A. Rutland, *The Birth of the Bill of Rights, 1776–1791*, 3d ed. (Boston: Northeastern University Press, 1991).

33

Fully alive now to the need for its approval, Mr. Jefferson had written to Mr. Madison on March 15, 1789, that "[t]he Bill of Rights is necessary because of the legal check which it puts into the hands of the judiciary." What he meant was a legal check against the *national* government—he was not worried greatly about the states, since they had their own bills of rights, restrictions that the framers considered comfortably satisfactory. The central government, however, was a different matter, and there is simply no doubt whatever that the overriding reason for the Virginians' authorship and sponsorship of the federal Bill of Rights was to place demonstrably far-reaching restraints on the fledgling central government. Indeed, the very first phrase of Article 1 of the approximately twenty-five assorted rights to be found in the Bill of Rights reads: "*Congress* shall make no law. . . ." Although the noun "Congress" reappears nowhere in the remainder of the eight articles that constitute the document at issue, the latter was unquestionably intended to be applicable against the national government only. Certainly that was the understanding with which the eleven states ratified the Bill of Rights—although Madison would soon come to believe that, once having become the law of the land, it ought to be applied against the states as well as against the national government. James Madison would quickly be joined by elements of the propertied community who advanced similar contentions. But, and one might well say appropriately, it would fall to our fourth chief justice, another renowned Virginian, John Marshall,[2] to be the first to adjudicate the question when, in 1833, in his thirty-third year on the Court, he authored the Court's landmark opinion in *Barron v. Baltimore*.[3] As was the case with the vast majority of the great nationalist's plethora of opinions, he spoke for a unanimous tribunal.

Mr. Chief Justice Marshall and Barron's Wharf. The basis for the litigation in *Barron v. Baltimore* was laid when the city of Baltimore, Maryland, began to pave some of its streets. In so doing its engineers found it necessary to divert several streams from their natural courses; near one, Barron's Wharf, this diversion resulted in deposits of gravel and sand which filled up the channel and prevented the approach of vessels. John Barron's fine wharf, previously the one with the deepest water in the harbor, was thus turned into little more than a useless inlet. Not amused, Mr. Barron obtained eminent legal counsel and went to court. He alleged that Baltimore's actions had violated that clause of the Fifth Amendment of the United States Constitution which expressly proscribes the taking of private property "for public use without just compensation." Although Barron won his argument at the level of the trial court, which awarded him $4,500 in damages, his joy was short-lived. Baltimore appealed the verdict to the Maryland State Court of Appeals, which reversed the decision. The un-

2. For an excellent biography of Marshall as chief justice, see Albert J. Beveridge, *The Life of John Marshall,* 4 vols. (Boston: Houghton Mifflin, 1919).
3. 7 Peters 243 (1833).

happy Barron then appealed his case to the United States Supreme Court on a writ of error.[4]

Marshall announced that "the question thus presented is, we think, of great importance, but not of much difficulty."[5] In a handful of pages he demolished Barron's fundamental contention that whatever is forbidden by the terms of the Fifth Amendment to the national government is also forbidden to the states, and that the Court therefore has an obligation to construe the Fifth Amendment's "guarantee in behalf of individual liberty" as a restraint upon *both* state and national governments. The chief justice's response was phrased in historical and constitutional terms:

> The Constitution was ordained and established by the people of the United States for themselves, for their own government, and not for the Government of the individual States. Each State established a Constitution for itself, and, in that Constitution, provided such limitations and restrictions on the powers of its particular government as its judgment indicated. The people of the United States framed such a government for the United States as they supposed best adapted to their situation, and best calculated to promote their interests. The powers they conferred on the government were to be exercised by itself; and the limitations on power, if expressed in general terms, are naturally, and, we think, necessarily applicable to the government created by the instrument. They are limitations of power granted in the instrument itself; not of distinct governments, framed by different persons and for different purposes.
>
> If these propositions be correct, the fifth amendment must be understood as restraining the power of the general government, not as applicable to the States. In their several constitutions they have imposed such restrictions on their respective governments as their own wisdom suggested, such as they deemed most proper for themselves. It is a subject on which they judge exclusively, and with which others interfere no further than they are supposed to have a common interest. . . .
>
> These statements [the Bill of Rights] contain no expression indicating an intention to apply them to the state governments. This court cannot so apply them. . . .
>
> This court . . . has no jurisdiction of the cause; and [it] is dismissed.[6]

Marshall had spoken, Barron had lost, and the Court's unanimous opinion that there was "no repugnancy between the several acts of the general assembly of

---

4. A discontinued writ. It served to bring the entire record of a case proceeding in a lower court before the Supreme Court for its consideration for alleged "errors of law" committed below.

5. *Barron v. Baltimore,* op. cit., at 247. It was the last constitutional law decision in which the great chief justice participated.

6. Ibid. at 247–48, 250, 251.

Maryland . . . and the Constitution of the United States"[7] became the law of the land. Citizens like Barron were destined to have no further recourse until the ratification in 1868 of the Fourteenth Amendment, probably the most controversial and certainly the most litigated of all amendments adopted since the birth of the Republic.

THE FOURTEENTH AMENDMENT

The Fourteenth Amendment[8] did not in and of itself overturn the *Barron* precedent: lively disagreement continues over the purpose of the framers of the amendment and the extent of its intended application, if any, to the several states. But certain evidence does exist and merits close examination.

Some Historical Facts. The *facts* surrounding the proposal and passage of the Fourteenth Amendment in the Thirty-ninth Congress (1865–67)—led by the Radical Republicans and their Committee of Fifteen[9]—are fewer than the resultant conjectures and analyses. We do know, however, that (1) the 52 U.S. senators (42 Republicans and 10 Democrats) and 191 representatives (145 Republicans and 46 Democrats) wanted to do something to ameliorate the lot of blacks; (2) de minimis, they intended to embody the provisions of the Civil Rights Act of 1866, forbidding "discrimination in civil rights or immunities . . . on account of race" in the amendment—although *political* rights (including jury service, for example) were excluded from that understanding; for "civil rights" were designed to relate to personal security and personal property only; (3) at least to some extent they were concerned with civil rights generally; and (4) they were interested in extending increased protection to personal property and personal security as well as to human rights.[10] We also know that (5) the amendment was intended to remedy the lack of a "citizenship" clause in the original Constitution—and the initial sentence of the first of its five sections makes this

7. Ibid. at 251.

8. For a collection of fine essays, including one by Chief Justice Warren, commemorating the amendment's centennial in 1968, see Bernard Schwartz, ed., *The Fourteenth Amendment: Centennial Volume* (New York: New York University Press, 1970).

9. Composed of twelve Republicans and three Democrats, it consisted of nine U.S. representatives and six U.S. senators, under the chairmanship of Republican Senator William Fessenden of Maine. It was essentially the congressional "policy committee," whose real leaders comprised four Radical Republicans: Representatives Thaddeus Stevens of Pennsylvania and John A. Bingham of Ohio, and Senators Jacob Howard of Michigan and Lyman Trumbull of Illinois.

10. Historians now generally agree that the word *person* instead of *citizen* was adopted by the Drafting Committee in the due process and equal protection clauses to extend protection to corporations as well as human beings. The Supreme Court officially adopted this point of view in 1886 in *Santa Clara County v. Southern Pacific Railroad,* 118 U.S. 394.

clear: "All persons born or naturalized in the United States, and subject to the jurisdiction thereof, are citizens of the United States and of the State wherein they reside." This, of course, would include blacks. We further know (6) from the language of the fifth and last section that there was some intention to provide Congress with the necessary power, if not the tools, to enforce the provisions of the amendment: "The Congress shall have power to enforce, by *appropriate legislation,* the provisions of this article."[11] We also know that (7) unlike the "privileges or immunities" and "due process of law" clauses, the "equal protection of the laws" clause of the amendment had no antecedent meaning but originated in the committee that drafted it—which could hardly have foreseen its subsequent controversial history and judicial application. And, finally, we know that (8) with respect to the matter of the reach of the Bill of Rights, both the heart and the greatest source of confusion and controversy of the famed amendment is the well-known phrasing of the second, lengthy sentence of Section 1, which was briefly composed by Republican Representative John A. Bingham of Ohio:

No State shall make or enforce any law which shall abridge the privileges or immunities of citizens of the United States; *nor shall any State deprive any person of life, liberty, or property, without due process of law;* nor deny to any person within its jurisdiction its equal protection of the laws.[12]

There is no disagreement that the italicized portion of the Fourteenth Amendment, which was lifted verbatim from the language of the Fifth Amendment, thus was intended to provide guarantees against *state* infringement supplemental to the Fifth's mandate against federal infringement. What does cause major disagreement, however, can be illustrated by two questions: First, *did* the framers of the amendment intend to "incorporate" or "nationalize" or "carry over" the *entire* Bill of Rights through the wording of its due process of law clause, thereby

---

11. In part thanks to this provision (italics supplied) and, by implication, to the almost identically worded Section 2 of Amendment Fifteen, Congress found authority to enact certain sections of the landmark Civil Rights Act of 1964. One of its most significant sections, that dealing with discrimination in public accommodations, was passed under the congressional power over interstate commerce and was specifically upheld by the U.S. Supreme Court in December 1964 (see *Heart of Atlanta Motel v. United States,* 379 U.S. 241; and *Katzenbach v. McClung,* 379 U.S. 294). Congress also utilized the "appropriate legislation" section of the Fifteenth Amendment to enact portions of the Voting Rights Act of 1965, which met and withstood two constitutional challenges in 1966 on the strength of the section's wording and intent (see *South Carolina v. Katzenbach,* 383 U.S. 301; and *Katzenbach v. Morgan,* 384 U.S. 641). The 1970 amendment lowering the voting age to eighteen was upheld as to federal elections but struck down as to state and local elections in a five-opinion, 184-page decision in *Oregon v. Mitchell,* 400 U.S. 112 (1970). The Twenty-sixth Amendment resulted as a direct consequence.
    12. Italics supplied.

making it applicable to the several states;[13] and, second, regardless of their intention, *should* the Bill of Rights be applied to the states, given the nature of the rights involved and the demands of the democratic society in which we live?

The Intention of the Framers. The Fourteenth Amendment was passed by Congress on June 16, 1866, ratified by the required three-fourths of the states—ten of these then being Southern Reconstruction governments under duress[14]—and was proclaimed in effect on July 28, 1866. The amendment had significant political overtones, for it was the key plank of the first Reconstruction platform drafted by the Radical Republicans, led by Thaddeus Stevens of Pennsylvania,

13. We realize that to use the terms "incorporation," "nationalization," "application," "carrying over," and "absorption" more or less synonymously and interchangeably is heresy to a good many members of the legal and academic community, if indeed it is not regarded as simply wrong. With all due respect and deference to those who do distinguish between these terms both literally and substantively (see, e.g., Justice Frankfurter's important "Memorandum" described *infra*) the basic issue involved clearly comes down to the answer to the following crucial question: Is a certain provision in the federal Constitution, is a specific right enumerated in the federal Bill of Rights, applicable to the states via the due process clause of the Fourteenth Amendment, or is it not applicable? If it is held to be so applicable by the judiciary, then it is "incorporated," "nationalized," "carried over," "applied," or "absorbed." To the affected litigants it does not matter what the process is called—what matters is whether or not it signifies state acquiescence with federal standards. This is not to say, of course, that we do not recognize basic historical and linguistic distinctions between the concepts of "incorporation" and "absorption," for example; and we have been fascinated and intrigued by the long-standing controversies that have engulfed them. But, given the judicio-legal developments of the past three or four decades—for example, the 1965 decision in the *Connecticut Birth Control Case (Griswold v. Connecticut,* 381 U.S. 479, discussed at length *infra*)—the distinctions are blurred. What matters constitutionally, to repeat, is whether a federal provision or standard, as interpreted and declared by the Court, does or does not apply to the states.

14. By March 1, 1867, there were thirty-seven states in the Union, including those of the old Confederacy. This meant that twenty-eight would have to ratify the amendment to bring it into effect. But by that time only twenty states had ratified, among them Tennessee as the sole southern state. Consequently, the congressional Radicals passed a law which in fact put the southern states on notice that they would not be readmitted to the Union "officially" unless they (1) ratified the Fourteenth Amendment and (2) extended the vote to adult males "of whatever race, color, or previous condition." This resulted in action by a sufficient number of southern states, where federal troops still attested to the Reconstruction era. President Johnson vetoed the act, but Congress passed it over his veto. The law accomplished its purpose: between April and July 1868 the legislatures of Arkansas, Florida, North Carolina, Louisiana, South Carolina, Alabama, and Georgia acquiesced, and the necessary figure (twenty-eight) had been attained. (Actually, in the interim New Jersey and Ohio had withdrawn their earlier ratifications—something they might no longer be able to do today, given the implications of the Supreme Court's 1939 decision in *Coleman v. Miller,* 307 U.S. 433—but Massachusetts, Nebraska, and Iowa had come aboard. Moreover, the secretary of state disregarded the former two states' withdrawal votes and proclaimed the amendment in effect, with Congress supporting his action by adopting a concurrent resolution to that effect.)

Roscoe Conkling of New York, and George Boutwell of Massachusetts. Indeed, the amendment's passage by Congress in June 1866 provided the Radical Republicans with a welcome, ready-made campaign issue for the November 1866 election campaigns. Attention directed to the amendment was almost wholly concerned with the political implications of bestowing full citizenship upon blacks. But there is no record of any campaign discussion or analysis of the matter of the application of the Bill of Rights to the states via its due process of law or any other clause. There was much talk of the amendment giving teeth to the Thirteenth Amendment and securing the "fundamental rights and fundamental freedoms of all men."[15]

In the face of the many disagreements on the "intent" of the framers, some argue that their intent no longer matters, for the "felt necessities of the time" (Justice Holmes's celebrated phrase) and the inevitable growth of the Constitution may a fortiorari dictate the application of the Bill of Rights to the several states regardless of the framers' intention. However, since it is preferable to have historical data to back one's contentions, both the proponents and opponents of total or even partial incorporation continue to invoke history. A great deal of published research on historical justification is available, yet there is no conclusive answer, for the evidence is not persuasive. Originally, those opposing the incorporation interpretation enjoyed a slight edge. Briefly, they contended that had the framers of the Fourteenth Amendment intended to "incorporate" or "carry over" or "nationalize" the Bill of Rights to the states, they would have spelled it out specifically rather than employ the general language of the due process of law clause. The proponents, on the other hand, argued and continue to argue that the famous clause was adopted as "shorthand" for the Bill of Rights, and that the framers utilized it both to broaden and to strengthen fundamental guarantees of rights and liberties. It is still possible to emerge with diverse conclusions, particularly in the light of the lengthy and heated congressional debates on the subject. What is certain is that since the Supreme Court first "incorporated" aspects of the Bill of Rights in 1925,[16] the process has been sporadic; it proved to be increasingly embracing as well as continuous over the next four decades—although it may well now have run its course.

Some Protagonists. The earliest spokesman for total incorporation of the Bill of Rights was Justice John Marshall Harlan (1877–1911), but his was a lonely voice. In his thirty-four-year career on the highest bench,[17] Harlan time and again unsuc-

---

15. The quotation is from a speech by Representative Lyman Trumbull of Illinois.

16. See text, this chapter, *infra* note 20, relative to the one earlier (1897) incorporation, namely, of *eminent domain* guarantees.

17. Harlan served longer than any other except Justice William O. Douglas (1939–75), Justice Stephen J. Field (1863–97), Chief Justice Marshall (1801–35), and Justice Black (1937–71).

cessfully championed that interpretation.[18] He was not even partially vindicated until 1925, when Justice Edward T. Sanford delivered his dictum in *Gitlow v. New York*,[19] albeit a case arguably could be made for the contention that the concept of *eminent domain* was applied formally to the states via Amendment Fourteen in a Harlan opinion in 1897.[20] And as late as 1947, in the famous *Adamson* case,[21] Justice Frankfurter rejected the concept of incorporation as one manufactured out of whole cloth. Both the concept itself and the term "incorporation" were anathema to him. Indeed, his last publication before his death in 1965 was an attack on "incorporation" and a defense of "absorption."[22] As he put it in a well-known passage:

> Of all these [43] judges [of the Supreme Court who passed on the question of incorporating the Bill of Rights via the "due process of law" clause of Amendment Fourteen] only one, *who may respectfully be called an eccentric exception,* ever indicated the belief that the Fourteenth Amendment was a shorthand summary of the first eight Amendments theretofore limiting only the Federal Government, and that due process incorporated those eight Amendments as restriction upon the powers of the States.[23]

The "eccentric exception" was, of course, Harlan—whose grandson by the same name became a Frankfurter ally on the incorporation question when he joined the Court as President Eisenhower's second appointee in 1955.[24]

18. See, e.g., his solo dissenting opinions in *Hurtado v. California,* 110 U.S. 516 (1884); *Maxwell v. Dow,* 176 U.S. 581 (1900); and *Twining v. New Jersey,* 211 U.S. 78 (1908). There were several others—he was a consistent advocate. See Henry J. Abraham, "John Marshall Harlan: The Justice and the Man," 46 *Kentucky Law Journal* 448 (Spring 1958), esp. pp. 469–70.

19. 268 U.S. 652. Gitlow lost, but the carryover principle was given its first public judicial notice. See later discussions.

20. *Chicago, Burlington and Quincy Railroad v. Chicago,* 166 U.S. 226. Yet in Footnote Four of his landmark *Palko* decision (see *infra*) Justice Cardozo suggested that its inclusion—like that of others—was due *not* to its enumeration in the Bill of Rights but because it is "included in the conception of due process of law." However that may be, some observers, including Justice Tom Clark, concluded that, in effect, the Harlan opinion in *Chicago, Burlington* "completely undermined" *Hurtado v. California,* 110 U.S. 516 (1884), although clearly not overruling it, and thus "laid the basis for *Gitlow v. New York.*" Yet while that was important, it was not the gravamen of the Court's intention: its overarching concern lay with the strengthening of the constitutional protection of property rights.

21. *Adamson v. California,* 332 U.S. 46 (1947).

22. "Memorandum on 'Incorporation' of the Bill of Rights into the Due Process Clause of the Fourteenth Amendment," 78 *Harvard Law Review* 746 (1965). For a highly contentious specific example of Frankfurter's perception of the issue, see William M. Wiecek, "Felix Frankfurter, Incorporation, and the Willie Francis Case," 26 *Journal of Supreme Court History* 53 (2001).

23. *Adamson v. California,* op. cit., at 62; italics supplied.

24. Eisenhower's first appointee was Earl Warren to succeed the deceased Chief Justice Fred M. Vinson in 1953.

Adamson v. California. It was Justice Black who became the leading proponent of incorporation—and he seized upon the aforementioned case of *Adamson v. California* to expound his views. At issue, briefly, was a provision of
California law that permitted court and counsel to comment upon the failure
of a defendant to explain or deny evidence against him, thus allowing the court
and the jury to consider it in reaching a verdict. Admiral Dewey Adamson,
who faced a sentence of death for first-degree and burglary murder, and who
had a record of convictions for burglary, larceny, and robbery,[25] not only called
no witnesses in his behalf but chose not to take the stand during his trial, a decision on which both the trial judge and the prosecuting attorney commented
adversely. (Such comments have been statutorily proscribed on the *federal*
level since 1878.) In his appeals, Adamson argued that the California law put
him into an impossible situation: if he testified, the previous convictions
would thus be revealed to the jury; and if he did not, comments by the judge
and prosecutor would, in effect, convert his silence into a confession of guilt.
(Only a few other states permitted the California procedure at the time. Interestingly, Britain adopted it in October 1933.) In short, he claimed that the adverse comments by the two officials violated his constitutional privilege
against compulsory self-incrimination under the Fifth Amendment of the federal Constitution, which he deemed incorporated and hence applicable to the
states under the "due process of law" clause of the Fourteenth Amendment. He
ultimately lost (5:4) at the bar of the Supreme Court. In an opinion written by
Justice Stanley F. Reed, and joined by Chief Justice Vinson and Associate Justices Robert H. Jackson and Harold H. Burton, the high tribunal held that the
self-incrimination clause of the Fifth Amendment was *not* incorporated or applicable and that the state of California "may control such a situation in accordance with its own ideas of the most efficient administration of criminal
justice."[26] Justice Frankfurter provided the decisive fifth vote in a long concurring opinion in which, as noted earlier, he took specific issue with the heart
of Justice Black's dissenting opinion.

   In his dissent, supported by a thirty-three-page appendix that quoted extensively from the congressional debates involving Amendment Fourteen, Black
was joined wholly by Justice Douglas and in part by Justices Murphy and Rutledge (who both, as we shall see later, wanted to go even beyond the Black position on incorporation—as indeed Douglas ultimately did too). Black's opinion
remains the most celebrated analysis of the intention of the framers of Section 1.
Elaborately researched, it insisted that one of the chief objects to be accom-

----

25. Adamson had a highly prolific and interesting prison record, involving hobbies that
included collecting the tops of women's stockings.
   26. *Adamson v. California,* 332 U.S. 46 at 57. (But see later discussion for its overruling in 1964.) Adamson was executed in San Quentin's gas chamber at the end of 1949,
following several additional unsuccessful appeals.

plished by the first section of the Fourteenth Amendment, "separately, and as a whole,"[27] was to apply the entire Bill of Rights to the states. In his own words:

> My study of the historical events that culminated in the Fourteenth Amendment, and the expressions of those who opposed its submission and passage, persuades me that one of the chief objects that the provisions of the Amendment's first section, separately, and as a whole, were intended to accomplish was to make the Bill of Rights applicable to the states. With full knowledge of the *Barron* decision, the framers and backers of the Fourteenth Amendment proclaimed its purpose to be to overturn the constitutional rule that case had announced. This historical purpose had never received full consideration or expression in any opinion of this Court interpreting the Amendment. . . .[28]

Responding to Justice Frankfurter's contrary views and call for more demonstrable proof (where Frankfurther believed none existed), Black observed: "I cannot consider the Bill of Rights to be an outworn Eighteenth Century 'straight jacket' . . ." and concluded:

> I believe [that] the original purpose of the Fourteenth Amendment [was] to extend to all the people of the nation the complete protection of the Bill of Rights. To hold that this Court can determine what, if any, provisions of the Bill of Rights will be enforced, and if so to what degree, is to frustrate the great design of a written Constitution.[29]

Justice Black, in his almost three and a half decades on the Supreme Court, never wavered from these basic convictions—convictions buttressed by the expansive support extended to them by Professor W. W. Crosskey of the University of Chicago in a major essay a few years after *Adamson*.[30] Black's staunchest historical-constitutional ally was Professor Horace Flack. After a careful study of the debates of the Thirty-ninth Congress, their newspaper coverage, and the election speeches of members of Congress in the fall of 1866, Flack concluded that Congress

> had the following objects and motives in view for submitting the First Section of the Fourteenth to the states for ratification. First, to make the National Bill of Rights applicable to the states; secondly, to give constitutional

27. Ibid. at 71. Periodically Black made it clear that, not withstanding his emphasis on certain occasions on one or the other of the specific sentences and phrases composing Section 1 of the Fourteenth Amendment, that amendment "*as a whole* makes the Bill of Rights applicable to the States. This would certainly include the language of the Privileges or Immunities Clause as well as the Due Process Clause" (from his 1968 concurring opinion in *Duncan v. Louisiana,* 391 U.S. 145 at 166, note 1).

28. *Adamson v. California,* op. cit., at 71–72.

29. Ibid. at 89.

30. Charles Fairman, "'Legislative History,' and the Constitutional Limits on State Authority," 22 *University of Chicago Law Review* 1 (1954).

validity to the Civil Rights Act [of 1866]; and thirdly, to declare who were the citizens of the United States.[31]

Black's opinion was soon challenged in almost every detail by Professor Charles Fairman of the Harvard Law School, a leading expert on constitutional law, in an article in the *Stanford Law Review*.[32] Fairman accused Black of deliberate distortion of the verities of the debates in the Thirty-ninth Congress to prove his point. In a companion article in the same issue,[33] Professor Stanley Morrison, of the Stanford University School of Law, seconded Fairman's rejection of Black's thesis. But Morrison did so with considerably less vehemence, and not so much on the basis of what was said during the congressional debates as on the strength of the judicial history of the clause following the amendment's adoption. Noting that only the elder Harlan had consistently supported Black's incorporation interpretation, Morrison sided with Frankfurter's analysis and statistics in his concurring opinion in the *Adamson* case.[34] He refers to the refusal of such "libertarian activist" justices as Holmes, Brandeis, Stone, Hughes (!), and Cardozo to incorporate the Bill of Rights per se and *seems* to score a telling point by recalling that Black himself did not dissent from, or write a separate concurring opinion to, Cardozo's famous majority opinion in the 1937 *Palko* case[35] (see *infra* this chapter). That Cardozo opinion established a hierarchy of basic human rights which would henceforth be considered applicable to the states via Amendment Fourteen—namely, those "implicit in the concept of ordered liberty"—while at the same time establishing a *nonapplicable* group.[36]

It is only fair to note at once here in Black's defense, however, that (1) he had just joined the Court a few weeks earlier; (2) thus he might well have believed that it would be ungracious as well as foolhardy to proclaim a new jurisprudential posture; (3) the Cardozo majority opinion did, after all, announce the incorporation of the most precious of all basic human freedoms, notably First Amendment rights; and (4), as Black himself had explained in his *Adamson* dissent: "[I]f the choice must be between the selective process of the *Palko* decision applying some of the Bill of Rights to the States, or the *Twining* rule applying none of them, I would choose the *Palko* selective process."[37] He reiterated in a

31. Horace Flack, *The Adoption of the Fourteenth Amendment* (Baltimore: Johns Hopkins University Press, 1908), p. 94.
32. "Does the Fourteenth Amendment Incorporate the Bill of Rights? The Original Understanding," 2 *Stanford Law Review* 5 (December 1949).
33. "Does the Fourteenth Amendment Incorporate the Bill of Rights? The Judicial Interpretation," 2 *Stanford Law Review* 5 (December 1949) at 140.
34. *Adamson v. California,* op. cit.
35. *Palko v. Connecticut,* 30 U.S. 319.
36. Among the latter were the Fifth Amendment's safeguards against double jeopardy (at issue in *Palko*) and compulsory self-incrimination (at issue in *Adamson*).
37. *Adamson v. California,* op. cit., at 89. He restated this position two decades later, one of the last times he spoke on "incorporation" (*Duncan v. Louisiana,* 391 U.S. 145 [1968] at 171).

footnote to his dissent in *Griswold v. Connecticut,* twenty-eight years after *Palko,* that he "agreed to follow" the *Palko* rule as a second-best method to "make [at least some of the] Bill of Rights safeguards applicable to the States."[38]

A sixth protagonist, Professor J. B. James of Georgia Wesleyan College, in his book *The Framing of the Fourteenth Amendment,*[39] agrees with Fairman and Morrison that Black's facile and sweeping interpretation of the congressional debates of 1866 is erroneous—but only *because* it is so sweeping and facile. With some reservations, James nonetheless does share Black and Flack's conclusion that, on balance, the amendment's framers did intend to incorporate the Bill of Rights. Although such a thought may have been entirely foreign to the collective majority who supported its passage, James, as did Flack—and Professor Jacobus ten Broek, who shares most of James's views on the entire matter"[40]—presents strong evidence that the amendment's floor managers indeed intended its incorporation.[41] This is particularly true of Representative John A. Bingham, the author of the pertinent provisions of Section 1, whom Black called "without extravagance . . . the Madison of [that section] of the Fourteenth Amendment."[42] Contrary to James's and other earlier belief, we now know that, significantly, Bingham was fully aware of the Supreme Court's decision in *Barron v. Baltimore*[43] when he led the debates on Amendment Fourteen in the House.[44] As a matter of fact, it was this ruling, he said, which made necessary "the adopting of the [Fourteenth] Amendment."[45] Certain in his belief that the Bill of Rights was designed to be *national* in scope, Bingham argued on the floor that had the Thirty-ninth Congress meant the Bill of Rights to be solely applicable to the *federal* government, the wording of the amendment's Section 1 would have so stated. James demonstrates quite convincingly that when Bingham and Republican Senator Jacob M. Howard of Michigan,

38. 381 U.S. 479 at 526, note 21.

39. (Urbana: University of Illinois Press, 1956).

40. See Jacobus ten Broek, *The Antislavery Origins of the Fourteenth Amendment* (Berkeley: University of California Press, 1951): "The rights sought to be protected," he asserted severally, "were men's natural rights, some of which are mentioned in the first eight amendments and some of which are not" (e.g., at 223).

41. E.g., James, op. cit., pp. 85, 130ff.

42. *Adamson v. California,* op. cit., at 74.

43. 7 Peters 243 (1833).

44. See *Congressional Globe,* 39th Cong., 1st sess. (Washington, D.C.: Blair and Rives, 1866), pp. 1088–90.

45. Ibid., p. 1089. In 1871, during a debate on the now-ratified amendment, Bingham observed that in 1865–66 he had closely "re-examined" Marshall's decision in *Barron,* wherein the chief justice had stated that "had the framers of these Amendments [One through Eight] intended them to be limitations on the power of state governments, they would have imitated the framers of the Original Constitution and have expressed their intention." Bingham then significantly added, "[A]cting upon this suggestion I did imitate the framers of the Original Constitution" (*The Globe,* 42nd Cong., 1st sess., 1871, Appendix, p. 150).

the amendment's floor manager in the upper house, spoke of the "fundamental rights of free men," they specifically meant the Bill of Rights. They wanted the proposed amendment to overrule *Barron v. Baltimore.*

Senator Howard, in fact, clearly insisted that the national Bill of Rights *in its entirety* was incorporated into Section 1, a section that in his judgment embodied not only the "privileges and immunities" of Article 4, Paragraph 2, of the Constitution but also all those rights guaranteed by the first eight amendments to the Constitution. Thus, in explaining the contents of the amendment, he stated: "To these privileges and immunities [Art. 4, Para. 2], whatever they may be for they are not and cannot be fully defined . . . to these should be added the personal rights guaranteed and secured by the first eight amendments to the Constitution." Enumerating these, he continued:

> [T]hese are secured to citizens solely as citizens of the United States, . . . they do not operate in the slightest degree as restraints or prohibitions upon state legislation. . . . The great object of the first section of this amendment is, therefore, to restrain the power of the states and compel them at all times to respect these fundamental guarantees.[46]

Nonetheless, Professor Fairman, with some support from Professor Morrison, still insists that the use of the phrase "fundamental rights" or "fundamental guarantees" was specifically intended to *exclude* the Bill of Rights. Fairman does admit that Senator Howard expressly stated that the "privileges or immunities" clause of Section 1 of the Fourteenth Amendment should be construed as embracing what Howard termed "the personal rights" of the first eight amendments of the Bill of Rights. But Fairman insists that Bingham merely "talked around the point." Fairman's position received highly vocal support as a result of the publication of Professor Raoul Berger's fascinatingly controversial book *Government by Judiciary: The Transformation of the Fourteenth Amendment.*[47] Berger, who called Bingham "a muddled thinker" and Howard "a reckless radical," concludes that his study of the "debates of the history of the period leads [him] fully to concur with Fairman," quoting approvingly Fairman's statement that the "freedom that states traditionally have exercised to develop their own systems of administering justice repels any thought that . . . Congress would . . . have attempted [to incorporate] the country would not have stood for it, the legislatures would not have ratified."[48] The historians Kelly and Harbison, on the other hand, side with Flack's, James's, Crosskey's, and Black's historical (and, incidentally, Black's con-

---

46. *The Globe,* op. cit., 39th Cong., p. 2765; italics supplied.

47. (Cambridge, Mass.: Harvard University Press, 1977); see especially chapter 8, "Incorporation of the Bill of Rights in the Fourteenth Amendment."

48. Ibid., p. 156. See also Berger's "Incorporation of the Bill of Rights in the Fourteenth Amendment: A Nine Lived Cat," 42 *Ohio State Law Journal* 435 (1982); and his *Death Penalties: The Supreme Court's Obstacle Course* (Cambridge, Mass.: Harvard University Press, 1982), especially chapter 2, "Incorporation of the Bill of Rights."

stitutional) interpretation and state flatly that Bingham and Howard agreed not only that the "privileges or immunities" clause "incorporated the entire federal Bill of Rights as a limitation upon the states" but that the "due process" clause was lifted from the Fifth Amendment and thus "became a guarantee against state action."[49] And independent scholarly investigations by such knowledgeable legal commentators as William Crosskey, Louis Henkin, Frank Walker, and Michael Kent Curtis[50] agree that there remains no genuine doubt that the framers of Amendment Fourteen intended it as a lever for the application of the Bill of Rights to the several states of the Union, with Curtis penning a learned point-by-point rebuttal of Raoul Berger's historical arguments. Curtis returned to the fray in a book-length treatment of the issue,[51] strongly arguing the case for full incorporation. Although his evidence may be neither new nor definitive, Curtis demonstrates persuasively that, given the antislavery movement's role in the genesis of the Fourteenth Amendment, its framers did indeed appear to intend to apply the provisions of the entire Bill of Rights to the several states. Moreover, he offers an intriguing analysis of, and a convincing exhortation to resurrect, the long-emasculated "privileges or immunities" ("P or I") clause of the amendment's Section 1.[52] He reiterated that posture with a major article in further support of that position as a result of the Court's 7:2 holding in *Saenz v. Roe*,[53] in which the majority, over dissents by Rehnquist and Thomas, relied in part on the "P or I" clause in a welfare travel case.[54] And, in his meticulously researched and lucidly presented work, Curtis presents a retort to attacks on the in-

49. Alfred H. Kelly and Winfred A. Harbison, *The American Constitution: Its Origin and Development,* 4th ed. (New York: Norton, 1970), p. 463; William W. Crosskey, "Charles Fairman, 'Legislative History,' and the Constitutional Limitations on State Authority," 22 *University of Chicago Law Review* 1 (1954).

50. Louis Henkin, "Selective Incorporation in the Fourteenth Amendment," 73 *Yale Law Journal* 74 (1963); Frank H. Walker Jr., "Constitutional Law—Was It Intended That the Fourteenth Amendment Incorporates the Bill of Rights?" 42 *North Carolina Law Review* 925 (1964); Michael Kent Curtis, "The Bill of Rights as a Limitation on State Authority: A Reply to Professor Berger," 16 *Wake Forest Law Review* 1 (1980); his articles "The Fourteenth Amendment and the Bill of Rights," 14 *Connecticut Law Review* 2 (1982), and "Further Adventures of the Nine Lived Cat: A Response to Mr. Berger on Incorporation of the Bill of Rights," 43 *Ohio State Law Journal* 89 (1982); Berger's response, "Incorporation of the Bill of Rights: A Reply to Michael Curtis," 44 *Ohio State Law Journal* (1983); and the latter's "Still Further Adventures of the Nine Lived Cat: A Rebuttal to Raoul Berger's Reply on Application of the Bill of Rights to the States," 62 *North Carolina Law Review* 3 (1984). John Hart Ely concludes that "this is an argument no one can win," in *Democracy and Distrust: A Study of Judicial Review* (Cambridge, Mass.: Harvard University Press, 1980), p. 25.

51. *No State Shall Abridge: The Fourteenth Amendment and the Bill of Rights* (Durham, N.C.: Duke University Press, 1986).

52. See his letter of August 27, 1997, to the senior author.

53. 526 U.S. 489 (1999).

54. "Historical Linguistics, Inkblots, and Life After Death: The Privileges and Immunities of Citizens of the United States," 78 *North Carolina Law Review* 4 (April 2000).

corporation doctrine, in particular Attorney General Edwin Meese III's controversial July 1985 statement to the American Bar Association, in which Meese
questioned that doctrine's "intellectually shaky" foundation and declared it to be
utterly lacking any constitutional justification.[55]

A Verdict? Regardless of personal intellectual and emotional commitments on the
basic question of incorporation, the various positions indicate how speculative history can be and may become. The German historian Leopold von Ranke's exhortation that it is essential to determine *"wie es eigentlich gewesen"* ("how it actually
was") is noble and human, but at times futile. However, such evidence as the history of the debates provides seems to substantiate Professor James's basic point
that we need not accept Justice Black's expansive evaluation, nor that advanced
six decades later by Professor Michael J. Perry,[56] of the events of the Thirty-ninth
Congress to side with his basic conclusion: there seems little doubt that the amendment's principal framers and managers, Representative Bingham and Senator
Howard, if not every member of the majority in the two houses of Congress, did
believe the Bill of Rights to be made generally applicable to the several states via
Section 1. And *no* member of that Congress, before he voted on the amendment,
contradicted Bingham's and Howard's final statements to that extent.[57]

   This conclusion does not, however, necessitate concurrence with the matter
of the *wisdom* of such an incorporation, nor with the judicial formulae devised

---

55. See also the interestingly imaginative article by Barry Latzer, calling for "selective
*dis*incorporation," "Toward the Decentralization of Criminal Procedure: State Constitutional Law and Selective Disincorporation," 87 *Journal of Criminal Law and Criminology* 1 (Fall 1996).

56. See his *We the People: The Fourteenth Amendment and the Supreme Court* (New
York: Oxford University Press, 1999).

57. Flack, op. cit., pp. 81, 87. On the entire controversy, see also Arthur A. North, S.J.,
"The Nationalization of the Bill of Rights," which is the third chapter of his book *The
Supreme Court: Judicial Process and Judicial Politics* (New York: Appleton-Century-
Crofts, 1966). For its specific relevance to the desegregation-segregation issues of the
1950s and 1960s, see the lengthy and learned chapter by Alexander M. Bickel "The Original Understanding and the Segregation Decision," in his *Politics and the Warren Court*
(New York: Harper and Row, 1965), pp. 221–61. Bickel's conclusion is that the authors
of the Fourteenth Amendment ultimately chose language which would be capable of
growth. It follows that "the record of history, properly understood, left the way open to,
in fact invited, a decision based on the moral and material state of the Union in 1954, not
1877" (p. 261). For an intriguing complementary—and wholly different—analysis of the
intentions of Bingham (and Senator Roscoe Conkling), namely, that the due process of
law clause was drafted to "take in the whole range of national economy," making corporations among the intended beneficiaries of the draft, see Howard Jay Graham, "The Conspiracy Theory of the Fourteenth Amendment," 47 *Yale Law Journal* 371 (1938); and
Charles A. Beard and Mary R. Beard, *The Rise of American Civilization* (New York:
Macmillan, 1927). See also Wallace Mendelson, "A Note on the Cause and Cure of the
Fourteenth Amendment," 43 *Journal of Politics* 152 (February 1981).

therefore.[58] Nor does it gainsay the fact that when Senator Howard's "privileges or immunities" clause (and his and Representative Bingham's incorporation contentions for it) had its first judicial test in the *Slaughterhouse Cases*[59] a mere five years after the adoption of the Fourteenth Amendment, it sustained a crushing and lasting defeat.

The Slaughterhouse Cases of 1873. These remarkable cases, also referred to as the *Dual Citizenship Cases,* delivered the second of the one-two knockout punches to the theory of a national applicability of the Bill of Rights, the first such punch having been *Barron v. Baltimore* forty years earlier. It will be recalled that in *Barron* the unanimous Court had ruled that the bill was *not* applicable to the several states, by either expressed or implied language. The *Slaughterhouse Cases* not only reconfirmed the *Barron* holding but went considerably further by ruling that the privileges or immunities clause of the Fourteenth Amendment did not, and was not intended to, protect the rights of *state* citizenship but solely those of *federal* citizenship. In the words of this never-to-date overruled decision written for the narrow 5:4 majority[60] by Justice Samuel F. Miller of Iowa by way of Kentucky: "It is quite clear, then, that *there is a citizenship of the United States, and a citizenship of a state, which are distinct from each other,* and which depend upon different characteristics or circumstances in the individual."[61] Thus the "citizens" protected by the "P or I" clause of Amendment Fourteen are such "citizens" only in their capacity as "citizens of the United States," *not* in their capacity or role as "*state* citizens."

The cases had arisen as a result of a statute regulating the livestock slaughtering business, which had been enacted by the Louisiana Reconstruction government in 1867. In the law, its "carpetbag"[62] legislature (unquestionably under corrupt influence) had conferred upon a single firm what, to all intents and purposes, constituted a monopoly of the New Orleans slaughterhouse business, preventing some one thousand firms and persons already established in the city from continuing in that activity. A number of the adversely affected parties filed suit in the courts of Louisiana, basing their complaint largely on alleged violation of their rights under the Fourteenth Amendment. Losing in the lower courts, they ultimately reached the state supreme court, which was equally unsympathetic to their claim and held that the contested Louisiana law was a valid and legal exer-

---

58. See *infra* this chapter.
59. *The Butchers' Benevolent Association of New Orleans v. Crescent City Live-Stock Landing and Slaughter-House Co.,* 16 Wallace 36 (1873).
60. With Miller were Associate Justices Nathan Clifford (Maine), David Davis (Illinois), William Strong (Pennsylvania), and Ward Hunt (New York).
61. Op. cit. at 74; italics supplied.
62. "Carpetbagger" denotes a Northerner who went south after the Civil War to obtain office or employment by morally questionable and often corrupt methods.

cise of the state police power.[63] The aggrieved litigants then appealed to the U.S. Supreme Court.

Although four main constitutional issues were raised by the opponents of the Louisiana monopoly statute, the chief concern of the Court in its majority opinion was with the appellants' crucial contention that the law constituted a prima facie violation of that portion of Section 1 of Amendment Fourteen which states that "[n]o State shall make or enforce any law which shall abridge the privileges or immunities of citizens of the United States. . . ."[64] In other words, the basic claim of the aggrieved businessmen was that the quoted clause clearly implied, indeed commanded, the protection of all civil rights and liberties *by the federal government* and that the several states could not, on pain of violating the Fourteenth Amendment, deny or abridge any rights accruing to citizens of the United States residing within their borders.

But the majority of five justices rejected this contention out of hand. They would have no part of this, or any related, notion of incorporating, of "carrying over," the prerogatives of the Bill of Rights so as to make them applicable to the states. Moreover, the Miller decision absolved the federal government from any obligation to protect "privileges or immunities" against state violation, a logical induction from the Court majority's basic premise that the *states* had the obligation to protect not only the rights guaranteed by their own bills of rights but the entire body of rights and liberties under the common law.

In short, the majority's decision meant that the "privileges or immunities" clause of the newly enacted amendment really *meant nothing at all* insofar as the states were concerned. As has been well pointed out by one close student of the *Slaughterhouse Cases,* the Court's distinction between state and national citizenship made of the P or I clause a mere tautology, since the rights of "citizens in the several states" could never have been *constitutionally* abridged by any state anyway. Thus, "the labors of the framers of the Fourteenth Amendment were nullified by a few strokes of Justice Miller's busy pen."[65] But *why?* The question is a natural one, given the history of the adoption of the amendment (no matter which version) and the general acquaintance of all the justices with the activities and debates in the Thirty-ninth Congress. In the opinion of most competent observers, the Court majority was simply unwilling to permit such a

---

63. Accruing to the states under Article 10 of the Bill of Rights, the "police power" is generally regarded as embracing and extending to the following concepts of state authority: (1) health, (2) welfare, (3) morals, (4) safety, and (5) regulation of business (and labor and agricultural) activities.

64. The other three were that the statute (1) created an "involuntary servitude" forbidden by Amendment Thirteen, (2) denied the appellants the "equal protection of the laws" under Amendment Fourteen, and (3) deprived them of their property "without due process of law," also safeguarded by Amendment Fourteen.

65. Loren P. Beth, "The Slaughterhouse Cases—Revisited," 23 *Louisiana Law Review* 487 (April 1963) at 492.

far-reaching alteration in the turbulent, beleaguered antebellum federal system—
the relation of state and federal governments—by an "ambiguous" amendment to
the Constitution.[66] Consequently, the majority of five expounded the at least
plausible conception of dual citizenship, by which practically all common private
rights were removed from the federal sphere of control. The majority also believed (and this idea was widely held at the time, as already noted) that the overriding, if not the sole, purpose of Amendment Fourteen was the protection of
blacks in exercising their *civil,* although not their political, rights.

But what, then, about existing "privileges or immunities" of *national* citizenship, which, by its own admission and by its creation of a "dual citizenship,"
the majority held to be protected against action by state governments, too? The
Miller opinion avoided precise definitions and limits, but, quoting from one of
his own 1868 opinions,[67] it suggested the appropriateness of the following
"rights" of the national citizen as bona fide "privileges or immunities":

> To come to the seat of government to assert any claim he may have upon
> that government, to transact any business he may have with it, to seek its
> protection, to share its offices, to engage in administering its functions . . .
> of free access to its seaports . . . to the subtreasuries, land offices, and courts
> of justice in the several states . . . to demand the care and protection of the
> Federal government over his life, liberty, and property when on the high
> seas or within the jurisdiction of a foreign government . . . the writ of habeas
> corpus . . . to use the navigable waters of the United States, however they
> may penetrate the territory of the several States.[68]

Also on Miller's list, significantly reemphasized as "rights of the citizen guaranteed by the *Federal* Constitution," were the "right[s] to peaceable assembly and
petition for redress of grievances. . . ."[69] This represents, of course, a line of reasoning typical of the nonincorporation argument, then and today: that the Fourteenth Amendment extended no "rights" to citizens of the United States; that most
of their rights had the same status as before, existing under *state* protection rather
than national protection; that the "citizens" presumably protected by the

66. Ibid. at 493. This is also C. Vann Woodward's view in his *Reunion and Reaction*
(New York: Doubleday-Anchor, 1956).

67. *Crandall v. Nevada,* 6 Wallace 36.

68. *The Slaughterhouse Cases,* 16 Wallace 36 (1873) at 73–75. These rights have been
originally identified as "privileges or immunities" in Justice Bushrod Washington's opinion in *Corfield v. Coryell,* 6 F. Cas. 546.

69. Ibid. Depending upon one's interpretation, "the right peaceably to assemble and
petition" was one of the "privileges or immunities" of U.S. citizenship—i.e., national, not
state—reconfirmed three years later in *United States v. Cruikshank,* 92 U.S. 542. But in
the key aspect of its holding by Chief Justice Waite, *Cruikshank* declared that Amendment
Fourteen "adds nothing to the rights of one citizen as against another. It simply furnishes
a federal guarantee against any encroachment by the States upon the fundamental rights
which belong to every citizen as a member of society" (at 554).

P or I clause are "citizens" only in the sense that they are "citizens" of the United States—emphatically not in their capacity as *state* citizens.[70] As pointed out before, this kind of reasoning renders the Fourteenth Amendment useless as a legal tool, for no state could ever *constitutionally* abridge or deny the rights of "citizens in the several states." Thus, all that seemed to remain of the amendment, given the majority's reasoning in the *Slaughterhouse Cases* a mere handful of years after its birth, was a vague, generally accepted understanding that it was intended to bring about citizenship for the Negro. In one participant's views, the Court's construction of the P or I clause had reduced it to "a vain and idle enactment."[71]

Of the three dissenting opinions by Associate Justices Noah H. Swayne—who pointedly accused the Court majority of having turned "what was meant for bread into a stone"[72]—Stephen J. Field, and Joseph P. Bradley, the most important was Field's, in which Chief Justice Salmon P. Chase concurred. But it should be noted that it is Bradley to whom goes the credit for being "first" to advocate "incorporation" via the P or I clause of all rights "specified in the original Constitution or in the early amendments of it."[73] Although Field had begun his long judicial career with a general inclination in favor of individual rights, this bias ultimately resolved itself into a "special emphasis on the sanctity of economic freedom."[74] Field's *Slaughterhouse* dissent is therefore deceptive in its overall implications, for it does argue angrily for an interpretation of the Fourteenth Amendment and its P or I clause that would insist upon man's "fundamental rights, privileges, and immunities which belong to him as a free man and a free citizen."[75] To Field, the citizenship clause made state citizenship both subordinate to and derivative of national citizenship. As a result of Section 1 of Amendment Fourteen, he argued, "a citizen of a state is now only a citizen of the United States *residing* in that state."[76] But Field's cardinal argument against the majority decision was based not so much on the cause of basic human freedoms as it

70. James Wilson, one of Pennsylvania's delegates to the Constitutional Convention of 1787, had made a point of calling the attention of his fellow delegates to the fact that the Constitution, if ratified, would create a dual citizenship—but the significance of this was both overlooked and misunderstood.

71. Justice Field's categorization, dissenting in *The Slaughterhouse Cases,* op. cit., at 96.

72. *The Slaughterhouse Cases,* op. cit., at 129.

73. Ibid. at 118. Field, whose longevity in service on the Court (almost thirty-five years) stood as a record until Douglas (who would serve thirty-six and a half) overtook him in 1975, will be remembered in the annals of constitutional law and development primarily as the "spokesman of rugged American individualism and laissez faire" (Rocco J. Tresolini, *American Constitutional Law,* 2d ed. [New York: Macmillan, 1965], p. 742). Field had served on the California Supreme Court for six and a half years before his promotion by President Lincoln in 1863 to the U.S. Supreme Court.

74. Robert G. McCloskey, *American Conservatism in the Age of Enterprise* (Cambridge, Mass.: Harvard University Press, 1951), pp. 122–23.

75. *The Slaughterhouse Cases,* op. cit., at 95.

76. Ibid.; italics supplied.

was on the doctrine of vested property rights—a cause he was to espouse throughout his long tenure with consistency, self-assurance, and emotion. For Field, *the* "privilege" and/or "immunity" that was at issue here was the absolute right to engage in the business of butchering. Louisiana's statutory interference with that right was to Field the crime par excellence of a governmental roadblock in the path of Darwinian-Spencerian economics.[77] For him, as McCloskey observed, "the property right is the transcendent value; political ambition ranks next when it is relevant; and the cause of human or civil rights is subordinate to these higher considerations."[78] Field's dissenting opinion was thus of but limited comfort to those who looked toward a "nationalization" of basic human rights and liberties. When he spoke of the "equality of right" to labor freely, he looked toward that period of half a century when the Supreme Court would strike hard at any legislative (and administrative) action it deemed violative of the sanctity of property, and of the "freedom of contract" concept it was soon to read into the "due process of law" clause of both the Fifth and the Fourteenth Amendments.[79] Except for a handful of instances,[80] and particularly when they involved a charge against a state of "cruel and unusual" punishment,[81] Field found no such justification for protection of the basic freedoms of the Bill of Rights, however—and he was clearly disdainful of his longtime colleague John Marshall Harlan's ad-

77. Oversimplified, perhaps, this was Field's philosophy of the survival of the fittest in terms of classical nineteenth-century capitalism.

78. McCloskey, op. cit., pp. 122–23. A considerably more charitable view of Field's stance is taken by Arthur A. North, op. cit., pp. 91–96. He flatly states that not only Harlan but also Field and Brewer "accepted the theory" of incorporation (p. 96). North appears to have arrived at that conclusion chiefly because of Field's posture in the 1892 case of *O'Neil v. Vermont* (see notes 74–76 and accompanying text). But Field resigned from the Court five years later, and his nephew Brewer, a fellow dissenter in *O'Neil*—as was Harlan, of course—changed his views on the matter, with only Harlan thus remaining as an "incorporationist."

79. To Field's great satisfaction, the word *person* in the latter clause was extended to corporations in 1886 as a result of an announcement from the bench by Chief Justice Waite, in *Santa Clara County v. Southern Pacific Railroad Co.,* 118 U.S. 394—in no small measure due to the interpretative efforts of Roscoe Conkling, who had been a member of the Joint Congressional Committee that had drafted the Fourteenth Amendment.

80. *Neal v. Delaware,* 103 U.S. 379 (1880); *Bush v. Connecticut,* 107 U.S. 110 (1882); *In re Kemmler,* 136 U.S. 436 (1890); *McElvaine v. Brush,* 142 U.S. 155 (1891); and *O'Neil v. Vermont,* 144 U.S. 323 (1892).

81. In the last-named case he noted the following in his dissent: "While, therefore, the ten Amendments, as limitations on power, and, so far as they accomplish their purpose and find their fruition in such limitations, are applicable to the Federal Government and not to the States, yet, so far as they declare or recognize the rights of persons, they are rights belonging to them as citizens of the United States under the Constitution; and the Fourteenth Amendment, as to all such rights, places a limit upon state power by ordaining that no State shall make or enforce any law which shall abridge them. If I am right in [t]his view, then every citizen of the United States is protected from punishments which are cruel and unusual" (at 363).

vocacy of total incorporation. Indeed, when the Court, seven years after *Slaughterhouse,* held unconstitutional racially based discrimination in jury impaneling by Virginia and West Virginia, Field entered a vigorous dissent, contending that the "equal protection of the laws" clause "did not prevent the outright exclusion of blacks" by states acting under their elective authority.[82]

Nonetheless, the Field dissent dramatized both the interest in the meaning of the most important of the Civil War amendments and its possible role as a catalyst in a "nationalization" of basic rights and liberties. The *Slaughterhouse* holding of "dual citizenship" has never been overruled per se,[83] and the P or I clause of Amendment Fourteen, which then Judge Benjamin N. Cardozo in a letter to his friend Judge Learned Hand categorized as "a chaos of words carefully designed to avoid any definite commitment to any rule you can cling to,"[84] has become "practically a dead letter," although, as noted above, the 1999 case of *Saenz v. Roe*[85] resurrected it, in part. The P or I clause has been more or less outflanked ever since *Slaughterhouse.*[86] But emphatically not so the "due process of law" and the "equal protection of the laws" clauses, however—which in fact have become a "second" Bill of Rights. And, of course, Congress has begun to make use of the potentially far-reaching provisions of Section 5 of the amendment, which gives it "power to enforce, by appropriate legislation," the amendment's aforementioned provisions.[87] Ergo, arguably, the P or I clause, in effect, is no longer needed.

To the "due process of law" clause of the former and the incorporation problem we can now return, noting en route the criticism of *Slaughterhouse* by one of the earliest American political scientists, John W. Burgess, who pronounced the decision "entirely erroneous" from whatever view he regarded it, be that "historical, political, or juristic."[88] As he wrote in 1890 in his classic two-volume work *Political Science and Comparative Constitutional Law:*

> I say that if history has taught us anything in political science, it is that *civil liberty is national in its origin, content and sanction.* . . . [I]f there is but a

---

82. See ex parte Virginia and *Strauder v. West Virginia,* 100 U.S. 339; and 100 U.S. 303 (1980), respectively.

83. After the Reconstruction government was turned out of office in Louisiana, the *Slaughterhouse* statute was promptly repealed. Then the monopoly went to court, claiming violation of its due process of law under Amendment Fourteen. But, with Justice Miller again writing the opinion, the due process claim here lost 9:0 (*Butcher's Union Slaughter-House v. Crescent City Live-Stock Landing Co.,* 111 U.S. 746 [1884]).

84. "BNC" to "LH," Learned Hand Papers, July 8, 1927 (Harvard University).

85. See *Saenz v. Roe,* op. cit., *supra.*

86. See Morrison, op. cit., note 34, at 144.

87. E.g., sections of the Civil Rights Act of 1964. Congress has also resorted to the almost identically worded provision of Section 2 of the Fifteenth Amendment—as in the Voting Rights Acts of 1965, 1970, and 1975.

88. *Political Science and Comparative Constitutional Law* (Boston: Ginn, 1890), vol. 1, p. 226.

single lesson to be learned from the history of the United States, it is this: Seventy years of debate and four years of terrible war turn substantially upon this issue, in some part or other; and when the Nation triumphed in the great appeal to arms, and addressed itself to the work of readjusting the forms of law to the now undoubted condition of fact, it gave its first attention to the nationalization in constitutional law of the domain of civil liberty. *There is no doubt that those who framed the Thirteenth and Fourteenth amendments intended to occupy the whole ground and thought that they had done so.* The opposition charged that these amendments would nationalize the whole sphere of civil liberty; the majority accepted the view; and the legislation of Congress for their elaboration and enforcement proceeded upon that view. In the face of all these well known facts it was hardly to be doubted that . . . [the Supreme Court] *would unanimously declare the whole domain of civil liberty to be under its protection against both the general government and the commonwealths.* Great, therefore, was the surprise . . . when the decision in the *Slaughterhouse Cases* was announced. . . .[89]

Whatever one's conclusions regarding the intent of the framers of the Fourteenth Amendment, and its role as a vehicle for the applicability of the Bill of Rights to the several states, we know that there has been piecemeal "incorporation" or "nationalization" or "absorption" of the Bill of Rights by judicial interpretation and, as we shall see later, it came about at a steadily accelerating rate following Justice Sanford's limited initial acceptance of the concept in 1925. Thus, we now turn to the historical evolution of the incorporation issue, followed by a consideration of the various judicial "positions" on, and the wisdom of, incorporation itself.

THE EVOLUTION OF "INCORPORATION"

Pre-1937 Developments

The 1833 *Barron v. Baltimore*[90] decision firmly shut the judicial and constitutional door on any notions of incorporation until the passage of the Fourteenth Amendment appears to have opened it in 1868; the *Slaughterhouse Cases*[91] relocked it in 1873; and matters seemed to be settled, res judicata[92] — reconfirmed in 1899, with the Court reiterating that "the first ten Amendments to the Federal

89. Ibid., pp. 225–26; italics supplied.
90. 7 Peters 243.
91. 16 Wallace 36.
92. Res judicata connotes authoritative, settled law. In other words, it represents *the* essential law involved.

Constitution contain no restrictions on the powers of the state, but were intended to operate solely on the Federal government."[93]

Justice Harlan. Only Harlan, the onetime Kentucky slaveholder,[94] continued to raise the incorporation problem with both conviction and consistency. He would never fail in appropriate cases—of which there really were not very many—to write impassioned opinions in dissent, urging his associates to accept the principle of the nationalization of the Bill of Rights.

Harlan's solitary dissenting opinions from three well-known decisions demonstrated his unshakable belief that the Fourteenth Amendment was intended to incorporate the *entire* Bill of Rights—if for no other reason than that he regarded all of the rights in the Bill of Rights as "fundamental" and therefore applicable to the states via the "due process of law" clause of Amendment Fourteen. The first of these, *Hurtado v. California* (1884),[95] turned on the question of whether California's 1879 substitution of the practice of "information"[96] for indictment by a grand jury constituted a violation of the "due process" guarantees of the Fourteenth Amendment because of the requirements of the Fifth Amendment. Joseph Hurtado was tried on the basis of "information," convicted of the murder of one José Antonio Estuardo, and sentenced to be hanged. His appeal to the U.S. Supreme Court accordingly alleged deficient procedural due process. But the Court, in an elaborate 7:1 decision delivered by Justice Stanley Matthews, rejected that contention, ruling that the substitution of "information" for a grand jury indictment did not violate due process of law because it was merely a "preliminary proceeding" and thus not essential to due process; that, in any event, the Fourteenth Amendment's language simply did not contain, and did not mandate, a grand jury provision—had that been the intention, contended Matthews, it would have stated so specifically. Harlan's scholarly dissent not only disagreed with the majority's analysis but argued at length his belief that the Bill of Rights is incorporated via the due process clause of Amendment Fourteen. It meant, he insisted, that "there are principles of liberty and justice lying at the foundation of our civil and political institutions which no state can violate con-

93. *Brown v. New Jersey,* 175 U.S. 172 at 174. The Court, speaking through Justice Brewer, was unanimous, Harlan, perhaps somewhat surprisingly, concurring separately without opinion.

94. See the Harlan symposium in the spring 1958 issue of the *Kentucky Law Journal;* Henry J. Abraham, "John Marshall Harlan: A Justice Neglected," 41 *Virginia Law Review* 871 (November 1955); and the excellent essay by Jacob Landynski, "John Marshall Harlan and the Bill of Rights: A Centennial View," 49 *Social Research* 899 (winter 1982).

95. 10 U.S. 516.

96. "Information" is a common law practice whereby the prosecuting officer merely submits his charges in the form of an affidavit of evidence, supported by sworn statements, to a trial court. It is still used widely by the states and, to a much lesser degree, by the federal government in civil and noncapital criminal cases at the district-court level.

sistently with that due process of law required by the 14th Amendment in proceedings involving life, liberty or property."[97]

The second case, *Maxwell v. Dow,*[98] came sixteen years later. Not only was the matter of the substitution of "information" for a grand jury indictment—this time by Utah—again present, but a far more important collateral issue was at stake: Charles Maxwell's trial by a Utah jury of eight instead of twelve. Convicted of the crime of armed robbery, Maxwell argued that he had been deprived of both "due process of law" and, especially, his "privileges and immunities" as a U.S. citizen; that the Bill of Rights' Fifth and Sixth Amendments, guaranteeing grand jury indictment and trial by jury in criminal cases, respectively, were incorporated by means of Amendment Fourteen. "No, not at all," said the Supreme Court, with Justice Rufus W. Peckham writing for the 8:1 majority. Peckham, relying heavily on the *Slaughterhouse* precedent, admonished his colleagues to look to the amendment's language rather than its proponents' speeches. Not only did he see no violation of due process by the procedures employed by Utah, but neither the due process nor the P or I clause comprehended the rights listed in the federal Bill of Rights. In short, any thoughts of incorporation were to be rejected logically:

> [W]hen the Fourteenth Amendment prohibits abridgment by the states of those privileges and [*sic*] immunities which [the individual] enjoys as such citizen, it is not correct or reasonable to say that it covers and extends to certain rights which he does not enjoy by reason of his citizenship, but simply because those rights exist in favor of all individuals as against Federal government powers.[99]

Harlan, the sole dissenter, was not impressed by this reasoning; scoffing at what he regarded as deliberate blindness and verbal gymnastics, he reiterated his *Hurtado* view that, indeed, the Fourteenth Amendment intended to incorporate the entire Bill of Rights. Pointing to the Court's firm 8:1 decision in favor of property rights pronounced just three years earlier,[100] he warned that "no judicial tribunal has authority to say that some of [the Bill of Rights] may be abridged by the States while others may not be abridged."[101] To him, each one of the rights was fundamental and ergo applicable to the states, for he regarded *all* federal rights possessed by citizens *prior* to the adoption of Amendment Fourteen as being among the "privileges or immunities" which were secured against encroachment by the states.

97. *Hurtado v. California,* op. cit., at 546. Hurtado died in his jail cell of a pulmonary embolism one month after the Supreme Court's decision.

98. 176 U.S. 581 (1900).

99. Ibid. at 595–96.

100. *Chicago, Burlington and Quincy Railroad v. Chicago,* 166 U.S. 226 (1897).

101. 176 U.S. 581, op. cit., at 616. Maxwell's sentence was commuted in 1903, but he was killed in a gunfight not long thereafter.

The last pertinent example of Harlan's lone stand on the issue was the 1908 case of *Twining v. New Jersey,*[102] which involved the controversial constitutional guarantee against compulsory self-incrimination. The president of the Monmouth Safe & Trust Company, Albert C. Twining, and its treasurer, David C. Cornell, had been indicted by a New Jersey grand jury for having deliberately and knowingly displayed a false paper to a bank examiner with full intent to deceive him as to the actual condition of their firm. At the trial the two defendants neither called witnesses nor took the stand in their own defense. Very much in the fashion of the trial judge in *Adamson v. California*[103] four decades later, the *Twining* trial judge, Wilbur A. Heisley, commented adversely and extensively from the bench on the defendants' failure to take the stand. His charge to the jury contained the following statements: "Because a man does not go upon the stand you are not necessarily justified in drawing an inference of guilt. But you have a right to consider the fact that he does not go upon the stand where a direct accusation is made against him." The jury returned a verdict of guilty as charged against both defendants, who ultimately appealed to the U.S. Supreme Court, contending, first, that the exemption from self-incrimination is one of the privileges or immunities of citizens of the United States which the Fourteenth Amendment forbids the states to abridge and, second, that the alleged compulsory self-incrimination constituted a denial of due process of law. This time Justice William H. Moody spoke for another 8:1 majority that rejected, again, not only the specific contentions but the larger issue of the incorporation of the Bill of Rights. However, citing *Chicago, Burlington and Quincy Railroad v. Chicago,*[104] he significantly now granted the "possibility" that due process meant that "some of the personal rights safeguarded by the first eight amendments against national action may also be safeguarded against state action"[105]—yet only if an affirmative response to the following question is called for: "Is it a fundamental principle in liberty and justice which inheres in the very idea of free government and is the inalienable right of a citizen of such a government?"[106] Moody answered his rhetorical question by declaring it inapplicable in the instant *Twining* case because he regarded the privilege against self-incrimination as "not fundamental in due process of law, nor an essential part of it."[107] John Marshall Harlan predictably repeated his plea for incorporation, based on what he continued to regard as the commands of the Constitution. Until he died in 1911, he endeavored to convince at least a bare majority of his colleagues of the correctness of his position. But he was not to see the victory that was to come only

102. 211 U.S. 78.
103. 332 U.S. 46 (1947).
104. 166 U.S. 226 (1897).
105. *Twining v. New Jersey,* op. cit., at 99.
106. Ibid. at 106.
107. Ibid. at 110.

from future judicial interpretations—one that was all but total by the late 1960s. Well might one of his biographers write that Harlan had always "maintained an unswerving faith in the role of the Supreme Court as defender of the citizen's liberties and guardian of American constitutional ideals. . . ."[108] So he had indeed, and not only in the realm of incorporation (as we shall have occasion to see later).[109]

The Gitlow Case. Despite the rising concern expressed for civil rights and liberties by Justices Holmes and Brandeis, who joined the Court in 1902 and 1916, respectively, incorporation of the Bill of Rights seemed a lost cause until June 8, 1925, when it received its first official judicial recognition, on an at least *partial* basis, in the famous case of *Gitlow v. New York.*[110]

Benjamin Gitlow, an active exponent of extreme left-wing causes and a member of the most radical wing of the Socialist Party, had run afoul of New York State's Criminal Anarchy Act of 1902—which was passed in the wake of President William McKinley's assassination in late 1901. He was tried and convicted—after forty-five minutes of jury deliberations—for having "advocated, advised, and taught the duty, necessity, and propriety of overthrowing and overturning organized government by force, violence, and unlawful means by certain writings" (the "Left Wing Manifesto" and "The Revolutionary Age"). Appealing his conviction through the appropriate tiers of the New York State courts to the U.S. Supreme Court, he alleged that the New York statute violated both the Fourteenth Amendment's due process clause and the freedom of speech guarantees of the First Amendment. Gitlow lost on his basic claims, the Court ruling 6:2—Justice Stone not participating—that the statute violated neither due process in general nor free speech in particular. However, while clearing Mr. Gitlow's path to a New York jail by ruling that the latter's writings did not constitute the advocacy of abstract doctrine but embodied "the language of direct incitement,"[111] Justice Sanford, the author of the Court's majority opinion, made judicial history by the first formal embrace of incorporation of provisions of the Bill of Rights, speech and press:

108. Alan F. Westin, "John Marshall Harlan and the Constitutional Rights of Negroes: The Transformation of a Southerner," 66 *Yale Law Journal* 710 (1957).

109. See, for example, the most famous of all his dissents in *Plessy v. Ferguson,* 163 U.S. 537 (1896).

110. 268 U.S. 652. A case can be made for the contention that a number of earlier 1920s cases had "moved" the Court to its *Gitlow* position—e.g., *Gilbert v. Minnesota,* 254 U.S. 325 (1921), but by dictum only—although Brandeis's dissenting opinion in the case could well be credited with a clarion call for incorporation; *Prudential Insurance Co. v. Cheeks,* 259 U.S. 530 (1922); *Meyer v. Nebraska,* 262 U.S. 390 (1923); and *Pierce v. Society of Sisters,* 268 U.S. 510 (1925). See Klaus H. Heberle, "From *Gitlow* to *Near:* Judicial 'Amendment' by Absent-Minded Incrementalism," 34 *Journal of Politics* 458 (1972).

111. *Gitlow v. New York,* op. cit., at 665.

For present purposes we may and do assume that freedom of speech and of the press—which are protected by the First Amendment from abridgement by Congress—are among the fundamental personal rights and "liberties" protected by the due process clause of the Fourteenth Amendment from impairment by the States.[112]

This renowned Sanford dictum[113] was fully subscribed to by all of his colleagues, including, of course, Justices Holmes and Brandeis. That the two dissented here in one of Holmes's most celebrated opinions was not because of the incorporation announcement but, as we shall have occasion to assess later in connection with freedom of expression in chapter 5, because they simply did not believe that Gitlow's action presented any "clear and present" danger[114] to the state of New York. Drawing the kind of line discussed in chapters 1 and 2, Justice Holmes pointed out that "every idea is an incitement," that "eloquence may set fire to reason. . . ." But regardless of Benjamin Gitlow's defeat—in later days he became a well-paid informant for the government in subversive activities matters[115]—the "carryover" doctrine concerning the Fourteenth Amendment had been officially enunciated.

The Doctrine Confirmed and Expanded. That the *Gitlow* incorporation development was neither a fluke nor a passing pronouncement in dictum soon became apparent. Only two years later, the Supreme Court, again speaking through Justice Sanford, confirmed unanimously the nationalization of *freedom of speech* in the case of *Fiske v. Kansas.*[116] Here, for the first time, it upheld a personal-liberty claim under the Fourteenth Amendment, ruling specifically that a Kansas criminal syndicalism statute—very similar to the New York one in *Gitlow* (although Sanford did not discuss *Gitlow*'s issues and decision at all)—did indeed violate the due process clause of the Fourteenth Amendment as applied to Harold Fiske, because of the free speech strictures of the First Amendment. It has long been argued,[117] with considerable persuasiveness, that a more elaborate and more defin-

---

112. Ibid. at 666. Many had long treated it as such.

113. Properly known as obiter dictum, it is a statement of opinion by a judge that is not necessary to the conclusion on the merits of the case.

114. That famous doctrine, first enunciated in *Schenck v. United States,* 249 U.S. 47 (1919), by Holmes and Brandeis, will be treated in detail in chapter 5.

115. He was especially busy in the 1940s and 1950s when he was usually paid fifty dollars a day. He had served three years of a five-to-ten-year sentence, being pardoned by Governor Al Smith, who opined that Gitlow had been "sufficiently punished for a political crime" (*New York Times,* December 12, 1925, p. 1). Gitlow died in 1965, aged seventy-three, having become a confirmed anti-Communist.

116. 274 U.S. 380 (1927). Fiske was sponsored by the IWW. Indeed, all cases involving the incorporation of the First Amendment were group-sponsored.

117. See Heberle, op. cit. He insists that "the question of incorporation was not settled until the decisions in *Stromberg* and *Near,*" with the Court there relying "on *Gitlow, Whitney [v. California,* 274 U.S. 357 (1927)] and *Fiske*" (at 477).

itive, and hence more clearly precedent-setting, case for the incorporation of speech is the 1931 Hughes opinion in *Stromberg v. California*.[118] There, nineteen-year-old Yetta Stromberg, a member of the Young Communist League, had led forty ten- to fifteen-year-old children in a summer camp pledge of allegiance to a red flag and found herself in multiple violation of a California statute prohibiting the display of such flags. The chief justice, speaking for a 7:2 majority (Justices Butler and McReynolds in dissent), admonished: "It has been determined that the concentration of liberty under the due process clause of the Fourteenth Amendment embraces the right of free speech (citing, among others, the *Gitlow* and *Fiske* cases)."[119] In any event, incorporation of freedom of the press followed not long thereafter in the well-known 1931 prior-censorship case of *Near v. Minnesota*.[120]

In *Near,* this time speaking for a majority of five, Hughes declared unconstitutional, as "an infringement of the liberty of the press guaranteed by the Fourteenth Amendment," the so-called Minnesota Gag Law, which permitted prior restraint from publishing under certain circumstances. He wrote: "It is no longer open to doubt that the liberty of the press and of speech is safeguarded by the due process clause of the Fourteenth Amendment from invasion by state action. It was found impossible to conclude that this essential personal liberty of the citizen was left unprotected by the general guarantee of fundamental rights of person and property."[121]

Less than a year later, the incorporation doctrine moved out of the realm of the First Amendment and, for the first time, into the area of the guarantee of a fair trial, in general, and *counsel in capital criminal cases*, in particular. The vehicle was the first of the notorious *"Scottsboro Cases," Powell v. Alabama*,[122] which was destined to become a cause célèbre in the records of applications of due process of law to black defendants. Writing for a majority of seven, Justice George Sutherland overturned the conviction in the Alabama courts of seven indigent, ignorant, minor blacks who had been falsely charged with the rape of two white girls and convicted in a one-day trial in a mob-dominated atmosphere without the benefit of proper defense counsel. Reversing and remanding their conviction to the trial court with a stern call for a fair trial, the Court held that

> the right to counsel . . . provided in the Sixth Amendment [as applied to this case] is of such a character that it cannot be denied without violating those "fundamental principles of liberty and justice which lie at the base of all our civil and political institutions."[123]

118. 283 U.S. 359.
119. Ibid. at 368.
120. 283 U.S. 697 at 723.
121. Ibid. at 707.
122. 287 U.S. 45 (1932). So termed because the accused were all apprehended near the Alabama town of Scottsboro.
123. Quoting from *Hebert v. Louisiana,* 272 U.S. 312 (1926) at 316.

[It] is obviously one of those compelling considerations which must pre-vail in determining *whether it is embraced within the due process clause of the Fourteenth Amendment, although it is specifically dealt with in another part of the federal Constitution.* . . . [T]he necessity of counsel was so vital and imperative that the failure of the trial court to make an effective ap-pointment of counsel was likewise a denial of due process of law within the meaning of the Fourteenth Amendment. . . .[124]

Sutherland hinted of the applicability of the new role of law to noncapital crim-inal cases as well but chose to state that it was not necessary to determine that question "now."[125] In any event, new ground had been broken, with Justices Pierce Butler and James C. McReynolds as the sole dissenters from the incorpo-ration phase of the case.

The fourth aspect of the Bill of Rights to be thus nationalized was the First Amendment's guarantee of *free exercise of religion.* This was determined in 1934 in the interesting and important case of *Hamilton v. Regents of the University of California.*[126] All students at the University of California, a public state institu-tion, were then required to take military drill on pain of expulsion. But one among them, Albert Hamilton, holding religious convictions against the bearing of arms, refused to participate in the program and was consequently expelled. He filed suit, contending that his religious beliefs entitled him to exemption by virtue of both Amendments One and Fourteen. When the case reached the U.S. Supreme Court, Justice Butler, speaking for his unanimous colleagues, ruled that Hamilton's religious convictions were indeed safeguarded by the Bill of Rights and that freedom of religion was henceforth to be regarded as incorporated via the "due process of law" clause of Amendment Fourteen.[127] However, the Court went on to rule that, despite its holding on incorporation, Hamilton was *not* en-titled to an exemption from the state requirement of military training because, after all, he was not *compelled to attend* the University of California. Since he

124. Ibid. at 71. Sutherland also took the occasion to reaffirm the incorporation of "freedom of speech and of the press" (at 67). In January 1989 the last of the seven "Scotts-boro Boys," Clarence Norris, died at age seventy-six. On the run for thirty years, he had at last been cleared in 1976.

125. The Court's ruling in *Betts v. Brady,* 316 U.S. 455 (1942), restricted its applica-tion to capital criminal cases, yet *Gideon v. Wainwright,* 372 U.S. 335 (1963), extended it to all criminal cases, save certain misdemeanors. But that holding was later interpreted as comprehending all nontraffic misdemeanors involving any imprisonment (*Argersinger v. Hamlin,* 407 U.S. 25 [1972]; and *Scott v. Illinois,* 440 U.S. 367 [1979]).

126. 293 U.S. 245.

127. Some observers, including North, op. cit., regard this statement of incorporation as well as a similar one made in the case by Justice Cardozo's concurring opinion (ibid. at 265) as dicta. They prefer to point to *Cantwell v. Connecticut,* decided six years later, as the "incorporator" by rule of law rather than dictum of the free exercise clause (310 U.S. 296 at 303).

had readily chosen to attend that institution of his own free will, his due process of law was in no sense being violated by a requirement to comply with the university's (i.e., the state of California's) rules and regulations while in attendance.

In 1937, a few months earlier than the landmark incorporation case of *Palko v. Connecticut,*[128] the First Amendment's freedom of assembly and, by implication, its freedom "to petition the Government for a redress of grievances" became the fifth and sixth segments of the Bill of Rights to be "carried over." *De Jonge v. Oregon*[129] again involved a state criminal syndicalism law: Dirk De Jonge had been convicted in Oregon's Multnomah County under such a statute, which made it a criminal offense to advocate "crime, physical violence, sabotage, or any unlawful acts or methods as a means of accomplishing industrial change or political revolution." There was no record that De Jonge had advocated what the statute proscribed, nor did the indictment charge him specifically with having done so. The sole charge against him was that he had participated in an advertised political meeting of the Communist Party, of which he was an admitted member. The meeting, concededly peaceful, had been held by the Portland section of the Party to protest alleged brutality and unlawful activity by the Portland police and conditions at the county jail. Speaking for his unanimous Court, Chief Justice Hughes pointed out that "peaceable assembly for lawful discussion, however unpopular the sponsorship, cannot be made a crime," and that "the holding of meetings for peaceable political action cannot be proscribed." Further declaring that the right of peaceable assembly "is a right cognate to those of free speech and free press and is equally fundamental," he proceeded to hold that assembly, too, is thus one of "those fundamental principles of liberty and justice" that are made applicable to the states via the due process clause of the Fourteenth Amendment.[130]

Hence, when the *Palko* case appeared on the Court's calendar for decision, the entire First Amendment and the right to counsel provision of the Sixth Amendment (at least in capital criminal cases) had been firmly incorporated. But what was needed was a more thorough discussion that would deal with the theoretical as well as the practical issues involved in "nationalizing" the Bill of Rights. Appropriately, it fell to the eloquent Justice Benjamin N. Cardozo to perform that task. His all too brief six-year tenure on the Court culminated in *Palko v. Connecticut.*

The Doctrine Spelled Out: Cardozo and *Palko*

Frank U. Palko had been indicted by the state of Connecticut for *first-degree* murder in the fatal shooting of two policemen. The trial jury—as juries have

128. 302 U.S. 319.
129. 299 U.S. 353 (1937).
130. Ibid. at 364.

been known to do with predictable unpredictability—found him guilty of *second-degree* murder, however, and he was accordingly sentenced to life imprisonment with a recommendation that he never be paroled. Pursuant to a statute of 1866, however, and with the permission of the trial judge in the case, the state of Connecticut then appealed the conviction on the lesser count to the highest state court, the court of errors. In its petition Connecticut charged that the action in the trial court constituted an "error of law to the prejudice of the state"; the court of errors agreed, reversing the judgment below, and ordered a new trial. Although Palko objected that the second trial would place him twice in jeopardy for the same offense—an action forbidden by the terms of the Fifth Amendment and, as he urged, consequently forbidden also by those of the due process clause of the Fourteenth Amendment—his retrial took place soon thereafter.

This time the trial jury returned a verdict of murder in the first degree, and the judge sentenced Palko to death. Having exhausted his judicial remedies at the state level, Palko then appealed to the U.S. Supreme Court; again he contended that "whatever is forbidden by the Fifth Amendment is forbidden by the Fourteenth also."[131] For reasons to be outlined presently, the Supreme Court, speaking through Justice Cardozo, ruled against Palko's claims on all counts; Justice Butler dissented without opinion (an intriguing but not very helpful practice).[132] Frank Palko was subsequently executed by electrocution. Macabre though it may be, a cynic could comment that, given the importance of his case for the future of civil rights and liberties, he did not die in vain.

The "Honor Roll of Superior Rights." Justice Cardozo's opinion was recognized immediately as a judicial landmark for several reasons: (1) It established a yardstick by which to measure the incorporation problem and thus to govern judicial action. (2) It provided official judicial recognition for the formerly unpredictable claim that, under certain conditions and in certain areas—based upon a hierarchy of values—the several states are beholden to the commands of the federal Bill of Rights under the Fourteenth Amendment. (3) It laid the groundwork for the support of both the theory and the practice of a judicial double standard in the interpretation of basic human rights.[133] Practically speaking, what the Cardozo opinion accomplished was to deny or reject any *general* rule of overall incorporation, while acknowledging that there are, and indeed must be,

---

131. Ibid. at 322.

132. Robert Lewis Shayon told the senior author in November 1966 that he had discussed the *Palko* case in considerable detail with Frank Palko's court-appointed attorney, David Goldstein, a distinguished Bridgeport, Connecticut, lawyer. According to Goldstein, Butler's reason for dissenting—even without opinion—was based on his conviction that the state of Connecticut had in effect denied Palko's due process of law. During oral argument Butler was "very tough" on the state's attorney, at one point shouting, "What do you want? Blood?"

133. See the discussion *supra* in chapter 2.

some rights in the Bill of Rights that are fundamental enough to require "incorporation" or "absorption."

Justice Cardozo's *Palko* opinion thus established the "Honor Roll of Superior Rights," to which his lifelong admirer and ultimate successor on the Supreme Court, Felix Frankfurter, so irreverently referred as the "slot machine theory . . . some are in and some are out." Although he refused to regard the due process of law clause of the Fourteenth Amendment as "shorthand" for the Bill of Rights, Cardozo nonetheless set himself the task of distinguishing those basic rights that he and his supporters viewed as "of the very essence of a scheme of ordered liberty" from those without which "justice would not perish" and which were not therefore "implicit in the concept of ordered liberty." Explaining his rationale further, he wrote movingly of "those fundamental principles of liberty and justice which lie at the base of all our civil and political institutions," and of principles of justice "so rooted in the traditions and conscience of our people as to be ranked as fundamental."[134] (It is significant to note the recurrent use of the concept of "fundamental" rights in juxtaposition to what, as we shall see later, are termed "formal" rights on the scale of basic rights and liberties.)[135] Recognizing the difficulties of evaluation and interpretation inherent in his dichotomy, and anticipating both the criticism and some of the problems that would follow, Cardozo resorted to the "freedom of thought and speech" as his cardinal illustration: "Of that freedom one may say that it is the matrix, the indispensable condition, of nearly every other form of freedom. With rare aberrations, a pervasive recognition of that truth can be traced in our history, political and legal. . . ."[136]

For the other group, these "formal" rights in the Bill of Rights without which "justice would not perish," Cardozo cited the right to trial by jury and the immunity from prosecution "for a capital or otherwise infamous crime" except as a result of an indictment, explaining that they may indeed have "value and importance," but

> they are not of the essence of a scheme of ordered liberty. To abolish them is not to violate a "principle of justice so rooted in the traditions and conscience of our people as to be ranked as fundamental." . . . Few would be so narrow as to maintain that a fair and enlightened system of justice would be impossible without them. . . .[137]

---

134. 302 U.S. 319 (1937) at 325.

135. The Court had established a dichotomy between "formal" and "fundamental" rights at the turn of the century in answering the question of how many, and which, of the rights in the Constitution were to be applicable automatically to possessions and territories. The "fundamental" ones only, held the Court in the series of *Insular Cases* from 1901 to 1905. See especially *Hawaii v. Mankiehi,* 190 U.S. 197 (1903); and *Rasmussen v. United States,* 197 U.S. 516 (1905). What is "fundamental" is of course a value judgment.

136. *Palko v. Connecticut,* op. cit., at 327.

137. Ibid. at 325.

Then, turning specifically to another right, the immunity from compulsory self-incrimination, he noted, "[T]his too might be lost, and justice still be done. . . . Justice . . . would not perish if the accused were subject to a duty to respond to orderly inquiry."[138] Cardozo thus insisted that in the realm of chiefly *procedural* rights, in general, and the protection against double jeopardy at issue in the *Palko* ruling, in particular, the question to be posed by the appellate tribunal must be, as Justice Harlan had phrased it decades earlier, all-embracing: "Does it violate those 'fundamental principles of liberty and justice which lie at the base of all our civil and political institutions'?" The answer, judged Cardozo, "surely must be 'no,'" for Connecticut "is not attempting to wear the accused out by a multitude of cases with accumulated trials. It asks no more than this, that the case against him shall go on until there shall be a trial free from the corrosion of substantial legal error."[139] In his view, Connecticut had sought no more than parity with the defendant in the right to continue a case "until there shall be a trial free from the corrosion of substantial legal error." A defendant was given the right to appeal errors adverse to him. "A reciprocal privilege . . . has now been granted to the state. . . ." And he concluded on a note of assurance: "There is here no seismic innovation. The edifice of justice stands, in its symmetry, to many, greater than before."[140]

A Caveat. It is essential to recognize at once that, despite the *Palko* dichotomy between the components of the Bill of Rights that are and those that are not "implicit in the concept of ordered liberty,"[141] Justice Cardozo made it clear that the several states would still be subject to the judicial test of whether or not a duly challenged law or action constituted a violation of the "due process of law" concept of the Fourteenth Amendment per se. In other words, simply because only some of the rights are ipso facto applicable to the states via the Fourteenth Amendment it does not mean that the states are free to violate the basic concepts of due process of law to which all persons in their jurisdictions are entitled. In such claims the judicial test then becomes the one so faithfully and ardently embraced by Justice Frankfurter during his career on the Supreme Court: does the alleged state violation constitute conduct that "shocks the conscience," or, in the less inhibited language of Justice Holmes, "does it make you vomit?" Given the

---

138. Ibid. at 326.
139. Ibid. at 328. An interesting 1997 decision dealt, as least partly, with the double jeopardy issue. In a narrow 5:4 ruling, penned by Justice Clarence Thomas, the Court held that states can commit sex offenders to mental institutions even though they have already served their full prison time, if they have been judged to be "mentally abnormal" or as having a "personality disorder" (*Kansas v. Hendricks,* 521 U.S. 346).
140. Ibid.
141. Louis Lusky protests that "ordered liberty is too vague to describe a national objective. . . . It is a vehicle for whatever meaning the Court gives it, and thus enables the Court to apply its own conceptions of public policy" (*By What Right?* [Charlottesville, Va.: The Michie Co., 1975], pp. 105, 107).

divergent status of consciences, and the different physiological responses to shock, it is obvious that the answer in individual cases is difficult and often unpredictable. We shall have occasion to return to this particular problem of drawing lines when we consider the various choices or "positions" on the incorporation question offered by justices of the Supreme Court and other knowledgeable participants in the search for justice.

Post-*Palko* Developments

The test devised by Justice Cardozo in *Palko* presumably permitted, if it did not indeed invite, subsequent alteration of the newly created incorporation "line." That line—*as of the famous Opinion Monday in* 1937—had created the dichotomy shown in Table 3.1.

As the limited number of *a*-marked items in the table indicates, Cardozo did not specifically cover each and every aspect of the Bill of Rights. But his language made quite clear that the underlying principles of our federal government structure demand that the states be permitted to follow their own practices and discretion in the realm of procedural due process so long as they provide a full measure of due process of law in each and every instance.

1947 and 1948: Two Additions. The Cardozo "Honor Roll" stood for almost a quarter of a century. During that period it was extended only twice: to include the concept of "separation of church and state" in the already incorporated exercise of freedom of religion and to require *public* trials. The vehicle for the former was the 1947 *New Jersey Bus Case*[142] (which we shall have occasion to discuss in considerable detail in chapter 6). Pertinent here is the unanimous Court's acknowledgment (despite its 5:4 split on the specific merits of the case) that a bona fide violation of the principle of the separation of church and state is constitutionally proscribed by *both* the terms of the First Amendment and the "due process of law" clause of the Fourteenth Amendment. The "public" trial requirement came with a 7:2 opinion by Justice Black (Justices Frankfurter and Jackson dissenting) in 1948 as a result of the secret sentencing of a Michigan citizen, William D. Oliver, by a judge serving as a one-man grand jury, a practice statutorily sanctioned in his home state's Oakland County.[143]

---

142. *Everson v. Board of Education of Ewing Township,* 330 U.S. 1. Justice Black preferred to think of *Murdock v. Pennsylvania,* 319 U.S. 105 (1943), as the vehicle of incorporation of separation of church and state.

143. *In re Oliver,* 333 U.S. 257 (1948). At first blush the case seemed to turn on simple due process considerations. But in later opinions the Supreme Court specifically (e.g., *Duncan v. Louisiana,* 391 U.S. 145 [1968]) referred to Oliver as having incorporated "public" trials. However, a 5:4 Court ruled in a hotly criticized 1979 decision that "members of the public have no constitutional right under the Sixth and Fourteenth Amendments to attend criminal trials" if the defendant, the prosecutor, and the presiding judge

Table 3.1. The Status of "Incorporation" as of *Palko* (1937)

Amendment	"Incorporated" (and Year)	Vote	Not "Incorporated"
One	Speech[a] (1925 and 1927) Press[a] (1925 and 1931) Free exercise of religion[a] (1934) Peaceable assembly[a] (1937) Right of petition (1937)	9:0 and 7:2 9:0 and 5:4 9:0 8:0 8:0	Separation of church and state
Two			Keep and bear arms
Three			No quartering of soldiers
Four			Evidence admitted as result of unreasonable search and seizure[a]
Five	Due process of law (as per Fourteenth) Eminent domain safeguards[b] (1937 and 1897, resp.)	9:0 and 8:1	Grand jury indictment[a] or presentment Double jeopardy[a] Compulsory self-incrimination[a]
Six	Counsel in criminal cases[a] (later judicially abridged to read "in capital" criminal cases only—but then reinterpreted to read "all criminal cases") Fair trial (1932 and 1937, resp.)	 7:2 and 9:0	Speedy and public trial Impartial jury trial in criminal cases[a] Nature and cause of accusation Compulsory process for appearance of witness Confrontation of accusers
Seven	Fair trial (1937)	9:0	Jury trial in civil cases[a]
Eight	Fair trial (1937)	9:0	Excessive bail and fines Cruel and unusual punishments

[a]Specifically mentioned in the *Palko* opinion by Justice Cardozo.
[b]Alluded to in his Footnote Four.

1961: The Cleveland Search and Seizure Case. The year 1961 heralded a new burst of judicial activity (some would say "activism"). It was the Fourth Amendment's guarantee against "unreasonable searches and seizures" that was next to be incorporated. The fruit of such seizures had long ago ceased to be admissible as evidence in *federal* court.[144] States, too, had been judicially forbidden to engage in *unreasonable* searches and seizures as of 1949 in the 6:3 *Wolf* deci-

---

agree to close the courtroom to press and public (*Gannett v. De Pasquale*, 443 U.S. 368). But see the more or less contrary 7:0 holding in 1980 (*Richmond Newspapers v. Virginia*, 448 U.S. 555), confining *Gannett* to pretrials; see also the 1982 follow-up holding in *Globe Newspaper Co. v. Superior Court*, 457 U.S. 596, and subsequent cases.

144. *Weeks v. United States*, 232 U.S. 383 (1914). The judicially created rule thus prohibits the admissibility in criminal trials of evidence seized in violation of Amendment Four.

sion,[145] but the traditions of common law—if the evidence is trustworthy (i.e., if it is "material, relevant, and probative"), it *is* admissible regardless of how it was acquired[146]—nonetheless were held to permit their "fruit" (i.e., their results) as admissible evidence in *state* court proceedings. The judicial rationale for this rather astonishing dichotomy was that the victim of such evidence could trigger "the remedies of private action"—namely, *sue* the procurer of the illegally obtained, but admitted, evidence for civil damages or call for criminal proceedings against officials engaged in unlawful searches. Demonstrably, the Court thus chose to regard the *exclusionary rule as an evidentiary rule, not as a constitutional provision.*[147] *Wolf* was reaffirmed narrowly (5:4) in a controversial 1954 California case in which Justice Tom C. Clark, the future author of *Mapp,* cast the decisive vote.[148]

As a result of her 1961 case, Ms. Dolree (Dolly) Mapp, a Cleveland woman of questionable reputation, catalyzed the carryover of the federal principle to the states. Acting on alleged information that Ms. Mapp, and possibly her daughter by an erstwhile marriage, were hiding (1) a fugitive and (2) "a large amount of policy paraphernalia" on the top floor of their two-story family dwelling, police forced their way into the house without a warrant of any kind—they feigned one by brandishing a blank white sheet of stationery—and found, after an unedifying struggle and a widespread search, some "obscene materials." On the strength of these, Ms. Mapp was convicted of the illegal possession of obscene materials in violation of an Ohio statute. The Ohio judiciary upheld her conviction, but the Supreme Court, on appeal, reversed it in *Mapp v. Ohio,*[149] in what

145. *Wolf v. Colorado,* 339 U.S. 25 (1949). Here the Court in effect announced the "incorporation" of the Fourth Amendment's pertinent guarantees but, as explained, at once neutralized or negated it by continuing to sanction admissibility of evidence so obtained by the states—in this state case, the confiscation of Dr. Wolf's appointment books. Thus, the *Weeks* rule (loc. cit.) did not yet apply to the states.

146. The courts of England and almost all those of the world's other lands still maintain that particular common-law approach to the acquisition of evidence, relying instead on civil, criminal, and disciplinary remedies against offending police officers. See J. David Hirschel, "What Can We Learn from the English Approach to the Problem of Illegally Seized Evidence?" 67 *Judicature* 9 (April 1984). For a discussion of English and American history in order to determine the sources and development of the Fourth Amendment, see Leonard Levy, "Origins of the Fourth Amendment," 114 *Political Science Quarterly* 79 (spring 1999).

147. In rejecting the application of the exclusionary rule in the state of New York in 1926, Cardozo, then a judge on its court of appeals, had asked the celebrated question whether "the criminal is to go free because the constable had blundered?" (*People v. Defore,* 242 N.Y. 13 at 19–25).

148. *Irvine v. California,* 347 U.S. 128. The others, like Clark, who joined Justice Jackson's reluctant majority opinion, were Chief Justice Warren and Justices Reed and Minton. Dissenters were Black, Douglas, Frankfurter, and Burton.

149. 367 U.S. 643 (1961). Actually, albeit upholding her conviction, the Ohio Supreme Court declared the pertinent Ohio statute unconstitutional by a majority vote of 5:2. How-

the *New York Times* appropriately termed "an historical step," and Harvard Law School dean—soon to be solicitor general of the United States—Erwin Griswold saw as requiring "a complete change in the outlook and practices of state and local police."[150] Speaking for the 6:3 majority—Justices Frankfurter, Harlan, and Whittaker dissenting—Justice Clark overruled the long-standing precedents, especially *Wolf,* and, not fully incorporating the Fourth Amendment's applicable guarantee, ruled that "all evidence obtained by searches and seizures in violation of the Constitution is, by that same authority [Amendment Four], inadmissible in a state court" and "since the Fourth Amendment's right of privacy has been declared enforceable against the States through the Due Process Clause of the Fourteenth [although not, as it held in 1984, to those in prison cells],[151] it is enforceable against them by the same sanction of exclusion as is used against the Federal Government."[152] Thus, in the words of a leading student of search-and-seizure problems, the *Mapp* decision "clearly catapulted the exclusionary rule into a position at the core" of the Fourteenth Amendment.[153] Yet 1974 witnessed a distinct dilution of its safeguards at the level of grand juries,[154] and considerable agitation for the rule's abridgment, if not its outright abolition, was manifest in Congress, segments of the judicial branch (encouraged by the chief justice of the United States), and the organized bar. Indeed, 1976 would see two 6:3 rulings sharply reducing the power of *lower* federal courts in habeas corpus proceedings to set aside *state* criminal convictions that relied on illegally obtained evidence, and another 6:3 one refusing to apply the

ever, since the Ohio Constitution permits only one dissenting vote on the seven-man Ohio Supreme Court in cases of declarations of unconstitutionality, the law survived (170 Ohio St. 427–28, 166 N.E.2d 387, 398). Ms. Mapp managed to run afoul of the law in subsequent years and, ironically, filed an appeal from a conviction for narcotics trafficking in New York in 1975 on the strength of the 1961 decision (*New York Times,* December 15, 1975, p. 35c).

150. June 20, 1961, p. 1, and as quoted in the *New York Times,* December 15, 1975, p. 35c.

151. *Hudson v. Palmer,* 468 U.S. 517.

152. *Mapp v. Ohio,* op. cit., at 655. Federal standards of "reasonableness" were specifically confirmed as applicable to the conduct of state police officers in *Ker v. California,* 374 U.S. 23 (1963).

153. Jacob W. Landynski, "Search and Seizure," in Stuart S. Nagel, ed., *The Rights of the Accused,* 23 vols. (New York: Sage, 1972), vol. 1, p. 47. For an enlightening analysis of Justice Clark's seminal role in *Mapp,* and his role perceptions as a member of the Court, see Dennis D. Doran, "Seize the Time: Justice Tom Clark's Role in *Mapp v. Ohio,*" in Victoria L. Swigent, ed., *Law and the Legal Process* (Beverly Hills, Calif.: Sage, 1982).

154. *United States v. Calandra,* 414 U.S. 338, in which the Court, by a 6:3 vote, wrote a significant exception into the rule by holding that grand juries may use illegally obtained evidence as a basis for questioning witnesses without violating their constitutional rights.

rule to *civil* cases.[155] In 1982 the Court, emphasizing a changed tenor with respect to the states' power over the administration of justice, ruled (6:3) that objections to state trial procedures must be raised at the time of the trial[156] and that there must be total exhaustion of the claim, below.[157] And 1984 would see a potentially far-reaching limitation of the exclusionary rule in two key decisions by establishing the "good faith" exception.[158]

1962 and Beyond: Cruel and Unusual Punishment. The next incorporation came scarcely a year after *Mapp.* California, a source of considerable litigation on constitutional questions, provided the vehicle that would bring about the nationalization of the Eighth Amendment's guarantees against the infliction of "cruel and unusual punishments" (a judicial action for which Justice Field had called seventy years earlier).[159] Because that issue itself was but fleetingly discussed and briefed, some doubt existed as to whether the Supreme Court actually intended to incorporate the provision; but the general assumption now is that Justice Stewart's language did, in effect, apply to the states those basic strictures of the last article of amendment in the Bill of Rights.[160] His allies in that interpretation were the chief justice and Justices Black, Douglas, and Brennan; Justice Harlan concurred, but on the narrower ground of violation of due process of law. Justice Byron R. White, joined by Justice Clark, wrote his first dissenting opinion on the bench in the case, accusing the Court of meddling unjustifiably with the state's criminal justice jurisdiction and discretion. At issue was a California statute making it a crime "to be under the influence of, or be addicted to narcotics, or to make unprescribed use of them"; "status" violations were punishable by a mandatory ninety-day jail sentence.

Walter Lawrence Robinson—who died a year before he won his case—had been arrested on a Los Angeles street by police, whom he told that he used narcotics; his arms bore what appeared to be hypodermic needle marks. (The case

---

155. *Stone v. Powell* and *Wolff v. Rice,* 428 U.S. 465, and *United States v. Janis,* 428 U.S. 433, respectively. (On the other hand, in 1979 the Court reconfirmed—albeit by a mere 5:4 margin—the federal courts' habeas corpus authority in cases of alleged racial discrimination [*Rose v. Mitchell,* 443 U.S. 545].) Two 1993 cases, both decided 5:4—arguably contradictorily—served to muddy these turbulent waters (see *Brecht v. Abrahamson,* 507 U.S. 619, and *Withrow v. Williams,* 507 U.S. 680). But see the Court's unanimous upholding of federal statutory limits of habeas corpus petitions in capital punishment cases (*Felker v. Turpin,* 518 U.S. 651 [1996]).

156. *Engle v. Isaac,* 456 U.S. 107. See also *United States v. Frady,* 456 U.S. 152 (1982).

157. *Rose v. Lundy,* 255 U.S. 509 (1982).

158. *United States v. Leon,* 468 U.S. 897; and *Massachusetts v. Sheppard,* 468 U.S. 981.

159. See *supra* this chapter.

160. *Robinson v. California,* 370 U.S. 660 (1962).

had nothing to do with the *sale* of narcotics.) He had been charged with violation of the statute and sentenced to jail. On appeal, Robinson's counsel successfully raised the "cruel and unusual punishment" issue on the ground that the law did not require *proof* of purchase or use of the drugs. Accepting this argument for the Court majority, Justice Stewart declared the statute unconstitutional as a violation of the Eighth and Fourteenth Amendments. As he viewed it, the law fell into the same category as one purporting to make it a criminal offense "for a person to be mentally ill, or a leper, or to be afflicted with venereal disease." Carrying over the pertinent provision of Amendment Eight, he held that "a state which imprisons a person thus afflicted as a criminal, even though he had never touched any narcotic drug within the state or been guilty of any irregular behavior there, inflicts a cruel and unusual punishment in violation of the Fourteenth Amendment."[161] In a significant concurring opinion, Justice Douglas regarded Robinson's conviction of being an addict, not his confinement, as *the* specific "cruel and unusual punishment." Addicts, suggested Douglas, should be cured, not jailed.

In the bizarre 1947 Louisiana "double electrocution" case, in which the "electric chair" malfunctioned on the first try but operated as intended on the second attempt to execute young Willie Francis, Justice Stanley Reed had voiced "the assumption, but without so deciding, that violation of the principles of the *Fifth* and *Eighth* Amendments, as a double jeopardy and *cruel and unusual pun-*

---

161. Ibid. at 666–67. But in 1968 the Court refused to extend the *Robinson* principle to chronic alcoholics, in a case involving one of Leroy Powell's one hundred (!) prior convictions for public intoxication. The Court held 5:4 that a Texas statute making it a crime to be "found in a state of intoxication in any public place" could not ipso facto be held to be "irrational" in line with the *Robinson* reasoning. For, wrote Justice Thurgood Marshall, Powell was not "convicted for being a chronic alcoholic, but for being in public while drunk on a particular occasion" (*Powell v. Texas,* 392 U.S. 514 at 532). And as the high tribunal ruled (4:3) in 1988, the Veterans Administration does not violate the Eighth Amendment when it denies disability benefits and others to most veterans disabled by alcoholism, for their condition is caused by "wilfull misconduct," not by "uncontrollable disease" (*Traynor v. Turnage,* 485 U.S. 535). The three dissenters were Blackmun, Brennan, and Marshall. The majority consisted of Rehnquist, Stevens, O'Connor, and White, who penned the opinion. Nor, held the Court per curiam (6:3), is a forty-year sentence for trafficking in marijuana "cruel and unusual punishment" (*Hutto v. Davis,* 454 U.S. 370 [1982]). Nor, as it ruled 5:4 in 1991—distinguishing a 1983 (5:4) precedent (*Salem v. Helm,* 463 U.S. 278)—is mandatory life imprisonment without parole a possibility for the possession of one and a half pounds, approximately 672.5 grams, of pure cocaine (*Harmelin v. Michigan,* 501 U.S. 957). But prison inmates who demonstrate that exposure to cigarette smoke is a threat to their health may invoke the cruel and unusual punishment safeguards of the Eighth Amendment in order not to be confined with a chain-smoking cellmate (*Helling v. McKinney,* 509 U.S. 25). Moreover, the Court in 1993 unanimously limited the federal government's power to seize homes and businesses used in illegal drug trafficking. It sharply rejected arguments that the Eighth Amendment does not apply to property forfeited in civil proceedings (*Austin v. U.S.,* 421 U.S. 990).

ishment, would be violative of the due process clause of the Fourteenth Amendment."[162] Yet it was a quarter century before the "cruel and unusual punishment" concept became the constitutional hook on which the Court, in *Furman v. Georgia*'s nine-opinion per curiam decision running to 243 pages, hung its 5:4 ruling, on the last day of the 1971–72 term, that capital punishment, as it was then administered under certain state laws, was unconstitutional.[163] When Congress and thirty-five states subsequently responded by enacting new laws, designed to meet the Court's objections but to retain capital punishment, a new judicial test on the latter's constitutionality loomed as a certainty. It came on July 2, 1976, in a series of twenty-four (!) opinions in five cases, led by *Gregg v. Georgia,* covering various capital punishment laws from five states. By a vote of 7:2 the high tribunal ruled in an opinion, announced by Justice Stewart, that the death penalty is *not* inherently cruel or unusual, at least not in murder cases, provided that judges and juries have been given "adequate information and guidance" for determining whether the sentence is appropriate in a particular case.[164] But the Court held (5:4) in 1976 that "mandatory" capital punishment laws in Louisiana that required the death penalty for every defendant convicted of one or more of five categories of murder may not be imposed, and it also disallowed a similar North Carolina law.[165] Louisiana tried to rescue the law by applying it only to anyone convicted of murdering a fireman or a policeman, but it, too, fell (5:4) in 1977.[166] Georgia's attempt to render rape a capital crime was struck down, also in 1977, by the Court (7:2) as constituting an impermissible cruel and unusual punishment.[167] As the Court put it (7:1) in 1978, "every conceivable mitigating factor" must be considered.[168] Thus, it overruled a conviction in 1982 involving the brutal, unprovoked murder of a traffic policeman by a sixteen-year-old using a sawed-off shotgun, holding 5:4 via Justice Powell that the accused's "uniqueness as an individual" had not been properly taken into account.[169]

The Court proscribed execution of insane prisoners, again 5:4, in *Ford v.*

162. *Louisiana ex rel. Francis v. Resweber,* 329 U.S. 459 at 462; italics supplied. For accounts of that grisly case, see the appropriate chapters by Barrett E. Prettyman Jr. in *Death and the Supreme Court* (New York: Harcourt, Brace, 1961); the detailed study by Arthur S. Miller and Jeffrey H. Bowman, "Slow Dance in the Killing Ground: The Willie Francis Case Revisited," 32 *De Paul Law Review* (fall 1982), as well as these two authors' *Death by Installments: The Ordeal of Willie Francis* (Westport, Conn.: Greenwood Press, 1988); and William M. Wiecek's excellent account, "Felix Frankfurter, Incorporation, and the Willie Francis Case," 26 *Journal of Supreme Court History* 53 (2001).

163. *Furman v. Georgia,* 408 U.S. 238 (1972).

164. *Gregg v. Georgia,* 428 U.S. 513 (1976).

165. *Roberts v. Louisiana,* 428 U.S. 335 (1976), and *Woodson v. North Carolina,* 428 U.S. 280 (1976), respectively.

166. *Roberts v. Louisiana II,* 431 U.S. 633 (1977).

167. *Coker v. Georgia,* 433 U.S. 584 (1977).

168. *Lockett v. Ohio,* 438 U.S. 586 (1978).

169. *Eddings v. Oklahoma,* 455 U.S. 104 (1982).

Wainwright (1986); and it narrowed application of the death penalty, with respect to juveniles under age sixteen, in *Thompson v. Oklahoma* (1988).[170] Yet it upheld the imposition of capital punishment in 1989 in two cases involving a sixteen- and a seventeen-year-old murderer and rapist, both by 5:4 votes, as well as in one involving a mentally retarded murderer-rapist, also by a 5:4 decision, in *Penry v. Lynaugh*[171] — a case redocketed as *Penry v. Johnson* for oral argument in the fall of 2001 and decided 6:3 in favor of Johnny Paul Penry because of the failure of prosecutors clearly to instruct jurors on how they could evaluate Penry's mental capacity.[172] It allowed (5:4) in 1987 the imposition of the death penalty for *accomplices,* even if the latter neither killed nor intended to kill.[173] And that same year in a dramatic 5:4 decision, *McCleskey v. Kemp,* written by Justice Powell, the justices ruled that a state's capital punishment system was constitutional despite the fact that killers of white people have been more frequently sentenced to die than killers of blacks.[174] The U.S. Supreme Court has increasingly imposed limits on the number and types of death penalty appeals it will hear. Thus, in 1993, in a 6:3 holding, it added more rules to appeals procedures for condemned prisoners, asserting that condemned inmates who have exhausted their appeals and then produce new evidence that could prove their innocence have *no* right to be heard by a *federal* court.[175] But one year later the Court ruled 7:2 that juries must be told whether "life in prison" means "no parole."[176] In 1998, by a 5:4 vote, the Court further curbed dealth penalty appeals based on trial error.[177] The next year the justices, again closely split (5:4), upheld the Federal Death Penalty Act of 1994 against its first challenge, pointing to "harmless error" at trial.[178]

However, the turn of the century would see a less favorable attitude on the high court's part toward the constitutional range and extent of capital punishment. Thus, in effect revising the first *Penry* case, it ruled 6:3 in June 2002 that executions of mentally retarded criminals violate the cruel and unusual punishment provisions of the Eighth Amendment.[179] Four days later the high court overturned (7:2) an Arizona death sentence because it had been pronounced by a

---

170. *Ford v. Wainwright,* 477 U.S. 399 (1986), and *Thompson v. Oklahoma,* 487 U.S. 815 (1988), respectively.

171. *Wilkins v. Missouri* and *Stanford v. Kentucky,* 492 U.S. 361 (1989), and *Penry v. Lynaugh,* 492 U.S. 302 (1989), respectively.

172. *Penry v. Johnson,* 532 U.S. 782 (2002).

173. *Tison v. Arizona,* 481 U.S. 137 (1987).

174. *McCleskey v. Kemp,* 478 U.S. 1019 (1987). See Barbara A. Perry, Donald L. Davison, and Michael Krassa, "Race and the Death Penalty," *JAI Research Annual on Law and Policy Studies* 189 (1991).

175. *Herrera v. Collins,* 506 U.S. 390 (1993).

176. *Simmons v. South Carolina,* 512 U.S. 154 (1994). See also *Felker v. Turpin,* 518 U.S. 651 (1996); and *O'Dell v. Netherland,* 521 U.S. 151.

177. *Calderon v. Coleman,* 67 LW 3391 (1998).

178. *Jones v. U.S.,* 67 LW 4508 (1999).

179. *Atkins v. Virginia,* 536 U.S. ___ (2002).

judge rather than the *jury*—echoing the Court's controversial 1999 *Apprendi v. New Jersey* decision[180]—prompting the Ginsburg-led majority to find the procedure in violation of the Seventh Amendment's trial by jury guarantee.[181] The number of executions since the 1976 *Gregg* decision reinstated the death penalty stood at five hundred as of mid-1999, with some thirty-five hundred individuals on death row.

1963: Clarence Earl Gideon's Right to Counsel Case. Of far greater significance, given the large numbers of individuals affected, is the celebrated case of *Gideon v. Wainwright.*[182] It is probably the most famous "incorporation decision" since *Palko.* In effect, it nationalized the right to counsel in *all*—save certain misdemeanor—criminal cases, *be they capital or noncapital.* As indicated earlier, a good many observers had quietly assumed that Justice Sutherland's language in the *Scottsboro Case*[183] had fully intended to incorporate the right to counsel in criminal cases generally. This understanding seemed to be confirmed by Justice Cardozo's choice of words in *Palko*—"the right of one accused of crime to the benefit of counsel"[184]—but the Court held to the contrary in the case of *Betts v. Brady*[185] in 1942. There, Justice Owen J. Roberts, speaking for a 6:3 majority, had ruled that the due process clause of the Fourteenth Amendment did *not* require counsel to be furnished by a state (here Maryland) in *noncapital* criminal cases unless "special" or "exceptional" circumstances, such as "mental illness," "youth," or "lack of education," were present. It was the *Betts* ruling that was specifically overturned by a unanimous Supreme Court, some twenty-one years later, with the opinion delivered with great conviction and satisfaction by the same man who had dissented in *Betts*—Justice Black.

The *Gideon* case, about which so much has been written,[186] and for good cause, reached the highest tribunal on a writ of certiorari as a result of a penciled petition in forma pauperis[187] composed with painstaking precision on lined prison-regulation paper by Clarence Earl Gideon. Without a lawyer and penniless, he had been committed to a Florida jail as a result of a criminal conviction for "having broken and entered a poolroom with intent to commit a misde-

---

180. *Apprendi v. New Jersey,* 530 U.S. 466 (2000).
181. *Ring v. Arizona,* 536 U.S. ___ (2002).
182. 372 U.S. 335 (1963).
183. *Powell v. Alabama,* 287 U.S. 45 (1932).
184. *Palko v. Connecticut,* 302 U.S. 319 (1937) at 324.
185. 316 U.S. 455.
186. The best full-length study—a superb account—is Anthony Lewis, *Gideon's Trumpet* (New York: Random House, 1964). Gideon died in 1972; his name has become a household word in the annals of justice. A gravesite service in Hannibal, Missouri, in 1984 honored him as "the catalyst for the U.S. Public Defender system."
187. "In the form of a pauper; as a poor man."

meanor"[188] on the strength of testimony by a man who later turned out to have been the culprit himself! Gideon's request for counsel to represent him at his trial had been refused because of Florida's then valid requirement under the *Betts* precedent that court-appointed counsel be reserved for capital criminal cases. To Gideon's warm plea in the courtroom—"Your Honor, the United States Constitution says I am entitled to be represented by Counsel"—Trial Judge Robert L. McCreary Jr. could only say, in accordance with his Florida mandate, "I am sorry, but I cannot appoint Counsel to represent you in this case."[189] Gideon thereupon acted as his own lawyer—but not too successfully: found guilty, he was sentenced to five years' imprisonment.

No knowledgeable observer of the judicial process and the Supreme Court was surprised that the Court overturned the *Betts* decision so decisively and unanimously[190] when Gideon managed to get his case "up"—his appeal before the Supreme Court briefed and argued by the Court-appointed, crack Washington attorney and future associate justice of the highest tribunal, Abe Fortas. Briefs amici curiae[191] from only two states—Alabama and North Carolina—supported Florida's plea to the Court that it leave *Betts v. Brady*[192] intact; yet twenty-three states argued, in Justice Black's words, "that Betts was an anachronism when handed down and that it should now be overruled." "We agree," concluded Black triumphantly, noting that in its *Betts* decision the Court had "departed from the sound wisdom upon which its holding in *Powell v. Alabama*[193] rested." Ruling squarely that a state's failure to appoint counsel in a noncapital case—whether requested to do so or not—deprived the indigent defendant in a criminal proceeding of due process of law under the Fourteenth Amendment, as comprehended by the right to counsel requirements of the Sixth Amendment, Black remarked that it was "an obvious truth" that "in our adversary system of criminal justice any person hailed into court who is too poor to hire a lawyer cannot be assured a fair

---

188. A misdemeanor is an indictable offense, not usually serious enough to be classified as a crime—but it is so in Florida and increasingly so elsewhere. In 1972, however, all imprisonable misdemeanors, beyond mere fine cases, were accorded full *Gideon* rights (*Argersinger v. Hamlin,* 407 U.S. 25), and they were unanimously made retroactive one year thereafter (*Berry v. Cincinnati,* 414 U.S. 29), as *Gideon* had also been in 1963 in *Pickelseimer v. Wainwright,* 375 U.S. 2. However, in 1979 the Court ruled (5:4) that *Argersinger* and *Berry* extend only to those instances in which there is a "likelihood" of actual imprisonment, as contrasted with a mere "possibility." Thus, a *fine* in a petty case would not trigger the *Gideon* or *Argersinger* right to assigned counsel (*Scott v. Illinois,* 440 U.S. 367).

189. *Gideon v. Wainwright,* op. cit., at 335–36.

190. Justices Douglas and Harlan wrote separate concurring opinions.

191. A brief amicus curiae (i.e., "friend of the Court") enables an interested third party to enter the case, with the consent of the other litigants and/or the Court.

192. 316 U.S. 455 (1942).

193. 287 U.S. 45 (1932).

trial unless counsel is provided for him."[194] Another long-overdue aspect of incorporation had thus been accomplished, one which, as will be determined in the next chapter, was to be significantly broadened in succeeding years.[195]

Moreover, for once Congress responded promptly and affirmatively by enacting the Criminal Justice Act (CJA) of 1964, designed to provide more adequate representation of defendants in federal courts in all nonpetty cases. Not only that, but within two years the legislatures and courts of twenty-three states took specific actions to implement the spirit as well as the letter of *Gideon*. As amended in 1970, the 1964 CJA authorizes both the creation of federal or community public defender organizations in "high-volume districts" and the necessary compensation for legal assistance at *every* step and stage of the criminal process, from the arrest to appeals, *including* postconviction and ancillary proceedings relative to the criminal trial. No wonder the *Gideon* case stands as a landmark! However, to limit cascading claims of "poor representation," the Court, in an interesting and important 8:1 decision in 1984—written by Justice O'Connor, with Justice Marshall in lone dissent—ruled that to prevail in such a claim a defendant must demonstrate that the lawyer's work fell "below prevailing professional norms" and that without counsel's professional errors the outcome would have been different.[196] Yet, perhaps believing a more broadly gauged standard to be apposite, for the first time the Court ruled (7:2) in a Brennan opinion one year later, over dissents by Burger and Rehnquist, that a criminal defendant has a "constitutional right to *effective* assistance by counsel on [the first] appeal"[197]—therewith opening a proverbial can of worms. (*But,* held the Court in 1989, in *civil* cases unwilling attorneys cannot be forced to represent indigents.)[198] And in the same term, a 5:4 majority ruled that indigent inmates on death row do *not* have a constitutional right to a lawyer "to assist them in a *second* round of *state* court appeals."[199] And it also held (8:1) that a state must provide an indigent criminal defendant with free psychiatric assistance in preparing an insanity defense if the defendant's sanity "at the time of the crime is seriously

194. *Gideon v. Wainwright,* op. cit., at 355. On remand to the Florida trial court, Gideon was quickly retried and acquitted with the aid of a local attorney.

195. See, e.g., these decisions liberalizing even further the right to counsel: *Massiah v. United States,* 377 U.S. 201 (1964); *Escobedo v. Illinois,* 387 U.S. 478 (1964); the series of June 1966 cases expanding the *Escobedo* decision, headed by *Miranda v. Arizona,* 384 U.S. 436; *Orozco v. Texas,* 394 U.S. 324 (1969); *Coleman v. Alabama,* 399 U.S. 1 (1970); *Argersinger v. Hamlin,* 407 U.S. 25 (1972); and *United States v. Henry,* 447 U.S. 264 (1980).

196. *Strickland v. Washington,* 467 U.S. 1267.

197. *Evitts v. Lucy,* 469 U.S. 387 (1985). However, one year later, the U.S. Court of Appeals for the District of Columbia interpreted *Evitts* to apply solely to "grossly inadequate" representation (*Watson v. United States,* 54 LW 2559).

198. *Mallard v. U.S. District Court,* 490 U.S. 296.

199. *Murray v. Giarantano,* 492 U.S. 1; italics supplied.

in question."[200] Obviously, the issue of "effectiveness" of counsel remains far from settled; it is a veritable hornet's nest. And just around the corner waited another contentious sector of the Bill of Rights: the Fifth Amendment's stricture against compulsory self-incrimination.

1964: The Self-Incrimination Cases. The frequently predicted and much publicized self-incrimination safeguards were incorporated in a significant dual decision in the last days of the 1963–64 term. In two cases[201] the Court dramatically overruled its 1908 decision in the *Twining* case,[202] thus adopting Justice Harlan's lone dissent therein to render another signal contribution to the broadening concept of criminal jurisprudence.

The first case was from Connecticut and concerned one William Malloy, who had been arrested during a gambling raid in 1959 by Hartford police. Pleading guilty to the crime of "pool-selling," he was sentenced to one year in jail and fined $500. Some sixteen months thereafter Malloy was ordered to testify in an official, court-sanctioned inquiry into alleged gambling and other criminal activities in the county. Asked a number of questions about events surrounding his own arrest and conviction, Malloy refused to answer any of them "on the grounds it may tend to incriminate me." He was held in contempt and incarcerated "until he was willing to answer the questions." His appeal via a writ of habeas corpus was rejected all along the judicial hierarchy in Connecticut, its highest tribunal ultimately ruling, inter alia, that the Fifth Amendment's privilege against self-incrimination was not available to a witness in a state proceeding and that the Fourteenth Amendment "extended no privilege to him." The Connecticut courts relied, of course, on past Supreme Court rulings to that effect. But they were now to fall. Over vigorous dissenting opinions by Justices Harlan and Clark, who firmly rejected nationalization of the Fifth Amendment, and by Justices White and Stewart, who questioned the propriety of the privilege's invocation in the instant case, a majority of five members of the Court extended the "incorporated" side of the Cardozo table. Speaking for the chief justice, Justices Black, Douglas, and Goldberg (who had replaced the retired Frankfurter two years earlier), and himself, Justice Brennan held that the Fourteenth Amendment, which assures all citizens due process of law, guaranteed the petitioner the protection of the Fifth Amendment's privilege against compulsory self-incrimination. In language redolent with appeals for a system of "nationalized" criminal justice, Brennan pronounced the *Twining*[203] and *Adamson*[204] decisions wrong constitutional law and announced that, "a fortiorari,"

200. *Ake v. Oklakoma,* 470 U.S. 68.
201. *Malloy v. Hogan,* 378 U.S. 1 (1964); and *Murphy v. Waterfront Commission of New York Harbor,* 378 U.S. 52 (1964).
202. *Twining v. New Jersey,* 211 U.S. 78 (see *supra* this chapter).
203. Ibid.
204. *Adamson v. California,* 332 U.S. 46 (1947). The specifics of *Adamson* (i.e., comments upon failure by the accused to take the stand) were overruled in *Griffin v. Califor-*

the Fourteenth Amendment secures against state invasion the same privilege that the Fifth Amendment guarantees against federal infringement—the right of a person to remain silent unless he chooses to speak in the unfettered exercise of his own free will, and to suffer no penalty . . . for such silence.[205]

The New York companion case turned on the refusal of William Murphy to give testimony to the New York Waterfront Commission, which was then investigating a work stoppage at certain New Jersey piers. Murphy had been promised immunity from prosecution in return for his testimony, but he refused this offer, fearing that his answers might incriminate him under *federal* law to which the grant of immunity did not purport to extend. Overruling its own precedents,[206] the Supreme Court, without dissent this time, categorically rejected "the established rule that one jurisdiction within our federal structure may compel a witness to give testimony which could be used to convict him of a crime in another."[207] Although two of the justices, in a concurring opinion by Harlan, joined by Clark, objected to the "mixing together" of the Fifth and the Fourteenth Amendments, the Court unanimously agreed with its spokesman, Justice Arthur J. Goldberg: "We hold that the Constitutional privilege against self-incrimination protects a state witness against incrimination under Federal as well as state law and a Federal witness against incrimination under state as well as Federal law."[208] While the case featured three separate opinions[209]—two of these concurring on different grounds—and the individual justices may have accepted the Goldberg conclusion for varying reasons, it nevertheless represented another broadening of the application of the Bill of Rights to the states.

1965 and 1967: The Texas Confrontation of Witnesses Cases. Next in line was the clause of the Sixth Amendment providing that "in all criminal prosecutions, the accused shall enjoy the right . . . to be confronted with the witnesses against him"—a right that existed as early as Roman law.[210] Did it also apply with equal

---

nia, 381 U.S. 957 (1965), Griffin's victorious counsel being the same attorney, Monis Lavine, who had lost in Adamson eighteen years earlier! In an elaborate "follow-up" decision in 1981 the Court held (8:1) that, upon a defendant's request, the presiding judge *must* instruct the jury not to draw an adverse inference from the invocation of the Fifth Amendment by someone on trial (*Carter v. Kentucky,* 450 U.S. 288).

205. *Malloy v. Hogan,* op. cit., at 8.

206. *United States v. Murdock,* 284 U.S. 141 (1931); *Feldman v. United States,* 322 U.S. 487 (1944); *Knapp v. Schweitzer,* 357 U.S. 371 (1958).

207. *Murphy v. Waterfront Commission of New York Harbor,* op. cit., at 77.

208. Ibid. at 77–78. The holding was extended (7:2) in 1979 to apply to testimony before a grand jury (*New Jersey v. Portash,* 440 U.S. 450).

209. Those by Justices Goldberg, White, and Harlan.

210. See Justice Scalia's opinion in *Coy v. Iowa,* 487 U.S. 1012 (1988).

effect to proceedings in state courts by virtue of the due process clause of Amendment Fourteen? Yes, held a unanimous Supreme Court, although the four opinions in the case were based on different grounds.

Granville Pointer (and a cohort, Earl Dillard) had been charged with robbing Kenneth W. Phillips of $375 "by assault, or violence, or by putting in fear of life or bodily injury."[211] At the preliminary hearing before a state judge, called the "examining trial" in Texas, Phillips gave detailed testimony, including an identification of Pointer, who, although present throughout the hearing, had no attorney and made no effort to cross-examine Phillips. At Pointer's trial the state submitted evidence that Phillips had recently moved to California and had no intention whatever of returning to Texas. The trial judge permitted the prosecution to introduce the transcript of Phillips's testimony at the preliminary hearing, over the repeated objections of Pointer's counsel. In each instance the trial judge overruled the defense objections on the ground that Pointer had had ample opportunity to cross-examine Phillips at the preliminary hearing stage. The Texas Court of Criminal Appeals affirmed Pointer's conviction—but the Supreme Court of the United States reversed it (9:0), though it was divided on the bases for its action.

Justice Black, speaking for the Court, referred to the spate of recent decisions holding applicable to the states various guarantees in the Bill of Rights, including the Sixth Amendment's right to counsel and the Fifth Amendment's guarantee against compulsory self-incrimination. He ruled: "We hold today that the Sixth Amendment's right of an accused to confront the witnesses against him is likewise a fundamental right and is made obligatory on the States by the Fourteenth Amendment."[212] Black then observed that the inclusion of "the right of confrontation" in the Sixth Amendment "reflects the belief of the Framers . . . that confrontation was a fundamental right essential to a fair trial in a criminal prosecution."[213] And he concluded that since the right of confrontation comprehended the right to cross-examine, reversal was mandatory. Henceforth, the same standards that protect litigants against federal encroachment of this right would be applicable and enforceable against the states. A precedent of more than six decades thus stood overruled.[214]

Three concurring opinions were filed, each dealing with the "incorporation doctrine." Justice Goldberg, evidently eager to go on record with *his* approach to the problem—for he had not been on the Court when the issue was joined in the *Adamson* case[215] in 1947—acknowledged that, on the record, the "incorporation

---

211. *Pointer v. Texas,* 380 U.S. 400 (1965).
212. Ibid. at 403.
213. Ibid. at 404.
214. *West v. Louisiana,* 194 U.S. 258 (1904). Unlike Clarence Earl Gideon, however, when Granville Pointer was retried below, he was convicted again (Phillips now appearing as the prosecution's star witness) and was sentenced to prison for five years to life.
215. 332 U.S. 46.

doctrine" had never really commanded a majority of the Court. However, he sternly rejected both the Frankfurter case-by-case "Was it due process?" approach and the *Palko* "Is it implicit in the concept of ordered liberty?" test. In effect, he embraced the applicability to the states of the *fundamental* guarantees of the Bill of Rights, and he clearly did not particularly care *how* this was done by the Court or by what name the process would be known—as long as those guarantees were indeed made obligatory for the states via the Fourteenth Amendment.[216]

Justice Harlan, while concurring in the result of *Pointer,* nevertheless reaffirmed his conviction that the majority's holding constituted "another step in the onward march of the long-since discredited 'incorporation' doctrine."[217] Exhorting the Court to return to a policy of "leaving room for differences among states," he wrote that *he* would have reversed Pointer's conviction on the basis that the procedure followed by Texas had deprived Pointer of due process of law guaranteed by the Fourteenth Amendment, "independently of the Sixth."[218] Harlan freely acknowledged that the right of confrontation is indeed "implicit in the concept of ordered liberty," which mandated its observance by Texas. But he lashed out at "incorporation" as being "incompatible with our constitutionally ordained federal system" as well as "unsound doctrine."[219] Once again he pointed to what he saw as the value of the states as "laboratories" that must not be "subordinated to federal power." Taking issue with that contention, Justice Goldberg wrote in his concurring opinion that while it was good that the states should be able to try social and economic experiments, he did not believe that this "includes the power to experiment with the fundamental liberties of citizens safeguarded by the Bill of Rights."[220]

In his brief concurring opinion, Justice Stewart took to task the Black opinion for the Court as a "questionable tour de force . . . entirely unnecessary to the decision of this case. . . ."[221] He said that *he* would have reversed Pointer's conviction on the simple ground that Pointer had been clearly deprived of liberty without due process of law in express violation of the Fourteenth Amendment— which, of course, constitutes the case-by-case approach to the applicability question. But on the same day the Court proceeded to apply the new ruling in reversing a conviction in a similar case.[222] While it would reconfirm that holding two decades later in *Coy v. Iowa* (see *supra* this chapter), involving "screened" confrontation and children, it qualified it dramatically (5:4) in 1990 by now ruling that states may shield victims of child abuse by permitting them

216. *Pointer v. Texas,* op. cit., at 414.
217. Ibid. at 408.
218. Ibid.
219. Ibid. at 409.
220. Ibid. at 413.
221. Ibid. at 410.
222. *Douglas v. Alabama,* 380 U.S. 415 (1965), with the same Court division, although Justice Brennan wrote the opinion here.

to testify on closed-circuit television rather than facing those accused of abusing them in open court.[223] And in 1967 it logically, and unanimously, extended the *Pointer* holding to cover compulsory process to obtain and thus to confront *favorable* witnesses, too (*Pointer* having dealt with *adverse* witnesses), in another Texas controversy.[224] Again, the Court was unanimous, its decision written by Chief Justice Warren—and again Justice Harlan's concurring opinion represented an important lecture on the basic incorporation controversy.

1965: "Incorporation" Reargued—The Connecticut Birth Control Case. As if to continue the "argument" among themselves on incorporation, which they had once again raised in the first *Texas Confrontation Case*[225] in 1965, the Supreme Court justices addressed themselves to it with gusto in their controversial six-opinion decision in *Griswold v. Connecticut,* now generally referred to as the *Birth Control Case*[226]—regarded as dangerous constitutional "hocus pocus" by Professor Wallace Mendelson, among others.[227] Our concern here is less with the merits of the decision than with the reasoning employed by the six opinion writers on the incorporation problem (which, depending upon one's analysis, either did or did not have something to do with the holding in the case itself). It suffices to note that the Court, by a 7:2 vote, invalidated an old and generally unenforced Connecticut statute that made it a crime for any person, married or single, to *use* any drug or other article or device for the purpose of preventing conception or to give information or instruction in their use. The Court's opinion was delivered by Justice Douglas, and its judgment of reversal of the defendants'[228] convictions was agreed to by the chief justice and Associate Justices Clark, Harlan, Brennan, White, and Goldberg. But only Clark fully accepted Douglas's reasoning (at least he wrote no opinion); Harlan, White, and Goldberg wrote separate concurring opinions, with the chief justice and Brennan joining in Goldberg's. Justices Black and Stewart wrote separate dissenting opinions, each specifically also joining the other's. There is now some fairly strong evidence that the godfather of the Douglas opinion was Brennan.

223. *Maryland v. Craig,* 497 U.S. 836.
224. *Washington v. Texas,* 388 U.S. 14. Jackie Washington's Sixth and Fourteenth Amendment rights were held fatally encumbered because, under an applied Texas rule, a codefendant was barred from appearing as a witness in his favor.
225. *Pointer v. Texas,* 380 U.S. 400.
226. 381 U.S. 479.
227. "Ninth Amendment Rights and Wrongs," 110 *Political Science Quarterly* 3 (fall 1995), pp. 405–15, at 414.
228. They were Estelle T. Griswold, executive director of the Planned Parenthood League of Connecticut, and Dr. C. Lee Buxton, a licensed physician teaching at Yale University's School of Medicine, who served as medical director for the league's New Haven center. They gave information and medical advice to married persons on means of preventing conception, were found guilty of violating the Connecticut statute at issue, and were fined $100 each. Their appeal was on Fourteenth Amendment grounds.

Douglas noted at the outset that the Court was here confronted with a bona fide controversy that it could properly decide, one involving "the constitutional rights of married people with whom [the defendants, leaders of the Planned Parenthood League] had a professional relationship."[229] He reviewed several Court decisions that, in his judgment, established "that specific guarantees in the Bill of Rights have *penumbras,* formed by emanations from those guarantees that help give them life and substance,"[230] penumbras that reached areas not specifically mentioned in the bill. He thereupon cited five different amendments, the "penumbras" of which "create zones of privacy," among them the First Amendment's protection of the right of association, the Third's prohibition of quartering of soldiers in homes, the Fourth's guarantee against unreasonable searches and seizures, and the Fifth's against compulsory self-incrimination. He added, in a potential trailblazing gesture, the Ninth Amendment, justifying its inclusion as a beacon to illuminate "the zone of privacy created by [the] several fundamental constitutional guarantees."[231] The 1973 *Abortion Cases* were just around the jurisprudential corner—the *Griswold* holding constituted their parentage.

Predictably, the concurring opinions raised the issue of "incorporation" and, specifically, whether—in the light of the expansive Douglas opinion—it was indeed limited to the Bill of Rights. Justice Harlan, in his separate concurring opinion, saw the issue in terms of the requirement of basic values that are "implicit in the concept of ordered liberty"—the *Palko* and case-by-case approach to the scope of the due process clause of the Fourteenth Amendment rather than "incorporation." He was persuaded that the Connecticut statute did unconstitutionally infringe the due process clause, which "stands . . . on its own bottom" and which is not dependent on "one or more provisions of the Bill of Rights . . . or any of their radiations. . . ."[232]

229. *Griswold v. Connecticut,* op. cit., at 481.
230. Ibid. at 484; italics supplied.
231. Ibid. at 485. Six years later, and this time squarely based on the equal protection clause as well as on considerations of "privacy," the Court, speaking through Justice Brennan—with only Chief Justice Burger in dissent—held (6:1) that Massachusetts could not outlaw the distribution of contraceptives to *single* persons when these are legally available to married ones (*Eisenstadt v. Baird,* 405 U.S. 438 [1972]). The vote declaring the ninety-three-year-old law unconstitutional was only 4:3, however. And five years thereafter (1977), a seriously divided Court struck down (7:2, 6:3, and 5:4) New York State's broad anticontraception advertising and distribution law on the following grounds: (1) it violated Amendment One (the state's proscription of the advertising or display of contraceptives), and (2) it violated due process of law because of the rights of privacy inherent in Amendments Fourteen and Nine (the state's limitations of sales to physicians, pharmacies, and drugstores). The Court once again invoked the recently found prerogatives of privacy emanating from due process considerations (the state's forbidding of the dispensing of contraceptives to those age sixteen or younger) (*Carey v. Population Services International,* 431 U.S. 678).
232. Ibid. at 488.

Justice Goldberg, whom the chief justice and Justice Brennan joined in his concurring opinion, made clear his conviction that the due process clause was neither limited to, nor necessarily so broad as, the Bill of Rights, but rather that it "protects those personal rights that are fundamental." In sweeping language, he emphasized the relevance of the Ninth Amendment to the Court's holding, contending that its language and history reveal that "the Framers of the Constitution believed that *there are additional fundamental rights,* protected from government infringement, which *exist alongside those fundamental rights specifically mentioned in the first eight constitutional amendments.*"[233] In other words, he viewed the Ninth Amendment—which Madison had proposed as a concession to Alexander Hamilton's and James Wilson's opposition to a Bill of Rights, opposition based on the fear that nonenumerated rights would be jeopardized—as a lever for the protection of all those "fundamental rights" not specifically protected by the first eight via the "liberty" component safeguard in the due process clauses of both the Fifth and the Fourteenth Amendments. The Ninth Amendment, he reiterated several times in his opinion—which was allegedly drafted by his clerk and future Supreme Court Justice Stephen G. Breyer—"is surely relevant in showing the existence of other fundamental personal rights now protected from state as well as federal infringement,"[234] a statement dramatically at war with the traditional conception of "Ninth Amendment privacy," namely, that the national government is limited to *delegated* powers and that, if it goes *beyond* those powers, it violates the right of the people, whether or not those rights are enumerated in the Constitution.

Goldberg thus rejected the Black approach to incorporation because it would *limit the rights eligible for incorporation to those specifically listed* in the Bill of Rights. For Black, the committed literalist, it had to be spelled out verbatim in the document to be applicable.

Justice White's relatively brief concurring opinion saw a clear-cut violation of substantive due process by the Connecticut statute because of its "too sweeping" provisions which entered "a realm of family life which the state cannot enter."[235] In short, incorporation or no incorporation, the crux of the matter to White was that the due process clause, which prohibits states from depriving any person of "liberty" without due process of law, was clearly violated by the restrictions of the Connecticut law.

233. Ibid.; italics supplied.
234. Ibid. at 493. Among the many scholars supporting this view is Bennett B. Patterson, the author of one of the few works on the Ninth Amendment, *The Forgotten Ninth Amendment* (Indianapolis, Ind.: Bobbs-Merrill, 1955)—although Patterson acknowledges that the Ninth Amendment may well simply be viewed as a "basic statement of the inherent natural rights of the individual" (p. 4).
235. *Griswold v. Connecticut* at 502. Since *Griswold,* a spate of Ninth Amendment litigation has been spawned. Among the claims and/or decisions: the Ninth does not grant a right to smoke marijuana (*People v. Glaser,* 238 C.A.2d 819, 48 Cal. Reptr. 427 [1965]);

In dissenting, Justice Black took pains to announce his complete agreement with all of the "graphic and eloquent strictures and criticisms" leveled at what his colleague Stewart, dissenting with him, termed "this uncommonly silly . . . asinine . . . law"—under which no one had ever been prosecuted—but he rejected the majority's collective reasoning. "[T]he law is every bit as [personally] offensive to me as . . . it is to my Brethren," he began his dissent.[236] Characteristically, he noted the absence of a *specific* constitutional provision that proscribed an invasion of privacy, which he styled "a broad, abstract, and ambiguous concept"— one he viewed merely as a "statement" of policy—and he warned that the Court's reliance on the Ninth Amendment together with the due process clause would give the "federal judiciary the power to invalidate any legislative act which the judges find irrational, unreasonable or offensive."[237] To accept such an approach, he believed, was to revive the "shocking" doctrine rejected by the Court three decades earlier under which it had for so long struck down—by virtue of a power "bestowed on the Court by the Court"[238]—federal and state statutes in the *economic* realm because of alleged violations of substantive due process of law based on such notions as the sanctity of contracts. "Privacy," he declared, "is a broad, abstract, and ambiguous concept" that can be readily expanded or shrunk by later decisions. This proved to be a prophetic statement, of course: in January 1973 down came the bombshell privacy-based, six-opinion *Abortion Cases,* with the Court holding (7:2) that the right of "privacy," derived largely from the "liberty" concept of due process of law under the Fourteenth Amendment, and partly from the Ninth (stare decisis *Griswold*), rendered unconstitutional all state laws (forty-six) that prohibited or restricted a woman's right to obtain an abortion during the first three months of pregnancy.[239] Lest he be misunderstood, Black reit-

---

to refuse army induction (*U.S. v. Uhl,* 436 F.2d 773, 9th Cir. [1970]); or to marry a person of the same sex (*Baker v. Nelson,* 489 U.S. 810 [1971]). The applicability of the Ninth Amendment to the long-hair syndrome remained guarded and clouded (cf. *Dawson v. School Board,* 322 F. Supp. 286 [1971]; and *Davis v. Firment,* 269 F. Supp. 524) for a number of years; but a 7:2 decision in 1976 in favor of the application of state authority under duly guarded police powers seems to have settled the matter, at least for the time being (*Kelley v. Johnson,* 425 U.S. 238). *Griswold,* of course, was parent to the 1973 *Abortion Cases* of *Roe v. Wade* and *Doe v. Bolton,* 410 U.S. 113 and 410 U.S. 179, respectively (see the following pages).

236. Loc. cit. at 507.

237. Ibid. at 509, 511.

238. Ibid. at 520.

239. *Roe v. Wade,* 410 U.S. 113; and *Doe v. Bolton,* 410 U.S. 179. The former case was brought by "Jane Roe," a pseudonym for Norma McCorvey, then pregnant for the third time. She became a celebrity and a heroine for abortion rights—but in 1995 she publicly renounced her role in the abortion rights movement and was baptized a born-again Christian (see Laurie Goldstein, "'Jane Roe' Renounces Abortion Movement," *Washington Post,* August 1, 1995, p. F1). Henry M. Wade was the district attorney named in the federal lawsuit. The holding was made retroactive in a 9:0 per curiam decision in 1975 in

erated his belief that the Court does have the power, "which it should exercise," to hold laws unconstitutional where they are forbidden by the Constitution, and that he fully believed, then as before, that the specifics of that document are incorporated and made applicable to the states via the due process clause of the Fourteenth Amendment. Yet, like Stewart in his dissenting opinion—who sarcastically commented that "to say that the Ninth Amendment has anything to do with this case is to turn somersaults with history"[240]—Black could find nothing in the Constitution and its amendments to forbid the passage of the Connecticut law. Quoting from his dissenting opinion in *Adamson v. California*[241] almost two decades earlier, he cautioned that

> to pass upon the constitutionality of statutes by looking to the particular standards enumerated in the Bill of Rights and other parts of the Constitution is one thing; to invalidate statutes because of application of "natural law" deemed to be above and underlined by the Constitution is another.[242]

Amplifying this position in his *Constitutional Faith* three years later, Black observed that "even though I like my privacy as well as the next one, I am never-

---

Louisiana State Bd. of Medical Examiners v. Rosen, 419 U.S. 1098—and both reconfirmed and indeed extended in 1976 in a series of cases headed by *Planned Parenthood of Central Missouri v. Danforth,* 429 U.S. 52, and in 1979 in *Bellotti v. Baird,* 443 U.S. 622, although a mite equivocally. But, as Black had warned, it has also proved at least partly "shrinkable." Thus, a trio of 1977 cases held that neither the Constitution nor federal legislation compels states to fund nontherapeutic abortions for women in financial need (*Beal v. Doe, Maher v. Doe,* and *Poelker v. Doe,* 432 U.S. 438, 526, and 519, respectively; see also *Colautti v. Franklin,* 439 U.S. 379 [1979]). And a six-opinion 5:4 decision in 1980 upheld the Hyde Amendment enacted by Congress, banning Medicaid financing by the federal government of abortions in all but a handful of cases (e.g., instances of promptly reported rape or incest or "where the life of the mother would be endangered if the fetus were carried to term") (*Harris v. McRae,* 448 U.S. 297). Cf. *H.L. v. Matheson,* 450 U.S. 398 (1981), backing 6:3 a Utah preabortion parental *notification*—but *not* interdiction— requirement for teenagers living at home. See also the trio of 1983 abortion decisions, broadly affirming *Roe* and *Doe;* the 1986 holding in *Thornburgh v. American College of Obstetricians and Gynecologists* (cited *supra* note 19 in chapter 1); the long-awaited decision in *Webster v. Reproductive Health Services,* which, while upholding Roe (or not addressing the crucial first-trimester issue) provided (5:4) considerably enhanced power to the states to regulate elective abortions (492 U.S. 490); the 1990 abortion decision, discussed *infra* in chapter 8; and the significant *Casey* holding of 1992, which refused to overturn *Roe* but substituted the "undue burden" test for Roe's controversial trimester schema, in upholding four of five restrictive Pennsylvania statutory provisions. See also *Stenberg v. Carhart,* 530 U.S. 914 (2000), the "late-term, partial-birth abortion" case, discussed in chapter 8, *infra,* and the 6:3 ruling in *Hill v. Colorado,* 530 U.S. 703 (2000), rejecting a constitutional First Amendment claim for a right to come within eight feet of abortion clinic patients to hand out literature or conduct discussions.

240. *Griswold v. Connecticut,* op. cit., at 527.
241. U.S. 46 (1947) at 90–92.
242. *Griswold v. Connecticut,* op. cit., at 525.

theless compelled to admit that government has a right to invade it unless prohibited by some specific constitutional provision." For he could "find in the Constitution no language which either specifically or impliedly grants to all individuals a constitutional right of privacy."[243]

Black's formula always was that the First Amendment protects freedom of *expression,* and it does that absolutely. Yet it does not protect "conduct" ("physical activities")—be that conduct a racial "sit-in"[244] or the use of contraceptive devices.[245] And he quoted with full agreement a famous statement by Judge Learned Hand on the matter of judicial invalidation of legislation offensive to the jurists' personal preferences: "For myself it would be most irksome to be ruled by a bevy of Platonic Guardians, even if I knew how to choose them, which I assuredly do not."[246] But in the footnote giving the preceding statement's citation, Black had to acknowledge that although he agreed with Hand's "criticism of use of the due process formula, I do not agree with all the views he expressed about construing the specific guarantees of the Bill of Rights."[247] Of course, Black could not; for, ironically, in his 1958 book *The Bill of Rights*[248]—which contains the "platonic guardians" statement so approvingly quoted by Black—Hand, rejecting any double-standard justifications between "economic" and "civil libertarian" rights, took considerable pains to contend that the Court, on which Black then served, had gone too far in a number of cases in holding legislation to be in violation of *specific* guarantees of the Bill of Rights.[249]

---

243. (New York: Knopf, 1968), p. 9. How subjective the concept of "privacy" is, and how vexatious its judicial application, may be illustrated by pointing to two 1970 lower court decisions which, both citing Griswold, struck down a Texas sodomy statute as an unconstitutional invasion of privacy while upholding a 1796 New Jersey statute proscribing fornication! (*Buchanan v. Bachelor,* 308 F. Supp. 729; and *Slate v. Lutz,* 57 N.J. 314). But late in 1977 the New Jersey Supreme Court did rule the old statute unconstitutional (5:2), as a violation of "the right to privacy" (*State v. Saunders,* 75 N.J. 200). To compound the "privacy" issue, the U.S. Supreme Court in 1986 upheld 5:4 Georgia's antisodomy statute, even as applied to consensual adults in private (*Bowers v. Hardwick,* 478 U.S. 168). Under that same 1832 law, James D. Moseley of DeKalb County (Atlanta) went to jail for nineteen months for having oral sex with his wife—who had turned him in. The couple later divorced (see *infra* chapter 4 for other cases). And in 1992 the Court denied review twice (113 S. Ct. 92) in cases that had held below that the proscription of consensual heterosexual oral sex is within the legislative purview and that such proscriptions violate no right of privacy (*U.S. v. Henderson,* U.S.C.M.A., 34 M.J. 174; and *Fagg v. U.S.,* U.S.C.M.A., 34 M.J. 179). In a totally different aspect of alleged privacy, the U.S. Supreme Court ruled unanimously in 2002 that the scoring by students of each other's tests, papers, and assignments did *not* constitute a violation of that right (*Owasso Independent School District v. Falvo,* 534 U.S. ___ [2002]).

244. See *infra* chapter 7.

245. *Griswold v. Connecticut,* op. cit., at 507–8.

246. Ibid. at 526.

247. Ibid., note 23.

248. (Cambridge, Mass.: Harvard University Press, 1958).

249. Ibid. pp. 35–45.

1966: Formally Incorporating the Right to Trial by an "Impartial" Jury. The first incorporation by the Court following its thorough reprise analysis and exposition of the basic issues in *Griswold* turned out to be something that had long been assumed to have been incorporated—the right to trial by an *impartial* jury. Indeed, the requirement of a *fair trial,* a cornerstone of the judicial process, would naturally assume trial by an *impartial* jury, provided a jury trial were granted in the first place, of course. (The right to a trial by jury per se was not incorporated until the *Duncan* case[250]—see later text—and it reached only criminal cases above the petty level.) However, although disposing of the matter in a per curiam opinion,[251] the Court evidently deemed it necessary and/or politic to inform the states that the Sixth Amendment's requirement for an "impartial" jury was indeed applicable to them as well as to the federal government. The case concerned a bailiff named Gladden who made the following statements to the sequestered jury trying one Lee E. A. Parker: "Oh, that wicked fellow, he is guilty. . . . If there is anything wrong, the Supreme Court will correct it."[252] The Court did—although hardly along the lines Bailiff Gladden could have expected!

1967: The Right to a Speedy Trial. With the right to a *public* trial by jury incorporated in 1948, it was only a question of time until the collateral Sixth Amendment requirement of a *speedy* trial—which had received recognition as early as 1166 in the Assize of Clarendon—would also be rendered applicable by the Court. Its vehicle became the case of a professor of zoology at Duke University, Peter H. Klopfer, who had been indicted by the state of North Carolina for criminal trespass after he took part in a sit-in at the then segregated Watts Motel and Restaurant in Chapel Hill. The controversy arose in 1964, and Professor Klopfer was indeed tried soon thereafter; however, the jury failed to agree on a verdict, and a mistrial was declared by Trial Judge Raymond B. Mallard, thus heralding a new trial. A year passed without a second trial, and when Professor Klopfer officially demanded either to be tried forthwith or to have his case dismissed, the judge granted, instead, State Prosecutor (District Solicitor) Thomas Cooper's motion for a nolle prosequi (which permits a prosecutor to place an indictment in an inactive status, without bringing the case to trial, but "retaining it for use at

250. *Duncan v. Louisiana,* 391 U.S. 145 (1968). See the discussion *infra.*

251. An unsigned, normally very brief, opinion for the Court, its authorship unknown to the outside world, applying res judicata (settled law).

252. *Parker v. Gladden,* 385 U.S. 363 (1966) at 364. In his excellent full-length study, *The Supreme Court and the Second Bill of Rights* (Madison: University of Wisconsin Press, 1981), Professor Richard C. Cortner disagrees with the above conclusion that *Parker* incorporated the impartial requirement of Amendment Six. Instead, he views *Parker* as a confirmation of the Sixth Amendment's confrontation and cross-examination rights. Justice Brennan for one, however, expressed agreement with my position in response to an oral quaere (January 15, 1969). The vote in *Parker* was 8:1, Justice Harlan dissenting (at 366).

any future time"—a procedure then permitted by thirty states). The exasperated Professor Klopfer appealed, arguing that this action denied his Sixth Amendment right to a speedy trial, which he regarded as applicable to the states. Denying his appeal, the North Carolina Supreme Court ruled in January 1966 that a defendant's right to speedy trial—which the tribunal readily acknowledged—does not encompass "the right to compel the state to prosecute him." In Klopfer's instance this meant that he would continue to be subject to a retrial at any time, at the discretion of the state, on the basis of the "suspended" trespass indictment. He appealed to the Supreme Court of the United States.

In another milestone decision in constitutional development,[253] the Court unanimously sided with the appellant. Speaking for six justices as well as himself, Chief Justice Warren called the North Carolina practice at issue an "extraordinary criminal procedure," noting that the North Carolina Supreme Court's position "has been explicitly rejected by every other state court which has considered the question."[254] Clearly, he concluded, the procedure served to deny Professor Klopfer "the right to a speedy trial which we hold is guaranteed to him by the Sixth Amendment of the Constitution of the United States"[255]—thus incorporating the requirement. Not surprisingly on the basis of his record on the matter, Justice Harlan, while voting to reverse the North Carolina decision—noting that he "entirely agree[d] with the result reached in the Court"—wrote a separate concurring opinion in which he again voiced his rejection of what he viewed as the "rigid uniformity" in state procedures brought about by "incorporation" or "absorption," explaining that *he* would have struck down the state's procedure because it was violative of the "fundamental fairness" guaranteed by the due process of law clause of Amendment Fourteen.[256] Justice Stewart simply noted that he concurred, but he did not elaborate. In 1974 Congress, led by the retiring Senator Sam J. Ervin Jr. (D.-N.C.), enacted the Federal Speedy Trial Act,[257] setting up a schedule to be implemented over a five-year period of time limits—ultimately (June 30, 1980) reaching a low of a hundred days—during which criminal charges

253. *Klopfer v. North Carolina,* 386 U.S. 213 (1967).
254. Ibid. at 219.
255. Ibid. at 222. It was on the grounds of denial of speedy trial that, in 1990, Green Beret doctor Jeffrey R. MacDonald found his conviction for the murder of his wife and two children overturned (2:1) by the U.S. Court of Appeals for the Fourth Circuit (*United States v. MacDonald,* 632 F.2d 258). However, he was reconvicted in a subsequent trial.
256. Ibid. at 226–27. On remand to the trial court, the charges against Klopfer were dismissed. Had Harlan lived to witness them, he would very likely have approved the Court's actions in two 1971 cases, in which—without dissent—it declined to review two lower court holdings which, based on the facts at issue, held (1) that an eighteen-month delay from arrest to trial did not necessarily deprive a defendant of his rights to a speedy trial (*Blevins v. U.S.,* 404 U.S. 823), and (2) that neither did a governmental delay for five years of an indictment after the alleged criminal offense took place (*Quinn v. U.S.,* 404 U.S. 850).
257. 18 U.S.C. 3161 et seq.

had to be either brought to trial or dropped. As to the precise nature of the time period to be considered, the Court ruled (7:1) in 1975 that it is the period between trial and *either* arrest or indictment, whichever comes first.[258]

1968: Gary Duncan's Right to a Trial by Jury in a Criminal Case. An appeal coming up from a decision by the Louisiana Supreme Court afforded the U.S. Supreme Court the long-anticipated occasion to incorporate *the right to be tried by jury in criminal cases* (above the petty level).[259] With the right to a "fair," a "public," an "impartial," and a "speedy" trial already established as incumbent upon the states, it was only a question of time until the Court would similarly deal with the fundamental right of a trial by jury per se, at least in criminal cases. Yet it took until 1968 and Gary Duncan's appeal of a conviction for simple bat-

---

258. *Dillingham v. United States,* 423 U.S. 64. (The chief justice dissented.) In 1977, in a speedy trial case ruling, a federal district court declared the statute unconstitutional as an "impermissible legislative encroachment on the judiciary" (*United States v. Howard,* 440 F. Supp. 1106). On appeal, the U.S. Court of Appeals for the Fourth Circuit affirmed on other grounds, finding that "the issue of constitutionality was not raised and therefore not properly before it" (ibid., 590 F.2d 564 at 568, note 4). The U.S. Supreme Court denied certiorari in 1979 (ibid., 440 U.S. 976). Thus, notwithstanding the trial court's holding—which may be viewed as a declaratory judgment (see Abraham, *The Judicial Process,* op. cit., pp. 354–55)—the act remains the law of the land, as amended and strengthened in 1979. Indeed, by 1980 some 96 percent of district criminal cases reached trial within one hundred days. In 1981, however, a federal district court once again declared the act ultra vires as "an unconstitutional encroachment upon the Judiciary" (*United States v. Brainer,* 515 F. Supp. 627 [Md.], at 630—only to see itself reversed by the Fourth Circuit Court of Appeals one year later: ibid., 691 F.2d 691). It is fair to conclude that, in effect, the speedy trial issue, *pace* the 1974 statute, is now still demonstrably governed by the Supreme Court's unanimous holding—two years prior to the Speedy Trial Act's birth—that the Sixth Amendment's speedy trial guarantee, in conjunction with the Fifth and Fourteenth Amendments' due process of law mandates, must be treated on a case-by-case basis; that, according to the unanimous opinion's author, Justice Powell (White, with Brennan, concurring separately), an "admittedly difficult" balancing test for determining a defendant's constitutional right to a speedy trial must be applied. Such tests, carefully applied, concluded Powell, would meet constitutional obligations vis-à-vis the state's defendants, and judicial obligations under the separation of powers (*Barker v. Wingo,* 407 U.S. 514). Further such balancing occurred in 1986 when the Supreme Court ruled (5:4) that the speedy trial requirement does not bar the federal government from prosecuting Indian activist Dennis Banks and three others on ten-year-old firearms charges (*United States v. Loud Hawk, et al.,* 474 U.S. 302). And in 1990 the U.S. Supreme Court unanimously upheld a six-month delay in civil jury trials in the state, saying the constitutional guarantees of speedy trials do not mean instant ones (*New York Times,* June 5, 1990, p. A24).

259. *Duncan v. Louisiana,* 391 U.S. 145 (1968). In 1996 the Court held 5:4 that defendants who are prosecuted in a *single* proceeding for *multiple petty* offenses, with the potential for a sentence exceeding a total of six months (the usual "line" for petty offenses) are not entitled to jury trial (*Lewis v. U.S.,* 64 LW 4581).

tery, which, under Louisiana law, was punishable by a maximum of two years' imprisonment and a fine of $300. Duncan, a nineteen-year-old black convicted in Plaquemines parish[260] court of slapping a white boy on the elbow and sentenced to sixty days in jail and a fine of $150, had sought a trial by jury. But because the Louisiana Constitution granted jury trials only in cases in which capital punishment or imprisonment at hard labor might be imposed, the trial judge denied Duncan's request, and the latter appealed to the Supreme Court, contending that the Sixth and Fourteenth Amendments to the federal Constitution secured the right of jury trial in state criminal prosecutions, such as his, where a sentence as long as two years could be pronounced. The Court agreed (7:2).

Speaking for the majority, Justice White, in a relatively brief opinion, reviewed aspects of the history of the judicially mandated application of the several provisions of the Bill of Rights to the states and concluded simply but firmly, after reviewing the specific nature of the controversy and the history of trial by jury:

> Because we believe that trial by jury in criminal cases is fundamental to the American scheme of justice, we hold that the Fourteenth Amendment guarantee, a right of jury trial in all criminal cases which—were they to be tried in a federal court—would come within the Sixth Amendment's guarantee. Since we consider the appeal before us to be such a case, we hold that the Constitution was violated when appellant's demand for jury trial was refused.[261]

Justice White pointed out that so-called petty offenses have traditionally been tried without a jury, and said this would continue to be true under the *Duncan* ruling. He noted that, in federal cases, a "petty" offense is one carrying a maximum penalty of six months' imprisonment and a fifty-dollar fine. Beyond that, he left for future decisions the delineation of "serious" from "petty" cases,[262] because, in the Court's view, the conviction of Gary Duncan[263] was clearly a "serious" one.[264]

Three other opinions were featured in the milestone case. Justice Black, joined by Douglas, took the occasion to reiterate the convictions and beliefs concerning incorporation he had first set out so prominently in the *Adamson*

260. This oil-rich parish was long bossed by the powerful, skillful political leader Leander H. Perez—a virulent segregationist and anti-Semite.

261. *Duncan v. Louisiana,* op. cit., at 149–50.

262. In 1989 a unanimous Court applied the "petty crimes or offenses" language in *Duncan* to hold that there was no right to a trial by jury in a prosecution for driving while under the influence of alcohol, where there was a minimum term of two days' imprisonment and a maximum of six months (*Blanton v. City North of Las Vegas,* 489 U.S. 538).

263. Because Louisiana refused to comply in its lower court hierarchy, Duncan was not free from the threat of further prosecution until the federal courts effectively enjoined Plaquemines parish by late 1971 (*Perez v. Duncan,* 404 U.S. 1017 certiorari denied).

264. See the 1970 decision in *Baldwin v. New York,* 399 U.S. 66.

case[265]—although he applauded the Court for reaching "almost" the same result via the "selective" incorporation approach (which he was thus "very happy to support" as a means to his desired end) and to dispute the stance again espoused in *Duncan* by his longtime opponent on incorporation, Justice Harlan. Black did so primarily because of Harlan's notable dissenting opinion, which may well have been the latter's most eloquent in the long incorporation debate. For, joined by Stewart, Harlan not only disputed the assertion that due process of law requires the application of federal jury trial standards, he also took pains to deliver another lecture against incorporation per se; against "selective" incorporation; and against the Court's reading of history, which, he charged, made "no sense"— thus once again opting for a case-by-case "fundamental fairness" approach. To Harlan, the 1833 holding of *Barron v. Baltimore*[266] was still good law: he never regarded it as having been overruled by the Fourteenth Amendment,[267] warmly pleading in conclusion for a return to Justice Brandeis's "celebrated dictum" of 1932 that it is "one of the happy incidents of the federal system that a single courageous state may, if its citizens choose, serve as a laboratory. . . ."[268] Until the day he left the Court in 1971, Harlan never failed to warn against "stifling flexibility in the States." He would have been pleased had he lived to see the Court's 5:4 ruling in 1976, which, seemingly narrowing the *Duncan* opinion, held that a state may indeed deny a defendant a jury in his initial trial on a criminal charge if it allows that defendant, through an appeal, to get a completely new (de novo) second trial in which there is a jury.[269]

And in a separate concurring opinion, siding with the White holding, Justice Fortas went on record as voicing his concern lest the ruling be regarded as "automatically [to] import all the ancillary rules which have been or may hereafter be developed incidental to the right of jury trial in the federal courts." He saw "no reason whatever," for example, "to assume that [the *Duncan* decision] should require us to impose federal requirements such as unanimous verdicts or a jury of twelve [a figure with a six-hundred-year history in Anglo-Saxon law] upon the States."[270] When the Court had an opportunity to rule in 1970 on Florida's six-man jury in noncapital cases, it upheld the practice (7:1).[271] Justice White again wrote the opinion; Justice Marshall dissented—contending that the Sixth Amendment requires a twelve-person jury.[272] Indeed it does, ruled a bare

265. See discussion *supra.*
266. See discussion *supra.*
267. *Duncan v. Louisiana,* op. cit., at 172.
268. Quoting from Brandeis's opinion in *New State Ice Co. v. Liebmann,* 285 U.S. 262 at 280, 311.
269. *Ludwig v. Massachusetts,* 427 U.S. 618.
270. *Duncan v. Louisiana,* op. cit., at 213.
271. *Williams v. Florida,* 399 U.S. 78. The issue promised to arise again in future terms of Court.
272. In a footnote White pointed out that the Court was not determining the minimum number permissible, "but we do not doubt that six is above that minimum" (ibid. at 91).

five-man majority two years later, *but* only in *federal* cases—Justice Powell providing the key vote in his concurring opinion, which, however, *upheld* (5:4) the right of Louisiana[273] to render 9:3 and that of Oregon[274] 10:2 and 11:1 verdicts in criminal cases. Powell insisted that the Sixth Amendment intended to require *federal* courts to employ the unanimous twelve-member jury of the English common-law tradition, but he did not view the due process of law clause of the Fourteenth Amendment as requiring similar unanimous verdicts in *state* criminal trials. Justice Blackmun, also in the majority, noted that he would have "great difficulty" in upholding a 7:5 verdict, however. Dissenting in both cases were Justices Douglas, Brennan, Stewart, and Marshall, who insisted that the federal standards apposite under Amendment Six are ipso facto incorporated. In 1973 down came the anticipated ruling by the Court regarding federal *civil* trials: in a 5:4 opinion, interestingly authored by one of the dissenters in the two aforementioned cases, Justice Brennan, the Court ruled that resort to fewer than twelve-member juries—long practiced and authorized at the level of the states—is not unconstitutional under the Seventh Amendment's guarantee of a trial by jury in civil cases if the value of the suit exceeds $20, nor is it proscribed statutorily.[275] (Here a six-member federal civil jury was utilized.) Justice Powell joined his colleagues Douglas, Stewart, and Marshall in dissent. In 1978 the Court drew a line on the size of juries in criminal cases; however, scattering all over the legal landscape in five separate opinions, it held (9:0) that a jury of *fewer* than six could not stand—here striking down Georgia's use of a five-member panel, although the latter's vote in the case had been unanimous (*Ballew v. Georgia*, 435 U.S. 223). Nor, said the Court (9:0) in 1979, could a 5:1 jury verdict stand—evidently thus drawing a firm line at six-member unanimous juries as the minimum constitutionally acceptable in state nonpetty offenses criminal cases (*Burch v. Louisiana*, 441 U.S. 130). On another significant aspect of the constitutional posture of juries, the Court held (5:4) in 1990 that the Sixth Amendment requires "not a *representative* jury" but "an impartial jury," thereby upholding peremptory challenges, even some involving race.[276] But, apropos of wholesale peremptory striking of racial groups by both the prosecution and the defense, note the Court's 1986 and 1992 rulings in *Batson v. Kentucky* (476 U.S. 79) and *Georgia v. McCollum* (505 U.S. 42), respectively. The Court accepted review in a case dealing with gender in 1993 (*J.E.B. v. Alabama ex rel. T.B.*, 511 U.S. 127) and ultimately ruled similarly.[277]

273. *Johnson v. Louisiana*, 406 U.S. 356 (1972).
274. *Apodaca v. Oregon*, 406 U.S. 404 (1972).
275. *Colgrove v. Battin*, 413 U.S. 149.
276. *Holland v. Illinois*, 493 U.S. 474.
277. Ibid., 62 LW 4219 (1994). But, as if to give peremptory challenges a new lease on life, the Court ruled 7:2 in 1995 that prosecutors do not have to give "a reason that makes sense" when they exclude a juror as long as their reason does not reveal any discrimination, such as race or gender (*Purkett v. Elem*, 514 U.S. 765).

1969: Applying the Constitutional Prohibition Against Double Jeopardy. The *Duncan* decision had left the Fifth Amendment safeguard against being "twice put in jeopardy of life or limb" as the most fundamental among the few still not incorporated. The Court had had a number of opportunities to come to grips with the problem,[278] but it was not until the case of *Benton v. Maryland*[279] that it found an appropriate one. Granting certiorari in 1968, it limited itself to the following two crucial questions: (1) Is the "double jeopardy" clause of the Fifth Amendment applicable to the states? (2) If so, was the petitioner twice put in jeopardy? Its affirmative response to both questions made Court history by incorporating the contentious provision.

John Dalmer Benton had been indicted and tried in 1965 in Prince George's County for burglary, housebreaking, and larceny. He was convicted of burglary and found not guilty on the larceny charge, and the state did not press charges on the housebreaking count. He was sentenced to ten years in jail on the burglary conviction. Subsequently, both his indictment and his conviction were set aside by the Maryland Court of Appeals under a ruling that struck down a section of the Maryland Constitution requiring jurors to swear their belief in the existence of God as a condition of jury service.[280] Reindicted and retried for both burglary and larceny, he was now convicted on *both* charges and sentenced to fifteen years for burglary plus five years for larceny, the sentences to run concurrently. Benton's convictions were affirmed in the appropriate Maryland courts, and he appealed to the highest court in the land in forma pauperis, arguing that the larceny conviction should be reversed on double jeopardy grounds, since he had been found innocent on *that* charge in his first trial. He also argued that the burglary conviction could not stand, on the theory that the jury was influenced by testimony on the larceny count.

Speaking for a 6:2 Court majority,[281] Justice Marshall held the double jeopardy provision to represent "a fundamental ideal in our constitutional heritage . . . that . . . should apply to the States through the Fourteenth Amendment." Adding that "[i]nsofar as it is inconsistent with this holding, *Palko v. Connecticut* is overruled," he explained:

> Our recent cases have thoroughly rejected the *Palko* notion that basic constitutional rights can be denied by the States as long as the totality of the circumstances does not disclose a denial of "fundamental fairness." Once it is decided that a particular Bill of Rights guarantee is "fundamental to the

278. E.g., *Cichos v. Indiana,* 383 U.S. 966 (1966), when it granted certiorari only to dismiss the writ as having been "improvidentially granted" (385 U.S. 76 [1967]).

279. 392 U.S. 925 (1968), certiorari granted.

280. *Schowgurow v. State,* 240 Md. 121 (1965).

281. *Benton v. Maryland,* 395 U.S. 784 (1969). Justice Fortas had resigned from the Court two months prior to this June 23, 1969, decision, which came on the very last day of Earl Warren's sixteen-year service as chief justice of the United States.

American scheme of justice," *Duncan v. Louisiana,* the same constitutional standards apply against both the State and Federal Governments. *Palko*'s roots had thus been cut away years ago. We today only recognize the inevitable. . . . The validity of [Benton's] larceny conviction must be judged, not by the watered-down standard enunciated in *Palko,* but under the Court's interpretations of the Fifth Amendment double jeopardy provision.[282]

Needless to relate, Justice Harlan was hardly prepared to "recognize the inevitable" so recognized by Marshall for the Court's majority. Joined by his frequent sympathizer in the incorporation cases, Stewart, he dissented sharply from the reversal of Benton's conviction because he did not think the Court should have "reached out" to decide the merits of the case. However, if those were to be reached, he made resolutely clear that he, too, would have been prepared to re-

---

282. Ibid. at 795–96. The Court apparently left undisturbed its long-standing policy of upholding separate state and federal prosecutions of the same offense, although a 6:3 ruling in 1977 seemed to open the door for its reconsideration (*Rinaldi v. United States,* 434 U.S. 22, based on *Petite v. United States,* 361 U.S. 529 [1960]). Res judicata reposes in two 1959 decisions: *Bartkus v. Illinois,* 359 U.S. 121, and *Abbate v. United States,* 359 U.S. 187. For an apparent narrowing of the protection against double jeopardy in the instance of the length (or brevity) of sentences, see Justice Blackmun's late 1980 opinion for a 5:4 Court in *United States v. Di Francesco,* 449 U.S. 117; the Court's 9:0 reaffirmation in 1981 of the constitutionality of imposing consecutive sentences for a single federal offense that violates two laws (*Albernaz v. United States,* 40 U.S. 333); and the 1982 holding (5:4 in *Tibbs v. Florida,* 457 U.S. 31) that the double jeopardy clause does not bar a retrial after a defendant's conviction had been reversed as being against the weight of the evidence. But cf. *Bullington v. Missouri,* 451 U.S. 430 (1981). See also *Grady v. Corbin,* 495 U.S. 508 (1990), in which the Court ruled (5:4) that the due process clause *bars* subsequent prosecution if, to establish an essential element of an offense charged in that prosecution, the government will prove conduct that constitutes an offense for which the defendant has already been prosecuted. The ruling featured dissents by Chief Justice Rehnquist and Justices O'Connor, Kennedy, and Scalia, with the latter accusing the Brennan-led majority of "ridiculous" answers. For a unanimous 1992 decision, distinguishing *Grady,* see *U.S. v. Felix,* 503 U.S. 378. But on the last day of the Court's 1992–93 term, *Grady* was overturned (5:4), thus clearing the way for successive prosecutions under some circumstances (*U.S. v. Dixon,* 509 U.S. 688). And at the end of the 1994–95 term, an 8:1 opinion by Justice O'Connor held that the double jeopardy principles do not bar prosecution for a crime even if that same criminal conduct has already been used to increase a defendant's prison sentence for a different *offense.* Only Justice Stevens dissented in *Witte v. U.S.,* 63 LW 4576 (1995). In 1996 the Court ruled that the government may prosecute drug dealers for criminal violations *and* seize their property, without breaching the constitutional guarantee against double jeopardy (*U.S. v. Ursery,* 518 U.S. 267). And it held 5:4 that property, owned at least in part by innocent people, may nonetheless be seized by the government when, as in this particular instance, it confiscated a Michigan woman's car used by her husband for sex with a prostitute. The majority decided that such forfeitures do not violate anyone's due process rights and do not amount to an unlawful governmental taking of private property under the Fifth or Fourteenth Amendment (*Bennis v. Michigan,* 517 U.S. 1163 [1996]).

verse the larceny conviction on constitutional ground—*but,* naturally, via the "traditional due process approach" of *Palko v. Connecticut*[283] (as he always viewed that)—rather than the majority's route of "incorporating" all of the details of the federal double jeopardy guarantee.[284] Once more he warned against the Court's "march" toward incorporation, expressing his "protest against a doctrine which so subtly, yet profoundly, is eroding many of the basics of our federal system."[285]

The Supreme Court of the United States, under Chief Justice William H. Rehnquist since 1986, has incorporated no further provisions of the Bill of Rights since *Benton* did so for the double jeopardy clause in 1969. But, in effect, only a few provisions still remained "out": grand jury indictment; trial by a jury in *civil* cases; excessive bail[286] and fines prohibitions; the right to bear arms; and the Third Amendment safeguards against involuntary quartering of troops in private homes. The close attention given during the sixteen years of the Warren Court's existence to problems of criminal justice, against the backdrop of fundamental concepts and concerns of due process of law, plus mounting legislative concern with such safeguards as bail,[287] may well leave those few that are indeed still "out" out. What is crucial is the increasing recognition and acceptance, both on and off the bench, that if there is anything at all "national" in scope and application under the U.S. Constitution, it is our fundamental civil rights and liberties.

LEADING POSITIONS ON INCORPORATION

It may be useful to summarize the major judicial positions taken on the question of incorporation of the Bill of Rights by representative past and present members of the Supreme Court. Although close students of the problem can determine as many as eight or nine such positions, one may eschew fine distinctions and point to four chief ones.

283. See discussion *supra.*
284. *Benton v. Maryland,* op. cit., at 808.
285. Ibid. Actually, the terms of the remand of the *Benton* case to the Maryland courts could not have completely displeased Harlan. For what the Supreme Court did was to send Benton's conviction back down for "re-examination," stating that it was "not obvious on the face of the record that the burglary conviction was affected by the double jeopardy violation" (ibid. at 809). In other words, although the provision was now incorporated, each case would still have to be examined to determine whether or not there was double jeopardy qua double jeopardy. And as a matter of fact, Benton's ten-year conviction for burglary in his first trial in 1965 did stand up.
286. The intriguing quaere as to whether the Constitution does, in fact, guarantee a "right to bail" (as contrasted with the acknowledged guarantee against its excessiveness when granted) was before the Court in 1982, but it "ducked" the issue by mooting the case (*Murphy v. Hunt,* 455 U.S. 478 [1982]).
287. See the important Federal Bail Reform Act of 1966.

The *first* position is probably, although arguably, still the current doctrine of a majority of the Court: selective incorporation, or the concept of the "Honor Roll of Superior Rights."[288] Since the *Palko* case in 1937,[289] this position has been adhered to by a majority of the members of the Court—a shifting majority, but a majority nonetheless. Among those who thus labored to "incorporate" the gradually increasing string of rights from the Bill of Rights without advocating total incorporation per se have been Chief Justices Hughes, Stone, and Warren (although it is possible to make a good, if inconclusive, case for the acceptance not only of total incorporation by the latter two but of total incorporation "plus") and Associate Justices Brandeis, Cardozo, Reed, Jackson, Burton, Clark, White, Blackmun, and Stevens (but almost all with some reservations in the area of criminal procedural safeguards). This majority position—now entering its seventh decade—possesses both the virtues of flexibility and compromise and the vices of selectivity and uncertainty. These properties would be applicable even if one were to view the Court's majority position as one more adequately described as "selective incorporation plus," given its recent repeatedly demonstrated willingness to broaden "due process" and "equal protection" understandings.

The *second* position on incorporation is the "fair trial" or "case-by-case" rule. This position was consistently and prominently advocated by Justice Frankfurter and faithfully continued, with some bows toward the Cardozo reasoning in *Palko,* but not toward the *Palko* doctrine itself, by "FF's" jurisprudential student and companion, the younger John Marshall Harlan—although Harlan's may well be viewed as a separate "fundamental rights" posture—and, after some initial uncertainty, by Stewart. To a lesser degree it was favored by Chief Justice Vinson and Justices Sherman Minton and Charles E. Whittaker. That also was the position of Chief Justice Warren Earl Burger and is that of his successor, William H. Rehnquist (who, however, categorically rejects the concept of incorporation per se),[290] and probably of Justices Sandra Day O'Connor, Antonin Scalia, and Anthony M. Kennedy. Its most articulate enunciator on the "Burger Court," however, soon became Justice Lewis F. Powell Jr., whose jurisprudence was closely akin to, and represented a blend of, that of Justices Frankfurter and Harlan. It is essentially a "case-by-case" approach which closely examines on its own merits each individual claim of violation of due process of law, determines whether or not the common law as well as statutory law principles of "a fair trial" were accorded to the petitioner, and tests his claim against the requirement of "due

---

288. For a scholarly view that the notion of "selective" incorporation is a misnomer and/or represents a "widespread misconception," see Jacob W. Landynski, "Due Process and the Concept of Ordered Liberty: 'A Screen of Words Expressing Will in the Service of Desire'?" 2 *Hofstra University Law Review* 1 (winter 1974).

289. *Palko v. Connecticut,* 302 U.S. 319.

290. See the perceptive study by Sue Davis, *Justice Rehnquist and the Constitution* (Princeton, N.J.: Princeton University Press, 1989), especially chapter 4.

process of law"—as that elusive concept may be viewed by a majority of the Court. It is here that the famous Frankfurter quaere, whether the governmental action does in effect "shock the conscience"[291] or violate "common standards of civilized conduct," is asked. If the answer is yes, the partisans of the case-by-case approach will then hold due process of law to have been violated. For the adherents to this group of justices, however, such a decision will be without any reference to incorporation of the Bill of Rights, wholly or partly. In short, the "fair trial" test adherents reject both the selective incorporation approach of the Cardozo test and the *total* incorporation approach of the elder John Marshall Harlan. They reject the total incorporation (and certainly total incorporation "plus") as an example of "judicial legislating," and as a clear-cut violation of the principles of federalism and the commands of the Constitution. They reject selective incorporation as an unwise and unworkable resort to the vague tenets of "natural law" as the "slot machine approach" whereby, in Justice Frankfurter's words, "some are in and some are out," and as the creation of a hopeless, artificial, and unfair distinction among our basic rights and liberties. Yet to Justice Black the "due process" approach was itself plainly a "natural-law due process" formula.[292]

Pertinent illustrations of the Frankfurter "fair trial" approach are the *Adamson* case,[293] discussed earlier in this chapter, and the *Rochin* case.[294] Reed's majority[295] simply had not seen a violation, and their consciences had not been shocked by California's statute that permitted official courtroom comment on the fact that the accused, Adamson, refused to take the stand in his defense. In *Rochin* the conduct of certain Los Angeles County police officers so outraged their standards and so shocked their consciences that the accused's conviction was unanimously reversed by the Court—although two justices, Black and Douglas, concurred on separate grounds: "incorporation" of the Bill of Rights safeguards involved in *Rochin.* Also, in the 1964 self-incrimination cases, Justice Harlan II and his supporters' consciences were *not* "shocked" by Connecticut's treatment of Murphy's compulsory self-incrimination claims,[296] but they *were* shocked by the New York Harbor Waterfront Commission's treatment of Murphy's compulsory testimony claims.[297] In *Malloy* Harlan's case-by-case ap-

---

291. That test was one of Justice Black's particular bêtes noires. "I do not wish," he once said to Edmond Cahn, "to have to pass on the laws of this country according to the degree of shock I receive! Some people get shocked more readily than others" ("Justice Black and First Amendment 'Absolutes': A Public Interview," 37 *New York University Law Review* 549 [1962] at 562).

292. E.g., *Harper v. Virginia Board of Elections*, 383 U.S. 663 (1966) at 677–79; and *Griswold v. Connecticut*, 381 U.S. 479 (1965) at 525.

293. *Adamson v. California*, 332 U.S. 46 (1947).

294. *Rochin v. California*, 342 U.S. 165 (1952). See *infra* chapter 4.

295. Reed and Frankfurter were joined by Chief Justice Vinson and Associate Justices Jackson and Burton.

296. *Malloy v. Hogan*, 378 U.S. 1 (1964).

297. *Murphy v. Waterfront Commission of New York Harbor*, 378 U.S. 52 (1964).

proach—one always exhortative of his consistently reiterated warning that the states should not be put into "a constitutional straitjacket"—thus enabled him to see due process accorded to the petitioner, while his five colleagues who constituted the Court majority here not only disagreed with his conclusions on the presence of due process but, going further, incorporated the Fifth Amendment's self-incrimination issue. In *Murphy,* on the other hand, Harlan did see a violation of the petitioner's due process, and he thus joined his unanimous brethren to reverse Murphy's contempt conviction. In *Argersinger,*[298] which applied the *Gideon*[299] incorporation of the right to counsel to incarceratable misdemeanors as well, Justice Powell joined in the Court's unanimous reversal of Argersinger's conviction but wrote an important, thoughtfully developed concurring opinion opting for the case-by-case approach. In 1978 he rearticulated his objection to "jot-for-jot" incorporation—this time in dissenting in a double jeopardy case, in which he was joined by Chief Justice Burger and Justice Rehnquist.[300] This Frankfurter-Harlan-Powell position has the virtues of extensive judicial discretion and minute individual examination and the vices of potential unpredictability and subjectivity.[301] Given the facts of all-but-total incorporation, the Court's approach may now, in effect, if not in theory, constitute the Court's practical position with regard to any future extension of incorporation.

The *third* judicial posture, total incorporation of the Bill of Rights, was, of course, ardently and faithfully advocated by Justice John Marshall Harlan, the elder—however he may have chosen to express it linguistically. It is a doctrine espoused after *Palko* most notably by Justice Black, with early support from Douglas, Murphy, and Rutledge, and later from Goldberg (all four of whom, however, wanted to go even beyond Black's incorporation to achieve maximum application of the federal Constitution to the states and eventually did so). Simply stated, the Black formula asserts not only that the due process of law and the privileges or immunities clauses of the Fourteenth Amendment mandate the total incorporation of the *specific* commands of the Bill of Rights[302] but that even if history does not provide a foolproof guide, the logic of life in democratic soci-

298. *Argersinger v. Hamlin,* 407 U.S. 25 (1972).
299. *Gideon v. Wainwright,* 372 U.S. 335 (1963).
300. *Crist v. Bretz,* 437 U.S. 28.
301. For an articulate and warm endorsement of the Frankfurter approach to the problem, see Henry J. Friendly, "The Bill of Rights as a Code of Criminal Procedure," in his *Benchmarks* (Chicago: University of Chicago Press, 1967). For Harlan's reiterated support, see especially his *Duncan* dissenting opinion, op. cit., 391 U.S. 145 (1968) at 171. The Frankfurter-Powell approach, with particular reference to the Burger Court period (1969–86), is ably chronicled and evaluated by Raold Y. Mykkeltvedt in his *Nationalization of the Bill of Rights: Fourteenth Amendment Due Process and the Procedural Rights* (Port Washington, N.Y.: National University Publications, 1983).
302. See his concurring opinion in *Duncan,* op. cit., at 166, note 1, for a firm reiteration of his credo just two years prior to his death.

ety in our times dictates such a position as a matter of minimum fairness and necessity. Yet it should be remembered that the Black position on nationalization in toto extends only to those guarantees *specifically spelled out in the Constitution and its amendments.* To Black, for whom any kind of "natural law" formula was anathema, the first section of the Fourteenth Amendment absolutely incorporated the specifics of the first eight amendments, but *it was also confined to them.* Time and again he made it clear that natural law may not be employed by the judiciary either to expand or to limit legislative powers beyond the commands of the Bill of Rights—to do so he regarded as an "incongruous excrescence on our Constitution."[303] This approach possesses the undeniable virtues of both simplicity and predictability and the vices of dogmatism and questionable interpretation of the Fourteenth Amendment in particular and the U.S. Constitution in general.

The *fourth,* and for our purposes last, position is really an extension of the third: namely, that the Bill of Rights in all its majestic guarantees may not suffice to ascertain full "due process of law," and that therefore it may be necessary to draw on a kind of total incorporation *plus* approach in order to do full justice to the allegedly aggrieved. Known as the "total incorporation plus theory," it was initially most notably expounded in the immediate post-*Palko* era by Justices Murphy and Rutledge. In their dissenting opinion in the famed *Adamson* case,[304] written by Murphy, the words and intent are clear—although they stopped well short of concise explication:

We agree that the specific guarantees of the Bill of Rights should be carried over intact into the first section of the Fourteenth Amendment. But [we are] not prepared to say that the latter is entirely and necessarily limited by the Bill of Rights. *Occasions may arise where a proceeding falls so far short of conforming to fundamental standards of procedure as to warrant constitutional condemnation in terms of a lack of due process despite the absence of specific provision in the Bill of Rights. . . .*[305]

Justices Black and Douglas, who had also dissented in *Adamson,* did not then address themselves to the issue raised by their two junior colleagues; they were simply content to advocate total incorporation. However, while Black would always resolutely reject the "incorporation plus" philosophy on the grounds that concepts of intrinsic justice may *be used neither to limit nor to expand* individual rights *beyond what is spelled out in the Bill of Rights,* Douglas rapidly drew closer to the Murphy-Rutledge position. In effect, not long after

---

303. *Adamson v. California,* 332 U.S. 46 (1947) at 75. See also *Griswold v. Connecticut,* 381 U.S. 479 (1965) at 511–13; and *Harper v. Virginia Board of Elections,* 383 U.S. 663 (1966) at 675–76.

304. *Adamson v. California,* op. cit.

305. Ibid. at 124; italics supplied.

Murphy's and Rutledge's untimely deaths in 1949, he wholly embraced the "incorporation plus" doctrine. "The Bill of Rights Is Not Enough" was the title of one of his essays,[306] symptomatic of this intriguing position, which might be called a "super fair-trial" rule. Justice Goldberg demonstrated his sympathy toward that constitutional posture with his important concurring opinion in the *Connecticut Birth Control Case,*[307] in which he was significantly joined by Chief Justice Warren and also Justice Brennan. Goldberg, it will be recalled, made a point of stating that the due process clause was "neither limited to nor necessarily as broad as" the Bill of Rights, but rather that it "protects those personal rights that are fundamental."[308] Despite the theoretical loophole for a contraction of incorporation in view of the "nor as broad as" phrase of the statement just quoted, the Goldberg position, embraced also by Warren and somewhat later, but then both enthusiastically and expansively, by Brennan and Marshall, constitutes the acceptance of "incorporation plus"—with the possibility of a retrenchment when deemed necessary (an unlikely assumption). Moreover, it accepts the spirit and letter of the Douglas position on the Ninth Amendment announced in the *Birth Control Case,* which is patently the most advanced of all positions on the basic issue[309]—one that would, of course, readily lend itself to a "selective incorporation *plus*" conceptualization for those unwilling to accept the "total incorporation *plus*" approach.

Some Guesses and a Judgment. Those very few federally ascertained rights that are still "out" of the mandatory due process of law concept of Amendment Fourteen are all likely to remain out, at least formally. Essentially, there are but five: one is the Fifth Amendment's provision for indictment by grand jury in a "capital, or otherwise infamous crime." Evidently deeming it neither vital nor fundamental as a necessary prerequisite for due process in all state cases, the Court again in 1968 denied certiorari in a case challenging its nonapplicability in certain criminal cases in Connecticut. There, one Edward R. Gyuro, convicted of breaking into a store and attempting to abscond with five fur coats, appealed his sentence of three to seven years in prison.[310] Like many other states, Connecticut utilizes "information" rather than grand jury indictment, under which the public prosecutor merely submits his charges against an accused in the form of an affidavit of evidence, supported by sworn statements, to a court of original jurisdiction for trial docketing.

A second provision not likely to be incorporated is the Seventh Amendment right to a jury trial in *civil* cases in controversies valued at more than twenty dol-

---

306. 38 *New York University Law Review* 207 (April 1963).
307. *Griswold v. Connecticut,* 381 U.S. 479 (1965).
308. Ibid. at 493.
309. Ibid. at 485.
310. *Gyuro v. Connecticut,* 393 U.S. 937.

lars. This is obviously even less of an essential due process guarantee than grand jury indictment—and, in fact, there has been little formal demand for its "nationalization." After having denied the application of the amendment to the states in 1916,[311] the Court had an opportunity to adjudicate the issue in 1968, but it denied certiorari in a case concerning a 1964 car-train collision in Grand Prairie, Texas, in which a seventeen-year-old University of Texas student was severely injured.[312] The student, Roger McBeth, had unsuccessfully asked for a jury trial rather than the summary judgment proceeding obtained in the Texas courts by the Texas and Pacific Railway. In 1973 the Court made it clear that it would not overturn its 1968 holding.[313] The issue rearose in 1987 in a case raising the question whether the Constitution guarantees jury trial in a lawsuit brought by the federal government under the Clean Water Act.[314]

Third is the matter of the Eighth Amendment exhortation against a requirement of "excessive bail . . . and fines." There is, of course, no *constitutional* guarantee of bail as such[315]—only one against "excessive" bail, if bail is granted in the first place, and what is excessive necessarily rests upon a judicial determination,[316] which also pertains to "excessive" fines.[317] However, the entire problem of bail became a very visible issue, given the late 1960s and 1970s preoccupation with the "law-and-order" syndrome, and it received considerable attention in both the legislative and the administration-of-justice arenas. Demands for bail reform were largely responsible for the Bail Reform Acts of 1966 and 1984. The latter, a response to considerable public clamor, provided for a measure of "preventive detention" legislation by enabling the denial of bail at the pretrial level to any defendant who seems to endanger public safety, although the statute levels a heavy burden on detention-oriented prosecution. By a 6:3 vote the Court upheld the controversial provision in 1987.[318] Whatever the ultimate fate of bail

311. *Minneapolis and St. Louis Railroad v. Bombolis,* 241 U.S. 211 at 217.

312. *McBeth v. Texas and Pacific Railway,* 390 U.S. 387 (1968).

313. *Colgrove v. Battin,* 413 U.S. 149 (1973).

314. *Tull v. United States,* 481 U.S. 412.

315. See, e.g., *Murphy v. Hunt,* 455 U.S. 478 (1982), with the Court ducking the issue by mooting it.

316. The leading decision here is *Stack v. Boyle,* 342 U.S. 1 (1951). The yardstick laid down by the Court is that fixing of bail must be based "upon standards relevant to the purpose"—that is, the "punishment" must fit the "crime."

317. In one of the very few Supreme Court cases on record involving fines, the high tribunal held in 1971 that it constitutes a violation of the equal protection clause of Amendment Fourteen to limit punishment to payment of a fine for those who are *able* to pay it, yet to convert a fine to imprisonment for those who are *unable* to pay it (*Tate v. Short,* 401 U.S. 395). But Justice Brennan's opinion emphasized that there are a number of ways to enforce judgments against those unable to pay (e.g., seven states—and England and Wales—allow installment payments; England and Wales also permit the garnishing of wages).

318. *United States v. Salerno,* 481 U.S. 739.

legislation and litigation, it does not seem likely that the Court will "incorporate" the antiexcessiveness proviso. When it does get cases relating to the problem, it is far more likely to adjudicate them on the basis of the broad and time-honored due process/fair trial requirements, as indeed it has done,[319] as, for example, in ruling 5:4 in 1998 that the federal government cannot always seize and keep all the money people try to take outside the United States without filing the proper reports.[320]

Fourth is the often purposely (by opponents of gun control legislation) incompletely quoted Second Amendment proviso: "A well-regulated Militia, being necessary to the security of a free State, the right of the people to keep and bear Arms, shall not be infringed." If any provision of the Bill of Rights seems to need no judicial protection, Amendment Two is it, so powerful have been the forces opposed to effective regulatory legislation. In the one fairly recent case on record that did reach the Supreme Court, the high tribunal denied review for want of a substantial federal question, the tribunal below having held categorically that Amendment Two does not apply to the states[321]—that, indeed, "as the language of the Amendment itself indicates, it was not framed with individual rights in mind";[322] and that "[e]nough has been said to differentiate the second amendment from those which protect individual rights and, as such, have been carried over into the fourteenth amendment."[323] There is simply no question that the basic historic purpose of the Second Amendment was to ensure the status of the state militia, as the Court made clear in 1939, ruling that Amendment Two was

319. Ibid. One federal court would, however, apply the provision to the states (*Pilkington v. Circuit Court,* 324 F.2d 45–46 [1963]). See *Murphy v. Hunt,* op. cit., at 107, note 250. Taking his cue from Pilkington, Justice Blackmun "assumed" in a 1971 opinion (*Schilb v. Kuebel,* 407 U.S. 357 at 365) that "the Eighth Amendment's proscription of excessive bail [applies] to the states through the Fourteenth Amendment," based on his reading of *Robinson v. California,* 370 U.S. 660 (1962) at 666. But neither the latter decision nor the Court as a whole seemed to share or substantiate his view, although Justices Stevens and O'Connor, in a partial concurrence/dissent in *Browning-Ferris v. Kelco Disposal,* 492 U.S. 257 (1989), claim (at 244), based upon *Schilb,* that the "excessive bail" and "excessive fines" clauses ought to apply to the states.

320. *United States v. Bajakajian,* 524 U.S. 321.

321. *Burton v. Sills,* 394 U.S. 812 (1969), appeal dismissed. A ban on the sale and possession of handguns by the town of Morton Grove, Illinois, was upheld by a U.S. District Court in 1981, over objections of alleged violations of Amendments Two and Fourteen (*Quilici v. Village of Morton Grove,* 532 F. Supp. 1169). In a 2:1 vote the U.S. Seventh Circuit Court of Appeals affirmed at the end of 1982 (ibid., 695 F.2d 261), ruling that the Second Amendment restricts federal authority in this area, not that of state and local governments, and concluding: "[T]he right to keep and bear handguns is not guaranteed by the Second Amendment." And the U.S. Supreme Court denied review one year later (ibid., 464 U.S. 863).

322. Ibid., 248 F.2d 521 (1968) at 526.

323. Ibid. at 528. See also *Presser v. Illinois,* 116 U.S. 52 (1886); and *United States v. Miller,* 307 U.S. 174 (1939).

designed to ensure the effectiveness of the military, *not* to guarantee a private right to possess firearms.[324] "What, sir," asked Elbridge Gerry during the debate on the amendment, "is the use of a militia? It is to prevent the establishment of a standing army, the bane of liberty." Some contemporary analyses of the militia and states' rights, however, differ from prevailing beliefs.[325] And Attorney General John Ashcroft has observed publicly: "Let me state unequivocally my view that the text and the original intent of the Second Amendment clearly protect the right of individuals to keep and bear firearms."[326] Yet no constitutional barriers exist to reasonable regulation of weapons acquisition and use[327] (a subject of accelerating federal legislation in the late twentieth and early twenty-first centuries)—as the Court made clear by unanimously letting stand a 1986 federal ban on the sale and manufacture of new fully automatic machine guns.[328] The prevailing judicial view has thus clearly long been that the Second Amendment guarantees the right to bear arms only in the context of maintaining a well-regulated—that is, a state-sponsored—militia. Indeed, *no federal* court has ever successfully invalidated a law regulating the private ownership of arms on Second Amendment grounds[329]—although a U.S. District Court arguably did so in *United States v. Miller* in 1939, only to see itself reversed on evidentiary grounds by the U.S. Supreme Court.[330]

Fifth, and last, is the seldom-perceived Third Amendment, which proscribes involuntary peacetime and illegal wartime quartering of soldiers in private homes. No record of any violations exists; no challenge under the amendment

324. *United States v. Miller,* 307 U.S. 174.

325. See, e.g., Glenn Harlan Reynolds and Don B. Kates, "The Second Amendment and States' Rights: A Thought Experiment," 36 *William and Mary Law Review* 5 (August 1995); and George Will, "Armed Against Terrorism," *Washington Post,* November 4, 2001, p. B7.

326. *Boston Globe,* July 16, 2001; and *Washington Post,* May 8, 2002, p. A1.

327. See the excellent article by David T. Hardy, "The Second Amendment and the Historiography of the Bill of Rights," 4 *Journal of Law and Politics* 1 (summer 1987). For a contrary point of view, see "A Critical Guide to the Second Amendment," 62 *Tennessee Law Review* 3 (spring 1995); and William Glaberson, "Right to Bear Arms: A Second Look," *New York Times,* May 30, 1999, Sec. 4, p. 3. Note the 1998 Supreme Court 5:4 holding broadly interpreting a federal law that adds five years to the prison sentence of anyone who carries a firearm while trafficking in illegal drugs (*Muscarello v. U.S.,* 524 U.S. 125).

328. *Farmer v. Higgins,* 498 U.S. 1047 (1991). With regard to handguns, in all of 1988 only 7 handgun murders were committed in the United Kingdom compared with 8,915 in the United States! In 1990, 22 such murders were committed in the former, 10,567 in the latter, 13 in Sweden, 91 in Switzerland, 87 in Japan, 10 in Australia, and 68 in Canada (*Washington Post,* December 21, 1993, p. A22).

329. See Neil A. Louis, "At the Bar," *New York Times,* May 5, 1995, p. B18; and Joan Biskupic, "Bearing Arms: A Personal 'Right' in the Mind, but Not in Court," *Washington Post,* May 10, 1995, p. A20, for two informative analyses.

330. See 26 F.Supp. 1002 and 307 U.S. 174 (1939), respectively.

has ever reached the Supreme Court; and the lower federal courts have seen just one, which was dismissed as being without merit.[331]

Reflecting upon these considerations involving the five "outs," perhaps it is just as well that they remain unincorporated. The "selective incorporation" concept—which, as suggested, should perhaps now be labeled as "selective incorporation plus"; the Court's increasingly "open-ended," omnipresent concern for "equal protection" and "due process of law," and their extension to heretofore only marginally covered groups;[332] the obvious presence of a "double standard" in favor of basic human rights;[333] and the Court's embrace of "suspect" and "almost suspect" fundamental rights categories, in which legislation must show a "compelling" state interest rather than mere legislative "rationality" in order to pass "close scrutiny" constitutional muster,[334] are now facts of constitutional law and interpretation. They all combine to render plausible the argument and plea that the federal principle might well continue to permit the states to pursue their own procedural standards in the remaining nonincorporated areas. If so, however, these standards obviously must scrupulously meet, reflect, and adhere to the demands of due process of law. In the words of the wise counsel of Justice Goldberg in his concurring opinion in *Pointer v. Texas,*[335]

[T]o deny to the States the power to impair a fundamental constitutional right is not to increase federal power, but, rather, to limit the power of both

331. *United States v. Valenzuela,* 95 F. Supp. 363 (1951).

332. Thus note the significant 1967 decision, *In the Matter of Gault,* 387 U.S. 1, which in effect extended most of the Bill of Rights to juvenile offenders (a notable exception being the right to a trial by jury—see *McKeiver v. Pennsylvania,* 403 U.S. 528 [1971]). An intriguing extension of far-reaching implications came with the Supreme Court's contentious 5:4 decision in 1975 in *Goss v. Lopez,* holding for the first time that young people are entitled by the Constitution's due process concepts to the same sort of protection against unfair interference with their education (here summary ten-day or less suspension from public schools) that adults enjoy when the government tries to deprive them of their rights (419 U.S. 565). And the same majority held shortly thereafter that school officials who unfairly discipline students cannot defend themselves against civil rights suits by claiming ignorance of the students' basic constitutional rights (*Wood v. Strickland,* 420 U.S. 308 [1975]). On the other hand, in 1977 the Court, in a 5:4 opinion written by Justice Powell, held that the spanking of schoolchildren by teachers or other school officials does not violate the Constitution's Eighth Amendment ban against cruel and unusual punishment, stressing the broad public acceptance of the practice (*Ingraham v. Wright,* 430 U.S. 651). And in 1984 it ruled (6:3) that laws (present then in all fifty states) under which juveniles charged with delinquency may be held in pretrial detention to prevent them from committing additional crimes are constitutional (*Schall v. Martin,* 467 U.S. 253).

333. See *supra* chapter 2.

334. Ibid.

335. 380 U.S. 400 (1964).

federal and state governments in favor of safeguarding the fundamental liberties of the individual. In my view this promotes rather than undermines the basic policy of avoiding excess concentration of power in government, federal or state, which underlies our concepts of federalism.[336]

336. Ibid. at 414. Although Goldberg's statement presumes that the states are adhering to a lower standard of civil rights and liberties, the increasing liberality of a good many state courts is demonstrable. For example, the supreme courts of New Jersey, Massachusetts, Florida, New York, California, and even Alabama and Mississippi have gone beyond federal parameters on a host of issues. Specifically, the supreme courts of Texas and Kentucky have willingly outpaced their federal counterparts in ordering their respective states to equalize financing of public schools—something the U.S. Supreme Court explicitly refused to do in the 1973 case *San Antonio Independent School District v. Rodriguez,* 411 U.S. 1 (see *infra* chapter 7). Of course, in many instances state jurists have the benefit of applying newer, and more liberal, *state* constitutional guarantees. See Justice Brennan's insistent claims to identify state supreme courts that have become more open to individual liberties claims (Brennan, "State Constitutions and the Protection of Individual Rights," 90 *Harvard Law Review* 489 [1977]). See also A. E. Dick Howard, "State Courts and Constitutional Rights in the Day of the Burger Court," 62 *Virginia Law Review* 873 (1976); for a different view, contrast Barry Latzer, "The Hidden Conservatism of the State Court 'Revolution,'" 74 *Judicature* 190 (December–January 1991).

4

The Fascinating World of
"Due Process of Law"

The concept "due process of law" has been an integral part of much of what we have been discussing. It is both subordinate and coordinate to any considerations of "values and lines" in the realm of civil rights and liberties. The presence or absence of no concept is mentioned more frequently in our judicio-legal process than "due process of law"; today its banner is raised in a host of appellate cases at the level of the U.S. Supreme Court, whereas that high tribunal decided but one case on due process grounds between 1789 and 1866! Its terminology, if not its clear meaning, is found in Amendments Five and Fourteen of the Constitution, both of which issue clarion calls to national and state governments, respectively, for the presence and maintenance of due process of law. In the words of Amendment Five, ratified on December 15, 1791: "No person shall . . . be deprived of life, liberty, or property, *without due process of law* . . .";[1] and in the words of Amendment Fourteen, ratified on July 23, 1868: "No State shall . . . deprive any person of life, liberty, or property, *without due process of law.* . . ."[2] Towering disagreements as to the meaning of that command have plagued us and will undoubtedly continue to do so, thus complicating seriously attempts at line drawing—as the aforegone analysis of the question of the incorporation of the Bill of Rights has demonstrated. Yet basic guidelines do exist, and, no matter how vexatious and hazardous the task at hand may well be, they do enable us to come to grips with the central meaning of due process of law.

SOME BASIC GUIDELINES

Although it may well be futile to attempt definitive interpretations of "due process of law," it is possible to delineate certain fundamentals. One basic re-

1. Italics supplied.
2. Italics supplied.

quirement of the concept due process of law is that government may not act in an "arbitrary," "capricious," or "unreasonable" manner in performing its task vis-à-vis the body politic. The judicial branch as the ultimate guardian of our Constitution-guaranteed civil rights and liberties has the delicate and difficult task of ascertaining the constitutional appropriateness of governmental action by weighing it against what amount to common-law notions of "arbitrariness," "capriciousness," or "unreasonableness"—although this adjectival test has been vehemently and consistently rejected as a usable measure by some prominent jurists, such as Justice Black, a dedicated Constitutional *literalist*.[3]

Suffice it to say that opinions differ widely on the meaning of these concepts. What may be "arbitrary" to some legislators and executives may seem "reasonable" to others; what may be "capricious" police behavior in the eyes of a prisoner may be "fair" in the eyes of the apprehending and prosecuting authorities; and what may well seem to be an "unreasonable" interpretation by an administrative agency in the view of an affected business concern or educational institution may appear "reasonable" to the agency's commissioners. Does the matter, then, become merely one of opinion, or are there ascertainable standards? The answer cannot be conclusive: there *are* standards, of course, but until they have been judicially tested and pronounced, they remain general standards based as much on civilized notions of fairness and decency—not infrequently widely personalized divergent ones—as on any written commands, whether statutes, ordinances, or even constitutions, federal or state. At the federal level, because of the specific exhortations of the Constitution and the centralizing tendency of having only one final arbiter, "due process" standards are generally both more predictable and more ascertainable than at the *state* level. Fifty separate units of government, despite the mandates and implications of the Fourteenth Amendment *and of their own bills of rights,* bring normally a more fluid, less predictable, and, in the main, less "generous" interpretation of due process of law to the individual than is customarily true at the federal level. However, given the post-1937 stance of the U.S. Supreme Court, the states, too, consequently have had to pay far more attention to the fundamental concepts of "fairness and decency," which are so vital to the presence of "due process of law"—and it is fair to say that they are "coming around" increasingly.

---

3. See, among others, his scathing lecture on the subject in his *A Constitutional Faith* (New York: Knopf, 1968), pp. 23ff. It probably represents the fullest statement of his due process philosophy. In essence, he hinged it to Lord Coke's understanding of *per legem terrae,* the "law of the land" provision of the Magna Carta, chapter 29, which to Black represented *already existing constitutional provisions; the Bill of Rights; plus all laws that had been passed pursuant to constitutional power at the time the alleged offense was committed.* To Coke, however, "by the due course and process of law" was almost certainly confined to *judicial proceedings*—not to substantive or contextual aspects of a statute.

A General Definition. Any general definition of due process of law must take into account the genesis of the concept. It was originally derived from English common law—probably during the reigns of Henry I (1100–1135) and Henry II (1154–89). Its more obvious antecedent is the Magna Carta of 1215, chapter 29 (chapter 39 in a later version), which declares: "No free man shall be taken, outlawed, banished, or in any way destroyed, nor will we proceed against or prosecute him, except by the lawfull judgment of his peers and by the law of the land." As Professor A. E. Dick Howard of the University of Virginia School of Law has pointed out in his commentary on the Magna Carta, as early as 1354 the words *due process* were used in an English statute interpreting the Magna Carta, and by the end of the fourteenth century "due process of law" and "law of the land" were interchangeable. The English colonists who established our courts brought the expression due process of law with them.[4] As it developed, "due process of law" restrained a head of government from arbitrarily depriving a member of his realm of life, liberty, or property. In due course this notion was embraced by all other departments of government as well; it has been an essential fact of governmental life on this side of the ocean since the Constitution's adoption in 1789.

Perhaps the best brief definition of due process of law was contained in the first Justice John Marshall Harlan's dissenting opinion in 1884, in *Hurtado v. California.*[5] Governments, he wrote, should be confined within the limits of those fundamental *"principles of liberty and justice,* lying at the foundation of our civil and political institutions, which no State can violate consistently with that due process of law required by the Fourteenth Amendment in proceedings involving life, liberty, or property."[6] This noble phrase, then advanced on the losing side of the judicial ledger, became firmly implanted on the majority side with its acceptance, clarification, and refinement by Justice Cardozo, more than half a century later, in *Palko v. Connecticut.*[7]

But what are those "fundamental principles of liberty and justice" that constitute the irreducible minimum of due process of law? We may discover them from a variety of sources:

the body of constitutions,

bills of rights,

4. A. E. Dick Howard, *Magna Carta: Text and Commentary* (Charlottesville: University of Virginia Press, 1964). See also Justice Black's commentary on the subject in his *Constitutional Faith,* op. cit., especially pp. 30–38. For a much more restrictive interpretation—which sees "due process" as wholly procedural—see Keith Jurow, "Untimely Thoughts: A Reconsideration of the Origins of the Process of Law," 19 *American Journal of Legal History* 265 (1975). Jurow thus sides with both Alexander Hamilton's interpretation of "due process of law" (see *infra* note 11) and Justice Frankfurter's (see later text).
5. 110 U.S. 516.
6. Ibid. at 546; italics supplied.
7. 302 U.S. 319 (1937). See *supra* chapter 3.

customs, conventions, and traditions,

legislative enactments,

executive ordinances, decrees, and practices,

judicial interpretations and precedents;

and significantly, from what one commentator aptly termed "current views of right and wrong which collectively have come to be accepted as a part of the established law of the land."[8] The concept of due process of law and its application to our federal and state governments is based on an extensive reservoir of *constitutionally expressed and implied limitations upon governmental authority,* ultimately determined by the judicial process, and upon those basic notions of fairness and decency which govern, or ought to govern, the relationships between rulers and ruled. Although Justice Frankfurter's record is, of course, based on the subjective case-by-case approach described earlier, rather than a clearly delineated one, he viewed this flexible concept of due process of law as "compounded by history, reason, the past course of decisions, and stout confidence in the democratic faith which we profess. . . ."[9] Yet in 1924, while professor of constitutional law at Harvard, he had written that "the due process clauses ought to go,"[10] a philosophical commitment he reiterated frequently from the bench.

SUBSTANTIVE AND PROCEDURAL DUE PROCESS OF LAW

Any explanation of due process of law must consider its two "types" or aspects— *substantive and procedural*—for judicial disposition of due process litigation necessarily turns on the *kind* of violation that is alleged by a petitioner. Although neither is as readily definable nor as clearly separable from the other as is sometimes claimed, it is essential to understand at least a general distinction between the two. We may view *substantive* due process as referring to the *content or subject matter* of a law or an ordinance; that is, whether what it deals with, what it is trying to accomplish, *contextually* conforms to due process of law. On the other hand, *procedural due process*—the more litigated of the two—refers to the manner in which a law, ordinance, administrative practice, or judicial task is carried out; that is, whether the procedures employed by those who are charged with the application of the law or ordinance violate *procedural* due process, regardless of the substance of the former. For nearly a century procedural due process

8. Jesse T. Carpenter, "Due Process of Law," in Edward C. Smith and Arnold J. Zurcher, eds., *Dictionary of American Politics* (New York: Barnes and Noble, 1955), p. 128.

9. *Joint Anti-Fascist Refugee Committee v. McGrath,* 341 U.S. 123 (1951), concurring opinion.

10. "The Red Terror of Judicial Reform," 40 *New Republic* 10 at 113.

was viewed in American jurisprudence as the *only* "due process" extant.[11] Substantive due process was not "discovered" formally by the judiciary as a viable "tool" until the now famed *Wynehamer* case in 1856,[12] in which New York's courts struck down a New York State liquor prohibition law. Here, then, for the first time, a court read "due process" to "prohibit, *regardless* of the matter of procedure, a certain kind or degree of exertion of legislative power altogether": due process, rather than merely protecting the "mode of procedure," was made to reach "the substantive content of legislation."[13] In both the substantive and procedural due process concepts the judicial test of constitutionality or legality has become more or less the same: Is the governmental action "arbitrary," "capricious," "unreasonable," "invidious," "irrelevant," or "irrational" either in content or in procedure?[14] If it is, the action by government and/or its agent will then fall—and on occasion *both* substantive and procedural violations have been present. To Justice Black, however, courts had *no* power whatsoever to pass on the "reasonableness" of state or federal legislation.[15]

Substantive Due Process

As the discussion of the post-1937 "double standard" has demonstrated,[16] the Supreme Court has largely abandoned substantive due process of law as a check on legislative *economic-proprietarian* regulation. This does not mean, of course,

11. Thus Alexander Hamilton: "The words 'due process' have a precise technical import, and are only applicable to the process and proceedings of the courts of justice; *they can never be referred to an act of the legislature*" (*The Papers of Alexander Hamilton* [New York: Columbia University Press, 1962], p. 35; italics supplied). Justice Frankfurter, deeply troubled by the increasing judicial resort to substantive due process rulings at home, was instrumental, upon being asked for his advice, in having India's Constitution of 1950 adopt in its Article 21 a concept of "due process of law" that reads that no one shall be deprived of due process of law "except in accordance with the *procedure* established by law"; italics supplied.

12. *Wynehamer v. People,* 13 N.Y. 358 (1856). Raoul Berger refers to *Wynehamer* as the locus classicus of substantive due process in his *Government by Judiciary: The Transformation of the Fourteenth Amendment* (Cambridge, Mass.: Harvard University Press, 1977), pp. 254–55. Wallace Mendelson finds it in an earlier New York case, however: *Taylor v. Sorter,* 4 Hill 140 (N.Y. 1843).

13. See Gerald Gunther, quoting Edward S. Corwin, in the former's *Individual Rights in Constitutional Law,* 4th ed. (Mineola, N.Y.: Foundation Press, 1986), p. 111, note 3.

14. These six adjectives were listed by Justice Black in his dissenting opinion in *Harper v. Virginia Board of Elections,* 383 U.S. 673 (1966) at 673, as the governing tests for claims of violations of the Fourteenth Amendment's equal protection of the laws clause.

15. See John Frank, "Hugo L. Black," in Leon Friedman and Fred L. Israel, eds., *The Justices of the United States Supreme Court* (New York: Chelsea House, 1980), p. 2330; and Tinsley E. Yarbrough, *Mr. Justice Black and His Critics* (Durham, N.C.: Duke University Press, 1988).

16. See *supra* chapter 2.

that legislatures are free to disregard the basic standards of substantive due process when legislating in the realm of the economy—indeed, the Court will permit no obvious violation.[17] But it does mean that in line with its latter-day double-standard canons of judicial self-restraint, the Court will generally bend over backward to uphold such legislation. In the area of civil liberties, however, judicial action in the substantive due process area is now frequent, and while the Court is called upon to pass judgment less often in that sphere than in the procedural one, no term passes without some challenges to governmental enactments on substantive due process grounds. Many of these fall into the area of the First Amendment freedoms,[18] in particular the freedom of expression[19] and religion, and, with steadily mounting frequency since the 1950s, Fourteenth Amendment egalitarian aspects (discussed in subsequent chapters). A pertinent illustration is sterilization legislation.

Carrie Buck Loses. Carrie Buck, an eighteen-year-old, purportedly feebleminded white woman from Charlottesville, Virginia, allegedly the illegitimate daughter

17. E.g., *Shapiro v. Thompson,* 394 U.S. 618 (1969)—alluding to the "very means to exist," namely, food, clothing, and shelter—and similar late 1960s and mid- and early 1970s judicial checks in the general area of welfare and poverty (when viewed as bearing upon individual constitutional rights). *Shapiro* has been heavily attacked, however—although tangentially reconfirmed, and even expanded, almost sixty years later, in *Saenz v. Roe,* 526 U.S. 489 (1999), a resurrection of aspects of the Fourteenth Amendment's "privileges or immunities" clause.

18. Space does not here permit a discussion of the following three basic substantive due process safeguards found in the body of the Constitution (Article 1): the writ of habeas corpus, ex post facto laws, and bills of attainder.

19. Thus, ready candidates for declarations of unconstitutionality—usually unanimously—are such patently vague enactments as "vagrancy," "loitering," and "public nuisance" laws. (E.g., *Papachristou v. City of Jacksonville,* 405 U.S. 156 [1972], which, among others, outlawed as "vagrants" and "rogues and vagabonds" persons who, among other things, "use juggling or unlawful games," are "common nightwalkers" or "habitual loafers," and who are able to work but habitually live upon the earnings of their wives or minor children." Plaintiff Papachristou had been convicted under that quaint statute of "prowling by auto." It fell unconstitutional, via Douglas, as vague under due process.) A "vague" statute, according to a classic 1926 definition by Justice Sutherland, is one which "either forbids or requires the doing of an act in terms so vague that men of common intelligence must necessarily guess at its meaning and differ as to its application, [and thus] violates the first essential of due process of law" (*Connally v. General Construction Co.,* 269 U.S. 385, at 391). See also Cincinnati's abortive law making it a crime for three or more persons to assemble on city sidewalks "and there conduct themselves in a manner annoying to persons passing by" (*Coates v. Cincinnati,* 402 U.S. 611 [1971]). Ditto Houston's statute making it a crime to oppose or "interrupt any policeman in the execution of his duty," the Court ruling 8:1 that the law was "unconstitutionally overbroad" (*Houston v. Hill,* 482 U.S. 451 [1987]). Also Chicago's 1992 antiloitering ordinance, which fell 6:3 in 1999 in a welter of six opinions as being too vague because it failed to draw a line between "innocent" and "sinister" lingering and failed to give police clear guidance as to appropriate dispersal (*Chicago v. Morales,* 527 U.S. 41).

of a state-proclaimed "maritally unworthy . . . shiftless, ignorant, and worthless" feebleminded mother, and herself the mother of a supposedly mentally defective, concededly feebleminded, illegitimate baby—the product of the rape by the nephew of her foster parents—was committed in 1924 to the Virginia State Colony for Epileptics and the Feeble-Minded—where her mother, Emma, probably the mother of two other illegitimate children, had also once been committed. A Virginia statute, enacted earlier in 1924, provided that the health of the patient and the welfare of society may be promoted in certain cases by the sterilization of mental defectives, under careful safeguard; that the sterilization may be effected in males by vasectomy and in females by salpingectomy, without serious pain or substantial danger to life; that the Commonwealth of Virginia "is supporting in various institutions many defective persons who if now discharged would become a menace but if incapable of procreating might be discharged with safety and become self-supporting with benefit to themselves and to society"; and that experience has shown that heredity plays an important part in the transmission of insanity, imbecility, idiocy, feeblemindedness, and epilepsy. The law was one of many sterilization statutes enacted in thirty of the fifty states, resulting in a total of 63,966 sterilizations during their existence.[20] Virginia's went on to state that whenever the superintendent of certain institutions, including the state colony at Lynchburg, where Carrie and her mother were committed, shall be of the opinion that it is for the best interests of the patient and of society, he may have the operation "performed upon any patient afflicted with hereditary forms of insanity, imbecility," and so forth, if he complies with the careful provisions by which the law protects the patient from possible abuse.[21]

Dr. J. H. Bell, the superintendent of the State Colony for Epileptics and the Feeble-Minded—prodded by the statute's author, Democratic Senator Aubrey Strode, and its leading philosophical proponent, Dr. Albert S. Priddy—recommended to his board of directors that Carrie Buck be sterilized. The board, in compliance with the apparently succinctly drawn law, ultimately so ordered. Carrie may have been feebleminded, but she understood what was about to happen to her. On her request for a lawyer, her guardian, Robert S. Shelton, chose a former colony director, and Strode's close friend, Irving Whitehead. He set in motion the elaborate appellate procedure provided under the act and applied to the county circuit court for reversal of the order, but it affirmed the sterilization decree. Carrie's less than enthusiastic petitioners then appealed to the Virginia Supreme Court of Appeals, which agreed with the conclusion reached below that the application of the sterilization law in the case would be a "blessing" for feeble-

---

20. *Charlottesville Daily Progress,* May 3, 2002, p. A9.

21. Act of March 20, 1924, ch. 394, 1924 Va. Acts 569. Specifically, the statute provided for sexual sterilization of any state hospital inmate who was "insane, idiotic, imbecile, feeble-minded or epileptic, and by the laws of heredity . . . the probable potential parent of socially inadequate offspring likewise afflicted."

minded patients like Carrie. The next legal step was an appeal to the Supreme Court of the United States, the constitutional issues raised by Whitehead being alleged denial of *substantive* due process and the "equal protection of the laws," both under the Fourteenth Amendment. The lawyer for the colony in the case was none other than Aubrey Strode! Carrie's attorney had no quarrel with the *procedural* aspects of the Virginia law, readily granting that they provided full due process of law; the attack was upon the *substance* of the legislation. In brief, Whitehead contended in a rather skimpy brief of eight pages (Strode's ran to forty-five) that not only was the sterilization order unauthorized on the existing grounds but that "in no circumstances could such an order be justified" under substantive due process of law; that it was on its face arbitrary, capricious, and unreasonable. Moreover, argued the attorney, Virginia had violated Carrie's, and similarly afflicted candidates', substantive due process and equal protection of the laws because the law reached only the "small number who are in the institutions named and is not applied to the multitude outside."[22]

Over Justice Butler's dissent[23] without a written opinion (an annoying idiosyncrasy), Justice Holmes upheld Virginia's statute and action, joined by Chief Justice Taft[24] and Associate Justices Van Devanter, McReynolds, Brandeis, Sutherland, Sanford, and Stone. Holmes reasoned that since the public welfare has more than once called, and may at almost any time call, upon the best citizens for their lives, it would be "strange if it could not call upon those who already sap the strength of the State for these lesser sacrifices often not felt to be such by those concerned, in order to prevent our being swamped with incompetence." Having established that premise the eighty-six-year-old Holmes—a confirmed Malthusian since boyhood—continued with an oft-quoted passage:

> It is better for all the world, if instead of waiting to execute degenerate offspring for crime, or to let them starve for their imbecility, society can prevent those who are manifestly unfit from continuing their kind. The principle that sustains compulsory vaccination is broad enough to cover cutting the Fallopian tubes. . . . Three generations of imbeciles are enough.[25]

---

22. *Buck v. Bell,* 274 U.S. 200 (1927).

23. Attributed by one close student of the case to Butler's Roman Catholic–based religious opposition to sterilization. See Paul A. Lombardo, "Three Generations of Imbeciles: New Light on *Buck v. Bell,*" 60 *New York University Law Review* 1 (April 1985), pp. 30–62 at 57, and his "The Lynchburg Story," an early 1990s documentary giving the historical background of *Buck v. Bell.* See also Stephen J. Gould, "Carrie Buck's Daughter," *Natural History,* July 1984, pp. 14–18, whose findings support Lombardo's, and "Case of Charlottesville Woman Sterilized 70 Years Ago Holds Lessons for Today," 24 *Inside UVA* 86 (December 2, 1994), p. 1.

24. In a letter to Helen Heron (May 6, 1927) he applauded: "[Holmes's] quickness and his powers of catching and stating the point succinctly are marvelous. His brilliance does not seem to abate at all" (Lombardo, loc. cit., at 57).

25. *Buck v. Bell,* op. cit., at 207 (1927).

As to the allegations of denial of the equal protection of the laws—that is, that the Virginia statute did not reach "the multitude outside" state institutions—Holmes commented that "it is the usual last resort of constitutional arguments to point out shortcomings of this sort." The answer to *that* argument, said the dedicated exponent of judicial self-restraint, is that the law does all that is needed when it does all that it can, indicates a policy, applies it to all within the lines, and seeks to bring within the lines all similarly situated so far and so fast as its means allow. Of course so far as the operations enable those who otherwise must be kept confined to be returned to the world, and thus open the asylum to others, the equality aimed at will be more nearly reached. Judgment affirmed.[26]

Almost sixty years after the 1927 decision in *Buck v. Bell,* painstaking research by Dr. Paul A. Lombardo of the Institute of Law, Psychiatry, and Public Policy of the University of Virginia[27] demonstrated with considerable conviction that the *Buck v. Bell* suit in fact "originated as a means of vindicating the moralism and private prejudices of three professional and political colleagues: the state-legislator (Strode) who drafted the law and defended it in court; the physician (Priddy) whose fervent belief that sterilization could rid society of undesirables spurred the statute's enactment; and the attorney (Whitehead) who represented Carrie Buck." It is Dr. Lombardo's conclusion that Carrie, her mother, and her daughter were not imbeciles but rather the unfortunate victims of an elaborate legislative and judicial campaign that resulted in the legally sanctioned sterilization of Carrie and thousands of other Americans—not only in Virginia but throughout much of the nation.

Although the underlying philosophy of *Buck v. Bell* has thus been subjected to heavy and trenchant criticism—arguably partly with the hindsight of sociomedical developments since the 1920s—it still serves to illustrate well some of the problems inherent in the concept of substantive due process of law: the *lawmakers'* prerogative to determine public policy, but presumably one permissible under the Constitution; the *judges'* responsibility ultimately to determine the legality and/or constitutionality of that public policy once the issue reaches them—without, however, substituting their own notions of wisdom and desirability for that of the lawmakers, to whom judicial deference is due under the so crucial institution of the separation of powers. Obviously, the line between "judicial judging" and "judicial lawmaking" is a thin and indeed a vexatious one. The courts had no problem with Virginia's sterilization law in *Buck v. Bell*—they upheld it all but unanimously. It is a valid question, however, whether they *should* have found constitutional barriers in the case. Almost certainly, they would have today. On the other hand, was the Supreme Court justified in striking down, on the basis of violations of substantive due process, legislation as that at issue in the

26. Ibid. at 208.
27. Lombardo, op. cit., note 23 and accompanying text.

aforediscussed case of *Griswold v. Connecticut*,[28] legislation that was as silly as it was unenforceable—but was there warrant to throw it out rather than have the people cause their legislators to alter it? Similar questions attend a veritable host of judicial decisions in a broad spectrum of legislative and executive actions—alluded to or analyzed throughout these pages—thus giving life to the omnipresent difficulties of delineating the appropriate parameters of judicial power.

Carrie Buck, her appeal to the U.S. Supreme Court for a rehearing having been denied,[29] was ultimately sterilized[30]—one of eighty-three hundred Virginians between 1922 and 1972, when Virginia decided to discontinue such sterilizations. The statute's most stringent features, especially those relating to *involuntary* sterilization, were repealed in 1974 and 1981.[31] But fifteen years after Carrie Buck's future chance of motherhood had thus been surgically terminated, one man *won* his battle against sterilization on both substantive due process and equal protection grounds, in a case often regarded as a sequel to *Buck v. Bell*. His name was Arthur Skinner—and he was not precisely a pillar of the community.

Arthur Skinner Wins. An Oklahoman habitually in trouble with the law, Arthur Skinner was convicted in 1926 of the crime of stealing three chickens and was sentenced to the Oklahoma State Reformatory. Three years later he was convicted of the crime of robbery with firearms and was again sentenced to the reformatory. In 1934 he was once more convicted of robbery with firearms and was sent to the penitentiary, where he was when, in 1935, Oklahoma enacted a new statute, known as the Habitual Criminal Sterilization Act. It was legislated in a burst of moralistic enthusiasm, with assurances not only of its wisdom but of its constitutionality. The law defined a "habitual criminal" as a person who, having been convicted two or more times for crimes "amounting to felonies involving moral turpitude" either in Oklahoma or in any other state court, is *thereafter* convicted of a *third* such felony in Oklahoma and duly sentenced to a term of imprisonment in an Oklahoma penal institution. The statute then provided that the Oklahoma attorney general could institute "a proceeding against such a person in

28. See the detailed discussion *supra*.

29. *Buck v. Bell*, op. cit. Carrie died in 1983; her daughter, Vivian, had died at age eight, fifty-one years earlier.

30. A challenge to a Nebraska statute similar to, but not identical with, Virginia's was dismissed by the Court well over four decades later (*Cavitt v. Nebraska*, 396 U.S. 996 [1970]). And in the 1973 *Abortion Cases* the Court reaffirmed its initial decision in Buck (*Roe v. Wade*, 410 U.S. 113 at 154).

31. Virginia began to conduct a massive media campaign in 1984 in an effort to reach those 1922–72 sterilizees who might still not know why they could not have children. And in May 2002 Virginia's Governor Mark R. Warner issued a public, formal apology for what he called "a shameful effort in which state government never should have been involved" (*Charlottesville Daily Progress*, May 3, 2002, p. A1).

the Oklahoma courts for a judgment that such person be rendered sexually sterile," and continued:

> If the court or jury finds that the defendant is an "habitual criminal" and that he "may be rendered sexually sterile without detriment to his or her general health," then the court "shall render judgment to the effect that said defendant be rendered sexually sterile" by the operation of a vasectomy in case of a male and of a salpingectomy in case of a female.[32]

The act went on to state that offenses arising out of the violation of "the prohibitory laws, revenue acts, embezzlement, or political offenses, shall *not* come or be considered within" its terms. In other words, one might commit a crime in these areas and *not* have them count as one of the three crimes that led to the knife for those who committed felonies[33] involving "moral turpitude."

Arthur Skinner was not so fortunate. He had already committed his three felonies involving "moral turpitude." Thus he was a perfect candidate when the sterilization statute became law. For a year he seemed to have escaped, but in 1936 the attorney general of Oklahoma began proceedings against him. Properly following every prescribed aspect of procedural due process of law under the statute, the state prosecutor steered the case through the various stages, challenged at each by Skinner's attorneys. But by a 5:4 decision, a judgment directing that the vasectomy be performed on Skinner was ultimately affirmed by the Oklahoma Supreme Court.[34] Now thoroughly frightened, Arthur Skinner appealed the statute's constitutionality to the U.S. Supreme Court.

Of the members of the Court that had sealed Carrie Buck's fate fifteen years earlier, all except Chief Justice Stone—who was then an associate justice—had died, resigned, or retired. Stone, who had sided with the 8:1 majority in that earlier case, now joined the unanimous 1942 Court, although he disagreed with certain aspects of the expansive opinion written by Justice Douglas.[35] Be it said at once that the Supreme Court did not *reconsider* its *Buck v. Bell*[36] decision— which still stands.[37] While, in a concurring opinion, Justice Jackson pointedly warned that there are "limits to the extent to which a legislatively represented majority may conduct biological experiments at the expense of the dignity and personality and natural powers of a minority,"[38] Stone, in his own concurring

---

32. *Skinner v. Oklahoma*, 316 U.S. 535 (1942).
33. A felony is a crime graver in general, or more serious in nature and penal consequence, than a misdemeanor.
34. *Skinner v. Oklahoma*, 198 Okla. 235, 115 P.2d 123.
35. *Skinner v. Oklahoma*, 316 U.S. 535.
36. 274 U.S. 200 (1927).
37. See *supra* note 29.
38. *Skinner v. Oklahoma*, 316 U.S. 535 at 546.

opinion, made it quite clear (he used the term "undoubtedly") that he still considered *Buck v. Bell* to have been properly decided.[39]

The Douglas opinion for the Court, joined by Justices Roberts, Black, Reed, Frankfurter, Murphy, and Byrnes, was actually less concerned with "due process of law" than with what it viewed as Skinner's denial by Oklahoma of the "equal protection of the laws." Still, the absence of substantive due process was clearly implied, since Justice Douglas, by continuous implication if not by language, demonstrated that, in fact, the law deprived Skinner of "a basic liberty" by its "inequality," one here involving "one of the basic civil rights of man."[40] And it was not difficult for him to find the manifold aspects of inequality that were indeed inherent in the act. Directing his attention to the provision that *included larceny* but *excluded embezzlement* as a crime leading toward sterilization, he wrote with indignation:

> A person who enters a chicken coop and steals chickens commits a felony . . . and he may be sterilized if he is thrice convicted. If, however, he is the bailee of the property and fraudulently appropriates it, he is an embezzler. . . . Hence no matter how habitual his proclivities for embezzlement are and no matter how often his conviction, he may not be sterilized.[41]

Douglas reminded Oklahoma and the nation that when the law "lays an unequal hand" on those who have committed intrinsically the same quality of offense and sterilizes one and not the other, it has made "as invidious a discrimination as if it had selected a particular race or nationality for oppressive treatment."[42] And he concluded that while there had been "saving features" in the *Buck v. Bell* circumstances, none were present in the *Skinner* case:

> Sterilization of those who have thrice committed grand larceny with immunity for those who are embezzlers is a clear, pointed, unmistakable discrimination. Oklahoma makes no attempt to say that he who commits larceny by trespass or trick or fraud has biologically inheritable traits which he who commits embezzlement lacks. . . . The equal protection [of the laws] clause would indeed be a formula of empty words if such conspicuously artificial lines could be drawn. . . .[43]

---

39. Ibid. at 544.
40. Ibid. at 541. "Marriage and procreation," added Douglas, "are fundamental to the very existence and survival of the race." But see *supra* note 29, and Justice Marshall's dissenting opinion, *joined by his colleague Douglas,* referring to *Buck* and *Skinner,* in *San Antonio Independent School District v. Rodriguez,* 411 U.S. 1 (1973) at 70ff.
41. *Skinner v. Oklahoma* at 539.
42. Ibid. at 541.
43. Ibid. at 541, 542.

To Stone, however, the most significant question of line drawing involved was not one of "equal protection" but "of whether the wholesale condemnation of a class to such an invasion of personal liberty . . . satisfies the demands for due process."[44] To him and to the entire Court, it clearly did not,[45] and Arthur Skinner escaped the surgical reaches of the statute, which was thus declared unconstitutional. Of course, there is a limit on the kind of laws regulating life, liberty, and property that a legislature can make.[46] Notwithstanding the high judicial regard for self-restraint vis-à-vis legislative activities—demonstrated again by the Court's upholding of the nation's first "Megan's Law," which allows the publication of the names and addresses of sex offenders[47]—the demands of due process of law (here substantive due process) will continue to require delineation.[48]

44. Ibid. at 544.

45. In 1965 the Supreme Court refused to rule whether sterilization of a California man violated the Eighth Amendment's ban on "cruel and unusual punishment" (*In re Miguel Vega Andrada,* 380 U.S. 953). He had agreed to the vasectomy, but he later charged it was coerced and "inflicted" as punishment in a misdemeanor case in which he was charged with failure to provide for his four children by his first wife. Having later resumed payments to his ex-wife, and having married his common-law wife (by whom he had had a child out of wedlock), he subsequently sought to have the vasectomy "undone," a feat successful in only 50 percent of such cases. On the other hand, in 1975 a Minnesota jury awarded $19,500 in damages to a couple whose eighth child was conceived six months after the husband underwent a vasectomy. The defendants in the case, brought by Mr. and Mrs. Eugene Sherlock, were the Stillwater, Minnesota, Clinic and Dr. John Stratte, a member of the clinic, who had performed the vasectomy (*New York Times,* June 11, 1975, p. 39c).

46. As of 1980, sterilization laws were present on the books of twenty-seven states—all of these *eugenic* in kind (and largely unenforced).

47. *E. B. v. Vernico,* 66 LW 1936 (1998). The law was enacted after the abduction, rape, and murder of seven-year-old Megan Kanka in 1994 by a neighbor twice convicted of sexual offenses involving young girls. Additional "Megan's Law" challenges appeared on the Supreme Court's 2002–3 docket with *Smith v. Doe* and *Connecticut Department of Public Safety v. John Doe* testing whether states can use Internet sites and comprehensive registries to publicize information about sex offenders who have served their sentences. "Yes," ruled the Court, 6:3 and 9:0, in early 2003 (538 U.S. ___).

48. A twist to the sterilization problem is illustrated by the case of one Nancy Hernandez, a twenty-one-year-old mother of two, who faced jail in California in 1966 because she refused to submit to sterilization as a condition of probation on a misdemeanor offense. She had pleaded guilty to a minor narcotics charge and was given a suspended sentence and freed on probation by Municipal Court Judge Frank P. Kearney provided she agreed to sterilization. She at first agreed but then changed her mind, and her court-appointed lawyer obtained a writ of habeas corpus. Judge Kearney's order was subsequently overruled as "arbitrary and outside the law" by Superior Court Judge C. Douglas Smith (see *New York Times,* June 9, 1966, p. 511; and *Time,* June 3, 1966, p. 32). On the other hand, a twenty-four-year-old unwed mother agreed to be sterilized in order to reduce her sentence for killing her four-day-old son (who was her fourth child born out of wedlock). The mother, who had an IQ of 62 and a mental age of twelve, was asked by Philadelphia Common Pleas Judge Raymond Pace Alexander if she understood the meaning of sterilization. "Yes, sir," Miss Francine Rutledge replied, "I don't want no more babies" (*Philadelphia Evening Bulletin,* June 1, 1966).

Procedural Due Process

Despite the recent cascading of litigation designed to achieve egalitarianism, the number of cases reaching the Supreme Court of the United States on grounds of alleged abridgment or denial of *procedural* due process of law still far outweighs those concerned with alleged *substantive* infringements. This is entirely natural, for it is in the execution, administration, and interpretation of the meaning of statutes and executive ordinances that actions of the agents of the governmental process are likely to be challenged on due process grounds, and courts are both better equipped and more role-justified in addressing situations involving *procedural* than substantive due process of law. "The history of liberty," once wrote Justice Frankfurter persuasively in a federal case, "has largely been the history of observance of procedural safeguards."[49] Indeed, due process of law, as already explained, was originally, and for nearly one hundred years after the birth of the Republic, interpreted as a *procedural* restriction upon government. It concerned itself, more or less, not with *what* government was doing but *how* it was doing it. Much is involved, of course, in the concept of procedural due process of law: it all but defies definition. It embraces a general standard of *fairness*. As a minimum, it denies to "governments the power to filch away private rights by hole-and-corner methods."[50] A host of practices fall into that category: for example, deliberately "stacked" juries; coerced confessions; lack of adequate notice; compulsory self-incrimination; denial of counsel at various stages in criminal justice; denial of counsel in criminal cases; questionable trial procedures;[51] and *unreasonable* searches and seizures. The difficulty arises, of course, in a consideration of the question when, for instance, a confession is coerced, or when a search and/or seizure is or becomes "unreasonable." The incorporation of federal standards in criminal justice cases has tended increasingly to narrow the scope of state violations of the standard of fairness, but lines must still be drawn. Among the mass of complex and contentious cases in the realms of search, seizure, counsel, notice, confession, and compulsory self-incrimination, the three to follow will illuminate both the difficulties involved and the differences of opinion on the meaning and requirements of procedural due process of law.

The Case of Antonio Richard Rochin. Rochin, habitually in trouble with the Los Angeles police—more often than not because of drugs—lived in a modest two-story house with his mother, common-law wife, and several brothers and sisters.

49. *McNabb v. United States,* 318 U.S. 332 (1943) at 347.
50. J. A. Corry and Henry J. Abraham, *Elements of Democratic Government,* 4th ed. (New York: Oxford University Press, 1964), p. 267.
51. See, e.g., *Lee v. Kenna,* 534 U.S. ___ (2002), in which a 6:3 decision, written by Justice Ginsburg, and surprisingly joined by Chief Justice Rehnquist, who is customarily "tough" on criminal defendants, found several debilitating errors by Missouri in Lee's trial. See also *Kelly v. South Carolina,* 534 U.S. ___ (2002), decided 5:4.

For some time the county had tried to "get the goods," literally and figuratively, on Rochin. In June 1949 the county received what its agents had reasonable ground to believe was reliable information that Rochin was selling narcotics. Hence, early on the morning of July 1, 1949, three deputy sheriffs appeared at the Rochin homestead. Finding the door open, they entered, called a soft "Hello," walked to the second floor, and forced open the door of Rochin's room. The deputy sheriffs had neither search nor arrest warrants. Inside his room Rochin was sitting partly dressed on the side of the bed, on which his spouse was lying. On the night table the deputies spied two morphine capsules. When they shouted, "Whose stuff is this?" Rochin quickly grabbed the capsules and put them in his mouth. The agents of the law thereupon "jumped upon him," kicking and pummeling him, in the mistaken expectation that he would relinquish the pills. He swallowed them. The officers then administered a thorough beating to the by then prostrate Rochin, hoping that he would vomit the desired evidence. Ultimately, the deputies tied and gagged Rochin and took him to Angelus Emergency Hospital, where they ordered a resident physician to administer to the immobile yet irate Rochin an emetic through a stomach tube that had been inserted forcibly. The procedure did have the desired effect: Rochin vomited the two morphine capsules, which the police agents presented as the necessary evidence at his trial. Over the defendant's objections that the police methods of obtaining evidence were not precisely in accordance with procedural due process of law, and despite the frank acknowledgment of the previously described facts by one of the participating deputies, Rochin was convicted and sentenced to a sixty-day prison stint.

He immediately appealed this conviction to the proper appellate tribunal, the California District Court of Appeals. To his chagrin and surprise, that tribunal *affirmed* the trial court's holding, despite its judicial finding that the officers "were guilty of unlawfully breaking into and entering defendant's room and were guilty of unlawfully assaulting and battering defendant while in the room [and] were guilty of unlawfully assaulting, battering, torturing and falsely imprisoning defendant at the alleged hospital. . . ."[52] What more is necessary to establish rank violation of procedural due process of law and a reversal of the conviction? On the *federal* level, the recovered morphine capsules indubitably would have been regarded as the fruit of an unreasonable search and seizure, forbidden by the Fourth Amendment and as a violation of the Fifth Amendment's guarantees against compulsory self-incrimination. But it was not until the dramatic and traumatic *Mapp* case[53] in 1961 that the U.S. Supreme Court ruled that all evidence obtained by searches and seizures in violation of the Fourth Amendment is inadmissible in state as well as federal courts in criminal trials.[54]

52. *People v. Rochin,* 101 Cal. App. 2d 140 (1950).
53. *Mapp v. Ohio,* 367 U.S. 643, *supra.*
54. But note its amendatory rulings in 1976, sharply reducing the power of *lower federal courts* in habeas corpus proceedings to set aside state court convictions that relied on

Since *Rochin* came almost a decade prior to *Mapp,* unless the defendant could demonstrate a violation of the due process of law clause of the Fourteenth Amendment he would have no case, for in 1952 neither the exclusionary rule of the Fourth Amendment nor the compulsory self-incrimination safeguards of the Fifth Amendment were held applicable to the states. And California, in line with standing traditions of common law then in use by roughly one-half of the states, did not bar the admission at the trial stage of evidence obtained illegally. It did enable the aggrieved party to *sue* the offending officers, with scant hope of success, needless to add, yet such an action in no manner affected his obligation to pay fines and go to jail. This accounts for the reasoning of the district court of appeals. Rochin next appealed to the California Supreme Court, which denied his petition for a hearing without opinion. But two of the seven justices dissented from this denial and, in doing so, expressed themselves in significant language. They contended that:

> a conviction which rests upon evidence of incriminating objects obtained from the body of the accused by physical abuse is as invalid as a conviction which rests upon a verbal confession extracted from him by such abuse. . . . Had the evidence forced from the defendant's lips consisted of an oral confession that he illegally possessed a drug . . . he would have the protection of the rule of law which excludes coerced confessions from evidence. But because the evidence forced from his lips consisted of real objects the People of this state are permitted to base a conviction upon it. [We two] find no valid ground of distinction between a verbal confession extracted by physical abuse and a confession wrested from defendant's body by physical abuse.[55]

When the unhappy Rochin then appealed to the Supreme Court of the United States, he was granted certiorari, and, in due course, his conviction was unanimously reversed on grounds of rank violations of the very rudiments of procedural due process of law. In what would soon be regarded as one of his most important and colorful opinions, Justice Frankfurter spoke for the Court. He not only outlined the "responsibilities" of both the state and federal courts and wrote a significant essay on the meaning of due process of law, but he restated his own case-by-case approach to the question of the applicability of the commands of the Constitution.[56]

"The vague contours of the Due Process Clause do not leave judges at

---

illegally obtained evidence (*Stone v. Powell* and *Wolff v. Rice,* 429 U.S. 465). Chief Justice Burger, the chief opponent of the exclusionary rule, commented in a concurring opinion that the rule's "function is simple—the exclusion of truth from the factfinding process" (at 496).

55. *People v. Rochin,* 101 Cal. App. 2d 140 at 149, 150; italics supplied.

56. See *supra* chapter 3.

large,"[57] Frankfurter explained; rather, they place upon the Supreme Court the duty of exercising a judgment "within the narrow confines of judicial power in reviewing State convictions, upon interests of society pushing in opposite directions . . . duly mindful of reconciling the needs both of continuity and of change. . . ."[58] He sternly lectured California that the proceedings by which its agents had obtained Rochin's conviction "do more than offend some fastidious squeamishness about combatting crime too energetically." Then came the sentence that represented his test, his creed, in determining the presence or absence of due process of law: *"This is conduct that shocks the conscience."*[59] And he continued to prove why it did:

> Illegally breaking into the privacy of the petitioner, the struggle to open his mouth and remove what was there, the forcible extraction of his stomach's contents—this course of proceeding by agents of government to obtain evidence is bound to offend even hardened sensibilities. They are methods too close to the rack and the screw to permit of constitutional differentiation.[60]

Although Frankfurter went out of his way to assure the states that they had considerable leeway in their administration and enforcement of justice, he reminded them that it is, and must always be, axiomatic that "[s]tates in their prosecution respect certain decencies of civilized conduct." Reversing Rochin's conviction for the unanimous Court, Frankfurter terminated his opinion in words symptomatic of his judicial posture on the entire incorporation problem:

> Due process of law, as a historic and generative principle, precludes defining, and thereby confining, these standards of conduct more precisely than to say that convictions cannot be brought about by methods that offend a "sense of justice."[61]

Precisely because of the vagueness of that "sense of justice" and, of course, because of their deep commitment to the underdog, Justices Black and Douglas, although naturally voting for the reversal of Rochin's conviction, wrote separate concurring opinions, contending that, while the case was rightly decided, it was decided on wrong grounds. In a judgment which has since been confirmed in the history of incorporation, the two justices held that the basic constitutional issue

---

57. Perhaps not, but there are more than a few observers who agree with Justice Douglas's frank avowal that "[d]ue process, to use the vernacular, is the wild card that can be put to use as the judges choose" (as quoted by Ray Forrester, "Are We Ready for Truth in Judging?" 63 *American Bar Association Journal* 213 [September 1977]). Douglas, of course, was a prime practitioner of that "wild card"! See Brennan's ABA address "The Fourteenth Amendment," August 8, 1986, for a contemporary all-out "wild card" plea.

58. *Rochin v. California,* 342 U.S. 165 (1952) at 172, 173.

59. Ibid. at 172; italics supplied.

60. Ibid.

61. Ibid. at 173.

involved in *Rochin v. California* was not at all the one Frankfurter expressed, that is, a violation of the procedural due process guarantees of the Fourteenth Amendment. Rather, held Black and Douglas, it was that California's agents had, in fact, clearly and unmistakably violated the *specific* command of the Fifth Amendment that "[n]o person . . . shall be compelled in any criminal case to be a witness against himself," a command which, in their view, extended to the states via the due process of law clause of the Fourteenth Amendment. To base the reversal of Rochin's conviction on a violation of procedural due process was constitutionally a Pyrrhic victory in the eyes of these two advocates of total incorporation of the Bill of Rights. The "Does it shock the conscience?" test, based on a case-by-case approach to the presence or absence of due process of law,[62] seemed a travesty of justice to Black and Douglas. As Black put it: "I long ago concluded that the accordion-like qualities of this philosophy must inevitably imperil all the individual liberty safeguards specifically enumerated in the Bill of Rights."[63] To him, the Frankfurter opinion was a testimonial to "what I object to most in what I consider to be an unwarranted interpretation of the Due Process Clause [for] the elaborate verbal standards offered . . . are to me merely high-sounding rhetoric[64] void of any substantive guidance as to how a judge should apply the Due Process Clause."[65]

Nonetheless, the case was decided, and Rochin owed the reversal of his conviction to considerations of procedural due process. Two related cases, decided five and fourteen years later, will illustrate both the assets and the liabilities of that due process test approach.

The Case of Paul H. Breithaupt. While driving a pickup truck on a New Mexico highway, one Paul H. Breithaupt collided with a passenger car. Three occupants in the car lost their lives; Breithaupt was seriously injured but eventually recovered. When the police arrived on the scene of the collision, they detected unmistakable alcoholic odors and, on investigating, not only found an almost empty pint bottle of liquor in the glove compartment of his truck but also thought they detected telling vapors on his breath. The three bodies were taken to the morgue; Breithaupt was taken to the nearest hospital.

---

62. E.g., a 1998 ruling held unanimously that police cannot be held responsible for injuries caused by high-speed chases, *unless* their actions are so egregious that they "shock the conscience" (*Sacramento County v. Lewis,* 66 LW 4407).

63. *Rochin v. California,* 342 U.S. 165 at 177.

64. "What in the world is that," he observed to his son, "but testing a law on the judges' notion of right and wrong?" (Hugo Black Jr., *My Father: A Remembrance* [New York: Random House, 1975], p. 104).

65. *A Constitutional Faith,* op. cit., pp. 29–30. Black felt similarly about the equal protection of the laws clause—as he demonstrated again in one of his last opinions prior to his retirement in 1971, when, writing in dissent, he warned: "The Equal Protection Clause is no more appropriate a vehicle for the 'shock the conscience' test than is the Due Process Clause" (*Bodde v. Connecticut,* 401 U.S. 371 at 394).

As he lay in the emergency room of the hospital, the smell of liquor on the unconscious man's breath was unmistakable, and one of the state patrolmen who had been at the scene of the accident requested that a sample of the patient's blood be taken. An attending physician, using a hypodermic needle, withdrew approximately twenty cubic centimeters of blood from the unconscious Breithaupt and turned the sample over to the patrolman in charge, who submitted it for the customary laboratory analysis. The analysis proved to contain 0.17 percent alcohol.

When Breithaupt was well enough to stand trial, the state charged him with involuntary manslaughter. The clincher proved to be the damaging sample analysis, which was submitted as New Mexico's chief evidence of the accused's culpability. An expert in toxicology and hematology testified that a person with 0.17 percent[66] alcohol in his blood was decidedly under its influence. Over Breithaupt's objection on procedural due process grounds, the trial judge admitted the blood test results into evidence, and Breithaupt was duly convicted. He accepted his conviction and sentence of imprisonment without appealing.

Later he had second thoughts and sought release by petitioning the Supreme Court of New Mexico for a writ of habeas corpus.[67] That tribunal did hear argument on his petition but denied the desired writ as being groundless. Breithaupt then petitioned the U.S. Supreme Court for a writ of certiorari, which the Court granted. In essence, Breithaupt contended that his conviction was a prima facie violation of procedural due process of law because it was based on an involuntary blood test taken while he was unconscious. No one had asked him for his consent, and he could not have responded in his "senseless condition" even if he had wanted to. Thus he pleaded violation of his liberty without the procedural due process of law guaranteed him by the Fourteenth Amendment. Relying on the Court's unanimous opinion in the *Rochin* case, he argued that the conduct of the state officers of New Mexico involved in his conviction offended that "sense of justice" of which the justices spoke in *Rochin;* that New Mexico's conduct here, just as much as California's there, represented, in Justice Frankfurter's test phrase, "conduct that shocks the conscience."

But two-thirds of the members of the Court disagreed. Seeing an important

66. In the vast majority of states, the "legally drunk" level is at a much lower percentage, usually between 0.08 and 0.15—in Virginia, for example, 0.08.

67. The "Great Writ"—the "highest remedy for anyone imprisoned"—dates at least to the Magna Carta of 1215. It is applicable "in all cases of a wrongful deprivation of personal liberty. Where the detention of an individual is under process for criminal or supposed criminal causes, the jurisdiction of the court and the regularity of the commitment may be inquired into." It is, to put it somewhat differently, "a writ directed to the person detaining another and commanding him to produce the body of the person or persons detained. . . . [Its] purpose . . . is to test the legality of the detention or imprisonment, not whether he is guilty or innocent" (*Black's Law Dictionary,* 5th ed. [St. Paul, Minn.: West, 1979], p. 638). The phrase *habeas corpus* is Latin for "you have the body."

distinction between the procedures utilized by agents of government in *Rochin* and *Breithaupt,* they were quite prepared to draw a line between the two cases. Speaking for the majority of six, Justice Clark began his explanation of the distinction by holding that there is nothing "brutal" or "offensive" in the taking of a sample of blood when done, as it was in this case, under the protective eye of a physician. He acknowledged that the driver of the death truck was unconscious when the blood was taken but that "the absence of conscious consent, without more, does not necessarily render the taking a violation of a constitutional right; and certainly the test as administered here would not be considered offensive by even the most delicate." Furthermore, Clark went on, endeavoring to explain the labyrinth of the due process test,

> due process is not measured by the yardstick of personal reaction . . . of the most sensitive person, but by that whole community sense of "decency and fairness" that has been woven by common experience into the fabric of acceptable conduct. *It is on this bedrock that this Court has established the concept of due process.* The blood test procedure has become routine in our everyday life.[68]

He proceeded to point out that

> as *against the right of an individual* that his person be held inviolable, even against so slight an intrusion as is involved in applying a blood test of the kind to which nearly millions of Americans submit as a matter of course nearly every day, *must be set the interests of society* in the scientific determination, one of the great causes of the mortal hazards of the road. And the more so since the test likewise may establish innocence, thus affording protection against the treachery of judgment based on one or more of the senses.[69]

Here again, we see the quest for the just line between the rights of an individual citizen and those of society at large—a line particularly difficult to draw when it comes to due process in general and *procedural* due process in particular. But three justices objected vigorously to the reasoning of the majority of six. Speaking for himself and Associate Justices Black and Douglas—the latter also wrote a separate dissent—Chief Justice Warren dissented on the ground that *Rochin* was not distinguishable at all but should, in fact, be controlling. He observed that the majority's opinion suggests that an invasion of private rights—that is, Breithaupt's body—is "brutal" or "offensive" only if the police use force to overcome a suspect's resistance. With deep feeling, the chief justice contended that he could not accept "an analysis that would make physical resistance by a prisoner

---

68. *Breithaupt v. Abram,* 352 U.S. 432 (1957) at 436; italics supplied.
69. Ibid. at 439; italics supplied.

[as in *Rochin*] a prerequisite to the existence of his constitutional rights."[70] Urging that Breithaupt's conviction be reversed, he asked rhetorically whether the taking of spinal fluid from an unconscious person would be condoned because such tests are commonly made and might be made as a scientific aid to law enforcement, and concluded that

> only personal reaction to the stomach pump and the blood test can distinguish them. To base the restriction which the Due Process Clause imposes on state criminal procedures upon such reactions is to build on shifting sands. We should, in my opinion, hold that due process means at least that law enforcement officers in their efforts to obtain evidence from persons suspected of crime must stop short of bruising the body, breaking skin, puncturing tissue or extracting body fluids, whether they contemplate doing it by force or by stealth.[71]

In his separate dissenting opinion, joined by his colleague Black, Justice Douglas stated as the crux of the whole matter his firm belief that, under our system of government, "police cannot compel people to furnish the evidence necessary to send them to prison."[72] To Black and Douglas a case such as *Breithaupt* merely confirmed the fears and reservations they expressed in *Rochin:* that the test of whether the conscience is shocked was so uncertain and so subjective that to render justice with an equal eye and an even hand was all but impossible. Their solution, of course, was to incorporate the entire Bill of Rights via the Fourteenth Amendment and thus make the former's specific provisions applicable to the states.

Yet *Breithaupt* was confirmed by a 5:4 majority in 1966 in *Schmerber v. California*[73] even in the face of the incorporation of the self-incrimination clause that had taken place two years earlier[74]—demonstrating the vital fact of constitutional life that incorporation does not obviate the need for line drawing but necessitates line drawing of a different genre. This has been particularly characteristic of the problems of searches and seizures[75] and compulsory self-incrimination. In the *Schmerber* majority opinion, written by Justice Brennan

70. Ibid. at 441.
71. Ibid. at 442.
72. Ibid. at 443.
73. 384 U.S. 757 (1966).
74. *Malloy v. Hogan,* 378 U.S. 1.
75. See, e.g., the "stop-and-frisk" and other "limited intrusion" cases: *Terry v. Ohio,* 392 U.S. 1 (1968); *Peters v. New York* and *Sibron v. New York,* 392 U.S. 40 (1968); *Davis v. Mississippi,* 394 U.S. 721 (1969); *Adams v. Williams,* 407 U.S. 143 (1972)—which held that the police may "stop-and-frisk" a suspect on any anonymous tipster's word that the suspect is carrying a loaded pistol; but see *Florida v. J.L.,* 529 U.S. 266 (2000), distinguising *Adams, infra* this chapter; *Terry's* extension to property in the 1983 automobile search case of *Michigan v. Long,* 463 U.S. 1032; the expansive 1973 decisions of *United States v. Robinson,* 414 U.S. 218, and *Gustafson v. Florida,* 414 U.S. 260; the "anti-rigid-time-limit" 1985 decisions in *United States v. Sharpe* and *United States v. Johns,* 470 U.S.

and joined by Justices Clark, Harlan, Stewart, and White, the Court held that the privilege against self-incrimination does not permit a driver to balk at giving a sample of his blood, taken by medical personnel in a medical environment, for a test to determine if he is drunk. (Schmerber had been arrested at a hospital where he had been taken for automobile accident injuries, incurred while he had been driving. At the direction of a police officer a sample of his blood was withdrawn. It showed a blood-alcohol level of 0.18 percent; California and most other states consider 0.15 percent as presumptive proof of drunkenness.) The Brennan opinion, relying in part on a 1910 opinion written by Justice Holmes,[76] declared that the Fifth Amendment protected an accused person from "the use of physical or moral compulsion" to extort "testimonial or communicative" evidence that could be used against him; but that "compulsion which makes the body of a suspect or accused the source of 'real or physical' evidence" that, like a blood sample, *did not involve personal communication or testimony,* did not violate the self-incrimination rule. He made it clear that arrested persons might be required by the police to submit to "fingerprinting,[77] photographing or measurements, to write[78] or speak[79] for identification, to appear in court, to stand, to assume a stance, to walk or to make a particular gesture."[80] In the majority's view the extraction of blood "performed in a reasonable manner," as here, thus did not offend that "sense of justice" of which the Court's majority spoke in *Rochin;* nor did it violate the protection now binding upon the states against unreasonable searches and

675 and 469 U.S. 478, respectively; and a 5:4 decision in 1999, which extended the 1968 "stop-and-frisk" cases by ruling that police may stop and frisk those who *flee* the scene at the sight of an officer, since such an action can lead to "reasonable suspicion," especially in a high-crime area, here drug trafficking (*Illinois v. Wardlow,* 528 U.S. 119). See also the *"Airport Profile" Security Cases* of *United States v. Mendenhall,* 446 U.S. 544 (1980); and *Florida v. Royer,* 460 U.S. 491 (1983).

76. Brennan paraphrased Holmes's point on obtaining evidence from the actual person of an accused, discussed in *Holt v. United States,* 219 U.S. 245 at 252–53: "The prohibition of compelling a man in a criminal court to be a witness against himself is a prohibition of the use of physical or moral compulsion *to extort communications from him,* not an exclusion of his body as evidence when it may be material"; italics supplied.

77. This includes the taking of samples from beneath the fingernails of a murder suspect (*Cupp v. Murphy,* 412 U.S. 291 [1973]).

78. Confirmed 6:3 (with Brennan in partial dissent) with regard to a grand jury witness who refused to furnish a specimen of his handwriting (*United States v. Mara,* 410 U.S. 19 [1973]).

79. Confirmed 6:3 (with Brennan again in partial dissent) with regard to a grand jury request to record a witness's voice for identification purposes (*United States v. Dionisio,* 410 U.S. [1973]).

80. *Schmerber v. California,* op. cit., at 764. (Many states employ other methods of detecting inebriation, such as the "drunkometer," or breathing apparatus. Twenty-one [1998] have "implied consent laws," meaning that anyone who drives there agrees to submit to a test of some sort or lose his road privileges. Some give drivers a choice between blood, breath, and urine tests.)

seizures because (1) there was "plainly probable cause" to arrest and charge Schmerber; (2) the arresting officer "might reasonably have believed" that he was confronted with an emergency, in which the delay necessary to obtain a warrant, under the circumstances, threatened "the destruction of evidence"; and (3) the test chosen to measure Schmerber's blood-alcohol level was "reasonable." The Constitution of the United States, Brennan concluded, "does not forbid the States minor intrusions into an individual's body under stringently limited conditions [such as these at issue in *Schmerber*]." (But in 1973, the Court, while affirming two California decisions, added the due process requirement that a suspect motorist *must be arrested* before a blood sample may be taken—else any subsequent conviction would fail to meet the basic strictures of the *Miranda* tests.)[81] And eighteen years after *Schmerber* its author would speak for a 9:0 Court in ruling that the forced removal of a bullet from the chest of an armed robbery suspect was *not* "reasonable," that it patently violated the amendment's intended safeguards.[82]

Dissenting opinions in *Schmerber* were written by the chief justice and Justices Black and Fortas, with Douglas joining Black's. (Warren, Black, and Douglas had been the three *Breithaupt* dissenters.) "To reach the conclusion," wrote Black, "that compelling a person to give his blood to help the state convict him is not equivalent to compelling him to be a witness against himself strikes me as quite an extraordinary feat."[83] With obvious feeling he concluded that he deeply regretted the Court's holding and that he would continue to believe "with the Framers that these constitutional safeguards broadly construed by independent tribunals of justice provide our best hope for keeping our people free from governmental oppression."[84] Yet with only Justice Marshall in dissent, an 8:1 opinion, authored by Justice Brennan in 1990, extended the *Schmerber* "nontestimonial" rationale to uphold the power of the police to videotape drunk-driving suspects and use evidence of their slurred speech at trial without first advising the drivers of their constitutional rights, because the responses of the suspect in the case (Inocencio Muniz) were *"nontestimonial"* and therefore did not require *Miranda* warnings.[85]

---

81. *California v. Hills* and *California v. Foreman,* 410 U.S. 908. *Miranda,* of course, refers to *Miranda v. Arizona,* 384 U.S. 436 (1966), discussed at length *infra.* In a related 1983 development, the Court upheld (7:2) a South Dakota law that gives the driver the right to refuse to take a blood alcohol test but explicitly provides that such a refusal can be introduced as evidence. Justice O'Connor's opinion for the majority rejected the defendant's Fifth Amendment claim by pointing to the inherent "free choice" he exercised (*South Dakota v. Neville,* 459 U.S. 553).

82. *Winston v. Lee,* 470 U.S. 753 (1985).

83. Ibid. at 773.

84. Ibid. at 778.

85. *Pennsylvania v. Muniz,* 496 U.S. 582.

The Dilemma

We know now, of course, that during the 1960s a majority of the Court gradually moved toward incorporation in a process that has come very close to totality. Thus, since *Breithaupt* in 1957, the following pertinent prohibitions and provisions of the Bill of Rights have been ruled applicable to the several states by way of the due process of law clause of the Fourteenth Amendment:

1961: unreasonable searches and seizures (Fourth Amendment);[86]

1962: cruel and unusual punishment (Eighth Amendment);[87]

1963: counsel in *all* criminal cases (Sixth Amendment),[88] (save certain non-imprisonable misdemeanors);[89]

1964: compulsory self-incrimination (Fifth Amendment);[90]

1965: confrontation by adverse witness (Sixth Amendment),[91] extended in 1967 to embrace favorable witnesses;[92]

1967: a speedy trial (Sixth Amendment);[93]

1968: trial by jury in nonpetty criminal cases (Sixth Amendment);[94]

1969: double jeopardy (Fifth Amendment).[95]

Admittedly, the incorporation of these various constitutional safeguards of procedural due process provides significant guidelines for the application of the adjectives "arbitrary," "capricious," and "unreasonable." Yet differentiation in posture, analysis, and interpretation is still permitted. Thus, it is one thing to *forbid* coerced confessions, to allude to an obvious can of worms, but it is quite another to standardize the *concept* of "coerced confession." We know that a forced confession *is* forbidden *when* it has been indeed proved to have been exacted and that the Supreme Court has provided both the states and the federal government with considerable directions in interpreting the concept, of which the most important is the test of "voluntariness." But at what point does a confession in fact become involuntary? Because no tests, decisions, or guidelines can really gain-

86. *Mapp v. Ohio,* 367 U.S. 643 (see earlier text for necessary elaboration).
87. *Robinson v. California,* 370 U.S. 660.
88. *Gideon v. Wainwright,* 372 U S. 355.
89. *Argersinger v. Hamlin,* 407 U.S. 25 (1972). But the holding accorded full *Gideon* rights to all likely imprisonables. *Not,* however, ruled the Court (8:1) in 1984, to prison inmates held in a special detention unit while under investigation for a crime *committed* in prison (*United States v. Gouveia,* 467 U.S. 180).
90. *Malloy v. Hogan,* 378 U.S. 1; and *Murphy v. Waterfront Commission of New York Harbor,* 378 U.S. 52.
91. *Pointer v. Texas,* 380 U.S. 400.
92. *Washington v. Texas,* 388 U.S. 14.
93. *Klopfer v. North Carolina,* 386 U.S. 213.
94. *Duncan v. Louisiana,* 391 U.S. 145.
95. *Benton v. Maryland,* 395 U.S. 784.

say the presence of procedural due process as a lodestar in both statutory and constitutional differentiation, the Court does need to test individual situations for the presence or absence of due process of law. This is a judicio-legal fact of the first magnitude, unless, of course, the alleged due process violation constitutes an outright violation of an established, identifiable principle about which there is no longer any doubt. For example, the Supreme Court's decision in *Gideon v. Wainwright*[96] left no room for future doubt in its ringing mandate that, henceforth *and* retroactively,[97] there exists an absolute right to have counsel in *all* criminal cases, be they federal or state—indigents must be provided with counsel. This is now a clear-cut, straightforward requirement of due process. Yet even the *Gideon* decision has raised numerous problems; for instance, *at what point* in the judicial process must counsel be provided?[98] Both the complexity of the problem and the philosophical justifications of the inherent line drawing need a much closer look, but first we shall attempt to summarize the current minimum requirements of procedural due process of law.

Basic Procedural Due Process Requirements. The Bill of Rights contains certain concepts inherited from common law that we have always viewed as basic to our government, be it federal or state. They are (more or less in the words of the Constitution, with the appropriate amendment indicated in parentheses):[99]

1. the right of people to be secure in their persons, houses, papers, and effects against *unreasonable* searches and seizures (Four);
2. the issue of a search and/or arrest warrant only upon *probable cause,* supported by oath or affirmation, and *particularly* describing the place to be searched and the person or things to be seized (Four);
3. *indictment* by grand jury for capital or otherwise infamous crime (Five);
4. no *double jeopardy* (Five);
5. immunity against *compulsory* self-incrimination (Five);
6. the right to *a speedy and public trial,* by an *impartial jury,* in the state and district wherein the crime was committed (Six);
7. the right to be *informed* of the nature and cause of the accusation (Six);

96. 372 U.S. 335 (1963). See *supra* chapter 3.

97. *Pickelsimer v. Wainwright,* 375 U.S. 2 (1963). But see above for a caveat.

98. See, among others, the three famous cases discussed *infra: Massiah v. United States,* 377 U.S. 201 (1964); *Escobedo v. Illinois,* 378 U.S. 478 (1964); and *Miranda v. Arizona,* 384 U.S. 436 (1966); and such other attempts at clarification as *United States v. Wade,* 388 U.S. 218 (1967); *Douglas v. California,* 372 U.S. 353 (1963); *Johnson v. Avery,* 393 U.S. 483 (1969); *Mempa v. Rhea,* 389 U.S. 128 (1967); *Orozco v. Texas,* 394 U.S. 324 (1969); *Coleman v. Alabama,* 399 U.S. 1 (1970); *Ross v. Moffitt,* 417 U.S. 600 (1974); *Argersinger v. Hamlin,* 407 U.S. 25 (1972); *Scott v. Illinois,* 440 U.S. 367 (1980); *Estelle v. Smith,* 451 U.S. 454 (1981).

99. Taken verbatim, or paraphrased, from the Bill of Rights, Amendments Four through Eight; italics supplied.

8. the right of the accused to be *confronted* with adverse and favorable witnesses (Six);
9. the right to compulsory process to *obtain witnesses* in the accused's favor (Six);
10. *counsel* in criminal cases (Six);
11. safeguards against *excessive bail, excessive fines,* and *cruel* and *unusual punishment* (Eight).

Although these safeguards, as outlined in the Constitution, are restrictions only upon the federal government, all but the third and the bail and fine aspects of the eleventh concept now also apply to the several states as a result of judicial interpretation. And even if a good many of the states do not provide all the specific safeguards inherent in those few remaining areas, they are expected to provide procedures that, in their sum total, amount to due process of law. In other words, the concept of a "fair trial" demands safeguards which may not fall below a certain minimum, even if it be that vague minimum of "due process." The freedoms from arbitrary arrest, questioning, and imprisonment, from unreasonable searches and seizures, from the third degree (be it physiological or psychological), from compulsory self-incrimination, from "stacked" juries, from "quickie" trials are as national in scope, at least in theory, as they would be if they had been derived from just one basic document rather than from fifty-one documents. In the words of Justice Black in his landmark 1940 opinion in *Chambers v. Florida*: "The requirement—of conforming to fundamental standards of procedure in criminal trials —was made operative against the States on [*sic*] the Fourteenth Amendment. . . ."[100] And, as Chief Justice Warren wrote at Christmastime of 1967: "The methods we employ in the enforcement of our criminal law have aptly been called the measures by which the quality of our civilization may be judged."[101]

Critical Reactions. Yet, precisely because our federal system is a multiple system of justice, particularly in the realm of criminal procedure, the U.S. Supreme Court has been increasingly called upon to adjudicate conflicting claims between individuals and society; and many public officials in most states have felt that, in so doing, the Court has made it increasingly difficult for them to bring accused violators of the law to bay. The federal judiciary, in particular the Supreme Court, has been bitterly assailed—often in intemperate language. Law enforcement officers, from longtime FBI head J. Edgar Hoover to the lowliest deputy sheriff, raising

---

100. 309 U.S. 227 at 241. The *Chambers* opinion contains one of *the* great Black exhortations: "Under our constitutional system courts stand against any winds that blow as havens of refuge for those who might otherwise suffer because they are helpless, weak, outnumbered, or because they are nonconforming victims of prejudice and public excitement" (ibid. at 241).

101. "Discriminating Against the Poor and the Fourteenth Amendment," 81 *Harvard Law Review* 435 (December 1967).

their voices in protest against what they have viewed as "undue sentimentality toward lawbreakers," have charged the judiciary with making the job of the police authorities not only difficult but well-nigh impossible.

Nor have these charges and complaints been confined to the executive-administrative and legislative segments of the government; members of the judiciary itself have gone on record as viewing with alarm the tough due process standards imposed by the Warren Court, particularly in the realm of procedure in criminal cases. In the Brune Report[102] thirty-six state chief justices protested what they considered "a dangerous development in Supreme Court adjudication." The report expressed general alarm over what the majority regarded as the "erosion of the federal system" and, exhorting the Court to return to the "greatest of all judicial powers—the power of judicial self-restraint," addressed itself censoriously to most of the controversies that have embroiled the Court in the recent past. The report particularly criticized the steady evolution by Court mandate of the due process and equal protection clauses of the Fourteenth Amendment as criteria with which the states must comply in exercising their authority; it concluded that, by assuming legislative authority and acting without judicial restraint, the Court had expanded national power and contracted the power of the states. This is not the place to discuss and attempt to rebut the specific charges thus flung—it has been well done by others[103]—but there is much to be said for Paul A. Freund's contention that all the Court has really demanded of the states under the due process concepts of Amendment Fourteen is that in order to "turn square corners" in dealing with sensitive areas of human liberty, they should follow procedures that are consistent with due process of law.[104] In his study of the Brune Report, Eugene V. Rostow concluded that its findings represent "not so much a protest against the Court as against the tide of social change reflected in the Court's opinions."[105]

Most vocal of all critics has been Congress. It came within a hair's breadth of drastically and dramatically restricting the appellate jurisdiction of the Supreme Court in a series of 1957–58 measures, generally known as the Jenner-Butler Bill(s).[106] And the Omnibus Crime statutes of 1968 and 1970 were clearly de-

102. Named after the chief judge of Maryland, who headed the Committee on Federal-State Relationships as Affected by Judicial Decisions of the 1958 Conference of Chief Justices. The Brune Report is reprinted in full in numerous legal journals, among others, the *Harvard Law Record* of October 23, 1958.

103. E.g., E. V. Rostow's biting attack on the report in chapter 3, "The Court and Its Critics," in his fine book *The Sovereign Prerogative: The Supreme Court and the Quest for Law* (New Haven, Conn.: Yale University Press, 1962).

104. *The Supreme Court of the United States: Its Justices, Purposes, and Performance* (Cleveland: World, 1961), p. 87.

105. Rostow, *The Sovereign Prerogative*, p. 111.

106. For an excellent account and analysis of the fascinating background of the fate of the Jenner-Butler measures, see Walter F. Murphy, *Congress and the Court* (Chicago: University of Chicago Press, 1962); also C. Herman Pritchett, *Congress Versus the Supreme Court* (Minneapolis: University of Minnesota Press, 1961).

signed to limit, if not necessarily roll back, some of the Court's most contentious holdings in the realm of criminal justice. In fact, three sections of the 1968 bill specifically endeavored to "overrule" the Court's decisions in the *Mallory* (arraignment), *Miranda* (confessions), and *Wade* (eyewitness/lineup) cases.[107]

Still, as we have seen, even some members of the Supreme Court itself have expressed serious alarm about the standards and requirements set by a majority of their fellow justices in certain instances, particularly in regard to procedural due process—for example, the angry dissenting opinion by Justice Byron White, joined by Justices Harlan and Clark, in *Massiah v. United States*.[108] It involved questions of the Fifth Amendment's protection against compulsory self-incrimination, the Sixth Amendment's right to counsel, and, by implication, the Fourth Amendment's safeguards against unreasonable search and seizure.

Winston Massiah and the Law. Massiah, a merchant seaman on the crew of the SS *Santa Maria* in 1958, was engaged in a narcotics traffic conspiracy and was about to transport a quantity of narcotics aboard the *Santa Maria* from South America to New York City. As a result of tips received by federal customs officers, the ship was searched on its arrival in New York. Parcels containing three and a half pounds of cocaine were found in the afterpeak of the vessel, and Massiah was connected with their presence. He was arrested, promptly arraigned, and then indicted for violating the federal narcotics laws; he retained a lawyer, pleaded not guilty, and was released on bail. All of these various steps[109] fully met the requirements of due process of law. Also indicted three months after Massiah as a coconspirator, and charged with the same substantive offense, was one Jesse Colson.

In November 1959, while free on bail, Massiah met Colson, who was also out on bail. The two men went for a ride in the latter's automobile and soon parked on a New York street. There, Massiah began a lengthy discussion regarding his part in the narcotics transportation conspiracy, making innumerable incriminating statements—incriminating, that is, if they had been made in the presence of public officials. But, or so Massiah had every reason to believe, Colson was a coconspirator—hardly a government agent!

---

107. Their citations, respectively, are *Mallory v. United States,* 384 U.S. 436 (1966); and *United States v. Wade,* 388 U.S. 218 (1967). In 1972 the Court did, in fact, itself overrule *Wade* insofar as it applied to pre–grand jury indictments (*Kirby v. Illinois,* 405 U.S. 951). Nor does *Wade* apply to the technique of photo-identifications in the absence of the suspect (*United States v. Ash,* 413 U.S. 300 [1973]). See also the 7:2 further widening of the eyewitness rule in 1977 (*Manson v. Brathwaite,* 432 U.S. 98).

108. 377 U.S. 201 (1964).

109. For a brief description of these "steps," from apprehension to trial and beyond, see Henry J. Abraham, *The Judicial Process: An Introductory Analysis of the Courts of the United States, England, and France,* 7th ed. (New York: Oxford University Press, 1998), pp. 148–50.

However, his "buddy" Colson, a few days after Massiah's indictment and subsequent bailing, had decided to cooperate with government agents in their continuing investigation of the kind of activities in which the two had allegedly been engaged. Hence Colson permitted a federal agent named Finbarr Murphy to install a radio transmitter under the front seat of the Colson car. By this means, Murphy, equipped with an appropriate receiving device, could overhear from some distance away conversations carried on in Colson's vehicle. And by prearrangement with Colson, Murphy was parked near the spot, but out of sight, of the Colson automobile. Murphy was an eager and accurate listener to Massiah's talkathon.

At the subsequent trial, agent Murphy was permitted by the U.S. District Court judge to testify regarding the Massiah statements he had overheard. Massiah's defense counsel vigorously objected on two distinct and independent grounds: the alleged violation of the Fourth Amendment's proscription against the admission of evidence obtained as a result of unreasonable searches and seizures, and the alleged violation of Massiah's rights established under the Fifth *and* Sixth Amendments because of the admission in evidence of the *incriminating statements* he had made in the car *after he had been indicted* and *in the absence of his retained counsel.* The jury convicted Massiah, and he was sentenced to nine years in prison. His conviction was affirmed by the U.S. Circuit Court of Appeals; he appealed to the U.S. Supreme Court, which granted certiorari.[110]

Addressing himself to the second argument and concentrating upon the italicized portions of the defendant's claims, Justice Stewart's majority opinion for six members of the Court did not reach the Fourth Amendment question at all, although it was implicit in the litigation, of course. Stewart, hardly a "bleeding heart," very simply pointed out for himself, the chief justice, and Associate Justices Black, Douglas, Brennan, and Goldberg that Massiah had been denied the basic protections of the Sixth and Fifth Amendments' guarantees of the right of counsel and against compulsory self-incrimination, respectively; the information that convicted him had been "deliberately elicited from him" by federal agents "*after* he had been indicted and in the absence of his counsel." Winston Massiah "did not even know that he was under interrogation by a government agent." Concluded Stewart: "*Fourth* Amendment problems aside . . . all that we hold is that a defendant's own incriminating statements, obtained by federal agents under the circumstances here disclosed, could not constitutionally be used by the prosecution as evidence against *him* at his trial."[111] And Massiah's conviction was thus reversed—which, since it had been based on what was now held to have been illegally obtained and illegally admitted evidence—meant that he went scot-free.

110. *Massiah v. United States,* 374 U.S. 805 (1963).
111. *Massiah v. United States,* 377 U.S. 201 (1964) at 207; italics supplied for "Fourth" only. See *Massiah*'s extension to a prison setting in 1980 (*United States v. Henry,* 447 U.S. 264).

The majority's reasoning infuriated Justice White. His lengthy dissenting opinion for himself and Justices Clark and Harlan asked precisely the sort of question a concerned observer of criminal justice might ask:

> Undoubtedly, the evidence excluded in this case would not have been available but for the conduct of Colson in cooperation with agent Murphy, but *is it this kind of conduct which should be forbidden to those charged with law enforcement?* It is one thing to establish safeguards against procedures fraught with the potentiality of coercion and to outlaw "easy but self-defeating ways in which brutality is substituted for brains as an instrument of crime detection."[112]

But in the *Massiah* case, he continued, there was no "substitution of brutality for brains, no inherent danger of police coercion justifying the prophylactic effect of another exclusionary rule." The petitioner, White went on, had not been interrogated in a police station, had not been surrounded by numerous officers, questioned in relays, or been forbidden access to others. "Law enforcement," he commented, "may have the elements of a contest about it, but it is not a game."[113]

The White dissent warned repeatedly against drawing the line in criminal justice between the rights of society and those of the accused too much in favor of the accused. It was a pungent attack on the whole approach of the Court's majority, not just in *Massiah* but in numerous other cases in this field of adjudication, in the judicial quest for a balance of interests in our federal system between fairness for the criminal suspect and adequate protection for the public at large. White expressed concern lest the *Massiah* decision discourage both the ordinary citizen and the confessed criminal "from reporting what he knows to the authorities and from lending his aid to secure evidence of crime. . . . Certainly after this case the Colsons will be few and far between, and the Massiahs can breathe much easier, secure in the knowledge that the Constitution furnishes an important measure of protection against faithless compatriots. . . ."[114] And, seconding a contention so frequently voiced by law enforcement officers, White warned that "meanwhile, of course, the public will again be the loser and law enforcement presented with another serious dilemma."[115] Less than five weeks later Justice White was to have occasion to become even more alarmed, although this time he gained the vote of Justice Stewart while retaining the support of Justices Clark and Harlan.

Danny Escobedo's Right to Counsel.[116] On the night of January 19, 1960, Manuel Valtierra, the brother-in-law of a twenty-two-year-old Chicago laborer

---

112. *Massiah* at 213; italics supplied.
113. Ibid.
114. Ibid. at 212.
115. Ibid.
116. *Escobedo v. Illinois,* 378 U.S. 478 (1964).

named Danny Escobedo, was fatally shot in the back. At 2:30 A.M. on the following morning Danny, his now-widowed sister Grace, and two of Danny's friends, Bobby Chan, seventeen, and Benni DiGerlando, eighteen, were arrested by Chicago police *without* warrants and questioned intensively at headquarters. Danny refused to make any statement whatever to his questioners. At 5:00 P.M. on that afternoon, after a full fourteen and a half hours of interrogation, he was released together with the others pursuant to an Illinois state court writ of habeas corpus obtained for him by attorney Warren Wolfson, who had once represented Escobedo in a personal injury case and had been called into the present case by Chan's mother. But on January 30, DiGerlando allegedly voluntarily confessed to his part in the crime and informed the police authorities that Danny was the one who had fired the fatal shots. Between 8:00 and 9:00 P.M. on the day of DiGerlando's assertions, Danny Escobedo was rearrested and, his hands manacled behind his back, taken to police headquarters together with the also rearrested Grace and Chan.

En route to the police station, one of the officers told Danny that DiGerlando had named him as the slayer of his brother-in-law. At his trial Danny swore—without any contradiction from the officers involved—that "the detectives said they had us pretty well, up pretty tight, and we might as well admit to this crime," to which, Danny testified, he replied, "I am sorry but I would like to have advice from my lawyer." On arrival at the police station around 9:00 P.M. Danny had been taken to the Homicide Bureau for questioning, after having been in the "lockup" for a while. In vain he asked to see his lawyer, Wolfson. The latter, having been told of the rearrest by Chan's mother, had immediately gone to the police station, where he arrived moments after Danny. Wolfson at once asked to see Danny, but the police told him, "Danny doesn't know you." Wolfson unsuccessfully repeated the request to see his client on some five or six separate occasions throughout the evening, but each was denied politely by the authorities, although he quoted to the Homicide Bureau's Chief Flynn the pertinent section of the Illinois Criminal Code which allows an attorney to see his client "except in cases of imminent escape." Wolfson and Danny did chance to catch a glimpse of each other "for a second or two" when the lawyer spotted Danny through a half-open door, waved to him, and was greeted by a similar wave by Danny—whereupon the door was quickly closed. At 1:00 A.M., realizing that he was not going to get anywhere, Wolfson signed an official complaint with Commissioner Phelan of the Chicago Police Department and left.

The interrogation of Danny Escobedo went on apace, despite his repeated unsuccessful pleas to see his attorney. At the trial the defendant and his interrogators disagreed on Danny's assertion that a Spanish-speaking interrogator, Officer Montejano, had offered to let his sister, Chan, and him "go home" if Danny "pinned it on DiGerlando." But the record showed that when DiGerlando and Danny were confronted with each other during the course of the night, Danny called DiGerlando a liar and said, "I didn't shoot Manuel, you did." In this manner, of course, Danny for the first time admitted to some knowledge of the crime, at least indirectly. Then, in the face of Montejano's alleged promise that a full statement would free him, Grace, and Chan, Danny further implicated himself as well as the other three accused in the murder plot. At this point an assistant state's attorney, Theodore J. Cooper, was summoned by the interrogating officers "to take" a full statement. Mr. Cooper, an experienced lawyer, not only failed to advise Danny of his constitutional rights before, during, or after "taking" the statement, but his questions were obviously carefully framed so as to assure admissibility into evidence at the trial. In any event, the record stands undisputed that no one during the interrogation advised Danny of his rights and that at no time during the long evening, despite repeated requests by Danny and Wolfson, was he allowed legal counsel. Danny, Grace, and Chan were all indicted for murder, but Grace was later acquitted for lack of evidence, and the charges against Chan were dropped. DiGerlando, who charged subsequently that his confession was beaten out of him, received a life sentence. As for Danny, his defense moved, both before and during his trial, that the incriminating statement he had given to Cooper be suppressed; but the trial judge ruled the confession to have been voluntary. Danny Escobedo, thus convicted of murder and sentenced to a twenty-year term in prison—he had a record of sundry previous arrests—appealed his sentence to the Illinois Supreme Court on several grounds of due process of law.

On February 1, 1963, that tribunal reversed Danny's conviction, holding that the defendant understood that "he would be permitted to go home if he gave the statement and would be granted an immunity from prosecution."[117] But the state successfully petitioned for a rehearing—resulting in a reversal and the sustaining of the conviction below. The court ruled: "[T]he officer [Montejano] denied making the promise and the trier of fact believed him. We find no reason for disturbing the trial court's finding that the confession was voluntary."[118] Danny Escobedo's counsel then appealed to the U.S. Supreme Court for review—his last hope—and won the first round when the Court granted a writ of certiorari in order to consider whether the petitioner's statement to Cooper was in fact constitutionally admissible at his trial.[119] On June 22, 1964, in the narrowest possible division (5:4), the Court responded "no," reversed Danny's conviction, and remanded it to the Illinois trial court "for proceedings not inconsistent with this opinion."[120] But the state of Illinois decided that it could not obtain a conviction without the now inadmissible statement and dropped the charges, and Danny was released from jail, where he had spent almost four and a half years.

To understand the Supreme Court's majority opinion by Justice Goldberg for himself, the chief justice, and Associate Justices Black, Douglas, and Bren-

---

117. Ibid. at 483.
118. Ibid. at 484.
119. *Escobedo v. Illinois,* 375 U.S. 902 (1964).
120. *Escobedo v. Illinois,* 378 U.S. 478 (1964).

nan, it is necessary to recognize not only the "toughening and tightening" of due process standards demanded of the states by the Warren Court, but also what it had done concerning both the right to counsel and the use of confessions between the day of Danny's arrest in 1960 and his appeal to the court of last resort in 1964. Regarding the right to counsel, the Supreme Court in 1961 had overruled the capital criminal conviction of Charles Clarence Hamilton on the *sole* ground, and for the first time, that the defendant had not been represented by counsel at the *arraignment,*[121] a "critical stage."[122] Two years later the *Gideon* case[123] was decided, which extended the absolute right of indigents to have counsel assigned in *all* criminal cases—save those involving certain misdemeanors[124]—by making the Sixth Amendment's requirements of "the Assistance of Counsel" obligatory upon the states via the due process of law clause of the Fourteenth Amendment. (On the same day, the Court extended the right to counsel to appeals.)[125] And two weeks after *Gideon,* the Court reversed the capital conviction of one Robert Galloway White *solely* because the defendant had not been represented by counsel at an even earlier stage than arraignment, namely, the "preliminary examination."[126] The *White* decision was based on the "critical stage logic" of the *Hamilton* case.[127] Regarding the problem of "voluntary confessions," which was so crucial in the *Escobedo* ruling, the Court had for some time shown increasing concern about their use as the basis for convictions in criminal cases. Until the late 1950s, the failure to bring an accused in promptly for a preliminary examination, the number of hours of interrogation, the refusal to allow communication with counsel, and long incommunicado detention had not in and of themselves been considered enough to violate due process of law on the *state* level.[128] However, by the beginning of the 1960s, the stringent new judicial approach had become readily apparent. One well-known instance of the reversal of

121. That stage of the proceedings in criminal justice when a prisoner is called to the bar of the court of jurisdiction to be identified, to hear the formal charges against him, and to make an appropriate plea.

122. *Hamilton v. Alabama,* 368 U.S. 52 (1961).

123. *Gideon v. Wainwright,* 372 U.S. 335 (1963). See *supra* chapter 2.

124. And these, except for nonimprisonable mere fine and traffic cases, were covered in a 1972 ruling (*Argersinger v. Hamlin,* 407 U.S. 25). But there must be a "likelihood" of imprisonment, as per the 1979 holding in *Scott v. Illinois,* 440 U.S. 367.

125. *Douglas v. California,* 372 U.S. 535. *But* in 1974 the Court held (6:3) that does not necessarily entitle anyone to free legal counsel to pursue a "discretionary" state appeal or a similar appeal to the U.S. Supreme Court beyond the initial "as a matter of right" appeal from a conviction (*Ross v. Moffit,* 417 U.S. 600).

126. *White v. Maryland,* 373 U.S. 59 (1963). In the "preliminary examination" stage, following arrest, the apprehended is brought before a magistrate or a commissioner to determine whether he shall be released or be held to answer for the alleged offense.

127. *Hamilton v. Alabama,* op. cit.

128. E.g., *Lisenba v. California,* 314 U.S. 219 (1941); *Crooker v. Calinia,* 357 U.S. 433 (1958); *Cicenia v. Lagay,* 357 U.S. 504 (1958).

a conviction based on a "voluntary confession" occurred in the case of Raymond L. Haynes, because the state of Washington authorities had refused to permit him to telephone his wife, who would then have called an attorney.[129] Then came the decision in *Massiah*.[130]

In overturning Danny Escobedo's conviction, the five-man Supreme Court majority stated the requirements for *early* implementation of the now "nationalized" right to counsel in all criminal cases *and* a confirmed, fundamental, judicially established distrust of confessions. The basic effect of Justice Goldberg's opinion for the slender majority was to cause "the adversary system, traditionally restricted to the trial stage, [to be] hauled back slowly into the earlier stages of criminal proceedings."[131] Goldberg's specific point in *Escobedo* was quite simply and unequivocally that a person can consult with a lawyer as soon as a police investigation makes him a prime suspect. Anticipating the heavy professional and lay criticism that was to come as a result of the decision, and combating the four dissenters, Goldberg concluded that the *Escobedo* decision did not affect the powers of the police to investigate "an unsolved crime," but when, as in Danny's case, "*the process shifts from investigatory to accusatory—* when its focus is on the accused and *its purpose is to elicit a confession—*our adversary system begins to operate, and, under the circumstances here, the accused must be permitted to consult with his lawyer."[132] Earlier, Goldberg had spelled out the majority's specific holding as follows:

> We hold, therefore, that where, as here, the investigation is no longer a general inquiry into an unsolved crime but has begun to focus on a particular suspect, the suspect has been taken into police custody, the police carry out a process of interrogations that lends itself to eliciting incriminating statements, the suspect has requested and been denied an opportunity to consult with his lawyer, and the police have not effectively warned him of his absolute constitutional right to remain silent, the accused has been denied "the Assistance of Counsel" in violation of the Sixth Amendment to the Constitution as "made obligatory upon the States by the Fourteenth Amendment" . . . and that no statement elicited by the police during the interrogation may be used against him at a criminal trial.[133]

The four dissenting justices, however, were not convinced, as they made clear in three separate opinions: one by Harlan, one by Stewart—who not only had been on the other side in *Massiah*[134] but had written its majority opinion—and one by

---

129. *Haynes v. Washington,* 373 U.S. 503 (1963).
130. *Massiah v. United States,* 377 U.S. 201 (1964).
131. *The Defender Newsletter,* November 2, 1964, p. 2.
132. *Escobedo v. Illinois,* 378 U.S. 478 (1964) at 492; italics supplied.
133. Ibid. at 490–91.
134. *Massiah v. United States,* 377 U.S. 201 (1964).

White, who was joined by Clark and, again, by Stewart. The overall tenor of the dissenting opinions was one of genuine concern, indeed conviction, that the decision would hamper criminal law enforcement. Harlan wrote that he regarded the new rule formulated by the majority as "most ill-conceived and that it seriously and unjustifiably fetters perfectly legitimate methods of criminal law enforcement."[135] Stewart reasoned that the decision would have an extremely "unfortunate impact" on the fair and adequate administration of criminal justice. He explained his *Massiah* stand on the basis of what he deemed the overriding fact that Massiah had already been arraigned and indicted, after which the incriminating evidence was elicited from him by trickery while he was free on bail.[136] The longest dissent was White's, who argued that the new ruling would cripple law enforcement and would render its tasks "a great deal more difficult." Bitterly, he asserted that from now on an accused's right to counsel would require "a rule wholly unworkable and impossible to administer unless police cars are equipped with public defenders and undercover agents and police informants have counsel at their side."[137] After pleading for more "reasonableness" and a more balanced approach that would eschew such a stringent and "nebulous" rule, the onetime deputy attorney general of the United States (under President John F. Kennedy) concluded wistfully:

> I do not suggest for a moment that law enforcement will be destroyed by the rule announced today. The need for peace and order is too insistent for that. But it will be crippled and its task made a great deal more difficult, all in my opinion, for unsound, unstated reasons, which can find no home in any of the provisions of the Constitution.[138]

Across the country the police and prosecuting authorities alike echoed the four dissenting jurists. Yet two years later many, although not most, of the nation's top prosecutors would concede that law enforcement had not suffered from *Escobedo.*

There is no question, however, that the *Escobedo* decision, far more than *Massiah,* presented both the legal profession and the police authorities with an enormous challenge. To interrogate a suspect behind closed doors in order to secure a confession not only was a concept based on the custom and usage of centuries, but it had become a deeply entrenched police practice, strongly supported by both "traditional" and "reform" elements in the ranks of those charged with the administration of criminal justice. Fully aware of this apprehensiveness and the general unpopularity of the decision, Justice Goldberg endeavored to put matters in their proper focus by appealing for a return to the obligations and commands of law enforcement by a government in democratic society:

135. *Escobedo v. Illinois,* 378 U.S. 478 (1964) at 493.
136. Ibid.
137. Ibid. at 496.
138. Ibid. at 499.

We have . . . learned the . . . lesson of history that no system of criminal justice can, or should, survive if it comes to depend for its continued effectiveness on the citizens' abdication through unawareness of their constitutional rights. No system worth preserving should have to *fear* that if an accused is permitted to consult with a lawyer, he will become aware of, and exercise these rights. *If the exercise of constitutional rights will thwart the effectiveness of a system of law enforcement, then there is something very wrong with that system.*[139]

The Miranda Bombshell. By January 1966 two U.S. Courts of Appeals had interpreted *Escobedo* in diametrically opposite ways. Duty-bound to referee such a conflict, the Supreme Court fully sifted 170 confession appeals and accepted for review four cases involving four individuals.[140] Known by its leading case, *Miranda v. Arizona,* the package decision consolidated the appeals of persons convicted on the basis of confessions made after extended questioning by officers of the law in which they were not informed of their rights to remain silent. The crimes of which they were found guilty included kidnapping, rape, robbery, and murder—all major felonies. Although *Miranda* is essentially a Fifth Amendment coerced confession case, it links naturally to the Sixth Amendment (and Fourth Amendment) problems raised by *Massiah* and, particularly, *Escobedo.*

Ernesto A. Miranda, a twenty-one-year-old Phoenix, Arizona, truck driver, had been convicted in the Arizona courts and sentenced to twenty to thirty years in prison for the kidnapping and rape of an eighteen-year-old girl. He was taken into custody, identified by the girl in a lineup, and questioned by two police officers. Two hours later the officers—following Miranda's oral confession admitting and describing the crime—also produced a handwritten one by him, on which was superimposed a typed statement that the confession was made voluntarily, without threats or promises of immunity, "and with full knowledge of my legal rights, understanding any statement I may make will be used against me." Over the objections of his defense counsel, Miranda's written confession was admitted into evidence and served as the basis for his conviction—and his appeal (plus the appeals of the similarly affected principals in the other three cases) to the highest tribunal in the land.

On June 13, 1966, in what must rank as the most bitterly criticized, most contentious, and most diversely analyzed criminal procedure decision by the Warren Court, came its 5:4 answer: the *Escobedo* rule was extended significantly to prohibit police interrogation of any suspect in custody without his consent, unless a defense attorney is present at the arrest stage. In effect, the Supreme Court

---

139. Ibid. at 490; italics supplied except for "fear."
140. *Miranda v. Arizona, Vignera v. New York, Westover v. United States, California v. Stewart*—all 384 U.S. 436 (1966).

thus answered two years of bitter criticism over its *Escobedo* ruling with a sweeping liberal opinion that mandated important changes in police interrogation as practiced in most of the states. While the Court did not outlaw voluntary confession, and stopped short of an *absolute* requirement that a lawyer be present before a suspect can be questioned, there is no doubt that the majority opinion intended to extend *Escobedo*. Written by the chief justice himself, who was joined by Justices Black, Douglas, Brennan, and Fortas, it was introduced with the dry and cautious comment, "The cases before us raise questions which go to the very root of our concepts of American criminal jurisprudence."[141] But its holding was dramatic, and it took Warren more than one hour to read the entire sixty-one-page opinion to a packed and hushed Court audience. Over the bitter dissents by Justices Clark, Harlan, Stewart, and White (Harlan, his face flushed and his voice occasionally faltering with emotion, denounced the decision orally from the bench on that Opinion Monday, terming it "dangerous experimentation" at a time of a "high crime rate that is a matter of growing concern," a "new doctrine" without substantial precedent, reflecting "a balance in favor of the accused"),[142] the Court, through the chief justice's opinion, in effect laid down the following rules which police (see also Figs. 4.1 and 4.2) must follow before attempting to question an *arrested* criminal suspect:

1. He must be told that he has the right to stay silent.
2. He must be told that anything he says may be used against him in court.
3. He must be told that he has the right to have an attorney with him before any questioning begins.
4. He must be told that, if he wants an attorney but cannot afford one, an attorney will be provided for him free.[143]
5. If, after being told this, an arrested suspect says he does not want a lawyer and is willing to be questioned, he may be, provided that he reached his decision "knowingly and intelligently."
6. If, after being told all his rights, a suspect agrees to be questioned, he can shut off the questions any time after they have started, whether or not he has an attorney with him.

Apprised of the Court's decision, Danny Escobedo commented, "I think it was very nice of them. Something good."[144]

---

141. *Miranda v. Arizona,* op. cit., at 437.
142. *New York Times,* June 14, 1966, p. 1, as reported by Fred P. Graham.
143. A warning in the language of the Court's opinion would thus read: "The law requires that you be advised that you have the right to remain silent, that anything you say can be used against you in a court of law, that you have the right to the presence of an attorney, and that if you cannot afford an attorney one will be appointed for you prior to any questioning if you so desire" (*Miranda v. Arizona,* op. cit., at 479). But "no talismanic incantation" is required (*California v. Prysock,* 453 U.S. 355, 1981).
144. *New York Times,* June 19, 1966, sec. 4, p. 1.

PHILADELPHIA POLICE DEPARTMENT
Standard Police Interrogation Card
WARNINGS TO BE GIVEN ACCUSED

We have a duty to explain to you and to warn you that you have the following legal rights:

A. You have a right to remain silent and do not have to say anything at all.

B. Anything you say can and will be used against you in Court.

C. You have a right to talk to a lawyer of your own choice before we ask you any questions, and also to have a lawyer here with you while we ask questions.

D. If you cannot afford to hire a lawyer, and you want one, we will see that you have a lawyer provided to you, before we ask you any questions.

E. If you are willing to give us a statement, you have a right to stop any time you wish.

75-Misc.-3
(10-9-67)

Figure 4.1

PHILADELPHIA POLICE DEPARTMENT
Reverse Side of Standard Police Interrogation Card
QUESTIONS TO BE ANSWERED BY ACCUSED

1. Do you understand that you have a right to keep quiet, and do not have to say anything at all?

2. Do you understand that anything you say can and will be used against you?

3. Do you want to remain silent?

4. Do you understand that you have a right to talk with a lawyer before we ask you any questions?

5. Do you understand that if you cannot afford to hire a lawyer, and you want one, we will not ask you any questions until a lawyer is appointed for you?

6. Do you want either to talk with a lawyer at this time, or to have a lawyer with you while we ask you questions?

7. Are you willing to answer questions of your own free will, without force or fear, and without any threats or promises having been made to you?

Figure 4.2

In February 1967 Miranda was tried and convicted again—for the Supreme Court had only reversed his first conviction, not quashed his indictment—this time on the basis of properly admitted testimony by his common-law wife, Twila Hoffman. She told the Arizona Superior Court Trial Judge Lawrence T. Wren in open court that Miranda had admitted committing the crime when she talked with him in jail—where he was serving a twenty-to-twenty-five-year sentence for robbery. Their conversation occurred[145] after the Supreme Court had handed down its original decision. Subsequently, having been found guilty by a jury deliberating eighty-three minutes, he was thus sentenced to the same twenty-to-thirty-year term in state prison. He appealed *that* case, too, but the Court refused to grant him a second hearing,[146] ditto a third one in which three Phoenix lawyers had filed a new appeal contending that a voluntary confession, given to police during an interrogation,[147] was no more valid as evidence than an *involuntary* one under such circumstances. Miranda was paroled in 1972, having served a total of nine years; but he again ran afoul of the law in 1974 (illegal gun possession and drug charges—subsequently dismissed because of Fourth Amendment violations); he was paroled later that year. Yet, all but magnetlike, he was returned to the Arizona State Prison for violations of his parole in early 1975—and once again released later that year. In early 1976, now thirty-four, he was slain in a Phoenix, Arizona, skid row bar in a quarrel over a card game. When the police arrested the prime suspect, they used a "Miranda Card" to read him his constitutional rights.

Reverting to the original 1966 decision,[148] despite public and private outcries that rivaled, if they did not exceed, those following such hotly opposed Warren Court decisions as the 1954 and 1955 *Public School Segregation Cases*[149] and the 1962 and 1963 *Public Prayer and Bible Reading Cases,*[150] *Miranda v. Arizona* was now the law of the land. Indeed, the remaining three years of the Warren Court were to see a number of extensions.[151] Guidance cards such as those advocated by the Philadelphia Police Department (reproduced here)

145. "When I visited him in jail," testified Mrs. Hoffman, "he admitted to me that he had kidnapped the girl and roped her up, then took her into the desert and raped her" (*Time,* March 3, 1967, p. 49).

146. *Miranda v. Arizona,* 396 U.S. 868 (1969).

147. Ibid.

148. *Miranda v. Arizona,* 384 U.S. 436 (1966). For a reflective, engagingly written look back twenty years later, see Liva Baker, *Miranda: Crime, Law and Politics* (New York: Atheneum, 1983).

149. *Brown v. Board of Education of Topeka, Kansas,* 347 U.S. 483 (1954), and the implementation decision, ibid., 349 U.S. 294 (1955).

150. *Engel v. Vitale,* 370 U.S. 421 (1963); and *Abington School District v. Schempp* and *Murray v. Curlett,* 374 U.S. 203 (1963).

151. E.g., to juveniles in most although not all of its aspects (*In the Matter of Gault,* 387 U.S. 1 [1967]); to the questioning of prison inmates when unconnected with the incarceration offense itself (*Mathis v. United States,* 391 U.S. 1 [1967]); to questioning of a

were introduced in many a jurisdiction even while the nationwide assault on the *Miranda* decision continued. It was capped, in a very real sense, by an (aforementioned) congressional response: Title II of the Omnibus Crime Control and Safe Streets Act of 1968. That heatedly debated title added a new section to the pertinent provision of the U.S. Code,[152] stating that in *federal* prosecutions a confession "shall be admitted in evidence if it is voluntarily given." Paraphrasing the five most pertinent subsections of the measure, Title II stated that judges need only consider "the totality of circumstances" in which a confession was obtained before they rule whether it was voluntary. Since that was, in effect, more or less the formula *before Miranda,* it was a foregone conclusion that the Court would find itself confronted with a test of the constitutionality of that aspect of Title II.

It fell to the Burger Court to reach the specific issue of the failure of police to give the required *Miranda* warnings in the 1971 *Harris* case.[153] There, in a 5:4 decision, the chief justice—joined by his fellow Nixon appointee Blackmun and by Justices Harlan, Stewart, and White (who had all been in dissent in *Miranda*)—stated that although an unwarned suspect's confession (such as Harris's) could not be admitted as *evidence,* it could henceforth be introduced in the courtroom by the prosecution in an endeavor to impeach an accused's testimony, on the central ground of the latter's *credibility,* if the accused had chosen to take the stand to testify in his behalf. In a sharp dissent, Justice Brennan, joined by his colleagues Black, Douglas, and Marshall, warned that the majority's decision in effect meant that police may now "freely interrogate an accused incommunicado," despite *Miranda.* A good many Court observers concluded that with the *Harris* decision—which, based upon what Justice White characterized as the need to "testify truthfully or suffer the consequences," was reconfirmed and perhaps even expanded in 5:4 rulings in 1980 and 1990[154]—the Court had clearly "sounded a retreat" from

---

subject at home rather than elsewhere (*Orozco v. Texas,* 394 U.S. 324 [1969]). The Burger Court would extend it to the "preliminary hearing stage" (*Coleman v. Alabama,* 399 U.S. 1 [1970]) and to postarrest questioning by psychiatrists in capital punishment cases (*Estelle v. Smith,* 451 U.S. 454 [1981]). But it refused to extend it to the traffic court level (*David v. Strelecki,* 393 U.S. 933 [1968]) or to indigent parents in civil proceedings involving the termination of their legal relationship with their children (*Lassiter v. Department of Social Services,* 452 U.S. 18 [1981]).

152. Section 3501, Ch. 18 U.S.C. Note especially 3501(b).

153. *Harris v. New York,* 401 U.S. 222.

154. *United States v. Havens,* 446 U.S. 620; and *Michigan v. Harvey,* 494 U.S. 344. The first case dealt with an Indiana lawyer who had smuggled cocaine into the country; the cocaine was seized without a warrant, and the defendant moved to exclude the evidence from the trial. His codefendant had pleaded guilty, and lawyer Havens's seemingly false answers to the prosecution's questions on cross-examination were, the Court ruled, "reasonably suggested" by the defendant's own direct testimony. The second case involved patently inconsistent testimony in court.

Miranda.[155] Further evidence had come with the Court's 1973 upholding of a guilty plea even though the defendant had not known that the confession he had—admittedly voluntarily—given would have been inadmissible at his trial under *Miranda.*[156] Then, in 1974, in a surprisingly lopsided 8:1 ruling—with only Justice Douglas in dissent—the Court held that the *Miranda* rules would not bar damaging evidence from a witness who, the defendant had told police questioners, would *corroborate* his alibi.[157] What defendant Tucker was entitled to, wrote Justice Rehnquist for the majority, was the barring of his *own* statements at the trial; but the testimony of his presumed friend could properly be used because it served the legitimate trial purpose of discovering the pertinent facts. Added proof that the Court no longer considered the prescribed *Miranda* warnings as a fundamental rock of criminal justice came in mid-1975: it held (6:2) that a defendant, who, once having been duly informed of his rights under the *Miranda* rules and having acknowledged understanding them, then made incriminating statements to the arresting officer in abeyance of access to his lawyer, could have these statements used against him on trial—but only to raise doubts as to his credibility after he gave *Harris*-like contrary testimony on the stand.[158] And the end of 1974 brought a 6:2 decision continuing *Miranda*'s reinterpretation: over bitter dissents by Justices Brennan and Marshall, who predicted "ultimate overruling of *Miranda*'s enforcement of the privilege against self-incrimination," the Court ruled that after a suspect exercises his right to remain silent about one crime, police may still validly question him about *another* (here after a two-hour interval).[159] Moreover, as the Court held in a less-than-crystal-clear mid-1976 multiple, although unanimous, opinion, the *Miranda* warnings need not be given to suspects called to testify before *grand juries.*[160] On the other hand, a 6:3 majority ruling later that year strengthened the *Miranda*-emphasized right to silence at the arrest stage by holding that a defendant's remaining silent, after being ad-

---

155. E.g., Abraham S. Goldstein, dean of the Yale Law School, in the *New York Times,* May 3, 1971, p. 351. But for a view that *Miranda,* though possessing significant educational value, may have been, in terms of tangible effects upon interrogation practices, "an act of judicial futility," see Otis H. Stephens Jr., *The Supreme Court and Confessions of Guilt* (Knoxville: University of Tennessee Press, 1973).

156. *Schneckloth v. Bustamente,* 413 U.S. 218.

157. *Michigan v. Tucker,* 417 U.S. 433.

158. *Oregon v. Hass,* 420 U.S. 741.

159. *Michigan v. Mosley,* 423 U.S. 96. But cf. *Edwards v. Arizona,* 451 U.S. 477 (1981), involving further questioning about the same crime in the absence of a lawyer, which went 9:0 the other way. The latter was extended 6:3 in 1986 by a ruling that barred the police, in the absence of a lawyer, from questioning a defendant who has made his request for counsel at an arraignment with a view primarily to representation in future court proceedings (*Michigan v. Jackson,* 475 U.S. 625).

160. *United States v. Mandujano,* 425 U.S. 564.

vised of his right to remain silent under questioning, could not be used against him in a trial.[161] And when the Court had a seemingly golden opportunity to overrule *Miranda* in the grisly Iowa child-murder *Williams* case in 1977, it demurred in an emotion-charged 5:4 decision that produced five opinions.[162] Obviously staking out a case-by-case course rather than attempting to draw a firm *Miranda*-application line, the high tribunal, three years later, distinguished its earlier Iowa decision in a not unsimilar Rhode Island case (6:3), but it now provided a definition of the meaning of "interrogation" to be used as a guide by police in criminal cases.[163] "Interrogation," explained Justice Stewart in his opinion for the majority, should be viewed neither to be limited to direct questioning of a suspect nor to be so expansive as to cover an offhand remark a police officer might make within the suspect's hearing. When the Iowa *Williams* case was remanded for a new trial, Williams was again found guilty of first-degree murder, carrying a mandatory life sentence in that state. He again appealed his conviction to the federal judiciary and scored a victory at the bar of the U.S. Court of Appeals for the Eighth Circuit in 1983. But when the Supreme Court reviewed the case in 1984, it overruled the lower tribunal (7:2), holding: "If the prosecution [as it has here] can establish by a preponderance of the evidence that the information *ultimately or inevitably would have been discovered by lawful means,* then the deterrence rationale [of the exclusionary rule] has so little basis that the evidence should be received."[164]

On the overarching question of "voluntariness" in confession cases, an issue so central to the *Miranda* rules, especially in the light of the aforementioned 1968 congressional statute supportive of voluntariness, the Court may well be on the road to the British case-by-case approach on the issue. That conclusion was strengthened by a 1977 holding (6:3) which was supportive of precustodial behind-closed-doors questioning, although the suspect had admitted committing the crime, thus presumably requiring custody and the full panoply of the *Miranda* rules; but he had been permitted to leave after questioning.[165] Further proof of the all but unavoidable case-by-case approach is provided by a 1979 decision (6:3) that apparently expanded the right to questioning in the absence of an attorney,[166] while one in 1980 reversed (8:1) the armed-robbery conviction of a Louisiana man because there was no evidence that he had

161. *Doyle v. Ohio* and *Wood v. Ohio,* 426 U.S. 610.
162. *Brewer v. Williams,* 430 U.S. 387 (known as the *Christian Burial Speech Case*). Attorneys general from twenty-one states had filed briefs amici curiae unsuccessfully supporting Iowa.
163. *Rhode Island v. Innis,* 446 U.S. 291 (1980). The Supreme Court's opinion was written by Chief Justice Burger, with Justices Brennan and Marshall dissenting.
164. *Williams v. Nix,* 700 F.2d 1164 (1983); and *Nix v. Williams,* 467 U.S. 431 (1984) at 444; italics supplied.
165. *Oregon v. Mathiason,* 429 U.S. 492.
166. *North Carolina v. Butler,* 441 U.S. 369.

Table 4.1. Rulings by the United States Supreme Court (Under Amendments Six and Fourteen) in Favor of the Guarantee of Counsel[a] in Criminal Cases, Arranged by Procedural and Chronological Stages

Votes of Justices (FOR: AGAINST)	Procedural State in Criminal Justice System	Procedural Order[b]	Chronological Stage by Cases (Citation and Year)	Chronological Order
9:0	Arraignment	7	*Hamilton v. Alabama,* 368 U.S. 52 (1961)	1
9:0	Trial	9	*Gideon v. Wainwright,* 372 U.S. 335 (1963)[c]	2
6:3	Appeal	10	*Douglas v. California,* 372 U.S. 535 (1963)	3
9:0	Preliminary hearing	6	*White v. Maryland,* 373 U.S. 59 (1963)	4
6:3	Postindictment	5	*Massiah v. United States,* 377 U.S. 201 (1964)	5
5:4	Preindictment confession	4	*Escobedo v. Illinois,* 378 U.S. 478 (1964)	6
5:4	Arrest	2	*Miranda v. Arizona,* 384 U.S. 436 (1966)	7
6:3	Lineup	8	*United States v. Wade,* 388 U.S. 218 (1967)[d]	8
		8	*Gilbert v. California,* 388 U.S. 263 (1967)[d]	8
9:0	Probation hearing	11	*Mempa v. Rhea,* 389 U.S. 128 (1967)	9
6:2	Quasi arrest	1	*Orozco v. Texas,* 394 U.S. 324 (1969)	10
6:2	Preindictment preliminary hearing	3	*Coleman v. Alabama,* 399 U.S. 1 (1970)	11
8:1	Revocation of probation or parole	12	*Gagnon v. Scarpelli,* 411 U.S. 78 (1973)	12
7:2	Counsel must be "effective" on appeal	10A	*Evitts v. Lucy,* 469 U.S. 387 (1985)	13

[a]In 1975, the Court ruled (6:3) that a defendant may move to waive the right to counsel in favor of self-representation, if recognized as "competent" to do so, and if the waiver is "voluntary and intelligent"—standards to be judge-decided (*Faretta v. California,* 422 U.S. 806).
[b]Number 1 represents the earliest and number 12 the latest stage in the criminal justice procedural process.
[c]Extended in 1972 (9:0) to cover all offenses involving possible imprisonment, whether they be classified as petty, misdemeanor, or felony, "absent a knowing and intelligent waiver" (*Argersinger v. Hamlin,* 407 U.S. 25). Interpreted in 1979 (6:3) as extending only to those offenses in which a defendant *was in fact sentenced* to a term of imprisonment (*Scott v. Illinois,* 440 U.S. 367 [1979]).
[d]Significantly narrowed in 1972 (5:4) so as to extend now only to post–grand jury indictment lineups (*Kirby v. Illinois,* 405 U.S. 951); and in 1973 (6:3) as *not* to apply to the photo-identification stage in the accused's absence (*United States v. Ash,* 413 U.S. 300).

"knowingly and intelligently" waived his rights before making the inculpatory statement.[167] Yet in addition to the Court's new approach represented by the *Nix* case,[168] it also held in 1984 that "overriding considerations of public safety" may justify immediate questioning without giving a suspect first the *Miranda* warnings against self-incrimination.[169] On the other hand, it ruled 5:4 that the *Miranda* doctrine applies to a suspect for any crime, no matter how minor, except for "ordinary roadside traffic stops."[170] And in 1986 the Court ruled 6:3 that a suspect's postarrest, post–*Miranda* warnings silence could not be used by the prosecution as evidence of his sanity.[171] But, as if to reemphasize the all but necessary ad hoc nature of passing judgment on *Miranda*-type cases, while stipulating 6:3 that the right to be represented by an attorney was the *suspect's* right, not the attorney's,[172] the Court in 1986 also explicitly reaffirmed its holdings in *Miranda* that police must inform arrested suspects of their rights to remain silent and to have a lawyer present, and that police must stop questioning any suspect who asks to see a lawyer. Yet a 5:4 ruling in 1989 permitted police, when advising suspects of their rights, to depart from the *exact* words set down in *Miranda,* provided that, in Chief Justice Rehnquist's words, the warnings given "touched all the bases required by *Miranda.*[173] And in 1990, with only Justice Marshall in dissent, the Court held that a law enforcement officer can pose as a prison inmate and elicit a confession from an actual inmate even though the officer gives no *Miranda* warnings about the inmate's constitutional rights. *Miranda,* wrote Justice Kennedy for the 8:1 majority, "does not confer a right to boast."[174]

However, to reunderscore the basic ad hoc nature of the *Miranda* syndrome, the Court, at the end of 1990, in a 6:2 opinion, surprisingly penned by Justice Kennedy, ruled in the *Minnick* case that police are barred from reinitiating interrogation after a lawyer has consulted with the suspect and departed, even if the *Miranda* rules had *again* been read to that suspect. The decision prompted a biting dissent by Justice Scalia, joined by Chief Justice Rehnquist.[175] But almost as if to "atone" for its *Minnick* decision, an early 1991 decision by a deeply divided (5:4) Court held that the use of a coerced confession in a criminal trial does not *automatically* invalidate a conviction; that, depending upon circumstances, it could be regarded as it was here as "harmless error."[176] In 2001 it held 5:4 that a

---

167. *Tague v. Louisiana,* 444 U.S. 469. For a summary article on aspects of the Fifth Amendment, see David M. O'Brien, "The Fifth Amendment: Fox Hunters, Old Women, Hermits, and the Burger Court," 54 *Notre Dame Lawyer* 26 (October 1978). See *supra* *Edwards v. Arizona* and *Estelle v. Smith.*
168. *Nix v. Williams, supra* note 164.
169. *New York v. Quarles,* 467 U.S. 649.
170. *Berkemer v. McCarty,* 468 U.S. 420 (1984).
171. *Wainwright v. Greenfield,* 474 U.S. 284.
172. *Moran v. Burbine,* 475 U.S. 412.
173. *Duckworth v. Eagan,* 492 U.S. 195.
174. *Illinois v. Perkins,* 496 U.S. 292.
175. *Minnick v. Mississippi,* 498 U.S. 146.
176. *Arizona v. Fulminante,* 499 U.S 270.

suspect who has a lawyer in one investigation cannot automatically have him present during police investigation for a related crime.[177] Another ruling narrowing *Miranda* came down 6:3 in 1991,[178] as did one by the Fourth Circuit U.S. Court of Appeals in 1999, that prosecutors may use a suspect's confession against him regardless of whether he was advised of his *Miranda* rights because of an obscure federal law (Section 3501 of the Criminal Code) designed to overrule the famed 1966 decision.[179] But in a major 7:2 decision, surprisingly authored by Chief Justice Rehnquist, the Court struck down Section 3501 as an impermissible interpretation of the Court's supervisory power over the federal courts in evidentiary and procedural criminal justice matters.[180] The ruling thereby upheld the governing precedent of *Miranda* emphasizing "the now established culture" regarding the admissibility of statements made during custodial interrogation in both federal and state courts. Nonetheless, Charles Dickinson was still sentenced in January 2001 to serve twelve years and eight months in prison for serving as the driver in a string of bank robberies. He planned to appeal. That, of course, brings us back to the basic dilemma of values and lines. The presence of lines and limits, and the need to draw them wisely and well, is at least as pressing and arguably more widely perceived in the realm of criminal justice than in any of the other areas under discussion in the civil libertarian spectrum.

DUE PROCESS OF LAW IN PERSPECTIVE

No one challenges the basic contention that both the individual and society are entitled to a full measure of due process of law. In the opinion of a good many observers, however, the balance shifted to the side of the potential or actual lawbreaker with the advent of the Warren Court. Thus, the Supreme Court and the lower federal judiciary have come under fire because of their tightening of due process concepts in the Court's decisions, particularly in the field of criminal justice. Has the judiciary, in particular the Supreme Court, gone too far—or not far enough? There is no answer that will please everyone, but it is possible to consider some fundamental points.

"The Criminal Gets the Breaks"

This caption in an article in the *New York Times Magazine,* written by Dean Daniel Gutman of the New York Law School[181] after *Escobedo,* but almost two

177. *Texas v. Cobb,* 532 U.S. 162.
178. *McNeil v. Wisconsin,* 501 U.S. 171.
179. *United States v. Dickerson,* 166 F.3d 667.
180. *Dickerson v. United States,* 530 U.S. 428 (2000).
181. November 29, 1964, pp. 36ff. (The New York Law School is not to be confused with the New York University School of Law.)

years prior to *Miranda,* has lost neither its pertinency nor its timeliness with the passage of years. Then, as Chief Justice Burger endeavored to drive home at every opportunity both on and off the bench,[182] Dean Gutman, with unassailable statistics demonstrating a continued upward trend in crime—a trend that persisted until the early 1990s—warned that "we do not solve the problem of dealing with those who make crime their business by providing procedural methods of escape for the guilty, to the detriment of the law-abiding who are victimized by the lawless." After reciting a number of the more controversial Supreme Court decisions "in favor of criminals"—among them the *Massiah* and *Escobedo* rulings—the author called for a series of steps to be taken "within the framework of the Constitution and the Bill of Rights" to remedy the situation. Among them were (1) legislation to permit wiretapping, pursuant to court order, for evidence of major crimes; (2) "recodification" of procedural requirements for search and seizure, "which are distinctive for ancient strictures no longer valid"; (3) extension of the right to detain and interrogate, with due safeguards against coercion or other violation of constitutional rights; (4) classification of the "extent and application" of the concept of right to counsel; and (5) "relaxation of the rule excluding all evidence improperly obtained, so as to vest discretion as to admission in the trial judge." Such a list prompts recognition of the paradox that the administration of justice poses to thoughtful and committed Americans like Dean Gutman, the members of the Supreme Court, and their respective supporters and detractors in the lay as well as the professional public. The basic issues are likely to continue to remain unresolved—notwithstanding the recurrent, variegated, earnest efforts of such qualified professional and lay, public and private groups as the American Bar Association; the President's National Commission on the Causes and Prevention of Violence; the Council of States; nationwide organizations of chiefs of police and district attorneys; Ralph Nader; Common Cause; local crime-fighting citizens' groups; educators; or, for that matter, the perpetual, if uneven, and not infrequently incomprehensibly self-defeating activity by Congress in the popular "law-and-order" realm.

Has the Court Been Too Lenient? It is entirely natural to ask whether the courts have not in fact tipped the balance of justice in favor of the criminal to the detriment of the public. Given a post-1938 rise in crime at a rate eight to ten times as fast as the growth of America's population, it is understandable that professionals and laymen alike should be fond of quoting Justice Cardozo's well-known observation that "justice is due the accused, but it is also due the accuser"; that the "concept of fairness must not be strained till it is narrowed to a filament,"

---

182. E.g., his annual "State of the Judiciary Messages" and his opinions in such opposite cases as *Bivens v. Six Unknown Named Agents,* 403 U.S. 388 (1971), and *Stone v. Powell,* 428 U.S. 465 (1976). In his 1981 message he pointed out that in 1980 Washington, D.C., with a population of 650,000, had more criminal homicides than Sweden and Denmark, with an aggregate population of more than 13 million!

coupled with the memorable Cardozo quaere whether the "criminal is to go free because the constable has blundered."[183] In the words of Justice Stanley Reed, the "purpose of due process is not to protect an accused against a proper conviction, but against an *unfair* conviction."[184] Or, as Justice Robert H. Jackson pointed out in a case involving the question of due process in connection with the composition of a "blue ribbon"[185] jury: "Society also has a right to a fair trial. The defendant's right is a neutral jury. He has no constitutional right to friends on a jury."[186]

Yet in insisting upon strict standards of decency and fairness in governmental lawmaking, law enforcing, and prosecuting, the courts simply perform the historic function of protecting the rights of the individual against the alleged unlawful acts of government. Justice Brennan once put the matter well in speaking for the 7:1 Supreme Court in a reversal of the conviction of union leader Clinton E. Jencks, a suspected perjurer of Communist persuasion, who had not been permitted to attempt to impeach testimony given to the FBI on the basis of which he had been found guilty and convicted in the trial court below: "[T]he interest of the United States in a criminal prosecution [and any of the several states] *is not that it shall win a case, but that justice shall be done.*"[187] There is no doubt that this philosophy is "hard to take" in specific instances—but can there really be any compromise with it under our form of government? The answer must be a firm "No!" True, indeed, that men and women like Rochin, Jencks, Mapp, Mallory,[188] Massiah, Escobedo, Robinson, Malloy, Murphy, and Miranda are neither paragons of citizenship nor likely to "stay out of trouble," despite their "victories" at the bar of the Supreme Court. Indeed, almost all of them did run afoul of the law again. That, however, is not the main issue; what is the issue is the need to provide justice in accordance with the commands of our constitutional principles, in this case due process of law—which, on the other hand, allows and should know limits, too.

But to devote some thought to certain of the specific attacks upon Supreme

183. *People v. Defore,* 242 N.Y. 13 (1926) at 19–25.

184. *Adamson v. California,* 330 U.S. 46 (1947) at 130; italics supplied.

185. A special jury which in some jurisdictions—for example, Manhattan—could be selected by the jury commissioner from those qualified as trial jurors on the basis of special or superior qualifications. With the enactment of the Federal Jury Selection Act of 1968 it is no longer *legal* on the *federal* level (but it has never been held to be *unconstitutional*).

186. *Fay v. New York,* 332 U.S. 261 (1947) at 288–89, upholding New York's "blue-ribbon" jury.

187. *Jencks v. New York,* 353 U.S. 657 (1957) at 668, quoting from Justice Sutherland's opinion in *Berger v. United States,* 295 U.S. 78 (1935) at 88; italics supplied.

188. Of the famed "Mallory Rule," under which the Court held in 1957 (*Mallory v. United States,* 354 U.S. 449) that officers must take an arrested person "without unnecessary delay" before the nearest available commissioner (Mallory had been held overnight and interrogated by the police for seven hours ere this was done)—thus reversing Mal-

Court rulings, *just which* of the more recent controversial issues would we have the Court or—failing its acquiescence to a hearing—the legislative branches alter, if not negate? The famed *Gideon* decision that guaranteed counsel in state criminal proceedings for indigent defendants in noncapital as well as capital criminal cases?[189] Or its subsequent extension to the preliminary hearing stage?[190] Or its further extension to the interrogation stage following arrest?[191] Can any member of a democratic society *honestly* argue the point that counsel in a criminal case is a luxury, that he who cannot afford it is not entitled to it? Or that, as in Danny Escobedo's situation, a request to consult with one's attorney prior to a police interrogation is somehow loading the dice against the government?

Or to consider an allied area of due process, are we really prepared to oppose or even reverse the Court's 1964 decision that the Fifth Amendment's tradition-heavy guarantee against compulsory self-incrimination is applicable to the states as well as the federal government?[192] Admittedly, there are matters of degree involved here—as there are in all of these areas—but there can hardly be any compromise with the elementary command that a suspect need not "sing" unless he so desires or unless he is given full statutory immunity.[193] The initial fears, and subsequent charges, that the *Miranda* decision would seriously inter-

---

lory's conviction and death sentence in a rape case. Mallory later went on to assault another woman and to burglarize a house and rape the housewife. Convicted on the latter two counts, he was ultimately sentenced to twenty-two years in the Pennsylvania State Penitentiary. After having served eleven and one-half years, he was released late in 1971. Soon thereafter, in July 1972, he was caught in the acts of robbing a couple and raping the woman and was shot fatally by Philadelphia Fairmount Park police when he tried to flee and pulled a gun on two officers. The *Mallory* "without unnecessary delay" rule became a focal point of congressional attacks on the Court and the subject of one of the "repealer" provisions in Titles II and III of the Omnibus Crime Control and Safe Streets Act of 1968 (discussed *supra*). A confession is now admissible if a judge rules that it was indeed voluntary and that the delay before the confession's presentation to a magistrate was not "unreasonably longer than necessary." (The outer limit seems to be six hours.) *Mallory* remains judicially untested specifically, but the Court appears to have more or less accepted it.

189. *Gideon v. Wainwright*, 372 U.S. 335 (1963).
190. *White v. Maryland*, 373 U.S. 59 (1963).
191. *Miranda v. Arizona*, 384 U.S. 436 (1966).
192. *Malloy v. Hogan*, 378 U.S. 1 (1964).
193. See *Ullmann v. United States*, 350 U.S. 422 (1956); *Murphy v. Waterfront Commission of New York Harbor*, 378 U.S. 52 (1964); and *New Jersey v. Portash*, 440 U.S. 450 (1979). The sufficiency of the protection provided by the "immunity bath" section of the 1970 federal omnibus crime statute, and almost identical state legislation, came under simultaneous constitutional attack in 1971 in both a state (*Zicarelli v. New Jersey State Commissioner of Investigation*, 406 U.S. 472) and a federal case (*Kastigar v. United States*, 406 U.S. 441). Both pieces of legislation—which provided a more limited type of immunity, known as *"use"* immunity rather than the normal complete or *"transactional"* immunity—were upheld in 5:2 opinions, written by Justice Powell, with Justices Douglas and Marshall in dissent (Brennan and Rehnquist not participating). The essential difference between

fere with the normal tendency to confess have not been borne out by resulting statistical evidence.[194]

Of course, it is revolting to find that obvious, confessed murderers go scot-free (indeed, the phrase "getting away with murder" applies here literally), as, for example, one Arthur Culombe did in a grisly, multiple murder case in Connecticut.[195] But the partially demented Culombe's confession had been *coerced* by Connecticut authorities in the most devious and patently illegal manner, involving the accused's family. True, one may well ask why the state was not justified

---

"use" and "transactional" immunity is that the latter covers *any and all aspects* of a matter for which a respondent is given immunity in return for waiving his rights against self-incrimination, whereas "use" immunity, while barring "investigatory leads" against an "immunized" respondent, does *not* prevent the prosecution from using evidence against him if such evidence is derived and developed from a source *wholly independent* of the "immunized" respondent's testimony—not an easy line to draw. See also, e.g., *Zicarelli v. New Jersey*, 401 U.S. 933; and *United States v. Hubbell*, 530 U.S. 27 (2000).

194. Following the uproar caused by this and the other *Miranda* rules, the findings of a major statistical study were disclosed by Evelle E. Younger, then district attorney of Los Angeles County (which has the largest caseload in the country) and later attorney general of California. The survey, which covered four thousand felony cases, and the results of which frankly "amazed" Mr. Younger, showed that confessions were needed for successful prosecution in fewer than 10 percent of the four thousand cases, and that 50 percent of the suspects were confessing despite the warning by the police. "The most significant things about our findings," commented Younger (a former FBI agent), "are that suspects will talk regardless of the warning and furthermore it isn't so all-fired important whether they talk or not" (*New York Times*, August 21, 1966, sec. 1, p. 52). The Younger study confirmed similar findings by Brooklyn Supreme Court Justice Nathan R. Sobel and by Detroit Chief of Detectives Vincent W. Piersante (see Sidney Zion, "So They Don't Talk," *New York Times*, op. cit., sec. 4, p. 13). An eighteen-month study of the effects of *Miranda* in Pittsburgh, Pennsylvania, reconfirmed the above: while confessions had dropped slightly since the June 1966 decision, the number of suspects who pleaded guilty had increased slightly as well (*New York Times*, December 31, 1967, sec. 1, p. 25). An eleven-week Yale University study in 1967 yielded similar results (ibid.). So did a May 1968 Washington, D.C., study (*New York Times*, May 14, 1968, p. 60), as well as a separate project observing custodial police interrogation in the District of Columbia (66 *Michigan Law Review* 1347–1422 [May 1968]). By 1970, after four years of close concern with the problem, Fred P. Graham concluded in a lengthy report that "despite evidence that crime has been steadily outstripping" the capacity of big-city law enforcement officers to control it, they "are becoming less disturbed by the Supreme Court's rein on their conduct towards suspects" (*New York Times*, April 6, 1970, p. 11). See also the report of the International City Managers Association, *Public Management*, July 1967, pp. 183–90, which confirms the preceding. The Yale and Washington, D.C., studies cited earlier, as well as similar compliance studies in Green Bay, Kenosha, Racine, and Madison, Wisconsin, showed that while implementation of *Miranda* was slow, grudging, and sometimes ineffective, overt flouting of the Court's norms by the police was a rarity. For the Wisconsin results see Neal Milner, "Comparative Analysis of Patterns of Compliance with Supreme Court Decisions: *Miranda* and the Police in Four Communities," 5 *Law and Society Review* (August 1970), pp. 119–34.

195. *Culombe v. Connecticut*, 367 U.S. 568 (1961).

in utilizing *any* methods that would bring such a criminal to justice. The answer is simple: because of our civilized standards of decency, fair play, and due process, our Constitution simply and resolutely proscribes such methods. In the words of Justice Clark in the 1961 *Mapp* case: "Nothing can destroy a government more quickly than its failure to observe its own laws, or worse, its disregard of the character of its own existence."[196] Which does not gainsay the frustrations of public officials such as Warren Earl Burger, who, just prior to his accession to the chief justiceship of the Supreme Court of the United States, wrote:

> The seeming anxiety of judges to protect every accused person from every consequence of his voluntary utterances is giving rise to myriad rules, subrules, variations and exceptions which even the most alert and most sophisticated lawyers and judges are taxed to follow. . . . We are approaching the predicament of the centipede on the flypaper—each time one leg is placed to give support for relief of a leg already "stuck," another becomes captive and soon all are immobilized. . . . We are well on our way to forbidding any utterance of an accused to be used against him unless it is made in open court. Guilt or innocence becomes irrelevant in the criminal trial as we flounder in a morass of artificial rules—poorly conceived and often impossible of application.[197]

The Fourth Amendment Can of Worms. There is neither time nor space to survey each of the various contentious and difficult areas in which the lines of private and public rights converge. But one last illustration: the complex matter of permissible search and seizure—which may well be *the* most complex to analyze as well as to adjudicate. Under the Fourth Amendment, *unreasonable*[198] searches and seizures are forbidden; out of this mandate grew the so-called exclusionary rule applied to the federal government as of 1914[199] and, as we noted in the *Mapp* case,[200] to the states as of 1961. But, ruled the Court (6:3) in a major case in 1990, the constitutional prohibition under the Fourth Amendment against unreasonable search and seizure does *not* apply to warrantless searches *abroad*—that,

---

196. *Mapp v. Ohio,* 367 U.S. 643 at 659.

197. As quoted in Alpheus T. Mason and William M. Beaney, *American Constitutional Law,* 5th ed. (Englewood Cliffs, N.J.: Prentice-Hall, 1972), p. xv.

198. An eternally controversial adjective!

199. *Weeks v. United States,* 232 U.S. 383. See Yale Kamisar's extensive supportive discussion of the rule, "Is the Exclusionary Rule an 'Illogical' or 'Unnatural' Interpretation of the Fourth Amendment?" 62 *Judicature* (August 1978), pp. 67–84. For a contrary view see Malcolm Richard Wilkey, "The Exclusionary Rule: Why Suppress Valid Evidence?" 62 *Judicature* 215 (November 1978). The rule has spawned an enormous amount of passionate as well as dispassionate commentary in books, journals, the press, other media, and the *Congressional Record.* See the Court's 1983 embarrassment on the issue in *Gates v. Illinois,* 462 U.S. 213.

200. *Mapp v. Ohio,* op. cit. See also *supra.*

thus, federal law enforcement agents do *not* need warrants when they go abroad to search the homes of foreign nationals.[201] The exclusionary rule now forbids the use of *any* illegally obtained evidence to convict an accused in *court,* although the as yet largely untested Organized Crime Control Act of 1970 contains a provision of questionable constitutionality, which sets a five-year statute of limitations on challenges by defendants of evidence from leads picked up by officers during *illegal* searches.[202] The basic exclusionary rule also means that an otherwise illegal search is not rendered legal simply by what it turns up; ergo, "fishing expeditions" on the part of police in search of evidence are thus out. Before asking for an arrest warrant,[203] the police officer must convince the warrant-issuing magistrate of his "personal knowledge" of "probable cause." To obtain a search warrant, the place to be searched and the object(s) to be seized must be described "particularly." When, surprisingly, the Supreme Court ruled (5:3) in 1978 that police can get warrants to make *un*announced searches of places owned or occupied by persons believed to be innocent of criminal activities,[204] Congress responded two years later by enacting the Privacy Protection Act of 1980, severely limiting such searches. And in 1995, in a unanimous opinion, penned by Justice Clarence Thomas, the Court ruled that the Fourth Amendment's protection against unreasonable searches and seizures includes a principle from the nation's common law and English roots that police officers "generally" must knock and announce their identity before entering a home with a search warrant. In 1997 the justices ruled unanimously that the Fourth Amendment also prohibits a blanket exception to the knock-and-announce requirement for felony drug investigations.[205] In any event, warrants are not issuable for "general" searches. Nor does a warrant to search a particular place *automatically* authorize the police to search anyone who happens to be there—as, for example, in a public bar.[206] But, as the Supreme Court ruled 8:1 in 2001, police waiting for a warrant to search a suspect's home may briefly prevent the suspect from going into the house, unless he has a police escort.[207]

There are, because there must be, situations in which the search of a per-

---

201. *United States v. Verdugo-Urquidez,* 494 U.S. 259.

202. It was upheld as to the questioning of grand jury witnesses (*United States v. Calandra,* 414 U.S. 338 [1975]).

203. It may be either a daytime or a nighttime warrant (*Gooding v. United States,* 416 U.S. 430 [1974]).

204. *Zurcher v. Stanford Daily,* 463 U.S. 547. "The critical element in a reasonable search," wrote Justice White in this highly controversial case, "is not that the owner of the property is suspected of crime, but that there is reasonable cause to believe that the specific things to be searched for and seized are located on the property" (at 556). Because the case involved the press, sundry First Amendment issues were also raised and disposed of.

205. *Wilson v. Arkansas,* 514 U.S. 927; and *Richards v. Wisconsin,* 520 U.S. 385.

206. *Ybarra v. Illinois,* 444 U.S. 85 (1979). But otherwise admissible evidence is not suppressible simply on the ground that it was unlawfully seized from a third party not before the court in a trial (*United States v. Payner,* 447 U.S. 727 [1980]).

207. *Illinois v. McArthur,* 531 U.S. 326.

son or the *immediate* surroundings is lawful *if* it is "incidental" to a legal arrest—that is, one authorized by an arrest warrant or on the basis of probable cause—but such an "incidental" search, to be considered "reasonable," must *really* be "confined to the immediate vicinity of the arrest . . . to the area within the arrestee's reach at the time of his arrest, the area from which he might gain possession of a weapon or destructible evidence."[208] *Mere* "suspicion," without more, is never enough to meet the constitutional commands, yet the concept of *"reasonable* suspicion" has been judicially justified in, for example, upholding "profile"-triggered airport[209] and Border Patrol[210] searches of drug traffic and hijacking suspects. And, of course, there are instances, other than the narrowly drawn "incidental" search rule, in which it is possible to search without a search warrant, *provided there is probable cause.*[211] Some examples would be: to seize evidence that is not listed in a search warrant but which is in plain view even if the discovery is not entirely "inadvertent" (the limits of a somewhat inconclusive 1971 test of constitutionality);[212] to discover weapons and/or prevent the destruction of evidence;[213] the common-law right of an arresting police agent to search when he has reasonable grounds to believe that a crime is being committed or that an individual on the scene is "armed and dangerous";[214] and, again always assuming the presence of "probable cause," in the case of *moving*

---

208. *Chimel v. California,* 395 U.S. 752 (1969) at 763, which "toughened" the standards of *United States v. Rabinowitz,* 399 U.S. 56 (1950). But cf. *Maryland v. Buie, infra* chapter 4.

209. *United States v. Mendenhall,* 446 U.S. 554 (1980), reconfirmed in *United States v. Sokolow,* 490 U.S. 1 (1989), with only Brennan and Marshall in dissent. But cf. *Reid v. Georgia,* 448 U.S. 438 (1980); and *Florida v. Royer,* 460 U.S. 419 (1983). Also, a traveler who puts his luggage in an overhead compartment on a bus expects it to stay private; hence a border patrol agent's physical manipulation of a carry-on bag was held 7:2 to violate the Fourth Amendment's proscription against unreasonable searches (*Bond v. United States,* 529 U.S. 334 [2000]). On the other hand, the Court ruled 6:3 that the Fourth Amendment does *not* require police officers to advise bus passengers of their right not to cooperate and to refuse consent to searches, here a routine drug and weapons interdiction effort (*United States v. Drayton,* 536 U.S. ___ [2002]).

210. *United States v. Arvisu,* 534 U.S. 279 (2002).

211. "Probable cause" is, of course, enormously difficult to define—and to disprove. The Court's most frequently quoted definition is taken from Justice Douglas's opinion in *Henry v. United States,* 361 U.S. 98 (1959): "Probable cause exists if the facts and circumstances known to the officer warrant a prudent man in believing that the offense has been committed" (at 102). See also the application of the "in plain view" doctrine, as rejected in *Arizona v. Hicks,* 476 U.S. 1156 (1987), in a 6:3 opinion written surprisingly by Justice Scalia—although the Court (including Scalia) seems to have adopted (7:2) a more permissive rule (see *Horton v. California, infra*).

212. *Horton v. California,* 496 U.S. 128 (1990).

213. *Agnello v. United States,* 268 U.S. 20 (1925).

214. See the several late 1960s and early 1970s "stop-and-frisk" cases cited *supra* in this chapter. See also *Pennsylvania v. Mimms,* 434 U.S. 106 (1977).

vehicles.[215] A police chase, ruled the Court (7:2) in a Scalia opinion, is not a "seizure" within the meaning of the Fourth Amendment.[216] Nor do police need a warrant to search the entire passenger area of an automobile after its occupants have been properly arrested.[217] And a unanimous Supreme Court upheld warrantless searches when convicted criminals signed away customary Fourth Amendment protections to gain probation. Mark James Knights had done so but now claimed unconstitutionality of the search.[218]

No such justifiable probable cause exists, however, the Supreme Court held (7:1) in 1979, in standard so-called police *spot* checks of automobile drivers' credentials on the public highways, *unless* the officer has some "articulable and reasonable suspicion that the motorist is unlicensed or [the auto] unregistered or [there is some other] violation of law."[219] That decision still allows the police to set up roadblocks for license and registration checks, however—prompting the dissenting Justice Rehnquist to observe that motorists, "like sheep, are much less likely to be 'frightened' or 'annoyed' when stopped en masse"; that, therefore, police can now stop "*all* motorists" but not "*less than all* motorists." The "stop them all at a roadblock" practice of Charlottesville, Virginia, was initially upheld by the Court in 1986,[220] and a 6:3 decision in 1990 made clear that the goal of apprehending drunk drivers justifies the "slight intrusion on privacy" sobriety checkpoints may cause.[221] And, as the Court made clear unanimously in 1981, police may indeed stop vehicles when "the totality of circumstances" suggests its occupants may be involved in a crime (here the transportation of illegal aliens in Arizona).[222] Indeed, in 1982 a 6:3 ruling in the *Ross* case announced that henceforth, if probable cause justifies the search of a lawfully stopped vehicle, it justifies the search of *every* part of the vehicle and its contents that could conceal the object of the search, including closed containers, *if* police have probable cause that they contain contraband.[223] Two May 1991 decisions (7:2 and 6:3, respectively) may, one hopes, devoutly, at last have settled the endemic car search syndrome. As of their holding, (1) a suspect who gives police permission to

215. *Carroll v. United States,* 267 U.S. 132 (1925).

216. *California v. Hodari D.,* 59 LW 4335 (1991).

217. *New York v. Belton,* 453 U.S. 454 (1981).

218. *United States v. Knights,* 534 U.S. 112 (2001).

219. *Delaware v. Prouse,* 440 U.S. 648.

220. *Lowe v. Virginia,* 475 U.S. 1084.

221. *Michigan Department of State Police v. Sitz,* 496 U.S. 444.

222. *United States v. Cortez,* 455 U.S. 923. See also the unanimously decided case of *United States v. Hensley,* 469 U.S. 221 (1984).

223. *United States v. Ross,* 456 U.S. 798. The Ross decision came in 1982. Less than two years earlier the Court had held that a warrant is needed for closed containers in a car's trunk (*Robbins v. California,* 453 U.S. 420 [1981]), in which it affirmed an earlier key (1977) holding on the vexatious issue (*United States v. Chadwick,* 433 U.S. 1), involving a locked footlocker.

search his car implicitly gives permission to search closed containers therein,[224] and (2) that police may search *warrantless* an automobile *and* containers within it *where they have probable cause* to believe contraband or evidence is contained.[225] That Blackmun-authored opinion, which he accompanied with a statement that henceforth there would be "one rule to govern all automobile searches," would at least *appear* to settle the contentious matter after sixty-six years of incomplete and conflicting rulings. That impression was strengthened by two unanimous decisions by the Court in 1996: The first held that police officers may stop motorists for minor traffic violations, even if the officers' real motive is to look for evidence of drug trafficking; the second upheld consensual police searches of cars during traffic stops—that is, the officers need not tell the stopped motorists that they are free to go before questioning them on other matters or searching their car for drugs. In 1997 the Court held 7:2 that police officers may automatically order passengers to get out of a car during a routine traffic stop.[226] And a significant 6:3 ruling in 1999, curtailing the privacy rights of automobile passengers, gave police officers broader powers to scour a car for drugs and other contraband, thus for the first time making passengers who are not suspected of wrongdoing subject to warrantless searches.[227] However, absent probable cause and/or a warrant, police may not conduct a full-blown search of motorists and their vehicles after pulling them over and ticketing them for speeding or other minor traffic violations (9:0).[228] And in a 1999 unanimous decision the Court curbed "ride along" practices by ruling that police can be sued for letting reporters and photographers accompany them on raids of private homes.[229]

Warrantless *aerial* searches of private areas were upheld (5:4) in 1986 in the instance of government investigators who used a plane to observe and photograph fenced-off areas where "pot" was grown in one case (confirmed 5:4 in a similar case in 1989: *Florida v. Riley*, 488 U.S. 445) and possible air pollution violations were suspected in the other.[230] Moreover, as it had ruled (6:3) in 1973, *if* there is "probable cause" to take a person into custody, "the fact of lawful arrest estab-

224. *Florida v. Jimeno*, 501 U.S. 429.
225. *California v. Acevedo*, 505 U.S. 565.
226. *Whren v. U.S.*, 517 U.S. 806 (1996), *Ohio v. Robinette*, 519 U.S. 33; and *Maryland v. Wilson*, 519 U.S. 408 (1997).
227. *Wyoming v. Houghton*, 526 U.S. 295.
228. *Knowles v. Iowa*, 525 U.S. 113 (1998). As Chief Justice Rehnquist explained, distinguishing *Whren, supra:* "Once Knowles was stopped for speeding and issued a citation, all the evidence necessary to prosecute that offense had been obtained."
229. *Wilson v. Lange* and *Hamlon v. Berger,* 67 LW 4329.
230. *California v. Ciraolo*, 476 U.S. 207; and *Dow Chemical Co. v. United States,* 476 U.S. 227. Also (6:2 in 1988) warrantless search of trash (*California v. Greenwood,* 486 U.S. 35). On the other hand, a 5:4 decision held in 2001 that sense-enhancing, high-tech monitoring devices, here a thermal-imaging one used to detect high-intensity lights utilized in growing marijuana, required a warrant before police scanning of a private home from the outside (*Kyllo v. United States,* 533 U.S. 27).

lishes the authority to search" the person "reasonably" (and not just in instances of suspected *serious* crimes;[231] nor does it have to be justified, like the *Terry* "stop-and-frisk" case,[232] which did *not* initiate an incident that led to an arrest but turned on the grounds of protecting the police officer from harm). The Court added (6:2) in 1976 that the Constitution does *not* require law enforcement officials to obtain warrants before they make arrests in *public places*—even when there is adequate time to obtain a warrant—provided there is probable cause that a felony has been committed.[233] In 1990 the Court ruled (6:3) that under the "totality of circumstances" rule police may stop and question suspects on the basis of anonymous telephone tips, given "reasonable suspicion" to justify investigatory stops,[234] and, of course, held the Court in 1997, for their own safety, police may order a passenger out of the car.[235] Also in 1990 it ruled (7:2) that police do not need "probable cause" for certain "protective sweeps" during an arrest when they have a "reasonable belief," based on "specific and articulatable facts," that the area searched "harbored an individual posing a danger to the officer or others."[236] Again in 1990 an O'Connor-authored 6:3 ruling allowed the practice of drug-seeking police to "work the busses," that is, that officers looking for illicit drugs may board buses and ask passengers *for permission* to search their bags without violating their constitutional rights.[237] A further extension of police search authority came with a 1993 unanimous decision holding that a police officer may seize drugs and other contraband felt through a suspect's clothing during a search for weapons. And, the Court ruled 5:4 in 2001, the Fourth Amendment does not forbid a warrantless arrest for a minor criminal offense, such as a misdemeanor seatbelt violation.[238] But a 6:3 majority cautioned that an officer may not go beyond the usual "pat down" necessary in a search for weapons and probe among a suspect's clothing for other items.[239] Yet as it had held in 1980, a warrant is needed for routine felony arrests in *private* homes, ab-

---

231. *United States v. Robinson* and *Gustafson v. Florida,* 414 U.S. 218 and 414 U.S. 260, respectively, and a contraband search warrant provided police power for "temporary detention" (*Michigan v. Summers,* 452 U.S. 692 [1981]).

232. *Terry v. Ohio,* 392 U.S. 1 (1968), an 8:1 decision written by Chief Justice Warren, Justice Douglas dissenting. See its extension to property, here the passenger area of a car in *Michigan v. Long,* 463 U.S. 1032 (1983), even if the suspect is out of the car and in custody. However, ruled a surprisingly unanimous Court in 2000, police may *not* stop and frisk someone based merely on an anonymous tip (*Florida v. J.L.,* 529 U.S. 266).

233. *United States v. Watson,* 423 U.S. 411. See *Donovan v. Dewey,* 452 U.S. 594 (1981).

234. *Alabama v. White,* 496 U.S. 325. But see *Florida v. J.L., supra.*

235. *Maryland v. Dennis,* 66 LW 3276.

236. *Maryland v. Buie,* 494 U.S. 325.

237. *Florida v. Bostick,* 500 U.S. 428. Cf. *Bond v. United States* and *United States v. Drayton, supra.*

238. *Atwater v. Lago Vista,* 532 U.S. 318 (2001).

239. *Minnesota v. Dickerson,* 508 U.S. 366.

sent "exigent circumstances,"[240] and not only must a confession thus obtained without a warrant be excluded, but the rule can be applied retroactively to 1980.[241] On the other hand, a 5:4 ruling in 1998 limited the privacy rights of guests invited to someone's home, rejecting the idea that visitors share their host's constitutional protection from unreasonable police searches. An *overnight* guest, however, may claim Fourth Amendment protection.[242] Frustrating as it may be, the constitutional rules must be observed—by the protagonists on both sides.

Drug Testing. What of the constitutionality of mandatory drug testing? The Court has been broadly supportive, heralded by two important 1989 decisions, both written by Justice Anthony M. Kennedy, that upheld two separate programs (7:2 and 5:4). The former applied to testing of railroad crews *after* accidents (*Skinner v. Railway Labor Executives' Association,* 489 U.S. 602), the latter to testing of applicants for certain top-level Customs Service drug enforcement jobs (*National Treasury Union v. Von Raab,* 489 U.S. 656). At the end of its 1988–89 term the justices ruled (7:2) that railroads are not required by federal labor law to bargain with their employees before seeking to impose drug testing programs (*Consolidated Rail Corporation v. Railway Labor Executives Association,* 491 U.S. 299). Early in the following term, the Court, without dissent, let stand a Boston police program requiring random drug testing for officers who carry firearms or are involved in drug interdiction (*Guinea v. Roache,* 493 U.S. 963 [1989]). In 1990, without comment, the Court refused to hear challenges to random drug testing programs brought by two groups of federal employees. One program applied to civilian drug and alcohol counselors employed by the army. The other applied to Justice Department employees holding top-secret clearances.[243] A 1995 6:3 opinion, penned by Justice Scalia, upheld random testing of public middle and high school *athletes* against Fourth and Fourteenth Amendment claims; in 1997 the Court confirmed that authority;[244] and in 2002 the Court upheld 5:4

---

240. *Payton v. New York,* 445 U.S. 573. For an excellent analysis—as of 1966—of the entire search-and-seizure syndrome, see J. W. Landynski, *Search and Seizure and the Supreme Court* (Baltimore: Johns Hopkins University Press, 1966). See also that author's work cited *supra* note 146, chapter 3. For a more recent study see J. D. Hirschel, *Fourth Amendment Rights* (Lexington, Mass.: D. C. Heath, 1979).

241. *United States v. Johnson,* 457 U.S. 537 (1980). And, going further, the Court ruled 6:2 in 1984 that the police are almost never justified in entering a private home without a warrant to arrest someone for a minor civil offense (here drunken driving) on the first infraction (*Welsh v. Wisconsin,* 466 U.S. 740).

242. *Minnesota v. Carter,* 525 U.S. 83.

243. *National Federation of Federal Employees v. Cheney,* 496 U.S. 936; and *Bell v. Thornburgh,* 493 U.S. 1056. See also the 1990 denial of certiorari in random drug testing of New York jail guards (*Seelig v. Koehler,* 498 U.S. 847; and *Bluestein v. Skinner,* 498 U.S. 1083 [1991]).

244. *Vernonia School District v. Acton,* 515 U.S. 646. See also *Todd v. Indiana,* 67 LW 3230.

the Oklahoma urinalysis testing of middle and high school students to participate in extracurricular activities.[245] But a 1999 refusal to grant certiorari in an Indiana case left intact a lower court decision striking down on privacy grounds a requirement that suspended students be subject to urine testing prior to returning to school.[246] Yet, also in 1999, the Supreme Court upheld a ruling by the Sixth Circuit Court of Appeals that applicants for a public school teaching job in Tennessee must take a drug test.[247] And in 1997 the Court struck down a Georgia law requiring drug tests of all candidates for certain high elective offices.[248] However, in the same year a one-sentence order allowed random drug tests for passholders of the Old Executive Office Building, located next to the White House.[249] But in 2000 the justices would not affirm Louisiana's random drug testing for its elected offices.[250] The next year a 6:3 vote held that a public hospital cannot administer drug tests to pregnant women without their consent and forward possible results to police.[251] Also in 2001 another 6:3 majority ruled that the police may not stop motorists *randomly* at roadblocks and search their cars with drug-detecting canines because such stops are specifically designed to catch criminals, and thus amount to unreasonable seizures banned by the Fourth Amendment.[252]

"Good Faith" and the Exclusionary Rule. Seventy years after *Weeks,*[253] thirty-five years after *Wolf,*[254] and twenty-three years after *Mapp,*[255] the heated and continuingly contentious controversy over the exclusionary rule came to a head in 1984. Dividing 7:2 and 6:3, the Supreme Court adopted the governmentally long-sought "good faith" exception to the rule. It held, speaking through Justice White, that the exclusionary rule should not apply when the police act in "objectively reasonable" reliance on a search warrant that at the time appears to be valid, even though it later proves defective. Over bitter dissents on Fourth Amendment grounds by Justice Brennan, who was joined by Justice Marshall in both cases and by Justice Stevens in the second,[256] White ruled that by suppressing "inherently trustworthy, tangible evidence," the exclusionary rule imposed "substantial social costs" that, at least in the context of a seemingly valid

245. *Pottawatomie County v. Earls,* 536 U.S. ___ (2002).
246. *Anderson Community School Corporation v. Willis,* 67 LW 3582.
247. *Knox County Education Association v. Knox County Board of Education,* 67 LW 3582.
248. *Chandler v. Miller,* 520 U.S. 305 (1997).
249. *Stigile v. Clinton,* 67 LW 2692 (1997).
250. *Foster v. O'Neill,* 68 LW 3792 (2000).
251. *Ferguson v. City of Charleston,* 532 U.S. 67 (2001).
252. *Indianapolis v. Edmonds,* 531 U.S. 32.
253. *Weeks v. United States,* 232 U.S. 283 (1914).
254. *Wolf v. Colorado,* 338 U.S. 25 (1949).
255. *Mapp v. Ohio,* 367 U.S. 643 (1961).
256. *Massachusetts v. Sheppard,* 468 U.S. 981 (1984) (7:2); and *United States v. Leon,* 468 U.S. 897 (6:3), respectively.

search warrant, outweighed the benefit achieved by deterring official misconduct. Legislation to accomplish the formal adoption of the good faith rule was introduced by Senator Strom Thurmond (R.-S.C.) in the spring of 1986, but it failed of adoption. Yet the Court itself expanded the "good faith" rule in 1987 by holding that evidence obtained in a search under an unconstitutional regulatory statute authorizing warrantless searches of certain businesses may be used if the police reasonably believed the law to be constitutional.[257] It is fair to conjecture that the Court will handle future exclusionary rule cases on an ad hoc basis and that the justices will continue to be closely divided on the rule's range, extent, and application. Indeed, Justice White, the author of the "good faith" rule, would provide the fifth and key vote—without explanation therefore—in a 1990 decision that reaffirmed the now seventy-five-year-old exclusionary rule in a complex testimonial case.[258] The exclusionary rule is, after all, a judge-made rule, not a constitutional requirement, and can be judge-altered, as it has been with the adoption of the "good faith" concept. That is what occurred in 1995, when a 7:2 Court, speaking through Chief Justice Rehnquist, with Justices Stevens and Ginsburg in dissent, reaffirmed the judicially created nature of the exclusionary rule. Specifically, it held that the rule does *not* require suppression of evidence seized in violation of the Fourth Amendment where the erroneous information resulted from clerical errors by lower court employees.[259]

That the Fourth Amendment line will continue to be a live, vexatious one is certain.[260] As Justice Brandeis mused six decades ago, the mind can hardly fore-

257. *Illinois v. Krull,* 480 U.S. 340. See also another 1987 confirmation of the vitality of the "good faith" rule in *Maryland v. Garrison,* 480 U.S. 79.

258. *James v. Illinois,* 493 U.S. 307. At issue was a ruling in a murder case by the Illinois Supreme Court that even if the defendant does not take the stand, the illegally obtained evidence could still be used to impeach the credibility of a defense witness. White joined the five-member majority opinion, reversing the Illinois tribunal, penned by Justice Brennan, and also embraced by Justices Marshall, Blackmun, and Stevens. The dissenting opinion by Justice Kennedy was joined by Chief Justice Rehnquist and Justices O'Connor and Scalia.

259. *Arizona v. Evans,* 514 U.S. 1.

260. Thus, the Court's 6:3 holding in *New Jersey v. T.L.O.,* 469 U.S. 325 (1985), established a "balancing approach" between individual and societal rights in the application of the Fourth Amendment to students in public schools. In the New Jersey case at issue, the Court approved warrantless searches of pupils on the school grounds during school hours on a case-by-case basis, with the test being the presence of "reasonable grounds" rather than the tougher one of "probable cause." Specifically, the case here involved the use and/or dissemination of controlled substances by students. In 1991, confronted with the need to define "prompt" for criminal suspects arrested without a warrant, the Court ruled (5:4) that "prompt" meant up to forty-eight hours, that is, that they may be jailed for as long as forty-eight hours before a judge determines the validity of the arrest (*County of Riverside v. McLaughlin,* 500 U.S. 44). And in 1997 it upheld, by denying certiorari, an Alabama public school's strip search of two second graders accused of stealing from a classmate (*Jenkins v. Herring,* 66 LW 3333).

see what scientific developments may lie in store for us—and they are certain to affect Fourth Amendment mandates.

The Case Study of Wiretapping. To illustrate the aforegone further, wiretapping, one of the most vexatious of the due process problems, is not unconstitutional— or at least the Supreme Court has never so held it. The famous 5:4 *Olmstead* case of 1928 set the tone,[261] Chief Justice Taft holding it *not* to be a Fourth Amendment violation because the telephonic messages at issue did not involve a physical intrusion into the defendants' homes or offices—the agents stationed off the premises had merely listened to statements no one had forced the bootleggers involved to make—nor was any "material thing" seized. Justice Holmes's vigorous dissent that it is "dirty business,"[262] and Justice Brandeis's prophetic warning about the "progress" of science, also rendered in a separate dissenting opinion— one of the great dissents in the Court's annals[263]—failed to command a majority. The response to *Olmstead* was the Federal Communications Act of 1934, which (like some state statutes) expressly forbade it; yet the FBI successfully qualified it with the interpretation that mere "interception" is not a violation of the act's famous Section 605 *unless there* is also *"divulgence"*—an interpretation that served as the agency's rationale for much of its wiretapping, despite the language of Section 605. Hence we had something that was proscribed yet went on constantly.

But does not wiretapping make the citizen prey to the very kind of "fishing expedition" which is theoretically forbidden under the Fourth Amendment? The modern scientific "advances" in the realm of detection, so perceptively predicted by Brandeis, are rapidly reducing privacy to a shibboleth. Thus, as was vividly demonstrated to a subcommittee of the U.S. Senate's Committee on the Judiciary,[264] we now have available such eavesdropping devices as tiny radio transmitters that can be concealed in a martini olive, with the toothpick serving as the antenna; in a woman's purse—even in the cavity of a tooth of an intimate associate! Then there is the laser, a device which can transmit a concentrated beam of light to a room several blocks away so as to reflect back a television picture of everything happening in the room, including the sound. Perhaps it was specters such as these that caused Justice Nathan R. Sobel of the New York

---

261. *Olmstead v. United States,* 277 U.S. 438.

262. "We have to choose," he observed, "and for my part I think it a lesser evil that some criminals should escape than that the government would play an ignoble part" (ibid. at 470–71).

263. Among its memorable language: "The makers of our Constitution . . . conferred, as against the government, the right to be let alone—the most comprehensive of rights and the right most valued by civilized men. . . . Men born to freedom are naturally alert to repel invasions of their liberty by evil-minded rulers. The greatest dangers to liberty lurk in insidious encroachment by men of zeal, well-meaning but without understanding" (ibid. at 478).

264. See *Life,* May 20, 1966, pp. 38–47.

State Supreme Court (Brooklyn Division) to declare unconstitutional on March 1, 1965, the New York State law that had authorized court-approved electronic eavesdropping on a suspect's private premises. In his thirty-two-page opinion, Justice Sobel held the law invalid because the eavesdropping orders it authorized could not, in his judgment, meet the standards required for the issuance of search warrants under the Fourth Amendment.[265] Just a year later, the Federal Communications Commission issued an order prohibiting private citizens from using radio devices to eavesdrop. Theoretically, the FCC order made illegal such equipment as the tiny radio transmitters described earlier (unless everyone present knew the equipment was being used). Yet it did not affect the use of a miniature tape recorder directly connected to a small camouflaged microphone, since no radio transmission was involved—although the same kind of eavesdropping may take place. Nor did the ban affect law enforcement agencies, such as the FBI, the Internal Revenue Service, or state and local police and similar authorities. However, in July 1967 the then attorney general, Ramsey Clark, in a dramatic order going far beyond any previously issued governmental limitations in the wiretapping and eavesdropping field, issued sweeping new regulations forbidding all wiretapping and virtually all eavesdropping except in national security cases. The new rules generated considerable controversy and opposition among federal agents and prosecutors,[266] and they were relaxed by the Nixon administration.

Indeed, by that time a number of legal experts had become convinced that the Supreme Court's *Griswold* ruling in 1965,[267] which, as noted in chapter 3, invalidated Connecticut's birth control statute by enunciating a new "right of privacy," had laid the basis for an eventual judicial outlawing of wiretapping and other forms of electronic eavesdropping. It was argued that the new right of privacy could be held to override the technical distinction of a physical intrusion that the Court made both in the *Olmstead* case[268] and in subsequent decisions involving other electronic eavesdropping,[269] and thus render all such intrusions un-

265. *People v. Grossman*, 257 N.Y.S.2d 266. The decision was reversed a year later by the appellate division, but he was more or less vindicated in 1967 when the U.S. Supreme Court declared the New York law unconstitutional in *Berger v. New York*, 388 U.S. 41.

266. Thus, FBI Director J. Edgar Hoover referred to Clark as the "worst Attorney-General" he had served under in fifty years in Washington, "even worse than Bobby Kennedy" (*Time*, November 30, 1970, p. 11).

267. *Griswold v. Connecticut*, 381 U.S. 479, *supra*.

268. *Olmstead v. United States*, 277 U.S. 438 (1928). The vote in that case, as noted earlier, was 5:4; the majority opinion was written by Chief Justice Taft and joined by Associate Justices Van Devanter, McReynolds, Sutherland, and Sanford. The dissenters, in addition to Holmes and Brandeis, were Justices Butler and Stone—all of whom wrote dissenting opinions.

269. E.g., *Goldman v. United States*, 316 U.S. 129 (1942); and *On Lee v. United States*, 343 U.S. 747 (1952). (*Lee* was reconfirmed [5:4], in 1971, in *United States v. White*, 401 U.S. 745.) Cf. *Silverman v. United States*, 365 U.S. 505 (1961).

constitutional.[270] On the other hand, it might well be asked, could not and should not the kind of search and seizure represented by wiretapping be authorized under our Constitution? Although wiretapping and electronic eavesdropping are clear-cut invasions of the basic rights of privacy, perhaps they are necessary in cases of subversive activities, seditious conduct, espionage, terrorism, kidnapping, and certain other major crimes. Perhaps a good case *can* be made for eavesdropping in the fields just mentioned when the act is duly requested *and judicially authorized before the fact,* notwithstanding the reprehensible nature of the incursions of privacy involved. However, it would be much harder to make a viable case for such intrusions on privacy in crimes like fraud, racketeering, prostitution, and gambling, or for the "investigation" of public and private employees in anything but highly secret positions.[271] In the final analysis, our response must turn first on the constitutionality of any such proposed action and second on its wisdom. And even assuming the former, any thoughts on the wisdom of such action must confront the basic issues raised by Justice Brandeis in his memorable dissent in the *Olmstead* case, an opinion that clearly endeavored to identify and promote a right of privacy, when he wrote:

> The makers of our Constitution undertook to secure conditions favorable to the pursuit of happiness. They recognized the significance of man's spiritual nature, of his feelings and of his intellect. They knew that only a part of the pain, pleasure and satisfactions of life are to be found in material things. They sought to protect Americans in their beliefs, their thoughts, their emotions and their sensations. They conferred, as against the Government, *the right to be let alone—the most comprehensive of rights and the right most valued by civilized men.* To protect that right, every unjustifiable intrusion by the Government upon the privacy of the individual, whatever the means employed, must be deemed a violation of the Fourth Amendment. . . .[272]

The Court—the recipient of so many governmentally, especially legislatively, "passed bucks"—in its 1967 catalytic *Katz* case[273] seemed to take a long

---

270. Such a ruling presumably would reach the so-called distinction between "wiretapping" and "bugging," a distinction that sees the latter as not proscribed. It was embraced by sundry law enforcement officials, apparently including the then ex–U.S. Attorney General Robert F. Kennedy (see David Lawrence, "Rightfully Bugging," *New York Herald Tribune* [international edition], July 9, 1966, p. 8).

271. An interesting case for such a balancing approach to the use of wiretapping and electronic eavesdropping was made by Alan Westin in his *Privacy and Freedom* (New York: Atheneum, 1967).

272. *Olmstead v. United States,* op. cit., at 478; italics supplied. Philippa Strum reports that one of Brandeis's working folders for *Olmstead* contains a 1928 clipping reporting on the development of "something called television." Brandeis, she comments, was a great believer in progress—"but not all progress was good." See her *Louis D. Brandeis: Justice for the People* (Cambridge, Mass.: Harvard University Press, 1984), p. 325.

273. *Katz v. United States,* 389 U.S. 347. The vote was 7:1, Justice Marshall not participating.

stride toward a possible solution of at least the eavesdropping ("bugging") aspect of the problem, and, by implication, of the entire privacy/intrusion dilemma. In that decision, with a solo dissent by Justice Black—who consistently rejected the contention that the specific safeguards of the Fourth Amendment, as spelled out therein, apply to eavesdropping, because the amendment speaks only of "persons, houses, papers, and effects"—the Court *eased curbs* on "bugging" *while adding safeguards* against it. Justice Stewart's majority opinion, noting that the Fourth Amendment should not "be translated into a general constitutional right of privacy,"[274] made it clear that the Constitution does not forbid electronic "bugging" by law enforcement officers if they first obtain warrants authorizing the eavesdropping—warrants being a basic requirement of the Fourth Amendment, of course. *But,* at the same time, with *Katz* the Court extended the reach of that amendment by holding that the search warrant procedure must be followed by the police officers even when they plan to eavesdrop on persons in semipublic places, such as a phone booth. Moreover, and significantly, the Court threw out its old "physical trespass" test by ruling that the trespass per se was not the crucial point, that the Fourth Amendment "protects people not places."[275] In effect, *Katz* thus overruled both the "material things seized" rationale of the *Olmstead* holding[276] and the "physical intrusion" distinction of the *Goldman* case[277] (which had come midway between the *Olmstead* and *Katz* decisions). The latter also lessened the effect of the Court's 5:4 decision in *Berger v. New York* a few months earlier in 1967,[278] when it had narrowly invalidated the aforementioned New York statute authorizing electronic eavesdropping because, as Justice Tom Clark—an ex–attorney general of the United States—wrote for the majority, the "statute is too broad in its sweep, resulting in a trespassory intrusion into a constitutionally protected area," and did not provide for "adequate judicial supervision or protective procedures."[279] What *Katz* did, then, was to enable the enactment of both wiretapping and eavesdropping ("bugging") statutes, provided the carefully delineated Fourth Amendment safeguards against unreasonable searches and seizures were

274. Ibid. at 350.

275. Ibid. at 351. See the Court's 7:2 majority emphasis of that crucial point in its 1977 striking down of a conviction obtained in a federal case involving a two-hundred-pound footlocker filled with marijuana (*United States v. Chadwick,* 433 U.S. 1). But the Court also pointed out three years later that the legality of a search is challengeable only if an accused can demonstrate "an expectation of privacy in the premises searched" (*United States v. Salvucci,* 448 U.S. 83 [1980]). See, too, the aerial surveillance cases, *supra* note 230.

276. *Katz v. United States,* op. cit., at 351.

277. *Goldman v. United States,* 316 U.S. 129 (1942), as distinguished by *Silverman v. United States,* 365 U.S. 505 (1961), in which the use of a "spike mike" was held to be an actual physical intrusion.

278. 388 U.S. 41.

279. Ibid. at 44, 60. It was Clark's valedictory opinion.

scrupulously observed by all branches of the government, both statutorily and procedurally.[280]

Against the backdrop of the rising controversy of the "law and order" issue, Congress took the *Katz* cue and enacted Title III of the Omnibus Crime Control and Safe Streets Act of 1968, headed "Wiretapping and Electronic Surveillance." It permits *court-approved* interceptions by both federal and state law enforcement officials in the investigation of a large number of listed crimes[281]—there were 648 such court-authorized, although not necessarily applied, orders in 1983 (440 state, 208 federal); 816 in 1971; 864 in 1973; 871 in 1974; 626 in 1977 (549 of these state and 77 federal); 578 in 1982 (130 of these federal); there were 340 federal court orders in criminal cases in 1992; in 1995 that number rose to 672; and the total for 1996 increased to over 700, only one application for a wiretap being denied by a judge during that year.[282] A majority of these involved alleged gambling offenses, which consistently lead the "tap" field, followed by those for drug-related crimes throughout the United States.[283] The above figures do not include "national security" wiretap orders, obtained under intelligence legislation, which have also jumped markedly. Replete with procedural safeguards—with an eye toward *Katz*—the law has a contentious "exemption" section in the case of "an emergency situation exist[ing] with respect to conspiratorial activities threatening the national security interest or to conspiratorial activities characteristic of organized crime."[284] Under its terms, and if the action at issue is so classified by either the U.S. attorney general or the principal prosecuting attorney of any state or its subdivisions, interception may proceed *without* court order, provided an application for an order is obtained and entered "within forty-eight hours after the interception has occurred or begins to occur."[285] Here, then, is the loophole—which may or may not be justifiable and constitutional.[286]

A different, and perhaps even more significant test, however, had come in 1971, when, breaking new ground in a surprisingly bold decision, U.S. District

280. See the analysis of privacy by David M. O'Brien, "Reasonable Expectations of Privacy: Principles and Policies of Fourth Amendment–Protected Privacy," 13 *New England Law Review* 663 (1978), and the same author's *Privacy, Law, and Public Policy* (New York: Praeger, 1979).

281. E.g., for the state level: murder, kidnapping, gambling, robbery, bribery, extortion, or dealing in narcotics, marijuana, or other dangerous drugs, and so forth (Section 2516[2]). Some of these also apply in the federal sector.

282. See the *National Legal Center for the Public Interest News,* July 1997, p. 3.

283. Based on annual reports by the U.S. attorney general and the Administrative Office of the United States Courts.

284. Section 2518(7).

285. Section 2518(7)(b).

286. By early 1997 lower federal courts had reached conflicting results, but no Supreme Court test had occurred. *United States v. Chavez,* 416 U.S. 562 (1974), in the eyes of at least some observers, seemed to approve the procedure tangentially in a 5:4 holding.

Judge Warren J. Ferguson ruled in Los Angeles that the federal government's "no-warrant-needed" national security wiretap policy, allegedly inherent in a perhaps even more contentious section of the 1968 statute than the one discussed earlier, which states that the law's provisions "do not restrict the constitutional powers of the President,"[287] was unconstitutional as applied to *domestic* cases (rather than foreign ones). As he put the issue:

> National security cannot be invoked to abridge basic rights. . . . To guarantee political freedom, our forefathers agreed to take certain risks which are inherent in a free democracy. It is unthinkable that we should now be required to sacrifice those freedoms in order to defend them.[288]

Shortly thereafter, Judge Ferguson's ruling was echoed in an even more strongly worded decision against the government's interpretation of its asserted authority under the 1968 Wiretapping Act by U.S. District Judge Damon J. Keith in a Detroit case.[289] The government appealed; lost (2:1) at the bar of the U.S. Court of Appeals for the Sixth Circuit in April, which held, inter alia, that there was not "one written phrase" in the Constitution or statutes to support the administration's view that federal agents might legally wiretap radical domestic groups without court order;[290] and took a further appeal to the Supreme Court.[291] In one of those decisions that render the study of the judicial process so fascinatingly unpredictable, down came the Burger Court's response in its next term: in an 8:0 opinion—Justice Rehnquist abstaining—written by Justice Powell, who, as a private citizen, less than three months theretofore had publicly *supported* the government's claim of constitutional authority for wiretapping of radical domestic groups sans warrant,[292] the unanimous justices declared the practice of doing so *without prior judicial approval* to be an unconstitutional invasion of Fourth Amendment guarantees, as well as being unauthorized under the 1968 statute![293]

---

287. Section 2511(3). Among other things, it states: "Nothing contained in this chapter . . . shall limit the constitutional power of the President to take such measures as he deems necessary to protect the nation against actual or potential attack or other hostile acts of a foreign power. . . ."

288. *United States v. Smith,* 321 F. Supp. 424.

289. *Plamondon v. Mitchell,* decided January 25, 1971 (see following footnote).

290. *United States v. United States District Court for the Eastern District of Michigan,* 444 F.2d 651 (1971).

291. A collateral issue had reached the Court in 1969, when it held that any criminal defendant had the right to see directly all transcriptions unexpurgated by a judge of his conversations picked up by an "illegal" police listening device. The purpose of the decision was to let defendants rest assured that no illegally obtained evidence was used against them—the government being forced either to turn the transcripts of the "illegal" tap over to defendants or to drop the case against them (*Alderman v. United States,* 394 U.S. 165).

292. Lewis F. Powell Jr., "Civil Liberties Repression: Fact or Fiction?—Law Abiding Citizens Have Nothing to Fear," *Richmond Times-Dispatch,* August 1, 1971.

293. *United States v. United States District Court for the Eastern District of Michigan,* 407 U.S. 297 (1972).

"The price of lawful public dissent," in Powell's words, "must not be a dread of subjection to an unchecked surveillance power. Nor must the fear of unauthorized official eavesdropping deter citizen dissent and discussion of government action in private conversation."[294]

The Court left open the statute's application to foreign groups suspected of subversive activity—a facet it refused (3:5) pointedly to explore when it had an opportunity to do so in 1974.[295] Four years thereafter, however, Congress—allowing for narrow exceptions—enacted legislation requiring federal court approval before the government can conduct electronic surveillance in foreign intelligence cases. Concurrently, Congress further narrowed the government's authority to obtain judicial warrants for *domestic* national security wiretaps and bugging. Chairman Birch Bayh (D.-Ind.) of the Senate Intelligence Committee hailed the measure as "a landmark in the development of effective legal safeguards for constitutional rights."[296] On a related matter involving the 1968 wiretapping law, it had administered another defeat to the government's attempts to use tapping more facilely: in two devastating, unanimous decisions in mid-1974, the Court threw out the convictions of two accused criminals[297] because of "shortcuts" under the 1968 statute taken by Attorney General John N. Mitchell some years earlier. While the justices acknowledged that the law had indeed vastly expanded federal investigative authority to tap, that authority hinged expressly on the personal approval in advance by the attorney general or by an especially designated assistant. But dozens of authorizations, including those involved in the two cases before the Court, had simply been initialed "JNM" by a minor Mitchell aide, Sol Lindenbaum, or sometimes even just by the latter's secretary! That irregularity, held the normally decidedly "pro" law-and-order Justice White, was no mere technicality: Congress had clearly and carefully required that "the mature judgment of a particular, responsible official" would be involved in any decision to tap. As a result of the Court's ruling, nearly two years of determined hard work by federal investigators was wiped out, and at least sixty cases involving no fewer than 626 accused gamblers, narcotic dealers, and other racketeers were imperiled.[298] Such, however, is the price of constitutional guarantees: shortcuts à la Mitchell's simply cannot be condoned, nor, it is to be hoped, will they be, so long as we are governed by our Constitution's letter and spirit. In that spirit Congress enacted in 1986 a modernization of the wiretapping statutes designed to protect the privacy of modern high-tech communications. Hence-

294. Ibid. at 314.

295. *Ivanov v. United States,* 419 U.S. 881 (1974).

296. *Washington Post,* October 26, 1978, p. A2. (The new legislation was in 18 USCS §2511.) See the Foreign Intelligence Surveillance Act of 1978.

297. *United States v. Giordano,* 416 U.S. 505; and *United States v. Chavez,* 416 U.S. 562.

298. See the account in *Time,* May 27, 1974, p. 57.

forth, in the absence of a warrant it will thus also be just as illegal to eavesdrop on someone's electronic mail, video conference call, conversation on a cellular phone, or computer-to-computer transmission as it continues to be to wiretap a telephone. Congressionally granted authorizations to law enforcement in 2002's antiterrorism "USA PATRIOT Act" (whose acronym stands for "Uniting and Strengthening America by Providing Appropriate Tools Required to Intercept and Obstruct Terrorism) may weaken privacy guarantees in computer and cellular-phone usage—all in the name of preventing future "9/11"-style attacks.

Law, Order, and Justice Reconsidered. Notwithstanding the great, and entirely understandable, public outcry to do something about the shockingly high level of crime in the 1970s and 1980s[299]—which saw millions of Americans set upon by violent criminals annually—and the war on terrorism in the wake of the September 11, 2001, attacks, theoretically, there are no shortcuts in democratic society to regulation, prosecution, and conviction. But it would be sophistry to gainsay the genuine concern, both lay and professional, over the contemporary broadening of judicial "supervision" in the realm of criminal justice and the resultant stringent new rules of procedure that have evolved. Given the constant presence of crime—much of which goes unreported[300]—are there alternatives to "easy" or "shortcut" apprehensions, prosecutions, and convictions that either circumvent, dilute, or disregard basic constitutional guarantees? Among them may well be such fundamental ones as deterrents and, arguably most significantly, the certainty of punishment. Because over the last thirty years statistics[301] have indi-

299. *Annual Reports* of the Federal Bureau of Investigation, 1970 and later. Its report for 1979 showed a 9.1 percent overall increase but an 11.0 percent increase in violent crime—the sharpest rise in four years. Violent crimes reported in 1988 increased 5.5 percent from 1987 to a new high, with murder rising 2.9 percent to 20,675. The District of Columbia led the nation in rate of murders and nonnegligent homicides; Detroit was second; Atlanta third; Los Angeles fourth (*Washington Post,* August 7, 1989, p. A12, quoting from the 1988 FBI *Uniform Crime Report,* signed by FBI Director William S. Sessions).

300. See the Bureau of Justice Statistics' annual National Crime Victimization Survey. In 2001 a total of 5,744,000 Americans reported being victims of violent crimes, down from 6,323,000 in 2000. The decline resulted primarily from the lower number of assaults reported. (Assaults are the most frequent form of violent crime perpetrated in the United States.) Only approximately half of the violent crimes reported in the survey were reported to police ("Rate of Violent Crimes Falls to Lowest Level Since '73," *Washington Post,* September 9, 2002, p. A18).

301. See James Q. Wilson's estimate of 87 percent in his *Thinking About Crime* (New York: Random House, 1985); among others, the President's Crime Commission's conclusion that 85 percent of those arrested for crimes more serious than a traffic offense had been arrested before, and that the average man who had been arrested once would be arrested seven more times (*New York Times Magazine,* May 11, 1969, p. 136). According to then–Chief Justice Burger, 65 percent of the two hundred thousand persons serving prison sentences in 1970 would be reconvicted (*Philadelphia Evening Bulletin,* February 23, 1970). In 1970 ex–Attorney General Ramsey Clark reported that 87 percent of the major

cated that between 65 and 92 percent of those booked on criminal charges were recidivists ("repeaters"), it seemed entirely reasonable to ask whether our courts had not been "too soft" on them and, instead, thus might well have been more severe in the type and length of sentences meted out to recidivists. The public has the right to be protected from habitual criminality; and perhaps longer, less readily commutable, and less easily parolable sentences[302] were in order. It seemed that trial judges and parole officers were often guilty of the kind of leniency in criminal cases involving "repeaters" that may be appropriate only for an initial offense; that the criminal was not infrequently regarded as the victim of society rather than society as the victim of the criminal; that, in the view of many onlookers, "there is more concern with the criminal than with the victim."[303] But there is another aspect to that suggestion.

Because "bigger and better" prison sentences will not solve the problem of crime, a plea for toughness in sentencing must join one for more effective efforts in prison rehabilitation; for more modern institutional facilities; and for more appropriately trained professional personnel. Revelations in 1969 and 1970 of conditions in prisons, styled "universities of crime" by President Nixon, gave shocking proof of the state of America's prisons—of which six that were still in

---

crimes that occurred in the United States were committed by youths who were previously convicted of an earlier offense (speech at Temple University, April 1970). The FBI's *Uniform Crime Report* of 1967 reported that of seventeen thousand randomly selected prisoners released in 1963, a total of 92 percent had been rearrested by 1967 (p. 28). According to the same source, almost 90 percent of those who were arrested for major crimes during 1967 had been arrested previously; 70 percent had been convicted; and 50 percent had served jail sentences of over ninety days (p. 23). "The public notion and the police idea of revolving door crime is thus borne out," reported Marvin E. Wolfgang, head of the Center for Studies in Criminology and Criminal Law at the University of Pennsylvania, in releasing a 1969 pilot study of 9,978 boys born in 1945. Six percent of those boys committed 5,305 crimes, nearly 9 apiece (release to the press, September 28, 1969). Of 14,214 adults arrested for major crimes in 1971, 69 percent had been arrested before and averaged 5.8 arrests each (*Philadelphia Inquirer,* April 1, 1972, p. 7). See Charles E. Silberman, *Criminal Violence, Criminal Justice* (New York: Random House, 1978; Vintage Books, 1980). The Bureau of Judicial Statistics reported a 75 percent recidivist rate for state prisoners in early 1985 (*New York Times,* March 4, 1985, p. A4). A 1989 federal study of inmates in eleven states found that 65 percent of those who were released from state prisons were rearrested within three years (Bureau of Judicial Statistics).

302. For a useful compendium on diverse criminal sentencing in the 1970s, see the special issue of 60 *Judicature* 5 (December 1976), entitled "Criminal Sentencing: A Game of Chance." And see 63 *Judicature* 4 (October 1979) for some fascinating, thought-provoking comparative data on the utilization of fines in lieu of imprisonment in sentencing in England and Wales.

303. As if to counter that "concern," in 1984 Congress enacted the Federal Victims of Crime Act (P.L. 98-473, Title II, Ch. 14), which established a Crime Victim Fund in the Department of the Treasury to be supported by fines levied in connection with federal criminal cases.

use in 1971 were built in the eighteenth century, and four prior to George Washington's inauguration.[304] In the last three decades, at least eight presidential commissions, dozens of legislative reports, and more than a thousand books and articles have pleaded for prison reform. Although we have witnessed some bona fide groping for such reform,[305] coordination and improvement of federal, state, and local systems is still vital. Of course, there is a limit to the type of rehabilitation that a prison can provide, but much more can be done than is done at present.

Some states, for example, which had experimented with mandatory minimum prison sentences in an effort to deter crime, have eliminated them for certain offenses. In 2000, and by 61 percent of the vote, California voters passed Proposition 36 that requires treatment rather than incarceration for nonviolent drug offenders. Most of these drug users eventually are placed on probation. Across the United States, almost 4 million people were on probation as of 2002, 2.8 percent more than in 2000. "The collection of reforms, from drug courts to treatment in lieu of incarceration to sentence reforms like getting rid of mandatory minimums and expanding community correction options, have the effect of redirecting people from prison to probation," noted Nick Turner, director of national programs for the Vera Institute of Justice, a nonprofit research group that partners with governments in addressing criminal justice matters.[306] As of 2002, the total numbers of Americans who were incarcerated (1.3 million) or on probation (4 million) indicate that "we've come to rely on the criminal justice system as a way of responding to social problems in a way that's unprecedented," observed Marc Mauer, assistant director of the Sentencing Project, a group that promotes alternatives to incarceration.[307]

Whether or not these various approaches might help us come to grips with important aspects of the problem and assuage the very real and justifiable[308] fears

---

304. *New York Times,* January 7, 1971, sec. 1, p. 1. See also "U.S. Prisons: Schools for Crime," *Time,* January 18, 1971, p. 48; and U.S. Senator William L. Armstrong's legislative policy paper, "Bursting at the Beams: America's Overcrowded Prisons," April 19, 1989.

305. E.g., the imaginative federal prison complex in Butner, North Carolina, which opened in mid-1976, designed and organized to try a new tack in penology. Another was the ultramodern federal minimum security prison at Eglin Air Force Base in Florida. "The best and most advanced prison ever built" was opened in 1982 in Oak Park Heights, Minnesota. The four-hundred-bed facility has a large gym, chapel, educational complex, and competent security control center. Each cell is a private room with a solid door, stainless-steel toilet, sink, mirror, desk, shelves, and a thickly mattressed bed.

306. Associated Press, "Record Number Under Eyes of Law," *Charlottesville Daily Progress,* August 26, 2002, p. A1.

307. Ibid.

308. From the 1960s to the early 1990s, robberies, forcible rapes, aggravated assaults, and murders increased sharply, as did property crimes such as burglary. As of the mid-1990s, the crime rate declined somewhat (down in 1997 for the sixth year in a row, with violent crimes showing the biggest decline since 1961), providing at least some encour-

of the lay and professional public—or whether such statutes as the Organized Crime Control Act of 1970, with its drastic provisions, the Violent Crime Control and Law Enforcement Act of 1994, or the controversial "three strikes and you're out" laws[309] have some answers—when it comes to the fundamental standards of due process of law under our Constitution, there should be no compromises, no shortcuts. "The interest of [the government]," to quote again Justice Brennan, ". . . is not that it shall win a case, but that justice shall be done."[310] There should be no reason whatsoever why, in our democratic society, well-trained, professional agents of the law cannot apprehend and convict alleged criminals without, in the process, becoming criminals themselves. As Arnold S. Trebach put it so well in his book *The Rationing of Justice*, the argument against greater protection for the rights of the accused "reduces itself to an argument *for* violation of the law in order to enforce it. It is a crime to violate the rights of *any* person," whether he be a criminal or a saint. Under our system, in the words of Chief Justice Warren to *New York Times* correspondent Anthony Lewis in 1969, the prosecutor "is not paid to convict people. He is there to protect the rights of the people in our community and to see that when there is a violation of the law, it is vindicated by trial and prosecution under fair judicial standards."[311] A poignant Warren trademark thus was to interrupt a learned counsel's argument citing precedent and book with the simple, almost naive-sounding quaere: "Yes, but was it fair?" Deeply concerned with social justice, that remarkable, if hardly uncontroversial, public servant once mused: "You sit there, and you see the whole gamut of human nature. Even if the case being argued involves only a little fellow and $50, it involves justice. That's what is important."[312]

---

agement to crime-fighting officials—although the rate of property crimes still stood at twelve million offenses in 1996. Experts attributed the decrease in violent crime throughout the 1990s to a healthy economy and tougher sentencing laws. "When people have jobs and poor neighborhoods improve, crime goes down," commented Ralph Myers, a criminologist at Stanford University ("Rate of Violent Crimes Falls to Lowest Level Since '73," op. cit.). Still, in 1993 nearly two thousand people were murdered in New York City alone, compared with just over three thousand in Northern Ireland during the entire quarter century since civil order broke down there in 1969. And 2001 saw an increase in the rate of murders in the United States of 3.1 percent ("Rate of Violent Crimes Falls to Lowest Level Since '73, ibid.).

309. See *Riggs v. California,* 67 LW 3456 (1999), in which the Court, with only Justice Breyer in dissent, declined to hear a shoplifter's "three-strikes" appeal. His third criminal violation, the theft of a bottle of vitamins from a supermarket, had triggered a twenty-five-year prison sentence. The high court agreed to take two other "three-strikes" appeals for its 2002–3 term (*Lockyer v. Andrade* and *Ewing v. California*). In both instances, it upheld them, 5:4 and 5:4 (538 U.S. ___ [2003]).

310. *Jencks v. United States,* 353 U.S. 657 (1957) at 668.

311. "A Talk with Warren on Crime, the Court, the Country," *New York Times Magazine,* October 19, 1969, p. 126.

312. From *Time*'s obituary essay, July 22, 1974, p. 66.

As he did so frequently, Justice Brandeis went to the heart of the matter in his dissent in the *Olmstead* case in 1928:

Decency, security, and liberty alike demand that government officials shall be subjected to the same rules of conduct that are commands to the citizen. In a government of laws, existence of the government will be imperilled if it fails to observe the law scrupulously. Our government is the potent, the omnipresent teacher. For good or for ill, it teaches the whole people by example. Crime is contagious. If the government becomes a lawbreaker, it breeds contempt for law; it invites every man to become a law unto himself; it invites anarchy. To declare that in the administration of the criminal law the end justifies the means—to declare that the government may commit crimes in order to secure the conviction of a private criminal—would bring terrible retribution. Against that pernicious doctrine this court should resolutely set its face.[313]

As the highest tribunal in the land, the Supreme Court should set its face "against that pernicious doctrine." Still, "courts should not blindly reach out, and find merit in a constitutional claim where none exists."[314] And the Supreme Court of the United States is obliged ever to be alive to the admonition by one of its most thoughtful and literate members, Justice Robert H. Jackson, that it must not en route "convert the constitutional Bill of Rights into a suicide pact."[315] Finding the balance between Brandeis's and Jackson's equally wise dicta will surely test the Court as it faces the inevitable litigation arising from new law enforcement methods of fighting global terrorism in the twenty-first century.

313. *Olmstead v. United States*, 277 U.S. 438 (1928) at 485. Chief Justice Warren would echo these haunting thoughts well in his opinion for the Court in *Spano v. New York*, 360 U.S. 315, three decades later: "The police must obey the law while enforcing the law; . . . in the end life and liberty can be as much endangered from illegal methods used to convict those thought to be criminals as from the actual criminals themselves" (at 320).

314. Dissenting opinion by Justice Matthew J. Jasen of the New York Court of Appeals in *People v. Rogers*, 48 N.Y.2d 167 (1979).

315. Dissenting opinion, *Terminiello v. Chicago*, 337 U.S. 1 (1949) at 37. See *infra* chapter 5 for a fuller discussion of that statement. For an echo see Chief Justice Burger's 1981 majority opinion in *Haig v. Agee*, 453 U.S. 280.

5

The Precious Freedom of Expression

If we Americans have, and practice, "ambivalence"[1] as our primary ideology, the realm of the precious freedom of expression is assuredly a case in point. The commonplace expression "It's a free country, isn't it—so I can darn well say what I please!" is in fact sincere, for its underlying philosophy is ingrained in the body politic's notion of what democratic America means. But its paradox is that throughout history we so often permit, wink at, even encourage, its violation in practice. Thus we have been quite willing to curb the "dangerous," the "seditious," the "subversive," the "prurient," the "obscene," the "libelous," and a host of other presumably undesirable modes and manners of expression that—at a particular time and place—seemed to justify repression. Yet, unless one accepts the absolutist approach advocated so consistently by Justice Black and his supporters (an approach that nonetheless still necessitates an answer to the basic question of just what "expression" *is*), the need to draw some line is primary, for, as Black observed in a famous 1941 dissenting opinion: "Freedom to speak and write about public questions is as important to the life of our government as is the heart of the human body. In fact, this privilege is the heart of our government! If that heart be weakened, the result is debilitation; if it be stilled, the result is death."[2] Justice Brandeis, whose last two years of service on the bench of the highest court coincided with Black's first two, tried to provide a memorable guideline when, in a concurring opinion joined by his colleague Holmes, he defended the "chance-taking" aspects of freedom of expression in ringing terms:

1. This was cogently suggested by Professor Robert G. McCloskey of Harvard University in "The American Ideology," in Marian D. Irish, ed., *Continuing Crisis in American Politics* (Englewood Cliffs, N.J.: Prentice-Hall, 1963).
2. *Milk Wagon Drivers Union v. Meadowmoor Dairies,* 312 U.S. 287 at 301–2.

[Those who won our independence] believed that freedom to think as you will and to speak as you think are means indispensable to the discovery and spread of political truth; that without free speech and assembly, discussion would be futile; that with them, discussion affords ordinarily adequate protection against the dissemination of noxious doctrine; that the greatest menace to freedom is an inert people, that public discussion is a political duty; and that this should be a fundamental principle of the American government.[3]

JUDICIAL LINE FORMULAE

The difficulty of any attempt to establish viable standards in the realm of freedom of expression is apparent. Yet, as five key example areas to be discussed below will indicate, attempts at judicial tests, doctrines, or formulae have been of lasting concern to the Court. Much depends on the definition of terms which determine a particular judicial decision. But—in addition to the self-evident one of "balancing" competing interests—we can isolate at least two, perhaps three, major judicial "tests," all of them post–World War I phenomena.

The "Clear and Present Danger" Test

Certainly the best known is the "clear and present danger" test. Credit for its authorship has generally been given to Justice Holmes, actively supported by Justice Brandeis, although there are some observers who would grant Judge Learned Hand of the U.S. Court of Appeals an important assist in the birth of the doctrine, if not with its central idea. It was first used in 1919 in the *Schenck* case.

Schenck v. United States.[4] In 1917 Charles T. Schenck, general secretary of the Socialist Party, and some of his associates sent out some fifteen thousand leaflets to potential and actual draftees under the Conscription Act, urging the young men—in impassioned language—to resist the draft. The leaflets' text intimated that conscription was despotism in its worst form and a "monstrous wrong against humanity, in the interest of Wall Street's chosen few." It urged them not to "submit to intimidation . . . from cunning politicians and a mercenary capitalist press" and referred to the Constitution as an "infamous conspiracy."

Under the Espionage Act of 1917, which had specifically proscribed the kind of activities in which Schenck and his colleagues had engaged, the federal government indicted them on three counts: (1) conspiracy to cause insubordination in the armed forces of the United States, and to obstruct the recruiting and

3. *Whitney v. California,* 274 U.S. 357 (1927) at 375.
4. 249 U.S. 47 (1919).

enlisting services; (2) conspiracy to use the mails for the transmission of matter declared to be nonmailable under the Espionage Act; and (3) the unlawful use of the mails for the transmission of the matter under (2). Schenck and his codefendants were convicted in a federal trial court over their objections that the pertinent provisions of the Espionage Act constituted a violation of the freedom of speech and press guaranteed by the First Amendment. Unanimously rejecting the petitioners' contentions, the Supreme Court, speaking through Justice Holmes, enunciated its new clear and present danger doctrine. As the then seventy-eight-year-old jurist explained in a memorable passage:

> We admit that in many places and in *ordinary times* the defendants in saying all that was said in the circular would have been within their constitutional rights. *But the character of every act depends upon the circumstances in which it is done.* . . . The most stringent protection of free speech would not protect a man in *falsely* shouting fire in a theatre and causing a panic. It does not even protect a man from an injunction against uttering words that have all the effects of force. . . . *The question in every case is whether the words used are used in such circumstances and are of such a nature as to create a clear and present danger that they will bring about the substantive evils that Congress has a right to prevent.* When a nation is at war many things that might be said in time of peace are such a hindrance to its effort that their utterance will not be endured so long as men fight and that no Court could regard them as being protected by any constitutional right.[5]

The doctrine was designed to draw a sensible and usable line between the rights of the individual and those of society at the point where the former's actions or activities tended to create a danger to organized society so "clear and present" that government, the servant of the people—here the representative legislative branch by way of a wartime emergency statute—had a right to attempt to prevent the individual's actions or activities in *advance*. Schenck and his associates deemed such a statute to be an unconstitutional invasion of their First Amendment rights. But the Court—here handing down its *first* ruling on a claim that an act of Congress violated freedom of expression per se—resorted to its new doctrine and concurred with the government that the exigencies of wartime provided sufficient justification for its passage; that, indeed, any government worthy of the name would protect itself against the danger "clear and present" of interference with the so basic element of conscription for military service. It would be difficult to quarrel with that contention. And just one Opinion Day

---

5. Ibid. at 52; italics supplied. For a book-length treatment of Schenck, see Jeremy Cohen, *Congress Shall Make No Law: Oliver Wendell Holmes, the First Amendment, and Judicial Decision-Making* (Ames: Iowa State University Press, 1989). He concludes, somewhat puzzlingly, that Holmes did not base his *Schenck* opinion on the First Amendment.

after *Schenck,* Holmes again was the author of two unanimous opinions for the Court upholding the act of 1917 anew, in which he again invoked the "clear and present danger" test, but without elaborating. One of the cases involved a pro-German newspaperman,[6] the other the famous Socialist leader Eugene V. Debs.[7] Not entirely happy with the nomenclature, Brandeis—as would Jackson in the *Dennis* case in 1951[8]—preferred to categorize the doctrine as a "rule of reason,"[9] which, of course, it has to be in order to be viable. As he saw the test, correctly applied it would preserve the right of free speech both from "suppression by tyrannous, well-meaning majorities, and from abuse by irresponsible, fanatical minorities."

Abrams v. United States.[10] As if to demonstrate almost immediately the difficulties inherent in the "clear and present danger" formula, its two leading champions found themselves in the minority in the celebrated *Abrams* case barely six months after the *Schenck* decision. This time the Sedition Act of 1918, which went considerably beyond its predecessor, the Espionage Act of 1917, was at issue. It made punishable what two subsequent observers justly called "speech that in World War II would have been deemed mere political comment."[11] It thus rendered punitive any "disloyal, profane, scurrilous, or abusive language about the form of government, the Constitution, soldiers and sailors, flag or uniform of the armed forces," and it also made unlawful any "word or act [favoring] the cause of the German Empire . . . or [opposing] the cause of the United States." Under the statute, Jacob Abrams, a twenty-nine-year-old self-styled "anarchist-Socialist," and four young associates (all aliens) were apprehended for distributing certain English- and Yiddish-language leaflets from rooftops on New York City's Lower East Side late in August 1918. These leaflets—headed "AWAKE! AWAKE, YOU WORKERS OF THE WORLD! REVOLUTIONISTS"—urged the "workers of the world" to resist the Allied and American military intervention against the Bolsheviks in Russia's Murmansk and Vladivostok areas during the summer of

6. *Frohwerk v. United States,* 249 U.S. 204 (1919). Frohwerk had inserted several articles in a Missouri German-language newspaper, challenging the purposes of the war as well as the merits and constitutionality of the draft.

7. *Debs v. United States,* 249 U.S. 211 (1919). Debs was charged with an attempt to cause insubordination in the army and to obstruct recruiting.

8. See Jackson's concurring opinion, discussed *infra* this chapter.

9. See his dissenting opinion in *Schaefer v. United States,* 251 U.S. 466 (1920): "If the words were of such a nature and were used under such circumstances that men, judging in calmness, could not reasonably say that they created a clear and present danger that they would bring about the evil that Congress sought and had a right to prevent, then it is the duty of the trial judge to withdraw the case from the consideration of the jury; if he fails to do so, it is the duty of the appellate court to correct the error" (at 483).

10. 250 U.S. 616 (1919).

11. Alpheus T. Mason and William M. Beaney, *American Constitutional Law,* 4th ed. (Englewood Cliffs, N.J.: Prentice-Hall, 1968), p. 495.

1918. They bitterly denounced President Woodrow Wilson for his decision to intervene and exhorted "the workers of the world" to a general strike in order to prevent future shipment of munitions and other war materials to the anti-Soviet forces. The English-language leaflet closed with the following observation: "P.S. It is absurd to call us pro-German. We hate and despise German militarism more than do your hypocritical tyrants. We have more reasons for denouncing German militarism than has the coward in the White House."[12]

Four of the five defendants were found guilty in the U.S. District Court for the Southern District of New York; the fifth was acquitted because of insufficient evidence. The judge[13] sentenced the three men, including Abrams, to the maximum of twenty years' imprisonment in a federal penitentiary and a $4,000 fine each; the lone woman, four-foot, nine-inch Mollie Steimer, received fifteen years and a $500 fine. (Four years later President Harding commuted their sentences on the condition that they all embark at once for their native Russia, which they did.) When their appeal reached the Supreme Court, Justice John H. Clarke, in a 7:2 opinion, agreed that the defendants had intended to "urge, incite, and advocate" curtailment of production deemed necessary to the conduct of the war effort, a crime under the Sedition Act and its predecessor statute. Clarke granted that the "primary purpose and intent" of the petitioners "was quite obviously to aid the cause of the Russian Revolution"—which was not forbidden per se under either of the statutes involved. But, he ruled,

> the plan of action which they adopted necessarily involved, before it could be realized, defeat of the war program of the United States, for the obvious effect of this appeal, if it should become effective, as they hoped it might, would be to persuade persons . . . not to aid government loans and not to work in ammunition factories.[14]

The question that arises at once, of course, is whether the advocacy of a general strike constituted the kind of direct threat to the war effort that the laws under which they were indicted and sentenced envisaged. A plausible case could certainly be made, as indeed it was made by Zechariah Chafee, that "interference with the war was at the most an incidental consequence of the strikes [they clamored for], entirely subordinate to the longed-for consequences of all this agitation, withdrawal from Russia," and should certainly *not* be made the main basis for punishments restricting open discussion.[15]

---

12. As quoted by Zechariah Chafee Jr. in his classic *Freedom of Speech in the United States* (Cambridge, Mass.: Harvard University Press, 1954), p. 110. See also Richard Polenberg, *Fighting Faiths: The* Abrams *Case* (New York: Viking, 1988).

13. Visiting Trial Judge Henry DeLamar Clayton of Alabama (as a member of Congress he was the author of the Clayton Anti-Trust Act of 1914). The other two convicted men were Hyman Lachowsky and Samuel Lipman.

14. *Abrams v. United States,* 250 U.S. 616 (1919) at 621.

15. *Freedom of Speech in the United States,* op. cit., p. 134.

And while the majority of seven saw a clear and present danger, the doctrine's authors *dissented* in an opinion written by Justice Holmes. With Brandeis concurring, Holmes penned the best that he (or anyone else, one may add) could say on the matter, to which the following impassioned excerpt testifies:

[W]hen men have realized that time has upset many fighting faiths, they may come to believe even more than they believe the very foundations of their own conduct that the ultimate good desired is better reached by *free trade in ideas*—that the best of truth is the power of the thought to get itself accepted in the competition of the market, and that *truth is the only ground* upon which their wishes can be safely carried out. That at any rate is the theory of our Constitution. *It is an experiment, as all life is an experiment.* Every year if not every day we have to wager our salvation upon some prophecy based upon imperfect knowledge. While that experiment is part of our system I think that we should be *eternally vigilant against attempts to check the expression of opinions that we loathe and believe to be fraught with death,*

—and here, of course, he draws the line—*"unless they so imminently threaten immediate interference with the lawful and pressing purposes of the law that an immediate check is required to save the country."*[16] Holmes and Brandeis saw no such interference in what Holmes called the "surreptitious publishing of a silly leaflet" by an unknown man. Assuredly, noted Holmes, this did in no sense constitute "a present danger of immediate evil," and he warned his fellow countrymen and their legislators that "[o]nly the emergency that makes it immediately dangerous to leave the correction of evil counsels to time warrants making any exception to the sweeping command, 'Congress shall make no law abridging freedom of speech.'"[17] Holmes was speaking not of *acts,* but of *"expressions of opinions and exhortations,* which were all that were uttered here." He concluded that beyond doubt they "were deprived of their rights under the Constitution of the United States."[18]

16. *Abrams v. United States,* op. cit., at 630; italics supplied. Justice Frankfurter wrote of those deeply moving (and provocative) words: "It is not reckless prophecy to assume that his famous dissenting opinion in the *Abrams* case will live so long as English prose retains its power to move" (*Justice Holmes and the Supreme Court* [Cambridge, Mass.: Harvard University Press, 1938], pp. 54–55). And Max Lerner commented that Holmes's language "has economy, grace, finality, and is the greatest utterance on intellectual freedom by an American, ranking in the English language with Milton and Mill" (*The Mind and Faith of Justice Holmes* [Boston: Little, Brown, 1943], p. 50).

17. *Abrams v. United States,* op. cit., at 630–31.

18. Ibid. at 631; italics supplied.

The "Bad Tendency Test"

If the *Abrams* majority did not theoretically modify the "clear and present danger" doctrine, it assuredly sidetracked it for all intents and purposes. The *official* modification came six years later in the *Gitlow* case.

Gitlow v. New York.[19] The facts and circumstances surrounding this famous decision have been amply outlined and discussed earlier.[20] However, we must examine here the Supreme Court majority's holding, over the dissenting opinion by Justice Holmes, in which once again Justice Brandeis concurred, that "certain writings" of Benjamin Gitlow constituted a *"bad tendency"* to "corrupt public morals, incite to crime, and disturb the public peace." The majority thus affirmed Gitlow's conviction under New York State's Criminal Anarchy Act of 1902, which prohibited the "advocacy, advising, or teaching the duty, necessity or propriety of overthrowing or overturning organized government [New York's] by force or violence" and the publication or distribution of such materials. Despite the fact that there was no evidence of any effect from the publication of Gitlow's "Left Wing Manifesto," Justice Sanford, speaking for the Court, contended that the "[s]tate cannot reasonably be required to measure the danger from every such utterance in the nice balance of a jeweler's scale"[21] and ruled that because a

> single revolutionary spark may kindle a fire that, smoldering for a time, may burst into a sweeping and destructive conflagration [the state] may, in the exercise of its judgment, suppress the threatened danger in its incipiency.[22]

Obviously, this was no longer the clear and present danger test. When the state is empowered to suppress a mere *threat* in its very *incipiency,* the line is being drawn on the basis of a bad tendency rather than on that of a clear and present danger. There was hardly anything very "clear" or "present" in Gitlow's activities, confined as they were to the written exhortations of a rather pathetic individual. As Professor Chafee, America's leading expert on freedom of expression during the second quarter of the twentieth century, commented: "Any agitator who read these thirty-four pages to a mob would not stir them to violence, except possibly against himself. This Manifesto would disperse them faster than the Riot Act."[23]

In asking itself whether Gitlow's activities had created or constituted a *"bad tendency" to bring about a danger* (a phrase from the *Schaefer*[24] decision five years earlier), the majority shifted the balance between the individual and the state toward the latter. Thundered Holmes:

19. 268 U.S. 652 (1925).
20. See *supra* chapter 3, on "incorporation."
21. *Gitlow v. New York,* op. cit., at 669.
22. Ibid.
23. *Freedom of Speech in the United States,* op. cit., p. 319.
24. *Schaefer v. United States,* 251 U.S. 466 (1920).

If what I think the correct test is applied it is manifest that there was no present danger of an attempt to overthrow the government by force. . . . It is said that this manifesto was more than a theory, that it was an incitement. *Every idea is an incitement.* It offers itself for belief and if believed it is acted on unless some other belief outweighs it or some failure of energy stifles the movement at its birth. The only difference between the expression of an opinion and an incitement in the narrower sense is the speaker's enthusiasm for the result. *Eloquence may set fire to reason.*[25]

Holmes pointed out, as he had in similar circumstances in his *Abrams* dissent, that the charges against the defendant alleged *publication,* and nothing more. And, calling a democratic spade a democratic spade, he commented:

If in the long run the beliefs expressed in proletarian dictatorship are destined to be accepted by the dominant forces of the community, the only meaning of free speech is that they should be given their chance and have their way.[26]

He was naturally confident, as was Justice Douglas in his dissenting opinion in the *Dennis* case[27] a quarter of a century *later,* that "the American people want none of Communism [whose] doctrine is exposed in all its ugliness . . . its wares unsold."[28] In a very real sense the issue for both Holmes and Douglas came down to a matter of faith in the ability of the American people to choose their destiny in the absence of demonstrable, overt, illegal *actions* or conduct.

Expanding Clear and Present Danger

Holmes and Brandeis recognized that some amplification of their clear and present danger test was needed to prevent its demotion to the bad tendency level. Their opportunity came some two years following the *Gitlow* decision in *Whitney v. California.*[29]

Whitney v. California. Miss Charlotte Anita Whitney, a niece of one of the pillars of laissez-faire American capitalism, Justice Stephen J. Field, was one of the

25. *Gitlow v. New York,* op. cit., at 673; italics supplied.
26. Ibid. In 1968 the Court would refuse to *review,* with Justice Douglas in a long dissenting opinion from that refusal, the conviction under the same statute of Marxist William Epton (*Epton v. New York,* 390 U.S. 29, appeal dismissed). In 1971, it also refused to review another New York case, which in 1969 had been construed below like *Gitlow* and *Epton* (*Samuels v. Mackell,* 401 U.S. 66); ditto a similar California case (*Younger v. Harris,* 401 U.S. 37 [1971]). But it had declared Ohio's criminal syndicalism law unconstitutional in 1969 in the significant *Brandenburg* case, discussed in connection with *Whitney, infra* (*Brandenburg v. Ohio,* 395 U.S. 444).
27. *Dennis v. United States,* 341 U.S. 494 (1951).
28. Ibid. at 588–89.
29. 274 U.S. 357 (1927).

band of disenchanted adventurers who, in 1919, helped to organize the Communist Labor Party of California. Motivated largely by her passionate espousal of the cause of the poor, she readily permitted herself to be elected as a member of the CLPC during its 1919 convention held in Oakland. The Party's constitution was quite clear on its affiliation with both the Communist Labor Party of America and the Communist International of Moscow. Miss Whitney's activities brought her into conflict with California's Criminal Syndicalism Act of 1919. She soon found herself indicted on five counts and subsequently convicted of one: that on November 28, 1919, she "did then and there unlawfully, willfully, wrongfully, deliberately and feloniously organize and assist in organizing, and was, is, and knowingly became a member of an organization, society, group and assemblage of persons organized and assembled to advocate, teach, aid and abet criminal syndicalism."[30]

On appeal, Miss Whitney protested, as she had during her trial, that at no time did she wish her party to engage in any acts of violence or terror, but the intermediate appellate tribunal affirmed her conviction, and the state supreme court refused to review her case, which then went on to the U.S. Supreme Court. At issue was the association between due process of law and First Amendment guarantees, against the basic charge of a criminal conspiracy—an activity that falls outside the protection of free speech. Again Miss Whitney lost. Justice Sanford, here writing the opinion for a unanimous Court that *included* Justices Holmes and Brandeis, agreed that the state of California had an inherent right to guard statutorily against the alleged conspiracy—and neither Holmes nor Brandeis disputed the Court's finding that there was sufficient evidence to point to the existence of such a conspiracy to violate the Criminal Syndicalism Act, that the group had transgressed the bounds of a political party and had in fact become a conspiracy to commit serious crime. However, in a highly significant concurring opinion, joined by Holmes, Brandeis rejected the majority's interpretation of a section of the law that made it a crime not only to advocate or teach or practice criminal syndicalism, or conspire to do so, but also to be in "association with those who proposed to teach it." Here Brandeis and Holmes saw a lurking and grave threat to the concept of clear and present danger as they had conceived of it; thus, with the *Gitlow* "bad tendency" doctrine in mind, the two jurists endeavored not only to resurrect their original clear and present danger concept but to strengthen it. In a ringing admonition (which reportedly so moved the then governor of California, C. C. Young, that he later pardoned Miss Whitney), Brandeis's concurrence—that, in effect, reads like a dissent[31]—attempted to clarify,

---

30. Ibid. at 358.

31. And so it was! *But* it had been written originally for *Ruthenberg v. Michigan*, 273 U.S. 782 (1927), a case mooted by Ruthenberg's death and dismissed that March. Brandeis subsequently seized upon the opportunity of *Whitney* to incorporate the central points of that dissent into what is his concurring opinion for *Whitney* (see Klaus H. Heberle, "From Gitlow to Near . . . ," 34 *Journal of Politics* 468 [1972]).

expand, and liberalize the doctrine by joining to its basic test the requirement of *"imminence"*:

> Fear of serious injury cannot alone justify suppression of free speech and assembly . . . there must be reasonable ground to fear that serious evil will result if free speech is practiced. There must be reasonable ground to believe that *the danger apprehended is imminent.* There must be reasonable ground to believe that the evil to be prevented is a serious one. . . . In order to support a finding of clear and present danger *it must be shown either that immediate serious violence was to be expected or was advocated, or that the past conduct furnished reason to believe that such advocacy was then contemplated.*
>
> Those who won our independence by revolution were not cowards. They did not fear political change. They did not exalt order at the cost of liberty. To courageous, self-reliant men, with confidence in the power of free and fearless reasoning applied through the processes of popular government, *no danger flowing from speech can be deemed clear and present, unless the incidence of the evil apprehended is so imminent that it may befall before there is opportunity for full discussion.* If there be time to expose through discussion the falsehood and fallacies, to avert the evil by the processes of education, the *remedy to be applied is more speech, not enforced silence.*[32]

In his and Holmes's opinion, "such . . . is the command of the Constitution."[33]

Brandenburg v. Ohio. Specific vindication of the Brandeis-Holmes view in their *Whitney* concurrence did not really come until they were long dead. It seemed to do so when a U.S. District Court declared the California Criminal Syndicalism Act unconstitutional in 1968 in *Younger v. Harris*—but the Supreme Court set the verdict aside on technical grounds two years later.[34] The Court, however, did dispose of Ohio's similar statute in the key 1969 *Brandenburg* decision,[35] in which it *specifically* overruled its 1927 *Whitney* holding. Clarence Brandenburg, a Ku Klux Klan leader, was convicted, fined, and sentenced to jail under the law at issue,[36] and challenged the latter on First and Fourteenth Amendment grounds.

32. Ibid. at 377; italics supplied.
33. Ibid.
34. *Younger v. Harris,* 281 F. Supp. 507; and *Younger v. Harris,* 401 U.S. 37 (1971), respectively.
35. *Brandenburg v. Ohio,* 395 U.S. 444 (1969).
36. Brandenburg had invited a television cameraman to a cross-burning ceremony, where he was filmed vowing "revengeance"against the nation's leaders and making slurring and vile remarks about "niggers" and "kikes," for example, that "the nigger should be returned to Africa, the Jew returned to Israel." During the "organizational meeting," some in the group of about twelve hooded Klansmen were seen brandishing firearms.

Pointing to a spate of intervening decisions,[37] the Court's unanimous but unsigned (per curiam) opinion, largely drafted by Justice Brennan,[38] reemphasized the

> principle that the constitutional guarantees of free speech and free press do not permit a State to forbid or proscribe advocacy of the use of force or of law violation *except* where such advocacy is directed to inciting or producing *imminent* lawless action *and is likely to incite or produce such action.*[39]

Mere advocacy is thus no longer punishable on pain of violating Amendments One and Fourteen, *but direct incitement to likely imminent action is.*[40] In effect, *Brandenburg* extended the clear and present danger test by adding the "likely to incite" requirement. That holding governs the Court's posture on the issue today.

Thus, we again see the basic dilemma inherent in the two approaches to freedom of expression in a democratic society. No matter what the language employed, no matter what the rationalization by individuals in specific situations, it comes down to a reading of the Constitution in its historical-evolutionary setting, against what Holmes called "the felt necessities of the time." And underlying the entire problem is, inevitably and necessarily, the faith one has in a free people's willingness and ability to experiment, to take chances, to govern itself in a democratic society.

"Preferred Freedoms" and Beyond. Chapter 2 noted that the Supreme Court in the late 1930s and much of the 1940s—in line with the Brandeis-Holmes philosophy expressed in *Whitney* and other cases—adopted the view that there should be "more exacting judicial scrutiny" of First Amendment freedoms. The Court thus identified a constitutionally protected area of "preferred freedom," based upon the famous footnote by Justice Stone in *United States v. Carolene Products*

---

37. E.g., *Dennis v. United States,* 341 U.S. 494 (1951); *Yates v. United States,* 354 U.S. 298 (1957); *Noto v. United States,* 367 U.S. 290 (1961); and *Bond v. Floyd,* 385 U.S. 116 (1966).

38. See Bernard Schwartz, "Justice Brennan and the *Brandenburg* Decision—A Lawgiver in Action," 79 *Judicature* 1 (July–August 1995), pp. 24–29.

39. *Brandenburg v. Ohio,* op. cit., at 444; italics supplied. Supported by Justice Black in separate concurring opinions, Justice Douglas restated the two liberals' firm faith, namely, that there is "no place in the regime of the First Amendment for any 'clear and present danger' test, whether strict and tight as some would make it, or free-wheeling as the court in Dennis rephrased it" (at 454). Judge Learned Hand's opinion in *Masses Publ. Co. v. Patten,* 244 Fed. 535 (1917), considered but rejected Holmes's future test as "too slippery, too dangerous to free expression." Instead he urged the adoption of a "strict," "hard," "objective" test, focusing on the speaker's words: if the language used was solely that of a direct incitement to illegal action, speech could be proscribed; otherwise it was protected. However, Hand evidently abandoned this approach a few years later and embraced the "clear and present danger" test.

40. For a pertinent later illustration, see *Hess v. Indiana,* 414 U.S. 105 (1973).

Co.,[41] where the future chief justice had called for a special niche for "legislation which restricts the political processes."[42] A concept enthusiastically embraced by Justices Black, Douglas, Murphy, and Rutledge when they served together with Stone from Rutledge's appointment in 1943 to the deaths of Stone, Rutledge, and Murphy, it was to be joined to the "clear and present danger plus imminence" doctrine.

But when Harlan Stone died in 1946, Fred Vinson replaced him as chief justice, foreshadowing trouble for the new "line" established by the civil libertarians. And when Murphy and Rutledge both died in the summer of 1949, their replacements, Justices Clark and Minton, together with the new chief justice and the "holdovers"—Justices Reed, Frankfurter, Jackson, and Burton—constituted a majority that almost at once departed from the philosophy of preferred freedom. "McCarthyism" had cast its long shadow. Indeed, in the landmark *Dennis*[43] internal security case even the clear and present danger doctrine underwent a rather dramatic transformation into what some observers viewed as a "grave and probable" test patterned upon Judge Learned Hand's lower court opinion,[44] on which Chief Justice Vinson leaned very heavily in his *Dennis* majority opinion.[45] Others felt that in fact the Court had adopted as its new freedom of expression doctrine a "possible and remote danger" test.[46] Unquestionably, bad tendency had taken over from clear and present danger. However, soon after Earl Warren became chief justice on Vinson's death in 1953, the Court returned to the clear and present danger test, even restoring its "imminence" appendage. Indeed, some even felt that the new Court adopted a "super-preferred" standard vis-à-vis claims of racial discrimination and due process standards of criminal justice. It did retain the bad tendency test in the national security field for a while longer, but, by the *late* 1950s, in cases such as *Yates v. United States,*[47] the Court, after some wavering and broken-field strategy, returned to the clear and present danger plus imminence test for the national security field also. With the advent of the Burger Court in 1969, Warren Earl Burger having replaced Earl Warren in the center chair, a change of direction could not be ruled out. However, there was no return to the Vinson approach. Indeed, despite some narrowing in the realms of "obscenity" and, arguably, aspects of freedom of the press,[48] freedom of expression was given generous interpretations by the Burger Court, notwithstanding the departures from the Court of its great champions, Justices Black and Douglas, in

41. 304 U.S. 144 (1938).
42. Ibid. at 152. See the extended discussion of *Carolene, supra* chapter 2.
43. 341 U.S. 494 (1951).
44. *Dennis v. United States,* 183 F.2d 201 (1950) at 212.
45. Op. cit., *supra* note 43 at 510ff.
46. Alfred H. Kelly and Winifred A. Harbison, *The American Constitution: Its Origins and Development,* 2d ed. (New York: Norton, 1955), p. 893.
47. 354 U.S. 298 (1957). See the discussion of the case, *infra* this chapter.
48. See the discussion of obscenity, *infra* this chapter.

1971 and 1975, respectively. Thus, a 1978 opinion by the chief justice strongly reaffirmed a tough clear and present standard upon any legislative attempts to bridle freedom of speech.[49] The Burger Court in fact emphasized an additional type of preferred freedom, the so-called suspect categories of race, alienage and national origin, and—although not quite so clearly—sex, which were accorded special judicial protection alongside other fundamental rights regarded as entitled to "close scrutiny" by the courts. If any retrenchment was in evidence, it was in the field of criminal justice, but even there the Court's record was not one-sided.[50] The same philosophy or policy has characterized the Rehnquist Court. On the other hand, it was obvious that none of the Nixon-Ford-Reagan appointees to the high bench[51] would be committed to the *absolutist* reading of freedom of expression brought to the Court by Black and Douglas for almost four decades.

SOME BASIC CONCEPTS

Since we cannot here attempt to cover all, or even most, aspects of "freedom of expression," we shall concentrate on those that illustrate the fundamental problem and are of enduring interest.

A Basic Definition. In its overall context, freedom of expression connotes the broad *freedom to communicate*—a concept that far transcends mere speech. It embraces the prerogative of the free citizen to express himself or herself—verbally, visually, or on paper—without *prior* restraint, and if the expression meets the test of truth, the prerogative necessarily extends to the postutterance period. It is vital to recognize at the outset that freedom of expression extends not only to speech and press but also to areas of *conduct* laced or tinged with expression such as those of press, assembly, petition, association, lawful picketing, and other demonstrative protests. To point to its diversity and range,

49. *Landmark Communications, Inc. v. Virginia,* 435 U.S. 829 (1978). He quoted a passage from Justice Brandeis's concurrence in *Whitney v. California* (op. cit., at 203ff.) that began: "A legislative declaration does not preclude enquiry into the question whether, at the time and under the circumstances, the conditions existed which are essential to validity under the Federal Constitution" (at 843–44).

50. See *supra* chapter 4.

51. In addition to the 1969 Burger-for-Warren switch, the following replacements had taken effect by late 1993: Blackmun for Fortas (1970); Powell and Rehnquist for Black and Harlan (1971); Stevens for Douglas (1975); O'Connor for Stewart (1981); Rehnquist as chief justice for Burger (1986); Scalia for the associate justiceship vacated by Rehnquist's elevation (1986); Kennedy for Powell (1988); Souter for Brennan (1990); Thomas for Marshall (1991); and Ginsburg for White (1993). In 1994 Breyer replaced Blackmun, and, as of 2003, the Rehnquist, Stevens, O'Connor, Scalia, Kennedy, Souter, Thomas, Ginsburg, and Breyer lineup had served together longer than any Supreme Court bench since the early nineteenth century.

freedom of expression now apparently extends also to independent individual or group *spending* by and for a candidate for federal elective office, but *not* in the form of unlimited *contributions;*[52] to purely "commercial speech,"[53] including even the right of professionals to advertise their fees (on a "limited, factual basis");[54] to the right to advertise alcohol content on beer labels and to advertising of liquor prices;[55] to television and radio advertising of commercial

---

52. See the complex six-opinion decision by the Court in 1976, replete with partial dissents and partial concurrences, in which it tested the Federal Election Campaign Act (FECA) of 1974 in *Buckley v. Valeo,* 424 U.S. 1, and the follow-up (7:2) in 1985 in *Federal Election Commission v. National Conservative Political Action Committee,* 470 U.S. 480, as well as the 1986 holding (5:4) that struck down as unconstitutional a regulation that prohibited political expenditures by nonprofit advocacy groups in *Federal Election Commission v. Massachusetts Citizens for Life,* 479 U.S. 238. The central reasoning in these cases was reconfirmed in 2000 in *Nixon v. Shrink Missouri Government PAC,* 528 U.S 377. Yet in 1990 it upheld (6:3) a Michigan restriction on corporate indirect expenditures of funds for public purposes (*Austin v. Michigan Chamber of Commerce,* 494 U.S. 652). Note its 1981 ruling (8:1), striking down a Berkeley, California, law that had limited campaign contributions by committees in referendum campaigns (*Citizens Against Rent Control v. City of Berkeley,* 454 U.S. 290). See also the related 5:4 ruling in *California Medical Association v. Federal Election Commission,* 453 U.S. 182 (1981), and the 1996 declaration of unconstitutionality of the law's (1974 FECA) prohibition of "independent" spending by political parties in congressional races (*Colorado Republican Party v. FEC,* 518 U.S. 604 [7:2]). But in a 5:4 ruling in 2001 the Court upheld strict limits on how much political parties can spend in coordination with their congressional candidates, the Souter-authorized opinion rejecting the argument that the restrictions on "hard money" violated the party's free-speech rights. *FEC v. Colorado Republican Federal Campaign Committee,* 533 U.S. 431. On related issues the Court rejected 7:2 a strong challenge to ballot initiatives (*Buckley v. American Constitutional Law Foundation,* 67 LW 4053 [1999]), and by the same vote struck down California's blanket primary as a violation of freedom of association (*California Democratic Party v. Jones,* 535 U.S. 567 [2000]).

53. *Virginia State Board of Pharmacy v. Virginia Citizens Consumer Council,* 425 U.S. 748 (1976). In 1993 the Court struck down (6:3) a Cincinnati, Ohio, ban on commercial news racks, ruling that the city's interest in nicer-looking and safer sidewalks did not justify the infringement on commercial advertisers' free-speech rights (*Cincinnati v. Discovery Network,* 507 U.S. 410).

54. *Bates v. Arizona State Bar,* 433 U.S. 350 (1977). It was significantly expanded in 1982 in *In re R.M.J.,* 455 U.S. 191, and, again, in *Shapero v. Kentucky Bar Association,* 486 U.S. 466 (1988), as applied to targeted mail solicitation. In 1995, however, *Bates's* basic principle was held 5:4 not to vitiate a Florida bar rule prohibiting personal injury lawyers from sending targeted direct-mail solicitations to victims and their relatives for thirty days following an accident or disaster. *Florida Bar v. Went For It, Inc.,* 515 U.S. 618.

55. *Rubin v. Coors Brewing Co.,* 514 U.S. 476 (1995); and *44 Liquormart, Inc. v. Rhode Island,* 517 U.S. 484 (1996). Both cases were decided 9:0. In the former, the Federal Alcohol Administration Act's prohibition against such labeling was declared unconstitutional, and in the latter Rhode Island's ban on advertising of liquor prices also fell as a violation of the First Amendment. But one year later the Court declined to hear a First Amendment challenge to Baltimore's 1944 ban on tobacco and alcohol billboards (*Anheuser-Busch, Inc. v. Schmoke,* 517 U.S. 1206).

casino gambling;[56] to pharmacies which advertise mixed products that have not been approved by the Food and Drug Administration;[57] to banks and business corporations making contributions or expenditures for the purpose of influencing votes on referendum proposals (even those not materially affecting their assets or property), of expressing their views on public issues, and of promoting their products (even by advertising or inserting them in customer utility bills);[58] to realtors posting "for sale" or "sold" signs in front of a home in a racially tense community and to door-to-door soliciting during reasonable hours;[59] to political messages on yard signs;[60] to persons marching in Nazi uniforms replete with the hated swastika symbol in a community peopled largely by survivors of Nazi concentration camps;[61] and to the right of members of the National Association for the Advancement of Colored People (NAACP) to engage in a political and economic boycott without being liable for damages suffered by targeted businesses.[62] Astonishingly, freedom of expression now even extends to the time-honored practice of dismissal, hiring, promotion, and transferring of most public employees because of their political beliefs, unless, as Justice Stevens explained ultimately, "party affiliation is an appropriate requirement for the effective performance of the public office involved."[63] A 1990 extension of these rulings (5:4) provided that the Constitution now prevents the use of partisan political considerations for hiring, promoting, or transferring public employees, as well as their firing, except for cabinet-level or policy-making posts.[64] The Court's rulings here have voided a "patronage" practice as old as the nation it-

---

56. *Greater New Orleans Broadcasting Association v. U.S.,* 527 U.S. 173 (1999).

57. *Thompson v. Western States Medical Center,* 536 U.S. ___ (2002) .

58. *First National Bank v. Bellotti,* 435 U.S. 765 (1978); and *Consolidated Edison v. Public Service Commission* and *Central Hudson Gas Co. v. Public Service Commission,* 447 U.S. 530 and 557 (1980), respectively.

59. *Linmark Associates v. Willingboro,* 431 U.S. 85 (1977); and *City of Watseka v. Illinois,* 479 U.S. 1048 (1987), respectively.

60. *Ladue v. Gilleo,* 512 U.S. 43 (1994). A local ordinance here had banned all yard signs except ten specified types (including realtors' signs)—an action the 9:0 Court deemed not "content neutral" and thus an unconstitutional abridgment of freedom of expression.

61. *Smith v. Collin,* 436 U.S. 953 (1978), the controversial Skokie, Illinois, case that caused problems of consistency for some of the most devoted exponents of freedom of expression. See Donald A. Downs, *Nazis in Skokie: Community and the First Amendment* (Notre Dame, Ind.: Notre Dame University Press, 1985).

62. *NAACP v. Claybourne Hardware Co.,* 458 U.S. 886 (1982).

63. *Elrod v. Burns,* 427 U.S. 346 (1976); and *Branti v. Finkel,* 445 U.S. 507 (1980). The former decision had confined its application to "below public policy-making levels," but the latter one expunged any such distinction, exempting only posts in which the hiring authority can demonstrate that party affiliation is an appropriate requirement for the effective performance of the public office involved. See also *O'Hare Truck Service, Inc. v. City of Northlake,* 518 U.S. 712 (1996).

64. *Rutan v. Republican Party of Illinois,* 497 U.S. 62.

self! In an arguably related case, a severely fractured ($5\frac{1}{2}$:$3\frac{1}{2}$) Court ruled in 1995 that below grade GS-16 government employees could not be forbidden to accept honoraria for speeches or articles. And in 2002 the high tribunal held 5:4 in a Minnesota case that candidates for judicial office could not be prohibited from announcing their views on disputed or political issues on pain of violating the First Amendment.[65]

Yet since, *pace* Justice Black, none of these freedoms can be absolute, any basic definition must consider the inevitability of limits—limits that recognize the rights of the minority in a majoritarian system without, however, subscribing to a philosophy of the "tyranny of the minority." Thus, the Court has repeatedly pointed out that the First Amendment does *not* "afford the same kind of freedom" to communicate *conduct* as to that which it extends to "pure speech."[66] There is no doubt that picketing, for example, is a vital prerogative of the freedom of expression; however, mass picketing; picketing that applies physical force to those who might wish to exercise their equal rights of freedom of expression by disregarding the picket line; certain kinds of picketing violative of a picketee's property rights or picketing utterly unrelated to a picketee's "operations"; or picketing in derogation of secondary boycott statutes is *not*.[67] Nor is the disregarding of reasonably established buffer zones in front of abortion clinics.[68] Screaming "Fire!" in a crowded theater—to use the famed Holmesian illustration—upon discovery of a blaze is not only "freedom of speech" but a dutiful exercise of citizenship; but if there is no fire, the call is not freedom of expression but license. Nor does freedom of expression extend to the construction of buildings and sleeping in parks near the White House, as the Court held (7:2) in 1984.[69] Nor

---

65. *Republican Party of Minnesota v. Minnesota Board of Judicial Standards*, 536 U.S. ——— .

66. E.g., see Justice Goldberg's opinion for the Court in *Cox v. Louisiana*, 379 U.S. 536 (1965) at 555, and the Court's striking down of a Los Angeles ordinance prohibiting all "First Amendment activities" in the city's main airport terminal (*Board of Airport Commissioners v. Jews for Jesus*, 482 U.S. 569 [1987]).

67. Compare and contrast *Thornhill v. Alabama*, 310 U.S. 88 (1940), with *Giboney v. Empire Storage and Ice Co.*, 336 U.S. 490 (1949); *Amalgamated Food Employees Union v. Logan Valley Inc.*, 391 U.S. 309 (1968), with *Lloyd Corp. Ltd. v. Tanner*, 407 U.S. 551 (1972), *Hudgens v. NLRB*, 424 U.S. 507 (1976); and *Pruneyard Shopping Center v. Robins*, 447 U.S. 74 (1980), *Carey v. Brown*, 447 U.S. 455 (1980), and *National Labor Relations Board v. Retail Store Employees Union*, 447 U.S. 607 (1980), with the last four aforementioned cases. There is patent need for more judicial clarifying of the problems created in picketing, notwithstanding a trio of disparate 1988 holdings: *De Bartolo Corporation v. Florida Gulf Trades Council*, 485 U.S. 568; *Boos v. Barry*, 485 U.S. 312; and *Frisby v. Schultz*, 487 U.S. 474. See also *NOW v. Scheidler*, 510 U.S. 249 (1994).

68. *Madsen v. Women's Health Center*, 512 U.S. 753 (1994); and *Schenck v. Pro-Choice*, 519 U.S. 357 (1997).

69. *Clarke v. Community for Creative Non-Violence*, 468 U.S. 288.

(9:0) is it an infraction of that freedom to require individuals to obtain a permit before conducting large-scale events in a public park.[70] Nor (6:3) to airport money solicitations from travelers by religious and political groups—*but* such groups' "leafleting" *is* (5:4) covered by the First Amendment's guarantees of freedom of speech.[71] So is the privilege of anonymity in people's refusal to sign leaflets or other campaign literature.[72] *Actual, overt* incitement of the overthrow of the government of the United States by force and violence, accompanied by the language of direct and imminent incitement, is not freedom of expression but a violation of Court-upheld legislation proscriptions; yet the theoretical advocacy of such overthrow, on the other hand, has been a judicially recognized protected freedom since 1957.[73] If a written work has "literary, artistic, political or scientific value," it is not proscribable as being "pornographic,"[74] but this safeguard may be vitiated by its publisher's "pandering."[75] A city may engage in an aggressive crackdown on strip clubs and pornography shops despite claims of First Amendment violations.[76] Publicly addressing someone as "damned Fascist" and "Goddamned racketeer" can hardly be considered freedom of speech—in fact, those terms have been judicially held to be "fighting words" that are proscribable if (and it is a big "if") the proscribing statute is carefully and narrowly drawn[77]—

70. *Thomas v. Chicago Park District,* 534 U.S. 316 (2002).

71. *International Society of Hare Krishna Consciousness v. Lee,* 505 U.S. 672 (1992).

72. *McIntyre v. Ohio Elections Commission,* 514 U.S. 334 (1995).

73. See *Yates v. United States,* 354 U.S. 298 (1957), particularly Justice Harlan's opinion for the 6:1 Court.

74. *Jenkins v. Georgia,* 418 U.S. 153 (1974).

75. *A Book Named "John Cleland's Woman of Pleasure" v. Massachusetts,* 383 U.S. 413 (1966).

76. *Amsterdam Videos and Hickerson v. City of New York,* 67 LW 3430 (1999).

77. *Chaplinsky v. New Hampshire,* 315 U.S. 568 (1942)—opinion for the unanimous Court by Justice Frank Murphy, then its leading civil libertarian. The New Hampshire statute had enacted the common-law "fighting words" doctrine: "No person shall address any offensive, derisive or annoying word [directly] to any other person who is lawfully in any street or other public place, nor call him by any offensive or derisive name." The state court had interpreted it to ban "words likely to cause an average addressee to fight," and "face to face words" likely to produce an immediate violent breach of the peace by the addressee. Although the "fighting words" test has continued to be relied upon, it has presented major problems when applied to the "profane," the "obscene," and the "libelous," as noted *infra.* By and large the Court's posture has been *one of focusing on* the specific "circumstances" in which the contested speech is uttered and, increasingly, on proof that the "fighting words" were intentionally, directly, and specifically addressed to an *identifiable individual rather than to a group.* See, e.g., its 5:2 distinction of *Chaplinsky* in the 1972 Georgia "bad language" case of *Gooding v. Wilson,* 405 U.S. 418, which disallowed (5:2) a Georgia statute as "on its face" unconstitutionally vague and overbroad. The law provided that any person "who shall without provocation use to or of [another person] opprobrious words or abusive language tending to cause a breach of the peace" was guilty of a misdemeanor. On the other hand, the same Court *declined* (8:1) to review a lower court decision that there is no "constitutional privilege to shout four-letter words on a pub-

but calling a duly convicted thief "thief" or "crook" presumably can be considered freedom of speech—at least until the epithet's target has paid his debt to society. Nor is there a constitutionally protected right to libel or slander, but what constitutes libel or slander, and what the exercise of First Amendment rights, has proved to be a veritable public-law snake pit. Broadly speaking, at least of this writing (mid-2003), the law seems to be that a public official or even a public "figure" or public "person" is not entitled to damages unless he or she can prove "actual malice," that is, proof that the defamatory statement was made "with knowledge that it was false or with reckless disregard of whether it was false or not"—which, rather than simple truth or falsehood, thus becomes the test.[78] Furthermore, only those false statements made with a "high degree of awareness of their probative falsity" may be the subject of either civil or criminal sanction[79]—which, however, does not mean that in *no* circumstances will a public official be judicially found to have been libeled.[80] Although the test is naturally less stringent in the instance of *private* or *quasi-private persons*,[81] who may win cases by proving carelessness, irresponsibility, or a similar "lapse," the

lic street" in a case in which a policeman arrested a man for disorderly conduct on the grounds that he had used obscene language (*Von Schleichter v. United States,* 409 U.S. 1063). For proof that the Court continues to find the *Chaplinsky* test extremely vexatious in application see Justice Powell's diverse, pained opinions in the 1972 "foul language trilogy" cases of *Rosenfeld v. New Jersey, Lewis v. New Orleans,* and *Brown v. Oklahoma,* reported as 408 U.S. 901, 913, and 914, respectively—all propounding definitional "overbreadth" and/or "vagueness" problems in the free-speech realm.

78. *The New York Times v. Sullivan,* 376 U.S. 254 (1964). This important test, since referred to as the "New York Times Rule," was initially expanded in *Ocala Star Banner v. Damron,* 401 U.S. 295 (1971), but then narrowed in *Time, Inc. v. Firestone,* 424 U.S. 448, a narrowing that was patently continued in two 8:1 holdings in 1979, in which the Court made clear that it would no longer be very generous in protective characterizations of "public"; that, to qualify for the "public" label, there would have to be proof that an individual made a deliberate, affirmative injection effort for the public limelight or be a policymaker. In other words, it would now no longer be neither so difficult to recover for an alleged libel nor so easy to hide under the "public" characterization (*Hutchinson v. Proxmire,* 443 U.S. 111; and *Wolston v. Reader's Digest Association,* 443 U.S. 157). See also the implications of the interesting verdicts against novelist Gwen Davis and her publisher, Doubleday, one year later (*Mitchell v. Bindrin* and *Doubleday v. Bindrin,* 444 U.S. 984, certiorari denied). An early 1981 Court refusal to review appeared designed to continue the narrowing of "public" characterization (*London Times-Mirror v. Arctic Co.,* 449 U.S. 1102). But cf. the 1988 ruling (8:0) in *Hustler v. Falwell,* 485 U.S. 46. See Rodney A. Smolla, *Jerry Falwell v. Larry Flynt: The First Amendment on Trial* (New York: St. Martin's, 1989).

79. *Garrison v. Louisiana,* 379 U.S. 64 (1964).

80. E.g., *Ginzburg v. Goldwater,* 396 U.S. 1049 (1970); *Indianapolis Newspapers, Inc. v. Fields,* 400 U.S. 930 (1970); and *Cape Public Co. v. Adams,* 434 U.S. 943 (1977).

81. See *Curtis Publishing Co. v. Butts,* 338 U.S. 130 (1967); *Matus v. Triangle Publications,* 408 U.S. 930 (1972); and *Patrick v. Field Research Corp.,* 414 U.S. 933 (1973). See also the cases noted *supra.*

line remains ambiguous.[82] Thus, while in 1971 the Court applied its free-press doctrine to news "about private individuals involved in matters of public or general interest,"[83] rendering collection of damages extremely difficult, it distinguished that decision three years later when it held (5:4) that an ordinary citizen "elevated to sudden prominence by news events" can sue any newspaper or radio or television station that circulated a false and defamatory account of his role in those events; that a publisher or broadcaster of *defamatory falsehoods* about a *private* individual's involvement in a public issue may not assert the 1964 "*New York Times* Rule" as protection against liability for actual damages, at least where "the substance of the defamatory statement makes substantial danger to reputation apparent."[84] Nonetheless, by 1974 the Court had drawn a *seemingly* sharp distinction between an ordinary citizen libeled by a news account and "public officials and public figures [who] have voluntarily exposed themselves to incurring risk or injury from defamatory falsehoods."[85] The new doctrine raised doubts about such famed past (1967) decisions as *Time, Inc. v. Hill*,[86] in which "newsworthiness" had narrowly triumphed over "privacy." However, in 1975 an 8:1 majority, striking down a Georgia law that made it a misdemeanor to print or broadcast the name of a rape victim, and barring the right of the victim or her parents to invoke "invasion of privacy" as a basis for a suit, held that the media cannot be subjected to either civil or criminal liability for disseminating *accurately* data that are available from public law en-

---

82. E.g., compare *Associated Press v. Walker,* 388 U.S. 130 (1967), with the three cases cited *supra* note 78, and *Greenbelt Coop. Pub. Assn. v. Bresler,* 298 U.S. 6 (1970). In 1990 the Court ruled 7:2 that the First Amendment does not *automatically* shield expressions of opinion from being found libelous; that the crucial question of where to draw the line in a particular libel suit between "pure opinion" and opinion that incorporates actionable assertions of fact is one that will have to be answered on a case-by-case basis (*Milkovich v. Lorain Journal,* 497 U.S. 1).

83. *Rosenbloom v. Metromedia,* 403 U.S. 29 (1971) at 44: "Voluntarily or not we are all public men to some degree," in Justice Brennan's words, at 48. See also *Edwards v. New York Times Co.,* certiorari denied, 434 U.S. 1002 (1977).

84. *Gertz v. Robert Welch, Inc.,* 418 U.S. 323 at 348 (but see text *infra* note 85).

85. *Gertz* at 345. That it was but a "seemingly" sharp one was demonstrated by its 5:3 narrowing of the "public *figure*" concept in 1976 when it upheld a $100,000 libel award won by a prominent Palm Beach, Florida, socialite, Mary Alice Firestone, whose notorious divorce proceedings had been publicized by *Time* magazine (*Time, Inc. v. Firestone,* 424 U.S. 448). The gravamen of Justice Rehnquist's opinion was that Mrs. Firestone was not a "public figure," since she had not assumed "any role of especial prominence in the affairs of society other than perhaps Palm Beach society," and because she had not thrust herself to the forefront of any particular public controversy in order to influence the resolutions of the issues involved in it (ibid. at 453). Room for doubt about that analysis of the facts persists, however.

86. 385 U.S. 374. It involved *Life's* review of the play *The Desperate Hours,* starring the young Paul Newman. Richard M. Nixon represented Hill (the loser); Harold Medina, *Time, Inc.* (the winner).

forcement records.[87] That holding was reaffirmed in a 6:3 decision in 1989 in a similar case involving a newspaper's publication of the name of a rape victim in violation of Florida law because the newspaper had lawfully obtained the victim's name from publicly available police records.[88] Moreover, the Court ruled (5:3) in 1976 that "reputation" is neither "liberty" nor "property" for purposes of an alleged civil rights violation.[89] Justices Black and Douglas, of course, never had difficulty in the realm of libel (nor did Justice Brennan): they considered an "unconditional right to say what one pleases about public affairs to be the *minimum* guarantee" under Amendments One and Fourteen.[90] They would have been aghast had they been on the Court in 1979 when it ruled (6:3) that, given the "malice aforethought" test-requirement of the *New York Times* case, a public official had a right to request reporters to testify on their "state of mind" in connection with their leveling of charges against him or her.[91] Nor would they have been amused in the face of the Court's 5:4 narrowing of the libel shield in 1985, when it ruled that the First Amendment does not protect against punitive damage awards *unless* the libelous statements involve "matters of public concern."[92] On the other hand, in a major victory for the news media, the Court ruled (5:4) in 1986 that people suing news organizations for libel must overcome the difficult burden of proving that the published statements about them were false.[93] Just a bit later in 1986 the Court held (6:3), in what seemed to be a major weakening of *Herbert v. Lando*,[94] that when examining a motion for summary judgment of a libel suit, judges must determine "whether the evidence presented is such that a reasonable jury might find that actual malice had been shown with convincing clarity."[95] But the justices made clear unanimously in 1991 that reporters may be sued for fabricating or deliberately and materially altering quotations[96] (although

87. *Cox Broadcasting Corp. v. Cohn*, 420 U.S. 469. The case involved the grisly rape and murder of a young woman whose grieving parents wanted privacy.

88. *Florida Star v. B.J.F.*, 491 U.S. 524.

89. *Paul v. Davis*, 424 U.S. 693.

90. See *The New York Times v. Sullivan*, op. cit., at 296, Justice Black's concurring opinion, for a comparative analysis of the right to denounce; italics supplied. For a fine account of the case and its background, see Anthony Lewis's *Make No Law: The Sullivan Case and the First Amendment* (New York: Random House, 1991).

91. *Herbert v. Lando*, 441 U.S. 153. The majority opinion in this contentious decision was written by Justice White, the dissenters being Justices Brennan, Stewart, and Marshall.

92. *Dun & Bradstreet v. Greenmoss*, 472 U.S. 749 (1985). See the two fascinating 1984 libel trials involving General William C. Westmoreland and Israeli General Ariel Sharon, both of whom were unsuccessful. Two excellent books dealing with them are by Bob Brewin and Sydney Shaw, *Vietnam on Trial: Westmoreland v. C.B.S.* (New York: Atheneum, 1987); and Uri Dan, *Blood Libel: The Inside Story of General Ariel Sharon's History-Making Suit Against Time Magazine* (New York: Simon and Schuster, 1987).

93. *Philadelphia Newspapers v. Hepps*, 475 U.S. 767.

94. See *supra* note 91 and accompanying text.

95. *Anderson v. Liberty Lobby*, 477 U.S. 242.

96. *Masson v. New Yorker Magazine*, 501 U.S. 496.

the case itself ended in a mistrial in 1993 because jurors deadlocked on the damages the *New Yorker* magazine should pay).

As a further illustration of the elusiveness of drawing the line for freedom of expression: petitioning and demonstrating against the draft are both bona fide manifestations of freedom of expression, but the burning of draft cards is not. "We cannot accept the view," wrote Chief Justice Warren in the leading case for his 7:1 Court, with only Justice Douglas in dissent, "that an apparently limitless variety of conduct can be labelled 'speech.'"[97] Justice Black, who drew the line at "conduct" rather than "expression," was in the majority here. And he strongly dissented from the Court's 7:2 holding, just a year later, that the wearing of black arm bands by high school students constituted constitutionally protected "symbolic" free speech.[98] Only Justice Harlan sided with him in what they viewed as a matter of proscribable *conduct.*

That line between speech and conduct in the realm of the First Amendment's freedom of expression received emotion-charged, widely debated attention in 1989 when the Supreme Court, in a 5:4 decision, upheld the right of one Gregory ("Joey") Johnson to douse the American flag with kerosene and set it afire. The Texan, a member of the Revolutionary Communist Youth Brigade, had torched the flag outside the 1984 Republican Convention in Dallas while chanting—in concord with a group of fellow protesters—"America, the red, white, and blue, we spit on you. You stand for plunder, you will go under." After Johnson was arrested, and subsequently convicted under a Texas flag desecration law, his appeal ultimately reached the Supreme Court of the United States. The latter, in a dramatic ruling that surprised a good many observers, upheld Johnson's act as a valid symbolic gesture of freedom of expression, guaranteed by the terms of the First Amendment. With two of the high court's most conservative members, Justices Scalia and Kennedy, moving over to the liberal trio of Justices Brennan, Marshall, and Blackmun, the Court thus declared unconstitutional flag desecration laws in forty-eight states and the federal government and set off a firestorm of protest. "If there is a bedrock principle underlying the First Amendment," wrote Justice Brennan in delivering the majority opinion, "it is that the Government may not prohibit the expression of an idea simply because society finds the idea itself offensive or disagreeable." The leading dissenting opinion was penned

---

97. *United States v. O'Brien* and *O'Brien v. United States,* 391 U.S. 367 (1968) at 376.

98. *Tinker v. Des Moines Independent Community School District,* 393 U.S. 503 (1969). The *Tinker* decision was confirmed in 1972 when the Court refused to review a lower tribunal's decision permitting a public school teacher of English to wear a black arm band on Vietnam Moratorium Day—despite his subsequent suspension for continued political activity and educational disruption (*Board of Education v. James,* 409 U.S. 1042). But cf. the 1986 "firm in his pants" case of *Bethel School District v. Fraser,* 478 U.S. 675, in which a 7:2 Supreme Court upheld a school district's punitive action involving a student speaker, and the 1987 ruling (5:3) in *Hazelwood School District v. Kuhlmeier,* 484 U.S. 260, upholding the censoring of sexual explicitness in a student newspaper.

by Chief Justice Rehnquist, who was joined by Justices White and O'Connor and, in a separate dissent, by the usually on-the-other-side Justice Stevens. "Flag burning," wrote Rehnquist, "is the equivalent of an inarticulate grunt or roar that, it seems fair to say, is most likely to be indulged in not to express any particular idea, but to antagonize others."

The Court's decision set off a wave of demands for federal remedial action, with Congress being asked to propose either a countermanding constitutional amendment or legislation to reverse *Texas v. Johnson*.[99] Congress complied with the Federal Flag Protection Act of 1989—only to see it struck down in June 1990 by the same vote as *Texas v. Johnson* with the identical Court lineup and reasoning as the latter.[100] Indeed, the issue had long been a troubling one for the Supreme Court, with a number of earlier cases pointing to the difficult nature of the controversy and frequently close divisions among the justices. For example, in 1969, dividing 5:4 (with the great First Amendment liberal, Hugo Black, in dissent), it upheld the public burning of an American flag by a Brooklyn bus driver, Sidney Street, who had thus vented his outrage at the news that civil rights activist James Meredith had been shot and wounded in an ambush.[101] In two 1974 cases, both decided 6:3, the Court overturned the convictions of Massachusetts and Washington State protesters. The former had sewn a small American flag to the seat of his trousers,[102] and the latter had affixed to the flag large peace symbols fashioned of removable tape and displayed the flag outside his apartment window.[103] Both men had been convicted under state flag desecration laws, which fell as a result of the Court's holdings. On the other hand, it has also upheld certain state regulatory measures designed to prevent purposeful flag mutilation, among them one Halter's insistence on a First Amendment right to imprint a flag representation on beer bottles[104] and one Kime's public burning of her privately owned flag on the sidewalk in front of the federal building in Greensboro, North Carolina.[105] Proposals to enact a constitutional amendment to give Congress the power to ban desecration of the American flag passed the House of Representatives by the necessary two-thirds vote in both 1995 and 2000, but the Senate failed to achieve the required two-thirds by three and four votes, respectively.

That the volatile free-speech issue gives every promise of remaining highly controversial, and that the Court's responses will always generate disagreement,

99. 491 U.S. 397.

100. *United States v. Eichman* and *United States v. Haggerty*, 496 U.S. 310.

101. *Street v. New York*, 394 U.S. 576 (1969). "We don't need no damn flag," Street had shouted. "I burned it! If they let this happen to Meredith, we don't need an American flag."

102. *Smith v. Goguen*, 415 U.S. 566.

103. *Spence v. Washington*, 418 U.S. 405.

104. *Halter v. Nebraska*, 205 U.S. 34 (1907).

105. *Kime v. United States*, 459 U.S. 949 (1982).

was made crystal clear in the Court's dramatic, far-reaching 1992 decision in *R.A.V. v. City of St. Paul,*[106] in which it unanimously struck down a St. Paul, Minnesota, ordinance directed against "hate crime laws" and, by strong implication, against campus speech codes designed to punish students for "offensive" remarks. All nine members of the Court joined in the controlling opinion by Justice Scalia, which held that *absolute content neutrality* is at the core of the First Amendment's guarantees; that, in other words, government may not *selectively* silence speech on the basis of its content. The Minnesota law at issue banned activities, such as cross burning—in which R.A.V. had engaged on the lawn of a black family—and the displaying of swastikas that "arouse anger, alarm or resentment in others on the basis of race, color, creed, religion or gender." Language of that breadth and vagueness, the Supreme Court held, is unconstitutional on its face—which does not mean, of course, that activities such as cross burning could not be validly reached under trespass, arson, property damage, or similar law-and-order statutes. Chief Justice Rehnquist and Justices Kennedy, Souter, and Thomas joined the Scalia opinion in full. But while acknowledging the unconstitutionality of the law because it reached beyond "fighting words"[107] to speech protected by the First Amendment, Justices White, Blackmun, Stevens, and O'Connor wrote separately to record their belief that the majority had pronounced too sweeping a proscription on governmental attempts to interdict bias-motivated crime; that the St. Paul ordinance should have been struck down simply on the far less sweeping grounds that *it* was written in too broad and sloppy a manner, but that its goals were worthy—only its means were flawed.

But one year later, a unanimous Court, speaking through its chief justice in *Wisconsin v. Mitchell,*[108] *upheld* a Wisconsin statute that imposes greater prison sentences and stiffer fines on assailants who choose their victims on the basis of race, color, disability, or sexual orientation. Distinguishing *R.A.V. v. St. Paul,* Rehnquist wrote that "a physical assault is not by any stretch of the imagination expressive conduct protected by the First Amendment." Thus he emphasized the *conduct* issue involved: here one Todd Mitchell and a group of other youthful blacks severely beat a fourteen-year-old white youth simply because he was white. The St. Paul ordinance had fallen because it proscribed a certain type of *expression,* "bias-motivated hatred," and as such violated the Constitution's fundamental First Amendment mandate against *"content-based"* speech discrimination. In contrast, the Wisconsin law is preeminently connected to underlying *conduct.*

On the other hand, an earlier Court had found no difficulty at all in unanimously declaring unconstitutional a part of a federal law that barred theatrical

---

106. 505 U.S. 377.
107. See *Chaplinsky v. New Hampshire, supra* and *infra* this chapter.
108. 508 U.S. 476.

performers from wearing a U.S. military uniform *if* their role was intended to discredit the armed forces;[109] the law had permitted performances that were laudatory! Appropriately, that classic symbolic freedom of expression opinion from 1970 was written by Justice Black. But it was by a mere one-vote margin (5:4) that the Court ruled in 1971 that the display on a jacket of the epithetical phrase "Fuck the draft" in a corridor of the Los Angeles courthouse is constitutionally protected speech and may not be made a criminal offense[110]—with the Court for the first time spelling out that Anglo-Saxon term (Justice Harlan, of all people, writing for the Court). Yet his colleague Black was one of three dissenters who saw "mainly conduct," very little "expression." As he frequently did, Black here evidently drew the proverbial line based on his belief that, in words he employed elsewhere, "a law which primarily regulates conduct but which might also indirectly affect speech can be upheld if the effect on speech is minor in relation to the need for control of the conduct."[111]

A unanimous 1995 decision, penned by Justice Souter, addressed another contemporarily controversial issue, holding that Massachusetts violated the First Amendment by *requiring* private citizens who organized a Saint Patrick's Day parade (here the South Boston Allied War Veterans Council) to include among the marchers a group, namely, the Irish-American Gay, Lesbian, and Bisexual Group of Boston (GLIB). The latter wanted to impart a message (i.e., homosexual pride) that the organizers did not wish to convey. GLIB was free to organize and march in its own parade, but it could not compel the state to order the Veterans Council to include them, on pain of infringing upon the council's freedom of expression.[112]

But when the village of Stratton, Ohio, promulgated an ordinance that, inter alia, prohibited "canvassers" from "going in and upon" private residential property to promote any "cause" without first obtaining a permit from the mayor's office by completing and signing a registration form, the Jehovah Witnesses went to court, alleging a violation of freedom of religion, freedom of speech and of the press, prohibited by the First Amendment. They lost in both lower courts but prevailed 8:1 in the U.S. Supreme Court, with only Chief Justice Rehnquist in dis-

---

109. *Schacht v. United States,* 398 U.S. 58.

110. *Cohen v. California,* 403 U.S. 15. White wrote a partly concurring dissent, Blackmun the lead dissenting opinion. Relatedly, see *Papish v. Board of Curators of University of Missouri,* 410 U.S. 667 (1973), which overturned (6:3) a student's expulsion for circulating "offensive ideas" in print in a campus publication that used the "M—— F——" expletive with obvious relish in connection with the trial and acquittal of the member of an organization called "Up Against the Wall, Motherfucker." (A headline story was entitled "M—— F—— Acquitted," and it printed a political cartoon depicting police raping the Statute of Liberty and the Goddess of Justice.)

111. Dissenting opinion, *Barenblatt v. United States,* 360 U.S. 109 (1959) at 141.

112. *Hurley v. Irish-American Gay, Lesbian, and Bisexual Group of Boston,* 515 U.S. 557.

sent. The Stevens majority opinion saw a clear violation of Amendment One as it applies to religious proselytizing, anonymous political speech, and the distribution of handbills.[113]

Throughout our history, lawmaking and judicial authorities have had to wrestle with these and similar questions—including such, perhaps less than earthshaking, ones as to the right of public school boards and other public agencies to prescribe the length of the hair sported by those under their aegis.[114] Limitations, today almost entirely of a statutory nature, are thus present on both the national and state levels of government—a phenomenon almost unknown prior to World War I. Thus, there is scant doubt that Congress has the authority to guard against sedition and subversion;[115] it has asserted it rather widely, especially in periods of national emergency and throughout the cold war, enacting three controversial pieces of legislation in less than fifteen years: the Smith Act of 1940, the Internal Security Act of 1950 (passed over President Truman's veto), and the Communist Control Act of 1954. The problem implicit in this legislation is, of course, where to draw the line between the individual's cherished right to espouse and express unpopular causes and the right of the community to protect itself against the overthrow of government. As the courts have ultimately been called upon to demonstrate time and again—as, for instance, in granting to members of the armed forces a lower degree of protection against the "chilling effect" which broad and vague regulations would normally be viewed as imposing upon the exercise of free expression[116]—democratic society has the right and duty to maintain concurrently *both* freedom of expression and national security.

To reallude briefly to another area, one in which the states have predominated, what of the matter of prohibiting the sale and dissemination of "obscene" literature? Statutes abound, yet many of these quickly run afoul of First and Fourteenth Amendment safeguards of freedom of expression. To what extent, then, may the community protect itself against "obscenity"? Do particular publications possess the "redeeming social value" which presumably underlies the exercise of responsible freedom? Is demonstrable obscenity a "civil right"? The anticipated negative chorus to these rhetorical questions must be discounted at least in part because of (1) hypocrisy and (2) the enormously difficult definition

113. *Watchtower Bible and Tract Society v. Village of Stratton,* 536 U.S. ___ (2002).

114. Although the Court has been on both sides of the issue in its decisions, and may well have to come down with a definitive one ultimately, by and large it has sided with duly constituted authorities, assuming reasonable rules are at stake. See, e.g., *Olff v. East Side Union High School District,* 404 U.S. 1042 (1972); *Jackson v. New York City Transit Authority,* 419 U.S. 831 (1974); and *Kelley v. Johnson,* 425 U.S. 238 (1976).

115. *Sedition* consists of publications, utterances, or other activities, short of treason, which are deemed to encourage resistance to lawful authority. *Subversion* comprehends participation in or advocacy of any organized activity to overthrow an existing government by force.

116. *Parker v. Levy,* 417 U.S. 733 (1974); and *Greer v. Spock,* 424 U.S. 828 (1976).

of the "obscene." Hence, here again the judicial branch has had to endeavor to draw lines—which it has done more than once by reading the allegedly "obscene" book and, especially, by screen-viewing the allegedly "obscene" film.[117] Some justices, as was ever true of Black and Douglas, have no problem here: not only do they not "go" to "those movies"—in Black's case, at least, cordially loathing them—but they do not have to: for any prior censorship of the visual (or the written) is regarded as a prima facie violation of freedom of expression.

The following capsule illustrations will indicate the at once fascinating and frustrating line-drawing problem involved in freedom of expression—one the Supreme Court, in particular, has been called upon repeatedly to solve amid the inevitable jeers and cheers.

DRAWING LINES: SOME BRIEF EXAMPLES

Press Freedom and Fair Trial and Prior Restraint

"The basis of our government being the opinion of the people, the first object shall be to keep that right; and were it left for me to decide whether we should have a government without newspapers, or newspapers without government, I should not hesitate a moment to choose the latter." So wrote Thomas Jefferson in 1787.[118] But even the embrace of that noble statement does not gainsay the need to face the reality of difficult and timely line drawing. Thus, where *does* one draw the line between the seminal right of a free press to comment and criticize and the fundamental duty of the judiciary to ensure a fair trial? Freedom and responsibility are sides of the same coin.[119]

Thus, the 1946 ruling in *Pennekamp v. Florida*[120] is a relatively early contemporary illustration of the ever-alive issue of the people's alleged "right to

117. E.g., the *"Miracle"* decision (concerning Roberto Rossellini's controversial movie) of *Burstyn v. Wilson,* 343 U.S. 495 (1952); that of the film *Lady Chatterley's Lover, Kingsley Corporation v. Regents of the University of New York,* 360 U.S. 684 (1959); and *Jenkins v. Georgia,* 418 U.S. 153 (1974), endeavoring to regulate the sexually suggestive *Carnal Knowledge.*

118. Letter to Edward Carrington in Paul Leicester Ford, ed., *Thomas Jefferson's Works* (New York: Putnam's, 1894), vol. 4, p. 359.

119. See A. E. Dick Howard, "The Press in Court," *Wilson Quarterly* (special issue) (1982).

120. 328 U.S. 331 (1946). Five years earlier, in what was long regarded as the leading case on the subject, the Court ruled through Justice Black's 5:4 opinion that highly intemperate published attacks upon the judiciary in pending cases by West Coast union leader Harry Bridges and editors of the *Times-Mirror* did not present a "clear and present danger" to the course of an orderly administration of justice (*Bridges v. California* and *Times-Mirror Co. v. Superior Court of California,* 314 U.S. 252 [1941]). What tied the two cases together was that both appellants challenged their contempt citations by the Superior Court of Los Angeles County on free-speech and free-press grounds.

know" versus the judicial duty to administer justice fairly. The publisher and the associate editor of the *Miami Herald* were fined for contempt because they had printed a cartoon and written an editorial designed to demonstrate that a Miami trial judge had, by certain rulings, favored criminals and gambling establishments. Their conviction was justified by Florida on the grounds that their actions had reflected upon and impugned the integrity of the trial court, had tended to create public distrust for it, and had obstructed the fair and impartial administration of justice of pending cases. In a unanimous decision, written by Justice Reed, the Supreme Court reversed the lower court, holding that the newspaper and its personnel's freedom of speech and press had been violated. Reed admitted that some of the *Herald*'s comments were directed at pending cases and, moreover, were not even truthful. But justifying his drawing a generous line here, he argued that

> in the borderline instances where it is difficult to say upon which side of the line the offense falls, we think the specific freedom of public comment should weigh heavily against a possible tendency to influence pending cases. Freedom of discussion should be given the widest range compatible with the essential requirement of the fair and orderly administration of justice.[121]

Not long thereafter, the Court, although splitting 6:3, reaffirmed the aforegone cases in *Craig v. Harney,*[122] which involved an intemperate and inaccurate attack on a lay judge who had directed a verdict in a civil suit. Reversing the resultant contempt citations by the judge against a Corpus Christi, Texas, publisher, editorial writer, and news reporter, the Court, although admitting that the "news articles were by any standard an unfair report of what had transpired," held through Justice Douglas:

> The vehemence of the language used is not alone the measure of the power to punish for contempt. The fires which it kindles must constitute an imminent, not merely a likely, threat to the administration of justice. The danger must not be remote or even probable; it must immediately imperil.[123]

And the Court sustained this general approach to the problem in a key case on the issue when it held (5:2) in *Wood v. Georgia*[124] that an elected sheriff in Bibb County, Georgia, could not be cited for contempt of court because, in "An Open Letter to the Bibb County Grand Jury" he expressed his "personal ideas" when he criticized a judge of the Superior Court who had instructed the grand jury in racially charged, intemperate tones. Over dissents by Justices Harlan and Clark,

---

121. *Pennekamp v. Florida,* op. cit., at 347.
122. 331 U.S. 367 (1947).
123. Ibid. at 376.
124. 370 U.S. 375 (1962).

Chief Justice Warren's opinion for the Court concluded that the majority agreed that Sheriff Wood's actions "did not present a danger to the administration of justice that should vitiate his freedom to express his opinions in the manner chosen."[125] Four decades later the high tribunal ruled 6:3 in a case raising media rights over privacy claims that the First Amendment protects the right of a Pennsylvania radio commentator to broadcast an illegally intercepted recording of a cell phone conversation by an unidentified person in which two local labor officials discussed a strike by public school teachers.[126]

Another facet of the vexatious issue is personified by the resolution of *Irvin v. Dowd*,[127] in which a unanimous Supreme Court struck down a state conviction solely on the ground of prejudicial pretrial publicity—a case that emphasizes the collateral question of the impact of broad press freedom on the individual on trial rather than its impact upon the tribunal itself. At the trial level of the case the jury panel consisted of 430 persons, 268 of whom were excused for cause as having fixed opinions of Irwin's guilt because of the pervasive trial publicity. Nothing happened to the offending newspapers or their "roving reporters" in Gibson County, Indiana, nor to the Evansville radio and television stations that blanketed the county with the news of petitioner Irvin's alleged crime of six murders in the vicinity of Vandenburgh County. But the accused's detention and death sentence were vacated and remanded in an opinion by Justice Clark, replete with criticism of an irresponsible press. Justice Frankfurter, concurring, administered a lecture to the news media, reminding them warmly that freedom implies responsibility:

> [T]his is, unfortunately, not an isolated case that happens in Evansville, Indiana, nor an atypical miscarriage of justice due to anticipatory trial by newspaper instead of trial in court before a jury. . . . But, again and again, such disregard of fundamental fairness is so flagrant that the Court is compelled, as it was only a week ago, to reverse a conviction in which prejudicial newspaper intrusion has poisoned the outcome. . . . This Court has not yet decided that the fair administration of criminal justice must be subordinated to another safeguard of our constitutional system—freedom of the press, properly conceived. The Court has not yet decided that, while convictions must be reversed and miscarriages of justice result because the

---

125. Ibid. at 395. On the other hand, as Justice Goldberg made clear in *Cox v. Louisiana*, 379 U.S. 559 (1965)—op. cit., note 66—a state has the right to enact a statute forbidding picketing or parades in or near a courthouse "with intent of interfering with [the] administration of justice or [of] influencing any judge, juror, witness, or court officer" (at 560, 567).

126. *Bartnicki v. Vopper*, 532 U.S. ___ (2001).

127. 366 U.S. 717 (1961). During voir dire 370 of 430 admitted believing Irvin guilty.

minds of jurors or potential jurors were poisoned, the poisoner is constitutionally protected in plying his trade.[128]

In other words, the Court's resolution here was (as it has often been the case) to effect a "compromise" under which both the press and the accused "win"—and society loses.

It is difficult enough to find the line when responsibility obtains, but how much more so when the press ignores its responsibility? Must we really continue to believe that there is an unlimited right to conduct ex parte public trials in the press, on the radio, and on television? The British have long since answered that fundamental question in the negative. There, any publication of information about a defendant in a criminal case *before* the trial starts leads to punishment for contempt of court. Nothing that might conceivably affect the attitude of a potential juror may be revealed unless and until it is formally disclosed in court. Large fines have been meted out to newspapers that have violated the so-called Judges Rules, some of which have been enacted into formal statutes. To cite some examples: a small weekly newspaper in Eastbourne (on England's south coast) was fined the equivalent of $500 for saying that a defendant wore a dark suit and glasses, had been married on New Year's Day, and was being held on a serious charge.[129] A Scottish newspaper, the *Daily Record* of Edinburgh, was fined $21,000 for using on its front page a picture of a soccer star charged with "indecent exposure." In addition, Chief Assistant Editor Robert Johnson—who was in charge when the issue went to press—was fined $1,400, and the only reason no individual was sent to jail for contempt was that the editor responsible had been at home sick that night. "How is a judge or jury to know," asked the presiding judge in the case, "that the witness is identifying the man seen on the occasion of the crime and not the man whose photograph has been blazoned on the front page of a newspaper?"[130] In general, it is British doctrine that from the moment the police announce that an individual will be charged to the final disposition of

---

128. Ibid. at 729, 730. We should note here that—perhaps as a precursor of the *Estes* decision (see notes 133–36 and accompanying text)—the Court, in *Rideau v. Louisiana,* 373 U.S. 723 (1963), voided on due process grounds the murder conviction of a defendant whose confession to a sheriff had been televised and thrice beamed at potential jurors throughout the area. Three seated jurors admitted to having viewed it. But thirty years later the justices ruled 5:4 that potential jurors exposed to pretrial publicity do not have to be questioned as to what they know about the crime at issue so long as they promise to be fair (*Mu'Min v. Virginia,* 500 U.S. 415 [1991]).

129. *New York Times,* March 22, 1974, p. 4.

130. As reported by the Associated Press in the *New York Herald Tribune,* February 12, 1960, p. 6. See also Anthony Lewis, "British Verdict on Trial-by-Press," *New York Times Magazine,* June 20, 1965, p. 31; the excellent comparative column by Richard Eder, "Curbs on Press Shield British Suspect," *New York Times,* March 22, 1974, p. 4; and Don Neuchterlein, "Press Freedom, Security Fight Waged in Britain," *Charlottesville Daily Progress,* January 29, 1984, p. E3.

the case—including appeals—nothing may be published about a defendant that might in any way influence the proceedings against him. Usually the only exception made is for information that comes out in the courtroom.[131]

Two significant U.S. Supreme Court rulings in 1965 and 1966 well pinpoint the omnipresent fact that, under our system, fundamental fairness cries out for a "balance" between freedom of the press and the right of the public to be informed, on the one hand, and the press's responsibilities and the right of the accused. The first ruling involved the conviction for swindling of Texas financier and "wheeler-dealer" Billie Sol Estes, who had been tried and convicted (among several other earlier convictions) in a Tyler, Texas, courtroom in 1962. During the pretrial hearing, extensive and obtrusive television coverage took place: "The courtroom," reported the *New York Times,* "was turned into a snake-pit by the multiplicity of cameras, wires, microphones and technicians milling about the chamber."[132] Estes's appeal to the U.S. Supreme Court alleged denial of his constitutional rights of "due process of law." In a six-opinion, 5:4 decision the Court laid down a rule that televising of "notorious" criminal trials is indeed prohibited by the "due process of law" clause of Amendment Fourteen, and it reversed Estes's conviction.[133] But it was a far from clear decision insofar as the basic problem of freedom of the press and fair trial goes. Four justices,[134] through Justice Clark, said that "the time honored principles of a fair trial" are violated when television is allowed in any criminal trial. A fifth, Justice Harlan—supplying the winning vote—agreed, but only because the Estes trial was one of "great notoriety," and he made clear that he would reserve judgment on more routine cases. Four dissenting justices[135] objected on constitutional grounds to the blanket ban at this stage of television's development, holding that there was insufficient proof that Estes's rights had here been violated.[136]

131. An average "allowable" report is this account from the *Daily Telegraph,* August 8, 1970, p. 9: "A man was . . . charged with the attempted murder of . . . two women. He will appear at Exmouth magistrates' court today."

132. June 9, 1965, p. 31c.

133. *Estes v. Texas,* 381 U.S. 532 (1965).

134. Clark, Warren, Douglas, and Goldberg.

135. Stewart, Black, Brennan, and White.

136. *Estes v. Texas* still provides the law, but the use of television in courtrooms had become much more frequent. By late 1991 all states permitted at least some form of television coverage in some of their courts, and the Supreme Court had almost eagerly confronted the issue in 1981 in what gave promise of becoming a seminal decision: *Chandler v. Florida,* 449 U.S. 560. Its 8:0 ruling, penned by Chief Justice Burger, with concurring opinions by Justices Stewart and White—Justice Stevens not participating—held that, notwithstanding objections by the defendant, states may permit the news media to televise, that is, to photograph and broadcast, criminal trials; that controlled televising (in Florida one camera and one cameraman) did not necessarily jeopardize the constitutional guarantees to a fair trial. While *Chandler* dealt only with a *state* trial, the extension of its gravamen to the federal sphere was a distinct possibility. But, as Chief Justice Burger announced

The second case involved the Court's striking down of the 1954 second-degree-murder conviction of a Cleveland, Ohio, osteopath, Dr. Samuel H. Sheppard, for the bludgeon murder of his pregnant wife.[137] Dr. Sheppard had been in jail until 1964, when a federal district judge in Dayton granted a writ of habeas corpus and released him from the Ohio penitentiary, ruling that prejudicial publicity had denied him a fair trial. Two years later the Supreme Court affirmed that action by a vote of 8:1, giving Ohio authorities a choice of retrying him or of dismissing the case against him. (Ohio decided to retry him on the murder charge; the jury acquitted him in November 1966 after a trial that was a model of courtroom decorum.) Justice Clark's majority opinion pointed to the circus atmosphere that attended Dr. Sheppard's sensationalized trial. For example, the trial judge, Edward Blythin, positioned the press inside the lawyer's rail so close to the bench that it was in effect impossible for defense attorneys to consult with either their client or the judge without being overheard. When the jurors viewed the scene of the murder at Dr. Sheppard's home, a representative of the press was included in the group, while other reporters hovered overhead in a press helicopter. Radio and television commentators, among them Bob Considine, Dorothy Kilgallen, and Walter Winchell, kept up a drumfire of accounts of alleged multiple illicit liaisons by the defendant. Television broadcasts spewed forth from the room adjacent to the jury deliberation chamber. Jurors were photographed and interviewed by the news media, as were witnesses. In setting aside Dr. Sheppard's conviction, Clark restated the Court's concern that had led it to void Billie Sol Estes's conviction just a year earlier, namely, that the presence of a large, ill-controlled news media contingent can deny a defendant that "judicial serenity and calm" which the due process of law guarantees of the Constitution mandate for a fair trial—even in the absence of proof that the jury was in fact prejudiced by the publicity. And Clark added significantly that although the various officials involved could probably stifle most sources of prejudicial trial pub-

---

again in 1984 and 1985, "There will be no cameras in the Supreme Court of the United States while I sit there." (*Washington Post,* November 13, 1984, p. A5). None had entered the Rehnquist Court by 1997, a carefully orchestrated 1989 video trial run by a group of television experts having proved unpersuasive. But most of the states and the U.S. Court of Military Appeals allowed cameras in their courtrooms under varying conditions (*New York Times,* November 1, 1989, sec. A, p. 23). Indeed, as of January 1, 1995, cameras were allowed in trial and/or appellate courts in forty-seven states on either a permanent or an experimental basis. (The exceptions were Indiana, Mississippi, and South Dakota, plus the District of Columbia.) However, a new trial run in selected U.S. Courts of Appeals and U.S. District Courts was agreed upon for 1991. In an interview on March 30, 1992, Chief Justice Rehnquist voiced ambivalence regarding the chances of any universal adoption at the federal level. When the aforementioned trial run had expired in 1994, the Judicial Conference voted 2:1 *against* any camera utilization in federal courts. But the Judicial Conference reversed itself in 1995 and provided the prospect of new pilot programs in the future.

137. *Sheppard v. Maxwell,* 384 U.S. 333 (1966).

licity, he would not rule out the possibility that *a judge could take direct action against a newspaper,* for example, if it persisted in violating defendants' rights.[138] The lone dissenting vote was cast by Justice Black—but without a written opinion, the record merely noting "Mr. Justice Black dissents."[139] In 1998 Sheppard's son, Sam Reese Sheppard, tried to have the case reopened once more to prove his father's innocence. He succeeded; yet in April 2000 a Cleveland jury ruled against the Sheppard family in a civil law suit. That May his lawyer filed an appeal for motion to set the jury's verdict aside. Ultimately, a jury found Dr. Sheppard "not guilty," but Sam Jr. had asked for an "innocent" rather that a "not guilty" verdict.[140]

The dilemma remains, but in *Estes* and *Sheppard* the Court probably gave a signal in the direction of considerably more concern for fairness to those on trial.[141] Such a trend was also indicated by the actions taken by bar associations and jurists in a number of states, among them New Jersey, New York, and Pennsylvania, and, perhaps most significantly, by a widely circulated 226-page report by the American Bar Association's Advisory Committee on Fair Trial and a Free Press. Known as the Reardon Report for its chairman, Massachusetts Supreme Judicial Court Justice Paul C. Reardon, it set out detailed rules aimed at drastically curtailing the flow of information about arrested persons that is made available to the press in most communities. Sharply tightening the canons of legal ethics, it also recommended that judges be given the power to punish newsmen for contempt.[142] The resultant uproar from the media was at least in part instrumental in the adoption of a new set of rules by the Judicial Conference of the United States, recommended by a special committee headed by Judge Irving Kaufman of the U.S. Court of Appeals for the Second Circuit. In part patterned upon the Reardon Report, the Judicial Conference rules attempt to discourage publicity that might influence a jury and result in an unfair trial but, unlike the Reardon-ABA code, do not attempt to define any standards for the news media or police working beyond the confines of the courtroom.[143] In particular, the "Kaufman Rules" do not include the three most controversial Reardon provisions: (1) exclusion, under some circumstances, of newsmen from preliminary

138. Ibid. at 357–62.
139. Ibid. at 363.
140. See James Neff, *The Wrong Man: The Final Verdict on the Dr. Sam Sheppard Case* (New York: Random House, 2001). Neff blames one Richard Eberling.
141. In October 1966 the Texas Court of Criminal Appeals reversed the murder conviction of Jack Ruby, who had been sentenced to death in 1964 for the slaying of Lee Harvey Oswald, the presumed assassin of President Kennedy. The court cited the rampant publicity (as well as inadmissible evidence) and, for Ruby's new trial, ordered a change of venue from Dallas County, where the shooting took place. But Ruby's fatal illness intervened.
142. For its text see *New York Times,* February 20, 1968, pp. 1, 35c.
143. For their text see *New York Times,* September 20, 1968, p. 32c.

hearings and other hearings held out of the presence of the jury; (2) extension to policemen of the curbs covering lawyers; and (3) recommendation that judges bring contempt of court citations against newsmen who publish material "wilfully designed" to influence a trial's outcome. Predictably, it was the Kaufman Committee's recommendations, not Reardon's, that seem to have become part of the rules, more or less, in every federal and many a state court in the nation. But, despite a helpful 1969 "Code of Professional Responsibility" for lawyers issued by the ABA,[144] and some encouraging signs that judges are indeed committed to the Kaufman Rules—with some prepared to go even beyond them toward those suggested by the Reardon Report[145]—the basic dilemma[146] of drawing lines between the right to a fair trial and that of freedom of the press remains. It was back before the highest court in 1976, involving a sensational Nebraska multiple-murder case in which Hugh Stuart, the trial judge, had imposed a very broad "gag order" sharply restricting pretrial coverage.[147] The Supreme Court's answer came quickly (9:0) and to the delight of the media—although the five different opinions delivered in the case[148]evinced considerable line-drawing difficulties: in general, judges may *not* impose such orders on the press that forbid publication of information about criminal cases—even if, in the judge's opinion, such an order would help to assure the defendant a fair trial by preventing prejudicial publicity.

The ABA entered the *Stuart* decision's spirit by adopting a new set of guidelines in late 1978 prohibiting a judge to seal off any portion of a trial or pretrial proceedings and from limiting comments to the press by attorneys—unless it could be shown that publicity would "create a clear and present danger" to a criminal suspect's ability to obtain an impartial jury, and unless other less restrictive alternatives, such as changing the location of the trial, would be impossible.[149] If these developments seemed to have a settling effect, it was a short-lived one, for down came the Supreme Court with its contentious, momentous 5:4 decision in the 1979 case of *Gannett Co. v. DePasquale*.[150] Two defendants in a New York State prosecution for second-degree murder, robbery, and grand larceny, arguing that their Sixth Amendment right to a fair trial had already been seriously threat-

144. See *Philadelphia Evening Bulletin,* September 10, 1969, p. 26.
145. Thus in 1973 the Supreme Court declined to review—Justice Douglas dissenting—the contempt of court convictions of two Louisiana reporters who had defied an order by a federal trial judge not to write articles about an open hearing in his court. The U.S. Court of Appeals for the Fifth Circuit had found the secrecy order unconstitutional but ruled that the reporters were subject to contempt proceedings anyway (*Dickinson v. United States,* 414 U.S. 979).
146. See the Alfred Friendly and Ronald L. Goldfarb proposals in their *Crime and Publicity: The Impact of News on the Administration of Justice* (New York: Twentieth Century Fund, 1967).
147. *Nebraska Press Association v. Stuart,* 427 U.S. 539.
148. By Chief Justice Burger and Justices Brennan, White, Powell, and Stevens.
149. Published August 25, 1978.
150. 443 U.S. 368.

ened by a redolent building up of pretrial publicity, moved at a *pretrial* hearing that the press and the public were to be excluded from the hearing during which the trial judge, Daniel DePasquale, was to hear arguments and rule on a defense motion to suppress certain physical evidence and alleged involuntary confessions. The New York district attorney did not oppose the motion, a reporter present said nothing, and the trial judge, granting the defense motion, held a closed hearing. When, on the following day, the reporter objected and requested access to any and all pertinent records of the hearing, the judge declined, contending that, at least at this stage of the proceedings, the defendants' Sixth Amendment rights to a fair trial outweighed any First Amendment rights of the press or the public to disclose the contents of the suppression hearing. The Gannett newspaper organization sought a writ of prohibition and mandamus against Judge DePasquale, and the Appellate Division of the New York Supreme Court vacated the closure order as an impermissible *prior restraint* in violation of Amendments One and Fourteen and an invasion of the public's interest "in open judicial proceedings." On further appeal, however, the highest New York tribunal, its court of appeals, upheld Judge DePasquale—who, ironically, in the meantime had made the suppression hearing transcripts available—and the U.S. Supreme Court promptly granted certiorari.

Regrettably, the Court's multidivided, five-opinion (four on the majority side) ruling, while upholding the suppression order, did little to clarify the gravamen of the basic controversy of the First versus the Sixth Amendment. Some among the five prevailing justices (Stewart, who authored the controlling plurality opinion, Burger, Powell, Rehnquist, and Stevens) seemed to confine their holding of suppressibility to the *pretrial* stage; others, such as Rehnquist, to both pretrial *and* trial; others, personified by the controlling plurality opinion by Stewart, seemed to leave the matter to another day by simply asserting that "members of the public have no constitutional right under the Sixth and Fourteenth Amendments to attend criminal trials."[151] All five on the prevailing side in effect thus agreed that these guarantees, hallmarked by the Sixth Amendment, mandated the right to a *public trial* only for the defendant—a right dating from eleventh-century England; that, however, it provides no such guarantee to the press or the public. Writing for his dissenting colleagues Brennan, White, and Marshall, Justice Blackmun, however, saw a clear-cut right of press access in the Sixth Amendment—except in "highly unusual circumstances . . . not present here"[152]—both at the pretrial *and* the trial stage of a criminal case, all events observed being publishable and reportable consistent with the First Amendment.

Given the multifaceted, quasi-confusing opinions in the DePasquale case, that "another day" was not long in coming—especially since some two hundred state and local judges had attempted to bar the press from their courts in the interim. At the very end of its 1979–80 term, the Court returned to the fray with its

151. Ibid. at 379.
152. Ibid. at 448.

eagerly awaited decision in *Richmond Newspapers v. Virginia.*[153] With native Virginian Justice Powell abstaining, the high tribunal now ruled firmly (7:1)— Justice Rehnquist in solitary dissent—that, "absent an overriding interest to the contrary," the trial of a criminal case must be open to the public. Six of the justices agreed—in what was a constitutional "first"—that there is a First Amendment guarantee of *access* to open trials; a seventh preferred to see it as a Sixth Amendment right. The controlling opinion (among seven rendered) written in twenty-four pages of ringing tones of support for press access by the press's latter-day villain, Chief Justice Burger, emphasized that the public and the press have a constitutional right to witness criminal trials—a right that is "implicit in the guarantees of the First Amendment for freedom of speech, of the press and of assembly" and in the Ninth Amendment's grant to "the people" of "certain rights" not specifically enumerated elsewhere.[154] Acknowledging that a trial may be closed in "rare circumstances" (that were unspecified), the chief justice held that, to have justice carried out, the process must also "satisfy the appearance of justice . . . that can best be provided by allowing people [and, of course, the press] to observe it."[155] It was clearly a watershed decision—a signal victory for freedom of communication. It was one that indeed was broadened two years later in a 6:3 holding, authored by Justice Brennan, that states (here Massachusetts) may not pass sweeping laws requiring that the press and public be barred from trials, even during testimony by juvenile (in this case below eighteen) rape or other sexual assault victims.[156] The chief justice plus Justices Rehnquist and Stevens dissented.

The post–*Richmond Newspapers* stance in favor of the press continued apace, notwithstanding an occasional "no." Thus, on the same Opinion Day in 1984, with Justice Powell writing for the 9:0 Court in both cases, the high tribunal ruled (1) that a Georgia judge could not keep press and public out of a hearing on the admissibility of wiretap evidence in a state gambling case, even though the defendant wanted an open hearing—for the judge's order was too broad and too vague by failing specifically to justify the reasons for closing the hearing without considering alternatives.[157] *But* (2) that a judge in Washington State acted properly when he ordered newspapers—in a *civil* suit—not to publish material they had obtained during pretrial "discovery" proceedings in a libel suit against them.[158] That the latter holding was patently an exception to the *Richmond Newspapers* rule was underscored by a far-reaching decision at the end of the Court's term in 1986, when a 7:2 vote, in an opinion written by the retiring

153. 448 U.S. 555 (1980).
154. Ibid. at 559.
155. Ibid. at 560.
156. *Globe Newspaper Co. v. Superior Court,* 457 U.S. 596 (1982).
157. *Waller v. Georgia,* 467 U.S. 39.
158. *Seattle Times Co. v. Rhinehart,* 467 U.S. 20.

Chief Justice Burger, made crystal clear that the press and public do indeed have a constitutional right to attend *pretrial* hearings as well as trials in criminal cases under most circumstances.[159] Burger, noting that "the preliminary hearing is often the final and most important step in the criminal proceeding," ruled that the press and public may be excluded from such hearings only if there is a "substantial probability" that a criminal defendant's right to a fair trial would be prejudiced by publicity and if that right could not be adequately protected through other means. The decision represented an extension of the 1980 *Richmond Newspapers*[160] precedent by, in effect, opening the entire criminal justice system in America to public scrutiny. To all intents and purposes, the 1979 *DePasquale* holding[161] was thereby overruled. And it was termed cable TV's "Bill of Rights" when a 9:0 Court declared that medium to be entitled to "nearly the same constitutional guarantees as newspapers and magazines." But note its limiting follow-up decision, involving the "must carry" rule in 1997, in *Turner Broadcasting Corp. v. FCC II*.[162]

The Pentagon Papers Case. Central to the embattled "free press versus fair trial" syndrome is, of course, the fundamental issue of *access by and to the media*—access without prior restraint, again involving that ubiquitous line between societal and individual rights. What had appeared at first glance to be a golden opportunity in 1971 for the Supreme Court to find and draw a significant portion of such a line, while concurrently enunciating a ringing defense of freedom of the press on First Amendment grounds, had in fact turned out little more than a qualified one, at best, on both counts. At issue were the now famous "Pentagon Papers," the publication—initially by the *New York Times* and then by several other leading newspapers—of a massive seven-thousand-page series of secret governmental documents dealing with the origins of the United States' involvement in Vietnam. These classified documents, compiled some years earlier by order of Secretary of Defense Robert S. McNamara, had been written by a team of distinguished experts; they had fallen into the hands of the *Times* through the instance of one of their authors, Daniel Ellsberg. Their publication became an immediate cause célèbre.

A series of legal maneuvers commenced instantly, with the U.S. government, through Attorney General John N. Mitchell, asking for an injunction against the *Times* and subsequently the *Washington Post* to suppress any further publication of the "Pentagon Papers" on the grounds of national security. It represented the first time in the history of the Republic that such *prior* restraint had

---

159. *Press-Enterprise Co. v. Superior Court of California*, 464 U.S. 501.
160. *Richmond Newspapers v. Virginia*, 448 U.S. 555.
161. *Gannett Co. v. DePasquale*, 443 U.S. 368.
162. *Turner Broadcasting Corp. v. FCC I*, 512 U.S. 622 (1994); and *TBS v. FCC II*, 520 U.S. 180 (1997).

been requested by the federal government.[163] Without going into the details of the legal maneuvers—all of which are carefully set forth in what became an instant all-time best-seller, *The Pentagon Papers*[164]—some federal courts granted, and some denied, injunctions in whole or in part. Inexorably, but with uncommon speed, what promised to be a major constitutional law case wound its way to the Supreme Court of the United States, which proceeded to delay its scheduled summer adjournment in order to hear oral arguments in the *Times* and *Washington Post* cases on June 27. The eagerly awaited decision was handed down three days later.[165]

The case had been expected to produce a landmark ruling on the circumstances under which prior restraint could be imposed upon the press, but because no opinion by a single justice commanded the support of a majority, only the unsigned per curiam opinion, read for his Court by Chief Justice Burger, will serve as a precedent. There was a judicial outpouring of *nine* opinions! Six of these[166] rejected the government's contention that the further publication of the "Papers" be enjoined on the grounds of national security, because, as the justices held variously, to do so in the circumstances at issue would impose an *unconstitutional prior restraint* upon the freedom of the press guaranteed by the First Amendment. The three dissenters,[167] on the other hand, held that courts should not refuse to enforce the executive branch's conclusion that material be kept confidential on matters affecting foreign relations—so long as a cabinet-level officer personally so decided.

163. The only time to date in which the federal government ever succeeded in obtaining a prior restraint order came in the 1979 "Hydrogen Bomb Article" case ("The H-Bomb Secret: How We Got It, Why We're Telling It"), *United States v. Progressive, Inc.* (467 F. Supp. 990). There U.S. District Judge Robert W. Warren, painfully and with the utmost reluctance, became the first federal jurist in our history to issue an injunction imposing prior restraint on the press in a national security case. However, in July 1980 the federal government decided to drop the litigation as a result of an agreement with the *Progressive,* under which thirty-eight of seventy-two impounded documents would be released in their entirety, along with parts of most of the others. Judge Warren readily agreed to dismiss the case. *Snepp v. United States,* 444 U.S. 507 (1980), was another controversial press decision. There the Court ruled (6:3) that an agreement requiring employees of the Central Intelligence Agency not to publish "any information" about the agency without specific prior approval is a judicially enforceable contract that applies to both classified and nonclassified information—and Frank W. Snepp, a former CIA officer who published his account of the fall of Saigon, *Decent Interval,* without such permission, was compelled to turn over to the CIA the entire earnings of the book ($142,090 by August 1980).

164. *New York Times,* based on investigative reporting by Neil Sheehan (New York: Bantam, 1971).

165. *The New York Times v. United States,* 403 U.S. 713 (1971); and *United States v. The Washington Post,* 403 U.S. 713 (1971).

166. By Justices Black, Douglas, Brennan, Stewart, White, and Marshall.

167. The chief justice and Justices Harlan and Blackmun. See Floyd Abrams, "The Pentagon Papers, a Decade Later," *New York Times Magazine,* June 7, 1981, pp. 22ff.

In effect, however, with the exception of Justices Black and Douglas, who restated their long-held absolutist belief that the First Amendment forbids *any* judicial restraint on speech and press, the difference of opinion among the justices turned on whether the government had *proved* that publication of the "Pentagon Papers" would constitute "immediate and irreparable harm to the nation." Only Chief Justice Burger and Justices Harlan and Blackmun believed that the government had made such a case; Justices Brennan, Stewart, White, and Marshall did not, although on varying grounds and in varying degrees. In brief, then, the highest tribunal of the land held (6:3) that the government had failed to meet the heavy burden it must in any attempt to block news articles *prior* to publication: namely, the presumption *against* the constitutionality of such an interference with basic First Amendment rights. Yet, fascinating though the denouement was, the Court's ruling was on narrow grounds—there was no "seismic innovation" here.

On a tangential question, however, the Court did rule (5:4) in 1972 that there was *no* First Amendment right to refuse to provide grand juries in *criminal* cases with the names of confidential sources and related information obtained by journalists in their line of duty[168]—a principle that was even extended to appropriate *civil* cases in 1977.[169] It was reconfirmed below in the much publicized 1978–79 litigation involving the refusal of Myron A. Farber, ace reporter for the *New York Times,* to turn over defense-requested notes in the sensational multiple-murder case of Dr. Mario E. Jascalevich. To date the Court has committedly adhered to its precedent—while adding to it (5:4) in 1991 press *liability* for breaking confidentiality based on promises of identity secrecy.[170] The Court also held (5:4) that congressional immunity did not prevent a grand jury from asking Senator Mike Gravel (D.-Alaska) or his aides certain questions about his version of the "Pentagon Papers"—including where he had obtained them.[171]

A further press-freedom-limiting decision by the same 5:4 majority[172] came in June 1973, when the Court sustained a Pennsylvania ordinance prohibiting

168. *Branzburg v. Hayes,* 408 U.S. 665. Reconfirmed in *Pennington v. Kansas,* 440 U.S. 929 (1979).

169. *Tribune Publishing Co. v. Caldero,* 434 U.S. 930.

170. Farber went to jail for forty days for contempt of court. The controversy ended when a jury acquitted Dr. Jascalevich. Farber's contention that New Jersey's press "shield law" vitiated any obligation to turn over his notes was rejected by the state's Supreme Court (*In re Farber,* 78 N.J. 259, certiorari denied, *New York Times Co. v. New Jersey,* 439 U.S. 997 [1978]). Yet two years later, in 1980, that same tribunal upheld, by a 6:1 vote, *Shrewsbury Daily Register* reporter Robin Goldstein's refusal to do likewise under the now amended law, which requires the utilization of "less intrusive" sources (*In the Matter of the Application of Robin Goldstein re: Subpoena,* 82 N.J. 446). The 1991 case was *Cohen v. Cowles Media,* 501 U.S. 663.

171. *Gravel v. United States,* 408 U.S. 697 (1972).

172. Chief Justice Burger and Associate Justices White, Blackmun, Powell, and Rehnquist. Dissenters were Justices Brennan, Stewart, Marshall, and Stevens.

newspapers from carrying sex-designated employment advertisements.[173] On the other hand, friends of freedom of the press rejoiced in June 1974, when, speaking through Chief Justice Burger, the Court unanimously struck down a Florida law requiring newspapers to print *replies*—as distinct from *retractions* from defamation—from political candidates attacked in their columns. "A responsible press is an undoubtedly desirable goal," wrote Burger, "but press responsibility is not mandated by the Constitution, and, like many other virtues, it cannot be legislated."[174] The aforegone *Tornillo* decision was not a surprise, of course: for while the Court's 1969 holding in *Red Lion Broadcasting Co. v. FCC*[175] appeared to recognize a *limited* ("contingent") right of access to the broadcast media under the commission's "fairness" doctrine, the Court concluded in its 1973 *CBS v. Democratic National Committee* ruling that neither the legislative requirement that the FCC act in the "public interest" nor the First Amendment itself required an FCC ruling that broadcasters accept paid editorial advertisements.[176] Nor does that amendment bar the FCC from prohibiting radio broadcasting of "offensive—indecent but not obscene—words," to wit, what the Court in its 5:4 ruling characterized as the "seven dirty words," used by comedian George Carlin in a twelve-minute monologue over station WBAI-FM New York.[177] Nor does the First Amendment prevent the federal government from shielding children from "dial-a-porn" telephone services by enacting a law that requires telephone companies to block access to the sexually explicit messages unless customers ask— in advance and in writing—to receive them.[178]

173. *Pittsburgh Press Co. v. Pittsburgh Commission on Human Relations,* 413 U.S. 376—obviously because of the Court's "close scrutiny" test (see *supra* chapter 2) applied to gender. See also a similarly intriguing line-drawing decision affecting competing interests, here race and religion, in *Norwood v. Harrison,* 413 U.S. 455 (1973). But cf. *Linmark Associates v. Willingboro, supra* note 59 involving expression and race. And the *Pittsburgh Press* case was distinguished in 1975 when the Court held (7:2) that Virginia had violated the First Amendment when it tried to punish a newspaper editor for publishing an advertisement telling of New York abortion services because abortions were illegal in Virginia (*Bigelow v. Virginia,* 421 U.S. 809). Justices White and Rehnquist dissented.
174. *Miami Herald Publishing Co. v. Tornillo,* 418 U.S. 241 at 256.
175. 395 U.S. 367. Strengthened in *CBS v. FCC,* 453 U.S. 367 (1981).
176. 412 U.S. 94. But it *must* sell time in federal campaign races.
177. *FCC v. Pacifica Foundation,* 438 U.S. 726 (1978). The words, characterized by the majority as "patently, offensively, referring to excretory and sexual organs and activities," were "shit, piss, fuck, cunt, cocksucker, motherfucker, and tits" (at 751–55). The Court's five-opinion lineup consisted of the chief justice and Justices Powell, Blackmun, Rehnquist, and Stevens in the majority, with Justices Brennan, White, Stewart, and Marshall dissenting. But the Court refused to review a (6:2) U.S. Court of Appeals decision in 1992 that a *round-the-clock* ban on "indecent" radio and television broadcasts violated the First Amendment. In *Pacifica* the time frame was confined to "family hours" (*FCC v. Action for Children's Television,* 503 U.S. 913, certiorari denied).
178. *Dial Information Services Corporation of New York v. Barr,* 502 U.S. 172 (1992). The FCC defines indecency as "language that depicts or describes in terms patently of-

Free Speech and Freedom from Noise

In a different although related form of the dilemma, during the 1948 presidential election, two interesting cases involving sound trucks caused the Court to draw two different lines between "freedom and order"—lines that are illustrative of the inherent complexities.

In the first case, *Saia v. New York*,[179] the petitioner was a minister of the Jehovah's Witnesses. Wishing to broadcast his gospel in Lockport, New York, Samuel Saia had run afoul of a city ordinance forbidding the use of sound-amplification devices except for "public dissemination of items of news and matters of public concern provided that the same be done under permission obtained from the Chief of Police." Refused a new permit on the grounds that complaints had been made about his prior sound-amplified speeches on religious (and not exactly very popular) subjects, Saia nevertheless decided to proceed to lecture, by means of loudspeakers, in a small city recreational park. He was convicted, fined, and sentenced to jail. Speaking for a closely divided Court (5:4), Justice Douglas held the ordinance "unconstitutional on its face, for it establishes a *previous restraint* on the right of free speech."[180] The right to be heard, concluded Douglas, was here placed impermissibly at the "uncontrolled discretion of the Chief of Police." However, to the four dissenting justices—Frankfurter, Reed, Jackson, and Burton—this was not a free speech issue at all, since no one, they contended, had stopped Saia from using his voice; rather, it was a question of the protection of society's unwilling listeners by a nonarbitrary, noncapricious, nondiscriminatory ordinance. But they lost.

They won, however, only eight months later in *Kovacs v. Cooper*,[181] with a ruling concerning the validity of a Trenton, New Jersey, ordinance. This time Henry Wallace's Progressive Party was involved. The case went 5:4 contra, Chief Justice Vinson switching sides and thus providing the key vote for the upholding of Trenton's law, which prohibited the use on the city's "public streets, alleys or thoroughfares" of any "device known as a sound truck, loud speaker or sound amplifier . . . [that] emits therefrom loud and raucous noises. . . ." Speaking for the new majority, Justice Reed, while emphasizing the "preferred position of free speech in a society that cherishes liberty for all," distinguished *Kovacs v. Cooper* from the *Saia* case on the grounds that the Trenton ordinance was carefully drawn and that the kind of discretionary power that the Court had found fatal to the Lockport ordinance was not present in Trenton's. In other words,

---

fensive as measured by contemporary community standards for the broadcast medium, sexual or excretory activities or organs."

179. 334 U.S. 588 (1948).

180. *Saia v. New York*, op. cit., at 559–60; italics supplied. Douglas was joined by Chief Justice Vinson and Associate Justices Black, Murphy, and Rutledge.

181. 336 U.S. 77 (1949).

Lockport's ordinance fell because of *prior restraint,* while Trenton succeeded because its case rested on *subsequent* punishment. The four dissenters (Black, Douglas, Murphy, and Rutledge, who, with the chief justice, had made up the majority in the *Saia* case) saw a rank violation of Charles Kovacs's right to freedom of expression under Amendments One and Fourteen.[182]

Freedom of Street Corner Exhortation

Two famous decisions, illustrating the importance of specific facts in particular court cases, were announced by the Supreme Court on the same day in 1951. The first favored free-speech claimant Carl Jacob Kunz, an ordained Baptist minister of rather unsavory reputation and long a thorn in the side of New York City police authorities because of his penchant for inflammatory addresses against Jews and Catholics in areas abounding with these two groups (minorities in most areas of the country, but certainly not in New York City). Preaching under the auspices of what he called the "Outdoor Gospel Work," of which he was the self-appointed director, Kunz had in 1946 asked for and received a permit under a New York City ordinance that made it unlawful to hold public worship meetings on the streets without first obtaining a permit from the city commissioner of police. Aware of what Kunz had done with his 1946 permit—which was revoked after a hearing—the commissioner several times refused a new one to Kunz, each time pointing to the fact that the 1946 revocation was based on clear evidence that Kunz had publicly ridiculed and denounced other religious beliefs in his meetings. In 1948 Kunz, having decided to hold one of his meetings *without* a permit, was arrested for speaking at Columbus Circle and fined ten dollars for violating the New York City ordinance in question. In an 8:1 opinion for the Court, Chief Justice Vinson addressed himself exclusively to the matter of prior suppression of free speech, concluding that "it is sufficient to say that New York cannot vest restraining control over the right to speak on religious subjects in an administrative official where there are no appropriate standards to guide his action."[183] There was a solitary, but lengthy and vigorous, dissenting opinion by Justice

---

182. The issue has a habit of recurring. Thus, in 1966 U.S. District Court Judge Alfred L. Luongo ruled that the city of Chester, Pennsylvania, was entitled to establish certain controls over operation of a sound truck but could not charge a twenty-five dollar fee for its operation. His decision came in a suit brought by the NAACP (*Philadelphia Evening Bulletin,* April 28, 1966). And in 1970 the Maryland Supreme Court struck down a Baltimore ordinance banning the use of loudspeakers without a permit. The law allowed the mayor and police commissioner to issue permits for "events of public interest"; it exempted newspapers, which were allowed to broadcast important news and sports items throughout the city. In effect, this accorded authorities the right to decide who would be permitted to exercise free speech! (For an account see 270 *Civil Liberties* 7 [July 1970].)

183. *Kunz v. New York,* 340 U.S 290 (1951) at 295.

Jackson. He pointed to the kind of "preachings" Kunz made, which, on his arrest in 1948 included the following observations:

The Catholic Church makes merchandise out of souls. . . . [Catholicism] is a religion of the devil. . . . [The Pope] is the anti-Christ. . . . The Jews . . . are Christ-killers. . . . All the garbage [the Jews] that didn't believe in Christ should have been burnt in the incinerators. It's a shame they all weren't.[184]

To Jackson, the chief American prosecutor at the Nuremberg war crimes trials, this public speech was too "intrinsically incendiary and divisive," given the delicate and emotional nature of the two subjects of "race and religion," to permit the type of constitutional protection claimed by Kunz and confirmed by Jackson's eight fellow judges. "The consecrated hatreds of sect," concluded the lone dissenter, "account for more than a few of the world's bloody disorders. These are the explosives which the Court says Kunz may play with in the public streets, and the community must not only tolerate but aid him. I find no such doctrine in the Constitution."[185]

Yet, on the same day of Court, just a few pages along in the same *United States Reports,*[186] the majority seemed to adopt the very ideas that Jackson alone expressed in the *Kunz* case! Involved here was the free-speech claim of one Irving Feiner, an adolescent Syracuse University student sidewalk orator who, using derogatory language about public officials and certain interest groups, had harangued a crowd of some seventy-five to eighty white and black persons in a predominantly black residential area of Syracuse, New York, in 1949. He was publicizing a "Young Progressives" meeting to be held that evening in a local hotel rather than in the public-school auditorium originally scheduled, because the permit granted for the latter had been revoked as a result of local pressure-group activities. In the course of his speech Feiner referred to President Truman as a "bum"; to Mayor Costello of Syracuse as a "champagne-sipping bum" who "does not speak for the Negro people"; to Mayor O'Dwyer of New York City as a "bum"; to the American Legion as "a Nazi Gestapo"; and in what the record described as "an excited manner," yelled: "The Negroes don't have equal rights; they should rise up in arms and fight for them."[187]

Feiner's statements "stirred up a little excitement," and one of the bystanders called out that if police did not get that "son of a bitch" off the stand, he would do so himself. (The police later admitted that there was "not yet a disturbance," but that there did occur "angry muttering and pushing.") At this point one of the two police officers detailed to the area stepped forward and arrested Feiner to "prevent [the events] from resulting in a fight," since Feiner—who had been

184. Ibid. at 296.
185. Ibid. at 314.
186. The official volumes reporting all Supreme Court decisions.
187. *Feiner v. New York,* 340 U.S. 315 (1951) at 330.

holding forth for over thirty minutes—had disregarded two earlier requests by the policeman to stop speaking. The New York State trial judge concluded that the police officers were justified in taking the action "to prevent a breach of the peace," and the intermediate appellate tribunal concurred. New York State's highest court, the court of appeals, then affirmed the findings below, stating that Feiner, "with intent to provoke a breach of the peace and with knowledge of the consequences, so inflamed and agitated a mixed audience of sympathizers and opponents that, in the judgment of the police officers present, a *clear danger* of disorder and violence was threatened."[188] Speaking for himself and five of his colleagues—Associate Justices Reed, Frankfurter, Jackson, Burton, and Clark— Chief Justice Vinson agreed with the findings of "three New York courts" that Feiner's free-speech claims were spurious: that, while his right to hold his meeting and utter the derogatory remarks was uncontested and uncontestable, the police officers were justified in making the arrest because they

> were motivated solely by a proper concern for the preservation of order and protection of the general welfare, and that there was no evidence which could lend color to a claim that the acts of the police were a cover for suppression of [Feiner's] views and opinions. Petitioner was thus neither arrested nor convicted for the making or the content of his speech. Rather, *it was the reaction which it actually engendered.*[189]

It was precisely from this last sentence that Justices Black, Douglas, and Minton dissented strongly in two separate opinions, Minton joining Douglas's and Black writing his own. In brief, the dissenters rejected the majority's two key points, namely, that danger of a riot existed and that Feiner had perpetrated a breach of the peace (for which he would serve thirty days in prison). They denied that the facts demonstrated "any imminent threat of riot or uncontrollable disorder"[190] and declared that the record merely showed "an unsympathetic audience and the threat of one man to haul the speaker from the stage. *It is against that kind of threat that speakers need police protection,*" concluded Justice Douglas,[191] pointing to what he and the other dissenting jurists viewed as the duty of the police: to, as Black put it, protect Feiner's "constitutional right to talk" rather than to arrest him.[192] And there, of course, lies the dilemma: At what point should speech be prohibitable? When it stirs to anger? When it creates opposition?

188. Ibid. at 318, note 2; italics supplied.
189. Ibid. at 319–20; italics supplied.
190. Ibid. Black, dissenting opinion at 325.
191. Ibid. dissenting opinion at 331.
192. Four decades later, Irving Feiner's daughter Susan Feiner, a professor of economics, made headlines in a well-publicized dispute with Virginia Commonwealth University, which had allegedly denied her promotion and tenure because of her avowed Marxist commitments and teachings (see Coleman McCarthy, "Free Speech and the Right to Teach," *Washington Post,* October 1, 1989, p. F9).

When it creates disorder? But who is to say that the latter cannot be artificially stimulated, even created? Could not, as Black, Douglas, and Minton tried to plead in *Feiner,* a strong point be made that the police have an obligation to protect the *maker* of the speech *against* a hostile audience? To raise these fundamental questions is to recognize the difficulty of any all-embracing response. Does it depend not only on the *content* of a speech but also on *how* it is *delivered?* And with what identifiable purpose and direction?[193] What of such emotion-charged issues as those that informed the wrenching 1978 Skokie, Illinois, Nazi Party activities?[194] What of the nature of the mass protests and demonstrations in the context of the contemporary youth and race "evangelism"? "Incitement," too, is a double-edged sword. After all, as Justice Holmes put it so perceptively in his memorable dissenting opinion in the *Gitlow* case,[195] "[E]very idea is an incitement. . . . The only difference between the expression of an opinion and an incitement in the narrower sense is the speaker's enthusiasm for the result. Eloquence may set fire to reason."[196] Whatever the elusive answer, democratic society demands that it be a generous one. If that means taking chances, so be it—but, as Justice Jackson put it so eloquently in his already alluded-to dissent in the *Terminiello* case, we are assuredly not obliged to be so doctrinaire and so devoid of practical wisdom as to "convert the constitutional Bill of Rights into a suicide pact."[197]

Free Expression and Association and Subversive Activity: The National Security Syndrome

The fact and concept of subversive activity and how to meet it have concerned the nation sporadically since its birth. From the hated Alien and Sedition Acts of

193. See *Chaplinsky v. New Hampshire, supra* note 77 and its subsequent interpretation.
194. See *Village of Skokie v. National Socialist Party,* 69 Ill.2d 605; 373 N.E.2d 21 (1978). See also *Smith v. Collin, supra* note 61 on the same case.
195. *Gitlow v. New York,* 268 U.S. 652 (1925).
196. Ibid. at 673.
197. *Terminiello v. Chicago,* 337 U.S. 1 (1949) at 37, an interesting and troublesome case, demonstrating that very problem. In *Terminiello* the Court, dividing 5:4, reversed the breach-of-peace conviction of a professional rabble-rouser (a suspended Catholic priest) who had *really* caused a riot. But the year was 1949—with Justices Murphy and Rutledge still on the bench (they both died later that year). And Douglas's majority opinion was based on a dubious procedural analysis: that the oral charge of the jury by the trial judge was ambiguous and imprecise in its explanation of the municipal ordinance defining "disorderly conduct" under which Terminiello had been tried and convicted. In fact, Douglas had initially voted to *sustain* the conviction—but then changed his mind and was assigned the writing of the opinion for the Court by Black (the senior justice on that side of the issue, Chief Justice Vinson being in dissent). Reed provided the decisive fifth vote, persuaded by Douglas's reasoning. (The other three dissenters were Frankfurter, Jackson, and Burton, with Jackson there penning his celebrated warning. Jackson's full statement was: "There is danger that, if the Court does not temper its doctrinaire logic with a little practical wisdom, it will convert the constitutional Bill of Rights into a suicide pact.")

1798 through the trying eras of the Civil War, World War I, the "red scare" of the 1920s, post–World War II, McCarthyism, and the cold war of the late 1940s and the 1950s, the legislative and administrative remedies adopted to deal with the problem of national security have often been dominant concerns. And the resultant statutes, executive orders, and legislative investigations have almost all, sooner or later, found themselves in judicial hot water, agitated by the friction between freedom of expression and association and national security and how to draw viable and allowable lines. Answers given by the judicial branch in this area—if answers they be—have understandably been perhaps more cautious and more circumspect than for any other aspect of the freedom at issue. Nonetheless, as the McCarthy-tinged late 1940s and the 1950s turned into the 1960s, the courts became increasingly sympathetic toward the individual's constitutional claims as against those of majoritarian society. Hence, for example, while necessarily recognizing the right and duty of the legislative branch to keep itself informed in order to legislate more wisely, both to "oversee" the executive branch and to inform the public, the Supreme Court has also recognized that there are, and must be, limits on the range and extent of the power to investigate. Among these are the witness's right to decline to respond by invoking the Fifth Amendment's privilege against compulsory self-incrimination, though in many areas he or she may be compelled to testify in return for immunity from prosecution;[198] to refuse to reply if the question is beyond the investigating committee's mandate;[199] and to have "explicit and clear" knowledge of the subject to which the interrogation is deemed pertinent.[200] Yet as other decisions of the Court have shown, great difficulties here are the matters of "pertinency"[201] and just what constitutes "exposure for the sake of exposure."[202]

Similarly troublesome has been the matter of "loyalty and security." The Court has been called upon repeatedly to draw lines between the rights of the individual under the Bill of Rights, which one assuredly does not surrender simply because he or she works for the government, and the rights of the state, which

198. E.g., *Ullmann v. United States,* 350 U.S. 422 (1955); and *Murphy v. Waterfront Commission of New York Harbor,* 378 U.S. 52 (1964).
199. E.g., *United States v. Rumely,* 345 U.S. 41 (1953).
200. E.g., *Watkins v. United States,* 354 U.S. 178 (1957).
201. E.g., *Barenblatt v. United States,* 360 U.S. 109 (1954).
202. E.g., *Braden v. United States,* 365 U.S. 431 (1961). Cf. *DeGregory v. Attorney-General of New Hampshire,* 383 U.S. 825 (1966). Most notoriously prominent in these investigations was "HUAC" (the House Committee on Un-American Activities). Restyled the Internal Securities Committee—its constitutionality upheld in 1968 in *Stamler v. Willis,* 393 U.S. 212—it was abolished in 1975 and its functions transferred to the House Committee on the Judiciary. The Senate's counterpart, the Judiciary Committee's Internal Security Subcommittee, was disbanded in 1977, but the Subcommittee on Security and Terrorism was constituted in 1981.

has a basic obligation to protect its citizenry from subversion by disloyal elements. Grave problems have surrounded the nature and meaning of the terms "loyalty" and "security," as well as the compatibility of appropriate security legislation and ordinances with the prerogatives of free citizens. Avoiding the constitutional issues whenever possible, the Court handed down several significant guidelines, chiefly by statutory interpretation. Thus, federal employee loyalty-security regulations, which initially seemed to have a rather free rein, found themselves increasingly confined in coverage and held to ever more strict requirements of procedural due process as of the mid-1950s.[203] At least one key aspect of the issue was more or less settled when a special three-judge federal court ruled in 1969 that the statute on which the then twenty-five-year-old *loyalty oath* requirement for federal employees was based was "unconstitutionally vague" not only as a violation of the Fifth Amendment's due process of law clause but also, in the ruling of the 2:1 majority opinion by Judges J. Skelly Wright and Harold Leventhal of the U.S. Court of Appeals for the District of Columbia, as a violation of the strictures against "odious test oaths" inherent in Article 6 of the Constitution.[204] When the U.S. Department of Justice decided not to appeal the decision to the Supreme Court, the Civil Service Commission quietly informed all federal departments and agencies that prospective employees would henceforth no longer have to sign the controversial affidavit stating that the applicant was neither a Communist nor a Fascist nor sought to overthrow the U.S. government by force and violence.[205]

The Warren Court did squarely face the constitutional issue in a related matter—namely, the government's policy of barring employment to otherwise qualified individuals *merely* because of their beliefs and/or associations. While never having wavered from basic erstwhile, and entirely logical, holdings that there is no ipso facto constitutional *right* to work for the *government,*[206] the Court nonetheless made clear in a series of cases in the late 1960s that the First Amendment is not vitiated simply because someone happens to be, or aspires to be, a governmental employee. Thus, speaking through Chief Justice Warren in the

203. *Peters v. Hobby,* 349 U.S. 349 (1955); *Cole v. Young,* 351 U.S. 356 (1956); *Service v. Dulles,* 354 U.S. 363 (1957); *Vitarelli v. Seaton,* 359 U.S. (1959); *Greene v. McElroy,* 361 U.S. 374 (1959).

204. *Stewart v. Washington,* 301 F. Supp. 610. Judge John Lewis Smith, the third member of the tribunal, agreed that the oath was invalid, but he did not agree that the wording of the law itself was unconstitutional.

205. *New York Times,* January 7, 1970, p. 1. And in late 1976 it ordered the elimination of all political loyalty questions on federal job application forms (*New York Times,* September 9, 1976, p. 1). Four years later, the Carter administration forbade government officials from inquiring into the sexual habits of employees or individuals seeking most federal jobs—an order that represented a major boost for the rights of homosexuals (*Washington Post,* May 14, 1980, p. C2).

206. *United Public Workers v. Mitchell,* 330 U.S. 75 (1947).

1967 *Robel* case, it declared unconstitutional (6:2)—as a violation of First Amendment rights of freedom of association—a provision of the Subversive Activities Control (McCarran) Act of 1950 that made it a crime for members of the Communist Party to work in defense plants, regardless of the "quality and degree" of that membership.[207] And the Court extended the aforegone ruling to the maritime industry early in 1968, holding unanimously that Herbert Schneider, a Seattle marine engineer and former Communist Party member who had applied for clearance in 1964, could not be barred from employment simply because of his beliefs or associations.[208] The government, wrote Justice Douglas for the Court, has every right to enact legislation to safeguard American shipping from subversive activity, but Congress had not, under the applicable statute—the Magnuson Act of 1950—given the executive branch the power "to ferret out the ideological strays."[209]

A host of state "loyalty" statutes and allied requirements have fallen on grounds of both substantive and procedural due process, often in concord with freedom of expression guarantees. Thus, while some practices have been upheld as valid exercises of the state police power—particularly *affirmative* rather than *disclaimer* loyalty oaths[210]—others have fallen, more often than not because of the "vice of vagueness": the sweeping implications of such terms as "subversive organizations," "subversive persons," or "sympathetic association with."[211] In fact, state loyalty oaths began to fall like veritable flies as of 1966, and by 1969 the vast majority of the disclaimer-type state oaths, as well as "mixed" disclaimer-affirmative types,[212] were a thing of the past.[213] And at-

207. *United States v. Robel*, 389 U.S. 258 (see discussion *infra*).

208. *Schneider v. Smith*, 390 U.S. 17. In that case, however, the Court applied statutory construction to the Magnuson Act of 1950 rather than hold it unconstitutional.

209. Ibid. at 26. Congress threatened to overturn the two decisions but never did.

210. *Garner v. Board of Public Works of Los Angeles*, 341 U.S. 716 (1951); *Gerende v. Board of Supervisors*, 341 U.S. 56 (1951); *Adler v. Board of Education of New York*, 342 U.S. 485 (1952), but overruled by *Keyishian, infra* note 212; *Knight v. Board of Regents of New York*, 390 U.S. 36 (1968); *Hosack v. Smiley*, 390 U.S. 744 (1968); *Lisker v. Kelly*, 410 U.S. 928 (1971).

211. *Wieman v. Updegraff*, 344 U.S. 183 (1952); *Shelton v. Tucker*, 364 U.S. 479 (1960); *Baggett v. Bullitt*, 377 U.S. 360 (1964).

212. *Elfbrandt v. Russell*, 384 U.S. 11 (1966); *Keyishian v. Board of Regents of New York*, 385 U.S. 589 (1967), overruling *Adler, supra* note 210; *Whitehill v. Elkins*, 389 U.S. 54 (1967).

213. E.g., *Rafferty v. McKay*, 400 U.S. 954 (1970), in which the Court affirmed a lower court holding that struck down California's loyalty oath for teachers by relying on *Baggett v. Bullitt*, op. cit. The oath at issue was the "mixed" type, reading: "I solemnly swear (or affirm) that I will support the Constitution of the United States of America, the Constitution of the State of California, and the laws of the United States and the State of California, and will . . . promote respect for the flag and . . . respect for law and order and . . . allegiance to the government of the United States." Had the oath stopped with "California" and before "and will," it undoubtedly would have been upheld as a simple affirma-

tacks, albeit unsuccessful,[214] were also launched against even the simple "positive" type.

Here, again, the advocates of maximum security and those who believe that democratic society must take risks for the sake of freedom are at loggerheads. It is far easier to criticize than to solve. And it has been understandably rare for the Court to be unanimous in any such cases unless the restrictions involved were clearly and patently unconstitutional.[215]

In the three major federal statutes that have been enacted since 1940 to combat subversion and increase national security, heavy judicial involvement was inevitable, given the nature of the controversy and the delicacy and difficulty of producing legislation that would achieve the desired goal without impinging upon fundamental individual liberties. The triumvirate of laws, in the order of their enactment, are the Smith Act of 1940, the Subversive Activities Control (McCarran) Act of 1950, and the Communist Control Act of 1954. We need not be concerned here with this last, hastily enacted, largely floor-legislated statute, since it has been more or less ignored by the Department of Justice as a basis for possible prosecution. Although it did figure tangentially in three cases in 1956, 1961, and 1970,[216] it had not been frontally adjudicated by the Court as of early 1988, and it is not likely to be.

Dennis v. United States. The first major test of anti-Communist legislation involved the Smith Act: the 1951 case of *Dennis v. United States.*[217] Here, in a 6:2 decision, featuring five separate opinions (the opinion for the Court by Chief Justice Vinson, two separate concurring opinions by Justices Frankfurter and Jackson, and two separate dissenting opinions by Justices Black and Douglas), the Supreme Court upheld the Smith Act's constitutionality. It did so against the contentions by Eugene Dennis and his ten coleaders of the American Communist Party that the statute infringed on First Amendment guarantees of freedom of expression, in addition to violating substantive due process guarantees under the Fifth Amendment because of vagueness. The eleven top leaders had been in-

tive oath. However, narrowly dividing 4:3, in 1972 the Court upheld a two-part Massachusetts loyalty oath which, in addition to the standard "uphold and defend" clause, requires public employees to pledge that they will "oppose" the overthrow of the federal and state governments by force, violence, "or by any illegal or unconstitutional methods" (*Cole v. Richardson,* 405 U.S. 676).

214. E.g., *Fields v. Askew,* 414 U.S. 1148 (1974).

215. E.g., *Wieman v. Updegraff,* op. cit., in which the Court unanimously struck down an Oklahoma loyalty oath law that made even innocent membership in a proscribed organization an offense.

216. *Pennsylvania v. Nelson,* 350 U.S. 497; *Communist Party v. Catherwood,* 367 U.S. 389; and *Mitchell v. Donavan,* 398 U.S. 427, respectively. In the 1961 case it ruled 9:0 (via Harlan) that the Communist Party could not be banned from state unemployment systems; in the 1970 case it pointedly declined to rule on the act's constitutionality.

217. 341 U.S. 494.

dicted and tried in U.S. District Court Judge Harold Medina's tribunal and after a sensational nine-month trial were found guilty of conspiracy[218] to teach and advocate the overthrow of the U.S. government by force and violence, and a conspiracy to organize the American Communist Party to teach and advocate the same offenses proscribed and rendered criminal by the terms of the Smith Act. Their appeal to the U.S. Court of Appeals for the Second Circuit had been unanimously rebuffed. In upholding the challenged segments of the act, the chief justice, speaking for himself and Associate Justices Reed, Burton, and Minton,[219] focused on what the majority regarded as the conspiratorial nature of the defendants' activities. Calling upon the "clear and present danger" formula—a judicial doctrine utilized in freedom of expression cases, to be discussed subsequently— Vinson ruled that these activities transgressed the permissible line between the exercise of individual rights of peaceful advocacy of change and the right of society to ascertain national security as viewed by the Smith Act. But in invoking the concept that the activities of the eleven did indeed constitute a clear and present danger which Congress had a right and duty to prevent, he added an important qualification originally expressed by Chief Judge Learned Hand in the case of the court of appeals below: "In each case [courts] must ask whether the gravity of the 'evil,' discounted by its improbability, justifies such invasion of free speech as is necessary to avoid the danger."[220] "We adopt this statement of the rule," the chief justice went on, because it is "as succinct and inclusive as any other we might devise at this time. It takes into consideration those factors which we deem relevant, and relates their significance. More we cannot expect from words."[221] Explaining the community's justification for its national security policy, he continued:

> The formation by [the convicted Communist Party leaders] of such a highly organized conspiracy, with rigidly disciplined members subject to call when the leaders, these petitioners, felt that the time had come for action, coupled with the inflammable nature of world conditions, similar uprisings in other countries, and the touch-and-go nature of our relations with countries with whom the petitioners were in the very least ideologically attuned, convince us that their convictions were justified on this score.[222]

"And this analysis," wrote the chief justice determinedly, "disposes of the contention that a conspiracy to advocate, as distinguished from the advocacy itself, cannot be constitutionally restrained, because it comprises only the preparation.

218. A conspiracy is commonly regarded as any combination of two or more persons to commit an unlawful act or accomplish some unlawful purpose by illegal means.

219. Justice Clark, who, as President Truman's attorney general, had brought the indictments in the case, did not participate.

220. *Dennis v. United States,* 183 F.2d 201 (1950) at 212.

221. *Dennis v. United States,* 341 U.S. 494 (1951) at 510.

222. Ibid. at 510–11.

It is the existence of the conspiracy which creates the danger."[223] Earlier, he had anticipated one objection by commenting that "clear and present danger" cannot mean that before the "[g]overnment may act, it must wait until the putsch is about to be executed, the plans have been laid and the signal is awaited."[224] And he rejected success or probability of success as a criterion.

Justice Frankfurter's concurring opinion was characteristic of his jurisprudential philosophy: to him, the decisive consideration was the Court's obligation to exercise judicial self-restraint by recognizing that the legislative assumption in passing the Smith Act was a reasonable one, consummated by reasonable representatives of the body politic. He was troubled by the law, however, and warned that "it is a sobering fact that in sustaining the conviction . . . we can hardly escape restriction on the interchange of ideas"; that without "open minds there can be no open society."[225] Yet he emphatically held to his creed that even "free-speech cases are not an exception to the principle that we are not legislators, that direct policy-making is not our province."[226] Only if the legislative determination on how competing interests might best be reconciled is clearly "outside the pale of fair judgment" would the Court be justified in exercising its veto. The obvious difficulty, of course, remains: how and when to judge what is "outside." On the other hand, Justice Jackson, in his concurring opinion, pursued a different tack; waving aside the intricate free-speech problem line per se (he rejected application of the clear and present danger doctrine "to a case like this"), he concentrated almost exclusively on what he chose to see as *the* crux of the case—a conviction of and for *conspiracy*—"as that is the case before us." Eleven times in two paragraphs of his opinion he used the noun *conspiracy,* commenting that the "Constitution does not make conspiracy a civil right."[227]

Justices Black and Douglas dissented vehemently. In separate opinions they *denied* the existence of a danger either clear or present enough to justify what they regarded as a rank invasion of the prerogatives of freedom of expression (although Douglas, unlike Black, granted that "freedom to speak is not absolute"); charged that the Court's majority had, in effect, introduced a formula far less "tough" for the government to cope with than the clear and present danger concept Chief Justice Vinson ostensibly employed; and fervently argued for "full and free discussion even of ideas we hate." Justice Douglas belittled the alleged internal strength and threat of the Communist movement, pointing out that in America "they are miserable merchants of unwanted ideas: their wares remain unsold."[228] Justice Black closed his opinion with the following observation:

223. Ibid. at 511; italics supplied.
224. Ibid. at 509.
225. Ibid. at 556.
226. Ibid. at 539.
227. Ibid. at 572.
228. Ibid. at 589.

Public opinion being what it now is, few will protest the conviction of these Communist petitioners. There is hope, however, that in calmer times, when present pressures, passions and fears subside, this or some later Court will restore the First Amendment liberties to the high preferred place where they belong in a free society.[229]

Yates v. United States. Whatever the substantive merits of the Black position, this statement proved to be correct both as an analysis and as a prophecy. By June 1957 the federal authorities had obtained 145 indictments and 89 convictions under the Smith Act. But then, a six-member majority of the Supreme Court[230]— with only Justice Clark in dissent—drastically and dramatically limited the application of the act by handing down a series of significant amendatory interpretations in the difficult case of *Yates v. United States.*[231] Writing an intricate opinion for the Court, Justice Harlan narrowed the meaning of the term "to organize"—one that Congress, clearly in retaliation, again broadened in 1962—and endeavored to establish an important legal distinction under the Smith Act between the *statement of a philosophical belief and the advocacy of an illegal action.* The Court took pains to make clear that the Smith Act still stood, and there was no attempt to overrule the *Dennis* case. But it was obvious that the federal government would now no longer be statutorily able to punish members of the American Communist Party, such as Oleta O'Connor Yates and her codefendant "second-string Communists," *for expressing a mere belief in the "abstract idea"* of the violent overthrow of the government. It would now have to prove that individuals on trial for alleged violations of the Smith Act had *actually intended,* now or in the future, to overthrow the government by force and violence, or to persuade others to do so. Moreover, the government would still have to demonstrate that the language employed by the advocates of actual overthrow was in fact "calculated to incite to action . . . to *do* something, now or in the future, rather than merely *believe* in something."[232] This, of course, it should be observed, was no longer the Vinson Court of 1951; the chief justice had died in 1953 and had been replaced by Earl Warren; Robert Jackson, who died a year later, was succeeded by John Marshall Harlan; and although they took no part in the consideration or decision of *Yates,* William Brennan and Charles Whittaker had supplanted the resigned Sherman Minton and the retired Stanley Reed. Remaining were Tom Clark, who had not participated in *Dennis* and now dissented in *Yates;* Felix Frankfurter and Harold Burton, who made up part of the *Yates* ma-

229. Ibid. at 581.
230. Justices Brennan and Whittaker did not participate in the case.
231. 354 U.S. 298 (1957).
232. Ibid. at 325. The Court did distinguish the cases of the fourteen petitioners in *Yates,* however, ordering the acquittal of five and remanding the case of the remaining nine for a new trial—based on the newly created *Yates* line.

jority; and the *Dennis* dissenters, Hugo Black and William Douglas—who concurred in the decision in part but also dissented in part because of their insistence that Amendment One renders any such legislation unconstitutional on its face. The public reaction to *Yates* was adverse; the line created by the Court between "theoretical" and "actual" advocacy did not assuage the uneasy feelings of both the opponents and the proponents that it would prove to be a vexatious distinction indeed. Hence it came as less than a total surprise that four years later the Court, in *Scales v. United States*,[233] the first test involving the so-called membership clause[234] of the Smith Act, upheld that clause in the face of stringent constitutional challenges on the grounds of First and Fifth Amendment infringements. Justice Harlan, speaking for the 5:4 majority, ruled that a person who was a "knowing, active" member of a subversive group, and who personally had a "specific intent to bring about violent overthrow of the government," could be convicted under the statute—and Junius Irving Scales, whose membership in the Communist Party the Harlan opinion categorized as "indisputably active," went to jail.[235] Yet in a companion case decided on the very same day, also testing the validity of a conviction under the "membership clause," Harlan, adhering to his *Yates* dichotomy between a philosophical belief and advocating an illegal action, *switched* sides, together with his four *Scales* supporters, to bring about a 9:0 vote *against* the culpability of one John Francis Noto.[236] Noto, held Harlan for the Court, including the chief justice and Justices Black, Douglas, and Brennan—who had all dissented from the *Scales* decision[237]—did not meet the "knowing, active" membership test necessary for conviction. Again we see the difficult and delicate case-by-case balancing problem in freedom of expression.

As if to demonstrate that fact of governmental and societal life, on the very day of the two decisions in *Scales* and *Noto,* a 5:4 verdict upheld the registration requirements of the second national security statute, the McCarran, or Subversive Activities Control, Act of 1950,[238] the Court's lineup being the same as in *Scales*. Under that statute, the Subversive Activities Control Board (SACB)

233. 367 U.S. 203 (1961).
234. The act, among other things, made a felony the acquisition or holding of knowing membership in any organization which advocates the overthrow of the government of the United States by force or violence (18 U.S.C. #2385, 18 U.S.C.A. #2385).
235. After having served fifteen months of his six-year sentence, he was pardoned by President Kennedy on Christmas Day 1962. Ironically, he had broken with the Communist Party four years before he went to jail.
236. *Noto v. United States,* 367 U.S. 290 (1961).
237. These four now concurred; they would have preferred to dismiss the indictment, not merely to reverse the conviction. Speaking for the four, Black wrote: "I cannot join in an opinion which implies that the existence of liberty is dependent upon the efficiency of the Government's informers" (at 302). He viewed the majority opinion as a clarion call to the government to maintain a permanent staff of informers who are prepared to give up-to-date information with respect to the Communist Party's present policies.
238. *Communist Party v. Subversive Activities Control Board,* 367 U.S. 1 (1961).

could, after a due hearing, order any Communist "action" or "front" group to register—and it had so ordered the American Communist Party. But for more than a decade the party had refused to register, and it challenged the order as a violation of freedom of expression and association and (in view of the Smith Act's criminal sanction) as compulsory self-incrimination under the Fifth Amendment. In one of the longest opinions in the Court's history, Justice Frankfurter, speaking also for his colleagues Clark, Harlan, Whittaker, and Stewart, upheld the forced disclosure of Communist Party members' names. With characteristic caution, and deference to the legislative branch, the Frankfurter opinion failed to consider the basic issue of compulsory self-incrimination under Amendment Five (or any of several other constitutional questions raised by the defense). Rather, he based his ruling strictly upon a judgment that the "registration requirement of #7 [of the McCarran Act], on its face and as here applied, does not violate the First Amendment."[239] Dissenting, Warren, Black, Douglas, and Brennan, in three separate opinions, not only flayed the Court majority for ducking the crucial self-incrimination issue but also exhorted it to recognize, in Justice Douglas's words, that "our Constitution protects all minorities, no matter how despised they are."[240]

Yet the Court's hand was forced on the compulsory self-incrimination issue just two years later, when the U.S. Court of Appeals for the District of Columbia *did* squarely meet that aspect of the registration issue by *reversing* the Communist Party's conviction in a federal trial court for its failure to register under the McCarran Act's commands. The reversal[241] was on narrow grounds and did not necessarily settle the self-incrimination matter,[242] but it did uphold the Communist Party's constitutional argument that since the Smith Act treats it as a criminal conspiracy, compelled registration would ipso facto be self-incriminating. Since "mere association with the party incriminates," ruled the unanimous intermediate appellate tribunal in its opinion by Chief Judge Bazelon, statutory registration would indeed force self-incrimination in the face of Fifth Amendment guarantees to the contrary. When the U.S. government appealed that holding to the Supreme Court, the latter eschewed the opportunity to expound on the problem and, by refusing without comment to review the decision, maintained the government's defeat.[243]

Two weeks later, however, the Court did come to constitutional terms with another section of the McCarran Act, which it had also purposely ignored in the

239. Ibid. at 105.
240. Ibid. at 190.
241. *Communist Party v. United States,* 331 F.2d 807 (1963).
242. "We hold only that the availability of someone to sign the forms was an element of the offense; that the officers, who should otherwise have signed, were unavailable by reason of their valid claim of the privilege against self-incrimination; that the government had the burden of showing that a volunteer was available; and that its failure to discharge this burden requires reversal of this conviction" (ibid. at 815).
243. *United States v. Communist Party,* 377 U.S. 968 (1964).

1961 decision: the denial of passports to members of the American Communist Party and its "fronts." In a 6:3 decision, written for the Court by its most junior member in point of service, Justice Goldberg, the majority ruled the provision "unconstitutional on its face" as a deprivation of liberty guaranteed by the "due process of law" concept of the Fifth Amendment because it "too broadly and indiscriminately restricts the right to travel."[244] The three dissenters, Justices Clark, Harlan, and White, contended with feeling that that right was not absolute and that its denial on national security grounds was entirely reasonable under the circumstances at issue. Subsequently, the Court granted certiorari in two cases again challenging the McCarran Act requirement that *individual members* of the Communist Party, rather than the Party itself, register with the government.[245]

It took until 1965, but when the Court's decision was announced, it was unanimous. Speaking through Justice Brennan, it held *unenforceable* the Justice Department orders requiring two alleged subversives, William Albertson and Roscoe Quincy Proctor, to register under the McCarran Act, ruling that such registration would expose them to prosecution under other federal laws "in an area permeated with criminal statutes."[246] The opinion stopped short of declaring the "individual membership registration" provision of the act *unconstitutional,* because a party member could waive his self-incrimination privilege and register. But the obvious effect of the Court's holding was to make the registration requirement governmentally unenforceable and thus unusable. In an area of freedom of expression in which unanimity is so demonstrably hard to attain, the Court thus stood as one with Brennan's holding that "the requirement to accomplish registration by completing and filing [the required form] is inconsistent with the protection of the self-incrimination clause [of the Fifth Amendment to the Constitution of the United States]."[247]

In 1968, faced with a now practically toothless Subversive Activities Control Board, Congress enacted a compromise measure designed to keep the SACB in business, notwithstanding the several damaging Supreme Court and lower court rulings affecting its functions. It provided that the SACB could hold hear-

244. *Aptheker v. Secretary of State,* 378 U.S. 500 (1964) at 514. The act's controversial Title II, its detention provision, was repealed by the Senate by unanimous vote in 1969; the House followed suit (356:49) in 1971. See also *Schneider v. Rusk,* 377 U.S. 163 (1964). But cf. *Haig v. Agee,* 453 U.S. 280 (1981).
245. *Albertson v. Subversive Activities Control Board,* 381 U.S. 910; and *Proctor v. Subversive Activities Control Board,* 381 U.S. 910 (1965). Earlier, the Court had vacated two orders requiring Communist "fronts" to register, ruling that the record in the cases was "too stale" for a serious constitutional adjudication (*American Committee for Protection of Foreign Born v. Subversive Activities Control Board,* 380 U.S. 503; and *Veterans of the Abraham Lincoln Brigade v. Subversive Activities Control Board,* 380 U.S. 513 [1963]).
246. *Albertson v. Subversive Activities Control Board,* 382 U.S. 70 (1965).
247. Ibid. at 76.

ings to determine whether individuals were Communists and whether organizations were either Communist "front" or Communist "action" groups. If it so determined, the SACB could then *itself* register them. The dubious constitutional provisions of the 1968 statute were tailor-made for a judicial test, and Simon Boorda, a Utah teacher ordered by the SACB to register, and then registered as "Communist" by the board itself upon his refusal to do so, brought suit in 1969. The U.S. Court of Appeals for the District of Columbia declared the registration procedures authorized under the 1968 law unconstitutional as a rank violation of the First Amendment's guarantee of freedom of association.[248] The Justice Department appealed, but the Supreme Court denied review, thus upholding the lower tribunal's decision.[249] President Nixon revitalized the SACB by executive order in 1971, indeed expanding its scope. Although Congress approved that move in 1972, it slashed the SACB's budget by 50 percent later, and the president's budget message for 1973 omitted all funds for it. It died a quiet death on June 30, 1973.

Foreshadowing its increasing strictness vis-à-vis legislative experimentations in the internal security realm, the Court had entered virgin territory in 1965 in the battleground between freedom of expression and national security by declaring unconstitutional for the very first time a congressional statute on grounds of First Amendment freedom of speech. While federal statutes had heretofore fallen on other grounds, frequently because of due process violation, for one, and many a state law had been struck down on the freedom of expression issue by its incorporation via Amendment Fourteen, this was a novel development. Unanimously, the Court now threw out a 1962 federal law that had required persons to whom "Communist political propaganda" from abroad was addressed to make a special request to the Post Office to deliver it. Under the statute—which did not cover sealed letters—the Customs Bureau gave the Post Office Department a list of countries from which printed Communist propaganda emanated. At the eleven entry points postal officials examined the material and, if they decided that it was "Communist political propaganda," intercepted it. The department then notified the persons to whom it was addressed that they could receive it only if they returned an attached reply card within twenty days; if they did not respond, the mail was destroyed! Justice Douglas's stern opinion concluded:

> [T]he act as construed and applied is unconstitutional because it requires an official act [returning the reply card] as a limitation on the unfettered exercise of the addressee's First Amendment rights. . . . The addressee carries an affirmative obligation which we do not think the Government may impose on him. . . . The regime of this *act is at war with the "uninhibited, robust, and wide-open" debate and discussion that are contemplated by the First Amendment.*[250]

248. *Boorda v. Subversive Activities Control Board,* 421 F.2d 1142 (1969).
249. *Subversive Activities Control Board v. Boorda,* 397 U.S. 1042 (1970).
250. *Lamont v. Postmaster-General* and *Fixa v. Heilberg,* 381 U.S. 301 (1965); italics supplied.

Perhaps more than any of the other examples of line drawing, that of the riddle of national security in the days of the cold war may serve to demonstrate that there are no easy answers to the problem of the balance between freedom of expression and the security requirements of the land. It is a demonstrable fact of life that dedicated democrats may well find themselves on opposite sides of the question.[251] A rather less vital but intriguing, titillating, and vexatious question concerns the line between freedom of expression and "obscenity."

What Is Obscene and When Is It?

The temptation to wallow a bit here is strong, but space demands confinement to some fundamental considerations. The obvious difficulty is again the problem of definition—Chief Justice Warren regarded obscenity, in retrospect, as the Court's "most difficult" area of adjudication.[252] What is "obscenity" to some is mere "realism" to others; what is "lascivious" in the eyes of one reader is merely "colorful" in those of another; what is "lewd" or "pornographic" to one parent may well be "instructive" to another. In one southern city the censorship board thus ruled "obscene" a movie which showed black and white children playing together in a school yard.[253] In cosmopolitan Chicago, the Police Board of Censorship held "obscene" Walt Disney's film on a vanishing prairie, which showed a buffalo giving birth in a snowstorm.[254] New York's Board of Regents—that state's official censor of movies—was never troubled by the charming little movie *The Moon Is Blue,* in which its actors used such commonplace terms as "pregnant" and "virginity"; but Maryland and the U.S. Navy deemed it "lewd" and "lascivious," and accordingly banned the showing of the film—lest it have dire effects on the viewers. On the other hand, New York banned the distribution of *Lady Chatterley's Lover,* charging that "the whole theme of this motion picture is immoral [under the applicable New York statute], for that theme is the presentation of adultery as a desirable, acceptable and proper pattern of behavior."[255] In unanimously reversing the New York action, the Supreme Court issued a number of

251. Carl Friedrich, a close student of the problem and convinced that it defies satisfactory solution by the judiciary—let alone the legislature—suggested that a constitutional amendment be passed specifically to deal with the security issue (see his "Rights, Liberties, Freedoms: A Reappraisal," 57 *American Political Science Review* 857 [December 1963]).

252. Interview, Sacramento, California, June 26, 1969, as quoted in the *New York Times,* June 27, 1969, p. 11. It did not take the Court's then newest and youngest member, Justice John Paul Stevens, long to observe in 1977 that its "thinking on obscenity is intolerably vague and makes evenhanded enforcement virtually impossible" (*Charlottesville Daily Progress,* March 2, 1977, p. A8).

253. *New York Times,* June 27, 1969, p. 11.

254. Ibid.

255. *Kingsley International Pictures v. Regents,* 4 N.Y.2d 349 (1957).

opinions,[256] but they turned, more or less specifically, on the vagueness of the concept "immorality" and the problem of censorship generally. In this concurring opinion, Justice Frankfurter stated the crux of the matter—differences of opinion as to the meaning of terms and differences of taste:

> As one whose taste in art and literature hardly qualifies him for the *avant-garde,* I am more than surprised, after viewing the picture, that the New York authorities should have banned "Lady Chatterley's Lover." To assume that this motion picture would have offended Victorian moral sensibilities is to rely on the stuffiest of Victorian conventions. Whatever one's personal preferences may be about such matters, the refusal to license the exhibition of this picture . . . can only mean that [the portion of the New York statute in question] forbids the public showing of any film that deals with adultery except by way of sermonizing condemnation or depicts any physical manifestation of an illicit amorous relation.[257]

In general, the trend has been to throw out, on constitutional or statutory grounds, most state visual prior censorship laws, or, if not the laws themselves, the *procedures* involved. And in 1975 *live theatrical productions*—here the musical *Hair*—were judicially recognized for the first time as enjoying the same kind of constitutional safeguards against prior restraints as do the press, books, and the movies.[258] Only a handful of states now have such statewide laws, and the *procedures* used by several have been declared unconstitutional.[259] A good many cities still do have censorship ordinances, but where the requirement is for licensing *in advance* of exhibition, only three were still enforced in 1980, Chicago's, for one, having been declared unconstitutional in 1968.[260] These statistics do not, however, cover state criminal statutes against the showing of ob-

256. *Kingsley International Pictures v. Regents,* 360 U.S. 684 (1959). Opinions were by Justices Stewart, Black, Frankfurter, Douglas, Clark, and Harlan—the last five all concurring in the result but on varying grounds.

257. Ibid. at 691–92.

258. *Southeastern Promotions, Ltd., v. Conrad,* 419 U.S. 892.

259. E.g., *Freedman v. Maryland,* 380 U.S. 51 (1965), where the law had provided no judicial participation in barring of a film, nor a time limit for the required administrative hearing. The Ohio obscenity statute fell unanimously in 1973 because it failed to provide a prior adversary hearing for an "obscenity" determination (*Hoffman v. United States District Court for Northern District of Ohio,* 414 U.S. 1021). And a Louisiana law, under which *Last Tango in Paris, The Stewardesses,* and several magazines had been banned as "lewd, lascivious, filthy or sexually indecent," was declared unconstitutional in 1974 on both substantive ("vague") and procedural (no "probable cause" had to be shown) grounds (*Louisiana v. Gulf State Theatres,* 417 U.S. 911). See also *F.W./P.B.S. Inc. v. Dallas,* 493 U.S. 215 (1990).

260. *Teitel Film Corp. v. Cusac,* 390 U.S. 139. Here the prescribed administrative process stretched from fifty to fifty-seven days, and it lacked a provision for judicial review. But compare the reasoning and result in the 1961 Chicago "submitted for review" case of *Times Film Corporation v. Chicago,* 365 U.S. 43, which had gone contrarily.

scene films *not subject to prior censorship;* these are still widespread and, of course, raise a different, no less difficult, issue. Moreover, when it comes to *general* antiobscenity laws, the federal government as well as all states except New Mexico had such laws on their books in the late 1980s.[261] Thus, while there is now fairly general consensus about the illegality of *prior* censorship, whatever the medium of expression, there still exists broadly general agreement that obscenity, at least in public, is at best of no redeeming social value and at worst actively corruptive of morals and must be both interdictable *and* punishable. The increase in printed smut throughout the country that seems to have accompanied judicial reversals of state obscenity convictions has thus given rise to fairly widespread outcries and demands for curbs—both genuine and hypocritical—from citizens and citizen groups. If only we could agree on just what is obscene! How can ideas and morality be protected concurrently? In 1968 President Johnson, in response to statutory authority, appointed a blue-ribbon eighteen-member Presidential Commission on Obscenity and Pornography. Its report, two years later, inter alia recommending the elimination of all restrictions on *adults* wishing to obtain sexually explicit books, pictures, and films, not only caused a storm of righteous controversy but was officially denounced and formally rejected by the pure U.S. Senate by a roll call vote of 60:5[262]—an action warmly endorsed by President Nixon, who agreed with the Reverend Dr. Billy Graham that the report was "one of the worst, most diabolical reports ever made by a Presidential Commission [that] no Christian or believing Jew could possibly support. . . ."[263] Almost two decades later, on the other hand, another Presidential Commission on Pornography, formed for President Reagan by Attorney General Meese, concluded in a lengthy public report that offered a twenty-six-page list of recommendations that most pornography sold in the United States is potentially harmful and can lead to violence. It strongly urged action against the "porno" industry.[264] The fundamental issue involved, whether certain forms of pornography are indeed harmful to the public and thus might be legitimately restricted by the government without violating the First Amendment, is unlikely to be settled by this—or any other—report. Ultimately, the Court will be called upon to do so—and it is not precisely anxious to comply.[265]

261. In 1971 the Supreme Court, by 7:2 and 6:3 votes, respectively, upheld the constitutionality of the federal statute that prohibits the knowing use of the mails for delivery of obscene matter and the right of customs agents to seize obscene "photographs, books, and advertisements coming into the country from abroad" (*United States v. Reidel* and *United States v. Thirty-Seven Photographs,* 402 U.S. 363).
262. The five courageous libertines who bucked the Puritan tide were Clifford Case (R.-N.J.), Jacob K. Javits (R.-N.Y.), George S. McGovern (D.-S.D.), Walter F. Mondale (D.-Minn.), and Stephen M. Young (D.-Ohio). Evidently neither political party had a corner on purity!
263. *New York Times,* October 14, 1970, p. 30.
264. *New York Times,* May 16, 1986, p. 13.
265. *New York Times,* May 18, 1986, p. B13; and *Time,* July 21, 1986, pp. 26ff.

Other democracies throughout the world have also wrestled with this problem, admittedly under different national and cultural traditions, and their solution has been far from easy. For example, the Chambre de Droit Publique of Switzerland's highest tribunal, the Tribunal Fédéral Suisse, had to deal with "indecency" charges against one Werner Kunz, a Zurich producer of three "naturalist" films who found himself censored because he had shown "nudism" on the beaches and on snow-covered mountains. Now, did this showing of nudity constitute "naturalist beauty" or "indecent character"? The seven jurists rendered a split decision on each count: yes (5:2), it was indecent to exhibit nudity publicly in the white snow; but no (4:3), it was not indecent to show it publicly on the beach.[266]

On the other hand, small and homogeneous Denmark—and the two preceding adjectives, particularly the second, are crucial to the modus operandi—decided to pioneer in 1967, when its *folketing* (the unicameral legislature) abolished all sanctions against the "production," import, export, and distribution of *written* pornography. The Danish Commission on Criminal Law, which had initially recommended both laws, had done so because it had been fully convinced by psychologists and sociologists that there was no *provable* nexus between pornography and corruption of sexual mores. The results were such that exactly two years later Denmark became the first state formally to abolish *every* legal sanction against pornography for *adults*. Its 1969 statute does continue to provide prison terms of up to six months for purveying pornography to children (defined as being under age sixteen), and the police do act against the "related" realms of brothels and narcotics.[267]

Turning back to the large and heterogeneous United States of America—and those two appropriate adjectives assuredly make a major difference in any attempted resolution of the problem, as all public and private sectors that have been brave enough to resolve it have repeatedly found out—most attempts to censor *written publications* have turned on the use of certain famous or infamous Anglo-Saxon four-letter words. Generally, books and allied media have enjoyed at least as much judicial protection against unbridled censorship as have movies. Obviously, obscenity or, more precisely, "hard-core pornography"—as it has been increasingly classified by the Court—may be forbidden, but the problems of classifications, sanctions, and punishment are indeed vexatious. Justice Stewart, for one, who backed censorship *solely* if the material represented "hard-core pornography," threw up his judicial hands when specifically asked its meaning in 1964, responding, "[All I can say is that] I do know it when I see it."[268] And

---

266. Chambre de Droit Publique, P110/CG, Séance du 7 décembre 1960, at 7–8. See Francis William O'Brien's perceptive account, "Movie Censorship: A Swiss Comparison," 3 *Duke Law Journal* (summer 1966), pp. 634–68.

267. See the account by Bernard Weintraub in the *New York Times,* January 26, 1976, p. 5.

268. *Jacobellis v. Ohio,* 378 U.S. 184, concurring opinion at 197. "Don't you mean, my Brother," rejoined a pixyish Justice Douglas from the bench, "you know it when you

he stuck to this position. Justice Harlan tried to be more precise when he explained that, to him, "hard core" signifies "that prurient material that is patently offensive or whose indecency is self-demonstrating"[269]—which is not crystal clear either, as definitions go.

One person's smut may well be another one's Chaucer! Or, as Harlan put it once, "One man's vulgarity is another man's lyric."[270] But, logically, as the Supreme Court held (8½-½)ustice Harlan concurred in part and dissented in part) in *Smith v. California,*[271] the proprietor of a bookstore cannot constitutionally be punished for offering an "obscene" book, here *Sweeter Than Life,* for sale—an act banned by the terms of a Los Angeles city ordinance—if he was *unaware* that the book was in fact obscene. And Eleazar Smith was thus absolved of the charges against him. Yet, it may be asked, if the book had already been adjudged "obscene" in another jurisdiction, could Mr. Smith really plead ignorance, or lack of *scienter,*[272] regarding continued sales of the volume? At least one student of the field observed that he certainly could not,[273] and fourteen years later the Supreme Court seemed to agree.[274] Actually, the Court ruled on the *scienter* matter in the *Smith* case only tangentially: the controlling point there was that the burden of proof of criminal violation was held to rest upon the state. To shift that burden to the individual constitutes an impermissible requirement, which the Court underscored again in 1971 when it declared two *federal* "mail block" laws unconstitutional because they had placed the burden of proof on the individual rather than on the government—the latter not being required to obtain a prompt judicial determination whether, in fact, the material was obscene.[275] The highest tribunal has gone further to condemn on constitutional grounds the kind

feel it given the definition of 'prurient,' i.e. to itch, long, lecher, lust?" In a postretirement 1981 news conference, Justice Stewart had definite second thoughts about his now legendary 1964 observation: "In a way I regret having said what I said about obscenity—that's going to be on my tombstone. When I remember all the other solid words I've written, I regret a little bit that if I'll be remembered at all, I'll be remembered for that particular phrase" (as quoted in the *Washington Post's* obituary, written by Al Kamen, December 8, 1985, p. A18).

269. *A Book Named "John Cleland's Woman of Pleasure" v. Massachusetts,* 383 U.S. 413 (1966), dissenting opinion.

270. *Cohen v. California,* 403 U.S. 15 (1971) at 25, majority opinion.

271. 361 U.S. 147 (1959).

272. *Scienter* means having such knowledge as charges a person with the consequences of his or her actions.

273. Paul G. Kauper, *Civil Liberties and the Constitution* (Ann Arbor: University of Michigan Press, 1962), p. 71.

274. In 1973 it thus dismissed 5:4 a challenge to a New York statute that created a presumption that the seller of obscene materials knows the character of its contents (*Kirkpatrick v. New York,* 414 U.S. 948). The four dissenters argued that the word *obscene* was impermissibly vague.

275. *Blount v. Rizzi* and *United States v. The Book Bin,* 400 U.S. 410.

of "informal censorship" practiced by the Rhode Island Commission to Encourage Morality in Youth, a unit statutorily created and empowered to educate the public "concerning any book, picture, pamphlet, ballad, printed paper or other things containing obscene, indecent or impure language, or manifestly tending to the corruption of the youth . . . and to investigate and recommend the prosecution of all violations of [the statute involved.]"[276] Such action, held Justice Brennan for the 8:1 Court, constituted "in fact a scheme of state censorship effectuated by extra-legal sanctions; they acted as an agency not to advise but to suppress."[277]

That the Court's search for a viable standard has been extremely difficult[278] is illustrated by some additional examples. In a well-known 1957 case, *Butler v. Michigan,* it held unconstitutional a Michigan law that forbade "any person" to sell or give away anything "containing obscene, immoral, lewd or lascivious language . . . tending to incite minors to violent or depraved or immoral acts, *manifestly tending to the corruption of the morals of youth.*"[279] Speaking for the unanimous Court, Justice Frankfurter set aside the conviction of Alfred E. Butler, who had sold such a book *(The Devil Rides Outside)* to another adult, here a policeman. (The book is a story of a young American's visit to a Benedictine monastery in France to study Gregorian chants. As a result of his observations of the monks he aspires to resemble them, particularly in the virtue of chastity, although he is obsessed by sex and indulges in several sordid amours.) The Court's ruling was on the ground that the state could not, under its police power, quarantine "the general reading public against books not too rugged for grown men and women in order to shield juvenile innocence. . . . Surely, this is to *burn the house to roast the pig.*"[280] Frankfurter, hardly a foe of reasonably drafted, tightly drawn[281] police-power legislation, continued:

276. *Bantam Books, Inc. v. Sullivan,* 372 U.S. 58 (1963) at 59–60.

277. Ibid. at 72. The lone dissenter was Harlan.

278. In the eleven-year period between the 1957 *Roth* and *Alberts* decisions and that of *Ginsberg v. New York* in 1968 (see later text for discussion and citation), the Court undertook a full-scale review of obscenity law in thirteen major cases. In those thirteen cases, members of the Court turned out fifty-five separate opinions. "The subject of obscenity . . . that intractable problem," as Justice Harlan observed laconically in 1968, "has produced a variety of views among the members of the Court unmatched in other courses of constitutional adjudication" (*Interstate Circuit v. Dallas,* 390 U.S. 676 at 704–5). It is no wonder, then, that Chief Justice Warren would regard it as the most vexatious of all lines to draw in the eternal contest between individual and societal rights. His successor found the going equally rough—the Burger Court dividing 5:4 in a bloc of eleven cases decided on a single 1973 Opinion Day, for example! Does smut perhaps lie "in the groin of the beholder"? (Clor, quoting Charles Rembar, *infra* note 295).

279. 352 U.S. 380 (1957); italics supplied.

280. Ibid. at 383; italics supplied.

281. E.g., see his opinion for the Court in *Kingsley Books, Inc. v. Brown,* 354 U.S. 436 (1957).

We have before us legislation not reasonably restricted to the evil with which it is said to deal. The incidence of this [law] is to reduce the adult population of Michigan to reading only what is fit for children. It thereby arbitrarily curtails one of those liberties of the individual, now enshrined in the due process clause of the Fourteenth Amendment, that history has attested as the indispensable conditions for the maintenance and progress of a free society.[282]

A few weeks later, a divided Court attempted to provide a viable yardstick, which has since proved to be but partly successful. In the combined *Roth* and *Alberts* cases,[283] featuring five opinions, the justices who joined in the majority's holding[284] did their best to "balance" the rights involved by establishing the "prurient interest" test[285]—and thereby at last abandoned the nineteenth-century standard, based upon an English case, *Regina v. Hicklin;* its test was "whether the *tendency* of the matter charged as obscenity is to *deprave and corrupt* those whose *minds are open* to such immoral influences and into whose hands a publication of this sort may fall."[286] Here, speaking through Justice Brennan—frequently called upon to write opinions in this sphere—the Court upheld both a federal statute forbidding the transportation through the mails of "obscene, lewd, lascivious, indecent, filthy or vile" materials *and* a state statute forbidding the sale or advertisement of "obscene or indecent matter" on the strength of the new "prurient interest" concept. This test, as elucidated by Brennan, was to determine *"[w]hether to the average person, applying contemporary community standards, the dominant theme of the material taken as a whole, appeals to prurient interests,"*[287] and whether, in addition, the material "goes substantially beyond the customary limits of candor." That Brennan cited "impure sexual thoughts" as one example of "prurient interests" ought to demonstrate the intriguingly difficult nature of the test. On the other hand, he made clear that by "obscenity" the Court had in mind only material that was *"utterly without redeeming social importance"*[288] (a concept-cum-test which, Justice

282. *Butler v. Michigan,* op. cit., *supra* note 279 at 383–84.
283. *Roth v. United States* and *Alberts v. California,* 354 U.S. 476 (1957).
284. Justices Brennan, Frankfurter, Burton, Clark, and Whittaker. The chief justice concurred separately; Justice Harlan concurred in *Alberts* but dissented in *Roth;* Justices Black and Douglas dissented in both.
285. *Prurient,* according to *Webster's,* signifies "itching; longing; of persons, having lascivious longings; of desire, curiosity, or propensity, lewd" (7th ed. [Springfield, Mass.: Merriam-Webster, 1969], p. 688).
286. L.R.3Q.B.360 (1868); italics supplied.
287. *Roth v. United States* and *Alberts v. California,* 354 U.S. 476 (1957) at 489; italics supplied.
288. On this point see his fine article, based on the 1965 Meiklejohn Lecture at Harvard University, "The Supreme Court and the Meiklejohn Interpretation of the First Amendment," 79 *Harvard Law Review* 1 (November 1965); italics supplied.

Black would write later, is "as uncertain, if not more uncertain, than is the unknown substance of the Milky Way").[289]

What Brennan himself regarded as the "difficult, recurring and unpleasant task" of setting a national moral criterion for a heterogeneous people such as the citizenry of the United States was accentuated by the wistful dissenting opinion of Justice Douglas, joined by his colleague Black. He questioned "prurience" as a viable standard, commenting that "the arousing of sexual thoughts and desires happens every day in normal life in dozens of ways."[290] He cited a questionnaire sent to female college and normal school graduates in the late 1920s which asked, "What things were most stimulating sexually?" Of 409 replies, 218 responded "man."[291] After a lengthy lecture on the First Amendment guarantees of free expression, Douglas concluded that he, for one, "would give the broad sweep of the First Amendment full support. I have the same confidence in the ability of our people to reject noxious literature as I have in their capacity to sort out the true from the false in theology, economics, politics, or any other field."[292] Yet the Court seemed to have created a line with its "prurient interest" test, which it further refined, perhaps liberalized, in 1962 in *Manuel Enterprises, Inc. v. Day*.[293] There, Justice Harlan, writing for the 6:1 Court majority—which was badly split, however, on just what was being decided—held not only that the matter challenged must be "so offensive as to affront current community standards of decency" but that the indecency must be "self-demonstrating." In other words, Harlan joined "patently offensive" to "prurient interest" in an attempt to find a more precise line.[294] Another explanation and refinement came in a multiple 1964 decision, in which it was Justice Brennan who, speaking for a majority of six, made it clear that the *Roth-Alberts* test reference to "contemporary community standards" was intended to establish a *national* standard rather than a "particular local community standard"[295]—an interpretation that would hold for a decade.[296]

289. Dissenting in *Ginzburg v. United States,* 383 U.S. 463 (1966) at 480. Seven years later the Court would abandon that test—but substitute a new one which would have been equally unacceptable to the now deceased champion of absolutist freedom of expression (*Miller v. California,* 413 U.S. 15; and *Paris Adult Theatre v. Slaton,* 413 U.S. 49, discussed *infra*).

290. *Roth v. United States* and *Alberts v. California,* op. cit., *supra* note 287 at 509.

291. Douglas quoted from Leo M. Alpert, "Judicial Censorship of Obscene Literature," 52 *Harvard Law Review* 40 (1938) at 73. Ninety-five young women said "books," forty "drama," twenty-nine "dancing," eighteen "pictures," nine "music"; others were scattered over a variety of subjects.

292. *Roth v. United States* and *Alberts v. California,* op. cit., *supra* note 287 at 514.

293. 370 U.S. 478.

294. Ibid. at 483.

295. *Jacobellis v. Ohio,* 378 U.S. 184 at 193. For an interesting study, which comprises a major appeal for reliance on the good sense of the *local* community, see Harry M. Clor, *Obscenity and Public Morality: Censorship in a Liberal Society* (Chicago: University of Chicago Press, 1968).

296. It fell—at least temporarily—in favor of *"local"* in *Miller* and *Paris Adult Theatre* in 1973.

Thus the Court by 1964 had established a basic constitutional requirement that material attacked on grounds of "obscenity," or any other similar concepts, *must be judged not by its isolated parts but by the dominant theme of the material as a whole.* The Court had made clear that freedom of expression carries with it the inherent privilege of "unconventional," "controversial," even "immoral" advocacy, *provided* the manner in which this is done is not "obscene" under the established guidelines. Moreover, the Court would obviously not permit loosely drawn administrative and/or legislative procedures, nor would it assume automatic *scienter* of possession of obscene matter on the part of the vendors.

However, in March 1966 along came the rather surprising *Ginzburg* decision.[297] There, in a welter of fourteen opinions by seven justices in three cases decided together,[298] the Court, narrowly dividing 5:4 in the lead case *(Ginzburg),* demonstrated that, notwithstanding its recent "liberalizing" decisions in the obscenity field, it was also by no means necessarily averse to "toughening" its *Roth-Alberts* test. Ralph Ginzburg, publisher of the magazine *Eros* and other erotic literature,[299] stood convicted on twenty-eight counts of violating the federal obscenity statute at issue in the *Roth* case, not because the material in itself was obscene but *because of the manner in which it was "exploited," that is, advertised*—advertisement permeated "with the leer of the sensualist."[300] As Justice Brennan, the Court's "obscenity expert," put the matter for himself, the chief justice, and Associate Justices Clark, White, and Fortas (with Justices Black, Douglas, Stewart, and Harlan dissenting in four separate opinions):

Where an exploitation of interests in *titillation by pornography* is shown with respect to material lending itself to such exploitation through pervasive treatment or description of sexual matters, such evidence may support the determination that the material is obscene even though in *other contexts* the material would escape such condemnation.[301]

In other words, in "close cases," evidence of pandering may be "probative with respect to the nature of the material."[302] But to Justice Black, the majority's stance fatally misinterpreted the First Amendment, for, as he put it: "I believe

297. *Ginzburg v. United States,* 383 U.S. 463.
298. Ibid. (decided 5:4); *Mishkin v. New York,* 383 U.S. 502 (6:3); and *A Book Named "John Cleland's Woman of Pleasure" v. Massachusetts,* 383 U.S. 413 (6:3).
299. *Eros,* a hardcover magazine of expensive format; *Liaison,* a biweekly newsletter; and *The Housewife's Handbook on Selective Promiscuity,* a short book. He also published the controversial magazine *Fact,* which figured in the *Ginzburg v. Goldwater* libel case.
300. *Ginzburg v. United States,* op. cit., supra note 297 at 468. After unsuccessfully seeking mailing privileges from the postmasters of Intercourse and Blue Ball, Pennsylvania. Ginzburg finally obtained them from Middlesex, N.J.
301. Ibid. at 475; italics supplied. Ginzburg's five-year sentence was eventually reduced to three. He did not begin to serve it until February 1972, and he was paroled and released that October.
302. Ibid. at 474. (Reconfirmed in 1977 in *Splawn v. California,* 431 U.S. 595.)

that the Federal Government is without power whatever under the Constitution to put any type of burden on speech and expression of ideas of any kind (as distinguished from conduct). . . . I would reverse this case and announce that neither Congress nor the states shall pass laws which in any manner abridge freedom of speech and press—whatever the subjects discussed."[303] The quest for a viable line continued apace after *Ginzburg,* and while no new rule emerged readily, there were definite signs that one would—sooner or later—and that it would attempt to distinguish between minors and adults, between private and public exposure, and between "captive" and "escapable audiences." It began to take shape with three decisions, known as the Redrup group,[304] that were rendered per curiam in 1967. As usual, the justices remained divided on the meaning of "obscenity" and sidestepped a great many issues. However, in this group of three cases involving ten "girlie" magazines and two paperbacks which had all been ruled "obscene" by state courts in Arkansas, Kentucky, and New York, the Warren Court, in joining the three cases and reversing the convictions in each, pronounced three identifiable "rules of thumb" (although still ducking such ticklish issues as just what is a "girlie magazine"). Rule 1 noted that in none of the three cases did the state law in question reflect a "specific and limited state concern for juveniles." Rule 2 explained that in none of the cases was there any effort of "pandering" à la *Ginzburg.* And Rule 3 pointed out that none of the materials in question was "forced" on an unwilling public.[305] These rules or

303. *Ginzburg,* op. cit., *supra* note 297 at 476; parentheses in original.
304. *Redrup v. New York, Gent v. Arkansas,* and *Austin v. Kentucky,* 386 U.S. 767. Shortly after these decisions, the Court upheld a conviction based on a public display of allegedly obscene sculpture in its owner's backyard, since it was "positioned" in a manner so obtrusive as to be unavoidable (*Fort v. City of Miami,* 389 U.S. 918 [1967]).
305. What of an outdoor movie screening of conceivably obscene movies visible from twelve to fifteen homes and passing motorists? Unless the obscenity statute involved explicitly gives fair and due notice concerning "context" or "location," its application, ruled a unanimous Court in 1972, is "impermissibly vague" under due process considerations (*Rabe v. Washington,* 405 U.S. 313). It affirmed this stance in 1975 when it struck down (6:3) as an unconstitutional interference with free speech a Jacksonville, Florida, ordinance making drive-in theaters criminally liable for showing films including nudity that are visible outside the theater grounds. Speaking for the majority, Justice Powell held that "the privacy interest of persons on the public streets cannot justify this censorship of otherwise protected speech on the basis of its contents" (*Erznoznik v. Jacksonville,* 419 U.S. 822). But zoning either concentrating or dispersing "adult" movies is constitutional (*Young v. American Mini Theatres,* 427 U.S. 50 [1976]). On the other hand, note *Schad v. Mount Ephraim,* 452 U.S. 61 (1981), in which the Court ruled 7:2 that communities which permit commercial activity may not use their zoning power to exclude live entertainment (here a nude dancer in a glass booth in a so-called adult bookstore). But in two 1986 decisions the Court, by lopsided 7:2 and 6:3 votes, upheld the power of communities to "zone in" certain "adult entertainment," either by confining the movie theaters concerned to one area or dispersing them in order "to preserve the quality of urban life" (*Renton v. Playtime Theatres,* 475 U.S. 41; and *Arcara v. Cloud Books,* 478 U.S. 697, respectively).

guidelines now began to be present in whole or in part, expressly or impliedly, in most of the important subsequent cases. Thus, in 1968, the Court in a very real sense seemed to "codify" its majoritarian conviction—with Black and Douglas always, and Stewart often, in dissent—that it would *not* strike down carefully drawn statutes aimed at the protection of juveniles. In the leading case of *Ginsberg v. New York* (no relation to *Ginzburg v. United States*) the Court ruled (6:3) that New York could indeed make it a crime knowingly to sell "to minors under 17 years of age material defined to be obscene to them whether or not it would be obscene to adults." Hence Sam Ginsberg, who in 1965 had sold two "girlie magazines" to a sixteen-year-old boy in Ginsberg's Bellmore, Long Island, "Sam's Stationary [*sic*] and Luncheonette," found himself in trouble with New York State's law on the subject and appealed his resultant conviction on First Amendment grounds. Speaking for the Court majority, Justice Brennan made it clear that New York's "prohibition does not bar parents who so desire from purchasing the magazines for their children," and of course, they were free to buy them for themselves—for they were *not obscene for adults*. Dissenting Justices Black, Douglas, and Fortas mocked this distinction, with Douglas angrily writing: "As I read the First Amendment, it was designed to keep the state and the hands of all state officials off the printing presses of America and off the distribution systems for all printed literature."[306] Yet the double standard of obscene-for-child-not-obscene-for-adult had been firmly embraced. And not only has it stood to date, it was reaffirmed by a 9:0 decision, authored by Justice White, upholding New York State's broad authority to combat *child* pornography by banning the production, sale, and distribution of such material—here showing children engaged in sexual conduct—whether or not it is legally obscene.[307] In 1994 the Court, 7:2, upheld a federal child pornography law, rejecting arguments that Congress had so vaguely worded the statute that it criminalized video and book sales in violation of the First Amendment, but in 1996 a seriously fractured Court, in six separate opinions and three distinct votes, struck down several provisions of the Cable TV Consumers Protection and Competition Act of 1992, which had been enacted to combat TV indecency and obscenity with particular attention to children.[308]

---

306. 390 U.S. 629 at 655. In a concurring opinion, Justice Harlan criticized the Court for avoiding a definition-cum-explanation of "girlie magazines." In a 5:4 decision in 1993 the Court ruled that the First Amendment was not breached when the government seized and destroyed adult magazines and videos that were part of a pornographic empire but not the basis of criminal charges. But collaterally, the Court held (9:0) that forfeiture of Alexander's estimated $25 million business, in addition to a prison term, might have breached the Eighth Amendment's excessive fines prohibition, and it remanded that issue to a lower federal tribunal (*Alexander v. United States,* 509 U.S. 544).

307. *New York v. Ferber,* 458 U.S. 747 (1982).

308. For the former decision, see *United States v. X-Citement Video, Inc., et al.,* 513 U.S. 30. The law at issue punishes anyone who "knowingly transports or ships . . . any

An additional principle was established, firmly and unanimously (although there were three separate opinions), in 1969 in the case of *Stanley v. Georgia.*[309] Federal and state agents, backed by a search warrant, had entered the Atlanta home of Robert Eli Stanley in 1967 to search for proof of suspected bookmaking. They failed to unearth any evidence of gambling, but they did find three reels of film that, as they later testified in court, depicted "successive orgies of seduction, sodomy, and sexual intercourse." Stanley was jury-convicted under a Georgia law that forbids *possession* of obscene material and was sentenced to a year in prison. Delivering the opinion for the Court, its then junior member, Justice Thurgood Marshall, agreed with Stanley's contention that his First and Fourteenth Amendment rights had been violated, for the mere *private* possession of obscene matter cannot constitutionally be made a crime. The Court took pains to note that its holding in no way infringes upon the right of states or the federal government to make possession of other items, such as narcotics, firearms, or stolen goods, a crime. But, in Marshall's words:

> Whatever may be the justifications for other statutes regulating obscenity, we do not think they reach into the privacy of one's own home. If the First Amendment means anything, it means that a State has no business telling a man, sitting alone in his own house, what books he may read or what films he may watch. Our whole constitutional heritage rebels at the thought of giving government the power to control men's minds.[310]

Hence it was entirely within that spirit that the Court, a year later, would uphold the right of individuals privately to show "stag" movies—even of women masturbating.[311] In 1990, however, a 6:3 Supreme Court majority seemed to limit severely its *Stanley* holding of three decades earlier by ruling that states may outlaw the possession or viewing of *child* pornography even in the privacy of one's home (except for materials possessed by the child's parents or used for a "bona fide" artistic, educational, or scientific purpose).[312] And, as the Court had ruled ingeniously (6:3) in 1972, states, acting under their authority derived from the Twenty-first(!) Amendment, may—without doing violence to the First Amendment—shut down state liquor-licensed bars that, in the words of Justice Rehn-

---

visual depiction [involving] the use of a minor engaging in sexually explicit conduct." For the latter ruling, consult *Denver Area Educational Telecommunications Consortium, Inc. v. FCC,* 518 U.S. 727 (1996). See also a 1996 decision in which the Court, rebuffing free-speech advocates, allowed federal regulators to confine smutty television and radio programs to late-night hours (between 10:00 P.M. and 6:00 A.M.), when children are less likely to tune in. *Pacifica Foundation v. FCC,* 64 LW 3465.

309. 394 U.S. 557.
310. Ibid. at 565.
311. *California v. Pincus,* 400 U.S. 922 (1970).
312. *Osborne v. Ohio,* 495 U.S. 103.

THE PRECIOUS FREEDOM OF EXPRESSION 243

quist's majority opinion, feature nude dancers and other "bacchanalian revel-ries."[313] Additionally, in 1991 the high Court upheld 5:4 Indiana's law banning nude erotic dancing unless at least pasties and G-strings were worn by the per-formers. Reaching the First and Fourteenth Amendment issues of freedom of speech and due process of law, the Rehnquist opinion thus sanctioned govern-mental strictures against public nudity.[314] Albeit fractured (five opinions), the Court reiterated that stance in a 2000 case involving an Erie, Pennsylvania, mu-nicipal regulatory ordinance on nude dancing,[315] and two years later it upheld (5:4) a Los Angeles law regulating multiple concentration of "adult establishments."[316]

In 1976 it had upheld a Virginia law that provided criminal penalties for committing adult, consensual, private homosexual acts;[317] a decade later it vali-dated Georgia's ban on sodomy, at least as applied to homosexual conduct.[318] Justice White's opinion for a five-justice majority rejected the notion of homo-sexual sodomy as a "fundamental right." In a notable victory for gay rights, how-ever, the Supreme Court voted 6:3 in 1996 to invalidate a Colorado constitutional amendment, which forbade laws protecting homosexuals from discrimination.

---

313. *California v. La Rue,* 409 U.S. 109. As Rehnquist delicately described the night-club's activities: "Customers were found engaging in oral copulation with women enter-tainers; customers engaged in public masturbation; and customers placed rolled currency either directly into the vagina of a female entertainer, or on the bar in order that she might pick it up herself" (at 111). See also *New York State Liquor Authority v. Bellanca,* 452 U.S. 714 (1982), which distinguished *La Rue* and affirmed the New York State Court of Ap-peal's declaration of unconstitutionality of the state's ban on topless entertainment.

314. *Barnes v. Glen Theatre,* 501 U.S. 560.

315. *City of Erie v. Pap's A.M.,* 329 U.S. 277.

316. *Los Angeles v. Alameda Books,* 535 U.S.___ (2002).

317. *Doe v. Commonwealth Attorney for the City of Richmond,* 425 U.S. 901 (1976). In November 2000 the Virginia Court of Appeals rejected an attack on the 207-year-old Virginia Sodomy Law by ten men who had been arrested for soliciting sex with under-cover police officers while "cruising" in Roanoke's public parks (*De Priest v. Common-wealth of Virginia,* 33 Va. App. 754). But cf. *Baker v. Wade,* 456 U.S. 1006 (1982).

318. *Bowers v. Hardwick,* 478 U.S. 186 (1986). Yet cf. *Watkins v. U.S. Army,* 847 F.2d 1329 and 1363, reconsidered (1988). Initially a 2:1 Ninth Circuit Court decision had found impermissible discrimination against Sergeant Watkins and had struck down the army's ban against homosexuals. But an eleven-member panel of that tribunal agreed to reconsider the former decision and set it aside pending its own review (June 10, 1988). The latter came one year later, with the tribunal ruling 5:4 that the army must allow Watkins to reenlist, *given the specific nature of his case*—he had been repeatedly allowed to reenlist with *scienter* of his status—*but* sidestepping the constitutional question 9:2 (*Walker v. United States Army,* 721 F.2d 687 [1989]). See also the implication of *Webster v. Doe,* 486 U.S. 592 (1988), that even national security considerations (here the CIA) do not ipso facto negate suits by federal employees for violation of their constitutional rights. But the Supreme Court, in February 1990, refused to review below-rejected constitutional challenges to the general ban on homosexuals serving in the army and navy by an army reservist lesbian and a navy reservist gay flight officer (*Ben-Shalom v. Marsh* and *Wood-ward v. United States,* 494 U.S. 1073).

Justice Kennedy's majority opinion in *Romer v. Evans* argued that no state may "deem a class of persons a stranger to its laws." Writing for his fellow dissenters (Chief Justice Rehnquist and Justice Thomas), Justice Scalia, calling Kennedy's opinion "long on emotive utterance and . . . short on relevant legal citation," angrily attacked its author for "imposing upon all Americans the resolution favored by the elite class from which the members of this institution are selected."[319] When Cincinnati's 1993 voter initiative, barring the city from enacting any policy that allows homosexuals "any claim of minority or protected status, quota preference or other preferential treatment," however, the Supreme Court denied certiorari and thereby upheld the Sixth Circuit Court of Appeals validation of the contested law, distinguishing the Colorado statute.[320]

But while several of the above landmark decisions settled, or at least seemed to settle, some of the major problems involved on the obscenity front, they did not settle—for they really could not—the basic problem of just what "obscene" means.[321] *Roth-Alberts, Ginzburg, Redrup, Ginsberg,* and *Stanley* had indeed provided some guidelines, but the very nature of the subject, and the public's understandable schizophrenic approach toward it, rendered additional litigation a certainty. And it was not long until the Court handed down a new—or perhaps another or additional—set of guidelines, intended to bring a degree of order into the vexatious subject.

Those new guidelines were announced in two 1973 cases.[322] Decided by the narrowest of margins (5:4), they were hardly conducive to future stability, yet they represented a significant development. Chief Justice Burger, speaking for himself and the three other Nixon appointees—Associate Justices Blackmun, Powell, and Rehnquist—plus Justice White, triumphantly noted that it was for "the first time" in sixteen years (referring to *Roth-Alberts*) that "a majority of this court has agreed on concrete guidelines to isolate 'hard core' pornography from expression protected by the First Amendment."[323] Designed to enable states and municipalities to ban books, magazines, plays, and motion pictures that are offensive to *local* standards, rather than the heretofore presumed prevalent single *national* standard, the five-man majority identified and promulgated the following trifold requirements as henceforth applicable guidelines for the obscenity law

---

319. 517 U.S. 620. But in 1997 the Court refused to hear another challenge to the military's "don't ask, don't tell" policy governing in-service individuals (*Selland v. Cohen,* 65 LW 3753).

320. *Equality Foundation of Greater Cincinnati v. Cincinnati,* 67 LW 3252 (1998).

321. For an excellent analysis and definition of the concept and application of "hardcore pornography," see William B. Lockhart and Robert C. McClure, "Obscenity Censorship: The Core Constitutional Issue—What Is Obscene?" 7 *Utah Law Review* 289 (1961). Their suggestion is that obscenity, in the constitutional sense, be limited to material *treated* like hard-core pornography by the primary audience to which it is addressed.

322. *Miller v. California,* 413 U.S. 15; and *Paris Adult Theatre v. Slaton,* 413 U.S. 49.

323. *Miller v. California,* op. cit., at 29.

of the land. In order to substantiate a charge of proscribable pornography: (1) "the *average* person applying contemporary [*local*, or, as later expanded, *state*] community standards" must convincingly demonstrate that the allegedly obscene work in question, *taken as a whole* (not by its isolated parts), appeals to prurient interests; (2) that the material depicts or describes, "*in a patently offensive way,* sexual conduct *specifically defined* by applicable state law"; and (3) that, taken as a whole, the work "*lacks serious literary, artistic, political, or scientific value*" (which quickly became known as the "LAPS value test").[324] In bitter, often sarcastic dissent, Justices Douglas, Brennan, Stewart, and Marshall predicted "raids on libraries"; contended that the new guidelines impinged seriously on free speech and free press; and warned that the necessary vagueness of any definition based on "local community" was redolent with censorship postures. Brennan, the author of seven major obscenity opinions *(Roth* and *Alberts, Jacobellis, Ginzburg, Ginsberg, Mishkin,* and *Memoirs),* clearly abandoning his "compromise" or "balancing" position in those decisions, now concluded with deep feeling that "the time has come to make a significant departure from that approach" and offered the following formula as the viable, sensible approach to the obscenity problem:

> [W]hile I cannot say that the interests of the State—apart from the question of juveniles[325] and unconsenting adults—are trivial or nonexistent, I am compelled to conclude that these interests cannot justify the substantial damage to constitutional rights and to this Nation's judicial machinery that inevitably results from state efforts to bar the distribution even of unprotected materials to consenting adults. . . . I would hold, therefore, that at least *in the absence of distribution to juveniles or obtrusive exposure to unconsenting adults,* the First and Fourteenth Amendments prohibit the state and Federal governments from attempting wholly to suppress sexually oriented materials on the basis of their allegedly "obscene" content.[326]

But he spoke for the minority. The Burger majority had indeed fashioned new interpretative guidelines that embraced two major changes in the heretofore applicable obscenity law: (1) the substitution of local or, at most, state for national standards; and (2) the adoption of the LAPS value test for the erstwhile one of "utterly without redeeming social value."

Those observers who were skeptical as to the clarity and finality of the now pronounced—though not retroactive[327]—*Miller* and *Paris Adult Theatre* guide-

---

324. *Miller v. California,* op. cit., at 24; italics supplied. Cf. *Pope v. Illinois,* 481 U.S. 497 (1987), *infra.*
325. Brennan joined the unanimous Court in 1982 when it upheld the double standard in instances involving juveniles (see *supra* note 301).
326. *Paris Adult Theatre v. Slaton,* op. cit., *supra* note 322 at 112–13; italics supplied.
327. *Marks v. United States,* 430 U.S. 188 (1977).

line triad did not have to wait long for confirmation of their analysis. Thus, notwithstanding its "old" (1971) guidelines vote (4:4), which upheld Maryland's highest court's 4:3 ruling that the controversial Swedish film *I Am Curious, Yellow* was obscene,[328] the "new" guidelines court ruled unanimously in 1974 that *Carnal Knowledge* was not obscene and could thus not be banned by Georgia.[329] Speaking through Justice Rehnquist, it emphasized that only material showing "patently offensive hard core sexual conduct" may be banned under the now applicable rules.[330] On the other hand, on the very same Opinion Day, an advertisement for an illustrated version of the report of the Presidential Commission on Obscenity and Pornography was held to be hard-core pornography, with Rehnquist now speaking for a 5:4 majority![331] To muddy the waters a mite further, the Court ruled (5:4) three years later that individuals are subject to the federal Comstock Act of 1873 ban on sending obscenity through the mail even if the state of their activity (here Iowa) has more permissive standards *and* despite the fact that the material's dissemination was wholly in-state.[332] Of course, it was not at all astonishing that the Court would run into a host of difficulty as to jury determinations of lines and limits governing the concepts of "average person" and "community standards";[333] the justices compounded the problem either by *adding* to their LAPS test rather than apply a "reasonable person" test to their "community standard" yardstick or by replacing the latter by the former entirely. The 5:4 majority opinion, written by White, was not exactly a model of clarity.[334] The Court was unanimous, however, in 1989 when it declared unconstitutional a major portion of the so-called Federal Anti-Dial-a-Porn law, because it failed to distinguish between "obscenity," which may be prohibited, and "indecency," which may not. A 7:2 Court in 1997 struck down, as a violation of the First Amendment, the Communications Decency Act, a law that rendered it a crime to make "indecent" or "patently offensive" material available to minors over the burgeoning Internet—thereby extending constitutional protection just as much to on-line systems as to newspapers and magazines.[335] Two years later, however, the Court, in a unanimous per curiam opinion, upheld another section of that law, aimed at limiting e-mail obscenity.[336] On the other hand, in a 5:4 2000 ruling the

---

328. *Grove Press, Inc. v. Maryland State Board of Censors*, 401 U.S. 480.

329. *Jenkins v. Georgia*, 418 U.S. 153. (The four *Miller* and *Paris Adult Theatre* dissenters concurred only in the judgment, in effect saying "we told you so," while reiterating their previous objections to the majority's doctrine.)

330. Ibid. at 160 (quoting *Miller* at 27).

331. *Hamling v. United States*, 418 U.S. 87 (1974). Similarly, see the White-written 5:4 decision in *Ward v. Illinois* in 1977 (431 U.S. 767).

332. *Smith v. United States*, 434 U.S 830 (1977).

333. *Pinkus v. United States*, 436 U.S. 293 (1977).

334. *Pope v. Illinois*, 481 U.S. 497 (1987).

335. *Sable Communication v. FCC*, 492 U.S. 115; and *Reno v. ACLU*, 521 U.S. 844.

336. *Apollo Media v. Reno*, 67 LW 3640 (1999).

Court declared Section 505 of the Telecommunications Act of 1996 unconstitutional for failing to address the admittedly "real problem" of time-restricting sexually oriented programs to children in "the least restrictive means."[337]And in 2002 a fractured 6:3 Court struck down two provisions of the Child Pornography Prevention Act of 1996 for being "overbroad and unconstitutional."[338] The law had been aimed at "virtual" child pornography. In the same term of Court (2001–2) the Child On-Line Protection Act of 1998, making it a crime to place material that is "harmful to minors" on a Web site available to those under seventeen, was placed on "hold" until further examination by the Third Circuit.[339]

In the visual media, such as movies, the problem is, of course, considerably less complicated than in the realm of the printed word. For one thing, the moviemaker is usually acutely conscious of what he or she perceives as the public consensus and the reaction of the public's pocketbook. Moreover, the American movie industry has tried to bestow its own formal or prerelease seal of approval.[340] Self-policing is not, of course, a guarantee of good taste, but it does lodge responsibility and judgment where it ought to lie: with the industry itself.[341] (The same may be said for the press.) The adult public, of course, should be free to patronize or to refuse to patronize the visual as well as the written media without governmental interference, or injunction by administrative or legislative fiat, or the censorial tactics of a powerful or vocal pressure group. If a movie is offensive to the sensibilities of a minority or majority group, that group is entirely free to advise and campaign against its patronization. But it is emphatically not free to prevent those who desire to patronize it from so doing. Freedom of expression is a two-edged sword. So is democracy.

Many of these considerations apply to the television industry. Responding to considerable parental as well as governmental pressures, industry executives

337. *United States v. Playboy Entertainment Group,* 529 U.S. 803.
338. *Ashcroft v. Free Speech Coalition,* 535 U.S. ___ .
339. *Ashcroft v. American Civil Liberties Union,* 535 U.S. ___ .
340. *The Man with the Golden Arm,* produced in 1955, dealing with the narcotics problem (producer Otto Preminger, United Artists Release), was the *first* movie released without that approval.
341. Perhaps partly copying the practices extant in, for example, the Scandinavian countries and in the United Kingdom, the movie industry published a much-heralded, simple Motion Picture Code of Self-Regulation late in 1968 which—amended early in 1970 and again in 1984 and 1990—did provide the public with the following (and for harried parents rather helpful) rating symbols:
G = All ages admitted.
PG = All ages admitted. Parental guidance suggested.
PG-13 = Special parental guidance for children under thirteen urged. (Adopted in 1984.)
R = Restricted. Children under seventeen require accompanying parent or adult guardian.
NC-17 = No children under seventeen admitted. (Adopted in 1990 to replace the erstwhile "X" rating.)

developed a ratings system, consisting of six broad categories for entertainment programs to become effective in January 1997, ranging from "TV-G" for shows suitable for all audiences to "TV-M" for those intended only for mature viewers. After repeated criticism from parents and others that the ratings were too vague, the television industry agreed to add symbols denoting programs with sex, violence, or strong language.[342]

Given the sizable number of federal and state statutes on the books, the obscenity question remains both current and vexatious in the absence of some such unlikely action as that taken by the Danes or that recommended by the abortive Presidential Commission on Obscenity and Pornography. This means, in effect, that we may expect continued, close, independent, case-by-case judicial scrutiny of findings of "obscenity," but with the aid of the new *Miller* and *Paris Adult Theatre* rules and guidelines, which were fashioned out of the experience of such earlier endeavors to determine lines and limits as those of *Roth-Alberts, Ginzburg, Redrup, Ginsberg, Ferber,* and *Stanley.* Censors will continue to find it difficult indeed to obtain judicial confirmation or support. On the other hand, it must not be assumed that the government has been, or is being, denied the authority to ban the sale and/or "pandering" of "hard-core pornography"—genuine smut—which, by self-demonstration, is patently offensive to current local or state community standards of decency, and thereby clearly appeals to prurient interests, particularly if advertised in "titillating" or "pandering" fashion. Presumably that type of filth and its method of dissemination would be classified as "hard-core pornography." Sex, which Justice Brennan—in his majority opinion in the key *Roth* and *Alberts* cases[343]—dubbed "a great and mysterious motive force in human life," has indeed, "indisputably been a subject of absorbing interest to mankind through the ages; it is one of the vital problems of human interest and public concern."[344] And, as he went on to point out, "sex and obscenity are not synonymous. On the other hand, obscene material is material which deals with sex in a manner appealing to prurient interests."[345] Moreover, to reiterate, since *Ginzburg* something need *not* have a "prurient appeal" to the public at large to be declared obscene. It can now be so judged even if it panders merely to a "clearly defined deviant sexual group," such as homosexuals or masochists.[346] A book is not obscene because of "isolated

342. The complete roster of the six categories is "TV-Y" (material suitable for children of all ages); "TV-Y7" (material suitable for children 7 and older); "TV-G" (material suitable for all audiences); "TV-PG" (parental guidance is suggested); "TV-14" (material may be inappropriate for children under 14); and "TV-M" (for mature audiences only). The ratings were greeted with less than enthusiasm by sizable segments of the public, so the industry agreed to add "S" (sexual material), "V" (violence), and "L" (strong language) to the ratings list effective October 1997. NBC said it would not use the three new categories but would utilize its own viewer advisories.
343. *Roth v. United States* and *Alberts v. California,* 354 U.S. 476 (1957).
344. Ibid. at 487.
345. Ibid.
346. *Mishkin v. New York,* 383 U.S. 502 (1966).

parts"; the work must be viewed "as a whole," based on its LAPS (literary, artistic, political, or scientific) values[347] as viewed by a "reasonable person."[348] But this anticensorship rule may be vitiated by evidence of a publisher's pandering.[349] Thus the history since *Roth-Alberts,* without settling the entire matter, has brought us closer to the possibility of drawing some lines, however serpentine they may well be. The lines inevitably deal with sex, a subject that, in Justice Black's dissenting words in the *Ginzburg* case, is "pleasantly interwoven in all human activities and involves the very substance of life itself."[350]

As the 1970s turned into the 1980s, four aspects of the obscenity puzzle seemed to be res judicata—notwithstanding the *Miller* and *Paris Adult Theatre* "retrenchment"—namely: (1) just about everything goes in the privacy of one's home—although the Court raised serious questions about that verity in 1976 when, by simply affirming (6:3) a 2:1 three-judge U.S. District Court decision below, it upheld a Virginia law that provides felony penitentiary sentences of one to three years[351] for committing consensual, adult homosexual acts *in private;*[352] and when it confirmed that stance in 1986 by ruling 5:4, in a much-praised and much-condemned decision, that Georgia's statute, making it a crime for anyone to engage in oral or anal sex, was constitutional even when applied to consenting adults in private—here homosexuals;[353] (2) *public* hard-core pornography is

347. *Miller v. California,* 413 U.S. 15 (1973) at 24.

348. *Pope v. Illinois,* 481 U.S. 497 (1987). See text *supra* this chapter.

349. *A Book Named "John Cleland's Woman of Pleasure" v. Massachusetts,* 383 U.S. 413 (1966).

350. *Ginzburg v. United States,* op. cit., at 481. For an anthology dealing with diverse viewpoints on sexuality and the law, see Note, School of Law, Duke University, "Sex Offenses," 25 *Law and Contemporary Problems* 214 (1960).

351. Va. Code §18.1-212 (Cum. Supp. 1974): "Crimes against nature.—If any person shall carnally know in any manner any brute animal, or carnally know any male or female person by the anus or by or with the mouth, or voluntarily submit to such carnal knowledge, he or she shall be guilty of a felony and shall be confined in the penitentiary not less than one year nor more than three years."

352. *Doe v. Commonwealth Attorney for the City of Richmond,* 425 U.S. 901 (1976), reconfirmed in *Enslin v. Bean,* 436 U.S. 912 (1978). The Court came under heavy criticism for deciding so privately crucial a matter without hearing oral argument and without issuing a formal opinion. (Four votes to hear the case were needed, but only Justices Brennan, Marshall, and Stevens voted in favor of oral argument on the merits.) Cf. the case of the dismissal of an admitted homosexual high school teacher in Washington State, *Gaylord v. Tacoma School District,* 434 U.S. 879 (1977). But see the supportive freedom-of-speech-and-assembly decision in the "campus recognition" of "Gay Lib" at the University of Missouri, *Ratchford v. Gay Lib,* 434 U.S. 1060 (1978). See also *People v. Onofre,* 451 U.S. 987 (1981), certiorari denied, and *Baker v. Wade,* 456 U.S. 1006 (1982).

353. *Bowers v. Hardwick,* 478 U.S. 168. Justice White penned the majority opinion, joined by Justice Rehnquist, Justice O'Connor and the chief justice, plus Justice Powell, who concurred separately and later publicly announced that he erred in voting as he did. Justices Brennan, Marshall, Blackmun, and Stevens dissented. Hardwick died of AIDS in 1991. Seven years later the Georgia Supreme Court overturned the conviction of one

not constitutionally protected;[354] (3) there now exists a judicially sanctioned "double standard" vis-à-vis obscenity legislation directed at minors and adults; and (4) while there is no judicially recognized *national* community standard, *local* (or *state*) standards, as viewed by a "reasonable person,"[355] are relevant[356] in obscenity litigation[357]—absent *federal* precedence.[358] The 1990s have embraced that quartet.

SOME CONCLUDING THOUGHTS

No other branch of our government is as qualified to draw lines between the rights of individuals and those of society as the Supreme Court of the United States. The legislative and executive branches yield all too easily to the politically expedient and the popular. Admittedly, the clear and present danger ap-

---

Anthony Powell for sodomizing his seventeen-year-old niece and struck down the law as an unconstitutional invasion of privacy (James Pilcher, Associated Press, November 23, 1998). But two years later Virginia's Court of Appeals upheld that state's 207-year-old sodomy ban (see *supra,* note 317). For its 2002–3 term the Supreme Court accepted an appeal by a gay couple from Texas challenging their state's law against homosexual sodomy and asking the court to overrule the 1986 *Bowers* precedent (Charles Lane, *Washington Post,* October 6, 2002).

354. Space does not permit a discussion of the fascinating clash between the competing constitutional values of freedom of expression and *privacy* that faced the Burger Court early in 1970. At issue was a 1967 federal antipandering law (enacted post-*Ginzburg*) which empowers any citizen to cut off the flow of mailed ads that he personally considers "erotically arousing or sexually provocative." The recipient simply notifies the Post Office, which then orders his name removed from the mailing lists. Unanimously, the Supreme Court upheld the law, Chief Justice Burger affirming every citizen's right "to be let alone." He added: "A mailer's right to communicate must stop at the mailbox of an unreceptive addressee" (*Rowan v. United States Post Office Department,* 397 U.S. 728). See also *U.S. Postal Service v. Council of Greenburgh Civic Assn.,* 453 U.S. 114 (1981).

355. *Pope v. Illinois,* 481 U.S. 497 (1987).

356. A flurry of activity by various communities, led by Cleveland, Ohio, commenced in 1977 to "determine" such obscenity standards and lines (often by way of questionnaires distributed by trash collectors!). Note, for example, the accounts in the *New York Times,* June 11, 1977, and June 26, 1977, p. 8E. The head of the Cleveland branch of the American Civil Liberties Union, doubting that the poll, if incorporated in a projected antismut law, would survive a serious court challenge, commented: "In our opinion it will probably wind up where it started—with the garbage men" (as quoted, June 26, ibid.).

357. For a view warmly praising the Burger Court for adding "clarity to the constitutional law of obscenity by drawing lines which are in most respects clearer than those of earlier cases," see Lane V. Sunderland, *Obscenity: The Court, the Congress and the President's Commission* (Washington, D.C.: American Enterprise Institute for Public Policy Research, 1974), pp. 114–15.

358. See *Smith v. United States, supra,* where the federal standard was ruled to govern (5:4).

proach to freedom of expression, however amended and augmented by the imminence requirement, is far from perfect. But the sole alternative to it would be an almost total absence of immunity in the face of legislative actions. Freedom of expression cannot be absolute; but it can be protected to the greatest degree humanly feasible under the Constitution. And there are giants of liberal democracy who bridle at any restraint on free expression. Thus we had Justice Black in his absolutist approach to the problem[359] and, almost as absolute, the late educator-philosopher Alexander Meiklejohn, who held that while the First Amendment "does not forbid the abridging of *speech* . . . it does forbid the abridging of *freedom of speech.*"[360]

For Meiklejohn, who, like Hugo Black, rejected the clear and present danger approach in favor of a more liberal standard, there is thus *never,* under the First Amendment, any right or reason to curb or abridge *freedom* of speech—at least not *public* speech (see later text); dangers, even in wartime, are irrelevant; and the time of danger is precisely the time to show people that one means what one says and has the right to say it:

> If, then, on any occasion in the United States it is allowable to say that the Constitution is a good document it is equally allowable, in that situation, to say that the Constitution is a bad document. If a public building may be used in which to say, in time of war, that the war is justified, then the same building may be used in which to say that it is not justified. If it be publicly argued that conscription for armed service is moral and necessary, it may likewise be publicly argued that it is immoral and unnecessary. If it may be said that American political institutions are superior to those of England or Russia or Germany, it may, with equal freedom, be said that those of England or Russia or Germany are superior to ours. . . . When a question of policy is "before the house," free men choose it not with their eyes shut, but with their eyes open. To be afraid of ideas, any idea, is to be unfit for self-government.[361]

This stirring language should serve as a beacon to us all; but the fact remains that there *are* limits to the precious freedom and that we do need some such doctrine as clear and present danger plus imminence. Meiklejohn, however, proposed a different solution: he created a dichotomy of *public speech* and *private speech,* "public" speech pertaining to any matter that concerns politics—that is, public policy and public officials. This type of speech, Meiklejohn held, is given *ab-*

---

359. E.g., his "Bill of Rights," 35 *New York University Law Review* 865 (April 1960); and his book *A Constitutional Faith* (New York: Knopf, 1968), especially chapter 11, "The First Amendment," pp. 43ff. (See also, generally, *supra* chapter 2.)

360. *Free Speech and Its Relation to Self-Government* (New York: Harper and Brothers, 1948), p. 19; italics supplied.

361. Ibid., p. 27.

solute protection, in the interests of a self-governing free and democratic society, by the First Amendment and the "privileges or immunities" clause of the Fourteenth Amendment, and cannot be abridged at all. "Private" speech, he contended, pertains to speech that concerns only private individuals in their personal, private concerns and can therefore be regulated or restricted—but only in accordance with the "due process of law" safeguards under the Fifth and Fourteenth Amendments. Noble as the Meiklejohn dichotomy may be,[362] it is burdened with what is clearly an unresolvable dilemma of its own: how to draw the line pragmatically between "public" and "private" speech. Much speech is private but has definite public ramifications—a viable line seems impossible to attain. Yet shortly before he died in 1965, Meiklejohn voiced the belief that the Supreme Court had, in effect, adopted his "public speech" approach because of its developing stance on litigation concerning libel, slander, and defamation of character, highlighted by the 1964 decision in *New York Times Co. v. Sullivan*.[363] There the Court held that a *public* official cannot recover libel damages for criticism of his official performance *unless he proves that the statement was made with deliberate malice*.[364] "It is an occasion for dancing in the streets," exclaimed Meiklejohn, according to Justice Brennan—who, however, preferred to leave to his readers "to say how nearly Dr. Meiklejohn's hope has been realized."[365]

Yet a staunch supporter of the Holmes-Brandeis "clear and present danger plus imminence" doctrine, Zechariah Chafee Jr., the aforementioned towering advocate of free expression, had publicly disagreed with his revered teacher and friend Meiklejohn in 1949. Reviewing Meiklejohn's *Free Speech and Its Relation to Self-Government*,[366] Chafee charged that Meiklejohn, in his repeated challenge

---

362. For a similar dichotomy see George Anastaplo, *The Constitutionalist: Notes on the First Amendment* (Dallas, Tex.: Southern Methodist University Press, 1970). He accepts "the First" as absolute in the "political" ("public business") area *but* denies it in the "private" sector, specifically "artistic expression" and "problems of obscenity." He confines his reading to the *First* Amendment, not reaching the states via the Fourteenth. Meiklejohn, of course, does not exempt the states. The two also differ somewhat on the meaning of "public."

363. 376 U.S. 254.

364. See discussion *supra* this chapter. Note that the Court has wavered on the degree of extending the "public" concept to "persons" and/or "figures" as well as "officials"—and on the question of what is "pure" versus "actionable" opinion. On the latter issue see *Milkovich v. Lorain Journal,* 497 U.S. 1 (1990), *supra* this chapter.

365. See William J. Brennan Jr., "The Supreme Court and the Meiklejohn Interpretation of the First Amendment," 79 *Harvard Law Review* (November 1965). Actually, the first to report Meiklejohn's "dancing in the streets" statement was Harry Kalven Jr. in "A New Look at the Central Meaning of the First Amendment," *Supreme Court Review* 191–221 (1964), pp. 191–221.

366. 62 *Harvard Law Review* 891 (1949). See also Meiklejohn's "charges which I would bring against the 'clear and present danger' theory," in another among his important works on the freedom of speech problem, *Political Freedom: The Constitutional Powers of the People* (New York: Oxford University Press, 1965), pp. 75–76.

to Holmes and the clear and present danger doctrine, simply showed no realization of the long uphill fight that Holmes had to wage in order to secure free speech. After all, as Chafee explained appropriately in his review, it was Holmes who

worked out a formula which would invalidate a great deal of suppression, and won for [free speech] the solid authority of a unanimous Court. Afterwards, again and again, when the test was misapplied by the majority, Holmes restated his position in ringing words which, with the help of Brandeis and [later, after he had become Chief Justice] Hughes, eventually inspired the whole Court.[367]

Of course, to support the clear and present danger doctrine, or that of clear and present danger plus imminence, is not to ignore its inherent dilemmas—as the preceding discussion demonstrates. The very adjectives *clear* and *present* raise problems of great magnitude. Still, in both its basic philosophy and its application, the doctrine's overriding tenets are realistic in approach and reflect an attitude which is both liberal *and* conservative in the classic connotations of those two misunderstood adjectives. It is simply not possible to get away from the concept of "balancing"—a contentious term in some quarters[368]—liberty and authority, freedom and responsibility.[369] But when "balancing" is called for, and in the absence of a danger clear, present, and imminent, we must presume the scale to be weighted on the side of the individual.

367. Op. cit., p. 901.
368. See, e.g., the intriguing law review debate between Laurent Frantz and Wallace Mendelson over the validity of "balancing" as a technique in free-speech cases: Laurent Frantz, "The First Amendment in the Balance," 71 *Yale Law Journal* 1424 (1962); Wallace Mendelson, "On the Meaning of the First Amendment: Absolutes in the Balance," 50 *California Law Review* 821 (1962); Laurent Frantz, "Is the First Amendment Law? A Reply to Professor Wallace Mendelson," 51 *California Law Review* 729 (1963); and Wallace Mendelson, "The First Amendment and the Judicial Process: A Reply to Mr. Frantz," 17 *Vanderbilt Law Review* 479 (1964). Speaking broadly, Professor Frantz was anti-, Professor Mendelson pro-"balancing"—but the reader is cautioned against oversimplification. See also the challenging article by Dean Alfange Jr., "The Balancing of Interests in Free Speech Cases: In Defense of an Abused Doctrine," 2 *Law in Transition Quarterly* 1 (1965). Note, too, Justice Black's scathing denunciation of "balancing" in his *Constitutional Faith,* op. cit., and *supra* chapter 2 of the present volume. To Black, of course, the "clear and present danger" doctrine—be it with or without the "imminence" requirement—was just another form of "balancing" and hence unacceptable under his reading of the absolutist commands of the First (and Fourteenth) Amendment. "[I]t has no place in [their] interpretation," as he admonished again shortly prior to the end of his long and distinguished career on the Court, in his concurring opinion in *Brandenburg v. Ohio,* 395 U.S. 444 (1968) at 449–50.
369. In his interesting position essay on the overall question, *Freedom of Speech: The Supreme Court and Judicial Review* (Englewood Cliffs, N.J.: Prentice-Hall, 1966), Martin Shapiro contends that although balancing "may still occasionally be useful in particular instances, it cannot be maintained as a general formula for a Court bent on fulfilling its First Amendment responsibilities" (p. 105). Issuing a clarion call for judicial activism,

The philosophical test[370] to be applied is clear: Will the forbidding of freedom of expression further or hamper the realization of liberal democratic ideals? The sole manner in which to moderate, remedy, or remove rankling discontent is to get at its causes by education, remedial laws, or other community action. Repression of expression will only serve to sharpen the sense of injustice and provide added arguments and rationalizations for desperate, perhaps reckless measures. Surely the loyalty of the mass of people to liberal democracy has been immensely strengthened by the right to free expression and the consequent feeling of a genuine stake in society, a society that allows the expression of our deepest and most rankling grievances. Hence repressive laws will fail to maintain "loyalty." While they may give a false sense of temporary security, since we would be excused from arguing the case for our ideals and for the carefully developed procedures for pursuing them, we must also recognize that freedom of utterance, even though it be rebellious, constitutes a safety valve that gives timely warning of dangerous pressures in our society. Committed to the principles of Western liberal democracy, we have a lasting obligation to leave open the political channels by which a governing majority can be replaced when it is no longer able to command popular support. However, to plead for a generous approach to freedom of expression is not to say that it is absolute. It is not; it cannot be. In the final analysis we must confidently look to the Court to draw a line based on constitutional common sense. No other agency of government is equally well qualified to do so.

---

he sees the "preferred freedom" position as the only viable formula, one that he insists must "again become the dominant First Amendment doctrine of the Supreme Court" (p. 172). Again and again calling for judicial activism, judicial policymaking, in the freedom of speech sphere, he argues that American democracy "not only permits but invites and requires a strong measure of judicial activism here."

370. See J. A. Corry and Henry J. Abraham, *Elements of Democratic Government,* 4th ed. (New York: Oxford University Press, 1964), pp. 262ff

6

Religion

If line drawing in the realm of due process is difficult because of the ambiguity of the concept, and if it is elusive in determining the parameters of freedom of expression, it is preeminently delicate and emotional in the matter of religion. Religion, like love, is so personal and irrational that no one has either the capacity or the justification to sit in judgment.[1] Any attempt by society to find and draw a line here is bound to be frustrating. Our own society is certainly no exception—although it is to America's credit that in probably no other area of civil rights and liberties have our agencies and agents of government maintained such a consistently good record. Even more than the freedom of the press has the freedom of religion been safeguarded from governmental interference. This is not to say, of course, that

1. Still, the senior author is tempted to profess a modicum of "expertise": a product of secular secondary schools, he spent one year at a Roman Catholic university; was graduated from an Episcopal college; married a Christian Scientist; has children who went to Quaker and Episcopal elementary and secondary schools (and to the same college as their father); and was for eight years a member of the board of trustees of an old Reform Jewish congregation. Although the junior author is not quite as ecumenical, her education included eight years in a Roman Catholic elementary school run by Dominican nuns, eight years of secondary and higher education in public institutions, graduate training abroad at a Church of England university, and doctoral studies steeped in the separationist philosophy of "Mr. Jefferson's University." She is currently a member of a Roman Catholic parish led by Dominican priests.

At the turn of the twenty-first century only one-half of the approximately 280 million inhabitants of the United States professed an avowed religious affiliation, to wit (in rounded figures): Roman Catholic, 62,000,000; Baptist (Southern and American), 21,500,000; Methodist, 10,500,000; Lutheran (Missouri Synod and Evangelical Lutheran Church of America), 8,000,000; Jewish, 6,000,000; Mormon, 4,500,000; Presbyterian, 3,000,000; Assemblies of God, 2,500,000; Episcopal, 2,300,000; and Muslim, 1,500,000 (estimate) (*Washington Post,* September 17, 2002, p. A3).

we have a perfect record; our early history is replete with both public and private discrimination against religious creeds, particularly Catholics, Quakers, and Jews. However, as we grew and developed as a nation, discrimination *by government* declined perceptibly and fairly rapidly. *Private* religious discrimination—which does still exist, and presumably always will to some degree—is no longer, if it ever was, sanctioned by government, and when it occurs it is preeminently of a "social" rather than a "religious" nature. The problems arise when attempts are made to commingle matters of religious belief with matters of state and to conduct policy in line with spiritual commitments.

The election of the first Roman Catholic president of the United States in 1960; the rise to public prominence and power of a host of members of religious minority groups; and the steadily increasing official proscription of public or quasi-public discrimination because of race, sex, religion, color, and national origin—brought to a dramatic climax in the Civil Rights Act of 1964, as amended—all augur well for a continuing increase in understanding and a continuing decline of the barriers built of religious discrimination. Nevertheless, problems of religious freedom still do arise, and lines must be drawn. Our concern here lies predominantly in the *public* sector, and in how and where lines are drawn between the prerogatives of the free exercise of religion, and all the concept entails, and the right of society to guard against activity that would infringe upon the rights of other members of that society. The distinction is compounded by the unique collateral problem of the constitutional command against the "establishment" of religion; *it* has proved to be a hornet's nest indeed!

SOME BASIC CONSIDERATIONS

Basic to our understanding of the problem are three constitutional facts.

The Proscription of Religious Tests in Article 6 of the Constitution. It is often forgotten that there exists in the body of our Constitution an important provision dealing directly with a crucial religious right, the forbidding of religious tests as qualifications for public office. The third section of Article 6, following the famed supremacy clause[2]—which constitutes all of Section 2—reflects the concern for religious liberty of four Virginians to whom, although they were not all participants in the Constitutional Convention, is due chief credit for our consti-

---

2. "This Constitution, and the Laws of the United States which shall be made in Pursuance thereof; and all Treaties made, or which shall be made, under the Authority of the United States, shall be the supreme Law of the Land; *and the Judges in every State shall be bound thereby, any Thing in the Constitution of Laws of any State to the Contrary notwithstanding*"; italics supplied.

tutional theory of freedom of religion: Thomas Jefferson,[3] James Madison, George Mason—who refused to sign the final draft of the Constitution because of the absence of a Bill of Rights—and, perhaps with an occasional aberration, Patrick Henry.[4]

The Journal of the Convention for August 30, 1787, bears the following entry: "It was moved and seconded to add . . . —'but no religious test shall *ever* be required as a qualification to *any* office or public trust under the authority of the United States'; which passed almost unanimously in the affirmative,"[5] only North Carolina voting against the adoption of this clause.[6] Later, referring to the clause's significance, Justice Joseph Story commented: "The Catholic and the Protestant, the Calvinist and the Armenian [*sic*], the infidel and the Jew, may sit down to the Communion-table of the National Council, without any inquisition into their faith or mode of worship."[7]

Although this ban against religious test oaths settled matters at once insofar as public office under the federal government was concerned, it did become an issue in state and municipal public employment and remained so for a good many years. Most states removed their mandated disqualifications against Jews and members of other theistic religions, but others, such as Arkansas, Maryland, Pennsylvania, and Tennessee, retained constitutional provisions compelling all would-be public officeholders to take an oath or make an affirmation of their belief in God. Inevitably, however, judicial nationalization of civil rights and liberties via the due process of law clause of the Fourteenth Amendment ultimately reached the area of religion.[8] And in 1961 the Supreme Court addressed itself specifically to the religious oath clause in *Torcaso v. Watkins.*[9]

In that case Roy Torcaso, an aspirant for the minor state office of notary public in Maryland, refused to abide by his state's requirement, embedded in a

---

3. Symptomatic of Jefferson's strong feelings about religious freedom is the following excerpt from a letter he wrote to Mrs. M. Harrison Smith on August 6, 1816: "I never told my own religion, nor scrutinized that of another. I never attempted to make a convert, nor wished to change another's creed. I have never judged the religion of others, and by this test, my dear Madame, I have been satisfied yours must be an excellent one to have produced a life of such exemplary virtue and correctness. For it is in our lives and not from our words that our religion must be read."

4. Anson Phelps Stokes and Leo Pfeffer, *Church and State in the United States,* rev. one-volume ed. (New York: Harper and Row, 1964), pp. 65ff.

5. Jonathan Elliot, *The Debates in the Several State Conventions,* 2 vols., 2d ed. (Philadelphia: Lippincott, 1854), vol. 1, p. 277; italics supplied.

6. With the substitution of a semicolon for the dash before *but* and of a period for the semicolon after *States,* it became the last phrase of Article 6, Section 3.

7. As quoted in Stokes and Pfeffer, op. cit., p. 91.

8. See *supra* chapter 3 and, inter alia, *Hamilton v. Board of Regents of California,* 293 U.S. 245 (1934); *Cantwell v. Connecticut,* 310 U.S. 296 (1940); and *Everson v. Board of Education of Ewing Township,* 330 U.S. 1 (1947).

9. 367 U.S. 488.

clause of its constitution, that all officeholders declare their belief in the existence of God as a part of their oath of office. On Torcaso's refusal to take the oath his application was denied, and he appealed to the Maryland courts for a reversal of that ruling, alleging violation of the religious liberty guaranteed to him by the U.S. Constitution. When the state courts sided with Maryland, Torcaso took his case to the U.S. Supreme Court, which not only agreed with Torcaso's contentions but declared the oath requirement unconstitutional as a violation of the free exercise of religion clause of the First Amendment of the federal Constitution. Unanimously, the Court, without any inquiry into what belief, if any, Roy Torcaso held—he was an atheist—declared that the state test oath constituted a clear invasion of freedom of belief and religion. Moreover, wrote Justice Black for the Court, in placing Maryland on the side of "one particular sort of believer," namely, theists—those who believe in the existence of God—the constitutional requirement imposed a burden on the free exercise of the faiths on *nonbelievers* in violation of the free exercise clause.[10] To emphasize this point, Black appended what has become a well-known footnote in constitutional law: "Among religions in this country which do not teach what would generally be considered a belief in the existence of God are Buddhism, Taoism, Ethical Culture, Secular Humanism and others."[11] In other words, the Court made categorically clear that not only were religious test oaths barred, but theistic belief could not be a requirement for religious belief.[12] Put somewhat differently, the Court affirmed what has been, or should have been, apparent all along: that the Constitution of the United States, in guaranteeing freedom of religion, by implication also guarantees freedom of *irreligion*. Four years later, the Maryland Court of Appeals specifically extended that guarantee to invalidate a requirement that all Maryland jurors declare a belief in God.[13]

The "Nationalization" of the Religion Clauses. As we already know from chapter 3, the wording of the First Amendment, of which the religion phrases constitute the opening statements, confined the inherent prohibitions against governmental action to the *federal* government. This made particular sense in the case of religion, for at the time of the adoption of the Constitution of the United States many of the original thirteen *states* had specific religious establishments or other restrictive provisos. In fact, in the earliest days of the fledgling nation only Virginia, led by Jefferson, Madison, and Mason, and Rhode Island conceded full, unqualified freedom; New York *almost* did.[14] Two states, Delaware and

10. Ibid. at 495.
11. Ibid., note 11. See the developing argument on "secular humanism," which reached the federal judiciary in 1987.
12. In this connection see the problem of the draft and conscientious objectors, discussed *infra.*
13. *Schowgurow v. State,* 240 Md. 121 (1965).
14. In addition to barring ministers from public office, New York required naturalized citizens to abjure allegiance in all foreign ecclesiastical as well as civil matters.

Maryland, demanded Christianity, Delaware also insisting on assent to the doctrine of the Trinity; four, Delaware, North Carolina, Pennsylvania, and South Carolina, called for assent to the divine inspiration of the Bible, with Pennsylvania and South Carolina further requiring a belief in heaven and hell, and South Carolina—the only one among the thirteen—still speaking of religious "toleration"; three, Maryland, New York, and South Carolina, excluded all ministers, even Protestants, from any civil office; five, Connecticut, Maryland, Massachusetts, New Hampshire, and South Carolina, insisted on "Protestantism," or "Christian Protestantism"; and six, Connecticut, Georgia, New Hampshire, New Jersey, North Carolina, and South Carolina, specifically adhered to religious establishments (Protestant).[15] Hence it is not surprising that the First Amendment was widely regarded as a protection of state establishments *against* congressional action. By 1833, however, following the capitulation of the Congregationalists in Massachusetts, the fundamental concepts of freedom of religion had, to all intents and purposes, become a recognized fact and facet of public law, with only minor aberrations, throughout the young United States of America.

It was thus but a matter of time for religious freedom and its attendant safeguards for the separation between church and state to become binding under our Constitution de jure as well as de facto. As the "incorporation," "absorption," or "nationalization" of the Bill of Rights guarantees achieved judicial recognition, beginning with the Sanford opinion in *Gitlow v. New York*[16] in 1925, it was but a question of time until the Court would address itself to religion. And so it did, first to the free exercise of religion in 1934 and 1940,[17] then to the separation of church and state in 1947.[18]

The Two Aspects of the Religion Clause. One of the difficulties in the interpretation of the religion clause is that its language speaks of both the "establishment" *and* the "free exercise" of religion, and many students of the issue contend that the two prongs be treated as a single precept, and that the First Amendment should be "religion blind," as Professors Leo Pfeffer and Philip Kurland long counseled. Certainly the two clauses are interrelated, but they are also separable.[19] The author

15. See Stokes and Pfeffer, op. cit., chapter 3, for a full account.

16. 268 U.S. 252. See *supra* chapter 3.

17. *Hamilton v. Regents of University of California*, 293 U.S. 245 (1934); and *Cantwell v. Connecticut*, 310 U.S. 296 (1940).

18. *Everson v. Board of Education*, 310 U.S. 1.

19. This is not to say that commentators and students have not at times been puzzled both as to the choice determined by the judiciary in specific cases and as to the viability of a distinction in others. Illustrative of the problem is the challenge brought in 1974 by four Roman Catholic students and priests against the University of Delaware's ban against religious services on its property. The university argued—ultimately unsuccessfully—that the establishment clause compelled it to ban such services; the students and priests argued

of the First Amendment, usually—although not always[20]—regarded as Madison, even separated the two by a comma: "Congress shall make no law respecting an establishment of religion, or prohibiting the free exercise thereof. . . ." When the Supreme Court first undertook to "nationalize" the religion clauses in the *Hamilton* case[21] in 1934, Justice Butler's opinion confined itself to Albert Hamilton's claim of free exercise; the matter of "establishment" or separation of church and state was not properly at issue. Nor did it play a meaningful role in the next great freedom of religion case to be decided by the Supreme Court, six years later, *Cantwell v. Connecticut,*[22] which elaborated upon the *Hamilton* rationale. It was not until the *New Jersey Bus Case,*[23] seven years after *Cantwell,* that the Court, speaking through Justice Black, held that the First Amendment's prohibition against legislation respecting an establishment of religion is also applicable to the several states by virtue of the language and obligations of the Fourteenth Amendment. Thus, by 1947, *both* aspects of the religion guarantee had been judicially interpreted to apply to *both* the federal government and the several states of the Union. Far more complicated, however, was the determination of the meaning, range, and extent of the two famous clauses—especially since the record shows that at the time of their adoption by Congress that august body debated the religion clauses but once (and that debate was neither long nor enlightening).

Attempting to Define "Religion"

To state the problem is to see its complications. Yet in a government under law, whatever an individual's personal idea of religion might be, formal definitions have to be ventured. Each individual does, of course, possess the basic right, now one universally guaranteed and protected under our Constitution, to believe what he or she chooses, to worship whom and how he or she pleases, always provided that it does not impermissibly interfere with the right of others. Hence, we have those who believe in nothing; those who believe but doubt; those who believe without questioning; those who worship the Judeo-Christian God in innumerably different ways; those who adhere to Muhammad's creed; those who worship themselves; those who worship a cow or other animals; those who worship several gods—to mention just a few of the remarkable variety of expressions of belief that obtain.

---

that the free exercise clause entitled them to hold such services. The Delaware courts upheld the latter's claim, and the U.S. Supreme Court declined to review the case, thereby leaving the state's judgment in force (*University of Delaware v. Keegan,* 424 U.S. 934).

20. See Donald L. Drakeman, "Religion and the Republic: James Madison and the First Amendment," 25 *Journal of Church and State* 427 (autumn 1983), for one who does not believe that Madison "drafted the language of the religion clauses" (at 431).

21. *Hamilton v. Regents of California,* op. cit.

22. 310 U.S. 296 (1940).

23. *Everson v. Board of Education of Ewing Township,* 330 U.S. 1 (1947).

Webster's New Collegiate Dictionary provides the following choices under the heading "religion":

1(a): the service or worship of God or the supernatural; (b): commitment or devotion to religious faith or observance; 2: a personal faith or institutionalized system of religious attitudes, beliefs, and practices; 3 (archaic): scrupulous conformity; 4: a cause, principle, or system of beliefs held to with ardor and faith.[24]

At best such a definition can offer a broad guideline of a nonbinding nature. The same is more or less true of the kind of psychological guideline furnished by such thoughtful commentators as Professor Gordon W. Allport, who wrote that religion encompasses a value that every democrat "must hold: the right of each individual to work out his own philosophy of life, to find his personal niche in creation as best he can."[25] He further elaborated: "A man's religion is the audacious bid he makes to bind himself to creation and to the Creator. It is his ultimate attempt to enlarge and to complete his own personality by finding the supreme context in which he rightly belongs."[26]

One may agree with Allport's approach to a definition or interpretation—or Alfred North Whitehead's that it is "what each individual does with his own solitariness"[27]—but the authoritative definition–cum–constitutional interpretation had to come from the Supreme Court, acting either upon a congressional definition or within the confines of its common-law responsibilities.

The Supreme Court Defines Religion. The classic Court definition was authored by Justice Stephen J. Field in an 1890 case in which the Court unanimously upheld a lower court judgment that one Samuel Davis, a Mormon residing in the then territory of Idaho, should be disqualified as a voter for falsifying his voter's oath "abjuring bigamy or polygamy as a condition to vote" since, as a Mormon, he believed in polygamy. Polygamy, then as now a criminal offense,[28] constituted a disqualification under territorial voting and other statutes. Field wrote for the court:

24. 8th ed. (Springfield, Mass.: G. and C. Merriam, 1975), p. 724, col. 1.
25. Gordon W. Allport, *The Individual and His Religion,* 2d ed. (New York: Macmillan, 1962), p. vii.
26. Ibid., p. 142.
27. "Religion in the Making," in F. C. S. Northrop and Mason W. Gross, eds., *Alfred North Whitehead: An Anthology* (New York: Macmillan, 1953), p. 472.
28. Utah's ban on polygamy, adopted in 1896 as a condition for attaining statehood, was reaffirmed in U.S. District Court in 1984. But it has seemed to persist in parts of Utah and small pockets of the American West. See Timothy Egan, "The Persistence of Polygamy," *New York Times Magazine,* February 22, 1999, pp. 51ff. And in a case eagerly covered by the media, an avowed Utah polygamist who appeared on television shows and flaunted his life with five wives and twenty-nine children was found guilty in a Provo, Utah, courtroom of four counts of bigamy and one count of nonsupport of his offspring (*Washington Post,* May 20, 2001, p. A2).

[T]he term "religion" has reference to one's view of his relations to his Creator, and to the obligations they impose of reverence for his being and character, and of obedience to his will. It is often confounded with the cultus or form of worship of a particular sect, but is distinguishable from the latter. . . . With man's relations to his Maker and the obligations he may think they impose, and the manner in which an expression shall be made by him of his belief on those subjects, no interference can be permitted, provided always the laws of society, designed to secure its peace and prosperity, and the morals of its people are not interfered with.[29]

Thus, although giving religion the widest feasible interpretation in terms of individual commitment, Field found that Davis had violated the reservation of the last qualifying clause.[30]

The "CO" Problem. This Supreme Court definition of religion was most often tested in cases dealing with military exemptions and conscientious objectors. Exemption from the draft and/or combat service for those who oppose war on religious grounds is deeply rooted in American tradition and history—although it was not really formalized until post–Civil War days. Much litigation has attended this problem, frequently involving the Jehovah's Witnesses, who contend that every believing Witness is a "minister" and as such ought to be exempt from military service. About four thousand of the six thousand "COs" to be sentenced to jail during World War II were Jehovah's Witnesses.[31] Both the Society of Friends (the Quakers) and the Mennonites have made pacifism a dogma. And, of course, there has been a continuous stream of individual conscientious objectors, coming chiefly from small Protestant sects but from other faiths as well—a stream that in the 1960s became a formidable river with our lengthy Southeast Asia involvement.[32] Congress has been generous in recognizing bona fide conscientious objectors and in exempting these from military service,[33] although it is not at all

29. *Davis v. Beason,* 133 U.S. 333 (1890) at 342.

30. See Jesse H. Choper, "Defining 'Religion' in the First Amendment," 1982 *University of Illinois Law Review* 3 (1982), in which the author suggests that the "seemingly intractable abstract question of what constitutes a religion need be answered in only a very limited way for constitutional purposes." He looks to other provisions of the First Amendment as disposing of "almost all other problems fairly considered," such as "freedom of expression and freedom of association."

31. Arlo Tatum, *Handbook for Conscientious Objectors* (Philadelphia: Central Committee for Conscientious Objectors, 1965), pp. 41ff.

32. In June 1970 alone, for example, 14,440 CO claims were officially filed (*New York Times,* July 25, 1970, p. 61).

33. A CO who first claimed conscientious objector status after he received an induction notice, when, he asserted, his CO views "matured," appealed unsuccessfully for Supreme Court review of his problem in 1967 (*Gearey v. United States,* 389 U.S. 959, certiorari denied).

clear that there exists a *constitutional* rather than a *moral obligation* to exempt conscientious objectors. It is quite possible to argue either—or both—sides of the issue. The Federal Conscription Act of 1864 as well as the two major draft statutes of this century, those of 1917 and 1940, both included exemption provisions. The 1917 law—which was unanimously upheld by the U.S. Supreme Court in 1918[34]—exempted from combat only members affiliated with "any well-recognized religious sect or organizations" such as "peace churches" or a "pacifist religious sect" like the Quakers. In 1940, however, Congress discarded *all* sectarian restrictions, so that conscientious objectors no longer had to belong to a church or other religious organization, provided their opposition to war was based upon "religious training and belief." The statute also provided for alternate civilian service for those COs who refused to perform noncombatant military service. Subsequent amendments to the 1940 statute, enacted in 1948 and 1951, expanded the prerogatives; but 1967 saw a distinct retrenchment.[35]

The problem in granting these exemptions has been, and is, the distinction between bona fide and not so bona fide claims. It is axiomatic in democratic society that men and women of abiding religious conviction who, either as individuals or as members of pacifist sects, hold creeds and beliefs that proscribe participation in war or related strife should neither be compelled to participate nor be jailed for refusing to do so. Yet what of those whose objections are not of a clearly identifiable, bona fide religious nature but are probably preeminently moral and/or sociological, philosophical, or even political? Where does personal "policy making" begin? Can it ever be given preference over duly enacted public policy, one that recognizes CO status in law but chooses to establish definite, limiting guidelines? And, to compound the inherent complexities, what of those whose conscientious objection is limited to a *particular* war, for example, that in Vietnam?[36]

34. *Arver v. United States,* 245 U.S. 366.

35. For an excellent, although now dated, treatment of the subject see Mulford Q. Sibley and Philip E. Jacobs, *Conscription of Conscience: The American State and the Conscientious Objector, 1940–1947* (Ithaca, N.Y.: Cornell University Press, 1952). A more recent and useful account of the comparative status of conscientious objection throughout the world is Charles C. Moskos and John Whiteclay Chambers, eds., *The New Conscientious Objection: From Sacred to Secular Resistance* (New York: Oxford University Press, 1993).

36. This issue faced the Court repeatedly as of the late 1960s, often coupled with a challenge to the legality of the undeclared Indochina involvement. On several occasions the Court denied review of the "legality" question involving individuals, e.g., twice in 1967, Justice Douglas dissenting from the denial in *both* cases, Justice Stewart in the second (*Mitchell v. United States,* 386 U.S. 972; and *Mora v. McNamara,* 389 U.S. 934); and, late in 1970, with the two dissenters joined by Harlan, it refused to entertain a lawsuit by the Commonwealth of Massachusetts which, based on a law it had passed, challenged the president's power to carry on the Vietnam War without a formal declaration of war (*Massachusetts v. Laird,* 400 U.S. 886). One year and again one and one-half years later, with

In 1965 the Supreme Court handed down a momentous decision in three cases involving the most recent provisions in the draft law exempting religious objectors from combat training and service. At issue was the restriction established by Congress in 1951 of exemption to "persons who by reason of religious training and belief are conscientiously opposed to any participation in war." The definition spelled out "religious training and belief" as follows:

Religious training and belief in this connection means an individual belief in relation to a Supreme Being involving duties superior to those arising from any human relation, but does not include essentially political, sociological or philosophical views, or a merely personal moral code.[37]

Three men were involved in these 1965 *Draft Act Cases,*[38] Daniel A. Seeger, Arno S. Jakobson, and Forest B. Peter. Seeger and Jakobson had been convicted by the U.S. District Court in New York, and Peter by the U.S. District Court in San Francisco, of refusing to submit to induction. Both New York convictions were reversed by the U.S. Court of Appeals for the Second Circuit, but the Appeals Court for the Ninth Circuit upheld the Peter conviction. Seeger had told the Selective Service authorities that he was conscientiously opposed to participation in war in any form because of his "religious" belief but that he preferred to leave open the question of his belief in a Supreme Being rather than answer "yes" or "no." Jakobson asserted that he believed in a Supreme Being who was "Creator of Man," in the sense of being "ultimately responsible for the existence of" man, and who was the "Supreme Reality" of which "the existence of man is the result." Peter said the source of his conviction was "our democratic American culture, with its values derived from the Western religious and philosophical

---

only Douglas and Brennan dissenting in both cases, it refused again (*Orlando v. Laird,* 404 U.S. [1971]; and *Da Costa v. Laird,* 405 U.S. 979 [1972]). A different effort, basing the appeal on the question of congressional power to appropriate funds for an undeclared war, also failed in 1972, Douglas and Brennan dissenting (*Sarnoff v. Schultz,* 409 U.S. 929); so did a similar one in 1973 (*Attlee v. Richardson,* 411 U.S. 94). On the matter of conscientious objection to a *particular* war—or, as it may also be styled, selective conscientious objection—the Court had a test case before it in 1970, but (1) the issue came up tangentially in connection with the more pressing one of "non-religious conscientious objection," and (2) a majority of 5:3 held that the case had been improperly appealed to it from the district court below (*United States v. Sisson,* 399 U.S. 267, an eighty-three-page decision). To make clear that it was not engaging in an artful evasion—something of which it is eminently capable, and often for excellent reasons—the Court granted two appeals by selective conscientious objectors, of which it disposed in March 1971 (*Gillette v. United States* and *Negre v. Larson,* 401 U.S. 437).

   37. 50 App. U.S.C.A., §456(j) (1951).
   38. *United States v. Seeger,* 380 U.S. 163 (1965). For a complete case study of *Seeger* (from start to conclusion), see Clyde E. Jacobs and John F. Gallagher, *The Selective Service Act: A Case Study of the Governmental Process* (New York: Dodd, Mead, 1967), pp. 138–89.

tradition." As to his belief in a Supreme Being, Peter added that he supposed "you could call that a belief in the Supreme Being or God. These just do not happen to be the words I use."[39]

In affirming the reversals by the Second Circuit Court of Appeals and in reversing the decision of that of the Ninth Circuit, the U.S. Supreme Court, while sidestepping constitutional questions, clearly broadened construction of the statutory provision quoted previously. The test of belief "in a relation to a Supreme Being," the Court held, is whether a sincere and meaningful belief which occupies in the life of its possessor a place *parallel* to that filled by the God of those admittedly qualifying for the exemption comes within the statutory definition. Applying this liberalizing test, the Court ruled that the beliefs expressed by the three men involved in the cases before it consequently entitled them to the exemption. Thus they created a new definition of the concept of religion under the Constitution, at least for pertinent statutory purposes. However, the Court, in a unanimous opinion written by its foremost religious layman, Justice Clark, added:

> We also pause to take note of what is not involved in this litigation. No party claims to be an atheist or attacks the statute on this ground. The question is not, therefore, one between theistic and atheistic beliefs. We do not deal with or intimate any decision on the situation in this case.[40]

Indeed, the Clark opinion and a concurring one by Justice Douglas read like a short course in theology, as the *New York Times* commented on the morning after.[41] Clark quoted Paul Tillich, the bishop of Woolwich, John A. T. Robinson, and the schema of the most recent Ecumenical Council at the Vatican to prove, as Clark put it, the "broad spectrum of religious beliefs found among us." These quotations, the opinion went on,

> demonstrate very clearly the diverse manners in which beliefs equally paramount in the lives of their possessors may be articulated. They further reveal the difficulties inherent in placing too narrow a construction on the provisions [of the particular sections of the Draft Act here at issue] and thereby lend conclusive support to the [broad] construction which we today find that Congress intended.[42]

Other than from Congress and the executive branch, there was astonishingly little criticism of this dramatic decision that recognized "a sincere and meaningful belief" as occupying a place "parallel to a belief in God." This abstemiousness differed markedly from the reaction which had greeted (if that is the word!) the

39. *United States v. Seeger*, op. cit., at 165.
40. Ibid. at 173, 176.
41. March 9, 1965, p. 431.
42. *United States v. Seeger*, op. cit., at 183.

Court's memorable decision in the *New York Prayer Case*[43] and the *Bible Reading Cases*[44] a few years before. What the 1965 *Draft Act Cases* proved conclusively is that there is less certainty in, and less emphasis on, a strictly construed traditional definition of religion. Instead, and without getting into the matter of distinctions between theistic and atheistic creeds and dogmas, a unanimous Supreme Court adopted broadened concepts of religious liberty and conscience by declaring that a conscientious objector need not believe in the orthodox concept of a Supreme Being. A "religious motivation," however vague or existential, was apparently still required, nonetheless.

On the other hand, neither the administration nor Congress was happy with the *Seeger* decision, especially not the House of Representatives, where the powerful, hawkish L. Mendel Rivers (D.-S.C.), then the chairman of the House Armed Services Committee, was livid with rage and threatened immediate revenge. At first he attempted to push through Congress a revised version of the 1951 CO provisions, which would have mandated the presence of a belief in an "organized" (and presumably "recognized") religion before an individual could qualify as "a bona fide CO." When his move failed, he proposed a new version of the 1951 language, which became law in 1967. Rivers was aided by his Senate counterpart, Chairman John Stennis (D.-Miss.), as well as a general wave of resentment against eligible draftees because of the spate of draft-card burnings. The 1967 provision—coded as Section 6(j)—reads: *"Religious training and belief does not include essentially political, sociological or philosophical views, or a merely personal moral code."* A quick comparison with the 1951 language of the provision will show that the term "Supreme Being" was deleted from the 1967 draft law amendment, and with it the Supreme Court's generous interpretation of the term in the *Seeger* case. Or at least so Representative Rivers and his supporters thought. But it was a short-lived triumph. The warnings voiced by a sizable number of Mr. Rivers's colleagues, that Congress was about to create a troublesome constitutional cul-de-sac,[45] proved to be prophetic. In 1969 and 1970 three different U.S. District Courts ruled the new provision unconstitutional, on a veritable smorgasbord of grounds, as violative of the establishment clause of the First Amendment and of its free exercise clause; of the due process of law clause of the Fifth Amendment; even of the equal protection of the laws clause of the Fourteenth Amendment, which is not applicable to the federal government.[46] The lead case came from Judge Charles E. Wyzanski's tribunal in

---

43. *Engel v. Vitale,* 370 U.S. 421 (1962).

44. *Abington School District v. Schempp* and *Murray v. Curlett,* 374 U.S. 203 (1963).

45. Fred P. Graham, "Again the Tough Issue of the C.O.," *New York Times,* April 6, 1969, sec. 4, p. 10.

46. *United States v. Sisson,* 297 F. Supp. 902 (D. Mass. 1969); *Koster v. Sharp,* 303 F. Supp. 836 (E.D. Pa. 1969); and *United States v. McFadden,* 309 F. Supp. (502 N.D. Cal. 1970).

Boston: *United States v. Sisson,*[47] alluded to earlier, concerned the refusal of one John H. Sisson, a "selective" Vietnam war objector, to be inducted into the armed forces. The colorful trial judge ruled that Sisson could not "constitutionally be subjected to military orders which may require him to kill in the Vietnam conflict." A jury had found him duly guilty of refusing to submit to induction, but Judge Wyzanski sustained two of Sisson's contentions: (1) a "broad," primarily free exercise claim "that no statute can require combat service of a conscientious objector whose principles are either religious *or akin thereto*"; and (2) a "narrower" assertion concerning separation of church and state, that "the 1967 draft act [Section 6(j)] invalidly discriminates in favor of certain types of religious objectors to the prejudice of *Sisson,*" excluding, for example, "atheists, agnostics, and the like. . . ."[48] Heavily relying on the Clark opinion in *Seeger,* Wyzanski concluded:

> In short, in the draft act Congress unconstitutionally discriminated against atheists, agnostics, and men, like Sisson, who, whether they be religious or not, are motivated in their objection to the draft by profound moral beliefs which constitute central convictions of their beings.[49]

The Supreme Court, for technical and procedural reasons, would not then deal with the key *Sisson* issue on its merits, but it docketed two cases on the "selective" conscientious objection problem,[50] and it did come to grips with at least some of the aspects of the basic "religious" problem in its 1970 decision in the case of *Welsh v. United States.*[51]

Elliott A. Welsh II, a twenty-eight-year-old Los Angeles commodities broker, had applied for draft exemption on CO grounds in 1964. In filling out the special form he took pains to cross out the words "religious training"—partly to demonstrate that he was opposed to war on broader historical, philosophical, and sociological grounds. His application was denied all along the line for want of proof of a "religious basis" for his beliefs; he refused induction; and he was sentenced to a three-year prison term. By a vote of 5:3, with Justice Black (a captain in the army in World War I) writing for four of the five justices on the majority side, the Court reversed his conviction. Justice White (a lieutenant commander in the navy in World War II) dissented sharply, joined by Chief Justice Burger and Justice Stewart (another naval officer in World War II). The Black opinion, which was joined by Justices Douglas (Student Training Corps in World War I), Brennan (an army colonel in World War II), and Marshall, was based on a broad and generous construction of the *Seeger* rationale of five years earlier. Welsh's

47. See *United States v. Sisson,* loc. cit.
48. Ibid. at 906; italics supplied.
49. Ibid. at 911.
50. See *supra* chapter 5.
51. 398 U.S. 333.

conviction, wrote Black, was inconsistent with the *Seeger* holding. He admitted that the draft law bars exemption based on "essentially political, sociological or philosophical views, or a merely personal moral code"—but he suggested that such views can readily be held so firmly as to be "religious" within the meaning of the law. According to Black's interpretation, then, the draft law actually exempts "all those whose consciences, spurred by deeply held moral, ethical or religious beliefs, *would give them no rest or peace* if they allowed themselves to become a part of an instrument of war."[52] In view of the explicit religious terminology in the crucial Section 6(j) of the statute, one might be pardoned for blinking a bit—and the three dissenters did more than blink. "Saving #6(j) by extending it to include *Welsh* cannot be done in the name of a presumed congressional will but only by the Court's taking upon itself the power to make draft-exemption policy,"[53] wrote Justice White.

To the majority, however, the key element had become Welsh's documented assertion that he believed "the taking of life—anyone's life—to be morally wrong." Because he held this belief "with the strength of more traditional religious convictions," he was, in the considered judgment of the four members joining in the Court's majority opinion, entitled to exemption under the statute. Justice Harlan (an air force colonel during World War II) wrote his own concurrence, agreeing that Welsh was entitled to exemption but for a dramatically different reason. In retrospect unhappy with the *Seeger* construction— although he had concurred in that decision, too—Harlan was even more unhappy with its expanded construction here. He now wanted to reach the constitutional question and, addressing it, urged that to deny Welsh an exemption *would show favoritism to religion* as opposed to nonreligion, and thus violate the First Amendment's ban against governmental "establishment of religion."[54] This, of course, raises again the fascinating quaere of whether Congress could be *compelled* to grant CO exemptions under the free exercise (conscience?) clause of the First Amendment in the face of the Harlan assumption—one held by many others—that to do so would constitute a violation of its "establishment" clause. White, in his dissent, while acknowledging that Congress could not be *compelled* to grant exemption on religious grounds, contended that it certainly could legislate to recognize free exercise values—thus rejecting the Harlan posture on establishment. Given *that* dilemma, the Black solution may well be the most viable suggestion for a usable line, after all. Yet to apply that line equitably throughout the land presented a dilemma—as the Selective Service director, Dr. Curtis Tarr, made clear, while valiantly attempting to issue guidelines

52. Ibid. at 344; italics supplied. In 1973, with Justices Douglas and Stewart dissenting, the Court declined to consider applying the decision retroactively (*Avery v. United States,* 414 U.S. 922).
53. Ibid. at 369.
54. Ibid. at 357.

to his 4,101 local draft boards.[55] There was much sympathy with his, and Congress's, unhappiness with the *Welsh* decision; but there was also much agreement with James Reston's poignant observation that, while recognizing the existence of what amounts to a "privileged sanctuary of conscience," there is

> something reassuring philosophically about the Supreme Court's support of ethical as distinguished from religious opposition to the war, something even exciting and ennobling about the American system that struggles with life's great imponderables.[56]

Those who were unhappy with *Welsh* would soon find themselves somewhat, if not totally, mollified, and those who were happy with *Welsh* would soon be somewhat, if not totally, disappointed in the face of the Court's momentous early 1971 decision in two cases that clearly raised the issue of "selective" conscientious objection. In other words, did the congressional, and judicially interpreted, provision for conscientious objection permit objection to only some wars, to "unjust" rather than "just" wars, to the Vietnam War rather than some other past, present, or future wars? The Court responded "No!" without equivocation in a joint 8:1 decision in *Gillette v. United States* and *Negre v. Larsen.*[57] Speaking for all members of the Court except the dissenting Justice Douglas, Justice Marshall held that Congress acted constitutionally when it ruled out "selective" conscientious objection by authorizing exemptions only for those men who were "conscientiously opposed to participation in war in *any* form," that the statutory provisions at issue did not unconstitutionally favor religious denominations that teach total pacifism and did not infringe upon the freedom of religion of those who believe that only "unjust" wars must be opposed. He acknowledged that Congress *could* create a "selective" exemption, but it was not required to do so, and it had not done so. Declaring that the "affirmative purposes underlying §6(j) are neutral and secular"; that the rule against "selective" conscientious objection was "essentially neutral" in its treatment of various religious faiths; that there were ample "neutral, secular reasons to justify the line that Congress has drawn"; and that any "incidental burdens" felt by particular draftees were justified by "the Government's interest in procuring the manpower necessary for military purposes,"[58] Marshall thus rejected both the free exercise of religion and the sepa-

---

55. The primary criterion for a CO henceforth, he told the boards, would be whether his beliefs were "sincere and deeply held," and not whether they were "comprehensible" to board members. A man must hold his "beliefs with the strength of traditional religious conviction," he wrote, and he must "demonstrate that his ethical or moral convictions were gained through training, study, contemplation or other activity, comparable in rigor and dedication to the processes by which traditional religious convictions are formulated" (*New York Times,* July 6, 1970, p. 11)

56. *New York Times,* June 21, 1970, p. 16e.

57. 401 U.S. 437 (1971).

58. Ibid. at 462.

ration of state and church claims lodged by the appellants. Douglas, on the other hand, saw a violation of both, especially of the former, and observed wistfully: "I had assumed that the welfare of a single human soul was the ultimate test of the vitality of the First Amendment."[59]

The government had readily conceded that Guy Porter Gillette and Louis A. Negre were sincere in their conscientious objection to the Vietnam War, but it insisted that they did not qualify for the CO exemption created by Congress because *they said that they did not oppose all wars.* Gillette, a rock musician, had told his draft board in Yonkers, New York, that his belief in the religion of humanism prevented him from serving in the military during the Vietnam War, which he considered unjust. The board denied him CO status because he frankly conceded that he would fight in defense of the United States or in a peacekeeping effort by the United Nations; he was convicted and given a two-year jail sentence for refusing to report for induction. Negre, a Bakersfield, California, gardener, a devout French-born Roman Catholic who had studied the writings of Saint Thomas Aquinas, Saint Augustine, and other Catholic theologians who taught that "unjust" but not "just" wars should be opposed,[60] had been drafted and had not reported for duty. However, when he was subsequently compelled to do so, he applied for a CO discharge; he was turned down, although the army granted that his objections to the Vietnam conflict were indeed sincere. The lower courts concurred, and Negre found himself transferred to Vietnam, where he began his quest for release.

Here, then—unlike the widespread protests that accompanied the successful appeal of his draft-evasion conviction by Cassius Clay, alias World Heavyweight Boxing Champion Muhammed Ali[61]—no one deemed questionable or "phony" the allegations or motivations of the two men involved, for they were obviously sincere in their opposition to the Vietnam conflict per se. But could they claim CO status under Section 6(j) of the Military Selective Service Act of 1967? In its firmly negative response, the eight-man majority dwelt at length on the government's assertions that its military capacity might be paralyzed if selective conscientious objection were recognized as a constitutional right. Justice Marshall pointed out that, among other touchy tasks connected with any such recognition, draft boards would be saddled with that of divining which draftees were sincere and which were having convenient attacks of selective conscience, inviting the very "real danger of erratic or even discriminatory decision-making in administrative practice."[62] Moreover, he opined, the nature of an unpopular

59. Ibid. at 469.

60. Later Protestant thinkers who supported the "just-war only" theory were Martin Luther, John Calvin, and Hugo Grotius.

61. *Clay v. United States,* 403 U.S. 698 (1971). That opinion, rendered per curiam (probably authored by Justice Stewart), relied heavily on a procedural aberration by the Department of Justice in its prosecution.

62. Op. cit., at 462–63.

war might change so that those who once considered it unjust would—or should—change their minds. It would be difficult to fault the logic of these basic contentions. Policymaking by individual draftees would create a chaotic situation: the Court-defined CO line, which Congress reluctantly accepted but soon made the law of the land, seems to be the most generous and most liberal obtainable in the light of our democratic society's constitutional fundamentals.[63]

THE FREE EXERCISE OF RELIGION

"Free exercise" brackets freedom of religious belief *and* freedom of religious action; it is linked closely with those other bastions of the First Amendment, freedom of speech, of the press, of assembly, and of petition. Indeed, any reading of the religion clause guarantee of the First Amendment that does not consider its dependence upon the other four guarantees spelled out in that provision of the Bill of Rights, and now carried over to the states via the Fourteenth Amendment, does a disservice to constitutional analysis and interpretation. The interrelationship is as real as it is significant.

A Basic Dilemma

The very language of the free exercise segment of the religion phrase poses a dilemma. It clearly militates against any governmental action "prohibiting the free exercise thereof." Unquestionably, the phrase is designed to mean what it says: Congress—and by interpretation the states—may not interfere with the sacred rights of freedom of religious "belief" and "exercise." Or, to put it somewhat differently, at a minimum the free exercise clause was intended to protect a wide range of religious observances from governmental interference. But as Justice Roberts pointed out in his opinion for a unanimous Court in the 1940 *Cantwell* case, while freedom of exercise embraces both the freedom to *believe* and the freedom to *act,* "the first is absolute but, in the nature of things, the sec-

---

63. That line has other limits, of course. Thus, in an 8:1 opinion, written by Justice Brennan in 1976, the Court rejected free exercise and due process appeals by an "alternate service" CO seeking "GI Bill" educational benefits, despite congressional statutory exclusion therefrom (*Johnson v. Robinson,* 415 U.S. 361, with Douglas in lone dissent). Nor, again 8:1—Douglas once more the only dissenter—can an employer withhold a lower rate from the income taxes due from COs who object to supporting the defense budget (*United States v. American Friends Service Committee,* 419 U.S. 7 [1974]). For a generally sympathetic analysis of selective conscientious objection, see Martin S. Sheffer, "The Free Exercise of Religion and Selective Conscientious Objection: A Judicial Response to a Moral Problem," 9 *Capital University Law Review* 6 (1979). For an even more supportive one see Walter S. Griggs Jr., "The Selective Conscientious Objector: A Vietnam Legacy," 21 *Journal of Church and State* 1 (winter 1979).

ond cannot be. *Conduct* remains subject to [governmental] regulation for the protection of society. The freedom to act must have appropriate definition to preserve the enforcement of that protection."[64]

In every case, Roberts continued, "the power to regulate must be so exercised as not, in attaining a permissible end, unduly to infringe the protected freedom."[65] This, of course, raises as many *practical* questions as it settles. But the general line is at least perceivable in *Cantwell,* and it remains a landmark chiefly for three reasons: it embraces the dual aspects of "belief" and "action"; it reaffirms the absorption or incorporation of the freedom of religion guarantees into the Fourteenth Amendment; and it emphasizes the close link of the free exercise of religion with the other freedoms spelled out in the First Amendment.

The Jehovah's Witnesses. The *Cantwell* case was the first freedom of religion case involving the Jehovah's Witnesses to be decided by the U.S. Supreme Court. Actually, the initial litigation concerning that fundamentalist sect had come two years earlier, but it was decided in reference to freedom of speech and press rather than to freedom of religion.[66] Not only have other so-called marginal religious groups increasingly proved victorious in free exercise claims, there has been a dramatic increase of late in the number of such cases filed.[67] The Jehovah's Witnesses have won over 90 percent of the host of significant First and Fourteenth Amendment cases which have come before the Court since the mid-1930s—their success due in considerable measure to the talents of their longtime chief legal counsel, Hayden C. Covington.[68] A dedicated sect of over 3 million members throughout the world who believe that Armageddon is imminent, the Jehovah's Witnesses base their creed on what they regard as utter obedience to the Bible. They accept the biblical prophecy that Satan will be defeated in the cataclysm of Armageddon, followed by eternal life for the righteous. Their movement began in 1872, largely as the result of the efforts of Charles Taze Russell, a Pittsburgh merchant, who had become disenchanted with his Congregationalist Church. Russell began to preach the Adventist doctrine that the imminent second coming

64. *Cantwell v. Connecticut,* 310 U.S. 296 (1940) at 303; italics supplied.
65. Ibid. at 304.
66. *Lovell v. Griffin,* 303 U.S. 444 (1938). The next Jehovah's Witnesses case, also decided under the freedom of speech and press guarantees, was *Schneider v. Irvington, New Jersey,* 308 U.S. 137 (1939)—one year prior to *Cantwell,* which was thus the third Supreme Court case involving the Witnesses.
67. From 56 cases in the decade ending in 1960 to 350 in that ending in 1980! See Frank Way and Barbara J. Burt, "The Free Exercise Clause and Marginal Religious Groups" (paper presented at the annual meeting of the Western Political Science Association, San Diego, Calif., March 26, 1982.
68. He was also Cassius Clay's (Muhammad Ali's) attorney in his aforementioned, eventually successful, battle to attain ministerial exemption as a Muslim. When apprised of his 8:0 per curiam victory in the Supreme Court, Ali told reporters that he "thanked Allah" (*Philadelphia Evening Bulletin,* June 28, 1971, p. 1).

of Christ will trigger Armageddon, which he finally pegged at 1914. With a rapidly increasing following, Russell incorporated in 1884 the Watch Tower Bible and Tract Society, now generally known as the Jehovah's Witnesses ("Ye are my Witnesses, saith Jehovah" [Isaiah 43:10]). They deem Abel the first Witness, Christ the Chief Witness, and themselves direct descendants—3.75 million worldwide, 946,000 in the United States—from whose ranks Jehovah will select 144,000 members who will reign in heaven after Armageddon.

An impressively organized hierarchy with totalitarian overtones, the Witnesses—who shun all political activity, even voting—are fiercely evangelistic, and publicly so. Although inevitably polite, they persistently solicit and proselytize, push their two journals, *Awake!* and the *Watchtower,* and, if given permission, play their tape recordings. To the Witnesses, the chief villains on earth are the leaders of organized religion in general, and the Roman Catholic Church in particular: the Witnesses' notorious record "Enemies" characterizes the Roman Catholic Church as "a great racket." It is no wonder, then, that they often find themselves in considerable litigation involving such matters as leaflet distribution, local and state censorship ordinances, parade permits, flag salutes, vehicular license plate inscriptions, license taxes, conscientious objection to the draft (indeed, they insist that, as "ministers," they are all entitled to military deferments so that they may go about their primary task of proclaiming the impending Kingdom), public meetings, and blood transfusion requirements.[69] The *United States Reports* for the past five decades list some fifty cases involving the Witnesses in one or more of the preceding problems. *Cantwell v. Connecticut*[70] was *not* one of the very few they lost.

Cantwell v. Connecticut. Newton Cantwell and his two teenaged sons, Jesse and Russell, approached three pedestrians on Cassius Street in New Haven, an area whose inhabitants were 90 percent Roman Catholic, and asked their permission to play them a record on their portable phonograph. Obtaining that permission, the Cantwells put on "Enemies." One portion of the record stated in particular that the Roman Catholic Church was an instrument of Satan that had for fifteen hundred years brought untold sorrow and sufferings upon mankind by means of deception and fraud. The three listeners were, according to their own testimony, "rather tempted to strike the Cantwells," but confined themselves to an exhortation to "shut the damn thing off and get moving"—which the Cantwells did

69. See, inter alia, *Minersville School District v. Gobitis,* 310 U.S. 596 (1940); *Cox v. New Hampshire,* 312 U.S. 569 (1941); *Martin v. Struthers,* 319 U.S. 141 (1943); *Jones v. Opelika,* 316 U.S. 584 (1942); *Prince v. Massachusetts,* 321 U.S. 158 (1944); *Marsh v. Alabama,* 326 U.S. 501 (1946); *Niemotko v. Maryland,* 340 U.S. 268 (1951); *Jehovah's Witnesses in the State of Washington v. King County Hospital,* 390 U.S. 598 (1968); *Wooley v. Maynard,* 430 U.S. 705 (1977); *Palmer v. Board,* 444 U.S. 1026 (1980); and many others. The listing here is representative, not exhaustive.
70. 310 U.S. 296 (1940).

forthwith. No violence of any kind occurred, nor was it alleged. Nonetheless, the Cantwells were arrested, indicted, charged with, and convicted of two separate violations of Connecticut law.

One count of a five-count indictment charged them with soliciting funds and subscriptions for the Witnesses' cause without obtaining in advance—as required by a 1917 statute—a "certificate of approval" from the secretary of the Connecticut Public Welfare Council, who was specifically empowered to determine, again in advance, whether the cause was either a "religious" one or one of a "bona fide object of charity." The second charge against the Cantwells was a breach of the peace, based on their stopping pedestrians on New Haven's public streets and asking them for permission to play the described phonograph record. The Cantwells appealed their convictions to the U.S. Supreme Court on both substantive and procedural grounds, alleging infringement of freedom of religion rights under both the First and Fourteenth Amendments on the first (substantive) count and violations of the Fourteenth Amendment alone on the second (procedural) ground. Agreeing, the Court reversed the convictions unanimously as constituting unconstitutional violations of the free exercise of religion, Justice Roberts authoring the opinion. It provided the Court with the opportunity to comment upon and endeavor to explain the difficulties of drawing the line between freedom of religious belief and proscribable action in the realm of the free exercise of religion.

Roberts emphasized that there can be no doubt that a state has the right to guard against breaches of the peace and thus punish those who would incite, or be guilty of, such breaches—even as a result of religious motivations or considerations. Yet just because an individual, in his religious fervor, resorts to exaggeration and even vilification, thereby arousing public anger and ill will, does not per se render him liable to punishment unless there is a demonstrably clear and present danger to public peace. In the instance of the Cantwells there was no such danger or menace: no assault took place; there was no intentional discourtesy, no threatening bearing, no personal abuse—their arrest was patently unconstitutional. The Connecticut statute, which gave such broad prior censorship powers to an official of Connecticut's government, was held to constitute on its face an impermissible infraction of free exercise of religion guaranteed by the First Amendment, as absorbed by the Fourteenth. The Court ruled that for religious groups such as the Jehovah's Witnesses, Connecticut's requirement, as applied here, represented a "censorship of religion as a means of determining its right to survive"—a clear violation of the basic guarantee. Roberts took pains to acknowledge that nothing he had said for the Court was "intended even remotely to imply that, under the cloak of religion, persons may, with impunity, commit frauds upon the public." Endeavoring to establish a viable line, he observed that, certainly, penal laws are properly available to punish such proscribed conduct, and he emphasized that even the exercise of religion may be at some slight inconvenience in order that the state may protect its citizens from injury:

Without doubt a State may protect its citizens from fraudulent solicitation by requiring a stranger in the community, before permitting him to solicit funds for any purpose, to establish his identity and his authority for the cause which he purports to represent. The State is likewise free to regulate the time and manner of solicitation generally, in the interest of public safety, peace, comfort or convenience. But to condition the solicitation of aid for the perpetuation of religious views or systems upon a license, the grant of which rests in the exercise of a determination by state authority as to what is a religious cause, is to lay a forbidden burden upon the exercise of liberty protected by the Constitution.[71]

The Cantwells had thus won an important victory not only for themselves but for the cause of religious liberty.

The Flag Salute Cases. But two weeks later, the next case to involve the Jehovah's Witnesses did not augur well in its decision for a continuing generous interpretation of the religious liberty clause. As a condition of attending the public schools of Minersville, Pennsylvania (population ten thousand), *all* children were required to salute the national flag as part of a daily school exercise. Twelve-year-old Lillian Gobitis and her brother William, aged ten, children of Walter Gobitis, a member of the Jehovah's Witnesses, were expelled from the public schools for refusing to do so. To them, any compliance with such a requirement would have been tantamount to paying homage to a graven image—a mortal sin under the precepts of the Witnesses.[72] For a while Walter Gobitis bore the burden of sending them to private schools that did not mandate the flag salute. Unable to sustain that expense, however, and seeing three more of his children expelled from public school, Gobitis sued to enjoin the public authorities from continuing to exact participation of Lillian and William in the daily flag salute ceremony as a condition of their public school attendance. To his surprise

---

71. Ibid. at 306.

72. The daily ceremony, in which all teachers as well as students participated, was a familiar one, with the following pledge recited in unison: "I pledge allegiance to my flag, and to the Republic for which it stands; one nation indivisible, with liberty and justice for all." While the words were spoken, teachers and pupils extended their right hands chest high in salute to the flag. In a letter to Superintendent of Schools Charles E. Rondabush, Lillian explained her three reasons for not saluting the flag: "1. The Lord clearly says in Exodus 20:3, 5 that you should have no gods besides Him and that we should serve Him. 2. The Constitution of [the] United States is based upon religious freedom. According to the dictates of my conscience, based on the Bible, I must give full allegiance to Jehovah God. 3. Jehovah is my God and the Bible is my creed. I try my best to obey the Creator." William wrote a similar letter (*Minersville School District v. Gobitis,* 310 U.S. 586 [1940] at 592). For a good recent work on the Jehovah's Witnesses, see Shawn F. Peters, *Judging Jehovah's Witnesses: Religious Persecution and the Dawn of the Rights Revolution* (Lawrence: University Press of Kansas, 2000).

and gratification, the U.S. District Court in Philadelphia granted his plea on the grounds that the expulsions violated the First, and through it the Fourteenth, Amendment's guarantees of religious liberty. Now it was the Minersville School District's turn to appeal, and it did so, first to the circuit court of appeals, which sustained the district court, and then to the Supreme Court, which granted certiorari. The nation awaited its decision with considerable interest; both the Committee on the Bill of Rights of the American Bar Association and the American Civil Liberties Union had sought, and been granted, permission to enter the case in behalf of the Witnesses as amici curiae.

But to the astonishment of many—including some of those who consider themselves experts on the Court and its personnel—the Court *reversed* the judgment below and upheld the Minersville flag salute requirements by a resounding 8:1 vote.[73] Delivering the Court's opinion, Justice Frankfurter contended that religious liberty does not exempt citizens from obedience to general laws applicable to all and not designed to restrict religious beliefs as such. Explaining that "we live by symbols," Frankfurter—Vienna-born, who came to the United States at the age of twelve—exhorted the country that the "flag is the symbol of our national unity, transcending all internal differences, however large, within the framework of the Constitution."[74] He rejected the plea that the Gobitis children should be excused from "conduct required of all other children in the promotion of national cohesion," adding that "we are dealing with an interest inferior to none in the hierarchy of legal values. National unity is the basis of national security. . . ."[75] Frankfurter acknowledged that many might well doubt the effectiveness of the compulsory flag salute in the promotion of national unity and loyalty, but he insisted—characteristically for one so committed to the doctrine of judicial self-restraint—that, lest the Supreme Court become "the school board of the country," this was a decision to be made by the elected school officials against the backdrop of the basic "legislative judgment." He continued: "But to the legislature no less than to the courts is committed the guardianship of deeply cherished liberties."[76] Joining the Frankfurter opinion were Chief Justice Hughes, Associate Justices McReynolds, Roberts, Reed, and—amazingly—Associate Justices Black, Douglas, and Murphy, whom prognosticators confidently expected to side with the sole dissenter, Justice Stone.

Conceding that the personal liberty guarantees under the Constitution are by no means "always absolutes," and that "Government has a right to survive," Stone's dissent nonetheless bitterly assailed the majority's opinion as doing vio-

73. *Minersville School District v. Gobitis,* 310 U.S. 586 (1940). The requirement was administrative, not legislative.
74. Ibid. at 596.
75. Ibid. at 595.
76. Ibid. at 598, 600.

lence to "the very essence of liberty . . . the right of the individual to hold such opinions as he will and to give them reasonably free expression, and his freedom, and that of the state as well, to teach and persuade others by the communication of ideas."[77] He contended that the very essence of the liberty, which the freedom of the human mind and spirit and the freedom of reasonable opportunity to express them guarantee, is

> the freedom of the individual from compulsion as to what he shall think and what he shall say, at least where the compulsion is to bear false witness to his religion. If these guarantees are to have any meaning they must . . . be deemed to withhold from the state any authority to compel belief or the expression of it where that expression violates religious convictions, whatever may be the legislative view of the desirability of such compulsion.[78]

His noble spirit simply could not see how any inconveniences that might attend what he called "some sensible adjustment of school discipline" would present a problem "so momentous or pressing as to outweigh the freedom from compulsory violation of religious faith which has been thought worthy of constitutional protection."[79] He did not have to wait long, however, to see his reasoning become the majority opinion of the Court and thereby the law of the land.

To attain that constitutional turnabout, some crucial developments took place—all significant elements in the judicial process. One was the retirement of Chief Justice Hughes in 1941 and his replacement by Attorney General Robert H. Jackson—although as an associate justice, President Roosevelt having seen fit to elevate Justice Stone to the chief justiceship. A closely related denouement was the resignation of Justice Byrnes late in 1942[80] and his replacement by the onetime dean of the University of Iowa School of Law, Wiley B. Rutledge. On paper, at least, the two new appointees could be expected to be more sympathetic to the Stone point of view than to that of Frankfurter. The third important development was a dramatic announcement by Justices Black, Douglas, and Murphy, who joined in a separate memorandum in a 1942 case[81] that upheld (5:4) the validity of a license tax on bookselling levied upon Jehovah's Witnesses, as well as other activities considered "commercial" by the city of Opelika, Alabama. (In 1943, just one year later, that ruling was reversed on rehearing[82] in conjunction with another decision favoring the Witnesses.)[83] Apparently authored by Black,

---

77. Ibid. at 604.
78. Ibid.
79. Ibid. at 607.
80. He had replaced Justice McReynolds, who had retired in 1941.
81. *Jones v. Opelika,* 316 U.S. 584 (1942).
82. *Jones v. Opelika,* 319 U.S. 103 (1943).
83. *Murdock v. Commonwealth of Pennsylvania,* 319 U.S. 105.

the six-sentence, one-paragraph memorandum—which followed two dissenting opinions[84] on the merits of the case—simply observed, inter alia, that "since we joined in the opinion in the *Gobitis* case, we think this is an appropriate occasion to state that *we now believe that it was also wrongly decided.*"[85] The test of these developments came but a few months later—appropriately, on Flag Day, June 14, 1943—when the Court overruled the *Gobitis* precedent in a new flag salute case, *West Virginia State Board of Education v. Barnette.*[86]

Following the Court's decision in *Gobitis*[87] three years earlier, the state of West Virginia legislature had amended its statutes to require all of its schools to conduct courses of instruction in history, civics, and both the federal and West Virginia constitutions "for the purpose of teaching, fostering and perpetuating the ideals, principles and spirit of Americanism, and increasing the knowledge of the organization and machinery of government."[88] In 1942, the board of education adopted a resolution based largely on *Gobitis,* which ordered the salute to the flag to become "a regular part of the program of activities in the public schools"; all teachers and pupils "shall be required to participate in the salute honoring the Nation represented by the Flag; provided, however [*sic*], that refusal to salute the Flag be regarded as an Act of insubordination, and shall be dealt with accordingly."[89] The "accordingly" meant expulsion—with readmission denied by the statute until compliance. Meanwhile, the expelled child was considered "unlawfully absent" and subject to delinquency proceedings, and his parents or guardians were liable to prosecution and punishment by fine and/or imprisonment. Members of the Jehovah's Witnesses, like the Gobitis family, Walter Barnette and his relatives, Paul Stull, and Mrs. Lucy Barnette Mc-Clure—the plaintiffs in the case—refused to comply and saw their seven children expelled from school for "insubordination." The crucial difference between their and the Gobitises' fortunes was that the Barnette families won. Indeed, they had begun to win at the lower federal tribunal level when a three-judge federal district court in West Virginia, in an opinion penned by Judge John

---

84. One was written by Chief Justice Stone, in which Justices Black, Douglas, and Murphy joined; the other was by Murphy, in which Stone, Black, and Douglas concurred.

85. 316 U.S. 584 at 623; italics supplied. Black elaborated some twenty-five years later in his great work *A Constitutional Faith:* "Reluctance to make the federal Constitution a rigid bar against state regulation of *conduct* thought inimical to the public welfare was the controlling influence that caused me to consent to the *Gobitis* decision. Long reflection convinced me that although the principle was sound, its application in the particular case was wrong, and I clearly stated this change of view in a concurring opinion in *Barnette* which Justice Douglas joined. Life itself is change and one who fails to recognize this must indeed be narrow-minded. . . ." (New York: Knopf, 1968), p. xv; italics supplied.

86. 319 U.S. 624 (1943).

87. 310 U.S. 586 (1940).

88. *West Virginia State Board of Education v. Barnette,* op. cit., at 625.

89. Ibid. at 626.

J. Parker, had enjoined the school board from enforcing the regulation against Jehovah's Witnesses.[90]

They won because the two new associate justices, Jackson and Rutledge, added to the three "mind changers," Black,[91] Douglas, and Murphy, and the one steady holdover from the *Gobitis* decision, the now Chief Justice Stone, constituted a new six-man majority. Three *Gobitis* holdovers, Associate Justices Frankfurter, Reed, and Roberts, continued to cling to their then majority reasoning in that case. The Barnettes had won a victory for a liberal construction of the line between the individual's freedom of conscience and the state's claims for conformance to majority policy in regard to symbols. It was a significant victory—one that is not likely to be overturned.

It would have been fitting had Chief Justice Stone assigned the majority opinion to himself, being the only member on that side of the decision who had consistently supported it. Yet he chose Justice Jackson,[92] who held that the guarantees of freedom of speech and conscience imply the freedom *not* to speak and *not* to make any other symbolic expression, even the saluting of the national flag. Jackson acknowledged that public officials did naturally have the right to foster national unity and might well employ a symbolic public ceremony to achieve this, but they might not render participation in such ceremonies compulsory. To the dissenters' contention that, if laws such as those of Pennsylvania and West Virginia were unwise, the manner to alter or abolish them was not through court action but through the electoral process—what Justice Frankfurter, the author of the dissenting opinion, was later on several occasions[93] to call the "searing of the legislators' conscience"—Jackson responded that it depended necessarily upon the type of claim involved. In situations like *Barnette,* judicial action was not only necessary but essential, because "[o]ne's right to life, liberty, and property, to free speech, a free press, freedom of worship and assembly, and other fundamental rights may not be submitted to vote; they depend on the outcome of no elections."[94]

The closing paragraphs of the Jackson opinion for the Court contain language both seminal and magnificent. Stressing the futility of compelling conformity and coherence in such sacred First Amendment guarantees as the freedom

90. *Barnette v. West Virginia Board of Education,* 47 F. Supp. 251 (D. W. Va., 1942) at 251–55.

91. Black wrote in his concurring opinion: "Words under coercion are proof of loyalty to nothing but self-interest. Love of country must spring from willing hearts and free minds" (ibid. at 644; see *supra* note 85).

92. See Glendon Schubert, *Dispassionate Justice: A Synthesis of the Opinions of Robert H. Jackson* (Indianapolis: Bobbs-Merrill, 1969), pp. 1–34.

93. Particularly on the "political question" in redistricting and reapportionment cases such as *Colegrove v. Green,* 328 U.S. 549 (1946); note especially his last signed opinion (appropriately in dissent—running to more than sixty pages) in *Baker v. Carr,* 369 U.S. 186 (1962).

94. *West Virginia State Board of Education v. Barnette,* op. cit., at 641.

of belief, conscience, and expression, the great stylist warned that "[t]hose who begin coercive elimination of dissent soon find themselves exterminating dissenters. Compulsory unification of opinion achieves only the unanimity of the graveyard." And he concluded memorably: "If there is any fixed star in our constitutional constellation, it is that no official, high or petty, can prescribe what shall be orthodox in politics, nationalism, religion, or other matters of opinion or force citizens to confess by word or act their faith therein."[95]

Predictably, and justly, the dissenting opinion was written by the author of the *Gobitis* majority opinion, Justice Frankfurter—and it was one of his most important and longest, representing, as it did, his passionate dedication to the creed of judicial self-restraint, the raison d'être of his judicial career. Probably quoted only slightly less than the Jackson passages outlined earlier are the opening passages of Frankfurter's exhortation:

> One who belongs to the most vilified and persecuted minority in history is not likely to be insensible to the freedoms guaranteed by our Constitution. Were my purely personal attitude relevant I should wholeheartedly associate myself with the general libertarian views in the Court's opinion, representing as they do the thought and action of a lifetime. But as judges we are neither Jew nor Gentile, neither Catholic nor agnostic. We owe equal attachment to the Constitution and are equally bound by our judicial obligations whether we derive our citizenship from the earliest or the latest immigrants to these shores. As a member of this Court I am not justified in writing my private notions of policy into the Constitution, no matter how deeply I may cherish them or how mischievous I may deem their disregard. . . . Most unwillingly, therefore, I must differ from my brethren with regard to legislation like this. I cannot bring my mind to believe that the "liberty" secured by the Due Process Clause gives this Court authority to deny to the State of West Virginia the attainment of that which we all recognize as a legitimate legislative end, namely, the promotion of good citizenship, by employment of the means here chosen.[96]

Frankfurter did not prevail, yet some school boards have continued to read his dissent as a majority opinion. Thus in 1966, almost a generation later, the New Jersey Supreme Court had to rule unanimously, quoting *Barnette,* that children cannot be suspended from school if they refuse to salute the flag on the grounds of conscientious scruples.[97] And in 1973 Mrs. Susan Russo had to fight all the

95. Ibid. at 642.
96. Ibid. at 646, 647. Associate Justices Roberts and Reed were the other two dissenters in the case. Philip Elman, a law clerk of Frankfurter's, argued vainly against the dissent, but his justice put his foot down: "This is my opinion, not yours" (as recounted to Israel Shenker, *New York Times,* October 22, 1977, p. 34).
97. *Holden v. Board of Education, Elizabeth,* 46 N.J. 281 (1966). In 1964 Governor Richard J. Hughes had vetoed a compulsory flag salute bill for all schoolchildren, enacted

way to the Supreme Court for reversal of her dismissal as a public school art teacher, which had come as a result of her refusal to recite the Pledge of Allegiance to the flag with pupils in her homeroom.[98]

A Catalog of Line Decisions. So manifold have been the Supreme Court's decisions concerning the free exercise of religion that it is impossible to detail them in the limited space available. But the following tables will at least serve to indicate a pattern—a pattern of demonstrable liberality on the part of the highest tribunal, a liberality based, in large measure, on the kind of basic convictions about individual freedom of conscience so well expressed by Justice Jackson in his *Barnette* opinion. Table 6.1 illustrates those instances in which the Court held *against* constitutional claims of freedom of religion and thus *in favor* of society's constitutional prerogative to promulgate and enforce the official statutes, ordinances, or practices involved. Table 6.2, in turn, demonstrates those instances in which the highest tribunal held in favor of the individual's contentions versus those of the state. Neither table is intended to be, nor could it be, exhaustive; rather, each will simply indicate the kind of values that America has embraced through the instrumentalities of the legislative and judicial processes.

The Dilemma Compounded

Before considering the far more intricate concept of the establishment of religion, its close relationship with the free exercise aspect may be demonstrated—following the tabular analysis—by pointing to at least one complex example,[99]

by the New Jersey legislature; other states have attempted similarly unconstitutional evasion and downright violation of *Barnette*.

98. The Court based its decision on freedom of speech, however (*Central School District #1 v. Russo,* 411 U.S. 932).

99. Space does not permit an examination of the tragic problem of drawing lines between the rights of parents and the right of the state, in loco parentis, when the parents' faith precludes or qualifies submittal to medical treatment. Since Christian Science practice, for example, is legal in every state of the Union, such parents have the statutory right to determine the nature of the medical care, if any, their minor children are to receive. What, then, if a Christian Science child dies as a result of the parents' deliberate decision not to submit the child to orthodox medical treatment? For a pertinent illustration see the case of *Commonwealth of Pennsylvania v. Cornelius, Philadelphia County* (Pennsylvania) Quarter Sessions, April Term, no. 105 (1956), which was *nolle prossed* at the request of the then district attorney, Victor H. Blanc. Numerous other examples could be readily cited, of course, involving particularly Jehovah's Witnesses and Seventh Day Adventists, who have frequently refused—with varying degrees of success—to submit to such standard medical practices and/or legal requirements as blood transfusions or compulsory smallpox vaccinations. For a case involving the latter see *Jacobson v. Massachusetts,* 197 U.S. 11 (1905). For one dealing with a Christian Scientist's successful refusal to take tranquilizers see *Winter v. Miller,* 404 U.S. 985 (1971), certiorari denied. See also the fascinating case of *Karen Ann Quinlan,* in which the New Jersey Supreme Court ultimately

namely, the Court's handling of the 1961 *Blue Laws Cases*[100] as seen against its decision, just two years later, in *Sherbert v. Verner*,[101] a case involving South Carolina unemployment compensation claims.

The Sunday-Closing Law Cases; Sherbert v. Verner and Beyond. The underlying principle of the manifold "Sunday" or "Blue Laws"—which still exist in several states in various forms and contain manifold inconsistencies and incongruities—is the right of a state, under its police power, to enact legislation providing for the

---

ruled unanimously—on privacy grounds—that the mechanical respirator that had kept her alive artificially for a year could be disconnected if her father so decided, subject to medical and hospital concurrence (*In the Matter of Karen Ann Quinlan,* decided March 31, 1976). The U.S. Supreme Court denied review (*Garger v. New Jersey,* 429 U.S. 922 [1976]). Similar actions followed elsewhere in the United States. Miss Quinlan lived for almost ten more years. Death, a friend, came at last on June 11, 1985. But other cases, e.g., those of Celia Cain and Rodney Poindexter, resulted in instantaneous death (Duval County, Florida, December 4, 1976; and Los Angeles, California, October 8, 1980, respectively). See Henry J. Abraham, "Religion, Medicine, and the State," 22 *Journal of Church and State* 3 (1980), and his "Abraham, Isaac, and the State: Faith Healing and Legal Intervention," 27 *University of Richmond Law Review* 5 (1993). In its first major "right to die" decision, the Supreme Court ruled 5:4 in 1990 that while there is a constitutional Fourteenth Amendment due process ("liberty") right to refuse life-sustaining medical treatment, states have the right to prevent family members from taking patients in a "persistent vegetative state" off life-support systems if there is no "clear and convincing" proof that the latter want the treatment ended. Here, Nancy Cruzan had provided no such proof (*Cruzan v. Director, Missouri Department of Health,* 497 U.S. 261). A few months after the U.S. Supreme Court's decision, a lower Missouri court judge found the evidence necessary to meet the state's standard, the life-support systems were removed, and Nancy Cruzan died on the day after Christmas 1990. (Her distraught father, Joe, suffering from constant depression following his daughter's tragedy, committed suicide by hanging in August 1996. The sixty-two-year-old exercised his own right to die in the carport of his home.) The Court had an opportunity to elaborate on its *Cruzan* holding in a 1996 Michigan case, but it denied review (*Martin v. Major,* 64 LW 3557). In a dramatic two-hour session, the justices heard oral argument in January 1997 on a burgeoning related issue: the constitutionality of an alleged right to physician-assisted suicide, claimed as both a privacy/due process of law and equal protection right. Distinguishing its *Cruzan* holding, the Court ruled in two cases unanimously that no such *federal* constitutional right exists (leaving the states free to act should they choose to do so) (*Washington v. Glucksberg* and *Vacco v. Quill,* 521 U.S. 702 and 521 U.S. 793). Even later that year the Court refused to hear a challenge to Oregon's 1994 physician-assisted suicide law (*Lee v. Harcleron,* 66 LW 3278 [1997]). Note also the "grandparents' rights" (due process) case of *Truxel v. Granville,* 530 U.S. 57 (2000), which cited *Washington v. Gluksberg*'s reasoning colaterally. In *Truxel* the 6:3 majority pronounced parents' fundamental right to rear their children. The grandparents in the case had charged the parents with compromising their allegedly agreed upon visiting rights.

    100. *McGowan v. Maryland,* 366 U.S. 420; *Two Guys from Harrison-Allentown, Inc. v. McGinley,* 366 U.S. 582; *Gallagher v. Crown Kosher Super Market of Massachusetts,* 366 U.S. 617; and *Braunfeld v. Brown,* 366 U.S. 599.

    101. 374 U.S. 398 (1963).

Table 6.1. "Free Exercise" Cases Decided Against the Individual or Group

Date	Case	Vote	Constitutional Issues Raised	Decision and Commentary
1878	*Reynolds v. United States,* 98 U.S. 145	9:0	Validity of congressional statute proscribing practice or advocacy of polygamy against claim of freedom of religious practice.	The first of the *Mormon* cases, holding religious beliefs not to justify polygamy. *(Reaffirmed repeatedly, most recently in Potter v. Murray, 585 F. Supp. 1126 [1984], with cert. denied, 474 U.S. 849 [1985].)*
1890	*Davis v. Beason,* 133 U.S. 333	9.0	Validity of Idaho territorial statute requiring an "oath abjuring bigamy or polygamy as a condition to vote."	Bigamy and polygamy regarded as crimes, not religious exercise. (Utah's subsequent ban of polygamy was again specifically upheld by the Court in 1984, in *Potter v. Murray,* 585 F. Supp. 1126.)
1890	*The Late Corp. of the Church of Jesus Christ of Latter-Day Saints v. United States,* 136 U.S. 1	9:0	Validity of 1877 congressional statute annulling charter of the Mormon church and declaring all its property forfeited save for a small portion used exclusively for worship.	Law came as a result of the continued defiance of the Mormon church regarding the practice of polygamy. Court saw no constitutional infirmities.
1929	*United States v. Schwimmer,* 279 U.S. 644	6:3	Denial of naturalization application to 50-year-old Hungarian Quaker woman for refusing to pledge to "take up arms" on behalf of U.S.	First of the naturalization cases. Holmes, Brandeis, and Sanford dissented from the Butler opinion upholding denial, asserting "we are a Christian people . . . acknowledging with reverence the duty of obedience to the will of God." (At 625.) *(Overruled in 1946.)*
1931	*United States v. Macintosh,* 283 U.S. 605	5:4	Denial of naturalization application to Canadian Baptist minister, a professor of theology and chaplain at Yale, for refusal to agree to defend U.S. by arms unless he were convinced of "moral justification."	Second of the naturalization denial cases. Hughes, Holmes, Brandeis, and Stone dissented from the Sutherland opinion. *(Overruled in 1946.)*
1934	*Hamilton v. Regents of the University of California,* 293 U.S. 245	9:0	Refusal of Hamilton (and others) on grounds of conscience to take state-required courses in military science and tactics at state university.	Concurring opinion by Cardozo, joined by Brandeis and Stone, warned against carrying compulsion too far, but joined in Court's decision in favor of California.

Table 6.1. (continued)

Date	Case	Vote	Constitutional Issues Raised	Decision and Commentary
1940	*Minersville v. Gobitis,* 310 U.S. 586	8:1	Validity of compulsory flag salute contested by Jehovah's Witnesses.	Discussed in detail in text above. *(Overruled in 1943.)*
1941	*Cox v. New Hampshire,* 312 U.S. 569	9:0	Validity of New Hampshire statute requiring a permit to hold a procession or parade on a public street, but considering only time, manner, and place of the parade.	Jehovah's Witnesses failed to apply for a permit; engaged in a parade. Court upheld the "exercise of local control over the use of streets for parades and processions."
1942	*Chaplinsky v. New Hampshire,* 315 U.S. 568	9:0	Validity of narrowly drawn New Hampshire law proscribing the "address [of] any offensive, derisive or annoying word to any other person who is lawfully in any street or other public place or call[ing] him by any offensive or derisive names."	Law upheld unanimously. A Jehovah's Witness called city marshal "God-damned racketeer" and "damned Fascist." Murphy wrote opinion. (See discussion in chap. 5, "The Precious Freedom of Expression.")
1942	*Jones v. Opelika II,* 316 U.S. 584	5:4	Validity of Opelika ordinance imposing license taxes on bookselling—here by Jehovah's Witnesses.	Stone, Black, Douglas, and Murphy dissented from upholding of law. *(Reversed in 1943.)*
1944	*Prince v. Massachusetts,* 321 U.S. 158	8:1	Validity of Massachusetts statute forbidding boys of under 12 and girls of under 18 to sell newspapers or periodicals on streets or in other public places. Jehovah's Witness Prince allowed her underage children and ward to help sell and distribute JW literature.	Freedom of religious exercise here must give way to state's interest and right to protect the health and welfare of children under the state's parens patriae position. Murphy dissented.
1945	*In re Summers,* 325 U.S. 561	5:4	Validity of Illinois's denial of admission to the bar of an otherwise qualified applicant who was a conscientious objector to war and who would therefore not serve in the state militia if called upon to do so under the state's constitutional provisions.	State's regulatory power upheld. Black, Douglas, Murphy, and Rutledge dissented, contending unsuccessfully that a state has no right to "bar from a semi-public position, a well-qualified man of good character solely because "of his religious conviction.

Year	Case	Vote	Issue	Comment
1949	State v. Bunn, 336 U.S. 942	No vote	Validity of North Carolina prohibition of handling of poisonous snakes in a "religious ceremony."	One of several such state laws upheld as valid exercise of police power via denial of writ of certiorari—most recently again in 1976. (*State ex rel. Swann v. Pack*, 424 U.S. 954.)
1951	Breard v. City of Alexandria, 341 U.S. 622	7:2	Validity of ordinance banning the practice of summoning occupants of a residence to the door *without prior consent* for the purpose of soliciting orders for the sale of goods.	Upheld. Distinguished from other solicitation cases because of the presence of the commercial element here. Similarly, *Heffron v Krishna Consciousness*, 452 U.S. 640 (1981), by involving state-fair soliciting.
1961	The *Four Sunday-Closing Law* cases:		Validity of a series of so-called state Blue Laws, variously forbidding sales on Sundays. Challenges were brought on several grounds, including "due process of law" and "equal protection" of the laws, and the individual facts and circumstances of the cases varied. However, in all cases both the religious liberty and the establishment of religion claims were raised, particularly the former, in the attacks on the statutes' constitutionality.	Laws upheld. Discussed in detail in text.
	a. McGowan v. Maryland, 366 U.S. 420	8:1		
	b. Two Guys from Harrison-Allentown, Inc. v. McGinley, 366 U.S. 582	8:1		
	c. Braunfeld v. Brown, 366 U.S. 599	7:2		
	d. Gallagher v. Crown Kosher Market, 366 U.S. 617	6:3		
1967	Garber v. Kansas, 389 U.S. 51.	6:3	Alleged constitutional right of the Amish to refuse to send their children to any state-accredited schools.	Per curiam opinion upheld Kansas's requirement, because Amish may have own schools and own teachers—simple *accreditation* being the sole state requirement. Warren, Douglas, and Fortas dissented.

(continued)

285

Table 6.1. *(continued)*

Date	Case	Vote	Constitutional Issues Raised	Decision and Commentary
1971	*Gillette v. United States and Negre v. Larsen*, 401 U.S. 437	8:1	Does the "free exercise" concept extend CO status to those whose opposition to war is confined to only "certain" or "just" wars rather than "unjust" wars, but not to *all* wars?	Rejection of "selective" conscientious objection claim is discussed in detail in text above.
1974	*Johnson v. Robinson*, 415 U.S. 361 (1974)	8:1	Does the performance of "alternate" instead of regular military service entitle a "CO" to educational benefits under the "G.I. Bill of Rights"?	With but Douglas dissenting, the Court, through Brennan, ruled that the statutorily authorized withholding of educational benefits to those who do not perform regular military service "involves only an incidental burden upon appellee's free exercise of religion—if indeed any burden exists at all."
1982	*United States v. Lee*, 455 U.S. 252	8:0	Although Congress exempted *self-employed* Amish from paying Social Security taxes, must Amish *employers* pay them and Unemployment Compensation for their *employees* (even if they consider paying such taxes a sin)?	Yes, for "the state may justify a limitation on religious liberty in cases [such as this] by showing that it is essential to accomplish an overriding governmental interest."
1983	*Bob Jones University and Goldsboro Christian School v. United States*, 461 U.S. 574	8:1	Validity of the IRS's decision to withdraw tax-exempt status from educational institutions that discriminate racially on grounds of their religious dogma.	Upheld because of the government's "fundamental overriding interest in eradicating racial discrimination in education," an interest that "substantially outweighs whatever burden denial of tax benefits places on petitioners' exercise of their religious beliefs."
1985	*Tony and Susan Alamo Foundation v. Secretary of Labor*, 471 U.S. 290	9:0	Does the First Amendment's free exercise component exempt an Arkansas-based religious group from complying with federal minimum wage laws?	"No," wrote Justice White, "it does not . . . unless, at a minimum, inclusion in the program actually burdens [the] freedom to exercise religious rights."

Year	Case	Vote	Question	Decision
1986	*Goldman v. Weinberger,* 475 U.S. 503	5:4	May an Orthodox Jewish rabbi and air force captain wear his yarmulke (skullcap) in the face of military dress codes to the contrary?	Notwithstanding petitioner's sincerely held religious beliefs, the military must be given a free hand to "foster instinctive obedience, unity, commitment, and esprit de corps," in Justice Rehnquist's 1987 majority opinion. (But note Congress's 1987 counteraction in effect reversing the Court.)
1986	*Bowen v. Roy,* 476 U.S. 693	8:1	May the government use Social Security numbers for citizens in its administrative procedures even if it conflicts with their religious beliefs?	Chief Justice Burger held that the Constitution's protection of freedom of religion "does not afford an individual a right to dictate the conduct of the government's internal procedures." (White dissented.)
1988	*Lyng v. Northwest Indian Cemetery Protective Assoc.,* 485 U.S. 439	6:3	May government harvest timber and/or build a logging road in a portion of national forest used as "sacred ground" by several Native American tribes?	"Yes," held O'Connor: The First Amendment does not give *any* citizens a veto power over public programs that do not *prohibit* the free exercise of religion.
1990	*Jimmy Swaggert Ministries v. Board of Equalization of California,* 493 U.S. 378	9:0	May California levy a sales tax on the sale of religious goods, such as pamphlets, tapes, records, and other items?	"Yes," ruled the Court, speaking through O'Connor, rejecting violation of First Amendment free exercise claims. She pointed out that the tax "is not a tax on the right to disseminate religious information, ideas, or beliefs, per se" but "rather . . . a tax on the privilege of making retail sales on tangible personal property."
1990	*Employment Division, Department of Human Resources of Oregon v. Smith,* 494 U.S. 872	6:3	May Oregon prohibit Native Americans from using peyote in their religious rituals without violating the constitutional guarantee of free exercise of religion? (Smith and others had been fired by a drug treatment center because they used peyote, *and they were denied unemployment compensation.*)	"Yes," held the Court, via Scalia—apparently abandoning the compelling state interest test—contending that nothing in the First Amendment prevents states from adopting "generally applicable" laws that have the *"incidental" effect of interfering with religious practices.* Over O'Connor's objection that the compelling interest test must stand—though she joined in upholding the Oregon statute—the five-member majority ruled that in cases of *"generally applicable prohibitions of socially harmful conduct"* the

(continued)

Table 6.1. (continued)

Date	Case	Vote	Constitutional Issues Raised	Decision and Commentary
	Employment Division, Department of Human Resources of Oregon v. Smith, 494 U.S. 872 *(continued)*			state need not demonstrate a *"compelling governmental interest"* (as, for example, they must do in race cases). Brennan, Marshall, and Blackmun dissented. Congress restored the compelling state interest test by *requiring* its utilization with the enactment of the Religious Freedom Restoration Act of 1993—which, in turn, was declared unconstitutional by U.S. District Court Judge Lucius D. Burton III of Texas as impermissibly invading judicial powers (*Flores v. City of Boerne,* 63 LW 257 [1995]). The U.S. Supreme Court heard the case on appeal in its 1996–97 term. (See below.)
1990	*Davis v. United States,* 495 U.S. 472	9:0	May a Mormon couple who provided money to support their sons while they served as missionaries for the church treat that financial outlay as a tax-deductible religious contribution?	"No," wrote Justice O'Connor for a unanimous Court. The activity is a free-will one, and the nondeductibility does not represent a burden on free exercise of religion.
1991	*St. Bartholomew's v. New York City and Seattle v. First Covenant Church,* 499 U.S. 901		May churches evade city landmark ordinances that prevent them from altering their buildings?	By refusing to review contrary rulings in the lower tribunals, the Court in effect said "No." (There were no dissents from the refusal.)
1997	*City of Boerne v. Flores,* 521 U.S. 507	6:3	Did Congress act within its powers when it wrote into the Religious Freedom Restoration Act of 1993 more protection for the free exercise of religion than the Supreme Court earlier had found in the Constitution? (See the *Smith* case above.)	No, Congress had usurped the Court's power to define constitutional protection of religion; had misapplied its power under Sec. 5 of the Fourteenth Amendment, which is limited to *enforcing* its provisions, not to creating new substantive and/or nonremedial rights; and had intruded on the business of the states, according to Justice Kennedy's majority opinion. O'Connor, Souter, and Breyer dissented.

Table 6.2. "Free Exercise" Cases Decided in Favor of the Individual or Group

Date	Case	Vote	Constitutional Issues Raised	Decision and Commentary
1892	*Church of the Holy Trinity v. United States*, 143 U.S. 226	9:0	Can a congressional statute prohibiting the importation of foreigners "under contract or agreement to perform labor in the United States" forbid, without violating "free exercise" of religion, a New York church from contracting with an English clergyman to migrate to the U.S. and act as its rector and pastor?	Marshaling much evidence that "we are a religious people," the Court held that such a restrictive intent as claimed could not be validly imputed to the statute by the government. Has overtones of church-state "separationist" problem in addition to "free exercise."
1940	*Cantwell v. Connecticut*, 310 U.S. 296	9:0	(a) Validity of Connecticut statute requiring certificate from state secretary of welfare before soliciting funds, to let him determine whether the "cause is a religious one." (b) Cantwell's conviction for breach of the peace.	Both aspects discussed in body of text above. First case under the "freedom of religion guarantees" clause decided by Court to be applicable to states as well as federal government. Jehovah's Witness Cantwell won on both counts (a) and (b).
1943	*Jones v. Opelika [II]*, 319 U.S. 103	5:4	Court's reconsideration of the *Jones v. Opelika* decision (see Table 6.1) of 1942, questioning validity of Opelika's ordinance imposing license tax on bookselling here by Jehovah's Witnesses.	Switch in favor of "JWs" was made possible largely by the new stance of Black, Douglas, and Murphy, the constancy of Stone, plus the replacement of the resigned Byrnes by Rutledge.
1943	*Murdock v. Commonwealth of Pennsylvania*, 319 U.S. 105 (See also *Follet v. McCormick*, 321 U.S. 573 [1944])	5:4	Validity of statute requiring payment of a tax ranging from $1.50 to $20.00 a day for three weeks for the privilege of canvassing or soliciting orders for articles, as here applied to Jehovah's Witnesses.	Douglas opinion, joined by Stone, Black, Murphy, and Rutledge, held statute inapplicable to Witnesses, for "a person cannot be compelled to purchase, through a license fee or a license tax, a privilege freely granted in the Constitution."
1943	*Martin v. Struthers*, 319 U.S. 141	5:4	Validity of Struthers, Ohio, ordinance forbidding knocking on door or ringing of doorbell of a residence in order to deliver a handbill to occupant without his invitation.	Ordinance declared an unconstitutional abridgment of freedom of religion as applied to Jehovah's Witnesses who distribute their literature in this way.

(continued)

Table 6.2. *(continued)*

Date	Case	Vote	Constitutional Issues Raised	Decision and Commentary
1943	*Douglas v. City of Jeanette,* 319 U.S. 157	9:0	Can public evangelism and proselytizing be stopped by police on Sundays, acting on numerous citizens' complaints?	Douglas's opinion held "no"—that Jehovah's Witnesses had right to do so; that these activities have the same claim to protection as the more orthodox and conventional exercises of religion. Angry Jackson concurrence exhorted community rights.
1943	*West Virginia State Board of Education v. Barnette,* 319 U.S. 624	6:3	Validity of West Virginia compulsory flag salute—upheld in *Minersville* case (see above)—again contested on free exercise grounds.	Famed overruling of the *Minersville* decision. (Discussed in detail in body of text above.)
1943	*Taylor v. Mississippi,* 319 U.S. 583	6:3	Validity of Mississippi statute making it unlawful to urge people, on religious grounds, not to salute the flag.	If the Constitution bans enforcement of a regulation to salute the flag, it also prohibits the imposing of punishment for advising and urging, on religious grounds, that citizens refrain from saluting the flag.
1943	*Jamison v. Texas,* 318 U.S. 413	8:0	Validity of Dallas ordinance prohibiting distribution of handbills in city streets.	A state may not prohibit distribution of handbills in city streets in the pursuit of a clearly religious activity merely because the handbills invite purchase of books or promote raising of funds for religious purposes.
1944	*United States v. Ballard,* 322 U.S. 78	5:4	May secular authority—in connection with alleged mail fraud—determine the truth of religious claims and beliefs, here the "I Am" movement?	No matter how "preposterous" or "incredible" they may be, religious beliefs are not subject to findings of "truth" by fact-finding bodies. (Seriously fractured Court.)
1946	*Girouard v. United States,* 328 U.S. 61 (See also *Cohnstaedt v. Immigration and Naturalization Service,* 339 U.S. 901)	5:3	Reexamination of the *Schwimmer* and *Macintosh* question (see Table 6.1) regarding denial of naturalization to conscientious objectors.	Court overruled its 1929 and 1931 decisions, adopting the then dissenting opinions of Justices Holmes and Hughes that religiously motivated refusal to bear arms does not manifest a lack of attachment to the U.S. Constitution.

Year	Case	Vote	Issue	Holding / Commentary
1946	*Marsh v. Alabama,* 326 U.S. 501 (See also companion case of *Tucker v. Texas,* 326 U.S. 517 [1946])	5:3	Validity of Alabama statute making it a crime to enter or remain on private premises—here the privately owned ship-building wharf of Chickasaw—after having been duly warned by the owner not to do so.	Distribution of religious literature by Jehovah's Witnesses cannot be banned even on the privately owned streets of a company town. First and Fourteenth Amendment guarantees apply here.
1951	*Niemotko v. Maryland,* 340 U.S. 268	9:0	Validity of city of Havre de Grace ordinance allowing use of public parks for public meetings, including religious groups, by custom requiring an advance permit to be issued by city council.	Denial of permit by city council to Jehovah's Witnesses, evidently based on "unsatisfactory responses" to questions concerning their views of flag salutes, military service, Roman Catholicism, etc., held to be prior censorship, violative of First and Fourteenth Amendments.
1953	*Fowler v. Rhode Island,* 345 U.S. 67	9:0	Applications of Pawtucket public park meetings ordinance that by interpretation, did not forbid church service in public parks to Catholics and Protestants, but did ban the Jehovah's Witnesses.	By treating the religious services of the Witnesses differently from those of other faiths, Pawtucket had unconstitutionally abridged the religious freedom commands of the First and Fourteenth Amendments.
1961	*Torcaso v. Watkins,* 367 U.S. 488	9:0	Validity of Maryland Constitution's provision of test oath of belief in the existence of God as prerequisite to holding public office.	Held a fatal invasion of freedom of belief and religion, violative of both the free exercise and establishment concepts. (See discussion above in body of text.)
1963	*Sherbert v. Verner,* 374 U.S. 398	7:2	Legality of South Carolina State's ruling that Seventh Day Adventist Sherbert's refusal to work on Saturdays (her Sabbath day), a refusal for which she was discharged by her employers, did not constitute "good cause" under the law, and therefore did not entitle her to unemployment compensation benefit payments.	Despite its 1961 precedents in the *Blue Law Cases* (see Table 6.1 and discussion below), the Court held that the denial of benefits to Sherbert constituted infringement of her constitutional rights under the First Amendment, because her disqualification imposed a burden on the free exercise clause by forcing her to choose between adhering to her religious precepts and forfeiting benefits for abandoning these precepts and accepting employment. (See text above.) But see *Thornton v. Caldor* (text below) for a different interpretation, finding a *mandatory* and *absolute* statutory deference to a Sabbatarian an impermissible "establishment of religion . . . by advancing a particular religious practice."

(continued)

Table 6.2. *(continued)*

Date	Case	Vote	Constitutional Issues Raised	Decision and Commentary
1965	*United States v. Seeger*, et al., 380 U.S. 1643	9:0	Validity of claim by Seeger and two others, alleging their exemptability under Draft Act provision governing conscientious objection "by reason of religious training and belief."	Delicate question of meaning of "an individual's belief in a relation to a Supreme Being" interpreted broadly and liberally by unanimous Court. (See discussion in text above.)
1970	*Welsh v. United States*, 398 U.S. 333	5:3	Does the *Seeger* decision and the Draft Act permit draft exemption as CO for purely moral and ethical reasons of conscience?	Broadening the "parallelism" of *Seeger* to extend to "strong beliefs about our domestic and foreign policy." (See text above.)
1971	*Winter v. Miller*, et al., 404 U.S. 985	9:0	May a Christian Scientist, involuntarily interred in a mental institution, be compelled to take tranquilizers in violation of her religion?	Court denied certiorari without comment. Court of Appeals below was divided, but upheld Ms. Miller's free exercise claim.
1972	*Wisconsin v. Yoder*, 406 U.S. 205	6:1	May the Amish, given their well-established belief that education beyond the eighth grade teaches worldly values at odds with their religious creed, be thus compelled to attend school nonetheless?	In what was the first Supreme Court holding that ruled a religious group immune from compulsory attendance requirements, Chief Justice Burger found a violation of the Amish's free exercise of religion but made clear that this holding would *not* apply to "faddish new sects or communes."
1977	*Wooley v. Maynard*, 430 U.S. 705	6:3	May New Hampshire require passenger automobiles to bear license plates with the motto "Live Free or Die" if contrary to Jehovah's Witnesses' religious creed?	Free exercise of religion (joined to freedom of expression), ruled the chief justice, includes "both the right to speak freely and the right to refrain from speaking at all." The New Hampshire law here compelled the JWs to be a "mobile billboard," objectionable to their beliefs. Rehnquist and Blackmun dissent.
1978	*McDaniel v. Paty*, 433 U.S. 618	8:0	May Tennessee disqualify members of the clergy from being legislators or constitutional convention delegates?	A welter of opinions seemed to agree that the answer was clearly "no," but the reasoning saw both free exercise *and* separation of church and state mandates for striking the statute down.

Year	Case	Vote	Question	Holding
1979	*International Assn. of Machinists v. Anderson,* 440 U.S. 960	7:2	Given the nondiscrimination provisions of the Civil Rights Act of 1964, may a Seventh Day Adventist, on free exercise grounds, refuse to pay union dues?	With but Justices Brennan and White wishing to review the case, the Court upheld lower court's holding that, absent the union's ability to demonstrate "undue hardship," religious freedom had preference over payment of union dues.
1981	*Thomas v. Review Board of the Indiana Employment Sec. Div.,* 450 U.S. 707	8:1	Denial of unemployment benefits for a Jehovah's Witness who quit his job because his religious beliefs forbade participation in the production of armaments. (He had been transferred against his will from an acceptable job making sheet metal to one producing tank turrets.)	Chief Justice Burger, writing for a near-unanimous Court, applied the *Sherbert* rule in arguing that Indiana had placed an unconstitutional burden upon religion and had failed to show that it had used "the least restrictive means of achieving a compelling state interest." (See Rehnquist's lone dissent for a cogent analysis of the modern tension between the two religion clauses in the First Amendment.)
1987	*Hobbie v. Unemployment Appeals Compensation Commission of Florida,* 480 U.S. 136	8:1	Denial of unemployment benefits to a Seventh Day Adventist who was fired by an Orlando, Florida, jewelry store for refusing to work on Friday evenings and Saturdays, her Sabbath.	Relying on the *Sherbert* precedent, Justice Brennan's majority opinion could find no compelling state interest served by denying Hobbie benefits, despite the fact that she had embraced her religious beliefs *after* her employment began at the store. (Dissent by Rehnquist.)
1989	*Frazee v. Illinois Department of Employment Security,* 489 U.S. 829	9:0	Does the Court's protection of religious liberty extend to personal religious beliefs that are in addition to those contained in formal religious doctrine?	"Yes," responded the justices in a case involving "a Christian's" refusal to work on Sundays. If belief is "sincere" and of a "religious nature," a refusal to labor on the Sabbath need not be based on "a tenet or dogma of an established religious sect."
1993	*Church of the Lukumi Babalu Aye v. Hialeah,* 508 U.S. 520	9:0	Does a city's ban on animal sacrifices breach the First Amendment's guarantees for the free exercise of religion?	"Yes," answered the Court, while split in its reasoning, distinguishing its 1990 *Oregon v. Smith* ruling above. It regarded the ban as a direct attack on a religious practice, rather than as a neutral law—like the Oregon one on the use of peyote—that only incidentally affects religious practice. Nor did the opinion find any compelling governmental interest.

Sunday closing of certain business enterprises while permitting others to remain open. Undoubtedly there must be some logic to such intriguing provisions as those that—under the very same state laws—ban the sale of hosiery in hosiery shops on Sundays yet do not forbid it in drugstores, or those that permit the sale of "antiques" but not "reproductions"; or those that require candy stores to be closed but permit roadside candy counters to be open; or those that allow clam digging but forbid oyster dredging![102] Such logic, if any, is difficult to detect and certainly subject to some question. It was just such questioning and reasoning that brought a spate of Sunday law litigation to the bar of the Supreme Court in the 1960s. In addressing itself to the basic constitutional question, the Court combined four cases, some of them reaching it with diametrically opposed judgments from lower federal tribunals. Two of them[103] involved owners of highway discount department stores that were open for business seven days a week; the other two concerned smaller stores, owned and operated by Orthodox Jews who, given their religious convictions, closed their establishments on Saturdays but wanted them open on Sundays.[104] The four cases came from three different "Blue Law states," Maryland, Massachusetts, and Pennsylvania, and in all of them the constitutionality of the several statutes involved was under attack on the grounds that they infringed upon religious liberty in violation of the First Amendment; that they contravened the First Amendment's constitutional proscription against the establishment of religion; and that they constituted an unreasonable, arbitrary, and capricious classification, thus denying to the merchant involved the equal protection of the laws guaranteed under the Fourteenth Amendment.

Depending upon how one wishes to count or number opinions that are listed as "concurring and dissenting in part," at least eight and perhaps a dozen separate opinions were handed down in these four cases by an obviously uncomfortable and unhappy Court. It suffices to point to the fact that the prevailing opinion in each one of the four cases was written by Chief Justice Warren, whereas Justice Douglas dissented in each. The other justices ranged across an opinion spectrum that varied from 8:1 to 6:3. It is clear that the Court did not believe that a demonstrable case for the laws' unconstitutionality had been made; nor did it wish to strike down legislation that, to such a large degree, was based upon either legislative discretion or popular demand, legislation that not only varied widely in character and substance but that also was enforced only sporadically for the simple reason that so many consumers evidently did not wish it en-

102. For an illuminating analysis of this—now declining—crazy-quilt pattern of exemptions and exceptions, see Richard Cohen, *Sunday in the Sixties* (New York: Public Affairs Committee, 1962).

103. *McGowan v. Maryland* and *Two Guys from Harrison-Allentown, Inc. v. McGinley,* op. cit.

104. *Gallagher v. Crown Kosher Super Market of Massachusetts* and *Braunfeld v. Brown,* op. cit.

forced—legislation that, moreover, was in some cases at least based upon popular referenda.[105] Hence, although avowedly recognizing the "religious origin" of Sunday laws, the chief justice, in his four opinions, hit hard upon the general theme that, in effect, their religious purposes were no longer present; that the present-day purpose of a legislature in enacting such laws was to set aside a day not for religious observance but for "rest, relaxation, and family togetherness," with the motivation thus being "secular rather than religious"; that—with an eye toward the Orthodox Jewish merchants—although the freedom to hold religious beliefs and opinions is absolute, what was involved in the cases at issue was not freedom to hold religious beliefs or opinions *but freedom to act;* and that such freedom, even when motivated by bona fide religious convictions, is not wholly free from legislative restrictions, duly enacted under the state police power. The chief justice indicated strongly that, although the Court would have wished that the states had passed "Sabbatarian" laws designating Sunday as a day of rest while providing an exemption, or the choice of another day (as some states have done), it obviously could not compel the states to adopt such legislation in their sovereign discretion. Wisdom could not be the issue; constitutionality was—and it was deemed to have been met in view of what the Court regarded as the overridingly secular nature of the various laws. To Justice Douglas and his supporters in dissent, however, there was a patent violation of both the free exercise and the establishment clauses. Rejecting the majority's finding of predominating "temporal considerations," Douglas contended with feeling that when the laws are applied to Orthodox Jews or to "Sabbatarians," their absence of justice is accentuated. As he put it:

> If the Sunday laws are constitutional, Kosher markets are on a five-day week. Thus those laws put an economic penalty on those who observe Saturday rather than Sunday as the Sabbath. For the economic pressures on these minorities, created by the fact that our communities are predominantly Sunday-minded, there is no recourse. When, however, the State uses its coercive powers—here the criminal law—to compel minorities to observe a second Sabbath, not their own, the State undertakes to aid and "prefer one religion over another"—contrary to the command of the Constitution.[106]

Whatever the realities of the Sunday closing laws, and their degree of enforcement, there can be little doubt that, as Justice Stewart wrote in dissent in the pertinent Pennsylvania case,[107] the Orthodox Jew is forced into "a cruel choice . . . between his religious faith and his economic survival . . . a choice which . . . no State can constitutionally demand. . . . [T]his is not something that can be swept

105. See the discussion by Murray S. Stedman Jr. in his *Religion and Politics in America* (New York: Harcourt, Brace and World, 1964), esp. pp. 71–74.

106. *McGowan v. Maryland,* 366 U.S. 420 (1961), dissenting opinion at 577.

107. *Braunfeld v. Brown,* 366 U.S. 599 (1961), dissenting opinion at 616.

under the rug and forgotten in the interest of enforced Sunday togetherness."[108] To Justices Stewart, Brennan, and Douglas this was a gross violation of the constitutional right to the free exercise of religion. In a sense, Pennsylvania responded by enacting a "Sabbatarian" law in 1967: it permits bona fide other-than-Sunday observers to remain open on Sunday, assuming they keep another Sabbath.

If the majority's reasoning in the *Sunday-Closing Law Cases* raised professional and lay eyebrows, they were *really* raised by the Court's opinion and decision in *Sherbert v. Verner*[109] two years later. As indicated earlier in Table 6.2, this free exercise of religion case was brought by Mrs. Adell H. Sherbert, a member of the Seventh Day Adventist church. For thirty-five years a loyal employee of the Spartan Mills, a textile mill in Spartanburg, South Carolina, she was on a five-day week when she formally joined the church in 1957, thus enabling her to have her Sabbath on Saturdays, in accordance with the church's precepts. In 1959 the firm changed the workweek to six days for all three shifts that operated in the mill. When she refused to work on Saturdays, she was fired. Finding herself unable to obtain similar work because she would not labor on Saturdays, she filed a claim for unemployment compensation under the South Carolina Unemployment Compensation Act. But the State Employment Security Commission ruled that Mrs. Sherbert's restriction upon her availability for Saturday work disqualified her for benefits under the act, which denies these to any insured workers who fail, "without good cause, to accept suitable work when offered by the employment office or the employer." The South Carolina Supreme Court sustained the commission's finding (4:1), for in its judgment no restriction was placed upon Mrs. Sherbert's freedom of religion, since she remained free to observe her religious beliefs in accordance with the dictates of her conscience.

In language that could have been applied in the *Sunday-Closing Law Cases* to obtain results *opposite* from those reached here, the majority of seven, speaking through Justice Brennan—who had been unhappy about at least two of the *Sunday-Closing Law Cases*[110]—now *reversed* the South Carolina authorities. It did so on the grounds that the denial of benefits to Mrs. Sherbert constituted a clear infringement of, and burden upon, her constitutional rights of free exercise of religion under the First Amendment:

> *The ruling forces her to choose between following the precepts of her religion and forfeiting benefits, on the one hand, and abandoning one of the precepts of her religion in order to accept work, on the other hand.* Government imposition of such a choice puts the same kind of burden upon the

108. Ibid. at 616.
109. 374 U.S. 398 (1963).
110. *Braunfeld v. Brown*, 366 U.S. 599; and *Gallagher v. Crown Kosher Market of Massachusetts*, 366 U.S. 617 (1961).

free exercise of religion as would a fine imposed against appellant for her Saturday worship.[111]

Any "incidental burden" on the free exercise of religion, Brennan wrote, invoking strict scrutiny, must be justified by a *"compelling"* state interest, rather than a mere "legitimate" one—a test that, in the majority's judgment, South Carolina failed.[112] Justice Stewart wrote a separate concurring opinion, and Justice Harlan dissented in an opinion joined by his colleague White.

The disappointed owners of the Braunfeld and Crown stores had much cause to wonder why the Brennan language—particularly the portions italicized earlier—did not also fit *their* cases. Yet although Justices Stewart, Harlan, and White did indeed believe that the *Sherbert* decision had the effect of overruling the *Braunfeld* and *Crown* judgments, Brennan's majority opinion *distinguished* the former on the ground that the same practical difficulties and considerations arising from the granting of exemptions in Sunday closing laws did not apply and were not present in the South Carolina unemployment insurance problem. It is quite obvious that what the Court did here was to try to draw a line: to balance considerations of public policy against infringement on religious liberty, based on the "compelling state interest" test. In the 1961 *Sunday-Closing Law Cases* the Court was not willing to make exemptions in laws of general application on grounds of claims of religious liberty versus economic hardship—in the 1963 *Sherbert* case it was. And this distinction was emphatically not due to changes in personnel, since Justices White and Goldberg, the successors to retired Justices Whittaker and Frankfurter, did not numerically or substantively affect the different results in the latter decision. Although the facts in the settings of the two

111. *Sherbert v. Verner,* op. cit., at 404; italics supplied.

112. Almost three decades later the Court—in a 5:4 opinion penned by Justice Scalia—would revisit *Sherbert* and dramatically reject the "compelling state interest" test as an overriding one in cases of a "generally applicable prohibition of socially harmful conduct" (*Employment Division, Department of Human Resources of Oregon v. Smith,* 494 U.S. 872 [1990]; see *supra* Table 6.1). But contrast *Church of Lukumi Babalu Aye v. Hialeah,* 508 U.S. 520 (1993), *supra* Table 6.2. And in 1993 Congress (led by ideological strange bedfellows Senator Orrin Hatch [R.-Utah] and Senator Edward Kennedy [D.-Mass.]) enacted the rather pretentiously titled Restoration of Religious Freedom Act, which *mandated* the application of the *Sherbert*-developed *compelling state interest test* in all apposite federal and state cases. Under that test: (1) The claimant must show that he or she is sincere in wanting to conform to the religious practice in question. (2) The claimant must demonstrate that the government's law poses a "cruel choice," i.e., it places more than a de minimus burden, direct or indirect, on the religious practice in question. (3) If points (1) and (2) are met, the claimant has established a prima facie case and will prevail, unless the government can meet its burden of producing evidence that (a) the societal interest in applying the law to the claimant is compelling; and (b) the government cannot achieve the same societal interest by means less restrictive to the claimant's religious practice. But the law fell in 1997. Some members of Congress support adding the "compelling state interest" test to the U.S. Constitution via amendment.

cases differed, the difference was surely one of rationalization rather than of substance. The conclusion is inevitable that the distinction made in the *Sherbert* case is neither very logical nor very convincing.[113] The distinction advanced by Brennan that in the applicable *Blue Law Cases* there was a "less direct burden upon religious practices" is highly questionable—or, as Justice Stewart put it in his concurring opinion, in which he strongly criticized the Brennan rationale, "[W]ith all respect, I think the Court is mistaken, simply as a matter of fact."[114] If anything, the secular purpose of the South Carolina statute was clearer than that of Pennsylvania's and Massachusetts's. The line the Court endeavored to establish here is simply not viable as a basic rule of law.[115] The Court's 1970 denial of certiorari in the case of a California Seventh Day Adventist construction worker who unsuccessfully attempted to invoke *Sherbert* below may represent some second thoughts—although the facts were rather different and his case did not involve similar hardship.[116] A 1981 case, however, relied on *Sherbert,* as did one in 1987, both by 8:1 votes in favor of the claimant.[117] A unanimous decision in 1989 went even further by ruling that if a person's belief is "sincere" and of a "religious nature," a refusal to work need *not* be based "on a tenet or dogma of an established church."[118]

In a sense, the Court was given "a hand" by virtue of a provision of Title VI of the Civil Rights Act of 1964, as amended, that—since the mid-1970s—requires employers "to make reasonable accommodations to the religious needs of employees [where] such accommodation can be made without undue hardship on the conduct of the employer's business." In the face of that provision's obvious judgmental flexibility, a 7:2 majority thus found in 1977 that Larry S. Hardison, a clerk at a large TWA maintenance base who had joined the Worldwide Church of God—a sect that proscribed work on Saturday—had not been deprived of his free exercise of religion, since TWA had made every good-faith effort to accom-

113. See the interesting analysis of this general problem in Paul G. Kauper, *Religion and the Constitution* (Baton Rouge: Louisiana State University Press, 1964), chapter 2, "Religious Liberty: Some Basic Considerations."

114. *Sherbert v. Verner,* op. cit., at 477.

115. For an interesting, perceptive analysis of the *Sherbert* decision see Warren L. Johns, "The Rights to Rest" 66 *Liberty* (January–February 1971) 1, pp. 7ff. See also his *Dateline Sunday, U.S.A.* (Mountain View, Calif.: Pacific Press Publishing Association, 1967).

116. *Stimpel v. California State Personnel Board,* 400 U.S. 952 (1970). A somewhat related subject matter was addressed by the Court in 1972 to the same result when it declined to review a lower court decision that required a member of the Seventh Day Adventist church to join a union, despite his religious belief in freedom of choice, since he was employed in a plant with a duly adopted union shop contract (*Hammond v. United Papermakers,* 409 U.S. 1028).

117. *Thomas v. Indiana Employment Security Review Board,* 450 U.S. 707 (1981); and *Hobbie v. Unemployment Appeals Commission,* 480 U.S. 136 (1987).

118. *Frazee v. Illinois Department of Employment Security,* 489 U.S. 829.

modate him. Hardison did not have enough seniority to select a non-Sabbath shift as a matter of right under the union agreement, and the union steward, at TWA's urging, had tried, but failed, to find someone who would exchange shifts.[119] That the 1964 provision's elasticity will indeed afford considerable leeway was demonstrated in 1985, when the Court declared unconstitutional (8:1) a Connecticut law that had mandated an *absolute* right for employees *not* to work on their chosen Sabbath.[120]

Yet if the results in *Sherbert* and some of its offspring signify a more generous interpretation of the free exercise phrase, it may be welcomed in the light of the fundamental question of whether more harm is done to the democratic process by permitting an eccentricity of personal code or behavior, so long as no valid law is broken, than by trampling upon the nonconformist in the interest of the power of majoritarianism.[121]

Because lines must be drawn along the way, and the drawing usually seems to fall to the Court, it is not surprising, then, that it would be guided on occasion, as it evidently was there, by certain judgments based on considerations of realistic subjectivity that inevitably characterize the political process. After all, the Supreme Court of the United States is a body at once legal, governmental, and political. Proof positive is the controversy triggered by the Court's opinion in *Oregon v. Smith.* Determined to overturn the Oregon peyote decision legislatively, and dictate guidelines to the high court, Congress enacted the Religious Freedom Restoration Act (RFRA) of 1993, *requiring* the "compelling state interest" test as a guarantee in "all cases where free exercise is substantially burdened." A dispute between a Roman Catholic parish near San Antonio, Texas, which wanted to expand its church, and the City of Boerne, which refused to

119. *Trans World Airlines, Inc. v. Hardison,* 432 U.S. 63. The dissenters were Justices Marshall and Brennan, who joined in an opinion by the former that was described by Justice White's majority opinion as including "hyperbole and rhetoric." Intriguingly, the provision at issue had been declared unconstitutional in 1977 by U.S. District Court Judge Manuel Real as a violation of the First Amendment's guarantee of separation of church and state (*Yott v. North American Rockwell Corporation,* 428 F. Supp. 763). But the U.S. Court of Appeals for the Ninth Circuit reversed Judge Real in 1979 (ibid. 602 F.2d 904).

120. *Thornton v. Caldor,* 472 U.S. 703.

121. But, needless to say, there are limits: thus, in 1973 the Supreme Court dismissed the appeal of defendants in a marijuana case who contended that the use of the drug was part of their religious beliefs, protected by the free exercise clause (*Gaskin v. Tennessee,* 414 U.S. 886). Dr. Timothy Leary, the stormy petrel of the 1960s and 1970s, had unsuccessfully endeavored to peddle a similar argument earlier (*Leary v. United States,* 383 F.2d 851 [1967]). See also the Oregon Native Americans' unsuccessful (3:6) attempt to have that state's prohibition of the use of peyote in religious rituals declared unconstitutional on free exercise grounds (*Employment Division, Department of Human Resources of Oregon v. Smith,* 494 U.S. 872 [1990]). On the other hand, contrast *Church of the Lukumi Babalu Aye v. Hialeah,* 508 U.S. 520, Table 6.2, *supra.* Finally, see Henry J. Abraham, "The Status of the First Amendment's Religion Clauses: Some Reflections on Lines and Limits," 22 *Church and State* 2 (spring 1980), pp. 215–31.

allow the expansion under the city's preservation law, brought a challenge under RFRA all the way to the U.S. Supreme Court in 1997. The parish, supported by 109 group and individual amici curiae briefs, maintained that Boerne's reliance on preservation laws did not provide the compelling state interest required under the 1993 congressional statute. The City of Boerne asserted that RFRA was unconstitutional, and six members of the Court agreed. In his opinion for the majority, Justice Anthony Kennedy argued that not only had Congress usurped the Court's power to define constitutional protection of religion and intruded on the business of the states, it had misapplied its powers under Section 5 of the Fourteenth Amendment *(City of Boerne v. Flores),* which he interpreted as being limited to *enforcing* its provisions, not to creating substantive and/or nonremedial rights.[122] With this background, we now turn to the Pandora's box of "establishment."

"ESTABLISHMENT": THE SEPARATION OF CHURCH AND STATE

If the clause "Congress shall make no law respecting an establishment of religion" is commanding in tone and clear in syntax, it is utterly unclear in its intention. What does it mean? What does it forbid? References to history only intensify the riddle. And because the establishment and free exercise clauses are closely related, the complexities of establishment simply cannot be understood if they are treated or considered in isolation from the central problem of religious liberty itself.

A Glance at History

Among America's revolutionary and postrevolutionary leaders, the persons who were initially responsible for the concept of nonestablishment and its incorporation into the Bill of Rights were Thomas Jefferson, James Madison, George Mason, Patrick Henry (on a somewhat different plane), and the Reverends Samuel Davies and John Leland.[123] Virginians all, they led and fought the good fight in the struggle that took place during Virginia's last days as a colony and early days as a state, a struggle similar to that which had taken place almost a century and a half earlier in Rhode Island and neighboring areas under Roger Williams. Williams, who has been appropriately called "the most advanced and effective advocate of religious freedom in colonial times,"[124] and his supporters

---

122. 521 U.S. 507. See Wilfred M. McClay, "The Worst Decision Since 'Dred Scott'?" *Commentary,* October 1997, pp. 52–54.

123. Of course, others who labored long before the Virginians (such as Roger Williams and the Reverend John Clarke) carved their niche in the history of religious liberty, but at a different moment in history, under different circumstances, and with different impact.

124. Stokes and Pfeffer, op. cit., p. 65.

fought less on the specific matter of "establishment" than on the general one of "freedom." Hence it is the Virginians who must receive chief credit for the notion and coinage of American theories of the separation of church and state. Their influence was decisive, and their debates and writings on establishment are indeed still valuable sources of reference, even though they can be differently interpreted. A matter on which there is agreement, however, is that they strived, above all, for separation of church and state in the sense that there should not be an established church—as the Episcopal (Anglican) Church was in Virginia at the time—and that there should never be "the preferred position of a favored Church." To achieve those minimum aims, Jefferson, Madison, Mason, and their allies struggled for more than a decade until they succeeded in bringing about the "disestablishment" of the Episcopal Church as the state church of Virginia. This they accomplished with the enactment, after a nine-year battle, of Mr. Jefferson's great Bill for Establishing Religious Freedom on December 15, 1785, by a 74:20 vote of the House of Delegates.[125] It became law on January 19, 1786. The effect of this legislation—hereafter commonly referred to as the Disestablishment Bill—was far-reaching: Virginia's victory over establishment decisively influenced not only the ultimate course of action of her sister states but also that of the federal government. No wonder that Jefferson requested notation of his role in the epic struggle for religious freedom on his tombstone at Monticello, along with the other two achievements he considered of greater significance than his eight-year presidency.[126]

Moreover, Madison's widely circulated and highly influential "Memorial and Remonstrance Against Religious Assessment" of 1784–85, against the proposal of Virginia's House of Delegates to provide, through assessments, for teachers of the Christian religion, is as classic a statement as may be found in support of the separation of church and state. Supported by Jefferson, the eloquent and lengthy fifteen-point document—the centerpiece of Madison's works on the separation of church and state—argued persuasively that the state as the secular authority must have jurisdiction over *temporal* matters, that such authority does not extend over *spiritual* matters, which lie in the domain of private belief and the churches (note: "churches," not "church"). He warned persuasively that once they look to government for the achievement of their various purposes,

125. Its heart read: "Be it enacted by the General Assembly that no man shall be compelled to frequent or support any religious worship, place or ministry, whatsoever, nor shall be enforced, restrained, molested, or burthened in his body or goods, nor shall otherwise suffer on account of his religious opinions or belief; but that all men shall be free to profess, and by argument to maintain, their opinions in matters of religion, and that the same shall in no wise diminish, enlarge, or affect their civil capacities."

126. "And not a word more" were his instructions for the epitaph he composed: "Here was buried Thomas Jefferson. . . ." First he listed his authorship of the Declaration of Independence, next that of the "Statute of Virginia for Religious Freedom," next "Father of the University of Virginia."

the churches invite the sacrifice of their spiritual independence; and that when government enters upon the religious scene, it, in turn, enters into competition with the churches in seeking favors—thereby incurring the risk of ecclesiastical domination, with the attendant dangers of coercion of belief and persecution of dissenters.

Thus, to Jefferson and Madison, "children of the Enlightenment [who] represented the secular and humanistic view that supported religious liberty and the separation of church and state,"[127] the principle of separation was absolutely indispensable to the basic freedoms of belief, conscience, and dissent. They were in no sense hostile to religion—far from it; they simply regarded it as an entirely private matter. Overridingly determined to keep religion out of the domain of public affairs,[128] they were as much concerned with freedom *from* religion as with freedom *of* religion—a concern still reflected in Virginia's constitution today (the 1971 revision retaining it in full).[129]

Difficulties of Historical Application to Contemporary Problems. Following the obvious intent of Jefferson and Madison, it is clear that there can be neither an *official* church nor even an especially *favored* church in the United States or in any of its constituent subdivisions. Or, to put it somewhat differently, at a minimum the establishment clause prohibited the national government *both* from founding or perpetuating a state religion *and* from favoring any one religion or religions. What is far less clear, however, is the matter of state *aid* to religious activities, and state *cooperation.* If government treats *all* religions with an equal eye and an even hand, may it not, wholly in conformity with the Jefferson-Madison injunction, aid in furthering the spiritual development of Americans, whom the Supreme Court has repeatedly styled "a religious people"?[130] Is the government, in the words of an experienced student of philosophy and politics, "furthering a legitimate purpose when it acts to encourage, support, or aid the institutions of religious life," or is it "precisely the point of the 'no establishment' clause that it

127. Kauper, op. cit., p. 48.

128. As president, Madison successfully vetoed a congressional "Act incorporating the Protestant Episcopal Church in the town of Alexandria, the District of Columbia" (February 21, 1811). See 22 *Annals of Congress* 982–83. But Jefferson supported, for example, government-paid chaplains, government use of religious symbols and mottoes, and government grants of land and funds for Christian and public schools using the Bible and nondenominational religious instruction.

129. The tough prohibitory language of its Bill of Rights bars "any appropriation of public funds, or personal property, or any real estate to any church, or sectarian society, association, or institution of *any kind whatever,* which is *entirely or partly,* directly or indirectly, controlled by any church or sectarian society" (Article 1, Section 16; italics supplied).

130. E.g., Justice Douglas's majority opinion in *Zorach v. Clauson,* 343 U.S. 306 (1952) at 313.

precludes government action to this end"?[131] How authoritative and decisive can the intent of men who wrote and lived almost two centuries ago be regarded when applied to the current scene (though we do know that Madison, for one, opposed tax exemption for churches, and even publicly opposed chaplaincies other than military ones)? Notwithstanding the historical fact that the debates of the First Congress on "establishment" read like negotiations and eventual compromise among opposing factions,[132] the principle of "separation" *is* demonstrably present in both the spirit and the letter of the Constitution. Once again, then, we are faced with the line-drawing problem; once again we must look to the Court, even if its role has evolved as much by default as by affirmation.

A Solution That Is No Solution. Striving for a solution, the Court seized upon Jefferson's concept of the "wall of separation between Church and State," which he expressed in a letter to the Danbury (Connecticut) Baptist Association in January 1802. (It appears nowhere else in Jefferson's works.) The idea that the clause against establishment of religion by law was intended to erect "a wall of separation between Church and State" was initially expounded in the *First Mormon Polygamy Case*[133] in 1879 by Chief Justice Waite, who wrote for a unanimous Court. The "wall of separation" clause reappeared in a far more significant, highly contentious, opinion by Justice Black for a 5:4 Court in the *New Jersey Bus Case*[134] in 1947, when the narrow majority found that "wall" had *not* been breached by granting state subventions of $354.74 for bus fares to parents of twenty-one children in Ewing Township's four nonpublic, if nonprofit (which here meant Roman Catholic), parochial schools as well as to public school children. As we shall have occasion to note again, Black reaffirmed the "wall" principle but ruled that it had *not* been breached here. His colleague Frankfurter, however, was not so sure and saw the "wall" "not as a fine line easily overstepped"; Justice Jackson quipped that that "wall" may become as winding as

131. Joseph Tussman, *The Supreme Court on Church and State* (New York: Oxford University Press, 1962), p. xv.

132. See Jonathan Elliot, *Debates in the Several State Conventions on the Adoption of the Federal Constitution* (Philadelphia: Lippincott, 1854).

133. *Reynolds v. United States,* 98 U.S. 145 (1879) at 164. Actually, that case rested essentially on the free exercise question.

134. *Everson v. Board of Education of Ewing Township,* 330 U.S. 1 (1947). The case was brought as a taxpayer's suit by Arch R. Everson, executive vice-president of the New Jersey Taxpayers' Association, an economy-in-government group. The litigation was in fact sponsored and paid for by the Junior Order of United American Mechanics, a Protestant fraternal organization active in New Jersey (personal correspondence, Professor Daryl R. Fair of Trenton State College, December 13, 1974). Professor Fair has authored a fascinating background study of the statute and the several court cases involved: "*Everson v. Board of Education*: A Case Study of the Judicial Process" (paper presented at the annual meeting of the New Jersey Political Science Association, Trenton, N.J., April 12, 1975).

Jefferson's celebrated "serpentine wall" of single bricks on the grounds of his beloved University of Virginia at Charlottesville; and Justice Reed objected to drawing a rule of law from what he viewed as "a figure of speech." Fifteen years later, Reed's point was echoed by Robert M. Hutchins: "The wall has done what walls usually do: it has obscured the view. It has lent simplistic air to the discussion of a very complicated matter. Hence it has caused confusion wherever it has been invoked. . . . The wall has been offered as a reason. It is not a reason: it is a figure of speech."[135] And, to compound the basic problem for generations yet unborn, one of the five "wall" upholders in that *New Jersey Bus Case,* Justice Douglas, seized upon the opportunity of the *New York Bible Case*[136] to announce from the bench that he *now* (1962) believed the *Bus Case* to have been wrongly decided by him and his four colleagues who then (1947) constituted the majority.[137] Obviously, then, that famous "wall of separation" seems to be made of different stuff and be of rather different height depending on its viewers, be they Supreme Court justices, other jurists, or subjective or objective commentators, lay or professional.[138] As Harold Hammett put it intriguingly in his essay "The Homogenized Wall," for the wall to function properly "one must not be able to climb over, dig under, break through or sneak around to the other side."[139] Accordingly, he suggested not one wall between church and state but two: with church on one side, state on the other, and joint functions permitted by the First Amendment in the middle.[140] Justice Black—a pillar of the Baptist Church in his native Alabama, who had taught Sunday school for sixteen years—had firmly insisted that in the instance of the New Jersey bus subsidies to children attending the township's nonprofit parochial schools, the "wall" stood high and unbreached:

135. *Christian Century,* December 4, 1963, p. 1512. See also "The Future of the Wall," in Dallin Oaks, ed., *The Wall Between Church and State* (Chicago: University of Chicago Press, 1963), p. 19.

136. *Engel v. Vitale,* 370 U.S. 421 (1962) at 443.

137. Writing in 1967, William A. Carroll, in a lengthy article, called the Everson definition "untenable . . . a sham" and urged that it be discarded for the sake of "ordered coherence" (see "The Constitution, the Supreme Court, and Religion," 51 *American Political Science Review* 663 [September 1967]).

138. For an admirable historical summary see Robert M. Healey, "Thomas Jefferson's 'Wall': Absolute or Serpentine?" 30 *Journal of Church and State* 8 (autumn 1988).

139. 53 *American Bar Association Journal* 929 (October 1967).

140. In one observer's interesting judgment, Jefferson had not meant his "wall" to effect a complete and absolute separation of church and state so that no religious influence would be permitted in state-sponsored activities and laws. His chief aim was to foster freedom of religious expression—and if that objection would be best served through statutory cooperation between church and state, Mr. Jefferson appeared willing to endorse it within appropriate constitutional guidelines and safeguards. See Daniel L. Driesbach, unpublished article funded by the Virginia Historical Society and the Religion and Public Policy Research Fund, July 1990, p. 143.

The "establishment of religion" clause of the First Amendment means at least this: Neither a state nor the Federal government can set up a church. Neither can pass laws which aid one religion, aid all religions, or prefer one religion over another. Neither can force or influence a person to go or remain away from church against his will or force him to profess a belief or disbelief in any religion. No person can be punished for entertaining or professing religious beliefs or disbeliefs, for church attendance or nonattendance. No tax in any amount, large or small, can be levied to support any religious activities or institutions, whatever they may be called, or whatever faith they may adopt to teach or practice religion. Neither a state nor the Federal Government can, openly or secretly, participate in the affairs of any religious organizations or groups and vice versa. In the words of Jefferson, the clause against establishment of religion by law was intended to erect a "wall of separation between Church and State."[141]

In the light of the preceding manifesto, Black's concluding passage in his opinion must have come as a bit of a surprise to some of his readers as well as some of his colleagues: "The First Amendment has erected a wall between church and state. The wall must be kept high and impregnable. *We could not approve the slightest breach. New Jersey has not breached it here.*"[142] Had it not? In a lengthy, troubled dissent (in which his colleagues Frankfurter, Jackson, and Burton joined), and to which he appended Madison's "Memorial and Remonstrance Against Religious Assessment,"[143] Justice Rutledge found, on the contrary, that the "wall" had been breached, flagrantly and inexcusably. According to Justice Murphy's notes, Rutledge had already stated bluntly in the Justices' Conference on the case: "First it has been books, now buses, next churches and teachers. Every religious institution in [the] country will be reaching into [the] hopper for help if you sustain this. We ought to stop this thing at [the] threshold of [the] public school."[144] Now, writing his dissenting opinion, and rejecting the majority's so-called child-benefit and/or public-purpose theory—namely, that New Jersey's subsidy was meant for, and went to, the *child* rather than to the church—Rutledge warned the majority that separation must be strictly construed. It is only by rigidly observing the prohibition against establishment, he contended, that

141. *Everson v. Board of Education of Ewing Township,* op. cit., at 15–16.

142. Ibid. at 16; italics supplied. The Court thus *affirmed* the judgment of the tribunal whence the case had come, the New Jersey Court of Errors and Appeals, which in turn had reversed a lower New Jersey court.

143. Rutledge called it "at once the most concise and the most accurate statement of the views of the First Amendment's author concerning what is an 'establishment of Religion'" (at 37).

144. Murphy Papers (located at the Michigan Historical Collections, University of Michigan, Ann Arbor), docket notes and conference notes, No. 52, Box 138. See also J. Woodford Howard Jr.'s illuminating biography of Murphy, *Mr. Justice Murphy: A Political Biography* (Princeton, N.J.: Princeton University Press, 1968), p. 448.

the state can maintain its neutrality and avoid partisanship in the dissensions inevitable when sect opposes sect over demands for public moneys to further religious education, teaching or training in any form or degree, *directly or indirectly.*[145]

And in response to the many who have argued long and persistently that such aid would be no more than simple equity to atone for the fact that people whose children go to nonpublic schools must pay public taxes and often tuition too, Rutledge observed:

Like St. Paul's freedom, religious liberty with a great price must be bought. And for those who exercise it most fully, by insisting upon religious education for their children mixed with secular, *by the terms of our Constitution the price is greater than for others.*[146]

In another well-known dissent, Justice Jackson argued—quite plausibly—that the Black opinion was inconsistent with the Black decision, and that he (Jackson) was reminded of Julia, who, according to Lord Byron's account, "whispering, 'I will ne'er consent,' consented."[147] And, referring to the Rutledge warnings, Jackson noted that "Catholic education is the rock on which the whole structure [of the church] rests."[148] The divergent views of such devotees to the Constitution and the basic freedoms of mankind as Justices Black,[149] Douglas, Rutledge, and Jackson are proof positive that the doctrine of the "wall" is no solution per se.[150] It fails because the necessary line depends overridingly on public policy considerations—and on the interests of contending groups[151]—even if one believes, as did Senator Sam J. Ervin (D.-N.C.), "in a wall between Church and State so high that no one can climb over it."[152]

Some Principal Theories of Separation

Since the "wall" approach is hardly definitive, let us analyze those principal theories of separation that have made themselves felt in the interpretation of the

145. *Everson v. Board of Education of Ewing Township,* op. cit., at 59; italics supplied.
146. Ibid.; italics supplied.
147. Ibid. at 19.
148. Ibid. at 24.
149. See Barbara A. Perry, "Justice Hugo Black and the 'Wall of Separation' Between Church and State," 31 *Journal of Church and State* 1 (winter 1989), pp. 55–72.
150. For some interesting data concerning the justices' maneuverings and misgivings on Everson, see J. Woodford Howard Jr., "On the Fluidity of Judicial Choice," 52 *American Political Science Review* 43 (March 1968).
151. Withal, *Everson* continues to be reaffirmed; e.g., in late 1971 the Court refused to disturb a New Jersey law providing for free school transport for many private and parochial school students (*West Morris Regional Board of Education v. Sills,* 404 U.S. 986).
152. As quoted in *Time,* March 8, 1971, p. 30.

First Amendment. Again, in considering them we ought to keep in mind that a strict segregation between the "establishment" and "exercise" clauses of the First Amendment is not only an oversimplification but misleading and a disservice to the discussion of the basic problem. A close reading of the major Supreme Court opinions specifically governing the issue of establishment or separation of church and state,[153] rather than the specific issue of free exercise (assuming that dichotomy can ever be thus clearly delimited), presents three more or less identifiable Court theories[154]—depending upon one's count. (One can find more.)

The Strict Separation or "No Aid" Theory. Presumably incorporating the "wall" approach to the problem, this theory holds that there must be a strict separation of church and state, and that government may not constitutionally provide support to religion or religious interests. The theory was demonstrably applied in the "released time" case of *McCollum v. Board of Education,*[155] where the Supreme Court ruled (8:1)—the majority opinion written by Justice Black, the dissenting one by Justice Reed—that the "no aid" concept had been violated. At issue was Mrs. Vashti Cromwell McCollum's challenge[156] to the constitutional validity of a practice by the board of education of Champaign, Illinois, which enabled the interfaith Champaign Council on Religious Education to offer classes in religious instruction to public school children on public school premises. The religious classes were attended from thirty to forty-five minutes on Wednesdays by those public school students whose parents submitted written authorizations. Teachers were provided by the council at no charge to the board, but they were subject to the approval of Champaign's superintendent of schools. The classes were conducted in the regular school classrooms during school hours; those students who did not wish to stay for the religious sessions were required to go elsewhere in the building to pursue "meaningful secular studies." Evidently, these were not very meaningful in the case of those few students—such as young James Terry McCollum, whose family were professed agnostics—who did not stay for the Protestant, Catholic, or Jewish classes. Attendance at both the religious and lay classes was enforced strictly by secular teachers.

153. These major opinions are indicated in *infra* Tables 6.3 and 6.4. Probably the most significant ones for our present purposes are the *Everson, Zorach, Allen, Walz, McCollum, Earley, Lemon, Tilton, Nyquist, Engel, Schempp, Roemer, Wolman, Regan, Mueller, Marsh, Lynch, Jaffree, Thornton, Grand Rapids, Aguilar, Kiryas Joel Village, Agostini, Santa Fe, Mitchell,* and *Zelman* cases (see tables for citations).
154. These are discussed in detail in Kauper, op. cit., chapter 3. See also Richard E. Morgan, *The Supreme Court and Religion* (New York: Free Press, 1972), chapter 3ff.; and J. C. Choper, "The Religion Clauses," 41 *University of Pittsburgh Law Review* 4 (summer 1980). The latter two present other theories.
155. *Illinois ex rel. McCollum v. Board of Education,* 333 U.S. 203 (1948).
156. See her interesting book on the case, *One Woman's Fight* (Boston: Beacon Press, 1961).

Strongly reiterating the "wall" principle that he had pronounced as the author of the majority opinion in the *Everson Bus Case*, Justice Black here found clear violations of the First and Fourteenth Amendments. He rejected the board of education's argument that, if the Court were to hold that a state cannot consistently, under these two amendments, utilize its public school system to aid any or all religious faiths or sects in the dissemination of their doctrines and ideals, then the Court would "manifest a governmental hostility to religion or religious teachings." Black pointed to *Everson*, repeating its—his—language: "[T]he First Amendment has erected a wall between Church and State which must be kept high and impregnable." Because there was much lingering doubt as to just what had really happened to that "wall" in *Everson*, Black evidently felt constrained to spell out his conclusions on the violation of separation of church and state again, and he closed his opinion with this admonition:

> Here [in *McCollum*] not only are the State's tax-supported public school buildings used for the dissemination of religious doctrines. The State also affords sectarian groups an invaluable aid in that it helps to provide pupils for their religious classes *through use of the State's compulsory public school machinery*. This is not separation of Church and State.[157]

On the other hand, Justice Reed, in solitary dissent, believed that the principle of *Everson* could accommodate the facts in *McCollum*. Sounding the frequently voiced argument that "devotion to the great principle of religious liberty should not lead us into a rigid interpretation of the constitutional guarantee that conflicts with accepted habits of our people," he observed sadly that here was "an instance where, for me, the history of past practices is determinative of the meaning of a constitutional clause not a decorous introduction to the study of its text."[158] Justices Reed and Black had been on the same side in the *Everson* case, although it will be recalled that Reed, perhaps sensing the expansiveness and uncertainty of the "wall" doctrine, and reflecting the fear of those who well recognized that it could "give" in either direction, had there objected to "drawing a rule of law from a figure of speech."

In the light of his position in the separation cases that were yet to follow,[159] and which would be consistent with his *McCollum* reasoning, Black's position in the *New Jersey Bus Case* can best be explained in terms of a distinction he was willing to make under the strict separation theory between "incidental" aid to religion and "direct" aid. The situation in the *Bus* case was for him an entirely viable example of *incidental* aid—which, to him, constituted "*no* aid." He reasoned

157. *Illinois ex rel. McCollum v. Board of Education*, 333 U.S. 203 (1948) at 212. The supplied italics point to Black's key objection (as he would have cause to point out five years later in the *Zorach* decision, discussed *infra*).
158. Ibid., dissenting opinion at 256. In an interview with Francis W. O'Brien (December 2, 1955), Reed confided that no opinion had ever won for him such a number of favorable letters as his *McCollum* dissent—"ten times more than any other."
159. See discussion and Tables 6.3 and 6.4, *infra*.

that since the purpose of the New Jersey ordinance was to provide nothing more than the *general public purpose* one of safe transportation of schoolchildren who were attending school under compulsory education laws, the fact that they happened to attend Roman Catholic parochial schools was not constitutionally fatal. For Black and his (then) supporters, the purpose of that aid was "secular" and "incidental" to the requirements of the compulsory school attendance statute, *hence appropriately directed to secular objectives.* In other words, the financial assistance given to the parochial school students was not the kind of "aid" forbidden under the "wall" doctrine of the *Everson* decision itself.

The Governmental Neutrality Theory. Under this theory, the establishment clause is viewed as requiring government to be resolutely "neutral" regarding religious matters. So neutral, in fact, that, in the interesting interpretation and application of the theory advanced by Professor Philip B. Kurland, government cannot do anything which *either aids or hampers religion*[160]—that there must be, in other words, *a secular legislative purpose and primary effect that neither advances nor inhibits religion.* Professor Kurland reads the freedom and separation segments of the religion phrases as "a single precept that government cannot utilize religion as a standard for action or inaction because these clauses prohibit classification in terms of religion *either to confer a benefit or to impose a burden.*"[161] This, of course, leaves us with the delicate and intriguing question as to the meaning not only of "benefit" and "burden" but of "neutral"—and, in the final analysis, of *religion* itself. It also leaves us with the suspicion that the suggested doctrine might well be rather hard on individual religious dissenters, which is something Kurland seems to acknowledge but does not quite concede.[162]

It was Justice Black who spoke for the Court's invocation of the neutrality theory most obviously, when he authored—fifteen years after the *Everson* and *McCollum* cases—what quickly became one of the most contentious and most misunderstood opinions of our time, the *New York Prayer Case.*[163] Here, writing for a 6:1 majority, Black endeavored to make clear that the principle of the separation of church and state could not permit the recitation in the public schools of a rather innocuous, twenty-two-word, nondenominational daily prayer that had been drafted by the New York State Board of Regents, a state agency composed of state officials. The prayer read as follows: "Almighty God, we acknowledge our dependence upon Thee, and we beg Thy blessings upon us, our parents, our teachers, and our country." It was recommended, although not re-

160. He has expressed this thesis frequently and in various media. See, e.g., his essay "The School Prayer Cases," in Dallin H. Oaks, ed., *The Wall Between Church and State* (Chicago: University of Chicago Press, 1963), p. 160.
161. Ibid., note 83; italics supplied.
162. See his *Religion and the Law* (Chicago: Aldine, 1962), esp. pp. 40ff.
163. *Engel v. Vitale,* 370 U.S. 421 (1962). Justices Frankfurter and White did not participate in the case.

quired, for viva voce reading by teachers and students in the classrooms of the New York State public schools at the beginning of each school day. Numerous school boards adopted the recommendation, among them that of New Hyde Park, Long Island, which did so in 1958. Five parents[164] of ten children attending the school involved brought suit on the ground that the use of the official state-composed prayer in the public schools violated both separation of church and state and freedom of religion. In his neither very lengthy nor very complex opinion for the Court, Justice Black agreed with the contentions of the parents and held the practice unconstitutional as a violation of the First and Fourteenth Amendments' ban on establishment of religion. "We think," he wrote,

> that by using its public school system to encourage recitation of the Regents' prayer, the State of New York has adopted a practice wholly inconsistent with the Establishment Clause. *There can, of course, be no doubt* that New York's program of daily classroom invocation of God's blessing as prescribed in the Regents' prayer is a religious activity. It is a solemn avowal of divine faith and supplication for the blessings of the Almighty.[165]

Anticipating the public outcry that was to follow the ruling—and it proved to be quite an outcry, one that has hardly subsided, giving rise to a host of proposed constitutional amendments designed to overturn the decision (some three hundred in the ensuing twenty-five years!)—he tried hard to put into words that the public might accept, and perhaps even appreciate, the manifold problems of personal commitments and drawing lines in cases of majority-minority religion that continue to bedevil these controversies. Thus, he explained,

> [T]he constitutional prohibition against laws respecting an establishment of religion must at least mean that in this country it is no part of the business of government to compose official prayers for any group of the American people to recite as part of a religious program carried on by government.[166]

And over the objections of the one dissenter, Justice Stewart, who contended that the Court "has misspelled a great constitutional principle" by ruling that "an 'official religion' is established by letting those who want to say a prayer say it,"[167] Black concluded on a frank, terse, and hardly illogical note:

> It is neither sacrilegious nor antireligious to say that each separate government in this country should stay out of the business of writing or sanction-

---

164. One Unitarian, one nonbeliever, one a member of the Ethical Culture Society, and two Jews.

165. *Engel v. Vitale,* op. cit., at 424; italics supplied.

166. Ibid. at 425.

167. Ibid., dissenting opinion at 445. Bills, designed to strip the federal courts of jurisdiction over state-authorized voluntary prayers in public schools, passed the Senate 61:30 and 51:40 in 1979 but died in the House.

ing official prayers and *leave that purely religious function to the people themselves and to those the people look to for religious guidance.*[168]

In an important footnote (no. 21), unfortunately largely ignored by the news media, Black tried to make clear—as he also did in two additional remarks he made orally from the bench on that Opinion Monday in June 1962—that, contrary to his colleague Douglas's concurring opinion, he in no sense of the term intended his opinion for the Court to extend to ceremonial functions and observations with religious mottoes or religious characteristics.

Just one year after the controversial *Engel* decision, the Supreme Court reemphasized its resort to the neutrality theory in two "follow-up" cases, the *Bible Reading Cases* of 1963, *Abington School District v. Schempp* and *Murray v. Curlett.*[169] Briefly, the *Schempp* portion of the two cases—which were decided together in a 144-page, five-opinion compendium—challenged the validity of a Pennsylvania law requiring the reading without comment of at least ten verses from the King James or Douay version of the Bible[170] on the opening of public school each day, although provision was made for a child to be excused from the

168. Ibid. at 435; italics supplied.

169. 374 U.S. 203. A later (1968) prominent example of resort to the neutrality doctrine is the Court's unanimous declaration of unconstitutionality of the Arkansas "monkey law," which prohibited the teaching in its public schools and universities of the theory of evolution (*Epperson v. Arkansas,* 393 U.S. 97). But note that its new 1982 law, which, like Louisiana's of the same year, required public schools to balance the teaching of "evolution" with the theory of the "creation by a supreme power," was promptly declared unconstitutional by a federal court in *McLean v. Arkansas Board of Education,* 723 F.2d 45 (1982)—even as at least eleven other states were planning to enact similar legislation. In December 1986 the U.S. Supreme Court bit the proverbial bullet in the issue by hearing oral argument in *Edwards v. Aguillard,* 482 U.S. 578. A packed courtroom witnessed spirited debate between opposing counsel, closely questioned by the justices, sprinkled with references to the Bible, Aristotle, St. Thomas Aquinas, and Spinoza, and with echoes of the Scopes "monkey trial" of the 1920s. The eagerly anticipated decision, handed down in June 1987, evoked inevitably strong feelings pro and con. In a lengthy opinion penned by Justice Brennan, the Court ruled 7:2 that the Louisiana statute was unconstitutional because "the pre-eminent purpose of the Louisiana Legislature was clearly to advance the religious viewpoint that a supernatural being created humankind," and thus violated the First Amendment's ban against any law "respecting an establishment of religion." Justice Scalia's dissent, which was joined by Chief Justice Rehnquist, denounced the decision as a "repressive" and "illiberal" action that prevented the people of Louisiana from having "whatever scientific evidence there may be against evolution presented in their schools" (ibid.). Another, somewhat altered try by the parish fell 6:3 in 2000 in *Tangipahoa Parish Board of Education v. Freiler,* 68 LW 2771. See Thomas Vincinerra, "In a Louisiana Parish, Dim Echoes of the 'Monkey Trial,'" *New York Times,* June 25, 2000, p. WK7.

170. Bible reading has always engendered emotional reaction. One of the most tragic on record came in 1842 after Francis Kenrick, the Roman Catholic bishop of Philadelphia, asked that *either* the Catholic (Douay) or the Protestant (King James) Bible be read in the public schools; or, alternately, that Catholic public school children be excused from Bible reading. Rumors began to sweep the city that "Catholics were trying to drive the Bible

exercises on the written request of a parent or guardian. The Schempps, whose son, Ellory, was the catalyst for the suits, were faithful Unitarian Universalists; Mrs. Madalyn E. Murray and her son, then seventeen-year-old William J. Murray III, a student at Baltimore's Woodbourne Junior High School, on the other hand,[171] were avowed atheists, contesting a rule by the Board of Commissioners of Baltimore City that required reading of a Bible chapter "and-or recitation of the Lord's Prayer" at daily opening exercises in the public schools. Students could be excused upon request, but William shunned that proviso. He had apparently been subjected to taunts and even physical assault with a switchblade in school because of his consistent opposition to these morning exercises.[172] (An interesting, al-

---

from the schools." In May and July 1844 the worst riots in the city's history erupted over the Bible issue, leaving a dozen persons dead and two Catholic churches, a seminary, and fifty houses in Kensington in ruins (*Philadelphia Sunday Bulletin,* April 21, 1968). A direct result was the development of a strong, separate Catholic school system.

171. In 1970 the now Mrs. M. M. O'Hair unsuccessfully sought Supreme Court review of her contention that the reading of the Bible from outer space (by astronauts) violated the establishment clause (*O'Hair v. Paine,* 397 U.S. 531, appeal dismissed). Another attempt by the tenacious Mrs. O'Hair failed in 1971 (ibid. 401 U.S. 955). But she did win her claim to tax-exempt status of an atheist library she set up in 1972—the IRS agreeing to her demands rather than do battle in a lawsuit she was about to bring (*New York Times,* June 12, 1972, p. 19c). In 1976 she announced her "resignation" as leader of "the American atheist community" (*New York Times,* March 26, 1976, p. 28). But, denounced as a "demon-directed damsel," she returned to the fray in 1978, filing suits to have the motto "In God We Trust" removed from the coin on which the image of suffragist Susan B. Anthony—alleged by Mrs. O'Hair to have been an atheist—appears, and indeed to have that motto expunged from all U.S. currency. She and her supporters also established a "Dial-an-Atheist" telephone message service in English and Spanish in New York and Chicago, designed to counter the "Dial-a-Prayer" inspirational message service long available in cities across the country. And in 1981 she filed an unsuccessful suit to stop the U.S. Court of Appeals for the Fifth Circuit from using its standard opening prayer, "Oyez, oyez, God save our nation and this honorable court."

172. Two decades later, William Murray—after a troubled life as a husband, father, adulterer, and alcoholic—found God, quit his job, and set about making friends, embraced as a prodigal son. Surrounded by fundamentalist ministers and right-wing congressmen, he publicly broke with, and indeed scathingly condemned, his mother in a dramatic, well-advertised appearance before a large "In God We Trust" sign at the U.S. Capitol (*Washington Post,* May 21, 1980, p. C1). In 1992, now preaching at Capital Baptist Church in Annandale, Virginia, he made a point of redenouncing Madalyn Murray O'Hair, concluding: "She blamed God and mankind for her personal sins and inadequacies rather than herself" (as quoted in the *Washington Post,* October 31, 1992, p. D9). By 1995 he was in the forefront of the movement to restore prayer in the public schools. In August of that year his mother, then seventy-six, his brother, Jon Garth Murray, and his daughter, Robin Murray-O'Hair, disappeared (with $600,000 in gold coins). The authorities suspected foul play, with suspicion centering on O'Hair's former office manager and an accomplice, both with long histories of violent crimes. The triple murders of the three O'Hairs were confirmed through forensic evidence in early 2001 (*Washington Post,* January 29, 2001, p. A13).

though not uncommon, by-product of the two cases involved was that the two different lower courts, through which the cases passed to the U.S. Supreme Court, had reached opposite conclusions on the same constitutional issues.)

The chief justice assigned the writing of the decision to Justice Clark, a devout Presbyterian active in his church, who delivered an opinion redolent with diplomacy and acknowledgment of the significant place religion is presumed to hold in American society. He clearly endeavored to avoid the hostile, however uninformed, outcries that followed the Black opinion in the *Engel* decision. In the 8:1 ruling—from which only Justice Stewart dissented but, unlike his *Engel* dissent, now rather heavily on *procedural* grounds and over widespread outcries, such as Senator Barry Goldwater's, that the Court had "ruled against God" and the contention by other legislators that it "had no business taking God out of public schools"—Clark chose to rest both the decision and the burden of the opinion on a different plane, that of *governmental neutrality*. How well he succeeded is perhaps tellingly illustrated by the fact that dozens of newspapers selected as the decisive segment of opinion the following explanation and exhortation by Clark:

> The place of religion in our society is an exalted one, achieved through a long tradition of reliance on the home, the church and the inviolable citadel of the individual heart and mind. We have come to recognize through bitter experience that *it is not within the power of government to invade that citadel, whether its purpose or effect be to aid or oppose, to advance or retard. In the relationship between man and religion, the state is firmly committed to a position of neutrality.*[173]

Not only was the opinion written by a devout Protestant, but among the five lengthy, separate concurring opinions was one delivered by that Court's Roman Catholic, Justice Brennan (whose comments embraced seventy-seven pages), and one by its Jewish member, Justice Goldberg. All five authors took great care to acknowledge the hallowed place of religion, yet all five firmly, and indeed repeatedly, referred to governmental neutrality as the sine qua non of the problem. Thus, the Court's emphasis was clearly on the theory of neutrality, a requirement based—as Justice Clark put it—on the possibility that "powerful sects or groups might bring about a fusion of governmental and religious functions or a concert or dependency of one upon the other."[174] The language, although evidently not the full intent, of the application of the principle of neutrality thus becomes that advanced by Professor Kurland, which asks whether the "purpose or primary effect" of an enactment is "either the enhancement or inhibition of religion":

173. E.g. (from the conclusion of the opinion), "Quotation of the Day," in *New York Times,* June 18, 1963, p. 39l; italics supplied. The citation is from 374 U.S. 203, op. cit., at 226.

174. *Abington School District v. Schempp* and *Murray v. Curlett,* 374 U.S. 203 (1963) at 222. Clark acknowledged that "the state may not establish a 'religion of secularism' in the public schools," but he insisted that the kind of neutrality required by the Court here would not bring about the establishment of such a "religion" (ibid. at 225).

[T]o withstand the strictures of the Establishment Clause there must be a *secular legislative purpose and a primary effect that neither advances nor inhibits religion.* . . . [And] the fact [advanced by Pennsylvania and Maryland] that individual students may absent themselves upon parental request . . . furnishes no defense to a claim of constitutionality under the Establishment Clause.[175]

The religious practices authorized by Pennsylvania and Maryland, and challenged by the Schempps and Murrays, thus failed to meet the demands of the "neutrality" test, a test under which *both* religion clauses of the First Amendment place the government in a "neutral position" with regard to religion. As for the allegation that a logical concomitant of that "neutrality" policy would be, in effect, to render government hostile to religion, Justice Clark explained that the Court, and through it the country's constitutional framework,

cannot accept that the concept of neutrality, which does not permit a State to *require* a religious exercise even with the consent of the majority of those affected, collides with the majority's right to free exercise of religion. While the Free Exercise Clause clearly prohibits the use of state action to deny the right of free exercise to *anyone,* it has never meant that a majority could use the machinery of the State to practice its beliefs.[176]

What Clark says here is surely a basic premise of our government under law: that majorities, even near-unanimous ones, cannot violate the Constitution! Thus, when Florida attempted to continue required prayers and Bible reading in its public schools, a practice approved by its state supreme court, the U.S. Supreme Court, without even hearing argument, promptly reversed the tribunal by an 8:1 vote one year later.[177] When in 1965 the principal of P.S. 184 in Queens, New York, ruled that not even a "voluntary" recitation of a nursery school prayer in public schools could be said, the Supreme Court upheld him by refusing to review an appeal from his ruling.[178] The Court even let stand a 1968 lower court ruling that a verse recited by *public* kindergarten children in De Kalb, Illinois, represented a violation of the separation principle, notwithstanding the deletion of the word *God,*[179] Justice Stewart dissenting. In 1971 the Court agreed (7:2) with the New Jersey courts that to use the prayers in the *Congressional Record*

---

175. Ibid. at 222, 224; italics supplied.

176. Ibid. at 225–26; italics supplied.

177. *Chamberlin v. Dade County Board of Instruction,* 377 U.S. 402 (1964). Justice Stewart dissented.

178. *Stein v. Oshinsky,* 382 U.S. 957. The prayer, said before eating cookies and drinking milk: "God is great, God is good, and we thank him for our food, Amen."

179. The prayer: "We thank you for the flowers so sweet; We thank you for the food we eat; We thank you for the birds that sing; We thank you for everything." A principle, alas, is a principle (*De Kalb v. De Spain,* 390 U.S. 906 [1968]).

as "voluntary devotional exercises" in the public schools constituted an impermissible "subterfuge."[180] Late in 1975 it declined an opportunity to consider whether public school children have a right to "pray aloud voluntarily" while in school, as the mother of a Massachusetts girl had sought unsuccessfully in the courts below.[181] Undaunted—and in concert with the actions by numerous other states, for example, New Jersey and New Hampshire—Massachusetts enacted a law in 1980 that permitted ritual prayer, with provisions for abstention, in its public schools, only to see it struck down as "an unconstitutional sponsorship of religion," the twelve-page opinion citing the U.S. Supreme Court precedents.[182] In 1982 the Supreme Court unanimously affirmed the declaration of unconstitutionality by a lower federal court of Louisiana's daily voluntary school prayer in its public schools,[183] and in 1984 down went a similar statute by New Mexico.[184]

But a good many of the states—encouraged by supportive congressional manifestations—refused to give up and now increasingly commenced to concentrate on "silent prayer" rules for their public schools. The bellwether was Alabama, whose U.S. District Court Judge William Brevard Hand proved to be an important ally with a string of "proreligion," "proaccommodation" holdings—including one in 1987 that banned forty-four textbooks from Alabama public schools because, he ruled, they promoted the "religion" of "secular humanism." He was overturned unanimously by the U.S. Court of Appeals for the Eleventh Circuit.[185] In 1984 Judge Hand, citing historical evidence, had upheld Alabama's statute authorizing a one-minute period of silence in all public schools "for meditation or prayer." He ruled there, inter alia, that since the Fourteenth Amendment did not incorporate any of the guarantees of religious freedom contained in the First, "the establishment clause of the First Amendment to the United States Constitution does not prohibit the state from establishing a religion"[186]—a conclusion

---

180. *Board of Education of Netcong, N.J. v. State Board of Education,* 401 U.S. 1013.

181. *Warren v. Killory,* 423 U.S. 929 (1975). An attempt by an Albany, New York, student group, Students for Voluntary Prayer, to hold prayer meetings in a public school came to naught on separation grounds in a late-1980 unanimous twenty-three-page opinion by the U.S. Court of Appeals for the Second Circuit (*Brandon v. Board of Education of Guilderland Central School District,* 487 F. Supp. 1219). The U.S. Supreme Court subsequently denied certiorari (454 U.S. 1123 [1981]).

182. Massachusetts Supreme Judicial Court, March 13 and 27, 1980, opinions by Justices Herbert P. Wilkins and Benjamin Kaplan (*Kent v. Commissioner of Education,* 402 N.E.2d 1340, 1980 Mass. Adv. Sh. 803, 1980).

183. *Treen v. Karen B.,* 455 U.S. 913.

184. *New Mexico v. Burciaga,* 464 U.S. 982.

185. *Smith v. Bd. of School Commissioners of Mobile County,* 827 F.2d 684. The six hundred Christian fundamentalist parents who had brought the suit decided not to appeal. And in another defeat for fundamentalists, the Court let stand a lower court ruling that parents do not have the right to insist that their children be excused from classes whose textbooks offend their religious beliefs (*Mozert v. Hawkins County Board of Education,* 56 LW 2142 [1988]).

186. *Jaffree v. Wallace,* 554 F. Supp. 1004.

the Supreme Court later termed "remarkable." Not astonishingly, the U.S. Court of Appeals reversed Hand, and the Supreme Court affirmed that decision (6:3) in *Wallace v. Jaffree* in 1985.[187] The case featured a notable dissent by Justice Rehnquist in which he again spelled out his basic point of view that the Founding Fathers never required "that the government be absolutely neutral as between religion and irreligion" and that the only things the establishment clause forbids are the "establishment of a national religion" and "preference [or discrimination] among religious sects of our democratic nation." The Court left open the possibility—arguably even the likelihood—that it would *uphold* the constitutionality of a statute that authorized a minute of *silence* but made no mention of *prayer.*[188] The issue reached the high tribunal in a New Jersey case late in 1987, but following a U.S. District Court's declaration of unconstitutionality of New Jersey's practice of observing one minute of silence at the opening of each school day "for private contemplation or introspection."[189] But it managed to duck the explosive problem by ruling unanimously that state lawmakers favoring the law had no legal authority to present their case—that is, that they lacked proper standing to sue.[190]

That the volatile, emotion-charged issue of public school prayer does not subside is manifested not only by the continuing efforts of states to come up with legislation that will pass judicial muster, and by the demonstrable fact that a plethora of communities still defy or ignore the now established law of the land, but also by repeated efforts in and by Congress to "overrule" the highest court in the land. Thus, both constitutional amendments and statutes have been introduced en masse with predictable regularity. Although none had passed both houses of Congress as of mid-1987, the U.S. Senate, trying a new approach, in 1979 had voted 49:37 and 51:40 *to deny appellate jurisdiction* to the Supreme Court of the United States in *Engel*-type and *Schempp*-type cases—obviously realizing that the Court would not reverse itself on the merits. The House failed to concur on both occasions, yet the 1980 and 1984 presidential election campaigns rang with clarion calls to "put God back into the lives of our school children." Indeed, the Senate, late in 1981, had voted 70:12 to endorse "programs of voluntary prayer" in public schools. Four years later it approved a constitutional amendment to permit organized silent prayer in the public schools, but the amendment failed to pass in the House. In the election atmosphere of 1984 Congress not only endorsed a silent prayer bill (as an amendment to one extending a variety of educational programs), it also passed the Equal Access Act of 1984, which makes it unlawful for any public *secondary* school receiving federal fi-

187. 472 U.S. 38.
188. Ibid. See especially the opinions by Justices Powell and O'Connor.
189. *May v. Cooperman,* 572 F. Supp. 1561 (D. N.J. 1983), affirmed 780 F.2d 240 (3d Cir. 1985).
190. *Karcher v. May,* 484 U.S. 72 (1987).

nancial assistance "and which has a limited open forum to deny equal access or a fair opportunity to, or discriminate against, any students who wish to conduct a meeting within that limited open forum on the basis of religious, political, philosophical, or other content of the speech at such meetings."[191] The Court, in an 8:1 ruling penned by Justice O'Connor, with only Justice Stevens in dissent, upheld the statute in 1990, rejecting arguments that it breached the constitutionally required separation between church and state.[192]

The retirements of centrist Justice Powell and liberal Justices Brennan and Marshall in 1987, 1990, and 1991, respectively, and their replacement by presumably conservative Justices Kennedy, Souter, and Thomas gave rise to a general expectation that a new Court majority would look more favorably upon prayers in public schools. Yet when a major case, involving a benediction by a rabbi at graduation ceremonies in a Rhode Island high school, reached the high tribunal in 1992, it ruled—to widespread surprise—that even nonsectarian benedictions and invocations (a staple at graduation ceremonies in public school systems nationwide) would violate the First Amendment's bar against governmental establishment of religion.[193] The 5:4 opinion, astonishingly authored by Justice Kennedy, who had been on the "other" side in the two *Allegheny County* cases two and a half years earlier,[194] was joined by his colleagues Blackmun, Stevens, O'Connor—and Souter, with the latter's concurring opinion contending intriguingly that "original intent" renders such prayers unconstitutional. In an acerbic, sarcastic dissent, Justice Scalia, joined by the chief justice and Justices White and Thomas, flayed the majority for a holding "as senseless in policy as it is unsupported in law." Yet just one year later, the Court, without comment, let stand a federal appeals court decision permitting prayer at a public school graduation because it was led and planned by *students*.[195]

In 1995 the justices dismissed the Ninth Circuit Court's ban on student-led and student-initiated prayers at public school graduation ceremonies.[196] And in late 1997 it, without comment, rejected a challenge to Indiana University's custom of having a clergy member offer two prayers at the school's graduation ceremony each May.[197] Evidently, the Court distinguished between colleges and universities and grade and high schools, as well as between *officially sponsored* and *student-led and student-sponsored* prayers (although the latter was not clear). Be that as it may, the Supreme Court expanded its presumed prohibition against religious activities *in the public schools* by striking down in 2001 a Texas

191. For a conveniently analyzed text of the key provisions of the Equal Access Act, see *New York Times,* July 26, 1984, p. A16.
192. *Board of Education of Westside Community Schools v. Mergens,* 496 U.S. 226.
193. *Lee v. Weisman,* 505 U.S. 577.
194. See *infra* this chapter.
195. *Jones v. Clear Creek Independent School District,* 61 LW 3819 (1993).
196. *Joint District No. 241 v. Harris,* 63 LW 3899.
197. *Tanford v. Brand,* 66 LW 3248.

school district's policy that allowed an elected student representative to deliver a public invocation before home high school football games. The 6:3 decision, authored by Justice Stevens, saw a *school-sponsored* practice that the majority deemed a violation of separation of church and state. Chief Justice Rehnquist and Justices Scalia and Thomas dissented.[198] But as if to muddy the waters further, the Court, by denying certiorari on Virginia's "One Minute of Silence" law requiring that public school children start their days with a silent minute "to meditate, pray or engage in other silent activity," in effect upheld the Fourth Circuit Court of Appeals' holding that the 2000 Virginia statute did *not* violate the First Amendment.[199] And two months after its contrary ruling in the 2001 Santa Fe case, it refused to review an Eleventh Circuit Court of Appeals decision permitting Duval County, Florida, schools to allow public high school students to elect a classmate to deliver a "message"—at graduation ceremonies.[200]

The concept of governmental neutrality can be interpreted in various ways, depending upon the interpreter and his philosophy. Thus, to Professor Wilbur G. Katz, it means that in order to be truly neutral, the government is in some instances *obliged* to give aid to religion in order to avoid restricting the complete enjoyment of religious liberty.[201] To some, anything but total neutrality is anathema;[202] to others, a neutrality that prevents a "just measure of governmental aid" is a violation of "the old American principles" of freedom of religion;[203] and to still others, it signifies that since government and religion both have roles to play in public life and the public order, and since they share some overlapping concerns and functions, neutrality can only mean that government policy must place religion at neither a *special advantage* nor a *special disadvantage.*[204] Professor Robert L. Cord maintains that genuine neutrality would encompass a restoration of the "no preference" doctrine of the First Amendment; that is, that aid to religious institutions is entirely acceptable as long as no preference is accorded to any one religion.[205] Professor William A. Carroll suggests that the "neutrality" definition and test assume a *complementary* interpretation of the religion clauses to the end that religion be defined "neutrally" so as to include "both belief and non-belief in God in regard to both the free exercise and the establishment

198. *Santa Fe Independent School District v. Doe,* 530 U.S. 290, overturning the contrary ruling by the Eleventh Circuit Court of Appeals in *Chandler v. Siegelman,* 230 F.3d 313 (2000).

199. *Brown v. Gilmore,* 534 U.S. ___ (2001).

200. *Adler v. Duval County School Board,* 534 U.S. ___ (2001).

201. *Religion and American Constitutions* (Evanston, Ill.: Northwestern University Press, 1964).

202. E.g., Professor Leo Pfeffer.

203. John Courtney Murray, S.J., "Law and Prepossessions?" 14 *Law and Contemporary Problems* 23 (1949).

204. Kauper, op. cit., chapter 3.

205. See, e.g., his "Church-State Separation: Restoring the 'No Preference' Doctrine of the First Amendment," 9 *Harvard Journal of Law and Public Policy* 1 (winter 1986).

clauses."[206] That the principle be applied with "benevolence" when applied to religious liberty in the public schools is urged by Professor Ellis M. West.[207]

How, then, does the "no aid" theory expounded in the *Everson Bus Case*[208] differ from the "neutrality" theory expounded in the *Public School Prayer Cases*?[209] Although the response depends upon interpretation, one can with some assurance say that the "no aid" test inquires whether government is acting *in aid of religion* (in *Everson* the Court found that New Jersey's subsidy aided the *child* rather than the *church*), whereas the "neutrality" test inquires whether government is placing religion at a patent advantage or disadvantage (which the Court answered in the former in the *Public School Prayer Cases*).[210] There remains the third theory, which frankly recognizes governmental "accommodation"—to which an interesting "bridge" might be Richard E. Morgan's controversial proposition that "there is no anomaly in banning even modest prayers in the common public schools, while financially aiding specialized independent parochial schools where sectarian prayer is routine."[211]

The Governmental Accommodation Theory. In his very lengthy concurring opinion in the *Public School Prayer* (Pennsylvania/Maryland)[212] decisions, Justice Brennan, while acknowledging that the accommodation theory had no place in the particular cases at issue, was moved to explain that only a concept such as that of "accommodation" could effectively reconcile the natural clash between the free exercise and separation clauses; that *some* accommodation between government and religion and between church and state could and should be ac-

206. Carroll, op. cit., pp. 664ff.; see esp. pp. 664–66 and 673–74.

207. "The Supreme Court and Religious Liberty in the Public Schools," 25 *Journal of Church and State* 87 (winter 1983).

208. *Everson v. Board of Education of Ewing Township,* 330 U.S. 1 (1947).

209. *Engel v. Vitale,* 370 U.S. 421 (1962); and *Abington School District v. Schempp* and *Murray v. Curlett,* 374 U.S. 203 (1963).

210. An interesting aspect of the problem of the Bible in the public schools was presented in New Jersey in 1953, in *Tudor v. Board of Education of Rutherford,* 14 N.J. 31, where the New Jersey Supreme Court held unconstitutional the state law sanctioning free distribution of Gideon Bibles (the King James version) at a group of public schools.

211. Morgan, op. cit., p. 207. See also Choper, op. cit., for a different approach that propounds a line that would forbid governmental action only if its religious purpose "is highly likely to result in coercing compliance or influencing religious beliefs." See also Paul J. Weber and Dennis A. Gilbert, who in their *Private Churches and Public Money: Church-Government Fiscal Relations* (Westport, Conn.: Greenwood Press, 1979) propose a doctrine of "fiscal neutrality." It would be based on an equal protection doctrine that protects free exercise without supporting establishment by taxing religious groups like all other groups (unless exempt under the eleemosynary umbrella) while permitting them freely to participate in the political process. Thus, "fiscal neutrality" would treat religious and nonreligious groups equally. George Anastoplo's essential "line" test is the answer to what he views as a simple yet logical quaere: Does the *community* benefit?

212. 374 U.S. 203 (1963) commencing at 230.

cepted.[213] Readily granting that Pennsylvania and Maryland had gone beyond "accommodation" with their Bible-reading and public prayer legislation, thereby violating the basic concept of governmental neutrality required by the Constitution, he cataloged activities that could *not,* in his opinion, be held to be constitutional violations,[214] activities that, although religious in origin, have ceased to have religious meaning—such as the motto "In God We Trust" on currency and the belief expressed in the Pledge of Allegiance that the nation was founded "under God";[215] provisions for churches and chaplains in the armed forces and in penal institutions; draft exemptions for ministers and divinity students; the recital of invocational prayers in legislative assemblies; the appointment of legislative chaplains; inclusion of prayers in public school commencement programs;[216] teaching *about* religion in the public schools, that is, the *study* of the Bible and other religious literature; *uniform* tax exemptions incidentally available to religious institutions;[217] other public welfare benefits which government

213. In 1971 there were still sixteen states that provided no "accommodation." By mid-1982 that number had shrunk to three (Florida, Georgia, and Oklahoma). See Albert R. Papa, *Auxiliary Services to Religious Elementary and Secondary Schools: The State of State Aid* (Washington, D.C.: Americans United for the Separation of Church and State, 1982). For a brief symposium on accommodation see 37 *DePaul Law Review* 3 (spring 1988), with essays and responses by Arlin M. Adams and Sarah Barringer Gordon, Jeffrey M. Shannan, and Charles R. Strain. For an imaginative justification of "noncoercive, nonpreferential" governmental aid to religion, see Gary C. Leedes, "Rediscovering the Line Between the Establishment Clause and the Fourteenth Amendment: The Citizenship Declaration," 26 *Indiana Law Review* 3 (1993).

214. Ibid. at 296–303.

215. Indeed, in 1964 the Court refused to review—and thereby let stand—a ruling by the Appellate Division of the New York Supreme Court that upheld the use of the words *under God* in the Pledge of Allegiance (*Lewis v. Allen,* 379 U.S. 923). The issue may well come before the high court yet again, for in the summer of 2002 a divided (2:1) U.S. Ninth Circuit Court of Appeals panel ruled that the "Pledge, as currently codified, is an impermissible government endorsement of religion because it sends a message to unbelievers 'that they are outsiders, not full members of the political community, and an accompanying message to adherents that they are insiders, favored members of the political community'" (nytimes.com/national). The decision generated such heated opposition (with members of Congress rising en masse to recite the Pledge, including its "impermissible" passage)—all eagerly reported by the media—that the Ninth Circuit panel stayed its ruling, pending an en banc hearing, which upheld the panel in 2003.

216. *Wood v. Mt. Lebanon Township School District,* 342 F. Supp. 1293 (W.D. Pa., 1972), affirmed 412 U.S. 967 (1974).

217. In 1966 the Supreme Court seemed to reaffirm that sensitive issue by declining to review a unanimous decision by the Maryland Court of Appeals that the time-honored state tax exemptions for church buildings were not an unconstitutional "establishment of religion" (*Cree v. Goldstein,* 385 U.S. 816; and *Murray v. Goldstein,* ibid.). And in 1970, in the *Walz* case, with Justice Douglas in lone dissent, the Court specifically upheld the tax exemption of property used exclusively for religious purposes. Chief Justice Burger, contending that "there is room for play in the joints productive of a benevolent neutrality which will permit religious exercise to exist without sponsorship and without interfer-

makes available to educational, charitable, and eleemosynary groups that *incidentally* aid individual worshipers; excuse of children from required school attendance on their respective religious holidays; the temporary use of public buildings by religious organizations when their own facilities have become unavailable because of disaster or emergency.

As if to indicate the difficulty of drawing such lines, Justice Douglas in *his* concurring opinion in the *Pennsylvania/Maryland* decisions essentially reiterated his strong stand in the *New York Prayer Case*, where he had said that the "First Amendment . . . prevented secular sanctions to *any* religious ceremony, dogma, or rite."[218] But lest he be misunderstood, he emphasized his now firm conviction that the concept of the "wall" brooked no infraction or circumvention, whatever the circumstances, whatever the rationale:

> [T]he First Amendment does not say that some forms of establishment are allowed; it says that "no law respecting an establishment of religion" shall be made. What may not be done directly may not be done indirectly lest the Establishment Clause become a mockery.[219]

ence"—provided there results no "excessive entanglement" with religion—held for his 7:1 Court that there was no relation between tax exemption and establishment, and explained: "The grant of a tax exemption is not sponsorship since the government does not transfer part of its revenue to churches but simply abstains from demanding that the church support the state" (*Walz v. Tax Commission of the City of New York,* 397 U.S. 664 at 669–70). To Douglas—and many another observer—however, "a tax exemption is a subsidy" pure and simple (at 704) and assuredly a far cry from the "wall of separation." It was the *Walz* case, and the Burger opinion therein, that in effect spelled out in detail the now widely accepted "three-pronged" test of constitutionality under any "accommodation" scheme, namely: (1) there must be a primary secular legislative purpose; (2) its effect must neither inhibit nor advance religion; and (3) its result must not foster an "excessive entanglement" of government and religion (at 674, 675).

The question of whether tax exemption could also be granted to church-owned property that is used for business purposes was answered by the Court in the negative in 1972 (6:1). See *Diffenderfer v. Central Baptist Church of Miami,* 401 U.S. 412. See also the 1990 decision (9:0) affirming the taxability of the sale of religious goods (*Jimmy Swaggert Ministries v. Board of Equalization of California,* 493 U.S. 378).

The tax exemption issue was back before the Supreme Court in 1988 in a case raising the intriguing matter of the use of tax-exempt funds in political campaigns, here involving the abortion problem (*United States Catholic Conference and National Conference of Catholic Bishops v. Abortion Rights Mobilization,* 487 U.S. 72). But it appeared doubtful that the Court was eager to reach the merits of the case amid indications that it might decide it on "standing" questions. Indeed, the Court, in an 8:1 opinion in mid-1988, "ducked" the substantive issue and remanded the case to the U.S. Court of Appeals to consider the conference's objection to the ABA's standing before a decision on the suit itself (ibid.).

218. *Engel v. Vitale,* 370 U.S. 421 (1962) at 442, note 7.

219. *Abington School District v. Schempp,* op. cit., at 230, concurring opinion. He took pains publicly to reiterate that posture in 1964 in the *Chamberlin* case, cited in *supra* note 177.

This stand, of course, rejects *any* "theory of accommodation." Ironically, Justice Douglas had not only provided the necessary fifth vote that upheld New Jersey's public funds subsidy to students attending Catholic parochial schools, a position he then publicly repudiated in *Engel v. Vitale*[220] and would again attack in the *New York Textbook Case* in 1968;[221] it was he who had written (a decade prior to the *Public School Prayer Cases*) the majority opinion in *Zorach v. Clauson*, the *New York Released Time Case*,[222] which well illustrates the accommodation theory that he now in effect rejected.

Zorach v. Clauson presented a situation ostensibly different from the one that had faced the Court in the *Champaign, Illinois, Released Time Case*[223] four years earlier, in 1948. It will be recalled that the Court's 8:1 decision in that Illinois case struck down as a clear-cut violation of the separation of church and state the Champaign School Board's practice of permitting the use of its public school facilities for weekly "released-time" religious classes. The New York released-time arrangement differed on its face principally in that those public school students whose parents requested in writing their attendance at religious instruction classes were in fact *released* from classes at school to journey outside to the site of the religious classes. Those who did not participate in the released-time program were required to remain in the public school buildings for instructional or study hall purposes. Theoretically, the public school teachers took neither public notice nor attendance of the student releases, but under the regulations promulgated by the board of education, the religious teachers did have to take attendance and file it with the individual's homeroom teacher or the principal, who was required to keep an attendance record.

The Supreme Court's six-man majority,[224] per the Douglas opinion, found critical differences between *McCollum* and *Zorach*. Douglas, while acknowledging that the public school teachers "cooperated" with the program to the extent of enabling voluntary attendance of the religious classes, held that the New York program, unlike that struck down in Illinois, involved neither religious instruction in the public school classrooms nor the expenditure of public funds per se. He insisted that the Court was indeed following the *McCollum* case, but he added that this did not mean that the Court had to read into the Bill of Rights a "philosophy of hostility to religion." Musing that the constitutional standard of the separation of church and state, like many problems in constitutional law, "is one of degree," he declared that church and state need not be hostile to each other. Although granting that "[g]overnment may not finance religious groups nor undertake religious instruction or blend secular and sectarian education nor use sec-

---

220. 370 U.S. 421 (1962).
221. *Board of Education v. Allen*, 392 U.S. 236.
222. 343 U.S. 307 (1952).
223. *McCollum v. Board of Education*, 333 U.S. 203 (1948).
224. Douglas, with Chief Justice Vinson and Justices Reed, Burton, Minton, and Clark.

ular institutions to force one or some religion on any person,"[225] he added in language that ultimately came to haunt him in light of his concurring opinions in the *Public Prayer Cases* of 1962 and 1963: "But we find no constitutional requirement which makes it necessary for government to be hostile to religion and to throw its weight against efforts to widen the effective scope of religious influence."[226] The First Amendment, he had said earlier in his opinion, "does not say that in every and all respects there shall be separation of Church and State";[227] and he elaborated later in a phrase much quoted by those opposed to later decisions by the Court, in general, and Douglas opinions, in particular, that "we are a religious people whose institutions presuppose a Supreme Being."[228]

But three dissenters, Justices Black, Frankfurter, and Jackson, not only regarded the majority's findings as going far beyond any constitutionally permissible "accommodation," they also saw no difference "even worthy of mention" (in the words of Justice Black, the author of the *McCollum* opinion) between the Illinois and New York programs, except for the use of public school buildings. Black especially objected to what he regarded as the compulsory process aspects of the New York practice: "New York," he wrote angrily, "is manipulating its compulsory education laws to help religious sects get pupils. *This is not separation but combination of Church and State.*"[229] As for the different use of the school buildings, Black noted: "As we attempted to make categorically clear, the *McCollum* decision would have been the same if the religious classes had *not* been held in the school buildings."[230] He concluded his opinion with an impassioned warning:

> State help to religion injects political and party prejudices into a holy field. It too often substitutes force for prayer, hate for love, and persecution for persuasion. Government should not be allowed, under cover of the soft euphemism of "co-operation," to steal into the sacred area of religious choice.[231]

To Justice Frankfurter, "the pith of the case" was that under New York's program, formalized religious instruction is instituted for other school activity which those who do not participate in the released-time program are *compelled* to attend. He suggested that this coercion might well be met, and met constitutionally, if the public schools were to close their doors completely for an hour or two, leaving the pupils to go where they will, "to God or Mammon." This practice,

---

225. *Zorach v. Clauson,* 343 U.S. 306 (1952) at 314.
226. Ibid.
227. Ibid. at 312.
228. Ibid. at 313.
229. Ibid. at 318; italics supplied.
230. Ibid. at 316; italics supplied.
231. Ibid. at 320.

known as "dismissed time," was then in vogue in three states, and had been readily upheld by the courts. Caustically, Justice Jackson, the third dissenter, commented that "my evangelistic brethren confuse an objection to compulsion with an objection to religion."[232] In his view the New York program operated to make religious sects beneficiaries of the power to compel children to attend secular schools, holding that the public school thereby "serves as a temporary jail for a pupil who will not go to Church."[233] He cautioned that "the day this country ceases to be free for irreligion it will cease to be free for religion—except for the sect that can win political power."[234] He ended his dissent on a note of combined alarm and sarcasm:

> [T]he *McCollum* case has passed like a storm in a teacup. The wall which the Court was professing to erect between Church and State has become even more warped and twisted than I expected. Today's judgment will be more interesting to students of psychology and of the judicial processes than to students of constitutional law.[235]

The *Zorach* decision, however, has *not* only not been overruled[236]—none of the above have, no matter which theory they might reflect—but the "accommodation" approach received further impetus when the Court in 1968 upheld New York's controversial 1965 law that *requires* public school systems to *lend* textbooks to students in private and parochial schools.[237]

In that *New York Textbook Case* the Court ruled (6:3)—in a case that appeared to open ever wider the door of accommodation—that the law directing school districts to lend $15 worth of textbooks each year to each pupil in grades seven through twelve in nonpublic schools, which then cost the state circa $25 million annually, was an entirely permissible "student benefit" rather than an impermissible "school benefit" program, and hence not violative of the First Amendment's strictures against establishment. In the majority opinion, Justice White—joined by Chief Justice Warren and Justices Brennan, Harlan, Stewart, and Marshall—thus clearly adopted the "child benefit" rationale of the *Everson* decision of two decades earlier.[238] He agreed that it would be unconstitutional for the state to purchase the books and *give* them gratis to parochial school students, but he noted that the law forbids that and merely requires the state to *lend* them. Underlying the legislature's action and the rationale of the earlier "child benefit" cases, contended White, "has been a recognition that private education has

232. Ibid. at 324.
233. Ibid.
234. Ibid. at 325.
235. Ibid.
236. Presented with a golden opportunity to reconsider it in 1976, the Court pointedly refused to do so (*Smith v. Smith,* 429 U.S. 806, certiorari denied).
237. The *New York Textbook Case* (*Board of Education v. Allen,* 392 U.S. 236).
238. *Everson v. Board of Education of Ewing Township, N.J.,* 330 U.S. 1 (1947).

played and is playing a significant and valuable role in raising national levels of knowledge, competence, and experience."[239]

But three opinions by three dissenters, Justices Black, Douglas, and Fortas, saw matters quite differently. Douglas pointed out that, in fact, the "statutory system provides that the parochial school will ask for the books that *it wants,*"[240] with the local public school board then simply (or not so simply) having to decide whether to veto the selection made by the parochial school. And, he asked, with rather difficult-to-refute logic: "Can there be the slightest doubt that the head of the parochial school will ask for the book or books that best promote its sectarian creed?"[241] Black, passionately contending that his *Everson* line had been not only overstepped but utterly misinterpreted—for he saw all the difference in the world between *bus* aid and *book* aid, the first being "incidental" or "ancillary" to the educational process, the latter being crucial to and an integral part of that process—warned (with a wary eye toward the Federal Aid to Education Act of 1965, discussed later in the text, and its presumed impending judicial tests):

> It requires no prophet to foresee that on the argument used to support this law others could be upheld providing for state or federal government funds to buy property on which to erect religious school buildings or to erect the buildings themselves, to pay the salaries of the religious school teachers, and finally to have the sectarian religious group cease to rely on voluntary contributions of members of their sects while waiting for the Government to pick up all the bills for the religious schools.[242]

To him the program constituted a "flat, flagrant, open violation" of the establishment clause.[243]

Fortas, in what would be one of his last decisions prior to his resignation from the bench in 1969, categorically stated that *Allen* was simply and patently *not* within the principles of *Everson,* for:

> Apart from the differences between textbooks and bus rides, the present statute does not call for extending to children attending sectarian schools the same service or facility extended to children in public schools. *This statute calls for furnishing special, separate, and particular books, specially, separately, and particularly chosen by religious sects or their representatives for use in their sectarian schools. This is the infirmity.*[244]

But there were six votes on the majority side—cast by justices who evidently believed the New York textbook law to fit into the now widely accepted "child ben-

239. *Board of Education v. Allen,* 392 U.S. 236 (1968) at 247.
240. Ibid. at 256; italics supplied.
241. Ibid.
242. Ibid. at 253.
243. Ibid. at 250.
244. Ibid. at 271; italics supplied.

efit" syndrome, who were willing, in White's words, to stipulate "evidence that parochial schools are performing, in addition to their sectarian function, the task of secular education."[245]

While the thrust of the times, the evolving nature of governmental aid to education, seemed then clearly to be on the side of the majority's reasoning in *Allen,* and while the latter's principle of the constitutionality of textbook *loans* was reaffirmed in 1973, 1975, and 1977 (in cases that, however, disallowed certain other state-devised attempts to "accommodate"),[246] there are obvious limits: thus, as the Court ruled unanimously in 1973—in a not necessarily overly convincing Burger opinion that professed to distinguish *Allen*—such free textbook aid may not constitutionally be extended to private academies (here under the terms of a 1940 Mississippi law) that have racially discriminatory admission policies.[247] Nor (6:3) does *Allen* by any means sanction state forays that would provide *funds* for the purchase of textbooks to *parents* of nonpublic school students.[248]

That there are constitutional limits to "accommodation," even when the 1968 *Allen* textbook case decision appeared to have made these academic, had been made crystal clear by two 8:0 and 8:1 decisions handed down in 1971 that dealt with attempted aid going well beyond textbook loans or bus subventions. With only Justice White dissenting in the second, the Supreme Court, speaking through Chief Justice Burger (hardly a doctrinaire opponent of "accommodation"), declared unconstitutional as *"excessive entanglement* between Government and religion"—and therefore violative of the separation of church and state mandated by the First Amendment—programs enacted by Pennsylvania in 1968 and Rhode Island in 1969 that provided *public funds* for *direct aid* for instruction in "nonreligious subjects" to Roman Catholic and other church-related primary and secondary schools. The aid involved in the Pennsylvania statute included the partial payment of salaries of parochial school teachers by professing to "purchase secular services" for their teaching of such "secular" subjects as mathematics, physical education, physical science, and modern foreign languages (Latin, Hebrew, and classical Greek were expressly excluded) and also for the purchase of textbooks and instructional materials. Lower federal courts had subsequently declared the Rhode Island law, which provided for a 15 percent supplement to private school teachers of secular subjects using the same instructional materials as those in the public schools, unconstitutional as violative of the establishment clause, but Pennsylvania's statute had been upheld.

---

245. Ibid. at 248.

246. *Committee for Public Education and Religious Liberty v. Nyquist,* 413 U.S. 476; *Meek v. Pittenger,* 421 U.S. 349; and *Wolman v. Walter,* 433 U.S. 229, respectively.

247. *Norwood v. Harrison,* 413 U.S. 455. "The leeway for indirect aid to sectarian schools has no place in defining the permissible scope of state aid to private racially discriminatory schools" (at 464). The Norwood case was reaffirmed in 1974 in *Evangeline Parrish School Board v. United States,* 416 U.S. 970.

248. *Marburger and Griggs v. Public Funds for Public Schools,* 417 U.S. 961 (1974).

In agreeing with the Rhode Island and disagreeing with the Pennsylvania decisions below, the Supreme Court gave renewed firm notice that while it did not retreat from its earlier "accommodation" holdings—such as its bus and textbook decisions—there were definite limits to "accommodation" lest it violate the separation of church and state, that "excessive entanglement" would and could not be tolerated. Explaining that the Court was thus obligated to draw lines with reference to the three main evils against which the establishment clause was intended to afford protection, "sponsorship, financial support, and active involvement of the sovereign in religious activity," the chief justice ruled:

> In order to determine whether the government entanglement with religion is excessive, we must examine the character and purposes of the institutions which are benefited, the nature of aid that the state provides, and the resulting relationships between the government and the religious authority. . . . Here we find that both statutes foster an impermissible degree of entanglement.[249]

And, in concluding, he reiterated the basic dimensions of the new line:

> The merit and benefits of these schools . . . are not the issue before us in these cases. The sole question is whether state aid to these schools can be squared with the dictates of the Religious Clauses. *Under our system the choice has been made that government is to be entirely excluded from the area of religious instruction and churches excluded from the affairs of government.*[250]

Along the way, the chief justice had restated the governing three-pronged "cumulative criteria" as follows: "First, the statute must have a secular legislative purpose; second, its principal or primary effect must be one that neither advances nor inhibits religion; finally, the statute must not foster an excessive entanglement with religion."[251] But Justice White disagreed; he theorized that aid to a "separable secular function" of a church-related school was *not* unconstitutional, contending that it does not matter if religious interests "may substantially benefit" from the aid.[252]

As if to underscore future problems for the "excessive entanglement" doctrine, on the very same Opinion Day the chief justice, speaking for himself and

---

249. *Lemon v. Kurtzman,* 403 U.S. 602 (1971) at 615.

250. Ibid. at 625; italics supplied. Yet in a rather grotesque postscript, the Court—through the chief justice—held 5:3 two years later that Pennsylvania could and indeed should release the $24 million in special aid for those private sectarian schools which it had authorized and appropriated for the school year *preceding* the 1971 holding of unconstitutionality! (*Lemon v. Kurtzman,* 411 U.S. 192 [1973]).

251. 403 U.S. 602 at 612–13. See the editorial "Bureaucratic Governmental Regulation of Churches and Church Institutions," 21 *Journal of Church and State* 2 (spring 1979).

252. Dissenting opinion in *Earley v. Dicenso,* 403 U.S. 602 (1971) at 664.

Justices Harlan, Stewart, White, and Blackmun, *upheld* (5:4) the Federal Higher Educational Facilities Act of 1963, under which $240 million in federal funds were paid for the construction of academic buildings on the campuses of private colleges—*including* religious colleges.[253] Over a sarcastic dissenting opinion by Justice Douglas—which was also signed by Justices Black and Marshall—charging that evidently "small violations of the First Amendment over the years are unconstitutional while a huge violation occurring only once is *de minimus*,"[254] the chief justice distinguished the federal higher education case from the two state secondary and primary school cases under three headings: that precollege church schools are more involved in religious indoctrination than colleges; that there are fewer entanglements between church and state in the "one-time, single purpose construction grant than in continuing salary-supplement programs"; and that what he viewed as the evil of bitter political battles, which he regarded as fatally damaging and divisive at the state programs' level, "is not likely to erupt" over aid to colleges. (Five years later he would join Justice Blackmun's opinion, utilizing the same general distinctions between college and below-college levels, in the Court's 5:4 decision upholding Maryland's aid to higher educational facilities program.)[255] The only Roman Catholic on the Court, Justice Brennan, echo-

---

253. *Tilton v. Richardson*, 403 U.S. 672 (1971). The Court did strike down unanimously (via Chief Justice Burger) a provision of the law which enabled the colleges to use the buildings for any purpose twenty years after receiving the funds. The right of states to help private colleges and universities borrow money to build nonsectarian facilities, even those that are owned and operated by a religious sect, was upheld 6:3 in 1973 (*Hunt v. McNair*, 412 U.S. 734). See also *Roemer v. Maryland Public Works Board*, 426 U.S. 736 (1976) *infra* this chapter.

254. *Tilton v. Richardson* at 692.

255. See *infra* this chapter. For an interesting discussion of the dichotomy between aid to higher and precollege institutions, see Edward N. Leavy and Eric Alan Raps, "The Judicial Double Standard for State Aid to Church-Affiliated Educational Institutions," 21 *Journal of Church and State* 2 (spring 1979). See also the same "wave length" distinction-cum-dichotomy between the Court's 1981 decisions in *Brandon v. Board of Education*, 454 U.S. 1123, and in *Widmar v. Vincent*, 454 U.S. 263, involving on-site activities of religious groups in elementary schools and universities, respectively. But, as noted earlier (*supra* this chapter), in 1990 the Court upheld (8:1) the Federal Equal Access Act of 1984, which requires public *high* schools to allow students' religious and political clubs to meet on the same basis as other extracurricular activities (*Board of Education of Westside Community Schools v. Mergens*, 496 U.S. 226). And in 1993 the Court, in one of Justice White's last opinions, ruled unanimously that a public school district may not prevent a church group from using its classrooms after school hours, simply because of the group's religious purpose (*Lamb's Chapel v. Center Moriches Union Free School District*, 508 U.S. 261). For a further extension of the above reasoning, see the refusal of the University of Virginia's student council—an instrumentality of the state—to fund a Christian student newspaper, an action that the Court declared 5:4 to be an unconstitutional infringement of free speech (*Rosenberger v. University of Virginia*, 515 U.S. 819 [1995]), and the *Good News Club v. Milford Central School*, 533 U.S. 198 (2001), which extended the *Mergens* and *Widmar* decisions by ruling 6:3 that the Milford Central School could not

ing Jefferson's and Madison's warnings, dissented separately, deploring what he saw as the secularizing impact of public assistance on church schools. By accepting government funds, he reasoned, not only do the religious activities of a sectarian institution become compromised—for there must inevitably be "policing" by the secular authorities—but there is really no way to separate out the religious and secular functions. Brennan restated his deeply held conviction that "the establishment clause forbids the federal government to provide funds to sectarian universities in which the propagation and advancement of a particular religion is a function or purpose of the institution."[256]

Obviously, neither the "excessive entanglement" line nor the allegedly governing "three-pronged cumulative criteria" thus settled the establishment clause controversies—but they did serve notice to policymakers across the land that the First Amendment contained certain basic strictures against the commingling of church and state—especially on pedagogical levels *below* college. Hence, when Ohio passed a law for direct tuition grants of ninety dollars annually to all parents of children in private and parochial schools, the Court barred it (8:1), with once again only Justice White in dissent.[257] And down in three 1973 cases went sundry formidable, ambitious nonpublic school aid attempts by New York and—again—Pennsylvania, the votes ranging from 8:1 to 6:3.[258] Included among them were such attempts as direct grants for maintenance and repair, for full and/or partial reimbursement of tuition, for nonmandatory testing and record keeping, and for tax relief. Such an endeavor, wrote Justice Powell for the Court, "advances religion in that it subsidizes directly the religious activities of sectarian elementary and secondary schools"; and he specifically viewed the programs as constituting a crass violation of the injunctions against any programmatic *effect* of advancing religion.[259]

The controlling Powell opinion in the preceding three mid-1973 decisions demonstrated clearly that, at least as of that period of history, the applicable test on separation between church and state was the already repeatedly alluded-to "purpose-effect-entanglement" trilogy yardstick. In the five cases at issue in the New York and Pennsylvania litigation, the first ("purpose") passed muster; the

deny the after-school use of its building to the Good News Club (an evangelical Christian group for elementary school students), while allowing such use to nonreligious groups. The majority opinion, authored by Justice Thomas, saw in Milford's denial of access to the religious club an unconstitutional free-speech violation (on the basis of viewpoint), à la *Rosenberger.*

256. 403 U.S. 602, op. cit., at 689.

257. *Essex v. Wolman,* 409 U.S. 808 (1972).

258. *Levitt v. Committee for Public Education and Religious Liberty,* 413 U.S. 427; *Committee for Public Education and Religious Liberty v. Nyquist,* 413 U.S. 756; and *Sloan v. Lemon,* 413 U.S. 825.

259. *Committee for Public Education and Religious Liberty v. Nyquist,* op. cit., at 774. For reconfirmation of Nyquist's tax relief negation, see also the Court's summary disposition in *Byrne v. Public Funds for Public Schools,* 442 U.S. 907 (1979).

third ("entanglement") was but briefly discussed; the second ("effect") became decisive. When, undismayed, undaunted, and stubborn, Pennsylvania tried once more in 1975, with a host of provisions for state aid to private and parochial schools for such services as counseling, testing, remedial classes in speech and hearing therapy, and for instructional equipment like charts, maps, records, films, tape recorders, and projectors, as well as an additional textbook loan program, all, except—predictably—the last, which survived 6:3, fell 3:6. With Justice Stewart speaking for the majority, joined wholly or partly by his colleagues Douglas, Brennan, Powell, Marshall, and Blackmun—the chief justice and Justices White and Rehnquist dissenting, more or less—and again zeroing in on the *effect* of the multiple legislation plus what it regarded as patent "political [and] administrative entanglement," the Court, in a stern, broadly sweeping opinion, saw grave potential for conflict between church and state. Provision of such services, wrote Stewart, raises "the danger that religious doctrine will become intertwined with secular instruction"[260] and creates a "serious potential for divisive conflict over the issue of aid to religion"[261] as legislation providing financial support comes up in the legislature year after year. The program, which cost $12 million for nonpublic schools in 1972-73, "inescapably" results in the direct and substantial advancement of religious activity, Stewart held for the majority, "and thus constitutes an impermissible establishment of religion."[262]

In fine, what the Court held in that 1975 landmark decision of *Meek v. Pittenger* was—speaking somewhat oversimplifiedly but accurately—that tax-raised funds may plainly not be used to finance the operations of church schools. Few, if any, Court watchers seriously believed, however, that the determined and numerous supporters of aid to nonpublic schools would cease and desist. Indeed, the Court's docket for the following term contained a number of possible candidates for renewed church-state legal strife. And one of them—to the astonishment (and dismay) of a number of close students of the Court—may have done more than "open a small crack in the 'wall' of separation," as the *New York Times* put it.[263] In a 5:4 decision in the *Roemer* case, featuring a welter of opinions but *no* majority agreement (the five-man victorious side splitting two ways in its reasoning),[264] the Supreme Court upheld Maryland's program of *noncategorical* financial aid to church-related *colleges,* thereby, for the first time in history, approving a system of state *general-purpose* subsidies benefiting church-related educational institutions. Over the troubled, fervent, often biting dissents by Justices Brennan, Stewart, Marshall, and Stevens (Justice Douglas's recent replacement), who viewed the subsidies as demonstrably involving "the disease of

260. *Meek v. Pittenger,* 421 U.S. 349 at 370.
261. Ibid. at 372.
262. Ibid. at 366.
263. June 27, 1976, sec. 4, p. 7E.
264. *Roemer v. Maryland Public Works Board,* 426 U.S. 736 (1976).

entanglement," the five justices composing the high tribunal's marginal majority—Chief Justice Burger and his colleagues Blackmun, Powell, White, and Rehnquist—saw no constitutional violation for a variety of reasons. The decision seemed to be controlled by a less than totally persuasive rationale that had also governed in the 5:4 holding four years earlier in *Tilton v. Richardson*[265]—which upheld limited *federal* aid to higher educational facilities for construction purposes. The "character" of the colleges, the ability of these colleges "to separate their secular and religious functions," and the lower "impressionability" of college students[266]—as contrasted with students on the secondary and primary levels—were held to lessen the dangers of indoctrination and thus sufficed to meet the trifold requirements of nonreligious purpose, nonreligious effect, and avoidance of excessive entanglement. The controlling plurality opinion by Justice Blackmun did admit "entanglement," but since he and his supporters did not deem it "excessive," it was not viewed as constitutionally fatal to the program.[267]

Needless to relate, however, the *Roemer* holding and reasoning encouraged pro-parochial aid forces on all levels of the pedagogical and political ladder. Thus, a scant year later, in the 1977 *Wolman* case, when the justices split five ways in ruling on a welter of six "aid" issues and their votes ranged from 8:1 to 3:6, new authority to aid parochial education was established by another Blackmun opinion, which was joined in all of its aspects only by Justice Stewart. Among the *Wolman* rulings, the following were found acceptable: therapeutic, remedial, and guidance counseling services, if provided on "neutral" sites off school premises (7:2); diagnostic services "on ground" (8:1); and state-mandated standardized tests and test-scoring services (6:3)—but *not* the loan to either parents or children of classroom paraphernalia like wall charts, maps, globes, science kits, and slide projectors (3:6); nor subsidized field trips (4:5).[268] The justices' five opinions were hardly models of clarity! Indeed, they constituted a mishmash of interpretations, which naturally invited further litigation. That December, perhaps in an effort to send a message that its broadening *Wolman* decision earlier in 1977 had decidedly not pulled out all the proverbial First Amendment stops, the Court ruled unconstitutional (6:3) a New York law that had provided for *direct financial reimbursement* to parochial schools for record keeping and testing services,[269] the chief justice and Justices White and Rehnquist predictably dissenting.

---

265. 403 U.S. 672 (1971). See discussion *supra.*

266. For a different point of view see Howard L. Reiter, "Do Professors Persuade Students?" *News for Teachers of Political Science,* winter 1980, pp. 5–7.

267. And for Justices White and Rehnquist only the first two requirements were constitutionally mandated. The Court, without opinion, affirmed similar college assistance programs in North Carolina and Tennessee in 1977—although Justices Brennan, Marshall, and Stevens wanted to hear oral arguments (*Americans United for Separation of Church and State v. Blanton,* 434 U.S. 803).

268. *Wolman v. Walter,* 433 U.S. 229 (1977).

269. *New York v. Cathedral Academy,* 434 U.S. 125 (1977).

Although 1978 and 1979 passed without any significant new development on the church-state litigation front, the Court returned to the fray with a major decision in 1980, spawned by the 1977 *Wolman v. Walter* confusion.[270] The new case, *Committee for Public Education and Religious Liberty v. Regan,*[271] arose as a result of New York's revised 1974 version of its 1970 law that the justices had struck down (3:6) in the 1973 *Nyquist* decision.[272] Now, however, in an opinion by Justice White—the Court's most ardent and consistent champion of widespread accommodation—the Court distinguished the latter decision (5:4) by pointing to the fact that the 1974 statutory revision mandated that the state-required tests and supporting procedures, for which *all* schools were to be reimbursed, were *prepared by officials of the state* rather than by the schoolteachers themselves, as had been the case under the 1970 law. White's opinion, joined by his close allies on the issue, Chief Justice Burger and Justice Rehnquist, and "swing" Justices Stewart and Powell, contained numerous caveats and frankly acknowledged a course that "sacrifices clarity and predictability for flexibility."[273] Not surprisingly, the four dissenters, Justices Blackmun, Brennan, Marshall, and Stevens, perceived and warned against a demonstrable primary effect on advancing religion and an entanglement patently violative of the First Amendment's strictures.

Notwithstanding the broadening of the open door implications of its *Regan* ruling,[274] the Court continued to recognize limits, such as it had done in the same term with its proscription of New Jersey's attempt to provide *special income tax deductions* for parents who send their offspring to nonpublic schools.[275] Its 6:3 per curiam opinion again endeavored to make clear that neither tax credits nor tax deductions nor exemptions nor rebates, nor any form of *direct* financial aid to parents or teachers, would pass muster with six (Brennan, Stewart, Marshall, Blackmun, Powell, and Stevens) of the nine members of the Court, at least not in the absence of some permissible type of federal statutory sanction. Chief Justice Burger and Justices White and Rehnquist, on the other hand, appeared to be firmly on record as finding constitutional support for almost any type of "accommodation," provided they could detect *some* kind of secular purpose. In the instance of the chief justice, this posture obtained only so long as he did not perceive an entanglement that was "excessive." But Justices White and Rehnquist, especially the former, seemed to be concerned not at all about either the "primary effect" of the state involvement or the attendant "entanglement." If they saw a viable *secular* purpose, they would vote to uphold the measure or action. For them,

270. 433 U.S. 229, op. cit.
271. 444 U.S. 646.
272. *Committee for Public Education and Religious Liberty v. Nyquist,* 413 U.S. 476.
273. *Regan,* op. cit., at 653.
274. Ibid.
275. *Byrne v. Public Funds for Public Schools,* 442 U.S. 907 (1979).

the Court's three-pronged test on the establishment front had thus been reduced to the single one of the presence of a secular purpose as perceived by them.[276]

A major late June 1983 holding not only confirmed these "lineup" assumptions but gave demonstrable evidence of a further widening of the door on behalf of "accommodation." For that Court, on which Justice Sandra Day O'Connor had replaced the retired Justice Stewart one and a half years earlier, was now willing to sanction an across-the-board tax deduction of up to $500 for parents of *all* elementary, and up to $700 for parents of *all* secondary, schoolchildren for bona fide educational expenses, identified as "tuition, secular textbooks and instructional materials, and transportation." Distinguishing *Nyquist*,[277] and gaining not only Justice O'Connor's vote but, arguably surprisingly, that of Justice Powell, the 5:4 ruling,[278] authored by Justice Rehnquist—and, also predictably, supported by Chief Justice Burger and Justice White—contended that the Minnesota law withstood separation of church and state challenges because it was "neutral" in design: it enabled parents of public school children as well as those in parochial and other private schools to avail themselves of the annual deduction.

To the four dissenters, however, speaking through Justice Marshall—who was joined by Justices Brennan, Blackmun, and Stevens—that reasoning was akin to a bad joke. In their eyes, the small benefits conceivably made available to parents of public school children were a mere pittance: of 815,000 beneficiaries, only 79 paid public school tuition, for example. The dissenters insisted that the per se inclusion of public schools could not "alter the fact that the most substantial benefit provided by the statute is available only to those parents who send their children to schools that charge tuition." Thus, Marshall saw only a "distinction without a difference" between the New York *Nyquist* and the Minnesota *Mueller* decisions, concluding both sadly and angrily that Minnesota's provisions for "the tax deduction for tuition and other educational expenses necessarily results in aid to the sectarian school enterprise as a whole."[279] There could be but little doubt now that, absent changes in the Court's membership, the constitutional tilt for a considerably greater degree of commingling of church and state had thereby been Court-sanctioned by mid-1983. Indeed, in 2000 a differently

276. For an important scholarly advocacy of that point of view, see the extensive essay by George Anastoplo, "The Religion Clauses of the First Amendment," 11 *Memphis State University Law Review* 2 (winter 1981), pp. 151–230. His essential "line test" responds to the question whether the community benefits in any manner. If so, fine—no constitutional problems.

277. *Committee for Public Education and Religious Liberty v. Nyquist*, 413 U.S. 756 (1973).

278. *Mueller v. Allen*, 463 U.S. 388 (1983). Sixteen years later, the Court rejected two appeals on separate grounds, from an Arizona Supreme Court decision, upholding that state's law providing tax breaks to people who donate money for scholarships at religious schools (*Ketterman v. Killian*, 68 LW 3217 [1999]).

279. Ibid. at 416.

composed Court—with only Justices Stevens, O'Connor, and Rehnquist, the latter now chief justice, as holdovers—held 6:3 that, contrary to its rulings in the 1970s and 1980s on Chapter 2 of the Elementary and Secondary Education Act of 1965, taxpayer money now *can* be used to buy computers and other instructional materials for religious schools. The Court's plurality opinion, penned by Justice Thomas, and joined by Chief Justice Rehnquist as well as Justices Scalia and Kennedy, with separate concurrences by Justices O'Connor and Breyer, provided the six-justice majority. In passionate dissent were Justices Souter, Stevens, and Ginsburg.[280]

The assumption of a more favorable view toward "accommodation" had in fact been confirmed a decade and a half earlier, when the justices made it clear not only that *Mueller* was no aberration but that an apparently firm 5:4 majority was now in solid control of an expanded "accommodationist" approach: in March 1984, the justices, splitting 5:4 exactly as they had in *Mueller* and speaking through Chief Justice Burger, upheld against a church and state separation challenge the constitutionality of the sponsorship by the city of Pawtucket, Rhode Island, of a forty-year-old practice of displaying a crèche as an integral part of a Christmas display in a park owned by a nonprofit corporation in the heart of the city's shopping district.[281] Its expenses were defrayed by the city and a downtown retail merchants' association.

Seeing only an "indirect" religious effect by what he termed a "passive symbol," the Chief Justice's brief but forthright opinion frankly stipulated that "total separation" of church and state is neither "possible" nor "required." He called for the kind of "line drawing" that would "affirmatively mandate accommodation, not merely tolerance of all religions, and forbids hostility to any." There was little doubt that the Burger opinion's emphasis on "accommodation" heralded a shift in, if not perhaps a total abandonment of, the then thirteen-year-old *Lemon* "three part test" of constitutionality, notwithstanding his reiteration of it.[282] Indeed, Justice O'Connor's concurring opinion saw "no government endorsement or disapproval" of religion but merely a "traditional symbol of the holiday." She called for a "clarification of our Establishment Clause" doctrine so as to place at its center of constitutional gravity "what is crucial," namely, "that a government practice not have the effect of communicating a message of government endorsement or disapproval of religion. It is only practices having the effect," she continued, "whether intentionally or unintentionally, that makes religion relevant, in reality or public perception, to status in the political community."[283] But the two impassioned dissents, one penned by Justice Brennan, joined by Justices Marshall, Blackmun, and Stevens, and the other by Blackmun, in which Stevens joined, saw

280. *Mitchell v. Helms,* 530 U.S. 793.
281. *Lynch v. Donnelly,* 465 U.S. 668 at 670–74.
282. *Lemon v. Kurtzman,* 403 U.S. 602 (1971).
283. *Lynch v. Donnelly,* loc. cit., at 674–76.

a clearly proscribable "primary effect . . . that place[s] the government's imprimatur of approval on the particular religious belief exemplified by the crèche."[284] To the four dissenters, Pawtucket's action amounted to an impermissible governmental endorsement of a particular faith. But one year later, with Justice Powell not participating, a divided 4:4 ruling upheld a decision below that had *required* the village of Scarsdale, New York, to allow a nativity scene by a private group in a public park in the center of town, citing the *Lynch* precedent.[285] The issue came before the Court again in 1989 when, dividing 5:4 and 6:3, the justices held in two opinions authored by Justice Harry A. Blackmun that (1) displaying a Nativity scene on the grand staircase inside the Allegheny County Courthouse in Pittsburgh violates constitutionally required separation of church and state because it appears to endorse Christian principles; but that (2) a Hanukkah menorah, placed on the steps of the city-county building—a few blocks away—joined by a Christmas tree and a sign saluting freedom, was allowable because it was placed in a physical setting that, in Blackmun's words, "conveyed the city's secular recognition of different traditions for celebrating the winter holiday season."[286] Justice Kennedy, dissenting in (1) but concurring in (2), propounded his "line" test by declaring that "non-coercive governmental action within the realm of flexible accommodation or passive acknowledgement of existing symbols does not violate the Establishment Clause unless it benefits religion in a way more direct and more substantial than practices that are accepted in our national heritage." One year later without dissent, the Court denied certiorari in a case in which a private Jewish group had been refused the alleged constitutional right to display a menorah in a public park near the Burlington, Vermont, city hall.[287]

A tabular recapitulation of the more significant Supreme Court decisions on separation of church and state is given in Table 6.3 and Table 6.4, augmented by

284. Ibid. at 676–85. For a full treatment of *Lynch* see Wayne R. Swanson, *The Christ Child Goes to Court* (Philadelphia: Temple University Press, 1990).

285. *Village of Scarsdale v. McCreary,* 471 U.S. 83 (1985). But contrast *City of Birmingham v. American Civil Liberties Union,* 55 LW 3309 (1986), in which the Court affirmed 8:1 a lower court's ruling holding unconstitutional the display of a Christmas Nativity scene on the front lawn of Birmingham's city hall, styling it a "purely religious symbol," in isolation, and thus violating the First Amendment ban against "establishment of religion." And shortly prior to Christmas 1986, Richmond, Virginia, withdrew its sponsorship from the fifty-five-year-old Christmas Eve Nativity pageant to avoid violating the doctrine requiring the separation of church and state. But the city continued its support of the production of *Amahl and the Night Visitors* (*Charlottesville Daily Progress,* December 3, 1986, p. C6). Similarly, see Charlottesville, Va., Christmas 1987, *Smith v. Albemarle County,* 699 F. Supp. 549 (1988), in which Judge J. Harry Michael ordered the display's removal on violation of establishment grounds. He was upheld (2:1) by the U.S. Court of Appeals for the Fourth Circuit, F.2d (1989), and again (5:3) by the full circuit court, 859 F.2d 953 (1990). The U.S. Supreme Court subsequently denied certiorari (*Albemarle County v. Smith,* 895 F.2d 953 [1990]).

286. *Allegheny County v. Greater Pittsburgh ACLU,* 497 U.S. 573.

287. *Burlington v. Kaplan,* 496 U.S. 926.

the subsequent textual discussion. The tables are designed to demonstrate that of all the questions posed by the delicate and emotion-charged issue of establishment, the leading one has been on the type, degree, and conditions under which governmental aid may be constitutionally extended to nonpublic schools. To all intents and purposes, this means predominantly Roman Catholic schools. Regardless of which of the three theories of separation one may regard as most appropriate, there are no easy answers—on either procedural or substantive grounds. The facts of life, on the other hand, are plain: the parents of several million parochial school children,[288] the vast majority of which are Roman Catholic, are members of the body politic and wield political power. When all is said and done, the issue ultimately falls into the *policy field*, heavily surcharged with considerations of public welfare in a pluralistic society with a democratic base. The sole remaining question then becomes that of the *constitutionality* of such programs as government, be it state or federal, does choose to adopt. *Is* the program a violation of the pertinent aspects of the First and/or Fourteenth Amendments? In the realistic commentary of Donald L. Drakeman:

> Had the Founding Fathers possessed the foresight to predict the multitude of interpretations we have tried to read back into their minds, they might have given us carefully crafted dissertations covering everything from the nascent public school movement to public Christmas displays. Or they might never have reached any consensus (or even majority vote) on the form of an establishment clause if they had been forced to agree on what it really meant. The Founding Fathers simply did not think they were doing anything particularly noteworthy. In the modern argot, it was no big deal. There was no national disestablishmentarian movement or cohesive impetus for national nonestablishment clause. And we err the most when we assume that there was. No matter what the Supreme Court and modern commentators have found in "proof texts," there is no clear mandate and hardly any useful guidance to be found in the records of the adoption of the establishment clause.[289]

Obviously, the judiciary, and the Supreme Court of the United States in particular, has not provided a clear-cut response to the constitutional question. At times it has upheld certain policies; at others it has struck them down. It must never be forgotten, however, that an additional consideration at the bar of judicial decision making is the Court's strong predisposition to exercise judicial self-restraint vis-à-vis legislative enactments. The Court's avowed purpose, given at least some doubt about a measure's legitimacy, is to *save*, not to destroy. It is a

288. *Standard Educational Almanac 1987* (New York: Marquis Academic Media, 1987), p. 174.
289. *Church-State Constitutional Issues: Making Sense of the Establishment Clause* (New York: Greenwood Press, 1991), p. 72.

Table 6.3. "Separation of Church and State" Cases in Which the Court Found *No Constitutional Violation**

Date	Case	Vote	Constitutional Issues Raised	Decision and Commentary
1872	*Watson v. Jones,* 13 Wallace 679	5:2	Can decision by appropriate ecclesiastical tribunals as to which of two Louisville Presbyterian church factions had the legal right to possess and operate a local church be held binding on the civil authorities as well as the churches?	The U.S. Supreme Court recognized here that the freedom and independence of churches would be in grave danger if it or any other organ of civil government undertook to define religious heresy or orthodoxy or to decide which of two factions was the "true faith." (Reconfirmed, more than a century later, in a 7:2 decision: *Serbian Orthodox Diocese v. Milivojovich,* 429 U.S. 873 [1976], and, but somewhat more equivocally, in the 5:4 decided case of *Jones v. Wolf,* 443 U.S. 595 [1979].)
1899	*Bradfield v. Roberts,* 175 U.S. 291	9:0	May Congress appropriate funds ($30,000) for a District of Columbia hospital, operated by a sisterhood of the Roman Catholic church but chartered by Congress?	Peckham held for unanimous Court that the First Amendment was *not* violated, since the hospital, as a corporation chartered by Congress, is a "purely secular agency" and does not become a religious one merely because its members are Catholic nuns.
1908	*Quick Bear v. Leupp,* 210 U.S. 50	9:0	Could U.S. government legally disburse treaty and other funds of which it was trustee for Indians (their real owners) to private religious schools, at the designation of the Indians, to defray their tuition costs?	Arrangement held constitutional on grounds that the U.S. government is necessarily "undenominational" and cannot make any law respecting an establishment of religion. It merely held the funds in a fiduciary capacity for the Indians.

(continued)

Table 6.3. *(continued)*

Date	Case	Vote	Constitutional Issues Raised	Decision and Commentary
1930	*Cochran v. Louisiana State Board of Education,* 281 U.S. 370	8:0	Validity of a Louisiana statute providing for purchase and grant of *secular* textbooks for use by public *and* nonpublic, including parochial, school children.	Initial application of the *"child benefit"* approach. Here, through its new Chief Justice, Hughes, Court held that benefits went to the "children of the state," not to the "private schools per se." "Individual interests are aided only as the common interest is safeguarded." Decision based chiefly on due process.
1947	*Everson v. Board of Education of Ewing Township, N.J.,* 330 U.S. 1	5:4	Validity of New Jersey statute authorizing bus fare reimbursement to parents of private (nonprofit) and here parochial, as well as public, school children.	Statute upheld. The famed "wall" decision. (See body of chapter for discussion and analysis.) "Public purpose" "child benefit" doctrine applied.
1952	*Zorach v. Clauson,* 343 U.S. 306	6:3	Validity of New York's "released time" program in New York City's public schools.	Upheld due to its special circumstances. (See body of chapter for discussion and analysis.)
1968	*Board of Education v. Allen,* 392 U.S. 236	6:3	Constitutionality of 1965 New York State statute requiring local school districts to *lend* books gratis to seventh- to twelfth-grade children in private and parochial schools.	Sustained on basis of broad application of the "child benefit" theory. Stinging dissents by Justices Black, Douglas, and Fortas. (See discussion in text above)
1970	*Walz v. Tax Commission of the City of New York,* 397 U.S. 664	7:1	Constitutionality of tax exemption of property used exclusively for religious purposes.	Sustained on the basis of "benevolent neutrality," i.e., on grounds that *no particular religion* is singled out for favorable treatment, and partly on the historical grounds that church tax exemptions have been accepted without challenge in *all* states for most of the nation's history. But there are limits, as the Court's (9:0) refusal in 1984 to review the tax fraud conviction of Rev. Sun Myung Moon for tax fraud (and an 18-month jail sentence) demonstrates. Sun Myung Moon had alleged government interference with the internal affairs of a church. (*The Reverend Sun Myung Moon v. United States,* 466 U.S. 971.) See also *Jimmy Swaggert Ministries v. California Board of Equalization,* Table 6.1).

Year	Case	Vote	Subject	Disposition
1971	*Tilton v. Richardson,* 403 U.S. 672	5:4	Constitutionality of $240 million Federal Higher Education Facilities Act of 1963, which funds construction of academic buildings on private sectarian as well as secular colleges.	Narrowly sustained—except for its 20-year "quit-claim" provision, which fell 9:0—on grounds that the admitted "entanglement" of church and state was "not enough" to invalidate (unlike that in the *Lemon* and *Earley* decisions made on the same day). Saved as a "one-time, single purpose construction," rather than a "continuing" grant. Justices Black, Douglas, Brennan, and Marshall dissenting in two separate opinions.
1973	*Hunt v. McNair,* 413 U.S. 734	6:3	Validity of a South Carolina state bond issue designed to aid all types of institutions of higher learning in construction, financing, and refinancing of projects of nonreligious purpose buildings.	Upheld on the strength of *Tilton* precedent in the absence of any showing that the recipient Baptist College involved was "any more of an instrument of religious indoctrination" than the institutions involved in *Tilton.*
1975	*Meek v. Pittenger,* 421 U.S. 349	6:3	Constitutionality of that portion only of a Pennsylvania statute that authorized loan of secular textbooks to private and parochial as well as public schools.	Sustained preeminently on the basis of the *Cochran* and *Allen* precedents, above, respectively.
1976	*Roemer v. Maryland Public Works Board,* 426 U.S. 736	5:4	Validity of Maryland law providing general purpose funds for nonsectarian purposes to church-affiliated colleges and universities—even if religion and theology are mandatory courses there.	Upheld by seriously divided majority on grounds that the aid neither violates the three-pronged test of "purpose," "effect," and "entanglement," nor is "pervasively sectarian." Dissenters, however, saw grants as "the disease of entanglement" between government and religion that the Constitution expressly forbids. (Reconfirmed in 1977 in North Carolina and Tennessee cases.)
1977	*Wolman v. Walter,* 433 U.S. 229		Constitutionality of a compendium of Ohio law providing a host of services to nonpublic primary and secondary schools, upheld by votes ranging from 8:1 to 6:3.	Included were certain diagnostic and therapeutic testing services, "off-ground" or "neutral," as well as book loans. (See body of text for details. Some parts of law were struck down; see Table 6:4.)

(continued)

Table 6.3. (continued)

Date	Case	Vote	Constitutional Issues Raised	Decision and Commentary
1980	*Committee for Public Education and Religious Liberty v. Regan,* 444 U.S. 646	5:4	Validity of New York statute designed to overcome the constitutional defects found by the Court in *Nyquist.* (See text above and Table 6.4.)	Seriously divided Court reluctantly sanctions reimbursement for certain expenses incurred by nonpublic schools in connection with state-mandated record-keeping and testing requirements (the latter prepared by the state rather than the teachers). Strong dissents by Brennan, Marshall, Blackmun, and Stevens.
1983	*Mueller v. Allen,* 463 U.S. 388	5:4	Constitutionality of a Minnesota law permitting parents of *all* elementary and secondary school children to deduct up to $700 annually for educational expenses from their state taxes.	Law sustained (over angry dissents by Marshall, Brennan, Blackmun, and Stevens) as a permissibly "neutral" accommodation since parents of public school children may also benefit. (See text above.)
1983	*Marsh v. Chambers,* 463 U.S. 783	6:3	Constitutionality of the widespread, time-honored practice, with roots dating back to the First Congress, of having chaplains open legislative sessions with prayer (here by an ordained Presbyterian minister for 18 consecutive years).	Overturning a lower court decision to the contrary, and basing most of his opinion on historical practice, Chief Justice Burger ruled that to "invoke Divine guidance on a public body entrusted with making the law is not, in these circumstances, an 'establishment' of religion or a step toward [it but] simply a tolerable acknowledgment of beliefs widely held [by] the people."
1984	*Lynch v. Donnelly,* 465 U.S. 668	5:4	Constitutionality of the City of Pawtucket, R.I.–sponsored practice of displaying a crèche as part of a Christmas display in a park owned by a nonprofit corporation in the heart of the city's shopping district. Expenses were defrayed by the city and downtown retail merchants.	Upheld, over dissent by Brennan, Marshall, Blackmun, and Stevens, as having only an "indirect" religious effect via a "passive symbol" and that "total separation" of church and state is neither "possible" nor "required." Burger's opinion calls for a line that "affirmatively mandates accommodation." Dissenters saw a departure from precedents. (See text above)

340

1985	Village of Scarsdale v. McCreary, 471 U.S. 83	4:4	May the Village of Scarsdale be *required* (following *Lynch,* above) to allow a nativity scene by a private group in a public park in the village's center?	With Justice Powell absent, Court affirmed 4:4 per curiam the lower court's OK, in a one-sentence order citing *Lynch.* (But the tie decision set no national precedent.)
1986	Witters v. Washington, 474 U.S. 481	9:0	Does the First Amendment bar use of state vocational rehabilitation funds to finance religious studies by a partly blind student at a Christian college?	"Not necessarily," responded a badly split Court, which, while unanimous on the adverb, split 4:3:2 on the decision's actual meaning. They agreed, however, that because the assistance was paid directly to the student, where to expend it institutionally was up to him.
1988	Bowen v. Kendrick, 487 U.S. 589	5:4	Does the First Amendment bar governmental funding for private religious as well as nonreligious community programs that deal with the problem of teen pregnancy by encouraging abstinence, adoption, and other alternatives to abortion?	"No," not on its face, held the narrow majority opinion, penned by Chief Justice Rehnquist. The Adolescent Family Life Act of 1981 does not per se violate the separation of church and state, for it "has a valid secular purpose"—here to address and develop sex education programs for teenagers. *But* a crucial test must be the law's application and administration by those who teach under it. (The Court remanded the case to the trial court to determine that factual question.) The four dissenters were the same as those in *Mueller, Lynch,* and *McCreary:* Brennan, Marshall, Blackmun, and Stevens.
1989	Allegheny County v. Greater Pittsburgh ACLU, 497 U.S. 573	6:3	Does the display of a Hanukkah menorah, placed on the steps of the Pittsburgh City–County building, together with a Christmas tree and a sign saluting freedom violate Amendment One's separation command?	"No," ruled Blackmun for the majority, for the display "conveyed the city's secular recognition of different traditions for celebrating the winter holiday season." (But compare the second holding in this case, in this chapter and Table 6.4.)

(continued)

Table 6.3. *(continued)*

Date	Case	Vote	Constitutional Issues Raised	Decision and Commentary
1990	*Board of Education of Westside Community Schools v. Mergens,* 496 U.S. 226	8:1	May Congress enact the Equal Access Act of 1984, requiring public *high* schools to allow students' religious and political clubs to meet on the same basis as other extracurricular activities?	"Yes," responded the Court in an opinion by Justice O'Connor. If the school allows student activities not related to the curriculum, it is bound by the Equal Access Act not to discriminate against any student group on the basis of its religious, philosophical, or political viewpoint. Stevens, the lone dissenter, saw "a sweeping intrusion by the federal government into the operation of the public schools." The Court, however, tangentially reaffirmed its decision (by denying review) in a 1990 Pennsylvania case involving a public school's refusal to rent space to outside religious organizations, while allowing such access to nonreligious groups (*Centennial School District v. Gregoine,* 498 U.S. 899). See also the supportive 1993 decision in *Lamb's Chapel v. Center Moriches Union Free School District* (508 U.S. 384), above and Table 6.4.
1993	*Zobrest v. Catalina School District,* 509 U.S. 1	5:4	Does the Constitution forbid the use of government funds to pay for a sign-language interpreter to accompany a deaf child to a parochial school?	"No," wrote Chief Justice Rehnquist, joined by Justices White, Kennedy, Scalia, and Thomas, thus for the first time allowing a public employee to be, in effect, part of a religious school's instructional program. But the majority insisted that, at most, the benefit to the school would be "remote," and they relied in part on the 1986 blind-student aid *Witters* 9:0 holding (above). Strong dissents were delivered by Justices Blackmun, Stevens, O'Connor, and Souter, who saw a major breach of the separation of church and state requirement.

Year	Case	Vote	Question	Holding
1995	*Capitol Square Review Board v. Pinette,* 515 U.S. 753	7:2	Did Ohio violate the establishment clause when, pursuant to a religiously neutral state policy, it permitted the Ku Klux Klan to display a cross in front of the state's capitol?	Over separate dissents by Justices Stevens and Ginsburg, Justice Scalia's majority opinion held that the KKK had a free-speech right to erect a cross on the capitol grounds in Columbus, which Ohio operates as a public forum, open to a variety of private expression.
1997	*Agostini v. Felton,* 521 U.S. 203	5:4	May public school teachers provide remedial instruction for children in parochial schools under Title I of the Federal Aid to Elementary and Secondary Schools Act of 1965?	Yes, wrote Justice O'Connor in her majority opinion, which explicitly overturned the Court's opposite ruling twelve years earlier in *Aguilar v. Felton.* (See Table 6.4.)
1998	*Jackson v. Benson,* 67 LW 3322	8:1	May Wisconsin provide low-income parents $5,000 yearly to defray schooling expenses in *both* public and private schools?	In a one-line order (albeit without a formal written opinion on the merits), the Court allowed the law to stand in the face of "blatantly" unconstitutional challenges. Only Justice Breyer dissented.
1999	*Bagley v. Raymond School District,* 68 LW 325, and *Stroud v. Albanese,* 68 LW 3250		May Maine and Vermont subsidize students who attend *private* schools but exclude *religious* ones?	Without formal opinions or stances, the Court refused to accept the challenge to the Maine and Vermont laws.
2000	*Koenick v. Felton,* 68 LW 3459		May Maryland require public schools to close on Good Friday?	Rejecting a constitutional challenge to the Maryland law, sans comment, thus leaving intact a ruling by the Fourth U.S. Circuit Court of Appeals that had concluded that the holiday law had a "clear secular purpose," namely, to avoid holding school on days when many teachers and students would be absent.
2000	*Mitchell v. Helms,* 530 U.S. 793	6:3	Does Chapter 2 of the Federal Elementary and Secondary Education Act of 1965 permit the use of taxpayer funds to buy computers and other instructional materials for religious schools (in Louisiana)?	Notwithstanding a bevy of its rulings in the 1970s and 1980s, the Court's splintered decision thus enabled the expenditure of funds in "secular, neutral and nonideological" ways for parochial schools. Justice Thomas wrote for a plurality that included Rehnquist, Scalia, and Kennedy. Justices O'Connor and Breyer concurred with qualifications. Justices Stevens and Ginsburg joined Justice Souter's strong dissenting opinion.

(continued)

Table 6.3. (continued)

Date	Case	Vote	Constitutional Issues Raised	Decision and Commentary
2002	*Zelman v. Simmons-Harris*, 536 U.S. ___.	5:4	May Ohio enact a "voucher" law that provides tuition aid for financially needy students *both* for religious and nonreligious schools, the choice being entirely up to the parents?	"Yes," held a 5:4 majority in Chief Justice Rehnquist's opinion, joined by Justices O'Connor, Scalia, Kennedy, and Thomas, finding no violation of the separation of church and state. Three lengthy opinions in dissent were headed by Justice Souter's anguished and angry opinion denouncing the majority's "dramatic departure from basic Establishment Clause principles."

*Some "mixed" cases, such as the *Sunday-Closing Law Cases*, in which the "free exercise" issues predominated, are found in Table 6.1.

Table 6.4. "Separation of Church and State" Cases in Which the Court *Did Find* Constitutional Violation*

Date	Case	Vote	Constitutional Issues Raised	Decision and Commentary
1815	*Terrett v. Tyler,* 9 Cranch 43	5:0	Validity of Virginia recession statute that negated the charter of the Virginia Episcopal church as a corporation and directed that its parish lands be sold and its proceeds used for the poor of the parish.	Not *truly* a "separation" issue, for the case was decided under principles of general corporate law. Nonetheless, this case established the principle that a state cannot deny to members of a religious corporation the right to retain a corporate charter and continue to act as a corporation.
1925	*Pierce v. Society of Sisters of the Holy Names of Jesus and Mary,* 268 U.S. 510	9:0	Constitutionality of Oregon's Compulsory Education Act of 1922 requiring every child from eight to sixteen to attend *public* school. (The "Sisters" conducted a group of *private* schools, according to the tenets of the Roman Catholic church.)	The act held to interfere "unreasonably" with the liberty of parents and guardians to direct the upbringing and education of child under their control. (Also not purely a "separation" case issue—it was decided on due process grounds—but related to it.) Similarly, see *Meyer v. Nebraska,* 262 U.S. 390 (1923), and the free exercise case of *Wisconsin v. Yoder,* 406 U.S. 205 (1972).
1948	*Illinois ex rel. McCollum v. Board of Education,* 333 U.S. 203	8:1	Validity of Champaign, Illinois, arrangements permitting "released time" programs on public school property under attendance sanctions.	Struck down as violative of separation concepts inherent in Amendments One and Fourteen. (See body of chapter for discussion and analysis.)
1952	*Kedroff v. Saint Nicholas Cathedral,* 344 U.S. 94	8:1	Authority of New York State to deprive the Moscow hierarchy of the Russian Orthodox Church of control over all its church property in New York by forceful statutory transfer to the local "Russian Church in America."	A state is no more allowed than the federal government to enact a law impairing the separation of church and state. Government has no capacity to intervene in religious controversies or determine which is "the true faith."
1962	*Engel v. Vitale,* 370 U.S. 421	6:1	Constitutionality of New York State composed 22-word nondenominational prayer administered in public schools.	"The New York laws officially prescribing the Regents' prayer are inconsistent with both the purposes of the Establishment Clause and with the Establishment Clause itself." (See text above for full discussion.)

(continued)

Table 6.4. (continued)

Date	Case	Vote	Constitutional Issues Raised	Decision and Commentary
1963	Abington School District v. Schempp and Murray v. Curlett, 374 U.S. 203	8:1	Validity of Pennsylvania's statutory requirement of reading of 10 verses from Holy Bible in public schools and Maryland's practice of daily Bible reading and Lord's Prayer recitation in public schools.	All three procedures held to violate the establishment clause, following Engel. (See text above for discussion and analysis.)
1968	Epperson v. Arkansas, 393 U.S. 97	9:0	Constitutionality of Arkansas "monkey law," a statute that made it unlawful to teach the theory that mankind is ascended or descended from a lower order of animals.	Law violates establishment of religion clause by embodying the idea of a particular segment of religious beliefs and proscribing all others. (In 1982 U.S. District Court Judge Wm. R. Overton declared Arkansas's "creation science" law unconstitutional. McLean v. Arkansas Board of Education, 723 F.2d 45.)
1969	Presbyterian Church v. Mary Elizabeth Blue Hull Memorial Church, 393 U.S. 440	9:0	May civil courts award church property to dissident congregations on the grounds that the parent church has lost the faith?	"First Amendment values are plainly jeopardized when church litigation is made to turn on the resolution by civil courts of controversies over religious doctrine and practice."
1971	Lemon v. Kurtzman and Earley v. Dicenso, 403 U.S. 602	8:0 8:1	Constitutionality of direct aid to Pennsylvania and Rhode Island parochial schools, involving state "purchase" of secular "services" in sectarian schools, including the use of public funds to pay salaries of parochial school teachers.	Both statutes struck down as involving "excessive entanglement between government and religion." Chief Justice Burger also pointed to "divisive political potential" of the laws, an "evil" the First Amendment was designed to avoid. White, in the solo dissent, saw no "excessive entanglement," finding "separable" secular functions. (See text above.)
1972	Essex v. Wolman, 409 U.S. 808	8:1	Constitutionality of an Ohio plan for direct tuition rebates of $90 annually per child attending a private or parochial school.	Struck down as "excessive entanglement," as a violation of the establishment clause, because "the effect of the scheme is to aid religious enterprises."
1973	Levitt v. Commission for Public Education and Religious	8:1 6:3 6:3	Validity of several New York and Pennsylvania programs of diversely attempted financial aid to private, chiefly parochial, schools, including	All statutes involved fell as "eroding . . . the limitations of the establishment clause now firmly implanted." Powell's opinions stressed

Year	Case	Vote	Issue	Ruling
	Liberty, 413 U.S. 472; *Committee for Public Education and Religious Liberty v. Nyquist*, 413 U.S. 756; and *Sloan v. Lemon*, 413 U.S. 825		tuition reimbursement, tax relief, repairs and maintenance, nonmandated testing, remedial classes, instructional equipment, and counseling.	that the programs all advanced religion in that they directly subsidized "the religious activities" of sectarian schools. (See text above.)
1974	*Marburger and Griggs v. Public Funds for Public Schools*, 417 U.S. 961	6:3	Constitutionality of two New Jersey programs providing money to parents of parochial school students, and also providing supplies and auxiliary services to those schools at public expense.	Court, per curiam, affirmed declaration of unconstitutionality below on basis of absence of bona fide child benefit theory applicability and on the basis of its own 1973 *Nyquist* rulings.
1975	*Meek v. Pittenger*, 421 U.S. 349	6:3	Constitutionality of another Pennsylvania attempt to provide sundry auxiliary services to private and parochial as well as public schools, including counseling, testing, remedial classes, and equipment. (Textbook loan provision was upheld.)	Same majority as *Nyquist, Sloan,* and *Marburger* held such provisions raised "the danger that religious doctrine will be intertwined with the secular institutions" and created a "serious potential for divisive conflict over the issue of aid to religion." Dissents by Burger, White, and Rehnquist. (See text above.)
1977	*Wolman v. Walter*, 433 U.S. 220		Validity of certain services by Ohio to nonpublic primary and secondary schools. Some upheld (see Table 6.3); some struck down, 6:3 and 5:4.	While upholding four such services (see Table 6.3), Court struck down financial aid for field trips (5:4) and for certain class paraphernalia (6:3).
1977	*New York v. Cathedral Academy*, 434 U.S. 125	6:3	Constitutionality of New York's $11 million of *direct* reimbursement to parochial schools for record-keeping and testing services.	Over dissents by Burger, White, and Rehnquist, six members held law to be unconstitutional by providing either direct aid to religion or producing "excessive state involvement in religious affairs." (But cf. its 1980 *Regan* holding above and Table 6.3.)

(continued)

Table 6.4. *(continued)*

Date	Case	Vote	Constitutional Issues Raised	Decision and Commentary
1979	*National Labor Relations Board v. Bishop of Chicago,* 440 U.S. 490	5:4	May a sectarian institution, such as a Roman Catholic school, be required to bargain collectively with a union?	Ducking the First Amendment's constitutional issue(s), the narrow majority ruled that there was no clear-cut affirmative congressional intention ascertainable in the National Labor Relations Board that would extend its coverage to teachers in church-operated schools.
1979	*Byrne v. Public Funds for Public Schools,* 442 U.S. 907	6:3	Constitutionality of New Jersey statute providing a special income tax deduction for parents who send children to nonpublic schools.	In a one-sentence order, the Court here affirmed two lower federal courts that had held that the tax deduction had the "primary effect of advancing religion."
1980	*Stone v. Graham,* 449 U.S. 39	5:4	Constitutionality of a Kentucky law requiring posting of a copy of the Ten Commandments in every public school classroom in the state.	Although paid for with private rather than tax funds, the practice fell as not being a "permissible state objective under the establishment clause."
1981	*Hall v. Bradshaw,* 450 U.S. 965	9:0	Constitutionality of a North Carolina practice of publishing a "motorist's prayer" on its official highway map.	Denying review, the Court, without dissent, upheld a decision below that saw a patent violation of the Constitution's bar against state establishment of religion.
1981	*St. Martin's Lutheran Church v. South Dakota,* 451 U.S. 772	9:0	Are religious schools that are "integrated into a church's structure," and have no separate identity, obliged to pay unemployment taxes for their employees?	Ducking the First Amendment's constitutional issue, the Court ruled that Congress had not intended to reach such schools, in contrast to those that are church-related but not directly church-run.
1981	*Widmar v. Vincent,* 454 U.S. 263	8:1	May Missouri's statute prohibiting the use of university buildings or grounds "for purposes of religious worship or religious training" be applied to regulate the content of religious speech by a duly registered student religious group?	Over a strange dissent by White, the Powell-led majority chose to view Missouri's regulation as a "content-based discrimination against religious speech," violative of the First Amendment's strictures against impeding freedom of speech, thereby inferentially violating the religion clauses. (In 1984

Year	Case	Vote	Question	Commentary
				Congress responded by enacting the Equal Access Act, which legitimizes the right of students to conduct any "political, religious, or philosophical" meeting on the school premises. See its 1990 upholding in *Mergens*, Table 6.3.)
1982	*Larsen v. Valente*, 456 U.S. 229	5:4	May Minnesota exempt some religious groups from stringent fund-raising reporting requirements on charitable solicitations, while placing that burden on others?	"No," ruled Brennan (over dissents by Burger, White, Rehnquist, and O'Connor), because the rules "do not operate evenhandedly [and are] precisely the sort of official denominational preference the framers of the First Amendment forbade."
1982	*Larkin v. Grendel's Den*, 454 U.S. 1140	8:1	May Massachusetts statutorily allow churches to control whether nearby restaurants may have liquor licenses? The law literally allowed churches to exercise a veto.	With only Rehnquist dissenting, Burger held that giving the church the power of a government agency "enmeshes churches in the exercise of substantial governmental powers contrary to . . . First Amendment" strictures against establishment.
1985	*Wallace v. Jaffree*, 472 U.S. 38	6:3	Can Alabama's statute authorize a one-minute period of silence in all public schools "for meditation or voluntary prayer"?	Although the law was permissive in form, the Court found it to have a clearly sectarian purpose and therefore to be the kind of enactment specifically proscribed by the seminal 1962 ruling in *Engel v. Vitale*. (See text above.) Note the important dissent by Rehnquist, who embraces the "no preference" concept.
1985	*Grand Rapids School District v. Ball*, 473 U.S. 373	7:2 and 5:4	Are the school district's "Shared Time" and "Community Education" programs constitutional? They supplement the core curriculum offered students in private schools. School district pays personnel and furnishes supplies and materials for classes during regular school day in rooms located in and leased from the private schools. All but one of the 41 participating schools are religious schools.	Down went both programs, 7:2 and 5:4, respectively, for they were viewed as having the effect of promoting religion in several ways, indeed "the primary or principal" ones, and thus violate "the dictates of the Establishment Clause of the First Amendment." (White and Rehnquist dissent in both, Burger and O'Connor only in the first program.)

(continued)

Table 6.4. (continued)

Date	Case	Vote	Constitutional Issues Raised	Decision and Commentary
1985	*Aguilar v. Felton*, 473 U.S. 402	5:4	May New York City provide instructional services, funded under Title I of the Federal Aid to Elementary and Secondary Schools of 1965, to parochial schools on the latter's premises? Although instruction was by public school teachers, the city utilized a system for monitoring the religious content of such Title I classes.	"No," ruled the Court by a 5:4 vote (Burger, White, Rehnquist, and O'Connor dissenting), because the risk of "substantial state-sponsored indoctrination" oversteps the "constitutional line between allowable governmental accommodation of religion and direct financial aid," notwithstanding the worthy goals promoted by the federal program. (See *Agostini v. Felton*, Table 6.3, overruling *Aguilar* 5:4 twelve years later.)
1987	*Edwards v. Aguillard*, 482 U.S. 578	7:2	May Louisiana require the teaching of "creationism" to balance that of "evolution" in its public school curriculum?	"No," held Brennan's opinion, with Scalia and Rehnquist dissenting, striking it down as a crass violation of separation. Another try by Louisiana fell 6:3 in *Tangipahoa Parish Board of Education v. Freiler*, 68 LW 3771 (2000).
1989	*Texas Monthly v. Bullock*, 489 U.S. 1	6:3	May Texas exempt religious publications from a sales tax it applies to all other publications?	No," ruled the 6:3 Court, in a Brennan opinion "finding a clear violation of the establishment clause. Dissenters: Scalia, Rehnquist, and Kennedy.
1989	*Allegheny County v. Greater Pittsburgh ACLU*, 497 U.S. 573	5:4	May Pittsburgh and Allegheny Co., given the Court's holdings in *Lynch* and *McCreary* (Table 6.3), display a Nativity scene inside the Allegheny County courthouse?	"No," responded Blackmun for the Court—which, in a companion case, *upheld a different Christmas display* (Table 6.3)—because it appeared to endorse Christian principles and thus violates the First Amendment's establishment clause.
1992	*Lee v. Weisman*, 505 U.S. 577	5:4	Do nonsectarian benedictions and invocations at public school graduation ceremonies (here by a rabbi) violate the establishment clause?	"Yes," held Kennedy for the bitterly divided Court, joined by Blackmun, Stevens, O'Connor, and Souter. Dissenting, Scalia, Rehnquist, White, and Thomas styled the decision "senseless" and "unsupported in law." A year later, the Court, without comment, let stand a lower court ruling

Year	Case	Vote		
				upholding a *student*-led and *student*-planned prayer at a Texas public school graduation (*Jones v. Clear Creek Independent School District*, 61 LW 3819). And in 1997 it rejected a challenge to Indiana University's custom of having a clergy member offer two prayers at the school's graduation ceremony each May (*Tanford v. Brand*, 66 LW 3248).
1993	*Lamb's Chapel v. Center Moriches Free Union School District*, 508 U.S. 384	9:0	May public school districts prevent church groups from using their classrooms after hours simply because of the group's religious purpose?	In what was a victory for both religious organizations and free-speech advocates, the Court, albeit splintered in its reasoning, used much of the 1981 *Widmar* decision (Table 6.3) in finding *no* constitutional violation of the separation of church and state mandate of the First Amendment, but rather a distinct violation of its freedom of speech guarantees. See also the 2001 *Good News* ruling in this table.
1994	*Board of Education of Kiryas Joel Village v. Grumet*, 512 U.S. 687	6:3	May New York carve out a separate school district, following village lines, to accommodate a particular community of "highly religious Satmar Hasidic Jews" in order to avoid having the community's special needs/handicapped children attend the local public schools?	"No," responded a 3+1+1+1 plurality, with the lead opinion penned by Souter. Relying on *Larkin v. Grendel's Den*, op. cit., he held that "a State may not delegate its civic authority to a group chosen according to a religious criterion." Dissenting, Scalia, joined by the chief justice and Thomas, argued that the accommodation here at issue was primarily one of culture and not of religion; that New York's 1989 law was "facially neutral"; that the "neutrality demanded by the Religion Clauses requires the same indulgence towards cultural characteristics that are accompanied by religious belief." A few days after the Court's 1994 decision, New York—in an approach suggested by Justice O'Connor's concurring opinion in *Kiryas*—passed a *general* law, not

(continued)

Table 6.4. (continued)

Date	Case	Vote	Constitutional Issues Raised	Decision and Commentary
	Board of Education of Kiryas Joel Village v. Grumet, 512 U.S. 687 (continued)			limited to Kiryas Joel, but aiming to produce the same results as that produced by the invalidated specific law. In its first court test less than a year later, Justice Lawrence Kalin of the New York Supreme Court upheld the statute in Grumet v. Cuomo, N. Y. Sup. Ct., 3d Ind. Dist., Dock. #4210-94, March 8, 1995. However, four years later the U.S. Supreme Court, by a 6:3 vote, rejected New York State's third attempt to create a special school district for the disabled Hasidic Jewish children in the Kiryas Joel community (Pataki v. Grumet, 68 LW 3246).
1995	Rosenberger v. University of Virginia, 515 U.S. 819	5:4	May the University of Virginia's student council—an instrumentality of the Commonwealth of Virginia—deny funding to a Christian student newspaper (Wide Awake) simply because of the religious commitment of the sponsoring student organization?	Relying on its unanimous decision in Lamb's Chapel two years earlier (see above), the Court, speaking through Justice Kennedy, held that the University's action constituted an impermissible viewpoint violation under the First Amendment freedom of expression mandates.
2000	Santa Fe Independent School District v. Doe, 530 U.S. 290	6:3	May a public school district have a policy that allows an elected student representative to deliver a public invocation before home high school football games?	"No," said Stevens's majority opinion over a strong dissenting opinion by Chief Justice Rehnquist, joined by Justices Scalia and Thomas, noting that the election of a student did not alter the fact that the school district was actually sponsoring pregame prayers.
2001	Good News Club v. Milford Central School, 533 U.S. 198	6:3	May a school deny the after-hour use of its building to an evangelical religious club for elementary school students while permitting nonreligious groups to utilize the school?	With Justices Stevens, Souter, and Ginsburg seeing a violation of the separation of church and state, in passionate dissent, the Thomas-led majority saw an impermissible First Amendment violation (based on viewpoint), citing Rosenberger.

*Some "mixed" cases, such as Torcaso v. Watkins, involving both separation and free exercise issues, are found in Table 6.2.

recognition of this basic maxim of judicial self-restraint that will facilitate an understanding of decisions that, at least on paper, would seem to be diametrically opposite. Thus, we have witnessed three levels of approach which the Court has utilized.

Level 1. The Court *strikes down* a measure or practice as a clearly and demonstrably unconstitutional infringement of the no establishment clause—because, in whole or in part, it is simply and patently unconstitutional (and usually, although not always, so regarded by a large majority of the justices). Some pertinent examples are the *Illinois Released Time Case,*[290] in which the released-time programs were held on public school property (8:1); the *Oregon Compulsory Education Law Case,*[291] in which that state *required* attendance at public schools (9:0); the *New York Prayer Case,*[292] in which the public school prayer composed and administered by New York State was declared unconstitutional (8:1); the *Pennsylvania and Maryland Bible Reading Cases,*[293] in which statutes and practices requiring public school reading of Bibles and the Lord's Prayer met a like fate (8:1 and 8:1); the *Arkansas "Monkey Law" Case,*[294] in which the proscription of the teaching of evolution fell (9:0); the *Pennsylvania and Rhode Island "purchase of secular services and direct salary supplemental laws"*[295] and the *Ohio* direct tuition reimbursement grants statute,[296] which fell on grounds of "excessive entanglement" of church and state (8:0, 8:1, and 8:1); the five *New York* and *Pennsylvania* laws,[297] providing numerous forms of financial aid to nonpublic schools, and the renewed 1975 *Pennsylvania* statutory endeavors[298] to attain the same end, all of which fell in 1973 as having a primary *effect* of aiding religion (8:1, 6:3, 6:3). The Court also struck down *Ohio*'s renewed efforts to provide certain class paraphernalia (6:3 and 5:4);[299] *New York*'s move *directly to reimburse* parochial schools for record-keeping and testing services (6:3) and to carve out a special public school district to accommodate the needs of handicapped children of a highly religious Jewish Hasidic community (6:3);[300] *New Jersey*'s attempt to legislate income tax deductions for parents of parochial

290. *Illinois ex rel. McCollum v. Board of Education,* 333 U.S. 203 (1948).

291. *Pierce v. Society of Sisters of the Holy Names,* 268 U.S. 510 (1925).

292. *Engel v. Vitale,* 279 U.S. 421 (1962).

293. *Abington School District v. Schempp* and *Murray v. Curlett,* 374 U.S. 203 (1963).

294. *Epperson v. Arkansas,* 393 U.S. 97 (1968).

295. *Lemon v. Kurtzman* and *Earley v. Dicenso,* 403 U.S. 602 (1971).

296. *Essex v. Wolman,* 409 U.S. 808 (1972).

297. *Levitt v. Committee for Public Education and Religious Liberty,* 413 U.S. 472; *Committee for Public Education and Religious Liberty v. Nyquist,* 413 U.S. 756; and *Sloan v. Lemon,* 413 U.S. 825 (1973).

298. *Meek v. Pittenger,* 421 U.S. 349.

299. *Wolman v. Walter,* 433 U.S. 229 (1977).

300. *New York v. Cathedral Academy,* 434 U.S. 125 (1977); and *Board of Education of Kiryas Joel Village v. Grumet,* 512 U.S. 687 (1994).

school students (6:3);[301] the Alabama Period of Silence law (6:3), which authorized a one-minute period of silence for "meditation or prayer" in all public schools;[302] and two *Louisiana* statutes mandating the teaching of the creationist theory of man's origin alongside evolution in public schools (7:2 and 6:3).[303]

Although fully aware of the relative unpopularity of some of its decisions, especially in the third and fourth illustrations (which evoked an emotional, popular reaction that was often uninformed and sometimes absurd, given the clear limits of the decisions involved), the Court did not hesitate to do what it clearly considered its duty under the commands of the Constitution. And it did so with but 31 dissenting votes cast of the 158 cast above altogether, one of the former coming on procedural rather than substantive grounds.

Level 2. The Court, perhaps somewhat uncomfortably at times, and often severely divided, *upholds* a measure or practice because it believes that it can stand under the principle of "auxiliary" or "general public policy" rather than as "primary" or "specific" governmental aid to a nonpublic school—often rationalized under the controversial "child benefit" theory. Appropriate illustrations are the *Louisiana Textbooks to All Case,*[304] which enabled use of textbooks purchased with public funds by pupils of public *and* nonpublic schools (8:0); although that case was actually decided on "due process" grounds rather than on the religious issue per se, it was confirmed and expanded (6:3) by the 1968 *New York Textbook Case,*[305] which did deal with the establishment issue directly; it was the only provision that escaped (6:3) unconstitutionality in the 1975 Pennsylvania *Meek v. Pittenger* holding,[306] and it was upheld (6:3) in the 1977 Ohio *Wolman v. Walter* litigation;[307] the *New Jersey Bus Case,*[308] the famous "wall" decision, upholding public subventions for transportation of parochial as well as public school students (5:4); the *New York Released Time Case,*[309] where religious classes were held *outside* public school buildings during the school day for those wishing to attend, with the others continuing secular education (6:3); the tax exemption of wholly church-owned property in the *New York Tax Exemption Case* (7:1);[310] the *Federal Education Facilities Act Case,* narrowly (5:4) upholding construction grants to both sectarian and nonsectarian col-

301. *Byrne v. Public Funds for Public Schools,* 442 U.S. 907 (1979).

302. *Wallace v. Jaffree,* 466 U.S. 924 (1985).

303. *Edwards v. Aguillard,* 482 U.S. 578 (1987); and *Tangipahoa Parish Board of Education v. Freiler,* 68 LW 2711 (2001).

304. *Cochran v. Louisiana State Board of Education,* 281 U.S. 370 (1930).

305. *Board of Education v. Allen,* 392 U.S. 236.

306. 421 U.S. 349.

307. 433 U.S. 229.

308. *Everson v. Board of Education of Ewing Township,* 330 U.S. 1 (1947).

309. *Zorach v. Clauson,* 343 U.S. 306 (1952).

310. *Walz v. Tax Commissioners of New York City,* 397 U.S. 664 (1970).

leges;[311] the 1973 *South Carolina Aid to Education Case,*[312] which sanctioned (6:3) a scheme providing state bond aid to *all* educational institutions of higher learning; the 1976 *Maryland Aid to Church-Affiliated Colleges and Universities Case,*[313] which upheld (5:4) a program of general grants for nonsectarian use even in institutions where religion is mandatory; the 1977 *Ohio Multiple Primary and Secondary Aid to All Case,*[314] upholding such heretofore unapproved state services to nonpublic schools as certain mandatory testing, diagnostic, and therapeutic services (6:3, 8:1, and 7:2, respectively); and the *New York 1980 Aid to Parochial and Other Nonpublic Schools Aid Case,*[315] sanctioning (5:4) reimbursement for certain state-required administration and testing services, provided these were prepared by the state rather than by the teachers; the highly controversial 1983 *Minnesota Parental Tax Deduction Case,*[316] upholding (5:4) that state's law permitting parents of all elementary and secondary school children to deduct annually up to $700 for educational expenses, be the schools private or public; the practice of having ordained, taxpayer-paid clergy open legislative sessions with a prayer, upheld (6:3) in the 1983 *Marsh v. Chambers Legislative Chaplains Case;*[317] the 1984 *Pawtucket, R.I., Crèche Case,*[318] in which that city's financial support of a Christmas display, including a crèche, was upheld (5:4), the Court viewing it as a "historic symbol" rather than as a religious practice, and the related 1989 ruling in the *Allegheny County Case* (see *supra* this chapter).

Here, although much more sharply split, with 45 of 140 total votes cast by the justices in dissent (roughly one-third, compared with circa one-fifth in the Level 1 group), the Court believed itself justified in accommodating public policy that raised questions about, but was not regarded as violative of, separation of church and state.

Level 3. The Court, on the basis of the principle of judicial self-restraint or because it adjudges the matter res judicata, either refuses to accept a case for review or simply affirms the decision below. This judicial practice may well have the effect of sanctioning practices in one state that are unconstitutional in another, since in each separate instance they were so held by the state courts concerned, but considerations of federalism are far from absent in the judicial process. Some random instances are:

Despite its decision confirming Louisiana's, New York's, Ohio's, and Penn-

---

311. *Tilton v. Richardson,* 403 U.S. 672 (1971).
312. *Hunt v. McNair,* 413 U.S. 734.
313. *Roemer v. Maryland Public Works Board,* 426 U.S. 736.
314. *Wolman v. Walter,* 433 U.S. 229.
315. *Committee for Public Education and Religious Liberty v. Regan,* 444 U.S. 646.
316. *Mueller v. Allen,* 463 U.S. 388.
317. *Marsh v. Chambers,* 463 U.S. 783.
318. *Lynch v. Donnelly,* 465 U.S. 688.

sylvania's free loan of textbooks for parochial schools laws,[319] the Court denied certiorari in an Oregon case,[320] thereby upholding a 6:1 decision by the Oregon Supreme Court that school districts must *stop* providing free textbooks to parochial schools; it even reconfirmed that decision one year later; New Mexico's and South Dakota's highest courts ruled likewise; it affirmed (6:3) a New Jersey decision declaring unconstitutional two state programs that provided cash funds to parents of nonpublic school students for the *purchase* of textbooks, and further provided supplies and auxiliary services to such schools at public expense;[321] and the Court declined to review a Missouri Supreme Court decision invalidating a Missouri law that authorized textbook *loans* to children in church-related schools as well as those in public and nonsectarian private schools.[322]

Regardless of its decision in the *New Jersey Bus Case* of 1948[323] the Court has refused to review, or has simply summarily affirmed,[324] innumerable state court decisions declaring *unconstitutional,* as violative of the respective state constitutions, free transportation provisions for parochial as well as public school children in, among other states, Alaska, Iowa, Missouri, New Mexico, Oklahoma, Washington, and Wisconsin. In fact, all of these came after the *New Jersey Bus Case*—although by mid-1987 twenty-seven of the states provided some type of transportation aid to parochial schools, several of which had found state judicial approval (e.g., Connecticut)—and subsequent Supreme Court sanction by virtue of refusal to review (e.g., Pennsylvania).[325]

Despite other state precedents *to the contrary,* the Court refused to review,[326] and thereby upheld, a Vermont Supreme Court decision holding unconstitutional the use of public funds for tuition payable to children attending either public or private schools of their own choice in the instance of towns that had no high schools of their own. Again, despite other state practices to the contrary, the Court refused to review,[327] and thus upheld, a 4:3 Maryland Court of Appeals decision that declared unconstitutional as a violation of the *First* Amendment the subvention of matching state grants for construction purposes to two Maryland Roman Catholic colleges (Notre Dame and St. Joseph) and one Methodist college (Western Maryland), while upholding similar grants to Hood College. It had regarded Hood's character "essentially secular" but deemed the other three as

319. See *supra* notes 304–312.
320. *Dickman v. School District, Oregon City,* 371 U.S. 823 (1962).
321. *Marburger and Griggs v. Public Funds for Public Schools,* 417 U.S. 961 (1974).
322. *Reynolds v. Paster,* 419 U.S. 1111 (1975).
323. *Everson v. Board of Education of Ewing Township,* 330 U.S. 1.
324. *Luetkemeyer v. Kaufmann,* 419 U.S. 888 (1974).
325. See *Rhoades v. Washington,* 389 U.S. 11 (1967); and *Worrell v. Matters,* 389 U.S. 846 (1967).
326. *Anderson v. Swart,* 366 U.S. 925 (1961).
327. *Board of Public Works of Maryland v. Horace Mann League of U.S.,* 385 U.S. 97 (1966); and *Horace Mann League of United States v. Board of Public Works of Maryland,* 385 U.S. 97 (1966).

clearly projecting a religious "image" (only to reverse itself [5:4] a decade later!).[328] It summarily affirmed (6:3) a lower federal court decision invalidating a California law that authorized state income tax reductions for parents of parochial school students,[329] yet nine years later it would sanction Minnesota's that permitted such deductions in all schools.[330] And, as noted earlier,[331] the Court had affirmed a decision by Maryland that *upheld* state tax *exemptions* for church buildings.

Obviously, the issue was far from settled in the 1980s. Notwithstanding *constitutional* proscriptions in thirty-six states, fully forty-seven (!) provided some sort of aid to church-related schools in 1988—often in the face of these constitutional prohibitions. Thus, twenty-seven states provided pupil transportation; twenty-six, textbooks; twenty-three, health services; seven, "general auxiliary" services; and three still "purchased services" from nonpublic schools and paid salary supplements to teachers in these schools—notwithstanding Supreme Court holdings to the contrary in similar cases.

In terms of experience these three "levels" are readily explainable and just as readily serve to reemphasize the difficulty, if not perhaps the utter impossibility, of creating and drawing a viable, predictable line between the permissible and the impermissible in the realm of the establishment clause in general and in that of the subsection of public and private education in particular. Still, some outlines of the lines that can be drawn are perceptible in general terms—if not in specific Court judgments. They can be identified, although their application cannot be predicted safely.

Some Overall Policy Positions. A number of these outlines have clearly emerged and may be stated broadly as follows:

First, because it is intended to serve pupils of all religious faiths, a public school in democratic society is ipso facto a secular institution. This, of course, does not mean that the public school either is, should be, or is intended to be anti- or irreligious—and the judiciary as well as the legislature have made this amply clear.

Second, freedom of conscience in all its religious aspects and concepts must be, and is, protected.

Third, while it is axiomatic that it is incumbent upon the federal government to protect freedom of religion and to ascertain the separation of church and state in the several states of the Union, responsibility for public school curriculum and administration lodges with the state. Just as applicable provisions of the Civil

---

328. The issue had been revived in 1974–75, when Maryland, having reinstituted a somewhat revamped program, won a victory in a three-judge district court ruling, which was appealed to the U.S. Supreme Court; the latter sustained the lower tribunal in 1976 (*Roemer v. Maryland Public Works Board,* 426 U.S. 736).

329. *Franchise Tax Board v. United Americans,* 419 U.S. 890 (1974).

330. *Mueller v. Allen,* 463 U.S. 388 (1983).

331. See *supra* note 217.

Rights Act of 1964 and the Federal Aid to Elementary and Secondary Education Act of 1965, both as amended, have had far-reaching impact in altering that tradition, so indeed have they indubitably had at the level of higher education.

Fourth, notwithstanding the contemporary changes just described, public education in the several states is controlled preeminently by duly appointed and/or elected public state officials.

Fifth, although attendance of public schools is inevitably one of the hallmarks of the body politic in the several states, no state may compel school-age students to attend *public* as distinct from private or parochial schools, and no state has tried to do so since Oregon's defeat at the hands of a unanimous Supreme Court in the *Pierce* case[332] in 1925.

Sixth, on the other hand, a state constitutional provision (e.g., Missouri's) that *forbids* the expenditure of public funds to church-related schools does *not* violate the religious freedom (free exercise) of parents who choose to send their children to sectarian schools.[333] This posture was firmly reiterated by Chief Justice Burger for the Court in 1973: "Even assuming that the equal protection clauses might require state aid to be granted to private nonsectarian schools in some circumstances—health care or textbooks, for example—a State could rationally conclude as a matter of legislative policy that constitutional neutrality as to certain schools might best be achieved by withholding all state assistance."[334]

Seventh, either by constitutional provision or by statute, most states have endeavored to prevent the "direct" disbursement or subvention of any funds from the public state treasury to any parochial or otherwise denominational school—although at least some states have acted to "purchase services," pay salaries, and rebate taxes, sometimes called "parochaid," devices that were declared unconstitutional severally by the Supreme Court in 1971, 1973, 1974, 1975, 1977, 1979, and 1985.[335] Most states have permitted, or even encouraged, the providing of one or more, or even all, of the following "auxiliary" services to accredited nonpublic schools: tax exemptions; free lunches; free medical care; free protective services; free school nurse services; free textbook loans; free bus transportation; free driver education; certain diagnostic, testing, therapeutic, and record-keeping services; and other similar governmental aid, usually termed "indirect," "general," or "auxiliary." It should be noted again here, however, that many of these practices have been specifically forbidden in some states and/or held to be unconstitutional by their state courts, while the precise *opposite* has been held in others.[336]

332. *Pierce v. Society of Sisters of the Holy Names,* 268 U.S. 510.
333. *Brusca v. State Board of Education of Missouri,* 405 U.S. 1050 (1972).
334. *Norwood v. Harrison,* 413 U.S. 455 (1973) at 462.
335. See discussion on preceding pages and Table 6.4.
336. The controversy was demonstrated by the successful veto by Delaware Governor Charles L. Terry Jr. early in 1966 of a bill that would have provided free bus transportation for parochial and other private school students. At approximately the same time, Governor W. W. Scranton of Pennsylvania *signed* a similar measure. Both chief execu-

Eighth, even prior to the *Illinois Released Time Case,*[337] the type of denominational or sectarian teaching there at issue was specifically forbidden by most states. Yet a number always did, and still do, permit the kind of "released time" practiced in New York and upheld in the *New York Released Time Case.*[338]

Ninth, state-mandated religious observances in the public schools, such as prayers, Bible reading, and recitation of the Lord's Prayer, practiced widely in various states and banned in a good many others even *prior* to the New York, Pennsylvania, and Maryland 1962 and 1963 Supreme Court decisions,[339] are no longer legal. And as it has already demonstrated repeatedly,[340] the Supreme Court will make short shrift of any subterfuges—provided a case is appealed to it (which of course does not necessarily occur in all, or even most, instances). The collateral question of the observance *in the public schools* of Christmas and other religious holidays has not squarely reached the Supreme Court. At the state court level this matter—which raises such emotion-charged, difficult social issues—has seen one adverse[341] and one partly favorable and partly adverse ruling by courts and at least one adverse ruling by an attorney general.[342] But a 5:4 ruling by the Supreme Court in 1980 struck down a Kentucky law that required the posting of a copy of the Ten Commandments in every public classroom in the state.[343] Schools with a substantial Jewish enrollment have increasingly tried to deal with the problem either by diminishing, or even eliminating, the more theological aspects of Christmas, or by commemorating the Jewish holiday of Hanukkah, which usually falls at the same time of year.

tives acted—or at least professed to act—in accordance with constitutional mandates governing such aid.

337. *Illinois ex rel. McCollum v. Board of Education,* 333 U.S. 203 (1948).

338. *Zorach v. Clauson,* 343 U.S. 306 (1952).

339. *Engel v. Vitale,* 370 U.S. 421 (1962); and *Abington School District v. Schempp* and *Murray v. Curlett,* 374 U.S. 203 (1963).

340. See *supra* notes 163–90.

341. Florida: *Chamberlin v. Dade County Board of Public Instruction,* 143 So. 2d 21 (Fla., 1962). Yet baccalaureate services were upheld, albeit on a procedural judicial point, in the same-named case, but recorded as 160 So. 2d 97 (1964). The Supreme Court dismissed an appeal on the issue for want of a properly presented federal question (ibid. 377 U.S. 402 [1964]). And in late 1980 the Court affirmed summarily, with two dissents, a South Dakota ruling allowing the use of religious materials in public school observances of holidays, such as Christmas, here religious symbols, music, carol singing, and literature (*Florey v. Sioux City School District,* 449 U.S. 987).

342. *Baer v. Kolmorgen,* 14 Misc. 2d 1015 (N.Y., 1960) was the court decision; the attorney general's opinion, the first of its kind, was issued by Minnesota at the request of the Rochester (Minnesota) school district, 256 *Civil Liberties* 7 (July 1968).

343. *Stone v. Graham,* 449 U.S. 39. The unsigned 5:4 majority opinion observed that the "pre-eminent purpose [was] plainly religious" because the document is "undeniably a sacred text" for Jews and Christians. The dissenters were Burger, Stewart, Blackmun, and Rehnquist. See Derek Davis, "The Ten Commandments as Public Ritual," 44 *Journal of Church and State* 221 (spring 2002).

Tenth, the "secular purpose/effect/entanglement" triad has diminished in importance for the Court. Decisions in the *Roemer* (1976), *Wolman* (1977), *Regan* (1980), *Mueller* (1983), *Marsh* (1983), *Lynch* (1984), one of the *Allegheny County Cases* (1989), and *Jackson v. Benson* (1998)[344] render inevitable the conclusion that an erosion of church-state separation has taken place, especially given the 1997 *Agostini* and the 2002 *Zelman* "voucher" decisions. That there are limits is demonstrated by the Court's 6:3 interdictive rulings in *Cathedral Academy* (1977), *Byrne* (1979), *Jaffree* (1985), *Grand Rapids* (1985), and *Aguilar* (1985) and one of the 5:4 *Allegheny County Cases.*[345] Yet there is simply little doubt that in a host of areas, broadly describable as financial support for "auxiliary" governmental aid and services to parochial schools, a more permissive judicial attitude toward separation of church and state has become res judicata, albeit usually by the narrowest of 5:4 margins—*pace* some landmark decisions, such as the three 1985 holdings just noted above. Indeed, twelve years later, a new Court majority, consisting of Chief Justice Rehnquist and Justices O'Connor, Scalia, Kennedy, and Thomas—with Justices Stevens, Souter, Ginsburg, and Breyer dissenting—reversed the 1985 *Aguilar* decision.[346] Writing for the 5:4 majority, O'Connor (who had dissented in the 1985 case) acknowledged "depart[ing] from the rule" and held that public school teachers may now indeed provide remedial instruction for children in parochial schools under Title I of the Federal Aid to Elementary and Secondary Education Act of 1965. Presumably, public school teachers would no longer have to teach parochial school students in off-premises temporary establishments, such as vans parked nearby, as they had to do after the *Aguilar* ruling. Probably the most dramatic erosion of the separation concept, and with it another bow toward accommodation, came with the Court's last day of the 2001–2 term ruling in the Ohio voucher case.[347] Over bitter dissenting opinions by Justices Stevens, Souter, and Breyer, joined by Justice Ginsburg, the 5:4 Rehnquist-led majority upheld Ohio's Pilot Project Scholarship Program. It provides tuition aid, according to financial need, to parents for use in both religious and nonreligious schools. Where the aid is spent is entirely up to the parents, with the 1999–2000 school year seeing 96 percent of the students

344. *Roemer v. Maryland Public Works Board,* 429 U.S. 736; *Wolman v. Walter,* 433 U.S. 299; *Committee for Public Education and Religious Liberty v. Regan,* 444 U.S. 646; *Mueller v. Allen,* 463 U.S. 388; *Marsh v. Chambers,* 463 U.S. 783; *Lynch v. Donnelly,* 465 U.S. 688; *Allegheny County v. Greater Pittsburgh ACLU,* 497 U.S. 573; and *Jackson v. Benson,* 67 LW 3322, all discussed *supra* in this chapter.

345. *New York v. Cathedral Academy,* 434 U.S. 125; *Byrne v. Public Funds for Public Schools,* 442 U.S. 907; *Wallace v. Jaffree,* 472 U.S. 38; *Grand Rapids School District v. Ball,* 473 U.S. 373; *Aguilar v. Felton,* 473 U.S. 402; *Allegheny County v. Greater Pittsburgh ACLU,* 497 U.S. 573; *Agostini v. Felton,* 521 U.S. 203; and *Zelman v. Simmons-Harris,* 536 U.S. ___, all discussed *supra* and *infra* in this chapter.

346. *Agostini,* see *supra* note 345.

347. *Zelman,* see *supra* note 345.

participating in the scholarship program enrolled in religiously affiliated schools (primarily Roman Catholic). Sixty percent of the students were from families at or below the poverty line, most of them from impoverished inner-city Cleveland neighborhoods.

Separation and the Problem of Federal Aid to Nonpublic Schools

The preceding ten guidelines to policy on the separation of church and state vis-à-vis aid to nonpublic schools and/or recognition of sectarian practices therein are firmly established. But new complexities may well have been triggered with the enactment of the 1965 Federal Aid to Elementary and Secondary Education Act, which contains controversial provisions of potentially crucial importance to the meaning of the First Amendment.

The 1965 Federal Aid to Elementary and Secondary Education Act. The concept of federal aid to education is not, of course, new. What is new is the revolutionary departure from precedent embraced in the 1965 bill. Breaking historic ground, it provided subventions of *federal money for elementary and secondary instruction for children in both public and parochial as well as all other schools.* Sundry measures in the field of education, in which private schools and colleges participated, had been passed prior to 1965, but none of these had tackled the ticklish problem of instructional federal aid to nonpublic schools below the college level. Among the former were the "GI Bill," the National School Lunch Act, the Special Milk Program, subsidized college housing, the Higher Education Facilities Act, the National Defense Education Act, the College Housing Loan Program, the National Science Foundation Program, and Atomic Energy Commission Fellowships. But because of the lasting opposition of educators, lawyers, and churchmen, instructional aid was never included—and as a result no general federal aid to education measure was put forward effectively until the presidency of Lyndon B. Johnson, who submitted his bill in 1964 and saw it become law in 1965.

To the surprise of many, notwithstanding full recognition of the remarkable Johnson *domestic* political savoir faire, the bill went through both houses of Congress without a big church-state fight, without a conservative-liberal battle, without a racial row. Indeed, it passed without a single major change after it had been first introduced for the administration by Representative Carl D. Perkins (D.-Ky.). It passed because the president managed to convince most of those either involved or interested that the entire scheme would collapse if anyone were to tinker with his bill. Although it may well have pleased no one entirely, all the traditional protagonists supported the measure, or at least did not oppose it: the National Education Association, the National Catholic Welfare Conference, the American Federation of Teachers, the American Jewish Congress, Americans for Democratic Action, Baptists, Methodists, and a coterie of other religious, educational, labor, and civil rights organizations. Heretofore, every past effort to see a general federal aid to education bill pass Congress had faltered for three over-riding reasons: (1) the opposition of the hard core of anti-big-government, con-servative members of Congress; (2) that of the die-hard southerners whose districts were in need of the kind of financial aid only the federal Treasury could provide but who steadfastly opposed the legislation because of the perennial "Powell Amendment"[348] that barred segregated use of funds; and (3) the contro-versy engendered by the delicate religious issue, with almost all Roman Catholics opposed to any bill that bypassed their parochial schools, and most Protestants and Jews opposed to any bill that did *not* bypass aid to parochial schools.

President Johnson licked all three problems deftly. The first was eliminated by the drastic reduction of conservative senators and congressmen as a result of the landslide Johnson-over-Goldwater victory in the 1964 election. The race issue was bypassed by Title VI of the Civil Rights Act of 1964, which banned the use of federal funds for segregated activities. The religious issue was the most difficult, of course; yet the superb and experienced parliamentarian and tactician was equal to the task—one his Roman Catholic predecessor in office had been unwilling even to consider: for President Kennedy believed the inclusion of di-rect federal financial assistance to elementary and secondary schools to be un-constitutional, or at least he chose to give that impression publicly in the administration's 1961 Ribicoff brief.[349] And Senator Robert F. Kennedy publicly agreed with his murdered brother's posture during his tragedy-truncated presi-dential campaign in 1968.

Determined to get a general aid-to-education measure through the Eighty-ninth Congress, and given a two-thirds Democratic majority, President Johnson, however, was not to be stopped by the religious issue. He met it in several inge-nious ways. First, he drafted his program as one in line with the Supreme Court's "child benefit" approach. Second, the control of funds was to be in the hands of public authorities. Third, all aid was to be "categorical" rather than "general." Fourth, he more or less restricted the bill to the poor and needy; its primary ben-efits were assigned to counties and school districts with ten or more children of families with a yearly income of less than $2,000. Next, the U.S. Office of Edu-cation was initially authorized to allocate $100 million for grants to the states for the purchase of textbooks and library materials to go to church-controlled and

---

348. Named after then Representative Adam Clayton Powell (D.-N.Y.).

349. See its reproduction in the *New York Times,* March 29, 1961, p. 221. Inter alia, he said: "[T]he Constitution clearly prohibits aid to the . . . parochial schools. I don't think there is any doubt of that. . . . The Supreme Court made its decision in the *Everson* case by determining that the aid was to the child, not to the school. Aid to the school—there isn't any room for debate on the subject. It is prohibited by the Constitution, and the Supreme Court has made that very clear. And therefore there would be no possibility of our recommending it." Justice Douglas quoted this as "the correct constitutional position" in his dissent in *Tilton v. Richardson* in 1971 (403 U.S. 672).

other private nonprofit as well as public schools. The language of this particular provision was closely tailored to the principle of textbook *grants* to students, for example, Louisiana's statute[350] that survived subsequent constitutional on- slaughts, with the terms of the aid changed now to emphasize *loans* rather than grants.[351] To the irrefutable argument that some states expressly forbid that type of book grant or even loan, the administration's response was that it, rather than the states, would be the "owner" of the books and could, of course, lend them to the children concerned. The last aspect of the Johnson strategy in defeating or isolating the religious issue as a factor of opposition to the overall program was an on-the-record promise by the president to a number of balky, key northern urban and suburban members of Congress to go "all out" to alleviate the over- crowded classrooms and half-day sessions so prevalent there. In typically force- ful language he assured these critical legislators in March 1965 that he would "use every rostrum and every forum and every searchlight that I can to tell the people of this country and their elected representatives that we can no longer af- ford over-crowded classrooms and half-day sessions."[352] On the morning fol- lowing this clinching declaration, the House Committee on Education and Labor reported the bill out favorably. The House ultimately passed it by a vote of 263:153, and the Senate, where the bill had been entrusted to Senator Wayne Morse (D.-Ore.), followed suit early in April by a vote of 73:18. For the first time, both houses of Congress had thus approved a broad ($1.3 billion)[353] fed- eral program to aid elementary and secondary education, regardless of the school's secular or nonsecular character. The president triumphantly signed the bill into law on April 11, 1965.

The Constitutional Attack on the 1965 Act. Exactly two days later the first steps were taken to mount the anticipated constitutional attack on the revolutionary measure. The National Governing Council of the American Jewish Congress, which has a record of close alliance with liberal Protestant denominations on the church-state issue, announced that it would seek a court test of the three most controversial and most innovative provisions of the act. Urging that the "grave issues that have been raised during the long debate on the [statute] must be re-

---

350. Upheld in *Cochran v. Louisiana,* 281 U.S. 370 (1930).

351. See *Board of Education v. Allen,* 392 U.S. 236 (1968); *Meek v. Pittenger,* 421 U.S. 349 (1975); and *Wolman v. Walter,* 433 U.S. 229 (1977), all discussed *supra* in the text.

352. *Philadelphia Evening Bulletin,* April 9, 1965, p. 1.

353. Predictably, this relatively modest-sounding figure had risen to $2.4 billion for the three-year budget period of 1970–73, to over $8.3 billion for 1988, and to $11.0 bil- lion in 1995. This figure did not include other types of federal grants for state and local education—the total approaching $20 billion by the early 1980s. Not surprisingly, votes to renew now passed with overwhelming margins—a far cry from the initial vote a decade earlier. The legislation's principle, if not all its components, is no longer controversial. It has become a congressional bread-and-butter staple.

solved promptly—before the church-state separation guarantee in the Bill of Rights is eroded to the point of extinction,"[354] the AJC moved to ask for constitutional tests of the following:

1. The dual enrollment or "shared time" arrangements authorized under the bill—to the extent that these result in the "commingling" of public and parochial school faculties, facilities, and/or administration. (Under "shared time" programs the time of parochial school children is divided between public and parochial schools; that is, for "religiously neutral" subjects—such as languages and physics—the child goes to the former, for the social sciences to the latter.)

2. Those provisions under which public school teachers and public school equipment may be sent into parochial schools under the bill's program of "supplementary educational centers." (Under Titles I and III, $100 million was initially allocated for remedial instruction, teaching machines, and laboratory equipment, teachers, and other services to public *and* nonprofit private schools.)

3. The aforementioned provisions in Title II of the act under which textbooks purchased with an initial $100 million of federal funds were made available to Catholic, Protestant, and Jewish parochial schools—the vast majority to the first—as well as to public schools.

But in order to be able to mount the desired Court test, it would first be necessary to obtain the kind of *federal* taxpayer standing to sue that had been consistently denied by the Supreme Court as a result of a famous 1923 decision.[355] Matters looked hardly promising for a Court reversal of that posture, especially given the delicate subject at issue—but the would-be litigants received aid from a powerful quarter: Senator Sam J. Ervin Jr. (D.-N.C.), the Senate's leading constitutional authority and, conveniently, an implacable foe of aid to parochial schools. The senator would *himself* argue the case for Supreme Court reversal of the "standing to sue" issue here. And he did so successfully! On June 10, 1968, the Court ruled (8:1) in a suit requesting an injunction against the 1965 statute in

354. As quoted in the *Christian Science Monitor,* April 13, 1965, p. 4. The AJC, as noted *supra,* had not opposed passage of the statute but was eager for a rapid constitutional test.

355. There, in the case of *Frothingham v. Mellon,* 262 U.S. 447, the Supreme Court had held unanimously that a *federal* taxpayer lacked "standing" to sue and had not presented a bona fide "case or controversy" under the Constitution for federal court review of a challenge to appropriations under the federal Maternity Act of 1921. This holding did not then, nor has it since, applied to state "taxpayer suits" acting under state laws, but it is res judicata for federal cases. For a detailed examination of "standing" and "case or controversy," see Henry J. Abraham, *The Judicial Process: An Introductory Analysis of the Court of the United States, England, and France,* 7th ed. (New York: Oxford University Press, 1998), pp. 387–91.

Flast v. Cohen[356] that the 1923 decision was not a barrier to suits, contending that the government was infringing on *specific Bill of Rights guarantees,* here the First Amendment's religion clauses.[357]

Although that momentous decision did not address itself to the substantive merits of the separation of church and state problem per se, it opened the door to a direct challenge of the huge federal expenditures under the 1965 law. By February 1971 fully fifty-two cases were "in the mill"—although, perhaps surprisingly, only two of significance had reached the Supreme Court's decisional stage on the merits by 1988: in 1974 it upheld (8:1) the act's Title I provision for the sending of public school teachers into parochial (and other private) as well as public schools during normal school hours, a practice forbidden in Missouri, whence the case was appealed.[358] Justice Blackmun, speaking for the Court, pointed to the law's rationale, which was based on programs for special federal aid for *all* children classified as "disadvantaged," be they in public or nonpublic schools. Over Justice Douglas's solitary dissent, Blackmun told Missouri that a state was not required to engage in Title I programs of the kind at issue if state law prohibits same—but that a comparable program must be provided. Missouri's failure to do so triggered the statutorily mandated federal one. But in 1985, albeit by a mere 5:4 margin, the Court made it clear that there are limits: as noted earlier, it disallowed on separation of church and state violation grounds New York City's practice, under Title I of the federal statute, of providing instructional services, funded by that title, to parochial schools on their premises. The city, moreover, monitored the religious content of these Title I class services. The scheme, in the eyes of the controlling opinion, penned by Justice Brennan, rose to a level of an impermissible "excessive entanglement." Nonetheless, also as reported above, the Court, with a newly constituted majority, explicitly reversed the 1985 precedent a dozen years later and found no establishment clause violation in Title I's remedial instruction program.[359]

356. 392 U.S. 83.

357. The opinion by Chief Justice Warren, which "distinguished" rather than overruled the 1923 case (*Frothingham v. Mellon,* op. cit.,), with only Justice Harlan in dissent, went further, however, to open the door to any taxpayer's allegation that "congressional action under the taxing and spending clause is in derogation of those constitutional provisions which operate to restrict the exercise of the taxing and spending power" (*Flast v. Cohen,* op. cit., at 106). It did this by setting two conditions, a "two-part nexus" test: (1) the taxpayer must establish a link between his status and the statute attacked by alleging that an act of Congress is unconstitutional under the taxing and spending power; (2) the taxpayer must allege that the challenged enactment exceeds a specific limit placed on the exercise of the taxing and spending power.

358. *Wheeler v. Barrera,* 414 U.S. 908 (1974).

359. *Aguilar v. Felton,* 473 U.S. 402 (1985). Brennan was joined by his colleagues Marshall, Blackmun, and Stevens, plus Justice Powell's key concurrence. The four dissenters were Burger, White, Rehnquist, and O'Connor. *Agostini v. Felton* was the 1997 case that overturned *Aguilar,* see *supra* note 346.

As the country saw the twenty-first century dawn, federal aid to education on *all levels* of schooling and to all schools, public or private, was an established fact. It is highly unlikely that the Court would be willing to strike down provisions that form the very heart of a law such as the 1965 one at issue, which was passed, and consistently extended and renewed, by an almost two-thirds majority of the people's representatives in Congress. After all, had the latter not evidently been converted to the proposition that a price, even perhaps a questionably constitutional one, had to be paid to get the much-needed and much-sought aid to our schools as a matter of public policy? It must never be forgotten that in the long run the Court reflects even as it reveals the nature of American society; that although it is often an effective educator and teacher in the short run, there are limits to which it can go in the face of determined, overwhelming *long-run* opposition by the body politic—a body politic wedded to those pluralistic concepts of which diverse schools form such an important part. What the Supreme Court of the United States says and holds indeed "reflects not only the competing interests and values at stake, but also its own role in accommodating constitutional interpretation to the demands of a pluralistic society."[360]

To reiterate, this is not to say that there are not limits. The Court, as we have seen time and time again, does ultimately determine lines—however uncertain their future may well be. Moreover, as it has demonstrated throughout its history, no amount of popular reaction and vilification will stop the Court from speaking as it perceives the command of the basic law of the land. It is a role crucial to the survival of our constitutional system, one it must continue to exercise with resolve.

360. Kauper, op. cit., p. 79.

7

Race—The American Dilemma: The Evolving Equal Protection of the Laws

In theory, *race,* the dominant subject of this chapter, should not present the sort of difficult line drawing that has pervaded considerations of the topics already discussed. Surely, in the twenty-first century race could hardly, in an enlightened democratic society, determine the outcome of an individual's quest for equality before the law and equality of opportunity—nor should gender or ethnic origin or creed or religion, or any other immutable characteristics not relevant to egalitarian and libertarian imperatives. Yet theory does not necessarily govern practice, and although—beyond any rational question—we have seen enormous strides taken toward the egalitarian goals of black Americans, both under law and in the mores of society, racial discrimination is still a fact of life. That great progress has been achieved since World War II, especially since the late 1950s, in both the private *and* the governmental sphere, is obvious to any fair-minded observer. Yet ingrained sentiments and prejudices of segments of people in the North as well as in the South die hard—if indeed they die at all. And government, under the Constitution the great line drawer in the absence of voluntary action, has had to be cautious lest it move too far in advance of those sentiments and prejudices. For full enforcement of the civil rights of all, there must be mutual trust and respect—and although government can accomplish much to promote such trust and respect, it cannot be a finite panacea substituting for the slower processes of education. Still, as the race problem has shown well indeed, leadership by responsible public officials is not only desirable but crucial at all stages. When the race controversy attained a degree of no longer ignorable public concern at the highest governmental level in the late 1940s, it was the judicial branch of the government, with the Supreme Court at its apex, which led the other branches in tackling the problem. While it probably did not lead eagerly or joyously, a people's rightful claims could no longer be ignored merely because the political, in particular the legislative, branches refused then to become involved

367

beyond the most cursory of levels, and in fact consistently passed the problems on to the Court. It is an intriguing question how much strife might have been spared and how much understanding might have been engendered had the elective branches of the government provided the decisive leadership with which they are charged and, as subsequent events proved, of which they are capable when pressed.

As of the 2000 census there were some 31 million blacks in the United States—roughly 12.3 percent of a total population of 281,421,906. Segregation barriers had tumbled or were tumbling everywhere; the federal government and now also state governments—whether voluntarily or as a result of enforceable orders from the judiciary—had made crystal clear that race would no longer be permitted as a valid factor of adverse classification in any public or quasi-public sphere—and even the demonstrably private sector of society found itself under intense and mounting pressure to fall into line with the spirit of the times. The tough Civil Rights Act of 1964 and the equally tough Voting Rights Act of 1965, with their numerous subsequent amendatory extensions and expansions, were being vigorously enforced; desegregation of public educational facilities, on all levels, but particularly in the Deep South,[1] had advanced from the tokenism of two decades earlier to an all but complete stage—with exceptions still extant, however, largely because of housing patterns and ethnic clusters that do not readily lend themselves to rapid alterations (of which much more later in these pages); the increase in college and university enrollment of blacks had become so dramatic during the 1970s and 1980s—some 300 percent in five years—that by the late 1980s the U.S. Bureau of the Census could report that blacks were entering higher education in numbers *exceeding* their representation in the total population (although their dropout rate was significantly higher than that of whites).[2] Jim Crow[3] legislation was legally dead everywhere; public accommodations were open to all; registered black voters numbered close to 10 million—almost four times as many as in 1960; and over 8,000 blacks, including 1,800 women, held elective public office—an increase from but 72 in 1965 and 480 in 1967, with almost 3,000 black officials in the South (where the most dramatic gains took place). Nationally, as of 1991 there were 895 black judges, more than 10 percent of whom were appointed to the *federal* bench by President Carter between 1977 and 1981. In his two terms as president (1993–2001), Bill Clinton appointed 61

1. Generally speaking, five southern states are usually classified as the Deep South: South Carolina, Georgia, Louisiana, Alabama, and Mississippi. The six other members of the erstwhile Confederacy are commonly simply called southern: Virginia, North Carolina, Florida, Arkansas, Tennessee, and Texas. Six are normally classified as border states: Delaware, Kentucky, Maryland, West Virginia, Oklahoma, and Missouri (although the Bureau of the Census no longer includes Missouri).

2. See the bureau's *Annual Report* for the 1970s and 1980s.

3. A slang term applied to blacks, derived from the title of a minstrel song, popularized about 1835 by F. D. Rice: "Wheel About and Turn About and Jump, Jim Crow."

African-American federal judges (53 to the U.S. District Courts and 8 to the U.S. Courts of Appeals, including the first African-American judge on the Fourth Circuit, which includes, in addition to West Virginia and Maryland, three states of the old Confederacy, North Carolina, South Carolina, and Virginia, and which has the highest black population of any of the federal judicial circuits).[4]

High-ranking black officials were in evidence at all levels of government by the middle to late 1980s—including more than 400 mayors (early 1996). Thus, among others, the important cities of Los Angeles and San Francisco, California; New York, New York; Detroit and Grand Rapids, Michigan; Chicago, Illinois; Baltimore, Maryland; Washington, D.C.; New Orleans, Louisiana; Savannah, Georgia; Philadelphia, Pennsylvania; Gary, Indiana; Cleveland and Dayton, Ohio; and Newark and East Orange, New Jersey, had elected black mayors, and one of them, Hartford, Connecticut, chose New England's first black female mayor in 1987. Fifty-five of these cities had white majorities, and more than one-half of them were in cities of more than 100,000 inhabitants, none of which had a black mayor as late as 1966. The year 1969 saw the election of black mayors in the southern cities of Chapel Hill, North Carolina, and Fayette, Mississippi; and 1973 not only brought the same to Raleigh, North Carolina, but witnessed the first election of a black mayor for a southern metropolitan center, Atlanta, Georgia, in the person of thirty-three-year-old attorney Maynard Jackson, who was succeeded by another prominent black, Andrew Young, in 1982—who, in turn, was again succeeded by Jackson in 1990. Birmingham, a symbol of southern intransigence on race, elected a black mayor in 1980. Massachusetts had a black population of only 3 percent when it sent Republican Edward W. Brooke to the U.S. Senate in 1966 to replace retiring New England Brahmin Leverett Saltonstall. Brooke, the first black senator since Reconstruction—who had easily defeated a distinguished Massachusetts Yankee of unquestioned civil libertarian persuasion, Endicott Peabody—was reelected by a margin of better than 2:1 in 1972.[5] In 1992 Carol Moseley-Braun of Illinois was elected the first black female to serve in the U.S. Senate, but she lost her reelection bid in 1998 (leaving the Senate without a black member). The House of Representatives of the

4. See statistics provided regularly by the U.S. Bureau of the Census, the U.S. Bureau of Labor Statistics, *Statistical Abstract of the United States,* the Joint Center for Political and Economic Studies, the Judicial Council of the National Bar Association, the *Christian Science Monitor,* the *Washington Post,* and the *New York Times.* As of January 1, 1986, Mississippi had the largest number of elected black officials (521), followed by Louisiana's 488. See also Sheldon Goldman, Elliot Slotnick, Gerard Gryski, and Gary Zuk, "Clinton's Judges: Summing Up the Legacy," 84 *Judicature* 228 (March–April 2001), pp. 244, 249.

5. His record tainted by some questionable financial transactions, Senator Brooke was defeated in his quest for a third term in 1978 by white Democrat Paul E. Tsongas—a man with an even more liberal record, who in turn was replaced in 1984 by a still more liberal white figure, John F. Kerry, also a Democrat.

107th Congress (2001–2) contained thirty-four black members. L. Douglas Wilder, a grandson of slaves, elected as lieutenant governor of Virginia in 1985, became the highest popularly elected black executive official, and the first of his race to become governor, with his razor-thin victory in 1989. And Representative Mike Espy of Yazoo City became the first black to represent Mississippi in Congress since Reconstruction. (In 1993 President Clinton appointed him to be secretary of agriculture.) By January 1990 there were 13,955 black elected officials, a total that has since grown dramatically. Another noteworthy statistic, revealed by a 1997 Gallup poll, indicated that 93 percent of whites said they "would be willing to vote for a black candidate for president." In fact, more whites than blacks (91 percent) responded that they would vote for a black presidential candidate.[6]

In 1967 President Johnson had appointed Thurgood Marshall to the Supreme Court—the first black ever to receive this honor. In that same year, Robert H. Lawrence became the first black astronaut. President George H. W. Bush appointed General Colin L. Powell to the highest post in military service, that of chairman of the Joint Chiefs of Staff, in 1989, and President George W. Bush named Powell to be the first black secretary of state in 2001. In 1976 Alabama Democrats had elected the first black ever to serve as a member of the state's regular delegation to the Democratic National Committee; and neighboring Mississippi, which now led all southern states in the number of elected black officials, saw the installation of a black as the state's Roman Catholic auxiliary bishop. Vanessa Williams became the first black Miss America in 1983. There were 711 black delegates (18 percent of the total) at the 1984 Democratic Convention, many of them from the Deep South. In the fall of 1998, thirty-nine blacks were elected to the 106th Congress (1999–2001), almost six times the number (only seven then) that had served there at the height of Reconstruction, from 1873 to 1877. (The 106th Congress also held a record sixty-five women [up from twenty-seven in the 102d], twenty Hispanics, and seven Asian Americans. Hispanics held 4,202 elective offices at all levels of government as of late 1992.) In the realm of national law enforcement, in 1963 there were 1,600 whites for every black in the FBI, and as late as 1972 there were no women. By 1980 the ratio had dropped to 35:1, and 2 of the 59 special agents in charge were black, a figure that mounted steadily through the 1980s under Directors William Webster and William S. Sessions, totaling 883 black and Hispanic and 880 female agents (of a total of 9,649). Indeed, the catalog of accomplishments was proud and impressive. Moreover, between the Civil War and the Korean War the rate of Negro illiteracy had dropped from 90 percent to less than 5 percent. There was now a rising black middle class (family incomes upwards of $20,000–$25,000 annually, with more than 1,500,000 black families earning more than $25,000 as of 1984

---

6. See the annual reports of the Joint Center for Political and Economic Studies, and James C. Glassman, "The Divide Is Narrowing," *Washington Post,* June 17, 1997, p. A17.

and 264,000 more than $50,000). Despite the economic turndown during the middle and late 1970s, family incomes rose at a rate greater than that of whites, while—for the first time in many years—blacks generally were moving into the poverty class at a lesser rate than whites. The number of nonwhite professional workers had more than quintupled between the *Brown* decision[7] and 1987—thus while there were but 300 black engineers in 1940, there were 36,019 in 1980; life expectancy for blacks had commenced to increase markedly, accompanied by a striking reduction in black mortality rates under one year of age; black migration to the suburbs increased 45 percent during the 1970s and 1980s; and blacks had begun to feel sufficiently confident about the evident improvement in the South's racial climate to start to move *into* the South in greater numbers than *out* of it as of 1974—a phenomenon that has continued at an accelerated pace.[8] Indeed, by 2001 some 600,000 more had moved south than had moved north, with 60 percent now again living in the South, the black population there having grown by 3.6 million in the 1990s.

Yet while there was indubitably demonstrable and truly commendable progress at every level of public and private life, the picture was not universally bright. Although the median black family income in 1984 had maintained an annual increase of close to 9 percent, to reach almost $15,000, that figure was still only 75 percent as much as that earned by white families. At the same time, the number of black families with a female head of household (there were circa 3 million such families in July 1987) had jumped to a total of 40 percent of all black families, as opposed to 10 percent of all white families. The majority of these fatherless families are poor, their children especially vulnerable to delinquency, crime, and premarital pregnancy. There were dramatic income gains at all age levels during the 1960s, 1970s, and 1980s, with one-quarter of the black families' earnings reaching the $25,000 threshold, and real earnings of black

---

7. *Brown v. Board of Education of Topeka,* 374 U.S. 483 (1954).

8. See *New York Times,* June 23, 1974, sec. 4, p. 15; the 1975 report of the U.S. Bureau of the Census; "Geographical Mobility: March 1975 to March 1977," a release by the U.S. Bureau of the Census; Bernard E. Anderson, "The Black Middle Class," *Pennsylvania Gazette,* March 1979, p. 37; Robert Reinhold, "Progress of Blacks Traced," *New York Times* News Service; *Charlottesville Daily Progress,* July 1, 1979, p. B9; *The Daily Progress,* June 2, 1980, p. A12, November 22, 1985, p. A5, and September 4, 1986, p. A5; U.S. Department of Commerce, Bureau of the Census, P-23 *Current Population Reports* 80, "The Social and Economic Status of the Black Population in the United States: An Historical View, 1790–1978" (1980); *New York Times,* July 3, 1981; *Washington Post,* July 27, 1986, p. A8, September 7, 1986, p. A8, and August 9, 1987, insert, p. 2. See also *supra* note 4. Further, *International Herald Tribune,* June 14, 1989, p. 3; the massive study by the National Research Council, *A Common Destiny: Blacks and American Society,* 1989; Barbara Vobejda, "Blacks Moving to the South," *Washington Post,* January 29, 1998, p. A3; D'Vera Cohn, "Reversing a Long Pattern, Blacks Are Heading South," *Washington Post,* May 5, 2001, p. A10; and the annual reports of the Joint Center for Political and Economic Studies.

males increased 300 percent, compared with 163 percent for white men, during the forty-year period from 1940 to 1980. But the jobless rate for blacks in 1987 stood at 14.7 percent, versus 6.5 percent for whites. Upwards of 50 percent of all food stamp purchases were being made by black families. More than twice as many black women as white women were separated or divorced. Although by 1995 74 percent of blacks completed high school (compared with only 31 percent in 1970), the dropout rate for blacks was still almost 10 percent higher than that for whites.[9] Unquestionably, enormous, readily recognizable progress had been made on almost all fronts of the racial dilemma—yet much remained to be accomplished. Race continues to be a fundamental cleavage in American society.

Moreover, the demonstrable psychological toll inflicted on America's blacks over almost three centuries was clearly in evidence; impatience, however understandable, threatened to play havoc with the newly established lines of equality of opportunity. Not only was racial prejudice still a factor, but, because of the assertive and highly visible civil rights clamor, it was engulfing areas it had not hitherto reached, especially in northern urban and suburban areas. The frightful riots in the Watts section of Los Angeles in August 1965 lasted six days and resulted in 34 deaths, 1,032 injuries, the arrest of 3,952 persons, and $40 million in property damage (more than 600 buildings were damaged, 200 totally destroyed). Those around Detroit's Twelfth Street in 1967 constituted the bloodiest uprising in the country in half a century, and the costliest ever in terms of property damage: the five days of rioting, looting, burning, and killing resulted in 43 deaths, 347 injuries, 3,800 arrests, 5,000 persons made homeless, 1,300 buildings reduced to ashes, and $500 million in damages. Watts and Detroit—and the disorders that in subsequent years engulfed such northern centers as Washington, Newark, Buffalo, Kansas City, Cleveland, Chicago, St. Louis, San Francisco, and many others, reaching into Miami (16 deaths) and Chattanooga again in 1980 and ultimately striking Los Angeles once more with a record-setting death toll (56) in the 1992 riots that swept the city in the aftermath of the acquittal of four white policemen accused in the videotaped beating of black motorist Rodney King—served as shocking and costly reminders that the mere removal of legal barriers to equality was not enough. The principle of equality now included demands not only for economic and social equality but also for compensatory, preferential "affirmative action." Yet fear and lack of communication were still rampant, and frustration, engendered by rising expectations, could readily lead to anger and thence to blind unreasoned violence. The President's National Com-

9. For sources of statistics see those cited in *supra* notes 4, 6; plus "Decade of Progress," *Time,* April 16, 1973, p. 16; the annual economic surveys of the National Urban League; Paul Delaney, "Economic Survey Cites Black Loss," *New York Times,* July 29, 1975, p. 27c; the periodic reports of the U.S. Commission on Civil Rights; those of the Joint Center for Political and Economic Studies; and Nathan Glazer, *We Are All Multiculturalists Now* (Cambridge, Mass.: Harvard University Press, 1997), as reviewed in *Commentary,* May 1997, p. 62.

mission on the Causes and Prevention of Violence thus reported late in 1969 that extensive violence had occurred in 239 hostile outbreaks by blacks, which resulted in more than 8,000 casualties and 191 deaths.[10] Prejudice and poverty still stood in the way. And the bitter school-busing controversies that crested in the 1970s—of which more below—would demonstrate that resort to violence is not confined to either one race or one section of the land.

Thus, whereas the gulf of opportunity and achievement was clearly narrowing, it remained wide for a good many blacks, especially at the lower socioeconomic levels. And the desire to bridge it not only fully but rapidly, coupled with a demonstrable measure of success, gave rise to insistent and greater demands, not infrequently backed by what became known as "action in the streets" rather than in the courts or in legislative halls. This action, in turn, prompted considerable feeling on the part of the white community that what had hitherto been regarded as legitimate grievances based on legitimate demands had now become unreasonable and unjustifiable demands for "special" or "privileged" treatment— increasingly characterized as "preferential treatment" or "reverse discrimination." Public authorities thus found themselves faced with the problem of drawing lines particularly between *public* and *private* action and the attendant legal and governmental responsibilities, a difficult and uncomfortable task. Just how, where, and by whom could or should such a line be established? How to find accommodations between the twin basic rights of liberty and equality—*both* being constitutionally mandated? Is it purely—is it properly—a judicial function? A summary glance into the history of racial discrimination in the United States may serve as a prolegomenon to some answers, if we can speak of answers at all.

A GLANCE AT HISTORY

Although the Declaration of Independence had stipulated, as a self-evident truth, that "all men are created equal," it soon became obvious that, in the words of George Orwell, "some men are created more equal than others." The second section of the first article of the Constitution clearly recognized the existence of slavery in the United States by directing the inclusion of "three-fifths of all other persons," that is, the *slaves,* in the enumeration which was to form the basis for representative apportionment and taxation. True, Section 9 of Article 1 did make it possible to stop the "migration or importation" of slaves after 1808, provided Congress chose to do so then, and the Thirteenth Amendment was designed to settle the matter by outlawing slavery in 1865. But it was not really until the ratification of the Fourteenth Amendment in 1868, five years after Lincoln's Emancipation Proclamation, that the white-supremacy concept inherent in Article 1

10. James L. Campbell, "American Society and the Radical Black Militant," in *Law and Order Reconsidered: A Staff Report* (New York: Bantam, 1970), pp. 85–117.

was removed from the Constitution. In the language of the amendment's Section 2: "Representatives shall be apportioned among the several States according to their respective numbers, *counting the whole number of persons in each State, excluding Indians not taxed. . . .*"[11] Yet despite these enactments, despite the mandates of Amendment Fourteen (quoted subsequently), and despite the language of the Fifteenth Amendment of 1870, which on its face seemed to assure to blacks the privilege of the ballot, neither the myth of white supremacy nor the fact of color prejudice was wiped out. Section 1 of the Fourteenth Amendment, now so significant but then so ineffective, would have to wait more than eight decades for its triumphs on behalf of the black:

> *All persons born or naturalized in the United States, and subject to the jurisdiction thereof, are citizens of the United States and of the State wherein they reside. No state shall make or enforce* any law which shall abridge the privileges or immunities of citizens of the United States; *nor shall any State deprive* any person of life, liberty, or property, without due process of law; *nor deny to any person within its jurisdiction the equal protection of the laws.*[12]

The Emancipation Proclamation and these three Civil War amendments intended, above all, to ameliorate the lot of blacks by attacking the constitutional silence on federal protection of civil rights, a protection that had, until then, been left wholly to the several states. They proved to be ineffective. True, Reconstruction seemed to offer genuine hope: twenty-two Southern blacks went to Congress, and two became U.S. senators from Mississippi. True also that in the decade following the passage of the Thirteenth Amendment, Congress enacted five major civil rights statutes, spelling out the rights of the new black freedom and providing penalties for their denial.[13] But the South proved itself equal to the challenge of restoring the status quo ante via a host of ingenious and disingenuous devices. By 1910 every former Confederate state, for example, had succeeded in disfranchising blacks either by state statute—for example, the "white primary" and the "grandfather clause"[14]—by state constitutional amendment, or with the direct or indirect aid of such U.S. Supreme Court decisions as those in *United States v. Harris,*[15] the *Slaughterhouse Cases,*[16] and the *Civil Rights Cases.*[17] The Court's position, as noted earlier,[18] was that the Fourteenth Amendment did not place under fed-

---

11. Opening sentence; italics supplied.
12. Entire section quoted; italics supplied.
13. Among them were the "Anti-K.K.K." Act of 1871 and the Public Accommodation Act of 1875.
14. See *infra* this chapter.
15. 106 U.S. 629 (1882).
16. 16 Wallace 36 (1873).
17. 109 U.S. 3 (1883).
18. See *supra* chapter 3.

eral protection "the entire domain of civil rights heretofore belonging exclusively to the states," and that the protection offered by the Fourteenth and Fifteenth Amendments was *against state action only,* not against private action. And in 1896 the Court upheld the convenient discriminatory concept of "separate but equal" in the case of *Plessy v. Ferguson.*[19] To all intents and purposes the black was at the mercy of the states—there was no Warren Court to redress grievances. Indeed, until World War II the federal government assumed at most a highly limited role in the protection of civil rights on the state level.

Before 1910 almost 90 percent of America's blacks lived in the South and the border states (a figure that had declined to 70 percent in 1950, to 60 percent in 1960, and to 51 percent in 1978, but had edged up to 52 percent in 1988);[20] the core of racial discrimination was naturally found there, on both the public and the private level. Thus, *public* authorities at the state and local levels, usually under the guise of the Court-upheld separate but equal concept, enacted measures (sometimes taking the form of a constitutional provision) *permitting* or even *requiring* segregation of buses, streetcars, taxicabs, railroads, waiting rooms, comfort stations, drinking fountains, state and local schools, state colleges and universities, hospitals, jails, cemeteries, sport facilities, beaches, bathhouses, swimming pools, parks, golf courses, courthouse cafeterias, libraries, dwellings, theaters, hotels, restaurants, and other similar facilities—be these public, quasi-public, or private in nature; and interracial marriages were widely proscribed.[21] *Private* individuals and groups, on their own initiative, and not infrequently encouraged by state authorities, acted to deny blacks, and often other non-Caucasians as well, access to social clubs, fraternities and sororities, private schools, colleges, universities, churches, cemeteries, funeral parlors, hospitals, hotels, dwellings, restaurants, movies, bowling alleys, swimming pools, bathhouses, sporting events, comfort stations, drinking fountains, barber and beauty shops, employment agencies, and employment itself. There was nothing particularly secretive about either public or private discrimination; it was simply a way of life.

Yet the onset of World War II—which witnessed many blacks fighting side by side with whites and saw increasing migration of blacks northward—prompted the federal government to take notice of the problem. Although his administration recommended no civil rights legislation per se to Congress—which,

19. 163 U.S. 537.

20. *United States Department of Commerce News,* October 23, 1970, p. 5; and U.S. Bureau of the Census, 1979 (see also *supra* note 8). The decline appeared to have been arrested at the end of the 1970s, and a reversal began to take place (see *supra* text and note 8).

21. It was not until 1967 that this particular prohibition was unanimously declared unconstitutional as a violation of both equal protection and due process guarantees under Amendment Fourteen in *Loving v. Virginia,* 388 U.S. 1 (about which a TV movie was made and aired in 1996). See also its 1964 precursor, *McLaughlin v. Florida,* 379 U.S. 184, also decided 9:0.

needless to say, did not act on its own—President Franklin D. Roosevelt did take two far-reaching executive actions. In 1939, at the prompting of Attorney General Frank Murphy (who would soon be promoted to the Supreme Court), he created a Civil Liberties Unit[22] in the Criminal Division of the Department of Justice. Then, since Congress would not have passed such legislation, he established by executive order[23] the first Committee on Fair Employment Practices (to be known as the FEPC). The president created it largely at the behest of black leaders, other civil rights advocates, and, significantly, his spouse, Eleanor Roosevelt—whose entire life was dedicated to the eradication of injustice. Although its enforcement powers were severely circumscribed, and its domain was exclusively in the federal sphere, the FEPC did make some progress toward the elimination of discriminatory employment practices in those companies and labor unions that had government contracts or were engaged in activities connected with World War II. Yet Congress abolished the committee in 1946.

The end of the war brought increasing public pressure on the federal government to combat the various manifestations of racial discrimination. But the political power of entrenched southern forces, both in Congress and out, often combined with northern conservative elements, was able to prevent, or at least to delay, any meaningful legislative aid. The House of Representatives, by definition theoretically "closer to the people" and more sensitive to the currents and tides of change, did pass in 1946 and 1950 such potentially remedial measures as bills establishing a permanent FEPC, but both were rejected by the more tradition-bound Senate, in which southern influence was still decisive in such matters. Again, the House passed legislation designed to outlaw the poll tax in 1945, 1947, and 1949, yet in no instance would the Senate accept it. (It would take another thirteen years before Congress legislated against the poll tax in *federal* elections by way of the Twenty-fourth Amendment, which was ratified in 1964.) No action at all was taken on the host of antilynching proposals introduced at every session of Congress.

Winds of Change: President Truman. Because Congress was unwilling or unable to make progress on the race problem, President Harry S. Truman—a son of Missouri, with Confederate ancestors—determined to take matters into his own hands. In a sense, the catalyst for his first move was Congress's deliberate failure to include a widely backed antidiscrimination provision in the important Selective Service Act of 1948. Angry, the president issued a no-nonsense executive order[24] that specifically banned "separate but equal" recruiting, training, and service in the armed forces. While this did not affect the National Guard and reserve units under state aegis, it was an important step in an area of public activity in

22. Subsequently to be called the Civil Rights Section.
23. Exec. Order 8802, *Federal Register,* vol. VI (1941), p. 3109.
24. Exec. Order 9981, *Federal Register,* vol. XIII (1948), p. 4313.

which discrimination based on race was particularly heinous: military service for one's native land. President Truman was convinced that he had to move on his own, insofar as that was legal and possible, because of the fate that the report of his President's Committee on Civil Rights had suffered at the hands of Congress: in 1946 he had appointed a fifteen-member blue-ribbon committee[25] and charged it specifically with the careful investigation of the need for legislative and other procedures designed to further and protect civil rights and liberties. One year later, the committee reported that although civil rights were indeed better and more generally protected than ever before, there were still alarmingly widespread violations. In its broadly distributed report, *To Secure These Rights,* the committee made numerous recommendations designed to ensure that every violation of a civil right by any individual be treated as a criminal offense. Were these recommendations to be followed, the enforcement of civil rights would become a new and vigorous government activity on a much extended scale. Specifically, the committee's proposals included federal laws to forbid lynching; to outlaw discrimination in voting requirements; to create a permanent Fair Employment Practices Commission and a permanent Commission on Civil Rights; and to expand into a Civil Rights Division the small, undermanned Civil Rights Section in the Department of Justice that Attorney General Murphy had established eight years earlier.

Like all proposals for the extension of government activities, these quickly became a political issue. Still, President Truman committed himself to the implementation of the report as far as federal action was feasible—in the face of considerable risks to his party position and his campaign for reelection in 1948. Indeed, that campaign witnessed the bolting from the Democratic Party of four southern states[26] and their formation of the Dixiecrat Party under then Democrat Strom Thurmond of South Carolina. Nonetheless, the president made *To Secure These Rights* an issue throughout his campaign. He won reelection, but he did not obtain—as already noted—congressional acquiescence. In fact, Congress took no action during the remaining four years of the Truman administration, a hiatus that extended through the first four and a half years of the Eisenhower presidency. But Truman attempted to salvage what he could by executive order. Shortly before his 1948 order banning segregation in the armed forces, he had issued an executive order[27] establishing a Fair Employment Board to oversee announced policy that henceforth all federal jobs were to be distributed without any regard to "race, color, religion, or national origin." Three years later the president created the Committee on Government Contract Compliance, requiring any business holding a contract with the federal government not only to pledge but to provide bona fide fair em-

25. Exec. Order 9808, *Federal Register,* vol. XI (1946), p. 14153. The committee was headed by Charles E. Wilson ("Electric Charlie"), president of General Electric.
26. Alabama, Louisiana, Mississippi, and South Carolina.
27. Exec. Order 9980, *Federal Register,* vol. XIII (1948), p. 4311.

ployment policies and practices.[28] The tenor of these several executive moves gradually began to pervade much of the executive establishment.

President Eisenhower continued his predecessor's civil rights policies. Resorting to the technique of the executive order,[29] the new chief executive created the President's Committee on Government Contracts, headed by Vice-President Nixon. The committee was empowered to receive complaints alleging discrimination by government contractors, and to cancel contracts if necessary. Various cabinet departments and agencies continued the policy of earlier administrations against sundry types of obvious internal discrimination.

The Watershed. These activities were of course not lost on the several states. A good many northern states turned to the FEPC and similar devices to combat discrimination. The air was filled with the beginnings of change. Yet the South was determined not to budge, and in Congress it had a seemingly eternal ally. President Eisenhower did not recommend any new civil rights legislation until his administration's Civil Rights Bill of 1956. It failed to be enacted, but Congress did pass a modified version, the Civil Rights Act of 1957, the first major piece of civil rights legislation since Reconstruction. It is fair to say, however, that it would never have become law had not the Supreme Court swung into the fray with its monumentally significant ruling in the *Public School Segregation Cases*[30] on May 17, 1954.

That decision was one of the most far-reaching in our history in terms of its social impact.[31] It catalyzed the issue of racial discrimination; it focused responsibility for remedial action on government officials everywhere; and, especially, it pointed an accusing finger at that branch of government presumably responsible for social action: the legislature. Conscious of its position as a national moral goad as well as a teacher in a continuing national constitutional seminar, the Court had led. Recognizing the necessarily limited options open to the executive branch, and the immobility of the legislative on the issue, the Supreme Court had decided unanimously that it had to create a line. As Justice Jackson remarked laconically during oral argument in *Brown,* "I suppose that realistically the reason this case is here was [*sic*] that action could not be obtained from Congress."[32] After two and a half years of painful deliberation, the high tribunal chose to attack the concept of "separate but equal" in the field of public school education on the grounds that separate facilities are "inherently

28. Exec. Order 10308, *Federal Register,* vol. XVI (1951), p. 12303.

29. Exec. Order 10479, *Federal Register,* vol. XVIII (1953), p. 4899.

30. *Brown v. Board of Education of Topeka,* 347 U.S. 483 (1954); and *Bolling v. Sharpe,* 347 U.S. 497 (1954).

31. Chief Justice Warren ranked it in second place behind *Baker v. Carr,* 369 U.S. 186 (1962)—see *supra* chapter 2—in terms of the significance of cases his Court decided during the sixteen-year tenure from 1953 to 1969.

32. Oral argument in the Virginia and South Carolina segments of the suit, p. 244.

unequal," and that the very concept of "separate but equal" in matters of race violates the "equal protection of the laws" clause of the Fourteenth Amendment (on the state level) and the "due process of law" clause of the Fifth Amendment (on the federal level).[33]

"SEPARATE BUT EQUAL": RISE AND DEMISE

We know that the intent of the three Civil War amendments was to abolish the institution of slavery, to bestow the full benefit of American citizenship upon blacks, and to enable them to exercise the franchise. And for a brief period of roughly two decades, give or take a few years depending upon the individual state involved, blacks were indeed in a position to exercise their newly confirmed civil rights relatively effectively—backed, to be sure, by federal Reconstruction forces. But, as we also know—and as C. Vann Woodward, among others, has told us so well[34]—the dominant white elements in the old Confederacy were not about to grant blacks anything like genuine, lasting freedom and equality; indeed, they utilized every conceivable covert and overt device to bar the onetime slaves from attaining even the semblance of first-class citizenship. As the evangelism and fervor of Northern abolitionists began to subside, especially after the Hayes Compromise of 1877 had resulted in the withdrawal of the troops from the South, Southern leadership all but restored the status quo ante—with the overwhelming support of the Southern constituency. By 1900 the Southern black had been pushed back into second-class citizenship. Jim Crow, with certain refinements, again reigned supreme.

The Rise of Separate but Equal

Black leaders endeavored to battle this trend. Unable to expect any aid in their efforts from either the executive or legislative branches, they turned to the state judiciary. But it, too, quickly proved itself generally in sympathy with the point of view of the region's population and its leadership. The blacks' only hope thus hinged on the U.S. Supreme Court. And *it* proved for a long time to be a vain hope.[35]

---

33. *Brown v. Board,* op. cit., which involved four different states—Kansas, Virginia, Delaware, and South Carolina—and *Bolling v. Sharpe,* op. cit., which concerned the District of Columbia only.

34. See his *Strange Career of Jim Crow,* rev. ed. (New York: Oxford University Press, 1966).

35. For an account of the story of the Supreme Court of the United States and black petitioners, written by the son of a black slave and his white wife, see Loren Miller's book *The Petitioners* (New York: Pantheon, 1966).

An Ill Omen: Slaughterhouse. The famous *Slaughterhouse Cases,*[36] as handed down by the Court in 1873, foreshadowed a bleak future for the black cause. Ironically, blacks were *not* involved in that litigation, and the Court's language even seemed to give distinct comfort to them. There were ringing phrases regarding the purposes of the Civil War amendments: the achievement of "freedom for the slave race," the "security and firm establishment of that freedom," and the protection of the "newly made freeman and citizen from the oppressions of those who had formerly exercised unlimited dominion over him."[37] But, as noted in the earlier discussion[38] of these cases, the Court's *real* point was that there must be a careful distinction between the "privileges or immunities" of *United States* citizens and *state* (here Louisiana) citizens; that the only privileges attaching to national citizenship are those that "owe their existence to the Federal Government, its National character, its Constitution, or its laws";[39] that, in effect, a citizen of a state derived his "privileges or immunities" from *state* citizenship, a thing quite "distinct" from federal citizenship rights, which "depend upon different characteristics or circumstances in the individual."[40] In other words, if blacks had hoped to rely on the "privileges or immunities" clause of that amendment as a source of salvation in their struggle for equal rights, the Supreme Court's narrow construction of the clause—one never really altered to this day—rendered it of little value as a restraint upon state regulation. But what of the due process of law and equal protection of the laws clauses of the Fourteenth Amendment?

Another Hope Shattered: The Civil Rights Cases. Things seemed to look up when Congress, in an effort to aid blacks, passed the Civil Rights Act of 1875, which made it a *federal* crime for any owner or operator of, inter alia, a hotel, public conveyance, or theater to "deny the full enjoyments of the accommodations thereof" because of race or color. Various blacks were nonetheless denied access and brought suit in a series of five cases,[41] ultimately consolidated by the Supreme Court as the *Civil Rights Cases* of 1883.[42] The Court, in an 8:1 decision written by Justice Joseph P. Bradley, with only Justice John Marshall Harlan I in dissent, declared the act of 1875 unconstitutional. The Court did so on the grounds that the Fourteenth Amendment applied to state action only and did not give Congress authority to forbid discrimination by private individuals (a point

36. 16 Wallace 36.
37. Ibid. at 71.
38. See *supra* chapter 3.
39. The *Slaughterhouse Cases,* op. cit., at 79.
40. Ibid., majority opinion by Justice Miller at 74.
41. One each from California, Kansas, Missouri, New Jersey, and Tennessee.
42. 109 U.S. 3. Their story is well known and well told. See, e.g., Alan F. Westin, "The Case of the Prejudiced Doorkeeper," in John A. Garraty, ed., *Quarrels That Have Shaped the Constitution* (New York: Harper and Row, 1987), pp. 139–56.

it had already made a few months earlier in *United States v. Harris,*[43] in which it declared unconstitutional a section of the Ku Klux Klan Act of 1871 as being inapplicable to the acts of *private* persons); that if the state did not assist the discrimination of an individual against another individual, the matter is purely between the two as private persons. An intriguing effort to utilize the Civil Rights Act of 1871 to bar antiabortion blockades of clinics was rejected (6:3) by the U.S. Supreme Court in *Bray v. Alexandria Women's Health Clinic*[44] in 1993. Thus, not only had the Supreme Court sharply limited the "privileges or immunities" that had, seemingly, come with national citizenship, it now read the phrase "no state shall" in the Fourteenth and Fifteenth Amendments to mean solely and literally the actions of state government *officials.* The decisive Court majority refused to accept the contention that it was in fact state action when individuals and corporations *licensed by a state* to "serve all without discrimination" used race as a criterion. As for alleged violation of the Thirteenth Amendment, it regarded restrictive public accommodations as having nothing to do with slavery or involuntary servitude. Indeed, Bradley commented in an oft-quoted dictum that blacks should cease endeavoring to obtain "special treatment"; that there had to be a time when blacks stopped being "the special favorite of the law" and adopted "the rank of a mere citizen" (a refrain that became highly audible again in the face of the "affirmative action" programs of the 1960s and beyond).[45] Harlan, however, not only flayed Bradley for these comments but firmly voted to uphold the Civil Rights Act of 1875. He insisted that it was well settled that "railroad corporations, keepers of inns, and managers of places of public amusement are *agents or instrumentalities of the State*"[46] and that the act regardless could and should have been upheld under the congressional power over interstate commerce—foreshadowing the Civil Rights Act of 1964 and its quick, unanimous upholding by the Supreme Court.[47]

Gradually taking their cue from the *Slaughterhouse, Harris,* and *Civil Rights* decisions, most of the states of the old Confederacy not only closed their eyes to the steadily spreading segregation practices that either had sprung up or were revived within their borders, but in the four-year period between 1887 and 1891 alone, eight of them enacted legislation *requiring* railroads, for example, to maintain *separate* facilities for whites and blacks.

---

43. 106 U.S. 629 (1882).

44. 506 U.S. 263. Early in 1994 the Court, in a unanimous ruling authored by Chief Justice Rehnquist, provided a new federal weapon against violence at abortion clinics by holding that groups responsible for such activity are suable under the Racketeer Influenced and Corrupt Organization (RICO) Act, but reversed itself in 2003.

45. The *Civil Rights Cases,* op. cit., at 25. For an analysis of the "affirmative action"/"reverse-discrimination" syndrome see *infra* chapter 8.

46. Ibid. at 58; italics supplied.

47. See *infra* this chapter.

Enter Plessy v. Ferguson. There had been earlier legal skirmishes at the state level; indeed, the "separate but equal" concept had been heavily attacked, albeit unsuccessfully, by Charles Sumner when Massachusetts Chief Justice Lemuel Shaw adopted it almost half a century earlier in 1849 in *Roberts v. the City of Boston*[48] by ruling in favor of Boston's "police power" to segregate schools. But the issue was first joined at the highest federal level in the case of *Plessy v. Ferguson,*[49] which was destined to remain law for fifty-eight years. Before the Court was the constitutionality of Louisiana's Jim Crow Car Act of 1890, euphemistically entitled "An Act to Promote the Comfort of Passengers." It required that railroads "provide equal but separate accommodations for the white and colored races" and that "no person be permitted to occupy seats in coaches other than the ones assigned to his race. Here, then, it was: *equal* but *separate.* With the exception of an 1892 decision in which the Louisiana Supreme Court had held the new law to be inapplicable to an *interstate* passenger—a decision the state did not appeal—all prior tests of the 1890 act at the state level had ended in victory for the new doctrine. Now at last the Supreme Court would hear and adjudicate the problem of "separate but equal," a problem which had been brought to it through the efforts of a group of eighteen blacks who had formed a "Citizens' Committee to Test the Constitutionality of the Separate Car Law" and raised $2,982 for the litigation. As their attorney they selected Albion Winegar Tourgee of Maryville, then residing in New York, a leading white carpetbagger during Reconstruction who, an Ohioan by birth, had served in the Union army, in which he was twice wounded in battle, and then had moved to Greensboro, North Carolina, to practice law. There he became a leader of the Radical Republican Party and a confirmed advocate of black rights, took an active part in the creation of the state's radical constitution, and served as a judge of the superior court of his adopted state for six years. Tourgee, who was aided in the formulation and presentation of the case by James C. Walker, New Orleans attorney, had been chosen by the Citizens' Committee even prior to the 1892 Louisiana "victory," which he obtained. That case had not met the needs and aims of the Jim Crow Act's challengers. Homer Adolph Plessy's case did.[50]

---

48. Cush. (59 Mass.) 198 at 206. Sumner here unsuccessfully represented Sarah C. Roberts, a black child, who brought suit against the city of Boston under an 1845 statute that provided for recovery of damages from "the city or town" that supported instruction from which any child was unlawfully excluded. Sumner's argument—to the effect that segregation schools can never be equal—prophetically antedated the NAACP brief in *Brown v. Board of Education* (see *infra* this chapter).

49. 63 U.S. 537 (1896).

50. Plessy was tried before Judge Ferguson, who would ultimately become the named defendant in Lousiana's criminal court. For a lively and illuminating description of the case and its setting, plus an engaging sketch of the principals, see C. Vann Woodward, "The Case of the Louisiana Traveler," in John A. Garraty, ed., *Quarrels That Have Shaped the Constitution* (New York: Harper and Row, 1987), pp. 157–74.

Plessy, thirty-four years of age, was seven-eighths white—an "octoroon"; his one-eighth "African blood" was not apparent. The Citizens' Committee had seen to it that the East Louisiana Railroad knew of his background. Selected by the committee to test the statute, Plessy boarded in New Orleans, having purchased a ticket to Covington, Louisiana, and took a seat in the "whites only" coach; when the conductor requested that he move to the "colored only" section, Plessy refused, whereupon he was promptly arrested by Detective Christopher C. Cain and charged with violating the Jim Crow Car Act of 1890. Tourgee's defense contended that the Louisiana statute under which Plessy had been arrested and charged was null and void as a violation of both the Thirteenth and Fourteenth Amendments. The argument turned on the latter's proscription of the denial of the "equal protection of the laws." Partly because of the fundamental requirement inherent in the judicial process that all remedies "below" must be exhausted before the Supreme Court will consider an otherwise properly qualified case, and partly because of its own work load, the high tribunal did not hand down its decision until four years later. These intervening years saw a further attrition of black post–Civil War gains—and unless the Court were to strike down the "separate but equal" doctrine, Jim Crow would be perpetuated.

The opinion of the Court—with Justice David J. Brewer not participating— upheld the statute (7:1). Once again, the lone dissenter was John Marshall Harlan I, whose grandson and namesake was destined to help preside over Jim Crow's judicial demise in the Court six decades later.[51] The majority opinion in *Plessy* was written by Justice Henry Billings Brown, one of seven northerners then on the Court.[52] Brown's opinion, which, he later recalled, was "reached with little difficulty,"[53] frankly acknowledged Louisiana's action to have been "state action," thus falling under Fourteenth Amendment consideration; *but*, he held, the action was *not discriminatory*, since the whites were separated just as much from the blacks as the blacks were separated from the whites! As for the charge that the basis for the separation was race, Brown ruled that was not in and of itself a violation of the Constitution's equal protection clause, for a state had every right under that document to "classify" as long as that classification[54] was not capricious, arbitrary, or unreasonable. "Separate but equal" did not run afoul of

51. He joined the Supreme Court approximately one year after the 1954 *Public School Segregation Cases,* op. cit., and was on the bench when the Court handed down its implementation decision in the second *Public Segregation Cases (Brown v. Board of Education of Topeka,* et al., 349 U.S. 294 [1955]).

52. The southerners were Harlan and Justice Edward D. White of Louisiana.

53. See Charles A. Lofgren, *The Plessy Case: A Legal-Historical Approach* (New York: Oxford University Press, 1987), p. 199; and Clarence Thomas, "The Virtue of Defeat: *Plessy v. Ferguson,* in Retrospect," *Journal of Supreme Court History* 15 (1997).

54. For a discussion of "classification" see Jewell Cass Phillips, Henry J. Abraham, and Cortez A. M. Ewing, *Essentials of American National Government,* 3d ed. (New York: American Book Co., 1971), pp. 110ff.

these considerations, said Brown, since the claim that the concept intended to "stamp the colored race with a badge of inferiority" (a phrase that would be quoted and construed quite differently by Chief Justice Earl Warren fifty-eight years later) was "not by reason of anything found in the act, but *solely because the colored race chooses to put that construction upon it.*" And Brown could not forbear to add: "If one race be inferior to another socially, the Constitution of the United States cannot put them upon the same plane." He admitted that the Fourteenth Amendment was "undoubtedly designed to enforce the absolute equality of the two races before the law," but that "it could not have been intended in the nature of things . . . [to] abolish distinction based upon color or to enforce social, as distinct from political equality."[55]

In eloquent anger, Justice Harlan rejected what he viewed as the majority's social Darwinism. To him, as to many others who would follow, the line drawn here by his colleagues reflected "a compound of bad logic, bad history, bad sociology, and bad constitutional law."[56] Moreover, it flew in the face of recent precedent.[57] "The thin disguise of 'equal' accommodations for passengers in railroad coaches will not mislead anyone, nor atone for the wrong this day done," Harlan warned the majority. He attacked the decision as one redolent with sociological speculation: "The arbitrary separation of citizens on the basis of race, while they are on a public highway, is a badge of servitude wholly inconsistent with the civil freedom and the equality of the law established by the Constitution. It cannot be justified upon any legal grounds."[58] And in memorable language he went on to note that

> in view of the Constitution, in the eye of the law, there is in this country no superior, dominant, ruling class of citizens. There is no caste here. *Our constitution is color-blind, and neither knows nor tolerates classes among citizens.*[59] In respect of civil rights all citizens are equal before the law. The

55. *Plessy v. Ferguson*, 163 U.S. 537 (1896) at 551, 544.

56. Robert J. Harris, *The Quest for Equality: The Constitution, Congress, and the Supreme Court* (Baton Rouge: Louisiana State University Press, 1960), p. 101.

57. *Strauder v. West Virginia*, 100 U.S. 303 (1880), in which the Court had struck down on Fourteenth Amendment equal protection grounds a state law that limited jury duty to *white male* citizens — although it proved to be a Pyrrhic victory. See also *ex parte Virginia*, 100 U.S. 339 (1880), where the Supreme Court upheld the conviction of a county court judge for having excluded blacks from jury lists compiled by him, solely because of their race. He had acted in violation of a federal law specifically forbidding such discrimination. Both cases were decided 7:2, Field and Clifford dissenting.

58. 163 U.S. 537 at 562.

59. Almost eighty years later, with *Plessy* overruled twenty years earlier in *Brown v. Board*, Chief Justice Hale of the Washington Supreme Court, speaking in dissent in the reverse discrimination case of *De Funis v. Odegaard*, 507 P.2d 1169 (1973) at 1189, asked whether the Constitution may be color-conscious in order to be color-blind — an ironic denouement (see *infra* this chapter). He believed not, but events since seem to have demonstrated the contrary.

humblest is the peer of the most powerful. The law regards man as man, and takes no account of his surroundings or of his color when his civil rights as guaranteed by the supreme law of the land are involved.[60]

But this was a *dissenting* opinion. The separate but equal concept had not only been adopted; now it had been judicially sanctioned.[61] It proved to be most detrimental to the blacks' cause in education, public accommodations, the franchise, the administration of justice, housing, employment, and, needless to add, social relationships. White supremacy seemed to have triumphed; assuredly this was true in most of the states below the Mason-Dixon Line. For that matter, when Brown spoke in *Plessy,* not only the southern and border states, but a total of thirty states of the Union, including most of those in the West, as well as Indiana, Kansas, and New York, had separate but equal public school statutes.

Chipping Away at the Doctrine

Yet, however slowly and imperceptibly, the legal chisels were being readied; the chipping away at the "separate but equal" line probably began with the case of *Missouri ex rel. Gaines v. Canada*[62] in 1938. Actually, the *first* court-enforced admission of a black to a heretofore segregated higher institution of learning had come two years earlier, when the Maryland Court of Appeals—that state's highest tribunal—ordered Donald Murray admitted to the University of Maryland School of Law.[63] But it was *Gaines* which initially gave notice to the nation that the winds of change had begun to blow. That change had its practical roots in certain attitudes, both legal and social, which were growing partly as a result of what might be called a heightened egalitarian national conscience and partly because of the imminence of war. In any event, it manifested itself chiefly in the gradual but unquestionably progressive shift in rulings of the U.S. Supreme Court from acceptance of the separate but equal doctrine to a close examination of the alleged "equality" to, ultimately, the firm rejection of the constitutionality of the doctrine. It took almost two decades to proceed from stage one to stage three. Although the Supreme Court clearly led—and it did so despite vilification and abuse—it did have an important ally, however tenuous, in what might be called the national conscience.

60. Ibid. at 559; italics supplied. According to his colleague Brewer, Harlan "went to sleep with one hand upon the Constitution and the other on the Bible, and thus secured the untroubled sleep of the just and the righteous" (quoted in G. Edward White, *The American Judicial Tradition* [New York: Oxford University Press, 1976], p. 129).

61. Plessy pleaded "guilty" in Louisiana Criminal District Court to the charge at issue and was fined $25. The case cost $2,762 of the $2,982 that the Citizens Committee had raised to support its challenge to Jim Crow. The committee distributed $160 of the balance to Louisiana charities and used the remaining $60 to inscribe a "flattering testimonial" to Tourgee (Lofgren, op. cit., p. 208).

62. 305 U.S. 337.

63. *Pearson v. Murray,* 169 Md. 478 (1936). He was admitted and ultimately graduated.

The Gaines Case. Lloyd Gaines was a black citizen of Missouri who sought, but was denied, admission to the School of Law of the state-owned University of Missouri after his graduation from Lincoln University, an all-black Missouri institution. There was no claim of lack of qualifications—S. W. Canada, the university's registrar, simply pointed to a Missouri statute under which the two races were to be educated "separately but equally." Mr. Canada told Gaines that he could, of course, avail himself of another feature of Missouri law applying specifically to black law school applicants, whereby state funds were made available to qualified blacks for their legal education in schools of *adjacent states* that offered unsegregated facilities—for example, Kansas, Nebraska, Iowa, and Illinois. But, encouraged in his stand by the increasingly active and influential National Association for the Advancement of Colored People (NAACP), Gaines declined. What he wanted, he said, was what was his due as a full-fledged citizen and taxpayer of his home state of Missouri: the right to attend the state law school and to practice law in Missouri. Mr. Canada again refused. The NAACP then financed Gaines's appeal through the lower courts and ultimately to the Supreme Court of the United States. Chief Justice Charles Evans Hughes wrote the opinion, speaking also for Justices Brandeis, Stone, Cardozo, Roberts, Black, and Reed; only Justices McReynolds and Butler—the two surviving members of the so-called arch-conservative quads[64]—dissented, pleading for a continuation of a practice that, they agreed, was in the "best interests" of Missouri's people.[65]

The chief justice praised the state of Missouri for the financial arrangements outlined but held that since there was no law school for blacks in the entire state—Lincoln University had none—the equal protection guarantee of the Fourteenth Amendment was in fact denied Lloyd Gaines. Hughes, continuing to give comfort to the partisans of the separate but equal doctrine, explicitly stated that Missouri could have fulfilled its obligation to provide legal instruction to its black citizens "by furnishing equal facilities in separate schools, a method the validity of which has been sustained by our decisions."[66] In other words, he ruled that while the Constitution did not guarantee Gaines's admission to the School of Law of the University of Missouri, it did guarantee a legal education in Missouri substantially equal to that afforded by the state to members of the white race. That Gaines happened to be the only black wishing such an education was beside the point. The state subsequently decided to set up a separate law school for blacks at Lincoln University, but Lloyd Gaines, perhaps overcome by notoriety and pressure, chose to disappear shortly before the Court's decision was handed

64. The other two were Justices Van Devanter and Sutherland, replaced by Black and Reed in 1937 and 1938, respectively. Yet it is entirely plausible that—based on their records in the civil rights and liberties realm—the two departed justices would have joined the majority opinion.

65. *Missouri ex rel. Gaines v. Canada,* 305 U.S. 337 (1938), dissenting opinion at 353.

66. Ibid., majority opinion at 344.

down. While it remained for someone else, then, to test the separate but equal doctrine per se, the *Gaines* case had laid the foundations based on the equal protection of the laws clause of Amendment Fourteen.[67] It was this clause that would bring ultimate victory to the blacks' strivings·

Post-Gaines. Almost ten years of prewar, war, and postwar preoccupation elapsed before the Court dealt with the doctrine again. Inconclusively, but nonetheless pointedly, in 1948 it ordered the state of Oklahoma to provide a duly qualified, NAACP-backed black woman applicant with an equal legal education in a state institution—ultimately the University of Oklahoma College of Law, whence she received her degree in 1951.[68] The results were less than satisfactory in terms of the ultimate goal, but there was no longer any question that, at the very least, *equal* facilities would have to be state-provided.

Two years later, however, the Court handed down a set of decisions which made painfully clear to the South that while separate but equal might still not be unconstitutional, it was patently on its last legs. The two 1950 cases were announced on the same Opinion Monday, and both were decided unanimously in opinions written by Chief Justice Vinson. Although neither outlawed the "separate but equal" doctrine per se, the conditions posited by the Court for its continued constitutionality were now in fact unattainable. Both cases had once again been stimulated and backed by the NAACP's capable, increasingly active, legal team. One, *Sweatt v. Painter,*[69] concerned the University of Texas's statutorily sanctioned denial of H. M. Sweatt's request for admission to its law school solely because he was black. Sweatt, a Houston mail carrier aspiring to be a lawyer, had refused to attend the separate law school for blacks established by Texas as a result of the *Gaines* case. He argued that because it was inferior, it would deprive him of the equal protection of the laws. The second case, *McLaurin v. Oklahoma State Regents,*[70] dealt with an ingenious requirement by the Oklahoma legislature, which enabled qualified blacks, such as Professor G. W. McLaurin, to do graduate study (here toward a doctorate in education) at the state-owned University of Oklahoma *if* the university's authorities admitted them as candidates on a "segregated basis"—defined as "classroom instruction given in separate classrooms, or at separate times."

67. See "Personal Rights, Public Wrongs: The *Gaines* Case and the Beginning of the End of Segregation," 2 *Journal of Supreme Court History* 113 (1997).

68. S*ipuel v. Oklahoma,* 322 U.S. 631 (1948); and *Fisher v. Hurst,* 333 U.S. 147 (1948), successfully argued by Thurgood Marshall and decided per curiam. Ada Lois Sipuel, a twenty-two-year-old Langston University graduate from Chickashaw, Oklahoma, had become Mrs. Fisher in the intervening period. In 1992 Mrs. Sipuel-Fisher was gubernatorially appointed as a member of the University of Oklahoma's Board of Regents.

69. 339 U.S. 629 (1950).

70. 339 U.S. 637 (1950).

Sweatt's argument that the Texas State University for Negroes was simply "inferior" and hence *unequal* found willing listeners. The chief justice's brief but lucid opinion pointed not only to the obvious physical differences between the two schools—which alone would have made them sufficiently unequal—but, far more significantly, to those "qualities which are incapable of objective measurement but which make for greatness in a law school."[71] Among these qualities he noted "reputation of the faculty, experience of the administration, position and influence of the alumni, standing in the community, tradition and prestige."[72] Tongue in cheek, Vinson commented that it was indeed difficult to believe that one who had a free choice between the two law schools involved would "consider the question close."[73] And he went on to identify some of the intensely practical considerations that rendered the new law school for blacks so decidedly inferior:

> The law school to which Texas is willing to admit [Sweatt] excludes from its student body members of the racial groups which number 85 per cent of the population of the State and include most of the lawyers, witnesses, jurors, judges, and other officials with whom [Sweatt] will inevitably be dealing when he becomes a member of the Texas Bar. With such a substantial and significant segment of society excluded, we cannot conclude that the education offered [Sweatt] is substantially equal to that which he would receive if admitted to the University of Texas Law School.[74]

While the Court thus held that there was simply no way to make the two schools equal and yet separate, it still had stopped short of declaring the doctrine null and void. Yet its willingness to look at sociopolitical, philosophical, and psychological "intangibles" of the separate but equal doctrine inexorably pointed the way to the 1954–55 *Public School Segregation Cases.*

The circumstances surrounding McLaurin's case were just as unpropitious for the future of the separate but equal concept. After McLaurin had been ordered admitted to the University of Oklahoma's School of Education to work for his doctorate in education, and since he was the only black so admitted at the time, the university administration endeavored to comply with the state-mandated provisions for "segregated admission" by resorting to the following degrading devices: rather than arranging separate classes for him, the university required him to sit apart at a designated desk in what was variously described as a "hallway" or an "anteroom adjoining the classroom," where he and the instructor could see and hear each other, but from which vantage point he would presumably not contaminate the superior race of his fellow students. In the library he was assigned

71. *Sweatt v. Painter,* op. cit., at 634.
72. Ibid.
73. Ibid.
74. Ibid. Sweatt was duly admitted but failed to earn a degree.

a special desk on the mezzanine floor but was told that he could not use the desks in the regular reading room. In the school cafeteria he was directed to eat at a specifically designated table and to do so at a different time than his white fellow students. And, as the chief justice described it in his opinion:

> For some time, the section of the classroom in which [McLaurin] sat was surrounded by a rail on which there was a sign stating, "Reserved for Colored," but these have been removed. He is now [at the time of the litigation] assigned to a seat in the classroom in a row specified for colored students.[75]

This hocus-pocus, declared the unanimous tribunal, was neither "equal" nor constitutional—and McLaurin was promptly admitted to full student citizenship and the equal protection of the laws.

After the 1950 triumphs of Messrs. Sweatt and McLaurin—and that same year's U.S. Circuit Court of Appeals–ordered admission of twenty-six-year-old Gregory H. Swanson as the first black to the University of Virginia School of Law in order to pursue graduate studies there—the barriers prevalent in higher education in the border states and the South began to give way, however gradually. But it would take the death of the separate but equal doctrine and the employment of federal troops in Tuscaloosa, Alabama, and Oxford, Mississippi, thirteen years later, before every state in the heretofore segregated area would admit at least one black to at least one of its graduate or professional institutions of higher learning.

Although the effective catalyst would be the *Public School Segregation Cases* of 1954 and 1955, collateral developments[76] also assisted in chipping away at the separate but equal doctrine. Transportation was one of these. As early as 1941, a unanimous Court, speaking through Chief Justice Hughes, held that the treatment of a black on an interstate journey—denying him the right to use an available Pullman seat after he had paid a first-class fare, and requiring him to leave that car and ride in a second-class one—violated the Interstate Commerce Act. Moreover, the Court found that the accommodations for black passengers were inferior to those for white passengers.[77] And five years later, a Virginia segregation statute, as applied to interstate buses, was declared unconstitutional (7:1) in a Supreme Court opinion authored by Justice Stanley F. Reed.[78] Four years later, compulsory segregation on interstate trains was outlawed—first by another Supreme Court decision,[79] then by the Interstate Com-

---

75. *McLaurin v. Oklahoma State Regents,* op. cit., at 640.
76. See *infra* and *supra* this chapter.
77. *Mitchell v. United States,* 313 U.S. 80 (1941).
78. *Morgan v. Virginia,* 328 U.S. 373 (1946). The lone dissenter was Burton. It was actually the Irene Morgan of that case—not Rosa Parks eleven years later—who initiated defiance of segregated buses in 1944; but Mrs. Morgan did not receive full recognition of her action until decades later. See this chapter *infra,* note 267.
79. *Henderson v. United States,* 333 U.S. 816 (1950).

merce Commission, which particularly referred to sleeping and dining cars. Ultimately, the ICC ordered the cessation of all racial segregation on interstate buses and trains and their public waiting rooms in stations and terminals. To the advocates of segregation, if there was to be an effective last stand at all, it would have to come in intrastate matters—of which, they hoped, public schools would be one of the most important. Then, on what would be known to arch-segregationists as "Black Monday," May 17, 1954, came *Brown v. Board of Education of Topeka, et al.*[80] Powerful rearguard actions continued to be fought, but the separate but equal doctrine was lost as a legal force.

The Death of the Separate but Equal Doctrine

The *Public School Segregation Cases* of 1954, and their implementation decision one year later, transferred, in the words of one commentator, "the legal sanction and moral authority of the nation's basic law from the segregationist forces to the civil rights advocates."[81] It marked the end of an era and the beginning of a new one. In the words of Alpheus T. Mason: "On May 17, 1954, the Court initiated the greatest social revolution of this generation."[82] Most of the considerable political, economic, and social progress blacks have been able to achieve since 1954 stems demonstrably from *Brown v. Board* and its offspring—and much of the criticism of the Supreme Court's authority in that era was traceable to that decision and its results. It richly deserves explanation and analysis.

Some Groundwork. Following the *Sweatt* and *McLaurin* decisions, the NAACP's now highly encouraged lawyers, headed by Thurgood Marshall, bided their time in the hope that the South might show some disposition to comply with the spirit of those two decisions and embark upon some "gradualist" program of desegregation. It is idle to speculate whether more courageous leadership by southerners and nonsoutherners, in and out of government, might have brought about the desired change. The fact is that no such leadership of any consequence was forthcoming. The evolving southern strategy now seemed to follow the candid public statement of Governor James F. Byrnes of South Carolina that, indeed, the South had failed properly to facilitate the education of its blacks and that "to remedy a hundred years of neglect" a crash building program of fine new schools for blacks had to be started instantly. Byrnes readily admitted that the South would

---

80. 347 U.S. 483.

81. Alan F. Westin, in Emmett S. Redford, David B. Truman, Andrew Hacker, Alan F. Westin, and Robert Wood, eds., *Politics and Government in the United States* (New York: Harcourt, Brace and World, 1968), p. 588.

82. *The Supreme Court: Palladium of Freedom* (Ann Arbor: University of Michigan Press, 1962), p. 170. For a revisionist view of the Court as "constrained" in its role as social reformer, see Gerald N. Rosenberg's *The Hollow Hope: Can Courts Bring About Social Change?* (Chicago: University of Chicago Press, 1991).

have to act, and act at once, to preserve the separate but equal concept, lest the Supreme Court, as he—once (1941–42) a member of that tribunal himself—put it, "take matters out of the state's hands." When all overt and covert entreaties for a gradualist approach were rejected, particularly by Virginia and South Carolina, Marshall and his battery of attorneys determined that the time had come to wage an all-out battle in the courts against separate but equal. They had no difficulty in finding appropriate vehicles for the desired litigation, and five separate de-segregation suits were instituted in carefully selected parts of the country. Four were begun in the states of Delaware, Kansas (Topeka), South Carolina (Clarendon County), and Virginia (Prince Edward County), and one at the federal level in the District of Columbia. Each suit, painstakingly presented by NAACP attorneys, charged not only that the several local black schools involved were *inferior* to their white counterparts but that the separate but equal rule itself violated the equal protection of the laws clause of Amendment Fourteen.

To no one's great astonishment the suits lost everywhere, save in Delaware, where a limited victory was achieved. (The lower court adhered to the separate but equal precedent of *Plessy* but ordered plaintiffs admitted to the white schools because of their superiority to their black counterparts.) However, the Supreme Court granted certiorari during 1952, hearing extensive oral arguments from both sides that December. According to one source, the vote to grant review came by the requisite bare minimum of four.[83] Thurgood Marshall's forces, augmented by other friendly lawyers and buttressed by a brief amicus curiae brought by President Truman's Attorney General Edward T. McGranahan, were supported in their argument in what was to become a famous appendix to their brief. In it, thirty American social scientists of national and international reputation[84] not only supported the NAACP's fundamental charge of segregation as constituting discrimination but—even more significantly from the standpoint of the Court's ultimate opinion—contended at length that segregation as such was harmful to the psyche of *both* black and white children, causing irreparable damage to their development as members of a healthy heterogeneous community. Arguing—without fee—on behalf of the segregation status quo, as represented by the five cases, was one of America's foremost constitutional law experts, trial attorney John W. Davis, who not only had held numerous high-ranking jobs in government but had been the unsuccessful Democratic nominee for president in 1924. It would be the now eighty-year-old Davis's last appearance before the Court—to which he had declined a nomination by President Warren G. Harding in 1922.

Conscious of the significance of the issue at bar, the Supreme Court bided its time. In June 1953 it not only rescheduled the cases for *reargument* but sub-

---

83. Fred Rodell, "It Is the Earl Warren Court," *New York Times Magazine,* March 13, 1966, p. 93. Apparently Frankfurter, Douglas, Burton, and Minton.

84. Among them Kenneth Clark, Floyd Allport, Robert M. MacIver, Robert Redfield, and Alfred McC. Lee.

mitted a set of five fundamental Frankfurter-framed questions to opposing counsel with directions for appropriate responses, questions that dealt chiefly with the meaning and intent of the Fourteenth Amendment vis-à-vis segregation and certain practical aspects of desegregation. However hypothetically they were phrased, the nature of the Court's questions caused the hopes of the NAACP and its supporters to soar. But the battle was not yet won, and Marshall, especially in view of what seemed to be the controversial historical aspect of the Court's basic quaere,[85] once again turned to the academic community. In September 1953 he enlisted the expertise of some 130 distinguished, chiefly academic, specialists in constitutional history, law, and interpretation. The impressive array of scholars met, chiefly in New York City, and aided Marshall and his immediate lieutenants in the preparation of the new brief.[86] It was filed on November 15, 1953, and argued orally on December 8, 1953, before a new chief justice, Earl Warren, Vinson having died just prior to the reargument.[87] The brief's chief historical contention was that the framers of Amendment Fourteen had *intended* to ban segregation "as a last vestige of slavery"—a contention elaborately disputed by a good many historians.[88] Davis's response was geared to judicial self-restraint as much as to contrary history; neither the Supreme Court nor any other judicial body had the power, he argued, to declare unconstitutional or ultra vires on sociological or psychological bases a school system, a way of life, duly enacted by the people's representatives, that "has stood for three-quarters of a century." If there was change in the offing, it would have to come either by evolution or by the legislative process. The now Republican administration's attorney general, Herbert Brownell, although not quite so assertive in his support of desegregation as McGranahan had been, filed a brief amicus curiae in favor of desegregation. It did not accept the historical rationale of the main brief but called for a one-year

---

85. The Thirty-ninth Congress—the framers of the Fourteenth Amendment—denied almost to a man that the amendment's equal protection of the laws clause required the desegregation of public institutions; it applied the same reasoning to racial discrimination in the exercise of the suffrage. The latter was reached, of course, by the Fifteenth Amendment two years later.

86. Among them C. Vann Woodward, John Hope Franklin, Alfred H. Kelly, Robert E. Cushman, Robert K. Carr, Milton R. Konvitz, John P. Frank, Walter Gellhorn, Horace Bond, and Howard J. Graham. For an excellent description of their work see Alfred H. Kelly, "The School Segregation Cases," in John A. Garraty, ed., *Quarrels That Have Shaped the Constitution* (New York: Harper and Row, 1987), pp. 307–33.

87. "This is the first indication I have ever had that there is a God," nastily quipped Frankfurter (see Kluger, *infra* note 91).

88. One of these is Raoul Berger, most of whose mammoth and controversial *Government by Judiciary: The Transformation of the Fourteenth Amendment* (Cambridge, Mass.: Harvard University Press, 1977) is intended to demonstrate that the amendment's framers and supporters specifically rejected its application to segregated schools, to juries, to the Senate galleries, and to the franchise (e.g., chapter 15, "The Rule of Law," and chapter 20, "Conclusion").

transition period to permit the South to adjust its social and educational problems. Listening intently to these various arguments in the jammed Supreme Court chamber, the full bench of justices peppered counsel with searching questions.

May 17, 1954. Five months after oral argument, and four years after the *Sweatt* and *McLaurin* decisions, the Supreme Court of the United States rendered its decision.[89] It did not resort to the historical issue in which it had expressed so much interest; obviously, and quite wisely, it did not believe it to be either convincingly resolvable or necessary to the unanimous conclusion it would reach through its new chief justice, who, as he would recall two decades later, assigned himself to write the opinion, "for it seemed to me that something so important ought to issue over the name of the Chief Justice of the United States."[90] Evidently Warren had labored hard and long to get a unanimous opinion; there are reliable indications that two justices were inclined to dissent—albeit on differing grounds—for at least some time during the Court's deliberations;[91] that, indeed,

89. *Brown v. Board of Education of Topeka,* et al., 347 U.S. 483; and *Bolling v. Sharpe,* 347 U.S. 497. The "Brown" in the case was the Reverend Oliver Brown, a welder on the Rock Island Railroad, who filed suit on behalf of his daughter, Linda.
90. Lecture, University of Virginia Legal Forum, April 18, 1973. At a celebration of his ten years on the Court, Warren noted that when the decisions were announced, "the Clerk of our Court for weeks was beset by scores of requests for copies of the 'dissenting opinion.' When told that there was no dissenting opinion, many of them demanded to know by whose order the dissenting opinion had been abolished. Others, believing that there must be a dissenting opinion, threatened to have him investigated for suppressing it" (as quoted in Jacobus ten Broek, *Equal Under Law,* new enlarged edition [New York: Collier, 1965], p. 7).
91. See Rodell, op. cit. Apparently, they were Reed and Jackson. See the account by William H. Harbaugh, *Lawyer's Lawyer: The Life of John W. Davis* (New York: Oxford University Press, 1973), pp. 483–519. See especially Richard Kluger, *Simple Justice: The History of* Brown v. Board of Education *and Black Americans' Struggle for Equality* (New York: Knopf, 1976), esp. pp. 678–99. Kluger reprints a draft dissenting opinion by Reed and demonstrates conclusively that Reed intended to dissent until just two days prior to the rendering of the decision—despite twenty luncheons with the chief justice—when he yielded in the interest of "what was best for America" (at 698). Reed's inner struggle with his conscience and perceived judicial obligations in *Brown* is dramatically recounted by his then law clerk, John D. Fassett, in a 1966 talk, which he did not permit to be published until 1986 ("Mr. Justice Reed and *Brown v. the Board of Education,*" *Yearbook 1986* [Washington, D.C.: Supreme Court Historical Society, 1986], pp. 48–63). (It ought to be noted, however, that it was Reed who had authored the 1944 and 1946 majority opinions striking down the white primary [see *infra* this chapter] and state laws requiring segregated seating on interstate buses [see *supra* this chapter]). Jackson, while resigned to go along, initially insisted on writing a *concurring* opinion based on judicial self-restraint, warning that the Court "was declaring new law for a new day." He craved "positive Congressional action and involvement" rather than judicial lawmaking (see Jeffrey D. Hockett, "Justice Robert H. Jackson and Segregation: A Study of the Limitations and Proper Basis of Judicial Action," *Yearbook 1989* [Washington, D.C.: Supreme Court Historical Society, 1989], pp. 52–67). But he was struck down by a severe coronary thrombosis—which seemed to be the catalyst in his agreeing to desist from penning a separate opinion.

the initial, tentative, conference vote was 6:3.[92] Notwithstanding the complex background and the emotional impact of the issue at hand, the Warren opinion— of which, after his retirement, he said he had written "every blessed word"[93]— was amazingly brief (just eleven pages),[94] simple, and direct, although certainly controversial! "We must look to the effect that segregation itself has on public education," he noted in nearing the heart of his Court's decision:

> In approaching this problem, we cannot turn the clock back to 1868 when the [Fourteenth] Amendment was adopted,[95] or even to 1896 when *Plessy v. Ferguson* was written. We must consider public education in the light of its full development and its present place in American life throughout the Nation. Only in this way can it be determined if segregation in public schools deprives these [Negroes] of the equal protection of the laws.

92. See S. Sidney Ulmer, *Courts as Small and Not So Small Groups* (New York: General Learning Press, 1971), p. 24. Ulmer's (and Harbaugh's) claim that Frankfurter was the third holdout is vigorously rebutted by Kluger—whose account of *Brown's* denouement is the most recent, most complete, lengthiest, and most convincing. Indeed, Frankfurter was one of the architects of unanimity, second in importance only to Warren. Moreover, it was Frankfurter who staved off a potentially seriously divided or even negative vote in June 1953 by framing the five key questions for reargument. "F.F." did, however, have strong reservations regarding the judiciary's proper role here.

93. As quoted by John F. Simon, *In His Own Image: The Supreme Court in Richard Nixon's America* (New York: David McKay 1973), p. 55. The chief justice, by his own account, was determined to (1) get a unanimous vote, (2) write the opinion for the Court, and (3) "use low key unemotional language." He waited more than five months before calling for a final vote in conference; when he did, he had his unanimous Court: "We took one vote, and that was it" (*New York Times,* June 11, 1974, p. A35). But that did not occur until after the developments described in *supra* note 92. In a letter, exhibited at Harvard (October 21, 1977), commemorating Frankfurter's ninety-fifth birthday, "F.F." noted to Reed that there would have been four dissents had *Brown* been decided just one term earlier (Reed, Vinson, Jackson, and Clark).

94. Responding to a student's question, Warren recounted that he "purposely wrote such a short opinion so that any layman interested in the problem could read the entire opinion [instead of getting just] a little piece here and a little piece there. Hopefully this would not be the case with *Brown*. I think most of the major newspapers printed the entire decision." They did (University of Virginia Legal Forum, April 18, 1973).

95. Kluger, a strong and avowed partisan of the *Brown* decision, acknowledges that painstaking research by Alexander M. Bickel, then Frankfurter's clerk, demonstrated that there was "no evidence that the framers of the Amendment had intended to prohibit school segregation nor, as Wilson pointed our, jury segregation" (Kluger, op. cit., at 655). In effect, Bickel had reported to his justice that "it is impossible to conclude that the 39th Congress intended that segregation be abolished, impossible also to conclude that they foresaw it might be, under the language they were adopting" (ibid. at 654). Indeed, that Congress segregated not only the District of Columbia schools but also its own Senate gallery. The managers of the amendment clearly wanted to leave segregation of schools alone. Raoul Berger labeled Warren's "we cannot turn back the clock" statement as "a veiled declaration that the intention of the framers was irrelevant and that the Court was revising the Constitution to meet present day needs" (note 88, op. cit., at 131).

Today, education is perhaps the most important function of state and local government. . . . [Education] is the very foundation of good citizenship. Today it is the principal instrument in awakening the child to cultural values, in preparing him for later professional training, and in helping him to adjust normally to his environment. . . .

We come then to the question presented: *Does segregation of children in public schools solely on the basis of race, even though the physical facilities and other "tangible" factors may be equal, deprive the children of the minority group of equal educational opportunity? We believe that it does.*[96]

The chief justice then asserted: "Segregation of white and colored children in public schools has a detrimental effect upon the colored children. . . . A *sense of inferiority affects the motivation of a child to learn.*"[97] And, as Earl Warren had explained a few sentences earlier, to separate children in grade and high schools "from others of similar age and qualifications *solely because of their race generates a feeling of inferiority as to their status in the community that may affect their hearts and minds in a way unlikely ever to be undone.*"[98] Now followed the famous and controversial "social science" Footnote Eleven, which cited the writings of those social scientists, chiefly psychologists and sociologists, on whose findings the Court here relied. Among them were the noted black psychologist Kenneth B. Clark and the Swedish sociologist Gunnar Myrdal, whose celebrated *An American Dilemma*[99] had caused such an uproar in the South and the border states when it first appeared in 1944. Wrote Warren: "Whatever may have been the extent of psychological knowledge at the time of *Plessy v. Ferguson,* this finding is amply supported by modern authority. Any language in *Plessy v. Ferguson* contrary to this finding is rejected."[100] Thus, out went the ruling by Justice Brown for his 7:1 Court in 1896—and up went the lone dissent by Justice John Marshall Harlan I. All that remained for the decision of 1954—against which President Eisenhower allegedly had lobbied secretly with the chief justice[101]—was the dramatic conclusion that

96. *Brown v. Board of Education of Topeka,* et al., 347 U.S. 483 (1954) at 492; italics supplied.

97. Ibid. at 494; italics supplied.

98. Ibid.; italics supplied.

99. *An American Dilemma: The Negro Problem and Modern Democracy* (New York: Harper and Bros., 1944). Republished in 1946, and, in a revised edition, by Harper and Row in 1962. For a highly critical evaluation of the resort to "social science" evidence, see lawyer-anthropologist John Aron Grayzel, "Using Social Science Concepts in the Legal Fight Against Discrimination: Servant or Sorcerer's Apprentice," 64 *American Bar Association Journal* 1238 (August 1978).

100. *Brown,* op. cit., at 494.

101. See Ed Cray, *Chief Justice: A Biography of Earl Warren* (New York: Simon and Schuster, 1997), and the obituary of Warren's longtime personal secretary, Margaret McHugh, by Graeme Zielinski in the *Washington Post,* April 5, 2002, p. B17. As Mrs. McHugh is quoted by Cray: "Dwight Eisenhower was just completely opposed to the segregation decision, and the chief justice knew that."

in the field of public education the doctrine of "separate but equal" has no place. Separate educational facilities are inherently unequal. . . . The plaintiffs and others similarly situated for whom the actions have been brought are, by reason of the segregation complained of, *deprived of the equal protection of the laws guaranteed by the Fourteenth Amendment.*[102]

In other words, the equal protection of the laws clause of the Fourteenth Amendment now forbade the racially segregated education of public school children.[103] Indeed, the strong implication of the *Brown v. Board* ruling was that *any publicly* authorized or *publicly* permitted racial segregation would henceforth be unconstitutional.[104]

The Implementation Decision. Meanwhile, the 1954 decision would have to be implemented—and here the Court bowed to the counsel of Attorney General Brownell. Refraining from an immediate desegregation order, given the revolutionary nature of the decision, the Court stayed any enforcement mandate and ordered supportive argument in all five cases for April 1955—almost a year later. For that purpose, the Court invited all interested parties, specifically including counsel, the amici curiae, the solicitor general of the United States, and all state attorneys general, to file briefs and, if they so chose, participate in oral argument. Most of the southern states refused to do so, but Florida, North Carolina, Arkansas, and Texas, joined by the border states of Oklahoma and Maryland, did argue, dramatically and at length.[105] One month later, another unanimous Warren opinion (for the same Court members as its predecessor decision, except that John Marshall Harlan II had replaced the deceased Justice Jackson) announced the implementation or "mandate" decision.[106] Invoking an old principle of equity

102. Ibid. at 495; italics supplied.

103. Raoul Berger charges repeatedly and angrily that herewith Warren "revised the Fourteenth Amendment to mean exactly the opposite of what its framers designed it to mean, namely, to leave suffrage and segregation beyond federal control, to leave it with the states, where control over internal, domestic matters resided from the beginning" (op. cit., at 245). See also his p. 105 for voting statistics regarding the former, demonstrating that the House and Senate, by votes of 125:12 and 34:4, respectively, specifically rejected the amendment's application to suffrage.

104. The District of Columbia litigation had to be decided on the due process of law clause of Amendment Five, of course (*Bolling v. Sharpe,* 347 U.S. 497 [1954]). In effect applying a type of "reverse incorporation," the Court read the concept of equal protection of the laws into the due process of law clause of the Fifth Amendment—a policy it has embraced ever since.

105. The Court allowed fourteen hours of argument; the usual allotment is now one hour per case.

106. *Brown v. Board of Education of Topeka, et al.,* 349 U.S. 294 (1955); and *Bolling v. Sharpe,* op. cit. Thirty-five years later, Linda Brown Smith, now a forty-three-year-old grandmother, took the witness stand as an intervening plaintiff in that very case, charging that the public schools of Topeka still had not purged themselves of segregation. But U.S

law,[107] and thereby avoiding any immediate problem of overall enforcement, it mandated the *local federal courts* to direct and oversee the transition to a racially nondiscriminatory system of public school primary and secondary education "with all deliberate speed."[108] It directed these courts to order "prompt and reasonable start" but clearly left the door ajar for consideration of the manifold local problems involved. In fact, "wide open door" may be a more appropriate description of the *initial* judicial attitude, compared with what would be a much stiffer attitude as the fifties turned into the sixties. Inevitably the "child of its time," the Court had carefully separated the principle of integration—a word that appears nowhere in the decisions involved—from its actual implementation.[109] Just as the Supreme Court reflected the sociopolitical realities of a new day and age[110] in *Brown I,* so did it reflect the judicial-limitation realities in *Brown II.*[111] As the ensuing months and years would prove, the Court can be a leader and the conscience of the country—but in the political process of which, after all, it is a part, it has only "the power to persuade: purse and sword are in other hands," as Alexander Hamilton stated so perceptively at the Republic's dawn in his *Federalist* No. 78.

District Court Judge Richard D. Rogers, in a strongly worded fifty-page opinion, resolutely disagreed (*Brown v. Board of Education of Topeka, Kansas,* 671 F. Supp. 1290 [1987]). In June 1989 the U.S. Court of Appeals overturned Rogers's decision, but, one month later, that tribunal withdrew its ruling without explanation, thus restoring Rogers's 1987 holding. The case was ultimately returned to the federal district court of jurisdiction for a decree to remedy any remaining segregation in Topeka (*Unified School District No. SD1, Shawnee County, Kansas v. Smith,* 61 113 S. Ct. 2994 [1993]). At last, in November 1999, after a twenty-two-year-old legal battle and a cost of $2 billion, U.S. District Court Judge Dean Whipple dismissed Kansas City's long-running case, ruling that the school district is making substantial progress toward providing equal education for black students (*Unified School District No. SD1, Shawnee County, Kansas v. Smith* [November 18, 1999, Docket no. 77-0420-CV-W-1, No. Dist. of Mo.]).

107. For a capsule explanation of equity see Henry J. Abraham, *The Judicial Process: An Introductory Analysis of the Courts of the United States, England, and France,* 7th ed. (New York: Oxford University Press, 1998), pp. 11–13.

108. The "all deliberate speed" formula was suggested by Justice Frankfurter—allegedly urged upon him by one of his clerks, Philip Elman—who found its source in a 1911 Holmes opinion dealing with monetary matters between states (*Virginia v. West Virginia,* 222 U.S. 17 at 20). Holmes identified it as "language of the English Chancery." For Elman's role, see "Philip Elman," *Washington Post,* December 5, 1999, p. B6.

109. See Ulmer, op. cit., pp. 23–26, for an illuminating account of the various options the Court perceived in *Brown I* and *II,* and the chief justice's leadership in the cases.

110. On this point see the interesting article by Charles L. Black Jr., "The Lawfulness of the Segregation Decisions," 69 *Yale Law Journal* 421 (1960).

111. Asked whether the justices ever considered "busing" in any of the implementation decision conferences, the chief justice replied, "No, I don't think we ever did" (University of Virginia Legal Forum, April 18, 1973). For a superb account of *Brown II* see J. Harvie Wilkinson III, *From Brown to Bakke* (New York: Oxford University Press, 1979), esp. chapters 1–9.

The Court would need immediate help from the executive branch. Overt or covert defiance became the rule rather than the exception in a good many areas, chiefly in the Deep South. While the District of Columbia, under direct federal control, did integrate its public schools immediately—Congress had permitted segregated schools there from 1864 onward—the response in the affected states ran from bowing to the inevitable in more or less good faith (e.g., in the District of Columbia, Delaware, and Kansas) through reasonably delayed action, to absolute refusal to obey. There was occasionally even avowed, outright defiance, accompanied by flurries of violence, in Arkansas, Virginia, South Carolina, Georgia, Florida, Louisiana, Alabama, and Mississippi. Many subterfuges were adopted by these states and others, such as the closing of all public schools in Prince Edward County, Virginia—where one of the five *Public School Segregation Cases* of 1954 originated.[112] Public feeling ran high indeed over what the majority of the white population in the affected sectors regarded as a threat to their way of life and the right of the states to govern themselves, the latter more often than not being a camouflage for the former. Some two hundred state segregation statutes would be enacted in the decade following the implementation decision.

Even Force. Still, a start, however halting and sullen, had been made; and enforcement of the decision continued to spread through a lengthy process of litigation, a host of patient efforts by many groups and individuals, courageous stances by the fifty-odd southern federal jurists who in many ways must be recognized as the heroes of the desegregation battles of the decade between 1955 and 1965,[113] the repeated affirmations of the basic decisions by the U.S. Supreme Court,[114] and, finally, a show of federal military force when deemed necessary as a last resort. President Eisenhower, for the first three years after *Brown,* had done his best to stay out of the battle and, indeed, had done nothing either to support the Supreme Court, so heavily under fire, or to explain, let alone defend, its decisions to the country. In the judgment of many, the enormously popular and influential national hero could have achieved something here if *anyone* could. But in the fall of 1957 he found his hand forced by Governor Orville Faubus of Arkansas. Faubus, following a lengthy desegregation battle with federal and state

112. *Davis v. County School Board of Prince Edward County, Virginia,* 347 U.S. 483.

113. Jack W. Peltason, *Fifty-eight Lonely Men: Southern Judges and School Desegregation,* rev. ed. (Urbana: University of Illinois Press, 1971), tells their story enlighteningly and engagingly.

114. Thus, Justice Hugo Black wrote for a unanimous Supreme Court in 1964, ultimately striking down the Prince Edward County school closing and related subterfuges: "There has been entirely too much deliberation and not enough speed in enforcing the constitutional rights which we held . . . had been denied" (*Griffin v. Prince Edward School Board,* 377 U.S. 218 at 229).

authorities,[115] called out the National Guard to prevent duly scheduled federal court–ordered public school desegregation in Little Rock, an order that involved only nine black children. When he was enjoined by the appropriate U.S. District Court from continued interference, he removed the guard, thereby encouraging the lawless. Riots and disorders promptly ensued. After a confrontation with Governor Faubus at Newport, Rhode Island, failed, an angry and reluctant President Eisenhower felt compelled to federalize the Arkansas National Guard and dispatch it[116] on September 25 to reestablish law and order and allow desegregation to proceed as judicially directed.[117] For an entire year the nine students had to be escorted to class by police. Four decades later the "Little Rock Nine" were awarded the Congressional Gold Medal.

Five years after Little Rock, in the fall of 1962, President John F. Kennedy deployed twenty-five thousand federal troops to overcome the opposition of Mississippi, led by its governor, Ross R. Barnett, to the federal court–ordered admission of black James Meredith[118] to the University of Mississippi at Oxford. A bloody all-

115. Well told by, among others, Wilson Record and Jane Cassels Record, *Little Rock U.S.A.* (San Francisco: Chandler, 1960).

116. These forces were under the command of Brigadier General Edwin Walker, who some years later became one of the must visible anti-integrationists and caused considerable difficulties for the federal authorities during the Oxford, Mississippi, confrontations (see *Associated Press v. Walker,* 388 U.S. 130 [1967]).

117. See the Court's unanimous, seminal decision—signed and authored jointly by all nine members of the tribunal—in *Cooper v. Aaron,* 358 U.S. 1 (1958), where it not only sternly ordered immediate compliance with the desegregation order by lower federal courts but reminded one and all that it is "emphatically the province and duty of *the judicial department* to say what the law is" (italics supplied). In 2002 U.S. District Court Judge William Wilson ordered the end of court desegregation monitoring of Little Rock schools, while observing that he will continue to track the school district's efforts to improve black students' academic performance. Arguing that the Little Rock schools have become resegregated (68 percent of the district's students were black), civil rights attorneys denounced Wilson's ruling ("Desegregation Monitoring Ends in Little Rock Schools," *Washington Post,* September 14, 2002, p. A22).

118. Meredith, a U.S. Air Force veteran with several years of college credit on his record, persevered through the hateful atmosphere that surrounded him on campus and received his degree from the University of Mississippi in 1963. Three years later, while on a march from Memphis to Jackson to dramatize the Negro registration drive in Mississippi, Meredith was shot and wounded in an ambush. Yet ten years later he would be the University of Mississippi's guest lecturer! (*New York Times,* April 22, 1972, p. 32c). And he ran, though unsuccessfully, for the Republican gubernatorial nomination in June 1972. By 1976, there were 475 black students on the Oxford campus. (*New York Times,* October 10, 1976, p. 16m). For the 2002 fortieth anniversary of Meredith's integration of "Ole Miss," the university, of which blacks form just above 12 percent of the student body, invited back to campus all the victors in the civil rights struggle that had embroiled the institution in 1962. Meredith, now sixty-nine years old, owns a used-car dealership in Jackson, Mississippi (Wil Haygood, "A Mississippi Odyssey," *Washington Post,* September 29, 2002, p. F1).

night battle was fought on and near the campus of "Ole Miss," with many wounded and two lives lost.[119] Eight months later President Kennedy again had to use troops, this time mobilizing the Alabama National Guard in order to overcome Governor George C. Wallace's defiance of the federal court–ordered admission of blacks Vivian Malone and James Hood to the University of Alabama at Tuscaloosa.[120]

Although even token integration was often resisted in the Deep South, mixed classes eventually became a reality on all levels of the public school system. "Mixed," of course, sometimes meant the presence of only one black student in an otherwise all-white classroom, but the principle was being established, and the tough financial penalties provided by Title VI of the Civil Rights Act of 1964 served to spur compliance in all but the most adamant situations. These last would be left to the judicial process; yet it was clear that in some instances, such as in Wallace-led Alabama, a course of "legal defiance," including a rejection of federal funds, would be at least temporarily pursued. In any event, on August 14, 1964, Mississippi became the last state to desegregate at least one school district when the Biloxi District bowed to a federal court order decreeing the desegregation of its first-grade classes. Less than six months later, the Greenville, Mississippi, School Board, facing the loss of $272,000 in federal aid-to-education funds if it failed to comply with the provisions of the Civil Rights Act of 1964 affecting such federal aid, voted unanimously to prepare a desegregation plan. Providing the first instance of non-court-ordered compliance by that state's authorities, Mayor Pat Dunne of Greenville endorsed the board's action, pointing out that there was no alternative: "Repugnant as the law is to all of us, it's a Federal law and it's either a case of comply or close the schools."[121] Decades later federal district courts, frustrated by what they viewed as intolerable delays in bona fide desegration by school districts would go so far as *compelling* local officials to increase property taxes—in the face of state laws contrary to nonlegislatively imposed hikes. The U.S. Supreme Court narrowly upheld (5:4) one of the most hotly contested such orders in 1990 in an opinion by Justice White. His colleague Kennedy's dissent accused the Court of allowing "an expansion of power in the federal judiciary beyond all precedent," that such "judicial taxation" was ultra vires.[122] Five years later, Kennedy found his point of view vindicated when a 5:4

119. See the important book by James W. Silver, a professor at the University of Mississippi, *Mississippi: The Closed Society* (New York: Harcourt, Brace and World, 1966); and, by his colleague Russell H. Barrett, *Integration at Ole Miss* (Chicago: Quadrangle, 1965).

120. Ten years later Wallace "crowned" the first black homecoming queen at the same university. Twenty years later he was reelected governor of Alabama with the decisive vote margin coming from the black community!

121. *New York Times,* January 16, 1965, p. 18l. (At the level of higher public education, the last bastions, Alabama and South Carolina, had already fallen two years earlier. Harvey Gantt, the first black to enter Clemson, became mayor of Charlotte, North Carolina, in 1983.)

122. *Missouri v. Jenkins I,* 495 U.S. 33.

Court, via Chief Justice Rehnquist's opinion, over a strong dissenting one by Justice Souter, joined by Justices Stevens, Ginsburg, and Breyer, ruled that lower federal courts had improperly ordered Missouri to help pay for state-of-the-art magnet schools and salary increases for teachers and support staff. The majority's holding cast doubt on the heretofore broadly open-ended assumed power of lower court judges to compel increasingly wide-ranging remedial reform.[123]

Enter Busing

Notwithstanding the very real and continuing desegregation progress described, the line between genuine and token *integration* has proved to be extremely difficult to draw[124]—even given such a clear mandate as that contained in the landmark October 1969 decision in the *Holmes County* case,[125] which announced the death of the "deliberate speed" concept in an 8:0 opinion, per curiam, highlighted by: "'All deliberate speed' for desegregation is no longer constitutionally permissible. . . . [T]he obligation of every school district is to terminate dual school systems at once and to operate now and hereafter only unitary school systems."[126] But even assuming good faith—not always a viable assumption—how much *busing* of students does the Constitution require in order to achieve the mandated "unitary" system?[127] How much, how far, and at what cost? What of

123. *Missouri v. Jenkins II*, 515 U.S. 70 (1995).

124. Thus, in May 1968, obviously having reached the end of its patience, a unanimous Court ruled that the so-called freedom of choice desegregation plans are inadequate if they do not undo southern school desegregation as rapidly as other available methods would. In what was its first detailed review of the adequacy of the means being used to implement the 1954 and 1955 *Brown* decisions, the Court—commencing a firm embrace of statistical evidence—declared that "delays are no longer tolerable"; that the "burden on a school board today is to come forward with a plan that promises realistically to work . . . *now*" (italics in original). It set out six factors, or "tests," all of which it henceforth required school boards (and judges) to address and weigh: student assignment, faculty, staff, transportation, extracurricular activities, and facilities (*Green v. School Board of New Kent County*, 391 U.S. 430 [1968] at 439). And in 1969, acting on the *first* school desegregation suit filed by the federal government in the North, U.S. District Court Judge Julius J. Hoffman (destined to become the much-embattled presiding judge in the "Chicago Eight" trial) ordered a suburban Chicago school district to desegregate its faculties and student bodies "forthwith" (*United States v. School District 151 of Cook County, Ill.*, 301 F. Supp. 201).

125. *Alexander v. Holmes County Board of Education*, 396 U.S. 19 (1969) at 20. Authorship has been attributed to Justice Brennan.

126. Ibid. For a copy of the text of the Supreme Court's order, see *New York Times*, October 30, 1964, p. 34.

127. As early as 1869, Massachusetts had authorized the expenditure of public funds to send children to and from school in horse-drawn wagons and carriages (see Wilkinson, *From Brown to Bakke*, op. cit., chapters 6–9, for a thorough discussion of the busing issue).

housing patterns, of fatigue factors, of the relationship of inner city and suburb, of the right of states to create administrative subdivisions?

In the face of a host of these vexatious questions, with their manifold political, economic, social, and psychological components, the Supreme Court considered the busing-to-integrate issue on its merits in an April 1971 decision of momentous significance for the entire country. Now thrust center stage, busing became the cardinal bone of contention in the continuing and expanding efforts to implement *Brown I* and *II*.

The 1971 *Swann* or *Charlotte-Mecklenburg* case,[128] as it became known popularly, headed a series arising from desegregation orders to a 105,000-student school district covering the Charlotte, North Carolina, metropolitan area that had a long history of maintaining two sets of segregated schools. By 1969, under court orders, half of the 30 percent of black students in the district were in formerly all-white schools, the others remaining in virtually all-black schools. The case squarely raised the seminal question, posed by attorneys for a group of white *and* black North Carolina parents, whether the *Brown* ruling required "color-blind" assignment of students and, if so, whether—among other devices that might be employed—busing to achieve integration was in effect unconstitutional. "We plead the same rights here that the plaintiffs pleaded in Brown," asserted the lawyers opposing busing—leaving to the Court another particularly complicated line-drawing problem, one charged with deep emotions.

These were not vitiated by the fact that, when the high tribunal handed down its decision on that April 20, it was unanimous—one of the last times all nine justices would be in agreement on racial matters.[129] Speaking for his Court, Chief Justice Burger's controversial opinion—which reportedly went through at least six[130] drafts, with the ultimate product largely the creation of Justice Bren-

---

128. *Swann v. Charlotte-Mecklenburg Board of Education,* 402 U.S. 1.

129. That long-standing unanimity—of almost two and one-half decades—ended on June 22, 1972, when the four Nixon appointees (Burger, Blackmun, Powell, and Rehnquist) dissented from a Supreme Court ruling that they characterized as requiring the imposition of "racial balance" rather than "desegregation." They protested that the majority of five (Douglas, Brennan, Stewart, White, and Marshall) had in effect equated racial balance with desegregation (*Wright v. Council of the City of Emporia,* 407 U.S. 451). According to one insider's account, the Court's unanimity in Swann was in fact deceptive: the initial vote had actually been 6:3 against forced busing (see Wilkinson, op. cit., pp. 146–50). See also Bernard Schwartz, *Swann's Way: The School Busing Cases and the Supreme Court* (New York: Oxford University Press, 1986)—the most detailed work extant on the controversial case.

130. Burger and Black wanted to *reverse* the district court, and Stewart and Blackmun wavered, but in order to prevent Douglas from assigning the case—which, as the senior justice on the majority side he would have been entitled to do—and seeing that he (Burger) lacked the votes to reverse, Burger did what he would also do two years later in *Roe v. Wade:* he joined the other side and, as chief justice, thereby earned the right to write the Court's opinion.

nan's persuasiveness—confounded Court watchers and the Nixon administration alike: for it specifically upheld not only *busing* but also *racial quotas, pairing* or *grouping* of schools, and *gerrymandering* of attendance zones, as well as other devices designed to remove "all vestiges of state-imposed segregation. . . . *Desegregation plans cannot be limited to the walk-in school*," he declared.[131] The Court stopped short of ordering the elimination of all-black schools or of requiring racial balance in the schools (and it made clear that its decision did *not* apply to northern-style segregation, commonly based on de facto neighborhood patterns). But it said that the existence of all-black schools created a presumption of discrimination and held that federal district judges—to whom it gave extremely broad discretion—may indeed use *racial quotas*[132] as a guide in fashioning desegregation decrees. On the busing issue, the chief justice, in a nod to that large

131. *Swann,* op. cit., at 15, 30; italics supplied.

132. This notwithstanding the on-its-face prohibition by Section 2000c-6 of Title IV of the Civil Rights Act of 1964, which *specifically* would seem to bar racial quota assignments. But the chief justice brushed that argument aside, invoking the judiciary's "historic equitable remedial powers" in the quest of attaining what he viewed as full compliance with the spirit as well as the letter of the equal protection of the laws clause of Amendment Fourteen. But he confessed that he found that in seeking "to define the scope of remedial power of the courts . . . words are poor instruments to convey the basic sense of fairness inherent in equity" (*Swann,* op. cit., at 31). He concluded, controversially, that "substance not semantics must govern"—whatever that may mean. In another portent of the Court's future posture on racial quotas, in 1977 it ruled 7:1—over a sharp dissent by Chief Justice Burger—in a "multiple plurality" decision that a state (here New York), drawing up a reapportionment plan in an effort to comply with the federal Voting Rights Act of 1965, as amended, may sometimes use racial quotas that are designed to assure that blacks and other nonwhites have majorities in certain legislative districts (*United Jewish Organizations of Williamsburg v. Carey,* 430 U.S. 144). But the Court refused (6:3) three years later to impose election by district in Mobile, Alabama, where the long-standing practice of at-large election of the three-member city commission had failed to produce a black commissioner, finding no intent to discriminate on racial grounds (*City of Mobile v. Bolden,* 466 U.S. 55). Yet in 1982 that same Court ruled 6:3 that Burke County, Georgia, could be lower court–required to switch to an election system using single-member districts, based on a finding that the erstwhile at-large system of electing its board of commissioners had been maintained for the purpose of discriminating against blacks (*Rogers v. Lodge,* 458 U.S. 613). See also the one-sentence upholding of a Mississippi district, drawn on *purely* racial lines to ensure black hegemony, based on the Court's reading of the Voting Rights Act, as amended in 1982 (*Mississippi Republican Committee v. Brooks,* 469 U.S. 1002 [1984]). And note especially the 1986 North Carolina decision in *Thornburg v. Gingles,* 478 U.S. 30, in effect embracing (5:4) the *results*-oriented concept, indeed coming perilously close to reading the Civil Rights Act of 1982 as requiring proportional representation in the realm of racial composition. Two unanimous 1993 Supreme Court voting decisions ruled that (1) the states are to be prime drafters of voting districts, federal courts thus being required to defer to local planners (*Growe v. Emison,* 507 U.S. 25), and (2) even more significantly, that race-conscious enclaves, designed to create majority-minority districts, are permissible (*Voinovich v. Quilter,* 507 U.S. 146). At least twenty new minority members of Congress had thus benefited in the November 1992

element among the populace favoring the neighborhood school concept, admitted that "all things being equal, with no history of discrimination, it might well be desirable to assign pupils to schools nearest their homes. But all things are not equal," he continued, "in a system that has been deliberately constructed and maintained to enforce racial segregation."[133] The sweeping *Charlotte-Mecklenburg* ruling represented a landmark along the road to full desegregation, yet there was little doubt that the problem would remain unsettled—as indeed it did until three decades later, when the U.S. Court of Appeals for the Fourth Circuit ruled that since the Charlotte schools no longer practiced intentional segregation, they could scrap the thirty-year-old court-ordered plan.[134]

That it was indeed not settled would promptly be demonstrated by two landmark decisions—the first school desegregation cases to reach the Court involving a major city outside the South. One came in a Denver, Colorado, case that squarely raised the crucial issue of "northern-style segregation," which—unlike *segregation by law*, typical of the South—was the product of *economic and social patterns*. In a surprisingly decisive 7:1 holding[135] (or $6\frac{1}{2}:1\frac{1}{2}$, depending upon one's analysis) and speaking through Justice Brennan—with only Justice Rehnquist in full dissent—the Court refused to discard the de facto–de jure distinction, as urged upon it by concurring Justices Douglas and, especially, Powell, who also took pains to abjure forced busing. But it demonstrably expanded the de jure scope by making it clear that even in the absence of statutorily authorized segregation policies—and none such existed in Denver or, for that matter, in Colorado, where in fact it had been statutorily *forbidden* since 1895—it was provable that the Denver School Board had in fact practiced segregation by manipulating school attendance zones and school sites and favoring a "neighborhood school" policy. The Court held it was necessary to demonstrate neither total or overall segregation nor the presence of a dual school system in order to find impermissible discrimination: it was sufficient to be able to point to segregation of "a substantial portion" of the

---

elections. A potentially significant caveat, however, came with the 5:4 O'Connor opinion in *Shaw v. Reno* in mid-1993 (509 U.S. 630), in which the majority ruled that white voters have the right to challenge a "bizarrely" drawn racially created North Carolina congressional district. See Barbara A. Perry, "Splitting the Difference: The Supreme Court's Search for the Middle Ground in Racial Gerrymandering Cases," in Christopher P. Banks and John C. Green, eds., *Superintending Democracy: The Courts and the Political Process* (Akron, Ohio: University of Akron Press, 2001).

133. *Swann*, op. cit., at 28. During the controversy surrounding the Charlotte-Mecklenburg school district, the North Carolina legislature enacted a law flatly forbidding any "busing assignment of any student on account of race or for the purpose of creating a racial balance or ratio in the schools." That provision, too, fell 9:0 on the same day *Swann* was decided (*North Carolina State Board of Education v. Swann*, 402 U.S. 43).

134. See *supra* this chapter.

135. *Keyes v. School District #1, Denver, Colorado*, 413 U.S. 189 (1973), rehearing denied, 423 U.S. 1066 (1976). Fifteen years later, the Court denied a renewed request to reopen the case (*Denver, Colorado v. Keyes*, 498 U.S. 1082 [1991]).

school district, with the Court thus strongly hinting that pockets of intentional segregation, be they such as a result of law, custom, or neglect, would be regarded as constituting cause for judicial proscription applicable to the *entire* district. This, of course, would mean busing—as an increasing number of cities in the North as well as the South were experiencing.

The Denver litigation had confined itself to a *single* school district, as had that involving Charlotte-Mecklenburg. But what of the manifold situations, particularly extant in the North, in which integration is in effect not accomplishable without *busing across district lines,* usually involving black cities and white suburbs? The *Charlotte-Mecklenburg* case had involved such cross-county (city-suburb) busing, but it dealt with a single school district. The explosive issue was joined in 1972, when U.S. District Court Judge Robert R. Merhige Jr., sitting in Richmond, Virginia, in a momentous 325-page opinion,[136] ordered a merger of that city's predominantly black public schools with those of two predominantly white suburban counties, Henrico and Chesterfield. A similarly contentious order was subsequently issued by U.S. District Court Judge Stephen J. Roth and was to involve the cross-county busing of three hundred thousand Detroit area children between that city and its suburbs.[137] There the similarity ended, for while the U.S. Circuit Court of Appeals for the Fourth Circuit *overruled* Judge Merhige (5:1),[138] Judge Roth's order was sustained (6:3) by the Sixth Circuit's Court of Appeals.[139] To the surprise of no one, both decisions were appealed to a somewhat less than eager U.S. Supreme Court.

Down came the Court, first with a "no-answer" answer in the Richmond case in a 4:4 one-sentence per curiam ruling, with Virginia's Justice Powell not participating: "The judgment is affirmed by an equally divided Court."[140] All eyes then turned toward Detroit, about which a decision was made in 1974. Speaking through the chief justice, the Court ruled (5:4) that whatever the situation in the city of Detroit itself might be or have been, the school systems in the surrounding suburbs had not been accused of unlawful segregation; that, absent proof of the latter, no constitutional power exists in the courts to decree relief balancing the racial composition of one community-wide segregated district (Detroit) with those of surrounding districts (the suburbs).[141] In bitter dissent Justices

---

136. *Bradley v. School Board of the City of Richmond,* 338 F. Supp. 67.

137. *Bradley v. Milliken,* 338 F. Supp. 582 (1972).

138. *School Board of the City of Richmond v. Bradley,* 462 F.2d 1058 (1972). Judge Harrison Winter dissented.

139. *Bradley v. Milliken,* 484 F.2d 215 (1973).

140. *Bradley v. State Board of Education of the Commonwealth of Virginia,* 411 U.S. 913 (1973).

141. *Milliken v. Bradley,* 418 U.S. 717. In the concurring Justice Stewart's words, "[T]he multidistrict remedy contemplated by the desegregation order was an erroneous exercise of equitable authority of the federal courts" (at 756). Joining Chief Justice Burger in the majority were Justices Stewart, Blackmun, Powell, and Rehnquist.

Douglas, Brennan, White, and Marshall accused the majority of taking "a giant step backward."[142]

What the Detroit landmark decision thus evidently conveyed was that the Court—recognizing the "deeply rooted" public education tradition of local control—would refuse to order cross-county or city-suburb integration, *unless* it could be proved that *intentional* segregation in one district leads to a "significant segregative effect in another district." Not surprisingly, numerous cross-county merger cases subsequently began to reach the Court, involving, among others, the areas around Louisville, Kentucky; Indianapolis, Indiana; Wilmington, Delaware; Atlanta, Georgia; Little Rock, Arkansas; and Buffalo, New York. In its actions the Supreme Court adhered to its announced test of whether proof of deliberate, intentional segregation had been provided. In a number of instances it so found and, for example, upheld lower court orders mandating interdistrict busing between the cities of Wilmington and Louisville and their respective suburbs, but it struck down an order directed to Atlanta and its suburbs.[143]

The busing issue[144] continued to smolder—and to create controversy of a magnitude rarely seen in the body politic. To illustrate: consistently having defied—or at least having but mildly obeyed—U.S. District Court orders to bus its children, the Boston community, led by South Boston (heavily white ethnic), was confronted with a series of drastic ultimata handed down by Judge W. Arthur Garrity Jr. Rejecting or downplaying these, the Boston School Committee, an elected, popular body, subsequently found itself deprived of many of its powers in December 1975; for example, some of its schools were placed in the hands of a court-appointed receiver. Widespread and intense pressures began to mount among the electorate: around the nation segregationist George C. Wallace was gaining support in the Democratic presidential race almost entirely on the busing issue; along with abortion, busing became a key concern of the 1976 presidential primary races in Massachusetts. But Boston's strife-torn public school system

---

142. Ibid. at 782.

143. *Evans v. Buchanan,* 423 U.S. 963 (1975); *Board of Education v. Newburg Area Council,* 421 U.S. 931 (1975); and *Armour v. Nix,* 446 U.S. 930 (1980), respectively. The Wilmington order was narrowly reconfirmed twice (4:3) in 1977 and (6:3) in 1980 (see *Delaware State Board of Education v. Evans,* 429 U.S. 973, and, ibid., 447 U.S. 916 rehearing denied). See also *Pulaski County v. Little Rock,* 488 U.S. 869 (1988); and *Arkansas State Board of Education v. Little Rock,* 476 U.S. 1186 (1988).

144. For some post-1970 literature on busing see the following: Robert H. Bork, *Constitutionality of the President's Busing Proposals* (Washington, D.C.: American Enterprise Institute, 1972); "The Agony of Busing Moves North," *Time,* November 15, 1971, pp. 57–64; John A. Morsell, "Busing Is Not the Issue," *Freedom at Issue,* May–June 1972, pp. 12ff.; Nicolaus Mills, ed., *The Great School Bus Controversy* (New York: Crowell, 1973); James Bolner and Robert Shanley, *Busing: The Political and Judicial Process* (New York: Praeger, 1974); Christopher Jencks, "Busing—The Supreme Court Goes North," *New York Times Magazine,* November 19, 1972, pp. 38ff.; and Lino A. Graglia, *Disaster by Decree* (Ithaca, N.Y.: Cornell University Press, 1976).

continued in effect to be administratively directed by Judge Garrity[145]—whose stern desegregation order was twice denied review, and thus upheld, by the U.S. Supreme Court.[146] Even stronger measures were taken by U.S. District Judge Frank J. Battisti in connection with his desegregation orders affecting the Cleveland, Ohio, school system. His orders included a citation for civil contempt of court in August 1980 for "incompetently administering" his program, and the appointment of an "administrator for desegregation" with power over every aspect of public education in Cleveland. The opposition to forced busing cannot simply be interpreted as merely prima facie evidence of racial discrimination or as racism; if it were that simple, evaluation as well as remedial action might be simpler. These labels do, of course, apply in the case of a good many opponents; but it is unquestionably also true that a good many other opponents of forced busing are neither racists nor antidesegregation obstructionists. They are opposed to busing qua busing for their children on understandable human grounds, and they do indeed prefer to embrace the thrust of Chief Justice Burger's *Swann* "all things being equal" hope: "assignment to schools nearest [the children's] homes"[147]—as do sizable segments of the black, the Hispanic, and almost all of the Chinese communities.

In what was indubitably a recognition of and response to majoritarian public sentiment on the issue, the congressional hoppers became replete with legislation endeavoring either to amend or to strike down busing practices and orders. Most failed of passage; but a number of "riders" to annual appropriation bills prohibiting the executive departments from using federal funds "to require, directly or indirectly, the transportation of any student to a school other than the school which is nearest the student's home, except for a student requiring special education,"[148] did become law—the judiciary making it quite clear, however, that it would continue to invoke its perceived powers of judicial equity in the contentious issue. A constitutional amendment to ban busing as a desegregation-integration tool failed (216:109) in the House in 1979; but late in 1980 both houses of Congress voted overwhelmingly to prohibit the Justice Department

---

145. Judge Garrity created a "Department of Implementation (administration of racial desegregation)," with an annual payroll of $473,559 for salaries alone (as of 1977). Note his April 2, 1987, comment about the role of the courts: "The honored place in our legal tradition has not been judicial restraint, but rather, its bedrock antecedent, judicial review" (*New York Times,* April 3, 1987, p. A1).

146. *White v. Morgan,* 426 U.S. 935 (1975); and *McDonough v. Morgan,* 429 U.S. 1042 (1976). In 1987 school officials finally regained some control (*Morgan v. Nucci,* 831 F.2d 313).

147. *Swann v. Charlotte-Mecklenburg School of Education,* 402 U.S. 1 (1971) at 28.

148. Section 208 of the Health, Education and Welfare-Labor Appropriations Act for fiscal year 1978 (see *New York Times,* March 31, 1978, p. A14). When a lower federal court upheld the rider, the Supreme Court refused to review the decision in 1978 (*Carroll v. Department of Health, Education, and Welfare,* 435 U.S. 904).

from using appropriated funds to pursue legal cases that would result in busing orders. Presidents Nixon and Ford had repeatedly called for remedial or statutory action; President Carter, however, firmly opposed such moves; when he pointedly threatened to veto the 1980 measure, Congress bowed reluctantly. Since the Republican platform for 1980 again contained a plank against forced busing, it was a foregone conclusion that the issue had been postponed, not resolved. A plethora of antibusing bills were introduced early in 1981, with at least tacit backing by the Reagan administration. One, the Helms-Johnston measure, passed the Senate (57:37) in 1982, only to die in the House, and a similar fate met a 1986 Helms bill, which passed the Senate (50:45).

How did the Court view the volatile issue that divided the nation? To employ a vernacular but apposite term, the justices' holdings were "clear as mud" on the dilemmas created by forced busing. Thus, they held (6:2) that if school authorities initially complied with a busing plan and thereby achieved a racially neutral student assignment scheme, the school authorities cannot be judicially compelled to readjust busing zones each subsequent year in an effort to maintain the same initial racial mix in the face of changing population patterns.[149] Concurrently, the Court unanimously declined to review, and thus in effect upheld, a lower federal appellate court ruling that school authorities in Chattanooga, Tennessee, need not redraft a desegregation plan to reflect population shifts that had taken place *after* busing and other desegregation measures had been duly and constitutionally adopted.[150] The justices also ruled unanimously that federal tribunals may order school districts to provide costly, far-reaching, broader-than-ever *remedial* educational programs—such as remedial reading classes, teacher training, counseling, and career guidance[151]—thus seemingly embracing a compensatory approach that would avoid the busing issue per se. When the Court also remanded three systemwide busing order cases[152] for reconsideration because they did not meet the "purpose and intent" standard it had developed in 1976–77 as a requirement for specific findings regarding alleged violations of equal protection of the laws, it seemed to have embarked upon a course that required proof of de jure rather than de facto segregation for judicially ordered redress. Yet such expectations of either a predictable or a consistent course were in vain (despite the fact that the same justices sat on the Court between 1975 and 1981), for 1979 and 1980 brought a series of bitterly divided compulsory-busing decisions.[153] They ranged in votes from 7:2 to 5:4 in upholding lower court bus-

149. *Pasadena City Board of Education v. Spangler,* 427 U.S. 424 (1976).

150. *Mapp v. Board of Education of Chattanooga,* 427 U.S. 911 (1976).

151. *Milliken v. Bradley II,* 433 U.S. 267 (1977).

152. *Dayton Board of Education v. Brinkman I,* 433 U.S. 406 (1977).

153. *Columbus Board of Education v. Penick,* 443 U.S. 449 (1979); *Dayton Board of Education v. Brinkman,* 443 U.S. 526 (1979); *Estes v. Metropolitan Branches of Dallas N.A.A.C.P.,* 444 U.S. 437 (1980); *Cleveland Board of Education v. Reed,* 445 U.S. 935 (1980); and *Austin Independent School District v. United States,* 443 U.S. 915 (1980). Jus-

ing plans and orders. Led by Justices Brennan, White, Marshall, and Blackmun, the Court had now developed a dramatic new test-cum-approach to the question of desegregation-integration, namely, that henceforth the test of compliance would be not a school board's *purpose* in acting to liquidate a dual system of education dating from pre-*Brown* days but its *effectiveness*. In the words of Justice White, the author of the Court's sweeping decisions on school busing orders for Dayton, Ohio (5:4), and Columbus, Ohio (7:2), there is an "affirmative duty" to eliminate the *effects* of *past* discrimination, even if there is no longer any discrimination practiced. Perhaps even more significantly, the Court adopted, albeit narrowly, a new test of the burden of proof in these school desegregation cases. Traditionally, a plaintiff alleging unlawful conduct has the burden of proof, but in accordance with the 5:4 Columbus holding, the burden of proof has now been shifted to the defendant school board—which in effect thus has to prove its innocence, rather than have the plaintiff prove a board's guilt. Yet in what the NAACP styled as "we won one and lost one," the Court seemed to signal more sympathy with antibusing forces shortly thereafter: while it narrowly struck down (5:4) a 1976 state of Washington initiative that barred busing beyond neighborhood schools,[154] it upheld (8:1) a 1979 California initiative that limited mandatory busing to the federal standard of intentional violation.[155] The Court's quizzicality was reconfirmed in two 1986 decisions, one of which went "pro" and the other "con" school board contentions of compliance.[156]

But five years later a 5:3 ruling, authored by Chief Justice Rehnquist, announced that henceforth formerly segregated school districts may be released from court-ordered busing once they have taken all "practicable" steps to eliminate the legacy of segregation. The chief justice explained that the likely reemergence of one-race schools as a result of local busing patterns was not necessarily a bar to lifting a busing order, as long as the housing patterns were a result of private choices and were not themselves "vestiges" of the era of official school desegregation.[157] The Court quickly returned to the fray by considering a DeKalb County, Georgia, case that raised similar questions. Its 8:0 ruling in 1992, featuring four opinions, generally gave hundreds of formerly segregated school districts a potentially new legal tool for returning to local control after decades of operating under federal court supervision. The gravamen of Justice Kennedy's controlling opinion was that "[r]acial balance is not to be achieved for its own sake. It is to be pursued when racial imbalance has been caused by constitutional

---

tice Powell's separate dissenting opinion in the first two cases cited represented a masterful analysis of the basic issue involved, including that of burdens of proof and the nature of the judicial function.

154. *Washington v. Seattle School District #1,* 458 U.S. 457 (1982).

155. *Crawford v. Board of Education,* 458 U.S. 527 (1982).

156. *Riddick v. School Board of Norfolk,* 479 U.S. 938; and *Board of Education of Oklahoma v. Dowell,* 423 U.S. 824, certiorari denied.

157. *Board of Education of Oklahoma City v. Dowell,* 498 U.S. 237 (1991).

violation." Ergo, where, as in DeKalb County, segregation is a product not of state action but of private choice, for example, voluntary demographic housing selection, "it does not have constitutional implications."[158] But in an 8:1 holding, penned by Justice White, with only Justice Scalia in dissent, the Court imposed a broad duty on states that once operated racially separate college systems, to eliminate the effects of their past discrimination. Such states (here Mississippi), wrote the senior associate justice, *"must do more than simply declare that the historically white and black colleges and universities are open to students of any race;* that the burden of justifying their policies is on the state that once operated a discriminatory system, not on those challenging it."[159]

Much of the thrust toward school desegregation implementation had been provided by a famed report written in 1966 by the distinguished University of Chicago sociologist James S. Coleman, who had then demonstrated with convincing statistical evidence that while home background tended to have a greater impact than the school on children's performance, the integration of a minority of disadvantaged youngsters (chiefly nonwhite) in classrooms dominated by middle-class children (chiefly white) tended to raise the poor children's achievements without hurting those of their more affluent peers.[160] The Coleman Report, widely distributed and meeting with general approbation in the academic and governmental communities, thus became a genuine catalyst in the desegregation-integration efforts that soon began to reach a crescendo. But in mid-1975—almost a decade later—Professor Coleman issued a bombshell "second thoughts" report in which he concluded that "programs of desegregation have acted to further separate blacks and whites rather than bringing them together"; that court-ordered busing and the instability created by the assignment of great numbers of disadvantaged children to middle-class schools in the big cities "have accelerated the white flight into the suburbs and have thus led to greater racial segregation in the schools." Still firmly committed to desegregation-integration, Dr. Coleman laid the blame at the doorstep of the judiciary, concluding that "it is ludicrous to attempt to mandate an integrated society. Integration must come through other means."[161] Primary attention, he pointed out, must focus on both education and

158. *Freeman v. Pitts,* 503 U.S. 467.

159. *U.S. v. Fordice,* 505 U.S. 17 (1992).

160. *Equality of Educational Opportunity* (Washington, D.C.: U.S. Government Printing Office, 1966).

161. *New York Times,* June 15, 1975, sec. 4, p. 16e; and *Time,* June 23, 1975, p. 60. The Court's 8:0 ruling in 1976 that federal courts are empowered to order the Department of Housing and Urban Development (HUD) to provide low-cost housing in a city's white suburbs to relieve racial segregation in housing within the city would prove to be a significant counterforce (*Hills v. Gautreaux,* 425 U.S. 284). In writing for the Court, Justice Stewart noted: "The critical distinction between HUD and the suburban school districts in *Millikin* [*supra* this chapter] is that HUD has been found to have violated the Constitution" (at 297).

environment; lack of special educational preparation and failure to maintain discipline would bring about, as he had warned in his 1966 report, a white backlash that had now taken the form of flight to the suburbs. As he concluded, "[A] large portion of that white flight has to do with the unresponsiveness of large school systems [in the inner cities], with the whole question of order and discipline in the schools, and with an undifferentiated sense of fear and disorder."[162] Readdressing the issue of "beneficial" versus "destructive" desegregation at the end of 1978, he cited "mandatory busing in large cities" as its "most destructive method" and called for its cessation forthwith.[163]

By the end of the century an increasing number of school districts found themselves freed from court-ordered desegregation, among them Cleveland, Denver, Norfolk—and Charlotte-Mecklenburg, the target of the *Swann* case thirty years earlier, with U.S. District Court Judge Robert Potter ruling that that school system, which is 40 percent black, remedied past segregation "quite some time ago."[164] Accordingly, in mid-2000 the Charlotte-Mecklenburg school board voted 6:3 to approve a new race-neutral school reassignment plan to comply with Judge Potter's ruling. Roughly a third of the school district's 105,000 students could attend different schools under the plan, which guarantees every student a seat in a school close to home. But a new suit was filed, and a 2:1 divided panel of the Fourth Circuit Court of Appeals refused to free the school system as of late 2000.[165] However, on rehearing en banc, the full appellate court vacated the earlier order and ruled 7:4 in 2001 that the thirty-year-old plan was dead. In the final analysis, society must find an answer to the basic problem of the elimination of inferior schools—it is *that* goal upon which the strategies of desegregation-integration must concentrate.

Some Other Post-*Brown* Developments

To revert to the days following *Brown I* and *II*, implementing the spirit of the *Public School Segregation Cases* beyond their specific educational substance became the foremost concern and task of a host of public and private groups, agencies, and individuals. In general, it was a painfully slow process. Gradualism characterized most progress. Even at the national level, the legislature and executive would thus wait, for all intents and purposes, until 1957, although President Eisenhower did move on the employee-hiring front in 1955 by issuing an executive order[166] to create the Committee on Government Employment Policy. This

---

162. *Charlottesville Daily Progress,* June 1, 1975, p. 1.
163. *Washington Post,* December 8, 1978, p. A19.
164. See "Judge Halts Charlotte Busing," *Washington Post,* September 11, 1999, p. A6; and George F. Will, "Busing's End," *Washington Post,* September 28, 1999, Outlook.
165. 233 F.3d 232.
166. Exec. Order 10590, *Federal Register,* vol. XX (1955), p. 409.

committee was charged with hearing individual complaints of alleged racial or religious discrimination in hiring or promotion by federal agencies. It became quite active and, on President Kennedy's assumption of office, merged with the Committee on Government Contracts (which had been created by President Truman in 1951), ultimately to become the Equal Employment Opportunity Commission (EEOC).[167] With Vice-President Johnson as its first chairman, it proved to be a far more significant body than its predecessor.

Civil Rights Act of 1957. By far the most important *legislative* action of the Eisenhower administration in civil rights, however, was the passage of the Civil Rights Act of 1957, the first major legislation of its kind since Reconstruction. Enacted largely owing to the bipartisan cooperation of Congress's Democratic leaders, House Speaker Sam Rayburn and Senate Majority Leader Lyndon B. Johnson[168] (both from Texas), it contained three or four significant provisions. One created the U.S. Commission on Civil Rights, which became a busy and assertive unit in the governmental struggle against racial discrimination. A second transformed the small and weak Civil Rights Section in the Department of Justice into the more effective Civil Rights Division, headed by an assistant attorney general.[169] A third and fourth not only authorized the federal government to obtain federal civil injunctions against actual or threatened interference with the right to vote (with or without the individual's consent) and to pay the costs for the litigation but also gave the appropriate U.S. District Courts jurisdiction over such suits without the normal requirement that all state judicial and administrative remedies be first "exhausted below."

Civil Rights Act of 1960. Despite considerable activity by the new Civil Rights Commission, however, the 1957 statute proved to be of only marginal value. Nevertheless, it served to focus and popularize aspects of the problem; and its weaknesses did prompt the Eisenhower administration to call for a new statute, which became the Civil Rights Act of 1960. No longer did the southern members of Congress have the necessary number of votes and allies to block such measures. The act of 1960 promised to be a far-reaching piece of legislation chiefly because, in an elaborate provision for appointment of federal "voting referees," it undertook to safeguard the black citizen's right to vote freely and without discrimination. The measure authorized federal district courts, through appointment

---

167. Exec. Order 10925, *Federal Register,* vol. XXVI (1961), p. 1977.

168. See Robert Caro's extensive examination of LBJ's legislative machinations in guiding the 1957 Civil Rights Act through the Senate (*Master of the Senate: The Years of Lyndon Johnson* [New York: Knopf, 2002]).

169. From a staff of 29 lawyers and 30 clerical workers in 1957 the Civil Rights Division had grown to a staff of more than 400 by 1982, and its caseload increased from 143 in December 1957 to 2,300 in July 1982 (*Washington Post,* January 16, 1983, p. A11).

of these referees, to enroll qualified voters for *all* state as well as federal elections in areas where local officials systematically denied them the right to register or to vote. And it enabled the federal Department of Justice to file suit to bring about this desired result. More than fifteen times as many suits were brought during the first three years following the act of 1960 as had been brought during any similar span of time under the previous statute.

Still, black leaders and other civil rights spokesmen regarded the act of 1960 as too slow, too costly to administer, and too cumbersome. Black restlessness and impatience were intensified; 1963 saw the peak of visible public protest movements. Reiterating their "loss of faith in the white power structure," blacks took to the streets in ever-increasing numbers throughout the United States. The summer of 1963 became known as the "long, hot summer," culminating late in August in a massive, peaceful, interracial march by some twenty thousand people in Washington, D.C. Billed as the March on Washington for Jobs and Freedom, its climax was Dr. Martin Luther King Jr.'s soaring "I Have a Dream" speech, delivered at the Lincoln Memorial. Other demonstrations were not so peaceful and orderly, especially some of those that took place in scattered cities in the Deep South where feelings ran high. Although not necessarily directly connected with the demonstrations, reprisals by white extremists resulted in forty-four violent deaths during 1963, 1964, and 1965.[170] The black riots in northern cities in the summer of 1966 led to a score more. Against this background of mounting anger, threats, and sporadic violence, President Kennedy had asked Congress twice in 1963 for new, strong, and expanded civil rights legislation. President Johnson again requested it when he first addressed Congress as the nation's new chief executive following the tragic assassination of President Kennedy on November 22. In the following June, Congress passed the Civil Rights Act of 1964.

Civil Rights Act of 1964. Demonstrably, that statute was the most comprehensive piece of legislation to be enacted by the federal legislature since the ill-fated measures of the 1870s. It cleared the House with relative ease (290:130). But its success in the Senate, by a bipartisan vote of 73:27, was delayed until the breaking of a seventy-five-day southern filibuster by the application of the Senate's debate-limiting cloture rule on the eighty-third day of debate by a vote of

---

170. *The Southern Regional Council Report,* released on January 30, 1966. Among these murders were those of Mississippi NAACP leader Medgar Evers in the driveway of his Jackson home; a pro–civil rights white Baltimore postman, William L. Moore, in northeastern Alabama; the bomb-murder of four black girls, eleven to fourteen years old, in the Sixteenth Street Birmingham Baptist Church (eleven years later, Chris McNair, the father of one of the murdered girls, was elected chairman of the Jefferson County, Birmingham, delegation to the Alabama House of Representatives); and, almost on the day of the passage of the 1964 act, the murder of three young civil rights workers, two white and one black, near Philadelphia, Mississippi. According to the SRC's report, eighty civil rights murders were committed between 1956 and 1966.

71:29.[171] It was the first time that cloture had been attained on a civil rights fili-buster since the adoption of the cloture rule in 1917.[172]

The principal provisions of the Civil Rights Act of 1964 extended the hereto-fore sharply limited life of the Civil Rights Commission for four years, to 1968 (extended periodically since then), and broadened both its duties and its powers; established a Community Relations Service to aid in the conciliation of racial dis-putes; forbade, in its crucial Title VII, discrimination because of race, color, sex, religion, or national origin either by employers or by labor unions in business concerns with one hundred employees or more, this number to drop by stages until it reached fifteen[173]—public employees were covered as of a 1972 amend-ment—and created the EEOC to administer that aspect of the act; prohibited vot-ing registrars from applying different standards to white and black applicants; required all literacy tests to be in writing, and rendered a sixth-grade education a "rebuttable assumption" of literacy; permitted the attorney general to bring suit, upon written complaint by aggrieved individuals, to secure desegregation of fa-cilities owned, operated, or managed by state and local governments; authorized, in its tough Title VI, the executive to halt any federal aid funds to either public or private programs "or activities" in which discrimination on grounds of race,

171. On the bill's final roll call, forty-six Democrats and twenty-seven Republicans voted in favor of it; twenty-one Democrats and six Republicans against. Voting to invoke cloture were forty-four Democrats and twenty-seven Republicans; opposed were twenty-three Democrats and six Republicans.

172. See Charles Whalen and Barbara Whalen, *The Longest Debate: A Legislative His-tory of the 1964 Civil Rights Act* (Cabin John, Md.: Seven Locks Press, 1985), for an ex-cellent account of the "how" and "why" of the legislation's genesis and enactment.

173. In the first interpretation of this provision as it relates to racial bias, the Supreme Court ruled 8:0 in March 1971 that it bars job tests by employers that screen out blacks without realistically measuring their qualifications to do the work (*Griggs v. Duke Power Co.,* 401 U.S. 424). On the other hand, the Court ruled 7:2 five years later, in the absence of proof of "racially discriminatory purpose," a statute or an official act is *not* unconsti-tutional just because it places a "substantially disproportionate" burden on one race (*Washington v. Davis,* 426 U.S. 229 [1976], involving a written qualifying test for mem-bers of the District of Columbia Police Department). Also, the Court refused to review an unsuccessful challenge by blacks of the Georgia bar exam, which blacks had traditionally failed in greater numbers than whites (*Tyler v. Vickey,* 426 U.S. 940 [1976]). Just prior to the end of its 1975–76 term, the Supreme Court held 7:2 and 9:0, in opinions written by its only black member, Justice Marshall, that Section 1981 of the Civil Rights Act of 1866 as well as Title VII of that of 1964 prohibit employers from discrimination against whites on the basis of their race in and to the same extent they prohibit racial discrimination against blacks (*McDonald v. Santa Fe Transportation Co.,* 427 U.S. 273 [1976]). And in 1978 it upheld 5:2 the use of the National Teacher Examination Test to determine hiring and promotion in a state, although the test results disqualified more than four times as many blacks as whites (*National Education Association v. South Carolina,* 434 U.S. 1026). See also the related, unanimous 1981 decision in *Texas Department of Community Affairs v. Burdine,* 450 U.S. 248.

color, or national origin (sex and age were added in 1972 and 1978, respectively[174]—note that "religion" is not included; it is in Title VII) is allowed to continue (a provision used since with considerable success—and increasingly accompanied by serious, and not inevitably rebuttable, charges of "preferential treatment" and "*reverse* discrimination"[175]—by governmental agencies,[176] coupled with Title IV grants available to state and local agencies to help them cope with problems stemming from school desegregation); outlawed, in its Public Accommodation Title II, discrimination because of race, religion, color, or national origin in hotels, restaurants, theaters, gas stations, and all other public accommodations that affect interstate commerce, as well as in all public facilities (Title II was specifically held constitutional in December 1964, the first test of any provision of the act of 1964 to reach the U.S. Supreme Court);[177] and empowered the attorney general to file enforcement suits against any owners of public accommodations who discriminate, and on behalf of any persons whose constitutional rights are deemed violated in school segregation or other instances.[178]

Understandably, the two most controversial provisions of the Civil Rights Act of 1964, both prior to and during the national debate that attended its conception and birth, were the two then most obviously concerned with delicate "line drawing": those dealing with fair employment practices[179] and with public

174. Broadly interpreted by the Department of Health, Education, and Welfare, for example, to *require* special assistance to non–English-speaking Chinese students— who were far from eager for such help—with the Court upholding the requirement in a multiple-opinion decision in 1974 (*Lau v. Nichols,* 414 U.S. 563).

175. E.g., see Justice Douglas's remarkable dissenting opinion in *De Funis v. Odegaard,* 416 U.S. 312 (1974)—the University of Washington reverse discrimination case, in which a majority of five ducked the delicate issue by ruling the case moot. Douglas wrote there: "The Equal Protection Clause commands the elimination of racial barriers, not their creation in order to satisfy our theory as to how society ought to be organized" (*De Funis* at 342). See also Mary K. Hammond, "May the Constitution Be Color Conscious to Remain Color Blind?" 1 *Ohio Northern University Law Review* 81 (1973), and the extensive discussion of the affirmative action/reverse discrimination issue, *infra.*

176. Until 1980 the latter two were part and parcel of the erstwhile Department of Health, Education, and Welfare.

177. *Heart of Atlanta Motel v. United States,* 379 U.S. 241; and *Katzenbach v. McClung,* 379 U.S. 294. Justice Clark's opinion for the unanimous Court rested the case for Title II's constitutionality on the congressional power over interstate commerce—although Justices Douglas and Goldberg, in concurring, contended that the equal protection of the laws clause of Amendment Fourteen and the latter's Section 5 (the "enforcement by appropriate legislation" power) also applied.

178. For a table excerpting, comparing, and contrasting the acts of 1957, 1960, and 1964, see John H. Ferguson and Dean E. McHenry, *The American System of Government,* 13th ed. (New York: McGraw-Hill, 1977), pp. 193–94.

179. With the recently sworn-in Justice John Paul Stevens not participating, the Court addressed itself, albeit obviously somewhat uncomfortably, to the long-smoldering inherent seniority issue in a landmark decision in 1976. Speaking through Justice Brennan, the 5:3 majority (consisting also of Justices Stewart, White, Marshall, and Blackmun) ruled

accommodations. For here the basic issues of individual rights and of societal obligations were patently joined. No other sections of the statute, not even its voting and educational segments, stirred so much controversy and debate or attracted so many negative votes. However, Title VI, too, was bitterly attacked and its application questioned even by such staunch northern liberals as Senate Majority Leader Mike Mansfield.[180] Indeed, given the implications of the aforementioned "preferential treatment" and "reverse discrimination," it was destined to become the focus of major national controversy during the early 1970s and into the 1980s, centering on legal and constitutional implications of the governmental role against the backdrop of the twin constitutional guarantees of liberty and equality.[181] After all, *both* are guarantees that are seminal to our society— and they do not readily lend themselves to facile line drawing.

---

that blacks who were denied jobs in violation of Title VII (see *supra*) of the 1964 statute must be awarded *retroactive seniority* once they succeeded in obtaining those jobs. The majority held that blacks must thus be given the same seniority they would have had if they had been hired initially, with all accompanying rights, including pension benefits— even if this means that some whites, hired after the blacks' initial job applications but *before* the blacks entered the jobs, would thereby now have less security and job protection (*Franks v. Bowman Transportation Co.,* 434 U.S. 747). Partly dissenting, together with Justices Powell and Rehnquist, Chief Justice Burger saw a clear-cut case of reverse discrimination, commenting that "I cannot join in judicial approval of 'robbing Peter to pay Paul'" (ibid. at 4366). But cf. the 1977 *Teamster* rulings (*Teamsters v. United States* and *TIME-D.C. Inc. v. United States,* 431 U.S. 324). Their gist was that unless a seniority plan *intentionally* discriminates among workers, it is not illegal under Title VII. The Court reconfirmed this posture 4:3 in 1980 in the instance of the California brewing industry system (*California Brewers Association v. Bryant,* 444 U.S. 598). Thus, "neutral" seniority systems might legally perpetuate favored employment for white males where, as in these cases, the seniority systems had been operative *before* the Civil Rights Act of 1964 took effect in 1965. In 1982 the Court came full cycle when it ruled 5:4 in *American Tobacco Co. v. Patterson,* 456 U.S. 63, that even those seniority systems emplaced after the Civil Rights Act of 1964, as a result of collective bargaining, may withstand racial or gender challenges, absent a showing of discriminatory *intent.* See also the 1984 *Stotts* and 1986 *Wygant* holdings, affirming bona fide seniority systems, discussed *infra.* Of course, seniority systems that *deliberately,* that is, intentionally, discriminate are illegal, whether they date from pre- or post-1964 days.

180. See John Herber's article in the *New York Times,* September 29, 1966, p. 11.

181. E.g., see the critical book-length treatments by Nathan Glazer, *Affirmative Discrimination* (New York: Basic Books, 1976); George C. Roche III, *The Balancing Act: Quota Hiring in Higher Education* (La Salle, Ill.: Open Court, 1974); and Thomas Sowell, *Affirmative Action Reconsidered: Was It Necessary in Academia?* (Washington, D.C.: American Enterprise Institute, 1975). For supportive works see Boris I. Bittker, *The Case for Black Reparations* (New York: Random House, 1973); Ronald Dworkin, *Taking Rights Seriously* (Cambridge, Mass.: Harvard University Press, 1977); and Robert M. O'Neil, *Discriminating Against Discrimination* (Bloomington: Indiana University Press, 1975). More or less "neutral" are works such as M. Cohen, T. Nagel, and T. Scanlon, eds., *Equality and Preferential Treatment* (Princeton, N.J.: Princeton University Press,

Toward the Civil Rights Act of 1968. Still more legislation was to come, legislation replete with provisions that promised to cause lively debate in and out of Congress. While conceding that the fruits of the 1964 act—and the Voting Rights Act of 1965 (see later discussion)—were already "impressively apparent," President Johnson sent Congress his third civil rights bill in three years in 1966, noting the obvious: that discriminatory practices "still exist in many American communities." In a tough attempt to further egalitarian goals, the most contentious provision of the Civil Rights Bill of 1966 would have outlawed discrimination on either racial or religious grounds in the "purchase, rental, lease, financing, use and occupancy" of *all housing.* Chiefly because of the so-called open housing provision, the bill, although it had passed the House in a watered-down version by a vote of 259:157, died on the floor of the Senate[182]—against a backdrop of black riots and demonstrations in cities throughout the land, now predominantly in the North, and the rise of resentment to the new "black power" slogan that began to characterize much of the civil rights activity of that year.

Undaunted, President Johnson submitted a new bill in 1967, emphasizing the controversial housing issue. It failed to pass but became law on April 10, 1968—six days after the assassination of Martin Luther King and one day after his burial. Styled "a memorial to the fallen leader" by the president, the 1968 act significantly broadened existing federal criminal laws dealing with civil rights, cataloging a whole range of federally protected activities; articulated Indian rights; and addressed itself to the rising tide of rioting and civil disobedience. But its most notable provision, certainly in terms of the yearnings of most blacks, was that on fair housing, which, with certain limited exemptions,[183] outlawed discrimination in the *sale or rental of all housing*—not just in public or public-aided housing—because of race, color, religion, or national origin. Gender was added in 1974. As if to confirm its legitimacy, even in advance of any litigation involving it on its docket, the Supreme Court, just two months later, ruled (7:2) that, under the almost-forgotten 102-year-old Civil Rights Act of 1866—enacted under the enforcement provisions of the Thirteenth Amendment—racial discrimination in the purchase, lease, sale, holding, and conveyance of real and personal property was expressly forbidden.[184]

1977); Allan P. Sindler, Bakke, De Funis *and Minority Admissions: The Quest for Equal Opportunity* (New York: Longman, 1978); and Ralph A. Rossum, *Reverse Discrimination: The Constitutional Debate* (New York: Marcel Dekker, 1980). See the discussion of the issue, *infra*.

182. Twice that September the Senate refused to shut off debate on the measure; the votes were 54:42 and 54:41—both short of the needed two-thirds.

183. See Sections 8803(b) and 807 of Title VIII of Public Law 90-284, 82 Stat. 73.

184. *Jones v. Alfred H. Mayer Co.,* 392 U.S. 409 (1968). In a stinging dissenting opinion, joined by Justice White, Justice Harlan flayed the majority for proceeding "with such precipitous and insecure strides." He doubted that the 1866 law's "goals could constitutionally be achieved under the Thirteenth Amendment" (at 476). In that connection see the Court's 1976 decisions in *Hills v. Gautreax, supra* note 161 and, especially, in *Runyon v. McCrary, infra*.

In 1988 Congress amended the law to toughen and speed the 1968 statute's available administrative enforcement powers significantly by giving the Department of Housing and Urban Development power to go to court to seek heavy fines, and it extended its provisions to handicapped persons and families with children.

THE QUEST FOR SUFFRAGE

A good many sincere as well as fair-weather friends of black equality prior to the decision to concentrate on education had insisted that it would be wiser to direct the thrust of the movement toward suffrage, arguing that effective suffrage would almost automatically rectify most, if not all, of the black grievances in the public sector, the private sector ultimately following. The feeling that NAACP strategists and their supporters committed a fundamental error persists in many circles to this day. Whatever the argument's merit, the suffrage problem was not really tackled until the Civil Rights Acts of 1957, 1960, and 1964 had become law—and not effectively until the passage of the Voting Rights Act of 1965.

Antecedents to the Voting Rights Act of 1965

Our nation's history is replete with systematic disfranchisement of blacks, particularly in the South and the border states. Although prior to the Civil War, especially in the early decades following the adoption of the Constitution, other groups, too, had experienced considerable difficulty in their quest for suffrage— for example, Quakers, Catholics, and Jews—blacks more than any other single minority group suffered second-class political citizenship. And, as we have seen, despite the enactment of the Civil War amendments—in particular the Fifteenth Amendment, which specifically and expressly provided, as the Fourteenth Amendment had not,[185] that the "right of citizens of the United States to vote shall not be denied or abridged by the United States or by any State on account of race, color, or previous condition of servitude"—blacks continued to find access to the ballot box difficult, and often impossible, in much of the old Confederacy. That access had been all but closed by the turn of the century, if not directly then indirectly by resort to assorted devices such as the "grandfather clause," the "white primary," the poll tax, interpretation clauses, understanding clauses, and sundry other registration requirements—a seemingly inexhaustible array of covert as well as overt tools of discrimination.[186]

185. See the discussion in Berger, op. cit., chapters 4 and 5.
186. For data on black registration and the denial of voting rights to blacks, see, among others, the 1959 *Report* and the 1961 voting study of the U.S. Commission on Civil Rights; subsequent annual *Reports;* and those by the U.S. Bureau of the Census.

Until the legislative activity in the 1950s, much of this discrimination was rendered feasible by our federal structure. An important distinction existed between the legal right to vote for *federal* officials and the legal right to vote for *local* and *state* officials. The latter vote stems from state constitutions and laws and is thus not on its face a federal right in the same sense and to the same degree as the right to vote for federal officers, such as members of Congress and presidential electors. Hence, at least until enactment of the four recent Civil Rights Acts and, more pertinently, the Voting Rights Act of 1965 and its subsequent strengthening amendments of 1970, 1975, 1982, and 1987, states were free to define their own qualifications for voting for state and local officials, and in part also for their federal representatives. This state power was subject only to the limitations of Amendments Fourteen, Fifteen, Nineteen, and Twenty-four and that intriguing Article 1, Section 4. The latter, while granting the "Times, Places, and Manner" of holding elections for federal officials to the states, also contains a clause that would become an important tool in the judicial arsenal of aid to blacks: "[B]ut the Congress may at any time by Law make or alter such Regulations, except as to the Places of chusing [*sic*] Senators."

When access to the ballot remained foreclosed to blacks because they continued to be denied their rightful influence in southern politics, and when Congress failed to come to their aid, they turned to the federal *courts* for redress. Initially they found little because of a then unsympathetic judiciary and the absence of appropriate precedent. When the Supreme Court rejected a promising challenge to the Mississippi literacy test in 1898,[187] matters looked bleak indeed. As recently as 1959, the literacy device was upheld unanimously by the Court in a North Carolina case,[188] in an opinion written by no less firm an exponent of black equality than Justice Douglas!

Light Ahead. Moving toward the 1950s and 1960s, when blacks were to win equal rights at least on paper and at the bar of the judiciary in all parts of the land, an important judicial tool proved to be the Fifteenth Amendment—although the crucial one, as in the education struggles, became the equal protection of the laws clause of Amendment Fourteen, notwithstanding its legislative history of excluding black suffrage from its intended reach.[189] Still, in 1915 the Supreme Court had based its decision on the clear-cut language of the Fifteenth Amendment when in a unanimous opinion by Chief Justice Edward D. White it struck down the Oklahoma "grandfather clause."[190] This transparent device, adopted in several southern and border states, provided a convenient loophole through which illiterate whites could escape the provisions of literacy tests. It exempted

187. *Williams v. Mississippi,* 170 U.S. 213 (1898).
188. *Lassiter v. Northampton Election Board,* 360 U.S. 45.
189. See Berger, op. cit., data in chapters 4 and 5.
190. *Guinn v. United States,* 238 U.S. 347.

from those tests all "persons and their lineal descendants" who were qualified to vote as of January 1, 1866, or any similarly convenient date prior to Amendments Fourteen and Fifteen, which would not apply to blacks. The words *Negro, black,* and *colored* did not appear anywhere in the various grandfather clauses because practically no blacks, if any, had voted or been able to vote before the Civil War.

After the failure of an attempt to resuscitate its spirit, if not its letter, in 1939,[191] the grandfather clause was indeed gone. But the poll tax, the "white primary," and a number of other devices remained available to those state officers bent upon the perpetuation of a pure or almost pure white suffrage. A windfall came their way in 1921 when a narrowly divided Supreme Court ruled—in a messy Michigan senatorial primary case, involving Henry Ford and Truman H. Newberry[192]—that Congress had no power, or at best highly dubious power, to regulate *primary* elections in the states, be they for federal or state or local office. Although the litigation itself dealt with fraud rather than racial discrimination, the decision was tailor-made for the devotees of the white primary. Hence, Texas went to work at once and passed the blatant Texas White Primary Law of 1924, which read: "In no event shall a negro be eligible to participate in a Democratic primary election in the State of Texas, and should a negro vote in a Democratic primary election, such ballot shall be void and election officials shall not count the same."

A black physician from El Paso, Dr. L. A. Nixon, took up the fight. Denied participation in the Democratic Party's primary under the terms of the Texas law, Dr. Nixon challenged its constitutionality. In a 9:0 opinion, written by Justice Holmes in 1927, the Supreme Court agreed. Without passing on the matter of primaries versus general elections, so importantly present in the Michigan decision,[193] the Court declared the Texas White Primary Law unconstitutional as a "direct and obvious infringement" of the equal protection of the laws clause of the Fourteenth Amendment. Here, then, that important clause entered the fray in the voting field—fully a decade prior to its first meaningful utilization in the area of educational segregation.[194]

Texas was not so easily discouraged, however: it repealed the 1924 statute and substituted a measure authorizing the State Executive Committee of every political party to "prescribe the qualifications of its own members." The state's Democratic Party then promptly "prescribed" that "only whites" shall be eligible in *its* primaries. When Dr. Nixon thus again was denied participation in the party of his choice, he returned to court with a constitutional challenge to Texas's enabling statute. The Supreme Court, speaking through Justice Cardozo, soon struck down this latest Texas device (albeit this time by the narrow-

---

191. *Lane v. Wilson,* 307 U.S. 268.
192. *Newberry v. United States,* 256 U.S. 232.
193. Ibid.
194. *Nixon v. Herndon,* 273 U.S. 536.

est of margins, 5:4) on the grounds that by setting qualifications the Democratic Party was usurping state law and that, consequently, the state of Texas had in fact *acted through* the party as its agent, thereby violating once again the equal protection of the laws clause of the Fourteenth Amendment.[195] Not to be outdone, Texas then (1932) *repealed* the authorizing clause of the above legislation. Its Democratic Party, in turn, acting through the *Democratic State Convention,* on its own authority and without any statutory sanction, adopted a resolution to render itself a "private group," permitting as members of this *private group* only *white* persons. When this arrangement also was challenged at the bar of our highest tribunal, the Court unanimously accepted (9:0) the constitutionality of this new loophole on the ground that the *state of Texas was not involved:* that the private group referred to was not a "creature of the state" but a *voluntary association* that had acted on its own. This appeared to settle the matter at issue, for, as Justice Roberts wrote for the Court, "private persons or groups cannot violate the Fourteenth Amendment," in the absence of state action per se.[196]

But this seeming triumph of the disfranchisers was short-lived. In 1941, just six years after the *"Private Group" Case* decision, the Supreme Court was confronted with a case of fraud in a Louisiana *federal* primary. A Louisiana election official, one Patrick B. Classic, had crudely transferred ninety-seven votes cast validly for two candidates in that primary to a third candidate—his own choice. In its 5:3 holding the Court, through Justice Stone, ruled that the previously mentioned Section 4 of the Constitution's Article 1 in fact authorized Congress to regulate *primaries* as well as *elections* because "primaries" in the words of the Constitution were tantamount to "elections" and, being "an integral part of the election machinery," were subject to congressional regulations.[197] This decision did not, to be sure, settle the question whether whites were legally at liberty to exclude blacks from primaries for state and local officials, for the race question was not involved. What the *Classic* decision did do—and it was a truly significant accomplishment in constitutional interpretation—was pave the way for federal regulation by overruling the *Newberry* (Michigan) holding, which had separated the concept of federal "primaries" from "elections."[198] The *Grovey v. Townsend "Private Group" Case*[199] still stood, however.

The White Primary Falls. Yet three years later, in the case of *Smith v. Allwright,*[200] the Supreme Court in an 8:1 opinion written by Justice Reed—a bor-

195. *Nixon v. Condon,* 286 U.S. 73 (1932).
196. *Grovey v. Townsend,* 295 U.S. 45 (1935) at 52.
197. *United States v. Classic,* 313 U.S. 299 (1941) at 318.
198. *Newberry v. United States,* 256 U.S. 232 (1921).
199. *Grovey v. Townsend,* op. cit.
200. 321 U.S. 649 (1944).

der state Democrat from Kentucky[201]—declared the Texas "private" white primary unconstitutional as a violation of the *Fifteenth Amendment.* Smith, a black, had been denied participation by a Texas election judge, Allwright, who relied on the "voluntary association" concept developed by the Court in the *Grovey* decision. But now that tribunal ruled that, in effect, the Democratic Party of the state of Texas was acting as an *agent of the state,* because of the character of its duties—such as providing election machinery—and was thus subject to the pertinent provisions of Amendments Fourteen and Fifteen, here the latter. In the *Classic* case,[202] the Court had set up two alternate or complementary "tests" to determine whether or not a primary was validly affected, and thus regulatable, by the provisions of federal authority under the Constitution: (1) Had the state law made the primary an integral part of the election machinery? and/or (2) Did the primary "effectively control the choice"?[203] Now in *Allwright* both tests applied. The Court admonished Texas and the nation that the constitutional right to be free from racial

> discrimination in voting is not to be nullified by a state through casting its electoral process in a form which permits a private organization to practice racial discrimination in the election. . . . It may be taken as a postulate that the right to vote in . . . a primary . . . without discrimination by the State . . . is a right secured by the Constitution.[204]

As had been true of the *Grovey "Private Group" Case,*[205] the controlling issue had to be the answer to the basic question: Had the black claimant involved thereby been barred from the primary by state action? The Supreme Court held that he had—and *Grovey* was thus overruled, nine years after it had become law. Only Justice Roberts dissented from the *Allwright* decision—and he did so as much on grounds of judicial "self-restraint"–cum–stare decisis as on the merits of the controversy, grumbling that "Supreme Court decisions are becoming in the same class as a restricted railroad ticket, good for this day and train only."[206]

The *Smith v. Allwright* decision did much to stimulate black participation in primary elections in the South and the border states; but the forces of exclusion were far from ineffective, and ingenuity was not lacking. For example, in an attempt to perpetuate white hegemony at the polls and, concurrently, to test the *Allwright* ruling further, South Carolina promptly *repealed* all of its 147 laws and

---

201. For a fascinating account, demonstrating that the case had originally been assigned to Justice Frankfurter but then reassigned for "strategic" reasons to Justice Reed, see Alpheus T. Mason, *Harlan Fiske Stone: Pillar of the Law* (New York: Viking, 1956), p. 615. It is also related in Abraham, *The Judicial Process,* op. cit., p. 230.
202. *United States v. Classic,* op. cit.
203. Ibid. at 318.
204. *Smith v. Allwright,* 321 U.S. 649 (1944) at 661, 664.
205. *Grovey v. Townsend,* op. cit.
206. *Smith v. Allwright,* op. cit., at 669.

one constitutional provision relating to the conduct of primaries. But a courageous U.S. District Court jurist, J. Waties Waring—a tenth-generation member of the South Carolina aristocracy—held in 1947 in *Rice v. Elmore*[207] that the South Carolina primaries, though denuded of state authorization per se, "effectively control the choice" of candidates for public office. This finding satisfied the second test of the *Classic* case,[208] and Waring ruled, consequently, that the denial to blacks of their right to vote in primaries was prima facie evidence of a violation of both the Fourteenth and Fifteenth Amendments. On appeal, the U.S. Court of Appeals for the Fourth Circuit sitting in Richmond, Virginia, sustained Judge Waring.[209] That opinion was written by Chief Judge John J. Parker—ironically, the same man who had been rejected as President Hoover's nominee to the U.S. Supreme Court in 1930, by a 41:39 vote, in part because of his alleged antiblack bias.[210] And the Supreme Court refused to review the *Elmore* case,[211] thus letting Waring's holding stand. As a result, thirty-five thousand blacks came to the polls in South Carolina's Democratic primary in 1948. Judge Waring, now harassed, pilloried, and isolated, found it necessary five years later to leave his old home and his beloved bench to move with his family to New York. "My ostracism was total," he recalled wistfully in a 1963 interview. "After my racial cases it got very lonely."[212]

Yet, undeterred by the decision in *Rice v. Elmore,* South Carolina sought to evade it by vesting control of primaries in private clubs to which blacks were not admitted. As a prerequisite to voting in primaries, these clubs required the taking of an oath that was particularly odious to blacks. Among other things, it was necessary to swear to a belief in the social and educational separation of the races. Predictably, this effort to continue disfranchisement of nonwhites also ran afoul of effective judicial vetoes in 1948 and 1949.[213] And in 1953 a much more elaborate and less obvious device used to keep blacks from voting in Fort Bend County, Texas, fell: the "preprimary primary," conducted by a group known as

207. 72 F. Supp. 516 (1947).

208. *United States v. Classic,* op. cit.

209. *Rice v. Elmore,* 165 F.2d 387 (1947).

210. See Abraham, *The Judicial Process,* op. cit., pp. 82–83. The next rejectees were President Johnson's 1968 attempted promotion of Abe Fortas to chief justice and Nixon's 1969 and 1970 nominations of Clement H. Haynsworth and G. Harrold Carswell, by votes of 55:45 and 51:45, respectively. See Henry J. Abraham, *Justices, Presidents, and Senators: A History of Supreme Court Appointments,* new and revised edition (Lanham, Md.: Rowman and Littlefield, 1999). The most recent rejection was President Reagan's 1987 nomination of Robert H. Bork (58:42).

211. *Rice v. Elmore,* 333 U.S. 875 (1948), certiorari denied.

212. *Greenwich (Conn.) Times,* August 30, 1963, p. 13, interviewed by Charles L. West. When he died in 1968, his Charleston, South Carolina, burial was attended by two hundred blacks and fewer than a dozen whites. See the sympathetic biography by T. E. Yarbrough, *A Passion for Justice: J. Waties Waring and Civil Rights* (New York: Oxford University Press, 1987).

213. *Brown v. Baskin,* 78 F. Supp. 933 (1948) and 174 F.2d 391 (1949).

the "Jaybird Democratic Association."[214] Few could continue to doubt that the federal authorities really meant business in the voting field. Still, the various shenanigans continued, often taking the form of "understanding" and "interpreting" clauses, which were destined to fall, too, sooner or later.[215] Then, of course, there was the poll tax—a device more difficult to indict: it had been specifically *upheld* by the Supreme Court in both 1937[216] and 1951.[217] While it was perhaps the best known of the several devices, it was the least important. When it was outlawed for *federal* elections by the Twenty-fourth, or Holland, Amendment,[218] ratified in January 1964, its southern presence was confined to Alabama, Arkansas, Mississippi, Texas, and Virginia. But even for *state* elections its days were numbered: when the question of the constitutionality of the Virginia state poll tax, as applied to state elections, reached the Supreme Court in 1966, the tax was given a prompt judicial burial.[219] Appropriately, it was Justice Douglas, the sole dissenter when the Court had upheld the Virginia tax fifteen years before,[220] who spoke for the six-man majority. Avoiding the First Amendment issue urged upon the Court by the then Solicitor-General Thurgood Marshall, Douglas leaned heavily on the Court's newly developed "one man, one vote" doctrine[221] for his authority that Virginia's $1.50 tax as a prerequisite for voting in state elections violated the equal protection of the laws guarantee of the Fourteenth Amendment. Interestingly, although the plaintiffs in the two cases before the Court were black, the majority's holding was based on *economic* rather than racial discrimination. "To introduce wealth or payment of a fee as a measure of a voter's qualifications," wrote Douglas, "is to introduce a capricious or irrelevant factor. The degree of the discrimination is irrelevant."[222] Justices Black, Harlan, and Stewart, on the other hand, while dissenting on varying grounds, all agreed that "nondiscriminatory and fairly applied" payment of a poll tax *could* be a reasonable basis for determining the right to vote.[223]

---

214. *Terry v. Adams,* 345 U.S. 461 (1953). For an explanatory article see Luther A. Huston, "High Court Upsets a Limited Primary," *New York Times,* May 5, 1953, p. 191.

215. E.g., *Schnell v. Davis,* 336 U.S. 933 (1949).

216. *Breedlove v. Suttles,* 302 U.S. 277, involving a *white* male Georgian.

217. *Butler v. Thompson,* 341 U.S. 937.

218. Named after U.S. Senator Spessard Holland (D.-Fla.), who "fathered" it.

219. *Harper v. Virginia State Board of Elections,* 383 U.S. 663 (decided March 25, 1966).

220. *Butler v. Thompson,* op. cit.

221. *Gray v. Sanders,* 372 U.S. 368 (1963) at 381. See *supra* chapter 2. Justice Stewart preferred the term "one voter, one vote"; Chief Justice Warren often used "one man, one vote," the most commonly employed terminology; Justice Douglas alternated between the nouns "person" and "man."

222. *Harper v. Virginia Board of Elections,* op. cit., at 668.

223. See the separate dissenting opinions by Justices Black and Harlan, ibid. at 670, 680. The former objected to what he viewed as the majority's "natural law" approach vis-à-vis "reasonableness"; the latter believed a constitutional amendment to be necessary.

The problem with the literacy test—in itself neither unreasonable nor discriminatory (something that could be said, at least in theory, of several of the devices used to disfranchise)—was its *application;* it was frequently used for gross discrimination against blacks. Its "non-discriminatory" principle was upheld by the U.S. Supreme Court as late as 1959,[224] and, as we shall see, when the Voting Rights Act of 1965 launched a selective assault upon the literacy test, almost one-half of the states of the Union were using a variety of such tests. Although it is perhaps easier to attack the concept of the literacy test as a necessary and desirable suffrage requirement than it is to attack the more essential requirements of residence[225] and registration, it would be unfair to condemn it on its face. There are other causes for nonvoting than racial discrimination; apathy, for example, is the chief cause of low participation by the American electorate—averaging barely 50 percent of those eligible to vote even in presidential elections. However, the privilege of voting also contains the privilege of abstinence, of course.[226]

The Voting Rights Act of 1965. Regardless of the weight one might assign to any one of the various factors that caused the demonstrably low black suffrage, mid-twentieth-century statistics serve well as an indictment of a state of affairs that cried out for government action above and beyond the Civil Rights Acts of 1957, 1960, and 1964. The presidential election year of 1948 saw barely 600,000 blacks registered in the eleven states of the South, a mere 12 percent of those of voting age; 1952 saw close to 1,000,000, some 20 percent; and 1956 roughly 1,250,000, or 25 percent. Sixty percent of the eligible whites were *registered* in the same region. Although the percentage of blacks registered continued to climb—reaching 27 percent by 1961 and 40 percent just prior to the enactment of the Voting Rights Act of 1965—the die-hard resistance to *any* registration in widespread and important areas of the South, particularly in most of Mississippi, much of Alabama, and a good many counties of Louisiana, continued to rankle civil rights leaders. As late as the summer of 1965, a mere 6.8 percent of eligible blacks had been registered in Mississippi, an increase of scarcely 2 percent after more than four years of activity and three federal statutes.[227]

---

224. *Lassiter v. Northampton Election Board,* 360 U.S. 45 (a North Carolina case).

225. Affirmed by the Court in a Maryland (one-year) test case in 1965 (*Deueding v. Devlin,* 380 U.S. 125). But see the 1970 federal statute, *infra* this chapter.

226. For a discussion of the problem of participation, including the issue of compulsory voting, see Henry J. Abraham, *Compulsory Voting* (Washington, D.C.: Public Affairs Press, 1955).

227. Statistics are obtainable from numerous sources, among them the Southern Regional Council, the *Race Relations Reporter,* various almanacs, the daily press, the *Statistical Abstract of the United States,* and annual compendia by the U.S. Commission on Civil Rights, the American Civil Liberties Union, the American Jewish Congress, and numerous other groups.

Counsels of patience were now clearly falling on deaf ears; the civil rights movement had begun to take to the streets in 1960; and then, in early 1965, the town of Selma, Alabama, became the catalyst for the new voting law. Civil rights leaders, headed by Dr. Martin Luther King, organized a well-advertised fifty-mile march from Selma to Montgomery in support of efforts to obtain greater black voter registration in the face of continued difficulty, defiance, and procrastination. The march began on March 7, only to be brutally broken up by Alabama state troopers, under orders of Governor George C. Wallace,[228] while it was still close to Selma. Employing whips, nightsticks, cattle prods, and tear gas, the troopers injured at least forty of the marchers. The scene flashed on the television screens of homes throughout the nation and the world. Widespread revulsion set in at once, and hundreds of additional civil rights supporters, many of them white clergy of all faiths, poured into the Selma area. Tragedy was not long in coming: a white Unitarian minister from Boston, the Reverend James J. Reeb, was fatally clubbed down on a Selma street by irate white natives. Civil rights leaders then rescheduled the march, and President Johnson ordered the Alabama National Guard into federal service to protect the marchers. Again led by Dr. King, the march was completed peacefully on March 25, with a crowd of thirty thousand gathering on the steps of the Alabama capitol in Montgomery. But on the same night a white woman from Detroit, Mrs. Viola Liuzzo, who was shuttling blacks back to Selma from Montgomery in her car, was shot and killed by a trio of white ambushers.

Ten days later, responding to public clamor for action following the Selma outrages,[229] President Johnson addressed Congress in an extraordinary joint session, calling for the enactment of the strongest voting rights legislation proposed in nine decades. "The time for waiting is gone," the president told his hushed audience; "outside this chamber is the outraged conscience of a nation—the grave concern of many nations—and the harsh judgment of history on our acts."[230] Against this background his administration submitted the Voting Rights Bill of 1965, based on the Fifteenth Amendment's exhortation that no person shall be denied the right to vote because of "race, color, or previous condition of servi-

228. Twenty years later, the very same Governor George C. Wallace cordially received the leaders of a three-thousand-member, peaceful Selma-to-Montgomery march in his capitol office. Times had changed indeed (see *Stars and Stripes,* March 9, 1985, p. 5). And in mid-1987 Selma's city council had its first black voting majority.

229. It is poetic justice that the 1972 elections—just seven years after Selma—would show that the greatest political gains for southern blacks had come in Alabama, generally, and in Selma, in particular: that year 117 blacks were elected to Alabama offices. Also in Selma—where the black registration had risen from 2.3 percent in 1965 to 67 percent (!) in 1972—five of the ten city council seats were won by blacks; and in 2000 that city elected its first black mayor, businessman James Perkins. Over 200 blacks held elective office in Alabama in 1976, double that number in 1986.

230. As quoted in the *New York Times,* March 16, 1965, p. 11.

tude," and giving Congress the power to enforce its provisions "by appropriate legislation."

The bill became law in August, and it was a tough one. It had passed the Senate by a vote of 79:18 and the House of Representatives by 328:74—an even more decisive margin than in the enactment of the Civil Rights Act of 1964—and contained the following key provisions: it barred literacy and other tests for voting deemed to be discriminatory, based on a rather complicated formula that affected six southern states (Alabama, Georgia, Mississippi, Louisiana, South Carolina, and Virginia); thirty-four counties in North Carolina; all of Alaska; and single counties in Maine, Arizona, and Idaho. (The formula concerning literacy tests extended only to those states where such tests were in force November 1, 1964, and where less than 50 percent of the voting-age population voted, or was registered to vote, in the 1964 presidential election.) It set up new criminal penalties for attempts to keep qualified persons from voting or to threaten or harm civil rights workers assisting potential voters. It directed the U.S. Department of Justice to begin court suits challenging the constitutionality of poll taxes still used in *state and local* elections. (Arkansas having by then abandoned the poll tax, this provision was directed at Alabama, Mississippi, Texas, and Virginia.)

Clearly, the fundamental purpose of the Voting Rights Act of 1965, the passage of which President Johnson termed a "proud moment for this nation," was to facilitate black registration and voting by the elimination, in those states where discrimination had been proved to be both most rampant and most persistent, of all requirements but the basic ones of age, residence, mental competence, and absence of a criminal record. Needless to say, this and some other provisions[231] of the act raised serious problems of constitutionality, given the somewhat murky division of responsibility for suffrage between the federal and state governments. South Carolina quickly brought suit, though it seemed hardly likely that the Supreme Court would strike down legislation that, however marginal in constitutional interpretation in some of its aspects, was still clearly based upon the let-

---

231. One of the most contentious was the Kennedy (Robert F.) amendment to the statute, which specifically granted the right to vote to Puerto Ricans, of whom 750,000 then lived in New York City, provided they had a sixth-grade education from a Puerto Rican school—in which Spanish is the principal language, of course. In effect, the amendment circumvented the then otherwise legal New York literacy test. A three-judge federal district court, one judge dissenting, declared that section of the Voting Rights Act unconstitutional in November 1965 (247 F. Supp. 196). However, in a 7:2 opinion, written by Justice Brennan with Justices Harlan and Stewart dissenting (they believed that the Court rather than Congress should have determined the constitutionality of the New York literacy law), the Supreme Court reversed the lower tribunal, concluding that Congress in passing the special Spanish literacy amendment to the bill had acted legally because it was "appropriate legislation . . . plainly adapted" to the enforcement of the equal protection of the laws clause of the Fourteenth Amendment and otherwise consistent with the letter and spirit of the "positive grant of legislative power" to Congress inherent in that amendment to the Constitution (*Katzenbach v. Morgan,* 384 U.S. 641 [1966]).

ter and spirit of the Fifteenth Amendment, adopted some ninety-five years before. The Court's answer came rapidly and, as anticipated, approvingly: with Justice Black dissenting in part (on the law's Section 5 appeals-cum-clearance procedure, which he viewed as treating the South as little more than a conquered province) and concurring in part, the Court upheld the seven major provisions of the act in a thirty-one-page opinion written by Chief Justice Warren. He based his ruling squarely on the act's constitutionality and, predictably, on the power of Congress to act under the provisions of the Fifteenth Amendment. The chief justice wrote that two points "emerge vividly" from the voluminous legislative history of the act: (1) that Congress felt itself "confronted by an insidious and pervasive evil which had been perpetuated in certain parts of our country by unremitting and ingenious defiance of the Constitution"; and (2) that Congress demonstrably concluded that the unsuccessful remedies which it had prescribed in the past would have to be replaced by "sterner and more elaborate measures."[232] "We may finally look forward to the day," summarized the chief justice, quoting verbatim the commands of Amendment Fifteen, "when truly the right of citizens of the United States to vote shall not be denied or abridged by the United States or by any state on account of race, color, or previous condition of servitude."[233]

The Voting Rights Act of 1965 had hardly become law when the Johnson administration commenced its enforcement with two steps. First, literacy tests were suspended as a prerequisite to voting in seven states (Alabama, Alaska,[234] Georgia, Louisiana, Mississippi, South Carolina, and Virginia), twenty-six counties of North Carolina, and one in Arizona; second, the Department of Justice, true to its mandate under the act, filed suits to abolish the poll tax in the four states that still had one: Alabama, Mississippi, Texas, and Virginia. Moreover, under the provisions of the law, some forty-five *federal voting examiners,* all employees of the U.S. Civil Service Commission, were standing by in the Deep South, waiting to move into fifteen to twenty counties that had a history of resistance to black voting. The examiners, working in teams, began to register eligible blacks that August within a matter of days. Results were almost immediately apparent: on the first supervised registration day under the new statute, 1,144 blacks were enrolled in nine counties with a history of rampant dis-

---

232. *South Carolina v. Katzenbach,* 383 U.S. 301 (1966). Black's statement is at 359, Warren's at 309.

233. Ibid. at 337.

234. On May 24, 1966, Alaska became the first state to be exempted from the act's literacy test suspension provisions when it convinced the Department of Justice that its literacy test had never been used to deny the right to vote on the basis of race or color. Virginia requested repeatedly to be exempted. Unsuccessful, it ultimately went to the Supreme Court (*Virginia v. United States,* 420 U.S. 901), which, however, without hearing oral argument, in 1975 affirmed (6:3) a lower federal court's decision denying Virginia's plea. Dissenting were Chief Justice Burger and Justices Powell and Rehnquist.

crimination in Alabama, Louisiana, and Mississippi—an increase of 65 percent! Extending their work to four other counties, the federal voting examiners had registered almost 20,000 blacks within ten days. In the first two months after the enactment of the new voting law, about 110,000 blacks were registered voluntarily by *local officials* and more than 56,000 by the federal examiners sent to areas designated by Attorney General Nicholas Katzenbach. It was in the May 1966 primaries that, for the first time, blacks voted in large numbers in the Deep South—and in six southern states they elected some of their candidates to office.

By March 1966, under pressure of the new law, federal examiners had enrolled 101,370 blacks, local registrars another 201,000. That November, the percentage of eligible blacks registered to vote in the South ranged from 27.8 percent in Mississippi and 49.9 percent in Alabama to 71.7 percent in Tennessee, averaging 50.1 percent. Although the apathy and fear by blacks about voting, which had been so firmly established by decades of white exclusionary rule, could not be eradicated overnight, southern black registration had now reached 2,671,514, fully 1,200,000 more than as of July 1960.[235]

The 1970 Amendments. The success of the 1965 statute heralded a fierce legislative battle to extend and amend it upon its termination five years later. Predictably, pro and con forces jockeyed to broaden and gut it, respectively. The resultant legislation was a compromise, but, by and large, the line was drawn in favor of the aspirations of the still unfranchised or underfranchised. Continued for five years, the amended statute, in its main provisions, extended the franchise in both federal *and* state elections to eighteen-year-olds;[236] extended the 1965 prohibition against the use of literacy tests as a condition to voting registration to *all* fifty states until 1975 (thus removing the "selective stigma" of the 1965 provision);[237] and established a thirty-day limit for residency requirements in *presidential* elections.[238] By fall 1971, the new voting laws had added 1.5 million

235. *New York Times,* July 27, 1966, p. 251, and November 27, 1966, p. 741. By September 1, 1966, a total of 1,147,236 blacks had registered in the five "black belt" states of Mississippi, Alabama, Georgia, Louisiana, and South Carolina, compared with 687,000 when the Voting Rights Act of 1965 became law one year earlier (*New York Times,* October 21, 1966, p. 11). An additional 210,000 had been added to the rolls three years later (*New York Times,* December 14, 1969, p. 11).

236. Late in December 1970 the Supreme Court upheld (5:4) the provision's *federal* applicability but struck down (5:4) the *state* aspect (*Oregon v. Mitchell,* 400 U.S. 112), Justice Black, the decision's author, providing the swing vote in both instances.

237. Upheld by the Court (8:1) in *United States v. Arizona,* 400 U.S. 112 (1970).

238. Upheld by the Court (9:0) in *United States v. Idaho,* 400 U.S. 112 (1970). In 1972 it extended this interpretation (6:1) to reach *state* and local elections (*Dunn v. Blumstein,* 405 U.S. 330). On the other hand, it upheld (6:3) the fifty-day preelection registration requirements for state and local elections in Arizona and Georgia (*Marston v. Lewis* and *Burns v. Fortson,* 410 U.S. 679). It also upheld (5:4) a New York State requirement of a preprimary registration period of eight to eleven months (October 22, 1974).

blacks and 6 million of the 11 million eighteen-to-twenty-one-year-old voters. By presidential election time in 1972 the figures for southern blacks had risen to 3,448,565,[239] reaching well above 3.5 million for the November 1974 "off-year" races.[240] The total of *all* blacks registered reached 8 million less than a year later.[241]

The 1975 Amendments. When the so demonstrably successful statute came up for renewal in 1975, the question was not whether it would be extended but to what degree it would be broadened even more. By thumping majorities Congress did both in mid-1975. Exactly ten years after President Johnson signed the original Voting Rights Act, President Ford affixed his signature to a new extension, this time for seven rather than five years, that substantially broadened the law by permanently prohibiting literacy tests anywhere; bringing Spanish, Filipino, Chinese, Japanese, and Korean Americans, American Indians, Alaskan natives, and other minorities under its coverage; bracketing additional states, or parts thereof—a total of thirty-five—under its preclearance provisions[242] in the case of any state-sponsored attempts to change existing voting laws (added were heretofore-not-included parts of *thirty* states, ranging from Arizona through Wyoming); allowing private citizens to file suit to bring their local jurisdictions under the law's protection; mandating bilingual ballots and election materials (or oral assistance in their absence) to the aforementioned minority groups;[243] and empowering the Justice Department to intervene in jurisdictions covered by the act when changes in voting procedures will result in minority voter dilution. By the beginning of the new decade, almost 10 million blacks were on the voting rolls, coming within 9 percent of the national figure of 70 percent for whites, and within 7 percent of the white voting turnout. By 1984 black voter registration had passed that of whites: 73 percent to 72 percent of those eligible.[244]

The 1982 Amendments. The new clout, and political realities, of the growing black vote clearly underlay the most dramatic extension of the Voting Rights Act

239. Charles V. Hamilton, *The Bench and the Ballot: Southern Federal Judges and Black Voters* (New York: Oxford University Press, 1973), p. vii.

240. *New York Times,* November 11, 1974, p. 30c.

241. U.S. Bureau of the Census, *Annual Report,* 1975.

242. Not applicable, however, if changes are formulated by the *courts* (see, e.g., the 1977 Mississippi reapportionment case of *Connor v. Finch,* 431 U.S. 407. But cf. the 1981 holding in *McDaniel v. Sanchez,* 452 U.S. 130).

243. By 1975 the government had already ordered 529 counties and towns in twenty-six states to comply with that provision; and in 1976 the Justice Department ruled that 513 political jurisdictions in thirty states were affected (*New York Times,* April 22, 1976, p. 25c).

244. See the quarterly and annual reports, *Current Population Reports* and *Population Characteristics,* published by the Bureau of the Census of the U.S. Department of Commerce.

in 1982. Heretofore, the 1965 statute had been extended for five, five, and seven years, respectively. Now, however, following a year of protracted, often heated, debate in Congress, the 1982 amendments extended the legislation by fully twenty-five years, key attention focusing on Section 5 (the preclearance requirement regarding any changes in electoral practices by the states and/or their subdivisions) and, most significantly, on Section 2 (pertaining to the utilization of the appropriate standard of proof for identifying laws or practices that "deny or abridge" the right to vote). Section 5 proved to be relatively easy to extend, once the initially proposed "indefinite" language was altered to read "25 years," and a "bail out" provision, effective as of 1985, was adopted. The latter enables jurisdictions now subject to the preclearance provision—affecting twenty-two states or subdivisions thereof—to "bail out" upon demonstrating a history of affirmative voting rights policies.[245]

The Section 2 changes, however, produced months-long emotional and constitutional arguments, for they were clearly designed to overturn the Supreme Court's 1980 ruling in *Mobile v. Bolden,*[246] which had determined that to demonstrate a denial of equal protection of voting rights plaintiffs would have to prove discriminatory *purpose (intent),* not merely discriminatory *result.* Under the leadership of Senate Majority Leader Bob Dole (R.-Kans.), the ultimately fashioned compromise provided:

> No voting qualification or prerequisite to voting, or standard, practice, or procedure shall be imposed or applied by any State or political subdivision in a manner which *results* in a denial or abridgement of the right of any citizen of the United States to vote on account of race or color, or in contravention of the guarantees [set forth in the law]. The fact that members of a minority group have not been elected in numbers equal to the group's proportion of the population shall not, in and of itself, constitute a violation of this Section. (Section 2 of the Voting Rights Act of 1982)

Obviously intended to change the *intent* standard the Court had adopted in the *Mobile* case to one of *result,* the amended Section 2 produced all but immediate results. Notwithstanding the explicit disclaimers to an entitlement to "proportional representation" based on race—and perhaps other group concepts—the judiciary commenced to strike down at-large and other multimember electoral systems in favor of single-member or single-unit district systems. When the Supreme Court applied the new standard, albeit by the narrowest of divisions (5:4), in the 1986 North Carolina case of *Thornburg v. Gingles,* there remained little doubt that the 1982 changes effected in Section 2 had demonstrably embraced the *result* test and that, arguably, something very close to an expectation of proportional representation based upon race had been judicially sanctioned. As

245. *Reno v. Bossier Parish,* 528 U.S. 320.
246. 446 U.S. 55.

Justice O'Connor, speaking also for Chief Justice Burger and Justices Powell and Rehnquist, saw the matter in dissent:

> Although the Court does not acknowledge it expressly, [the ruling] results in the creation of a right to a form of proportional representation in favor of all geographically and politically cohesive minority groups that are large enough to constitute majorities if concentrated within one or more single-member districts. . . . [The ruling] has disregarded the balance struck by Congress [in amending the Voting Rights Act of 1982]. That compromise was not designed to assure safe seats for minorities.[247]

But Justice Brennan's controlling opinion pointed to the "totality of the circumstances" and found in each district

> racially polarized voting; the legacy of official discrimination in voting matters, education, housing, employment, and health services; and the persistence of campaign appeals to racial prejudice [all of which] acted to impair the ability of black voters to participate equally in the political process and to elect candidates of their choice.[248]

Whatever one's perception may be, it became rapidly apparent that the 1982 law, as interpreted and applied, gave blacks a powerful tool to challenge and change election practices in cities and counties across the land, particularly in the South. Indeed, as if in response to that fact, the U.S. Department of Justice, in an abrupt reversal of earlier statements, issued new regulations in 1987 allowing its civil rights lawyers to reject proposed election changes simply on the basis of discriminatory *results,* rather than having to prove that local officials intended to discriminate against blacks or other minorities. And in 1991, in a 6:3 opinion that would eventually challenge the makeup of state courts, especially throughout the South, the Supreme Court, speaking through Justice Stevens, ruled that elected *judges* now also fall under the strictures of the 1982 statute's amendments to Section 2 of the Voting Rights Act of 1965—if the voting practices involved have the effect of discriminating on the basis of race, even in the absence of any *intent* to do so.[249] Indeed, as of mid-1995, challenges to judicial election and selection procedures had been mounted in fifteen states as a result of that interpretation of the law.[250] In 1996 the Court, in a 5:4 ruling regarding selection, told the Virginia

---

247. *Thornburg v. Gingles,* 478 U.S. 30 at 85, concurring opinion.

248. Ibid. at 80, majority opinion.

249. *Chisom v. Roemer,* 501 U.S. 380. But note the 6:3 holding in *Presley v. Etowah County Commission,* 502 U.S. 380 (1992), arguably limiting the impact and application of *Chisom.*

250. See Anna M. Scruggs, Jean-Claude Mazzola, and Mary E. Zang, "Recent Voting Rights Act Challenges to Judicial Elections," 79 *Judicature* 1 (July–August 1995), pp. 34–41.

Republican Party that it could not charge a mandatory fee to attendees of its nominating convention without federal approval.[251]

Moreover, the 1982 amendments became the tool for the creation of often bizarrely racially gerrymandered post-1990 census congressional districts, usually urged and sanctioned by the U.S. Department of Justice. At least fifty such majority-minority districts were drawn, resulting in twenty additional black representatives in the House of Representatives. The extreme nature of the racially drawn Twelfth District of North Carolina was subsequently challenged by white voters, the Supreme Court ruling (5:4) that the latter were entitled to do so under the Fourteenth Amendment.[252] Ultimately, that case returned to the Supreme Court in 1996, with the high tribunal ruling 5:4 that the Twelfth had indeed been unconstitutionally created in violation of the Fourteenth Amendment's strictures.[253] The presence of several voting rights cases on the Court's 1993–94 docket indicated that much litigation lay ahead. Two of these were handed down in 1994, both limiting the reach of the Voting Rights Act. In the first[254] (a consolidation of three cases) the Court ruled 7:2 in an opinion by Justice Souter that there is no right of increased minority political representation beyond "roughly proportional" numbers. In the second,[255] it held 5:4 that the *size* of a governmental body—here a single commissioner form—cannot be challenged under the Voting Rights Act as diluting the influence of minority voters because no standard exists for determining what would be a "fair" number of commissioners. In 1995, the Court moved closer to censuring practices of state redistricting that utilize race as a "predominant factor" in a closely divided 5:4 decision, written by Justice Kennedy. The ruling, which cast doubt on the future of sundry "majority-minority" racially drawn districts, especially in the Deep South, evoked widespread emotional pro and con reactions, heralding much future litigation.[256] Accordingly, the Court was called upon in 1996 to rule on the constitutionality of three majority-minority districts in Texas, as well as the aforementioned one in North Carolina. In all four instances, a majority of five justices, headed by Justice O'Connor, found them to be illegally and unconstitutionally race-based in violation of Amendment Fourteen. New York, Georgia, Louisiana, and Virginia, among others, were similarly affected in 1997, usually by the same consistent judicial reasoning and division.[257] However, a unanimous 1999 ruling, authored by Justice Thomas, directed judges to look deeply into apposite evidence ere deciding that state lawmakers have unconstitu-

251. *Morse et al. v. Republican Party of Virginia*, 517 U.S. 186.
252. *Shaw v. Reno*, 509 U.S. 630 (1993).
253. *Shaw v. Hunt*, 517 U.S. 899.
254. *Johnson v. DeGrandy*, 512 U.S. 997.
255. *Holder v. Hall*, 512 U.S. 874.
256. *Miller v. Johnson*, 515 U.S. 900.
257. *Shaw v. Hunt*, 517 U.S. 899 (North Carolina); *Bush v. Vera*, 517 U.S. 952 (Texas); and *Abrams v. Johnson*, 521 U.S. 574 (Georgia). See also *Johnson v. Board of Regents of the University System of Georgia*, 2000 WL 1121741 (S.D. Ga.).

tionally used race as a factor in drawing districts.[258] In an intriguing, arguably related, decision in 2000 the Court ruled 7:2 that the Hawaiian voting law restricting participation in certain elections to the descendants of the *original* inhabitants was an unconstitutional violation of the Fifteenth (*not* the Fourteenth) Amendment because it denied the vote on account of race.[259]

Justice Kennedy's reasoning in the Hawaii case's majority opinion presaged the justices' ruling a mere ten months later in *Bush v. Gore,* the stunning decision in which the U.S. Supreme Court effectively determined the winner in the deadlocked 2000 presidential election between George W. Bush and Al Gore. Via a per curiam opinion (undoubtedly drafted in large part by Kennedy), *Bush v. Gore,* like the Hawaii decision, struck down state voting procedures (here Florida's bizarre efforts to extend the ballot counting so as to assess the status of punch-card "chads") in the name of the equality of the citizenry in electoral politics. The nonuniform manner of Florida's manual vote counts was violative of the Fourteenth Amendment's equal protection clause, argued the same seven-justice majority that had shaped the Hawaiian voting procedures ruling. In addition to the troublesome lack of uniform standards for hand counting Florida ballots, the U.S. Supreme Court found that the inevitable time pressures, as the clock ticked toward the constitutionally prescribed date for certifying Florida's Electoral College votes, were not valid reasons for circumventing equal protection guarantees.[260]

New Tactics for Old Problems and New Ones

The evolving desegregation process, described in the preceding pages, underwent a major change following that Opinion Monday on May 17, 1954, when Chief Justice Warren announced the Court's decision in *Brown v. Board of Education.*[261] The change in tactics began with the Montgomery bus boycott in De-

258. *Hunt v. Cromartie,* 526 U.S. 541. And when the case surfaced again in 2000–2001, a 5:4 opinion by Justice Breyer, surprisingly joined by Justice O'Connor, held that the district's lines could stand because "race here closely correlates with political behavior" (532 U.S. 234).

259. *Rice v. Cayetano,* 528 U.S. 495.

260. *Bush v. Gore,* 531 U.S. 98. See Stephen G. Bragaw and Barbara A. Perry, "The 'Brooding Omnipresence' in *Bush v. Gore:* Anthony Kennedy, the Equality Principle, and Judicial Supremacy," 13 *Stanford Law and Policy Review* 19 (2002). An avalanche of books analyzing Election 2000 and the resulting litigation has appeared on the scene. A small sample includes Alan M. Dershowitz, *Supreme Injustice: How the High Court Hijacked Election 2000* (New York: Oxford University Press, 2001); E. J. Dionne Jr. and William Kristol, eds., Bush v. Gore: *The Court Cases and Controversies* (Washington, D.C.: Brookings Institution Press, 2001); Gerald M. Pomper, ed., *The Election of 2000* (New York: Chatham House, 2001); Richard A. Posner, *Breaking the Deadlock: The 2000 Election, the Constitution, and the Courts* (Cambridge, Mass.: Harvard University Press, 2001); and Larry J. Sabato, ed., *Overtime! The Election 2000 Thriller* (New York: Longman, 2002).

261. 347 U.S. 483.

cember 1955, although it became most dramatically evident with the Greensboro "sit-ins" early in 1960. Whatever its genesis, the protest movement was now clearly tired of delays, frustrated by creeping gradualism, angered by physical outrages. Militancy came to the forefront.

Thus, the initiative for change shifted from a relatively few professional desegregationists, in such traditional organizations as the NAACP and the Urban League, to large numbers of average citizens who concluded that they had no choice but to do battle against "the System" by direct action "in the streets." This development both stemmed from and gave rise to a coterie of new, formally organized protest groups,[262] particularly the Southern Christian Leadership Conference (SCLC), which had been created in 1956–57 under the leadership of Martin Luther King.[263]

The "sit-in" movement of 1960 had first illustrated the belief that only *action* would obtain results, a belief that became a firm conviction of these groups and their followers—action as a supplement or complement to the educational and legal means heretofore predominantly employed. Although the educational, and especially the legal, tools had produced significant results since World War II, they were nevertheless for Dr. King, other protest movement leaders, and their vast number of followers too slow in producing change. Turning then to "action," the black leadership rapidly discovered that the development of community "crisis situations," such as economic boycotts by black protest movements, was usually at least partly successful simply because the crises demanded a speedy resolution by community decision makers. Yet "activism" was certain to raise serious problems in and for society—problems of the limits of civil disobedience: problems, once again, of where to draw the line. Interestingly, Thurgood Marshall viewed some of King's tactics as "street

262. See the article by James H. Laue, "The Changing Character of Negro Protest," 357 *Annals of the American Academy of Political and Social Science* 119 (January 1965).

263. Others were the Congress of Racial Equality (CORE), established in 1943; the Student Nonviolent Coordinating Committee (SNCC), an "action" group founded in 1960; and the National Welfare Rights Organization (NWRO), established in 1968 (but dissolved after its founder, George Wiley, drowned in a boating accident in 1973). While SCLC under Dr. King's guidance steadfastly maintained its dedication to nonviolence, CORE and especially SNCC proved to be not averse to violent action, as demonstrated from 1965 on under the direction of such fiery young leaders as CORE's Floyd McKissick and SNCC's Stokely Carmichael and H. Rap Brown. But after having been the pacesetter in the civil rights movement for eight years, SNCC, with a rural southern origin, was largely displaced as of 1968 by the slum-born Black Panthers, a militant "black liberation" group: violence-prone and small but potent. Additional groups were organized, with varying degrees of success, throughout the 1970s, some featuring the rise of highly visible, influential leaders, such as the Reverend Jesse Jackson, head of the Chicago-based People United to Serve Humanity (PUSH), who would become a candidate for president of the United States in 1984 and again in 1988. More than a thousand delegates from thirty-four states formed a new organization, the National Black United Front, in mid-1980, "to pull together the diverse elements within black America, most of which have not succeeded" (*New York Times,* June 30, 1980, p. B13).

theatre" and as expensively counterproductive. "I think he was great as a leader," Marshall would later say of King. But "as an organizer he wasn't worth shit. . . . All he did was to dump all his legal work on us [the NAACP], including the bills."[264]

Illustrations of New Tactics. Of course, some "action" had accompanied the movement for quite a while: there were sporadic rallies, marches, boycotts, and picket lines, but almost none really attained major significance. Yet the Montgomery, Alabama, bus boycott, eighteen months after *Brown I,* did. It was a stubborn, 381-day-long boycott of the city's buses in protest against Montgomery's continued segregated seating practices. The action began on December 1, 1955, when Mrs. Rosa Parks, a forty-two-year-old black seamstress— who was to become a symbol of the civil rights movement—refused to give up her front-row black-section window seat to a white male rider on Bus No. 5726 and was fined ten dollars. Led by Dr. King, Montgomery's entire black community participated in the boycott. No longer willing to sit in the "Jim Crow" section, something they had done all their lives, they were ready to walk miles or wait hours for car pools. As one weary seventy-two-year-old black woman said with ungrammatical profundity: "My feets is tired but my soul is at rest."[265] Although Mrs. Parks and one hundred others were fingerprinted and charged with conspiracy, the boycott did not end until, over one year later, segregation was outlawed by a federal court injunction, followed quickly by a Supreme Court decision that struck down as a violation of equal protection of the laws the Montgomery statute that had required segregation on motor buses operated within the city.[266] It is not astonishing that the successful Montgomery boycott[267] set a precedent for similar actions in cities throughout the South, extending to retail stores, produce markets, and a host of other sales and service facilities. In 1999 the U.S. Senate voted 86:0, and the House of Representatives concurred separately, to award Rosa Parks, then eighty-six, Congress's highest civilian award, the Congressional Gold Medal.

Yet a boycott destined to be far more militant and far more controversial

---

264. As quoted by Louis Menand in *"Brown v. Board of Education* and the Limits of the Law," a review of James F. Patterson's Brown v. Board of Education: *A Civil Rights Milestone and Its Troubled Legacy* (New York: Oxford University Press, 2001), in the *New Yorker,* February 12, 2001, p. 96.

265. As quoted by Martin Luther King Jr., "Letter from Birmingham Jail," in his *Why We Can't Wait* (New York: Harper and Row, 1963), p. 99.

266. *Gayle v. Browder,* 352 U.S. 903 (1956).

267. For a thorough retrospective account, see Wolf Harrington, "A Person Who Wanted to Be Free," *Washington Post Magazine,* October 8, 1995, pp. 10–30. But see also Carol Morgan, "The Freedom Rider a Nation Nearly Forgot," depicting Irene Morgan's bus segregation defiance eleven years earlier (this chapter, *supra,* note 78, in connection with *Morgan v. Virginia,* 328 U.S. 373 [1946]).

began on February 1, 1960, when four black freshmen[268] at North Carolina Agricultural and Technical College began what at first was a spontaneous "sit-in" demonstration at the lunch counter of F. W. Woolworth's dime store in Greensboro. They had asked for cups of coffee, and had done so politely, but were refused service. They then simply continued to sit at the counter in protest—notwithstanding cursing, pushing, spitting, and catsup throwing by their white neighbors. Ultimately, the four filed out, formed a tight circle on the sidewalk, and recited the Lord's Prayer—and another group took over for them inside.

This example of nonviolent protest spread to six more North Carolina and forty-eight other cities as well as eight additional southern states within four weeks. Not only did the Greensboro sit-in set a precedent,[269] it led directly to the organization of the Student Nonviolent Coordinating Committee. The SNCC quickly began to serve both in the South and in the North as an organizer and backer for sit-ins and a large variety of other "ins," such as "stand-ins," "read-ins," "pray-ins," "wade-ins," "sleep-ins," and "lie-ins."[270] Thousands who had never before taken an active part in the protest movement now joined. Variously successful, the movement also gave rise to an intricate set of legal problems stemming from the action by the protesters themselves or by the local authorities, who, either by request or on their own initiative, would often arrest the "ins" for such common-law offenses as "breach of the peace" or "trespassing." When *statutes* compelling, permitting, or forbidding segregation were present, the legal setting was tailor-made for litigation, of course. But when the actions of the "ins" constituted action against *private* inhospitable hosts acting in their *private* capacity, line drawing would naturally be far more difficult; here, indeed, the Supreme Court's usually unanimous opinion on race discrimination issues would be bitterly split.

268. Joseph McNeil, David Richmond, Franklin McCain, and Ezell Blair Jr. (who later changed his name to Jibreel Khazan). Exactly twenty years to the day later (February 1, 1980), the four met triumphantly at the same counter to commemorate the historic event—which was widely covered by the media. And they would meet there again ten and fifteen years later. A plaque on a downtown street near the site reads:

SIT-INS
Launched the national
drive for integrated
lunch counters, Feb. 1, 1960,
in Woolworth
store 2 blocks south.

269. The first "sit-in" was reenacted on the same spot by David Richmond on February 1, 1985, a quarter of a century later.

270. The developing record of sit-in demonstrations in southern cities during the fourteen months from February 1, 1960, to March 27, 1961, was as follows (adapted from the

Other participants in "ins" movements, mounted largely by the Congress of Racial Equality (CORE), were the "freedom riders." Their chief target was transportation, supposedly desegregated for some time. The "rides" not only pinpointed but actually tested, often at the cost of imprisonment and violence, the still prevalent segregation practices in almost all interstate travel and terminal facilities in the Deep South. In general, these rides accomplished their purpose: the exposure of continued, rampant violation of what was now the declared law of the land.

The Birmingham Trigger. Yet it was Birmingham, Alabama, that was destined to become the center of the militant black activism of April and May 1963, with vast implications for the years to follow. Having failed to make headway in the quest for desegregation in the state's largest and most highly industrialized city, mass street demonstrations, involving thousands, including schoolchildren, were staged there by Dr. King and his faithful allies, the Reverends Ralph D. Abernathy and Fred L. Shuttlesworth. Some 150 demonstrators were arrested on the first day, but the protests continued with a march and a "kneel-in" in the face of a court injunction. When the three leaders were also arrested, the street demonstrations daily grew larger. So did the prison populace, reaching twenty-five hundred in a matter of days. Failing to obtain any concessions, the blacks continued to demonstrate and were now met by high-pressure water hoses, police dogs, and cattle prods. The entire nation was outraged, and the Birmingham authorities, under pressure from both the Kennedy administration and local business leaders, agreed

---

special report of the Southern Regional Council, *The Freedom Ride,* published in Atlanta in May 1961):

Date	State	City	Demonstrators	Arrests
Feb. 1, 1960	North Carolina	Greensboro	4,200	268
Feb. 11	Virginia	Hampton	11,000	235
Feb. 12	South Carolina	Rock Hill	4,000	947
Feb. 12	Florida	Deland	2,500	243
Feb. 13	Tennessee	Nashville	16,000	692
Feb. 25	Alabama	Montgomery	5,500	86
Feb. 27	Kentucky	Lexington	6,000	374
March 5	Texas	Houston	6,500	317
March 10	Arkansas	Little Rock	50	20
March 15	Georgia	Atlanta	7,000	292
March 28	Louisiana	Baton Rouge	10,000	71
March 27, 1961	Mississippi	Jackson	1,600	40
Totals			74,350	3,585

For further illustrative aspects of the matter see Table 4, "Peaceful Rights Demonstrations 1954–1968," in Jonathan W. Casper, *The Politics of Civil Liberties* (New York: Harper and Row, 1972), p. 90.

to a "truce," promising alleviation of black grievances in public accommodation, employment opportunities, and interracial committees. But Governor Wallace promptly denounced the agreement, and on May 11, after a series of bomb blasts directed against, among others, Dr. King and his brother, thousands of irate blacks resumed demonstrations. Within hours the streets were filled with uncontrollable rioters battling with the police. At this juncture President Kennedy, having experienced nothing but defiance from Wallace, dispatched three thousand federal troops to the area—but not to Birmingham itself. This seemed to achieve results; racial tensions gradually subsided. And although they were revived by Governor Wallace's infamous "schoolhouse door stand," which unsuccessfully tried to prevent the court-ordered admission of two blacks to the University of Alabama at Tuscaloosa, an important corner had been turned. After Wallace's interference with court-ordered desegregation of certain public schools was blocked by the federalization of the Alabama National Guard that September, a tenuous peace finally came to Birmingham. Tragically, it did so only after four little black girls had died in the wreckage of the bombed Sixteenth Street Baptist Church in 1963[271] and two black teenagers had been gunned down by white terrorists.

These 1963 events set off chain reactions throughout the country. In the seventy days following the Birmingham "truce," almost eight hundred racial demonstrations took place in the nation. They culminated in the mammoth, orderly Washington march of August 1963, in which, as already noted, more than two hundred thousand blacks and whites participated. Racial demonstrations continued during the ensuing six summers throughout northern cities.[272] Not even the new federal civil rights and voting statutes would lessen the now determined, often militant and impatient drive for black equality. It had obtained results! For most southerners and, indeed increasingly, northerners as well, adaptation to change had become a fact of daily life for state and local governments; racial incidents had to be avoided; and resistance to federal authority was, in the long run, futile. Still, the southern leadership was allowed to move slowly and, with some exceptions, to do nothing more than the bare minimum. "Tokenism" was still the rule of the day.

This attitude, however understandable it might be in terms of the practices and traditions of generations, continued to incite militancy on the part of the in-

---

271. See the retrospective essay by Howell Raines, "The Birmingham Bombing," *New York Times Magazine,* July 24, 1983, pp. 12ff. It was not until 2001 that a former KKK member, Thomas E. Blanton, was convicted of first-degree murder for the dastardly deed by a jury of eight whites and four blacks, which deliberated for just two hours and sentenced him to life in prison. Another former KKK member, Bobby Frank Cherry, was convicted by a mostly white jury in 2002 and was also sentenced to life in prison, thus closing the case almost forty years after the evil crime was committed (*Washington Post,* May 23, 2002, p. A1).

272. See *supra* this chapter for statistics and details. Few, if any, of the large centers were spared.

creasingly restive blacks—and now particularly those in the ghettos of the *northern* cities. They were tired of waiting, tired of gradualism, tired of tokenism. In effect, they demanded what was patently impossible: full equality "here and now"—and if that meant "favored treatment," so be it! But black poverty, both of means and of opportunity, and prejudice—always prejudice—could not be eradicated so quickly. The resultant frustration frequently generated overt belligerency, often referred to by the participants as "direct action," which was frequently, although by no means inevitably, counterproductive to the aims of the black cause and which, as indicated, provoked a serious split in the Supreme Court,[273] which heretofore had been supporting civil rights causes with unanimity.

While it is feasible to offer explanations for the wave of questionable and tragic actions, such as the riots that swept so many northern cities between 1963 and 1969, there could be no excuse for the looting, the burning, the destruction, the loss of lives—the reckless dedication to manifestations of hate. As a result, there was mounting fear among civil rights leaders and supporters that the days of wide national support for civil rights had come to an end, at least temporarily. It would ultimately prove to be a groundless fear, but the failure of Congress to pass the 1966 civil rights bill seemed to confirm it at the time. And as President Johnson—who had done so much for blacks—told a group of visiting bishops from the all-black African Methodist Episcopal Church in October of that year:

> We have entered a new phase. . . . What if the cry for freedom becomes the sound of a brick cracking through a store window, turning over an automobile in the street, or the sound of the mob? If that sound should drown out the voices of reason, frustration will replace progress and all of our best work will be undone.[274]

In any event, it was now clear that, even in the nonviolent sector of black protest, lines were becoming increasingly blurred: Had not the limits of civil disobedience in a free representative democracy now been reached, and sometimes exceeded? There is a difference between the exercise of constitutional rights that are inherent in the freedoms of speech, press, assembly, and petition and the kind of militant, often lawless, activities that were becoming frequent. The basic issues of racial discrimination, of the injustices of generations, were obvious; there could no longer be any doubt of the need for the acknowledgment, both legally

---

273. See, among others, *Bell v. Maryland,* 378 U.S. 226 (1964); *Hamm v. City of Rock Hill,* 379 U.S. 306 (1964); *Elton v. Cox,* 379 U.S. 536 (1965); *Brown v. Louisiana,* 383 U.S. 131 (1966); *Adderley v. Florida,* 385 U.S. 39 (1966); and *Cameron v. Johnson,* 390 U.S. 611 (1968).

274. As quoted in *Time,* October 7, 1966, p. 17. Appropriately, indeed, did leading civil rights activist Clarence M. Mitchell Jr. say of LBJ: "He was the greatest American President on civil rights" (as quoted in the *New York Times,* April 15, 1979, p. 28).

and morally, of full egalitarianism. Yet, it was also obvious that it would still take a long time to achieve it in the public sphere—and it would take infinitely longer in the *private* sector.

Since the means of amelioration of injustice in a representative democracy are patently lodged in the public sector, one of the great issues of the day thus became: Just what constitutes that "public" sphere, which *is* reachable by the authority of government under law? Just when does an action become "state action"—an action subject to the commands and sanctions of the Constitution in general and Amendment Fourteen in particular?

STATE ACTION AND BEYOND: A TRUE DILEMMA

The words of the famed second sentence of Section 1 of the Fourteenth Amendment concerning "state action" would seem to be quite clear:

> *No State shall make or enforce any law* which shall abridge the privileges or immunities of citizens of the United States; *nor shall any State deprive* any person of life, liberty, or property without due process of law; *nor deny to any person within its jurisdiction the equal protection of the laws.*[275]

What is proscribed here is *discriminatory state action* only; it does *not* extend to *private action* (unless, of course, it has been legislatively covered to extend to the private sector—as is significantly true, for example, of segments of the Civil Rights Acts of 1964 and 1968 and their progeny). And this is the interpretation the judiciary has quite naturally and appropriately given to the amendment. But at what point has a state, or its "agent," deprived an individual of life, liberty, or property without due process of law; or, more appropriately, since black litigants have relied predominantly upon the equal protection of the laws clause, when has a state, or its "agent," denied an individual that equal protection? The important question is not so much "state action" per se but whether, as Court opinions have demonstrated increasingly, "state action" denies "equal protection."

The Dilemma

Technically, *state action* is any action taken by legislative, executive, or judicial instrumentalities of the state.[276] *Private action* is any act or action engaged in or

---

275. Italics supplied.

276. See the intriguing 5:4 decision in 1988, denying state action presence in the NCAA's action against the University of Nevada–Las Vegas, involving certain questionable activities by its then basketball coach Jerry Tarkanian (*NCAA v. Tarkanian*, 488 U.S. 179).

perpetrated by any individual in his private capacity and association.[277] But six Supreme Court justices, in a highly significant set of racial violence cases in 1966,[278] warned that they would feel bound to uphold any appropriate law aimed at punishing *private* individuals who use violence to deny persons their Fourteenth Amendment rights. Of course, *state* activity causing or abetting racial discrimination would, under present-day interpretations by the courts, be regarded as patently violating the Fourteenth Amendment injunctions against discriminatory state action. It is thus that the "separate but equal" concept met its doom, along with the manifold instances of state-authored or state-enforced racial discrimination in education, transportation, housing, employment, voting, and a vast array of other areas. But *private* discrimination, or so it might be assumed, would be entirely legal, even though neither democratic nor just. Hence, until the passage of the federal Civil Rights Act of 1964, it was not considered illegal to refuse to serve or admit blacks in privately owned establishments, such as restaurants, hotels, motels, or theaters, so long as the owner was *really* a *private* person, acting in his *private* capacity, and, of course, provided that *state* law did not forbid such discrimination.

Even before the Civil Rights Act of 1964 extended the reach of governmental proscription of discrimination on racial, religious, ethnic, and other related grounds to such contentious areas as public accommodations and employment, however, the distinction between "public" and "private" under certain conditions had been legally questioned, although never really effectively challenged. Perhaps the first such instance to raise and at the same time to befuddle the basic issue at the bar of the judiciary was the *Restrictive Covenant Case, Shelley v. Kraemer.*[279] Briefly, in the lead case, J. D. and Ethel Lee Shelley, black citizens from St. Louis, Missouri, had "for valuable consideration" received in 1945 from one Josephine Fitzgerald a warranty deed to a parcel of land situated in an area restricted by common agreement of some thirty resident-owners to persons of "the Caucasian race." The restrictive covenant, originally sched-

277. One expert, Professor Louis Henkin, suggests three bases for holding the state legally responsible *when private discrimination is involved:* (1) "The state is responsible for what it could prevent, and should prevent, and fails to prevent." (2) "The state is responsible for discrimination which it encourages or sanctions." (3) "The state is responsible when its courts act to render discrimination effective." See his *"Shelley v. Kraemer:* Notes for a Revised Opinion," 110 *University of Pennsylvania Law Review* 481 (February 1962). Yet some of his arguments in this important and scholarly article would seem to cast doubt on his own tests.

278. *United States v. Price,* 383 U.S. 688 (1966); and *United States v. Guest,* 383 U.S. 746 (1966). Expressed in two concurring opinions, severally joined by Chief Justice Warren and Associate Justices Black, Douglas, Clark, Brennan, and Fortas. *Griffin v. Breckenridge,* 403 U.S. 88 (1971), unanimously confirmed and expanded the two earlier holdings via Amendment Thirteen.

279. 334 U.S. 1 (1948). A similar question was raised by a Detroit group and was decided concurrently.

uled to run from 1911 to 1961, specifically barred "people of the Negro or Mongolian race." Louis and Fern E. Kraemer, for the restrictive covenanters, attempted to block the Fitzgerald-to-Shelley sale in the appropriate Missouri State Circuit Court, but they lost—more or less on an interpretative technicality. The Supreme Court of Missouri, however, reversed the lower court's ruling and directed it to order the Shelleys to vacate their property.

Yet with Justices Reed, Jackson, and Rutledge taking no part in either the consideration or the decision of the case, the Supreme Court of the United States unanimously *reversed* the highest Missouri tribunal. Speaking through Chief Justice Vinson, the Court affirmed that orders by state courts *enforcing* restrictive covenants based on race and color are violative of the equal protection of the laws clause of the Fourteenth Amendment. Restrictive covenants drawn up by private individuals, reasoned the Court, are not in themselves a violation of the amendment's commands so long as they are completely private and voluntary, and, of course, do not breach some federal or state law or state ordinance (which restrictive covenants in the housing field would have done in a number of states even in the late 1940s; and since the enactment of the federal fair housing law of 1968 and the Supreme Court's decision in *Jones v. Alfred H. Mayer Co.,*[280] such covenants would be illegal anywhere in the country). "Here, however," the chief justice pointed out, "there was more," because the state of Missouri, through its judicial branch, not only *aided in the enforcement* of the restrictive covenant— which would in itself have constituted forbidden state action—but, in effect, rendered the agreements workable. "We have no doubt," concluded America's highest jurist, "that there has been *state action* in the full and complete sense of the phrase."[281]

In other words, *Shelley* presented the intriguing dichotomy of permitting private discrimination so long as no state aid in its implementation or enforcement was sought: the judiciary aid desired by Kraemer and his supporters was regarded as such state aid. The implications of the *Shelley* case became quickly apparent, and the decision evoked a flood of favorable, unfavorable, and tentative commentary by laymen and professionals alike.[282] But whatever one's feelings regarding either the equity of the decision or the viability of the dichotomy it enunciated, the decision brought the state action problem to the fore. In brief,

280. 392 U.S. 409 (1968). See the discussion regarding the statute and the *Mayer* decision *supra* and *infra* this chapter.
281. *Shelley v. Kraemer,* op. cit., at 13, 19. Attorney General Tom Clark and the solicitor general had written an amicus curiae brief on behalf of Shelley's petition.
282. E.g., Herbert Wechsler, "Toward Neutral Principles of Constitutional Law," 73 *Harvard Law Review* 1 (1959); Louis Henkin, "Some Reflections on Current Constitutional Controversy," 109 *University of Pennsylvania Law Review* 637 (1961); Henkin, "*Shelley v. Kraemer:* Notes for a Revised Opinion," op. cit.; and Louis Pollak, "Racial Discrimination and Judicial Integrity: A Reply to Professor Wechsler," 108 *University of Pennsylvania Law Review* 1 (1959).

444 FREEDOM AND THE COURT

the problem comes down to the crucial question of a free democratic society: how to reconcile the competing rights and claims of *equality and liberty*—a question as old as the ages. Where *does* the Constitution draw the line between the right to legal equality and to equality of opportunity, and the rights of liberty, property,[283] privacy, and voluntary association? Where *do* we draw it? Where *should* we draw it? Where *can* we draw it? It is, of course, a balancing problem. Yet "balancing" is a delicate matter, even regarded as unconstitutional in some quarters—particularly when applied to the Bill of Rights. Thus, notwithstanding his avowedly absolutist position on the First Amendment,[284] Justice Black was deeply disturbed over the implications of the broad interpretation of "state action" under the Fourteenth Amendment; in fact, he came to "balance" *here*— most notably in some of the sit-in and demonstration cases,[285] although he did *not* in the cases concerning bona fide freedom of expression under the First Amendment. A few additional illustrations of the problem of private and state action and rights may be helpful (although it ought to be noted that the problem is assuredly not confined to matters of race).

Popular Referenda and State Action: Reitman v. Mulkey. The housing field provides a number of fascinatingly complex state action cases—particularly when "state action" involves a linkage to what, presumably, is *the* most democratic expression of a free participating electorate: the "direct democracy" instrumentalities of initiative and/or the referendum. What if a state's electorate, in a free and open election, approves a constitutional amendment to a state constitution, duly initiated by that state's electorate, that was designed to repeal fair housing legislation previously passed by the state legislature? This is precisely what occurred in the case of "Proposition 14" in California in 1964, when that state's voters, by the almost 2:1 margin of 4.5 to 2.4 million votes, adopted the following seemingly neutral provision: "Neither the state nor any subdivision or agency thereof shall deny . . . the right of any person . . . to decline to sell, lease, or rent [real] property to such person or persons as he, in his absolute discretion, chooses." Ap-

---

283. In that connection see the interesting 5:4 Supreme Court decision in *San Antonio Independent School District v. Rodriguez,* which dealt, among other things, with the matter of "state action" and "equal protection" regarding the singular use of the property tax to fund public education (411 U.S. 1 [1973]). For a 5:4 holding on the other side of the entitlement scale, see the "Children of Illegal Aliens" case of *Plyler v. Doe,* 457 U.S. 202 (1982). But *Kadrmas v. Dickinson Public Schools,* 487 U.S. 450 (1988), followed *Rodriguez*'s holding. Two collaterally related alien-INS cases, both decided 5:4 in the face of heavy criticism in 2001, seemed to imply that the government has an obligation to apply the same standards to immigrants as to U.S. citizens (*Calcano-Martinez v. INS,* 533 U.S. 348; and *Zadvydas v. Davis,* 533 U.S. 678).

284. See the explanation and analysis of his position throughout the pages of this book, particularly in chapters 2, 3, and 5.

285. See *supra* note 273, and *infra* notes 301–7.

proved by an overwhelming majority, the provision became Section 26 of the California Constitution. *But* when a challenge to the newly adopted provision reached the California Supreme Court in 1966, that tribunal ruled it unconstitutional (5:2) as a violation of the equal protection of the laws clause of the Fourteenth Amendment, reasoning that "when the electorate assumes to exercise the law-making function [as it had done here by initiating and subsequently approving Proposition 14], then the electorate is as much a state agency as any of its elected officials."[286] This interpretation of the equal protection clause bewildered many observers and predictably went to the U.S. Supreme Court—which, by the narrowest of winning margins (5:4), upheld the California tribunal. Justice White's opinion, joined by Chief Justice Warren and Justices Douglas, Brennan, and Fortas, held that the amendment went beyond a mere repeal of the state's fair housing legislation and created "a constitutional right to discriminate on racial grounds in the sale and rental of real property."[287] He concluded that, in effect, the electorate's action constituted "state action"—state action that would impermissibly involve the state in private racial discrimination to an unconstitutional degree. In other words, both the state and the federal judiciary rejected the contention that the electorate's action had merely restored *neutrality;* they instead held that the "in his absolute discretion" clause ipso facto legislated discrimination. But in an angry dissenting opinion, joined by Justices Black, Clark, and Stewart, Justice Harlan pronounced Section 26 unquestionably "neutral" and "inoffensive on its face," that the "state action" required to bring the Fourteenth Amendment into operation must be "affirmative and purposeful"; and he warned, in what constitutes an intriguing exhortation of appropriate institutional roles, that

> By refusing to accept the decision of the people of California, and by contriving a new and ill-defined constitutional concept to allow Federal judicial interference, I think the court has taken to itself powers and responsibilities left elsewhere by the Constitution.[288]

The *Reitman* holding, notwithstanding its far-reaching implications concerning the range of state action under Amendment Fourteen, seemed to leave the door open, however, for straightforward "neutral" repealers of antidiscrimination legislation. Not only did the White opinion so hint, but during oral argument before the Supreme Court, A. L. Wirin, counsel for the Los Angeles chapter of the American Civil Liberties Union, which sponsored the challenge to Proposition 14, conceded during a colloquy with Justices Black and White that a referendum

---

286. *Reitman v. Mulkey,* 64 Cal. 2d 529 at 542.

287. *Reitman v. Mulkey,* 387 U.S. 369 (1967) at 376. For an excellent commentary on the case see R. E. Wolfinger and F. I. Greenstein, "The Repeal of Fair Housing in California: An Analysis of Referendum Voting," 62 *American Political Science Review* 753 (September 1968).

288. *Reitman v. Mulkey,* op. cit., at 396.

merely repealing California's fair housing statutes would not have been unconstitutional.[289] Yet along came the Court's 1969 decision in *Hunter v. Erickson*,[290] in which it held, with only Justice Black dissenting, that an Akron, Ohio, charter provision, adopted by the voters in a citywide referendum, violated the equal protection of the laws clause. That provision not only repealed a "fair housing" law that had been shortly prior thereto enacted by Akron's city council but, moreover, required that before any fair housing law could be restored to the books, it would have to be readopted *by a referendum vote*.[291] Speaking for the eight-man Court majority, Justice White reasoned that, by singling out fair housing laws as the only ones subject to such referendum votes—whereas the city council regularly and routinely legislates on such other housing matters as rent control and urban renewal—the voters of Akron in effect engaged in constitutionally proscribed state action; that the referendum requirement here "makes an explicitly radical classification." The majority denied Black's contention that it had made even a simple repeal of the legislation impossible—and it not only proved that point in a 1971 case, but it gave Black an opportunity to write the opinion. At issue was the constitutionality of a California referendum law—similar to that of a good many states—permitting a majority of the voters in a community to block the construction of low-cost housing. A lower federal court had declared it unconstitutional as a violation of the equal protection of the laws clause. Justice Black's majority opinion, joined by Chief Justice Burger and Justices Harlan, Stewart, and White, reversed (5:3) the decision below, declaring that the thrust of the Fourteenth Amendment was to outlaw legal distinction based on race; that there was no evidence that the California law was aimed at any racial minority; and that this "procedure for democratic decision making gives the people a voice in decisions that would raise their taxes, dilute the tax base, and affect the future development of the community."[292] But the dissenting opinion by Justice Marshall, joined by his colleagues Brennan and Blackmun, charged that the statute "explicitly singles out low-income persons" for unequal treatment. "It is far too late in the day," the Court's black member noted, "to contend that the 14th Amendment prohibits only racial discrimination; and to me, singling out the poor to bear a burden not placed on any other class of citizens tramples the values that the 14th Amendment was designed to protect."[293] Yet in a 6:3 ruling in 1976 the Court again sustained a referendum requirement—this time that of a city charter provision in Eastlake, Ohio,

289. *New York Times,* March 22, 1967, p. 1e, and oral argument at the Supreme Court, March 23, 1967.
290. 393 U.S. 385.
291. That provision of the charter (Section 137) required that any ordinance regulating real estate transactions "on the basis of race, color, religion, national origin or ancestry must first be approved by a majority of the electors voting on the question at a regular or general election before said ordinance shall be effective."
292. *James v. Valtierra,* 402 U.S. 137 (1971) at 143.
293. Ibid. at 144.

requiring land-use changes to be ratified by a 55 percent referendum majority as well as the city council.[294] And in 1977 it held (5:3) that it was not inherently unconstitutional for a suburb to refuse to change zoning restrictions, the practical effect of which is to block construction of racially integrated housing for persons with low and moderate income; that to be unconstitutional there must also be an "intent" or "purpose" to discriminate—which, however, does not mean that under no circumstances could a village, such as Arlington Heights, be *statutorily* required to rezone so as to provide such housing.[295]

Aspects of the "In" Syndrome. What of "private" versus "public" action inherent in the spate of "sit-in" demonstration cases that reached the Court prior to the Civil Rights Act of 1964?[296] The act settled the matter in terms of the constitutionality of the pertinent section, based on congressional power over interstate commerce, *provided* the establishment concerned came under the provisions of the statute governing "public accommodations"; but did it really settle the problem of liberty versus equality in philosophical terms? Justice Black had joined in the unanimous opinion in the two late 1964 cases upholding the law's public accommodations section,[297] yet obviously he did so only because he believed Congress to have had the power to legislate as it had *because* it *expressly* invoked its authority over interstate commerce. But, as he had noted orally from the bench in conjunction with his dissenting opinion in one of the sit-in cases a few months earlier in 1964, "[T]his Court has never said, in the school segregation decisions or any before or since, that the prejudice of individuals could be laid to the state."[298] And again, from the bench on the last day of the Court's 1963–64 term, Black commented that the idea that the Fourteenth Amendment *itself* prohibited segregation in public accommodations made "the last six months' struggle in Congress a work of supererogation"[299]—a reference to the prolonged debate that preceded passage of the legislation. As his longtime jurisprudential "adversary," the retired Justice Frankfurter, had done so often, Black then again admonished his country that "[t]he worst citizen no less than the best is entitled to equal protection of the laws of his state and of his nation."[300] And it was Black again, this

---

294. *Eastlake v. Forest City Enterprises, Inc.,* 426 U.S. 668.

295. *Village of Arlington Heights v. Metropolitan Housing Development Corp.,* 429 U.S. 252.

296. E.g., *Edwards v. South Carolina,* 372 U.S. 229 (1963); *Peterson v. Greenville,* 373 U.S. 244 (1963); *Lombard v. Louisiana,* 373 U.S. 267 (1963); *Griffin v. Maryland,* 378 U.S. 130 (1964); *Robinson v. Florida,* 378 U.S. 153 (1964); *Barr v. City of Columbia,* 378 U.S. 146 (1964); and *Bell v. Maryland,* 378 U.S. 226 (1964).

297. *Heart of Atlanta Motel v. United States,* 379 U.S. 241 (1964); and *Katzenbach v. McClung,* 379 U.S. 294 (1964).

298. *Barr v. City of Columbia,* op. cit.

299. As quoted in the *New York Times,* June 23, 1964, p. 161.

300. *Bell v. Maryland,* 378 U.S. 226 (1964), dissenting opinion at 328.

time joined by Harlan, Stewart, and White, who, having all voted to uphold the constitutionality of the contentious provision of the Civil Rights Act of 1964, took pains to emphasize on the very same Opinion Monday what should be obvious to all believers in law, order, justice, and the dignity of liberty: that the passage of the act did *not* authorize persons "who are unlawfully refused service a 'right' to take the law into their own hands by sitting down and occupying the premises for as long as they choose to stay."[301] Black's deep concern—one steeped in his high dedication to what he regarded as the prerogatives of home privacy and local control—continued to make itself known, albeit in the minority. Yet he carried three other justices—Clark, Harlan, and Stewart—with him when, in a public library "stand-in" case in 1966, he asked impassionedly:

> Can any provision of the United States Constitution tell any citizens—white or colored—they can march with impunity into a public library and demonstrate against some public policy? . . . It has become automatic for people to be turned loose as long as whatever they do has something to do with race. That is not the way I read the Constitution.[302]

A few pages earlier he had vigorously challenged the majority's position with the following exhortation:

> It is high time to challenge the assumption in which too many people have too long acquiesced, that groups that think they have been mistreated have a constitutional right to use the public streets, buildings, and property to protest whatever, wherever, whenever they want, without regard to whom such conduct may disturb.[303]

That spring the Court summarily *upheld* the conviction of twenty-five New York City racial demonstrators at a housing project[304] and the conviction of a CORE "stand-in" at the office of the police chief of Syracuse.[305] And on the last day of the 1965–66 term, Justice Clark formally provided the fifth vote for that point of view, and thus a Court majority. He joined his colleagues Black, Harlan, Stewart, and White in holding that twenty-nine persons arrested on various local charges arising from civil rights movements in 1964 in Leflore County, Mississippi, could not have their trials transferred from state to federal courts merely upon their contention that their rights of free speech might be infringed by prejudicial treatment in state courts.[306] Lest that decision be regarded as a procedural "fluke," or one based on a

---

301. *Hamm v. City of Rock Hill,* 379 U.S. 306 (1964), dissenting opinion at 318.
302. *Brown v. Louisiana,* 383 U.S. 131 (1966), dissenting opinion at 168.
303. Ibid. at 162.
304. *Penn v. New York,* 383 U.S. 969 (1966).
305. *Baer v. New York,* 384 U.S. 154 (1966).
306. *Greenwood v. Peacock,* 384 U.S. 808 (1966).

wavering majority, the same five justices again agreed late in 1966 in a case of particular significance in the fundamental freedom-versus-order clash because the civil rights demonstrations involved were directed against *public* rather than *private* property. Speaking through Justice Black, the five-man majority upheld the "willful-trespass" conviction of Harriet Adderley and thirty-one other Florida A & M University Negro students who had demonstrated outside the Leon County jail in Tallahassee, Florida.[307] The earlier decisions had involved prosecutions for *breach of the peace* rather than trespass. In attempting to draw the line between speech and *conduct,* Black wrote:[308]

> [N]othing in the Constitution of the United States prevents Florida from even-handed enforcement of its general trespassing statute against those refusing to obey the sheriff's order to remove themselves. . . . *The state, no less than a private owner of property, has power to preserve the property under its control for the use to which it is lawfully dedicated.*[309]

But to Justice Douglas, dissenting in a vigorously worded opinion in which he was joined by Warren, Brennan, and Fortas, the Black holding represented "a great break with the traditions of the Court." Now, he said, trespass laws could be used as a "blunderbuss" to suppress civil rights; the Court has, he concluded, "now set into the record a great and wonderful police-state doctrine."[310] Although two subsequent decisions intensified the concern voiced by Douglas and his supporting colleagues,[311] the Court unanimously made it clear in 1968 that it is unconstitutional for tribunals to delay public meetings—even when violence is threatened—without hearing testimony from those who wish to meet; that, in other words, there could be no ex parte injunctions.[312] And, also unanimously, it reversed in 1969 the 1965 conviction of civil rights leaders King and Shuttlesworth for parading without a permit in Birmingham in 1963, because that city's ordinance gave its commissioners "unfettered discretion" to reject permits.[313] Moreover, in a 1972 decision (*not* involving race) the Court unanimously declared unconstitutional a federal 1882 law that banned all "unauthorized" demonstrations on the grounds of the U.S. Capitol,[314] and in 1983 it invalidated

---

307. *Adderley v. Florida,* 385 U.S. 39 (1966). The Florida statute reads: "Every trespass on the property of another, committed with a malicious and mischievous intent . . . shall be punished."

308. See his discussion of that vexatious line in his book *A Constitutional Faith* (New York: Knopf, 1968), pp. 53–56.

309. *Adderley v. Florida,* op. cit., at 47; italics supplied.

310. Ibid., extemporaneous remark from the bench, November 14, 1966.

311. *Walker v. Birmingham,* 388 U.S. 307 (1967); and *Cameron v. Johnson,* 390 U.S. 611 (1968).

312. *Carroll v. President and Commissioners of Princess Anne County,* 393 U.S. 175.

313. *Shuttlesworth v. Birmingham,* 394 U.S. 147.

314. *Chief of Capitol Police v. Jeannette Rankin Brigade,* 409 U.S. 972.

on "public forum" grounds a part of one that banned picketing or the distribution of leaflets on the *sidewalks* surrounding the U.S. Supreme Court—although in 1991 it would refuse to hear a challenge to the same law's criminal ban against demonstrations on the marble plaza in front of the Supreme Court building, which it viewed as a "non-public forum."[315] Clearly, then, the line is drawn on the basis of each case's facts.

State Action or Routine Service? What of such services rendered by the state as *licensing* or the *probation of wills* that do involve the state but which had heretofore been regarded as *routine services* rather than as state action? If these services were to be construed as "state action," would not almost *everything* then be state action? Would anything remain in the private sphere at all?

Girard College. The matter of probation of discriminatory wills (of which there are innumerable examples) underwent its first important post-*Brown* litigation in the *Girard College Cases*,[316] involving Philadelphia's famed Girard College (actually a private elementary and high school for "male, white orphans," as provided in the generous will of Stephen S. Girard, an early-nineteenth-century Philadelphia merchant). The trust, established by Girard's will, was being administered by the Board of Directors of the City of Philadelphia when in 1957 the Supreme Court of the United States, citing the precedent of the *Public School Segregation Cases*,[317] ruled unconstitutional as a violation of the equal protection of the laws clause of Amendment Fourteen the municipality's described participation in the Girard trust's administration.[318] It was deemed "state action." But then an interesting turn of events took place: the Board of Directors of City Trusts asked the Orphans Court—the appropriate tribunal of jurisdiction—to *remove the municipal trustees and to substitute private trustees.* This the Orphans Court promptly did, and the Supreme Court of Pennsylvania upheld the action as not being violative of the equal protection clause's "state action" concept. In other words, the state judiciary did not regard either the administration of the trust by private individuals or the role of the two courts in facilitating it to be constitutionally proscribed. On the Pennsylvania attorney general's petition for a writ of certiorari, the U.S. Supreme Court denied review,[319] thus upholding the state tribunals.

---

315. *United States v. Grace,* 461 U.S. 171; and *Pearson v. United States,* 502 U.S. 380, respectively.

316. *Pennsylvania v. Board of Directors of City Trusts of the City of Philadelphia,* 353 U.S. 230 (1957) and 357 U.S. 570 (1958), certiorari denied. These two citations are confined to Supreme Court action. There was a host of lower federal and state case dispositions, of course.

317. *Brown v. Board of Education of Topeka,* 347 U.S. 483 (1954).

318. *Pennsylvania v. Board of Directors of City Trusts of the City of Philadelphia,* 353 U.S. 230.

319. Ibid., 357 U.S. 570 (1958).

The Girard issue continued to bubble, however, and became acute again fully eight years later when, following lengthy sparring between the NAACP and the school's board of trustees, U.S. District Court Judge Joseph S. Lord III ruled that blacks could not be excluded from Girard College *under Pennsylvania law.* Specifically *refusing to pass on the probate problem,* Judge Lord simply held that the Pennsylvania Public Accommodations Act of 1939—which threw open all *public* institutions and accommodations—applied to Girard College, for he classified it as a "public institution."[320] Shortly thereafter, he ordered the admission of seven black orphans if they were otherwise found to qualify.[321] The trustees appealed his decision to the U.S. Third Circuit Court of Appeals, which first stayed Judge Lord's order and then reversed him on the ground that the 1939 statute did *not* apply to Girard College.[322] The plaintiffs, armed with a different strategy, returned to Judge Lord in 1967. The latter, eschewing the Pennsylvania law as well as any probation of wills consideration, now ruled that Girard's refusal to admit the black applicants constituted a violation of the equal protection of the laws clause by virtue of being proscribable *state action* under the Constitution, since the college was sufficiently "public" (e.g., tax-exempt) to invoke the Fourteenth Amendment's state action strictures.[323] This time the U.S. Court of Appeals, in a three-opinion, 5:0 decision, affirmed Judge Lord's ruling. The principal opinion, written by Judge Gerald McLaughlin, turned predominantly on the quasi-public nature of the institution—which constituted sufficient "state action."[324] The Supreme Court declined to review the case,[325] and thus another attempt to make distinctions in the realm of the racial discrimination sector had succeeded. But could the distinction hold? What about "private" parks, deeded in a bequest, for example?

Bacon's Park. The Court soon confronted the question of whether such a privately owned park, here one in Macon, Georgia, could discriminate racially because of the terms of the original donor's will. In 1914 the hundred-acre park had been left in trust to the city of Macon by the will of a former Confederate general, Senator Augustus Octavius Bacon, stipulating that the park's use be reserved for "white women and children." As did parts of the Girard will, Bacon's bequest contained a number of features that were ultimately branded "state action" by civil rights leaders. The will had been drawn up under a Georgia law

320. *Commonwealth of Pennsylvania v. Brown,* 260 F. Supp. 323 (1966).
321. *Commonwealth of Pennsylvania v. Brown,* 360 F. Supp. 358 (1966).
322. Ibid., 373 F.2d 771 (1967).
323. Ibid., 270 F. Supp. 782 (1967).
324. Ibid., 392 F.2d 120 (1968).
325. *Brown v. Commonwealth of Pennsylvania,* 391 U.S. 921 (1968). For an engaging, albeit not unflawed, summary of the *Girard* case (and the eccentric Stephen S. Girard), see John Keats, "Legacy of Stephen Girard," 29 *American Heritage* 38 (June–July 1978).

that, unlike Pennsylvania's, *specifically permitted segregation* in charitable trusts. But, like Philadelphia, Macon appointed the trustees and, like Girard College, Bacon's Park was considered an eleemosynary institution and therefore tax-exempt. Similar to the Philadelphia actions regarding Girard, Macon withdrew as trustee in 1963 and transferred the fiduciary authority to private trustees after lower federal courts had ruled unmistakably that a municipality could not constitutionally operate a segregated park.

Six blacks, successful in getting the trustee transfer question before the Supreme Court, contended that Macon had become so intimately involved in the operations of Bacon's Park that to permit private individuals to take over and continue to discriminate racially would be tantamount to "unconstitutional state action." In a 6:3 decision, with Justice Douglas delivering the Court's opinion, the Supreme Court agreed with the six petitioners.[326] It held that Macon had become so "entwined" in the park's operation that the mere change of trustees could not constitutionally remove the command to desegregate. Joined by the chief justice and Associate Justices Brennan, Clark, and Fortas, Douglas held that park services are "municipal in nature" and in the "public domain." Under the circumstances, he ruled, "we cannot but conclude that the public character of this park requires that it be treated as a public institution" and therefore subject to the commands of the equal protection of the laws clause of the Fourteenth Amendment. As opposed to golf clubs, social centers, *private schools,*[327] and other similar organizations, a park, Douglas explained, "is more like a fire department or police department that traditionally serves the community. Mass recreation through the use of parks is plainly in the public domain."[328]

Justices Harlan and Stewart dissented, as did Black, but the latter did so on separate and largely jurisdictional grounds. To Harlan and Stewart, the Douglas contention was at best dubious. Noting that Douglas had specifically excepted private schools, Harlan was nonetheless alarmed, contending that the Douglas theory could "be spun out to reach privately owned orphanages, libraries, garbage collection companies, detective agencies, and a host of other functions *commonly regarded as nongovernmental though paralleling fields of governmental activity.*"[329] As for private schools, Harlan argued cogently that the "public function" of privately established schools and privately established parks is assuredly similar. If, Harlan continued, the majority really believed that its ruling left "unaffected the traditional view that the Fourteenth Amendment does *not* compel private schools to adapt their admission policies to its requirements," he certainly could not agree with their interpretation in the light of the *Bacon's Park* case. He regarded it as indeed difficult

326. *Evans v. Newton,* 382 U.S. 296 (1966).
327. See the discussion of private school developments in 1976; *infra* this chapter.
328. Ibid. at 302.
329. Ibid. at 322; italics supplied.

to avoid the conclusion that this decision opens the door to reversal of these basic constitutional concepts. . . . The example of schools is, I think, sufficient to indicate the pervasive potentialities of this "public function" theory . . . a catch phrase as vague and amorphous as it is far reaching.[330]

But, in one of those unpredictable Court actions, the Supreme Court ruled (5:2) four years later that Baconsfield (as Senator Bacon had called it) could be returned to the donor's heirs despite a federal court order to admit blacks to its use.[331] In thus siding with the Georgia Supreme Court, Justice Black—speaking also for Chief Justice Burger and Justices Harlan, Stewart, and White—concluded that no constitutionally forbidden state action was involved here; that the Georgia courts had merely carried out Senator Bacon's wishes and had not themselves acted to discriminate against Macon's blacks; and that the Fourteenth Amendment's crucial equal protection of the laws clause had not therefore been violated. Dissenting, Justices Brennan and Douglas, however, asserted that making the park private to frustrate desegregation *did* amount to discriminatory state action.[332] In any event, at least as of this writing—and buttressed by a 1975 holding, with only Justice Douglas in dissent[333]—it seems clear that the mere probation of a will falls outside the realm of the kind of "state action" governed by constitutional commands, which is not to say that a future Court may not read the Constitution differently.

Jackson's Pool. Demonstrating its capability of "surprises" and the dangers of attempting predictions as to its course of action, the Court, dividing 5:4, held in a contentious 1971 Mississippi litigation that public officials may close all of a city's public swimming pools rather than comply with a court order to desegregate them—the city having desegregated its public parks, golf courses, auditoria, and the city zoo.[334] Thus the majority opinion, written by Justice Black—who was joined by his colleagues Harlan, Stewart, Blackmun, and Chief Justice Burger—upheld the right of the city council of Jackson to shut its five community pools on the claimed grounds that to integrate them would be "uneconomical" and create a threat of violence. Refusing to be drawn into attempts to "ascertain the motivation, or collection of different motivations, that lie behind a legislative enactment," Black ruled:

330. Ibid. at 322.
331. *Evans v. Abney,* 396 U.S. 435 (1970).
332. The Court's sole black member, Justice Thurgood Marshall, disqualified himself from sitting in the case because he was once chief counsel for the NAACP Legal Defense and Educational Fund, Inc., which represented the blacks who began legal proceedings challenging the segregated park in 1963.
333. *Sutt v. First National Bank of Kansas City,* 421 U.S. 992. The Court here let stand a bequest to Protestant Christian hospitals in a single county to help care for native-born, white patients.
334. *Palmer v. Thompson,* 403 U.S. 217.

Neither the 14th Amendment nor any act of Congress purports to impose an affirmative duty on a state to begin to operate or to continue to operate swimming pools. . . . It is not a case where a city is maintaining different sets of facilities for blacks and whites and forcing the races to remain separate in recreational or educational activities.[335]

But in his heated dissenting opinion, Justice White, joined by his colleagues Brennan, Marshall, and Douglas—who also issued a separate one, based on his reading of the Ninth Amendment, which he viewed as incorporating freedom from racial, creed, or color discrimination by reason of the three Civil War amendments as "one of the 'enumerated rights,'"—accused the majority of turning back the clock seventeen years on racial equality, of adopting a policy tantamount to "apartheid." In White's words, "[A] State may not have an official stance against desegregating public facilities . . . implemented by closing those facilities in response to a desegregation order."[336] At the least, "an honest difference of opinion about what the Constitution says,"[337] as Black put it, underlay the Court's majority opinion—one replete with broad implications for future policy judgments and decisions (irrespective of the fact that Jackson *voluntarily* reopened its pools on an integrated basis in 1975).

Private Clubs. Perhaps not one of the most important on the scale of basic bread-and-butter values, but assuredly an intriguing one, and one replete with considerations of dignity and egalitarianism as well as freedom of association and liberty, is the matter of the exclusionary policies of private clubs. Even the tough provisions of the Civil Rights Act of 1964, which, among others, forbid places of public accommodation—and these have been broadly defined and construed by the courts[338]—to discriminate because of race, color, religion, or national origin, leave a specific loophole (in Title II) by *expressly* permitting private clubs to do so, thus testifying to Congress's belief that private clubs can, indeed, discriminate without violating the Constitution. But the courts, of course, are not ultimately bound by the beliefs and/or enactments of Congress, and they have been faced increasingly with difficult questions. When is a "club" a club; that is, when is a "club" a place of public entertainment or public "business" rather than a private club exempt under the Civil Rights Act? At what point, if at all, do the prerogatives the Court "found" in the Civil Rights Act of 1866 as of its 1968 fair-housing law decision[339] vitiate prevailing concepts of the rights of private

335. Ibid. at 220.
336. Ibid. at 240.
337. Ibid., oral comment from bench, June 14, 1971.
338. E.g., *Heart of Atlanta Motel v. United States,* 379 U.S. 241 (1964); and *Katzenbach v. McClung,* 379 U.S. 294 (1964). See also *supra* this chapter.
339. *Jones v. Alfred H. Mayer Co.,* 392 U.S. 409 (1968). See *supra* note 184 for the act's key provision on housing. See also the Court's important 1967 *Gautreaux* decision, *supra* note 161.

clubs? And, finally, and most important, at what point, if any, do a club's actions, and the services it receives, constitute proscribable "state action"? In the 1970s the Supreme Court began to face each of these questions.

Thus, as to when is a "club" a club, the Court ruled (7:1) in 1969 that so-called private recreational clubs cannot resort to subterfuge to bar blacks from membership when in fact they are *not* private.[340] The case involved a swimming, boating, and picnicking club near Little Rock, Arkansas (Lake Nixon); the establishment widely advertised that it charged but twenty-five cents for "membership" and had one hundred thousand "members" in a single year. While the lower federal courts, to whom two excluded blacks had appealed, found the "club" arrangements to be a sham, they held that blacks could nonetheless be excluded because Lake Nixon was a private, local activity, not covered by the Civil Rights Act's public accommodations provision. It took a bit of imaginative stretching, but the Supreme Court, speaking through Justice Brennan, with only Justice Black in dissent, found that the establishment *did* affect commerce and therefore came under the statute's reach.[341] How? Well, it solicited business where interstate travelers might respond; it leased canoes from an Oklahoma company; it used a jukebox and records manufactured outside of Arkansas; and ingredients of three out of four items served at the snack bar were shipped interstate. This reasoning was simply too much for Black,[342] but he had no supporters.

In 1969, too, the Court reached the question of whether those provisions of the Civil Rights Act of 1866 which, as explained earlier,[343] outlawed racial discrimination against anyone who wishes to *contract* to buy or lease real estate, extended to any "private club" rights. In a 5:3 decision, written by Justice Douglas—who was joined by his colleagues Black, Brennan, Marshall, and Stewart, with Justices Harlan, White, and Chief Justice Burger dissenting—the Court ruled that the 1866 statute prevented the exclusion of a black family, which had moved into a certain neighborhood housing development, from a swimming pool and a park owned by residents of the suburban community involved.[344] The

340. E.g., in 1976 the Court upheld a lower tribunal's ruling that health spas are "places of entertainment" within the meaning of the Civil Rights Act of 1964 and thus subject to the act's prohibition against racial discrimination (*Shape Spa for Health & Beauty, Inc. v. Rousseve*, 425 U.S. 911 [1976]).

341. *Daniel v. Paul*, 395 U.S. 298 (1968). Douglas wrote a separate concurring opinion.

342. As he put it: "This would be stretching the commerce clause so as to give the federal government complete control over every little remote country place of recreation in every nook and cranny of every precinct and county in every one of the fifty states. This goes too far for me."

343. See *supra* this chapter. The act's pertinent provision (42 U.S.C.A. Section 1982) reads: "All citizens of the United States shall have the same right, in every State and Territory, as is enjoyed by white citizens thereof to inherit, purchase, lease, sell, hold, and convey real and personal property."

344. *Sullivan v. Little Hunting Park, Inc.*, 396 U.S. 229 (1969).

excluded black applicant for membership, Dr. R. Freeman Jr., an official of the Department of Agriculture, had obtained a share in the pool and park with the lease of his house from its owner-member, Paul E. Sullivan. Not only did the development's board of directors refuse to admit Dr. Freeman, it also expelled Mr. Sullivan from membership when he protested the action. The Douglas opinion did not decide whether a club membership is "personal property" under the 1866 act, since the share in the development (Little Hunting Park) was part of the lease itself. The three dissenters objected that the majority unnecessarily propounded grave constitutional questions and that the fair-housing provisions of the Civil Rights Act of 1968 would have provided the same relief without reliance upon the vaguely worded 1866 law. The majority left undecided the broader question of whether private clubs that admit white applicants without selectivity may legally exclude blacks when *no* lease is involved—an issue it again dodged, perhaps quite understandably, four years later.[345]

But what of a private club or lodge that discriminates on racial—or, for that matter, on sexual or religious—grounds and *holds a state liquor license?* In the absence of "state action," even the tough provisions of the Civil Rights Act of 1964 specifically exempt *private* organizations from its nondiscrimination mandates. Is the grant of a state liquor license the sort of "state action" at issue, or is it, like probating of wills, merely a "service" that does not constitute proscribable state action? The judicial response to date has been rather equivocal, but, on the whole, the answer would appear to be negative, so long as a law does not specifically bar such discrimination as a condition for obtaining either a license or tax exemption—as Boston's licensing board, for one, did in 1987.

Thus, could the Loyal Order of Moose, for example, limit membership in its two thousand lodges to white adult Caucasian males—who, if married, are married to "white Caucasians" and are of "good moral character" and "mentally normal" and "express a belief in a supreme being"? If it is a truly private organization, receives no governmental aid, and pays its taxes, the answer would presumably be yes—for the liberty to associate privately, even if it be on a discriminatory basis, would appear to outweigh egalitarian commands, especially since the First and Fourteenth Amendments guarantee freedom of association and

---

345. Relying heavily on its 1969 decision, the Court, speaking through Justice Blackmun, held unanimously: "When an organization limits membership benefits to residency in a narrow geographical area, that decision infuses those benefits into the bundle of rights for which an individual pays when buying or leasing within the area" (*Tillman v. Wheaton-Haven Recreation Association,* 410 U.S. 431 [1973] at 437). The association drew *all* its members from *whites* living within three-quarters of a mile from its swimming pool, and it barred all *nonwhites* living in the same area. The Court refused to recognize the association as a "private club on any level." See also a similar stance in 1980 by the U.S. Court of Appeals for the Fourth Circuit, by overturning a lower court ruling that had dismissed a charge of racial discrimination (*Wright v. Salisbury Country Club, Ltd.,* 632 F.2d and 479 F. Supp. 378, respectively).

liberty as well as equality. The Harrisburg, Pennsylvania, Lodge No. 107 of the Moose, possessor of a state liquor license, refused to serve a meal and drinks to K. Leroy Irvis, the black majority leader of the Pennsylvania State House of Representatives, who had gone to the lodge as a guest of a Moose member. Evidently, the lodge did not discriminate selectively in its discrimination against blacks! After losing in Pennsylvania Commonwealth Court—which called the lodge's refusal to serve Irvis "morally indefensible and deficient in good manners and common sense,"[346] but held the lodge to be a private club exempt on grounds of privacy and association—Representative Irvis brought suit before a three-judge federal district court, contending that state regulation of liquor was "so detailed and pervasive" that to license a club that discriminated was tantamount to licensing discrimination. Unanimously, the three-judge tribunal ruled in Mr. Irvis's favor, agreeing that the holder of a liquor license was, indeed, clothed with "state action" under the Fourteenth Amendment.[347] Blurring the issues somewhat, however, the court added that the lodge could continue to discriminate on the basis of religion and national origin—it said nothing about sex—because it did not regard these characteristics to be protected by that Civil War amendment, which had been adopted primarily to prevent discrimination against blacks.

The lodge, in its resultant appeal to the U.S. Supreme Court, called that distinction "clearly fallacious" and pointed to the stipulated exemption of private clubs under the public accommodations provision of the Civil Rights Act of 1964. Moreover, it invoked freedom of association concepts under the First (and Fourteenth) Amendment. The high tribunal evidently agreed, at least in part: in a 6:3 opinion, written by Justice Rehnquist—Justices Douglas, Brennan, and Marshall dissenting—it ruled that *mere liquor regulation* does not involve the state in the kind of discriminatory state action forbidden by the Fourteenth Amendment's equal protection clause—"the State," in Rehnquist's words, "must have significantly involved itself with invidious discriminations . . . in order for the discriminatory action to fall within the ambit of constitutional prohibition."[348] However, the *Moose Lodge* decision did *not* mean that states could not make the receipt of a liquor license, or its continued retention, contingent upon the eschewing of racial discrimination—as fifteen Maine Elk lodges soon found out.[349]

346. *Commonwealth v. Royal Order of Moose,* 92 Dauph. 234 (1970) at 239.

347. *Irvis v. Scott and Moose Lodge #107,* 318 F. Supp. 1246 (1970) at 1251.

348. *Moose Lodge #107 v. Irvis,* 407 U.S. 163 (1972). But it ought to be noted that when—just two months after the Court's decision—the Pennsylvania State Human Relations Commission ruled that Lodge No. 107 had in fact turned itself into a *"public accommodation"* because it freely allowed guests, and thus could not ban blacks under state law, the state supreme court affirmed, and the U.S. Supreme Court dismissed the lodge's appeal, thus upholding the commission's ruling (*Royal Order of Moose v. Pennsylvania Human Relations Commission,* 409 U.S. 1052 [1972]).

349. *B.P.O.E. Lodge #2043 v. Ingraham,* 412 U.S. 913 (1973). Later that year the Elks dropped their "whites-only" rule.

On the other hand, in the absence of state laws prohibiting discrimination on the basis of *sex* as well as race in places of public accommodation—and in the absence of the adoption of an "Equal Rights Amendment"—the Court consistently refused, until the mid-1980s, to overturn lower tribunal rulings upholding the right of *private* clubs or other *private* organizations that were "male only" to obtain and/or retain liquor licenses, *provided* that they were *genuinely* private.[350]

Yet, to the delight of many women's organizations and civil rights and liberties groups, an alteration in the Court's stance on "all-male" clubs came clearly into view. Thus, in 1984 it applied Minnesota's public accommodation statute making it "an unfair discriminatory practice" to discriminate in public accommodations because of "race, color, creed, religion, disability, national origin, or sex" to the restrictive membership policies of the Jaycees, whose national organization bylaws limited that membership to young men between the ages of eighteen and thirty-five. While Justice Brennan's opinion for the unanimous (7:0) Court[351] conceded that "there can be no clearer example of an intrusion into the internal structure or affairs of an association than a regulation that forces the group to accept members it does not desire," and that freedom of association, protected by the First and Fourteenth Amendments, "plainly supposes a freedom not to associate," Brennan pointed out that "the right to associate for expressive purposes is not absolute." He rejected the Jaycees' contention that the Minnesota law posed "any serious burden on the male members' freedom of expressive association," and he seemed to set the constitutional parameters for future litigation of this nature by apparently distinguishing large associational groups like the Jaycees from those characterized by "relative smallness, a high degree of selectivity in decisions to begin and maintain the affiliation, and seclusion from others." Justice O'Connor, who concurred separately, as did Justice Rehnquist (Chief Justice Burger and Justice Blackmun recused themselves because of their

---

350. E.g., *Millenson v. New Hotel Monteleone,* 414 U.S. 1011 (1973); *Junior Chamber of Commerce of Rochester v. U.S. Jaycees,* 419 U.S. 1026 (1974); and *Junior Chamber of Commerce of Philadelphia v. U.S. Jaycees,* 419 U.S. 1026 (1974). See also the 1977 ruling by Federal Judge W. C. Conner upholding the right of the politically influential Town Club of Scarsdale, New York, to continue to bar women as it has done since 1905 (440 F. Supp. 607). The U.S. Supreme Court also refused to review a lower ruling upholding the right of the international Kiwanis organization to withdraw the charter of an affiliate for having admitted women to its membership (*Kiwanis Club v. Board of Trustees,* 434 U.S. 859 [1977]). In the same year the Illinois Appellate Court, under the Illinois Liquor Control Act, which specifically sanctions "exclusionary policy" for private clubs, held that private clubs may exclude women and members of minority groups as guests (*New York Times,* December 25, 1977, sec. A, p. 27). But cf. *Iron Arrow Honor Society v. Heckler,* 464 U.S. 67 (1983). The tax exemption issue remains murky in this connection: private, nonprofit fraternal clubs evidently can still enjoy that exemption, even if they discriminate, but all earned income becomes taxable (*McGlotten v. Connally,* 338 F. Supp. 448 [1972]).

351. *Roberts v. U.S. Jaycees,* 465 U.S. 455.

Minnesota ties), wanted to create a distinction resting solely between rights of *commercial* association and rights of expressive association. Because she viewed the Jaycees as primarily commercial, she concurred in regarding the associational challenge to be without merit.

Evidently the Court found its only female member's argument persuasive, for a major 1987 holding on the issue in a case involving California's Rotary Clubs was based upon Justice O'Connor's dichotomy. She, together with Justice Blackmun, recused herself because of a conflict of interest, but their seven brethren agreed unanimously, in an opinion written by Justice Powell, that the Constitution does not protect sex discrimination by most all-male clubs, and in particular not by those that are often used for business purposes or by nonmembers.[352] The Court did not define with precision how private and selective a club would henceforth have to be to mount a successful constitutional prerogative to exclude women—thus leaving the door open for other clubs to argue that they are indeed more private than the Rotary Clubs or the Jaycees.[353] But as for the nineteen thousand Rotary Clubs, with their nine hundred thousand members in 157 countries, the Powell ruling made clear that in the Court's considered judgment the evidence in the case indicated that the relationship among their members "is not the kind of intimate or private relation that warrants constitutional protection."

Private Schools. Perhaps the most significant and most emotion-charged area of the "private"-"public" dichotomy is that of the Fourteenth Amendment "state action" status, if any, of genuine *private schools.* We know, of course, that those otherwise private institutions of higher and lower learning that receive funds from the federal government have had to toe the proverbial "no discrimination"

---

352. *Board of Directors of Rotary International v. Rotary Club of Duarte,* 481 U.S. 537 (1987).

353. This argument promised to become a key aspect of putative litigation involving such presumably private clubs as the Century Club in New York City; the Burning Tree Club in Bethesda, Maryland; and the Cosmos Club in Washington, D.C. Late in 1987 the Supreme Court agreed to review New York City's law aimed at banning sex and race discrimination by all-male private clubs. Down came its decision on June 20, 1988: the Court ruled (9:0) that the latter statute was constitutional. It bars discrimination by all clubs, other than benevolent orders and religious ones, if such clubs have more than four hundred members; provide regular meal service for members and guests; and regularly get their members' dues paid by nonmembers, such as the members' employers (*New York State Club Association v. City of New York,* 487 U.S. 1). On the day before, the prestigious Cosmos Club had voted to admit women. The New York decision was implicitly confirmed in a 1989 case involving a Maryland statute (*Burning Tree Club v. Maryland,* 493 U.S. 816). A decade later, the Court, by a 5:4 vote, upheld the Boy Scouts of America's ban on homosexual Boy Scout leaders, ruling that the Boy Scouts, all Americans, have a right to freedom of "expressive association" (*Boy Scouts of America v. Dale,* 530 U.S. 640 [2000]).

line in accordance with the mandates of Titles IV, VI, VII, and IX of the Civil Rights Act of 1964, and that the rules laid down by the Departments of Labor, Education, and Health and Human Services have been so adamant and persistent that many aspects of compliance have arguably been justifiably characterized as "reverse discrimination" (of which more later). But what of the status of governmentally *non*-aided *private* schools? Because they are not covered by the Civil Rights Act of 1964 (and provided they do not fall under state civil rights statutes), may they not, being indeed private, discriminate in their admissions on whatever basis they may determine? In particular, on the basis of race?

That issue reached the highest court in the land in 1976, when it heard oral arguments in the case of *Runyon v. McCrary,* with the nation a fascinated and interested witness. The Court's decision was almost certain to lead to one of the most far-reaching judgments involving the clash between the private and public realms. Involved were two all-white private Virginia schools in the suburbs of Washington, the Fairfax-Brewster School and the Bobbe's School, organized in 1955 and 1958, respectively. Neither had ever admitted a black student. When two black youngsters, Michael McCrary and Colin M. Gonzales, were rejected in 1973, their parents filed suit in federal district court, citing Section 1981 of the now more than a century-old Civil Rights Act of 1866, which was enacted to provide for blacks the same right "to make and enforce contracts . . . as is enjoyed by white citizens." Judge Albert V. Bryan Jr. ruled firmly that private all-white schools cannot legally bar blacks from admission on the basis of race. No "state action" need be shown, he held: the cited provision of the 1866 Civil Rights Act amply covered the quest for redress.[354]

The schools appealed to the U.S. Circuit Court of Appeals for the Fourth Circuit, which, in a 4:3 decision, authored by Chief Justice Clement F. Haynsworth Jr.—of 1969 Supreme Court nomination-rejection fame[355]—narrowly affirmed Judge Bryan's holding.[356] A private school, he wrote, "may not refuse with impunity to accept an otherwise qualified black applicant simply because it declines to admit unqualified white applicants." In the bare majority's view, the pertinent provision of the 1866 law simply prohibited private schools from barring students solely because of their race. The two schools now took their case to the U.S. Supreme Court, where the U.S. Department of Justice submitted a brief amicus curiae on the side of the black applicants. The Court's answer came quickly in a historic 7:2 (5:2:2) decision[357] written by Justice Stewart, who was joined by his colleagues Burger, Brennan, Marshall, and Blackmun—Justices Powell and Stevens concurring separately and with

354. *McCrary v. Runyon,* 363 F. Supp. 1200 (1973).
355. See Abraham, *Justices, Presidents, and Senators,* op. cit., esp. chapter 2, pp. 10–11.
356. *McCrary v. Runyon,* 515 F.2d 1052 (1975).
357. *Runyon v. McCrary,* 427 U.S. 160 (1976).

considerable misgivings.[358] The Supreme Court upheld the lower courts, ruling that "private, commercially operated, non-sectarian schools" may not deny "admission to prospective students because they are Negroes." Over a strongly worded dissenting opinion by Justice White, who was joined by Justice Rehnquist, the Court majority based its ruling on the aforementioned section (§1981) of the Civil Rights Act of 1866—passed to enforce the Thirteenth Amendment's ban on slavery—which accords "all persons the same rights to make and enforce contracts as is enjoyed by white citizens." In response to the schools' contention that this interpretation and application of the statute violate constitutional guarantees of freedom of association, the right to privacy, and parental rights, the controlling opinion found no invasions of any of these safeguards, holding that they "do not provide easy or ready escapes" through which whites "can contravene laws enacted by Congress to enforce the Constitutional right to equality."

But Justice White viewed the legislative history and intent of the section of the 1866 statute at issue utterly differently than did the five-member majority. It confirms, he wrote in his dissenting opinion,

> that the statute means what it says and no more, *i.e.*, that it outlaws any legal rule disabling any person from making or enforcing a contract, but does not prohibit private racially motivated refusals to contract. . . . What is conferred by [the disputed section of the law] is the right—which was enjoyed by whites—"to make contracts with other willing parties and to enforce those contracts in court." . . . The statute by its terms does not *require* any *private* individual or institution to enter into a contract or perform any other act under any circumstances, and it consequently fails to supply a cause of action by respondent students against petitioned schools based on the latter's racially motivated decision not to contract with them.[359]

358. Ibid. at 186, 189. Their reluctant concurrences came almost solely because of what they viewed as the binding 1968 precedent of the *Mayer* decision (see *supra* this chapter), also citing the "*mores* of the day." Powell admitted that he would have sided with the dissenters "if the slate were clean," and Stevens, while acknowledging an almost certain misinterpretation of the Civil Rights Act of 1866 by the majority, pointed to the Court's need for and "interest in stability in orderly development of the law." The all-white Prince Edward Academy in Farmville, Virginia, which had been established in 1959 to avoid integration, admitted its first black students in the fall of 1986.

359. Ibid. at 195–96. In 1988 the Court ordered the case reargued to determine if its ruling should be "reconsidered" (*Patterson v. McLean Credit Union*, 491 U.S. 164). In June 1989 the Court upheld the important pro–civil rights precedent it had established in *Runyon* and reaffirmed the 1866 act's application as a tool in combating discrimination in the private sector at the *initial hiring stage. However,* it ruled in *Patterson* (5:4) that the statute could not be similarly applied regarding claims of *on-the-job* discriminatory treatment because, in Justice Kennedy's opinion for the majority, Congress had not intended the 1866 law's key Section 1981 to reach such allegations; but that, of course, other antidiscrimination laws are applicable and usable.

In language and philosophy reminiscent of Justices Harlan II and Frankfurter, he concluded by flaying his colleagues for undertaking the political task of "construing a statute . . . a task appropriate for the legislature, not the judiciary." Nonetheless, a bit more than a decade later the Court ruled unanimously that the 1866 Civil Rights Act protects not only racial groups—as it had blacks in the earlier private school case—but also what are now considered ethnic groups, namely, Jews and Arabs.[360]

Left intriguingly unanswered until a future day and Court by Justice Stewart's majority opinion were such tantalizing questions as the right of *sectarian* schools to discriminate on the basis of race and, conceivably, the application of the 1866 statute to *private clubs*. What was not difficult to predict was that there would be future litigation involving that fascinatingly vexatious line between liberty and equality. And an answer to the first issue came in mid-1983: two fundamentalist Christian educational institutions, one Bob Jones University, the other Goldsboro Christian School, had long practiced racial discrimination in admissions policy or internal rules of conduct or both—based on their professed religious creed and customs. Ultimately, the Internal Revenue Service withdrew their tax-exempt status, and the two schools, losing in lower federal courts on their First Amendment contentions, appealed to the Supreme Court. In an 8:1 opinion, authored by Chief Justice Burger, with only Justice Rehnquist in dissent on grounds of the absence of congressional action on the issue, the high tribunal ruled that the governmental interest in eradicating racial discrimination "substantially outweighs whatever burden denial of tax benefits places on petitioners' exercise of their religious beliefs."[361] Although he concurred with the Court's judgment that Congress had determined that the policy against racial discrimination in education should "override the countervailing interest in permitting unorthodox private behavior," he wrote separately to emphasize that "the balancing of these substantial interests is for *Congress* to perform. . . . It is not appropriate to leave the I.R.S. 'on the cutting edge of developing national policy.' The contours of public policy should be determined by Congress, not by judges or the I.R.S."[362]

Thus we return to the basic question of establishing a viable line between "private" and "state" action. Does the line *really* serve the desired purpose when it is applied to such utterly routine governmental services as business registration, licensing,[363] contract enforcement, or probation of wills? One may question

360. *Shaare Tefila Congregation v. Cobb,* 481 U.S. 615 (1987); and *Saint Francis College v. Al-Kkavraji AKA Allan,* 481 U.S. 604 (1987).
361. *Bob Jones University and Goldsboro Christian School v. United States,* 461 U.S. 574.
362. Ibid., concurring opinion at 612; italics in original. For an intriguing quaere on tax exemption involving the *Bob Jones* issue(s), see Dean M. Kelley's "Guest Editorial: A New Meaning for Tax Exemption," 25 *Journal of Church and State* 415 (autumn 1983).
363. See *Jackson v. Metropolitan Edison Co.,* 419 U.S. 345 (1974), in which the Court, dividing 6:3, held that a Pennsylvania electric company was not related closely enough to

the choice of the adjective "utterly" in conjunction with "routine services" yet still acknowledge that when services such as those indicated are categorized as "state action" the private sector becomes an anomaly. Perhaps this has happened, but it is doubtful that a majority of the American polity would subscribe to such a conclusion. In the second Justice Harlan's observation, "The times have changed [but] perhaps it is appropriate to observe that . . . the equal protection clause of [the Fourteenth] Amendment [does not] rigidly impose upon America an ideology of unrestrained egalitarianism."[364] For, as he had commented on an earlier occasion: "Freedom of the individual to choose his associates or his neighbors, to use and dispose of his property as he sees fit, to be irrational, arbitrary, capricious, even unjust in his personal relations, are things all entitled to a large measure of protection from governmental interference."[365] One can wholly support, encourage, fight for, and even die for the eradication of the fundamental injustices in the realm of racial and gender discrimination; equality before the law and of economic, educational, and cultural opportunity; the suffrage; access to the rewards and responsibilities of public office; the end of state-supported or state-permitted or state-enforced segregation—these are the aspects of the problem that should, and do, matter. Indeed, a general consensus exists here. But there is less agreement on wills, clubs, and societies. There *is* something to be said for privacy of association, no matter how silly, undemocratic, or puerile. While, generally, the equal protection clause does preclude state enforcement of private discrimination, there may thus well be, in the words of Professor Louis Henkin, one of the foremost students of the field—and a devoted libertarian—"a small area of liberty favored by the Constitution even over claims to equality. Rights of liberty and property, of privacy and voluntary association, must be balanced, in close cases, against the right not to have the state enforce discrimination against the victim. In the few instances in which the right to discriminate is protected or preferred by the Constitution, the state may enforce it."[366] Unquestionably, this stance raises as many problems as it professes to solve, but a dogmatic approach is no answer either.[367] In part, of course, such legislation as the public accommodations title of the Civil Rights Act of 1964, enacted by the nation's legislative representatives, and subsequently upheld by the Supreme Court, settles the matter in an orderly and legal fashion. So does the "open housing" section of the Civil Rights Act of 1968—whatever one's view of its wisdom.

Yet not all aspects of the vexatious public versus private problem can be conclusively settled by legislative action, nor should they be. There will always

the state government merely because it held a license to service, and that consumers were hence unable to raise due process of law claims.

364. *Harper v. Virginia Board of Elections,* 383 U.S. 663 (1965), dissenting opinion at 678.

365. *Lombard v. Louisiana,* 373 U.S. 267 (1963), dissenting opinion.

366. Henkin, "*Shelley v. Kraemer:* Notes for a Revised Opinion," op. cit., p. 496.

367. See the *Tarkanian* decision, *supra* this chapter.

be gray areas that should be treated with common sense—a common sense cognizant of our responsibilities as well as our ideals, a common sense that is conscious both of constitutional commands and of the need to strike a balance between liberty and equality. When all other avenues fail, the last word may well have to be given by the judiciary, that branch of our government that has proved itself more capable than any other of guarding our basic civil rights and liberties. As Justice Douglas once wrote, "The people should know that when filibusters occupy other forums, when oppressions are great, when the clash of authority between the individual and the State is severe, they can still get justice in the courts."[368] But in the final analysis all judicial actions must be grounded in constitutional authority.

368. *Bell v. Maryland,* 378 U.S. 226 (1964), concurring opinion at 242–45.

8

Gender and Race Under the New Equal Protection

In a host of ways, although superficially differing in kind, degree, and genesis, discrimination on the basis of sex—or, perhaps more appropriately termed, gender-based discrimination—is part and parcel of the American dilemma. Such discrimination is now constitutionally impermissible. Although there has long been a "women's movement," the issue of invidious discrimination in the realm of gender did not really impress itself upon the public conscience in majoritarian contemplation until the desegregation movement in the racial sphere evolved close to its crescendo in the middle to late 1960s. And, as has been so true of invidious racial discrimination, it would again preeminently be the judiciary that was called upon initially to articulate and to mandate the parameters of egalitarianism and equal opportunity in the realm of sex, broadly based upon the implicit and explicit commands of the equal protection of the laws—in its "new" model—and the due process of law clauses of the basic document.[1]

A GLANCE AT THE EVOLVING HISTORY OF GENDER DISCRIMINATION

That women have faced special obstacles deriving from their historically *subordinate* role in American society is axiomatic: sexually stereotyped, their economic, educational, and political opportunities subordinated to those of males—even their legal position suffered from a double standard. Moreover, while the strivings of blacks were directed against a legal tradition designed to retain them in a *subservient* status, women had to direct their struggle against a deeply ingrained tradition that was patently designed to accord them a *protective*

1. See *supra* chapter 2.

465

as well as a subordinate status. Thus, in 1908, in a constitutional landmark decision that upheld a 1903 Oregon statute limiting female workers in mechanical establishments, factories, and laundries to a ten-hour workday, the state's victory came clearly because of attorney—and future U.S. Supreme Court justice—Louis D. Brandeis's brilliant brief (which, incidentally, heralded the utilization of social science data in the judicial process). Here, in what would become known as the "Brandeis brief," the scholarly Boston lawyer attained a unanimous Court victory by disposing of the constitutional issues and precedents (chiefly apposite to the Fourteenth Amendment's due process of law clause) in two pages but devoting more than one hundred pages to statistical data on hours of labor, health, morals, and factory legislation abroad—all emphasizing the protected status of women. Accepting Brandeis's contentions, Justice David Brewer, speaking for the Court, justified its decision, inter alia, as follows:

> The two sexes differ in structure of body, in the functions to be performed by each, in the amount of physical strength, in the capacity for long-continued labor, particularly when done standing, . . . the self-reliance which enables one to assert full rights, and in the capacity to maintain the struggle for subsistence. This difference justifies a difference in legislation and upholds that which is designed to compensate for some of the burdens which rest upon her.[2]

Today's jurists would hardly be likely to employ such language!

Women's egalitarian movements existed prior to our days, but they were not generally or overridingly successful at any of the governmental branches, and especially not at the federal level, despite isolated victories such as Wyoming's grant of the right to vote to women in 1869, while still a territory. When Congress made noises about "this petticoat provision" in Wyoming's application for statehood in 1890, the territory's legislature responded that it would stay out of the Union a hundred years rather than enter it without women's suffrage.[3] Indeed, led by the pioneering West, more than one-half of the states had granted women the suffrage by the end of World War I. Yet, in the pithy comment by then United States Circuit Court Judge Ruth Bader Ginsburg, except for the Nineteenth Amendment—which, in 1920, granted women the right to vote in *all* federal and state elections—"the Constitution remained an empty cupboard for sex equality claims."[4] It would take another fifty years before the Supreme Court would bite the proverbial bullet and begin to strike at invidious gender discrimination. Surprisingly, it was not the Warren Court, which did so much, and so de-

---

2. *Muller v. Oregon,* 208 U.S. 412.

3. James McGregor Burns, J. W. Peltason, and Thomas E. Cronin, *Government by the People,* 11th ed. (Englewood Cliffs, N.J.: Prentice-Hall, 1981), p. 114.

4. "Employment of the Constitution to Advance the Equal Status of Men and Women" (paper presented at Hebrew University, Jerusalem, May 19, 1987), p. 4.

cisively, to attack racial discrimination, but the Burger Court that would recognize women's rightful constitutional claims as of the beginning of the 1970s. The Warren Court had maintained a passive stance, generally inclining to uphold gender-based legislative classifications by invoking the "reasonable man" or "rational person"[5] standard of adjudication—and women continued to be denied equal rights, equal pay, and a host of a priori justifiable legal claims. Disabilities imposed by both federal and state laws were endemic and rampant.

But, perhaps inevitably, the 1960s would witness a significant degree of legislative action on the federal level to commence the changes which many now take for granted. One of the catalysts in the now-no-longer-to-be-denied egalitarian movement on the gender front was feminist activist Betty Friedan's highly influential, widely noted, and eagerly read book *The Feminine Mystique,* which was published in 1963.[6] There is simply no doubt that her work served to raise women's consciousness far beyond the once so commonly accepted notion that a woman's place was essentially in the home, that by and large the proper and appropriate role was that of wife, mother, and housekeeper. That same eventful year saw some long-overdue action by Congress with the adoption of the Equal Pay Act as an amendment to the Fair Labor Standards Act, embracing the basic principle of equal pay for equal work, regardless of sex. And just one year later Congress enacted the seminal Civil Rights Act of 1964, Title VII of which prohibited discrimination on the ground of sex by employer, labor unions and organizations, and employment agencies. Its Title VI was amended in 1972 to include gender discrimination as a trigger for the denial of federal aid funds to any public or private program or activity, and Title IX, also adopted in 1972, made a point of ascertaining that equal athletic facilities opportunities were available to women—amid anguished wails by male coaches, especially those in contact sports. They appear to have survived, however. In 1997, the Supreme Court refused an appeal from Brown University, whose underrepresentation of female students in its athletic programs was found by the First U.S. Circuit Court of Appeals to constitute illegal discrimination under Title IX (*Brown University v. Amy Cohen,* et al., 65 LW 4283).

The ERA Struggle. The indisputable accretion and extension of rights to women, by both judicial and legislative action, seemed to herald relatively easy sailing for an "Equal Rights Amendment" (ERA). In fact, such an amendment had been in the congressional hoppers since 1923, but it had never garnered the necessary two-thirds majority for passage in both houses. Its operative clause read: "Equality of rights under the law shall not be denied by the United States or any State on account of sex." Resuscitated amid widespread support, led by the increasingly visible and influential National Organization for Women (NOW) and the

5. See *supra* chapter 2.
6. (New York: Norton).

National Women's Political Caucus, founded in 1966 and 1971, respectively, the ERA passed Congress overwhelmingly in 1972, by votes of 84:8 in the Senate and 354:24 in the House. Its future looked bright indeed.

That optimism seemed wholly justified when the legislatures of twenty-two states ratified the ERA within twelve months of its passage, almost always by huge margins. But three years later that enthusiastic reception had obviously slowed markedly, and two of the erstwhile ratifiers, Nebraska and Tennessee, voted to rescind their initial "aye" actions. By 1978, while thirty-five states had ratified, three had changed their minds; even not counting the rescissions, the ERA still lacked three votes; and March 22, 1979, the deadline for ratification, loomed on the horizon. In what was indubitably an action of highly questionable constitutionality, Congress, by simple majority vote, extended the ratification deadline to June 30, 1982[7]—but none of the fifteen state refusers would change their minds. The ERA was dead. In view of the significant progress of the women's movement and the Court's generous rulings in its favor, it may well be doubted that the ERA, or a similar measure, will become constitutional law. As James Q. Wilson succinctly summarized the reasons for its failure to do so: "The ERA became an issue that symbolized the conflict over a broad range of cultural values in the United States."[8] Since it is always difficult to obtain ratification by three-fourths of the states—and, except for unicameral Nebraska, both houses of each state legislature had to vote affirmatively—it was not surprising that well-organized, confirmed opposition groups such as the Mormons, the National Council of Catholic Women, other important segments of orthodox religions, and tireless crusading individuals, such as Phyllis Schlafly and her Eagle Forum, would triumph in blocking the ERA's enactment. But the Supreme Court proved to be a sympathetic interpreter of the Fifth and Fourteenth Amendments, and, arguably, the Court may well have achieved what the ERA was expected to accomplish (as the following text and Table 8.1 demonstrate).

The Court's Attack on Gender Discrimination. Two years after President Nixon had appointed Warren Earl Burger chief justice of the United States, the latter wrote an opinion on the gender discrimination front that heralded a new day for egalitarianism. As the front page of the *New York Times* announced in large type on November 23, 1971: "Court, for First Time, Overrules a State Law That Favors Men." Indeed, not since the Fourteenth Amendment's birth in 1866 and its ratification in 1868 had the Supreme Court of the United States provided a victory for women on the ground that a state had violated its equal protection of the

7. By two 9:0 votes the Supreme Court *mooted* pending suits in 1982 that had challenged the constitutionality of the majority vote extension *(NOW v. Idaho)* and that of the change-of-mind action *(Carmen v. Idaho),* both 459 U.S. 809 (1982).

8. *American Government: Institutions and Policies,* 3d ed. (Lexington, Mass.: D. C. Heath, 1986), p. 560.

laws mandate. Here, in the now memorable case of *Reed v. Reed,*[9] the Court *unanimously* struck down an Idaho statute that accorded men preference over women in administering deceased persons' estates. It marked the first time that the Supreme Court of the United States had invalidated a state law on grounds of sex discrimination.

In doing so the justices applied the traditional "rationality" test, which merely requires a judicial judgment whether or not rational or reasonable legislators could constitutionally enact legislation of the type under attack. Not wisdom, fairness, intelligence, or even democracy is thus an issue: the key is the law's "reasonableness." In the Idaho case, however, the Court, applying that test, found that its legislature had made an "arbitrary" decision to favor men over women, in order to spare trial judges from having to decide in each case who was best suited to administer each contested estate. The result, wrote the chief justice of the United States, was to divide men and women into separate classes "on the basis of criteria wholly unrelated" to the objective of efficient distribution of estates. And he thus concluded that, plainly, Idaho's women had been denied equal legal rights—even under the otherwise so deferential-to-legislative-action test of "reasonableness" or "rationality." But as the anti-gender-discrimination movement grew and matured, the judiciary was soon persuaded also to utilize tests that would be more generous to aggrieved plaintiffs. Soon the scrutiny the Court extended to allegation of gender discrimination thus commenced to embrace stricter standards, with the scrutiny ranging from "close" to "heightened," stopping just short of adopting the "suspect" plane standard that the Court had adopted for claims of racial discrimination.[10] The latter became a live issue with the Court's significant 8:1 ruling in the important 1973 case of *Frontiero v. Richardson.*[11]

In that litigation, Air Force Lieutenant Sharron Frontiero objected to a federal statute under which male officers automatically qualified for benefits for their wives, whereas female officers could obtain the same benefits only upon providing proof that their husbands were dependent upon them for support. Recognizing this injustice, the Court, in the plurality opinion written by Justice Brennan, with Justice Rehnquist in solitary dissent, declared that the federal government had failed to demonstrate the necessary "compelling interest" to justify the law's distinction between men and women; that laws such as the instant one "in practical effect . . . put women, not on a pedestal, but in a cage."[12] Indeed, joined by his colleagues Douglas, White, and Marshall, Brennan now

9. 404 U.S. 71 (1971). The chief justice was joined by Justices Douglas, Brennan, Stewart, White, Marshall, and Blackmun.
10. See *supra* chapter 2.
11. 411 U.S. 677. See also Justice Ruth Bader Ginsburg's concurring opinion in *Harris v. Forklift Systems,* 510 U.S. 17 (1993), alluded to *supra* and *infra.*
12. Ibid.

wanted to establish the application of the "suspect" category test to gender discrimination—just as it had already been judicially embraced for the realms of
race, alienage, and nationality. But he fell short of securing the necessary fifth
vote, the other four concurring justices—Stewart, Powell, Blackmun, and the
chief justice—contending in two separate opinions that it was "unnecessary . . .
to characterize sex as a suspect classification"; that *Frontiero* should be decided
on the basis of the "rationality" test utilized in *Reed;* and that "any expansion of
its rationale" should be reserved for the future.[13] Despite the appointment of the
first two women justices in the interim, the Court has declined to embrace the
"suspect" test for gender discrimination.

What it has done, on the other hand, is to adopt a "heightened" or "intermediate" scrutiny standard test, one it developed with considerable aplomb in *Craig
v. Boren*[14] in 1976. There, Oklahoma's 3.2 percent beer regulation law prohibited
the beverage's sale to males under the age of twenty-one but to females only under
age eighteen. Over dissents by Chief Justice Burger and Justice Rehnquist, who
regarded the state law as entirely sustainable under the "rationality" test, Justice
Brennan's opinion struck it down as invidiously discriminatory under the equal
protection of the laws clause of the Fourteenth Amendment. In therewith adopting its new "heightened scrutiny" test, the Court let it be known that it would no
longer sustain differential treatment of men and women that was merely *rationally*
related to some *permissible* government objective; that, instead, the Court would
henceforth strike down any gender classification absent a *substantial* relationship
to an *important* government objective.[15] Thus we see that, while the Court in gender cases has neither totally abandoned the "rationality" test nor embraced the
"suspect category" test, it has, in general, embraced the "heightened or 'intermediate' level of scrutiny" test developed in *Craig v. Boren* in 1976. And it is noteworthy that the victors in that case were *male,* just as Justice O'Connor's opinion
of the 5:4 majority in *Mississippi University for Women v. Hogan*[16] in 1982 held
in favor of *male* registered nurse Joe Hogan, who had been denied admission to
MUW's School of Nursing solely because of his sex. "That this statute discriminates against males rather than females," asserted the Court's first woman mem-

13. See the concurring opinion by Justice Powell, joined by Chief Justice Burger and
Justice Blackmun. Justice Stewart concurred separately.

14. 429 U.S. 190. For a description of attorney Ruth Bader Ginsburg's crucial role in
the Court's development of the "heightened scrutiny" standard for gender during her stint
in the 1970s as head of the Women's Rights Project of the American Civil Liberties Union,
see David Von Drehle, "Redefining Fair with a Simple, Careful Assault," *Washington
Post,* July 19, 1993, p. A1.

15. Ginsburg, op. cit., p. 15, note 4. For "a strategic account of [the] judicial decisions"
made among the justices in *Craig v. Boren,* based on a systematic study of the Brennan,
Marshall, and Powell papers, see Lee Epstein and Jack Knight, *The Choices Justices Make*
(Washington, D.C.: CQ Press, 1998), chapter 1.

16. 458 U.S. 718.

ber, "does not exempt it from scrutiny or reduce the standard of review." Chief Justice Burger, Justice Blackmun, and Justices Powell and Rehnquist dissented in three separate opinions, each of which in one degree or another maintained that Mississippi's policy of single-sex admission for what was the oldest state-supported all-female university in the nation was both "benign" and "compensatory" and was readily sustainable under the "rationality" test.

In the 1990s, the battleground shifted to two state-supported, all-male military academies—the Citadel in South Carolina and the Virginia Military Institute (VMI). The latter, founded in 1839, long revered by many Old Dominion citizens for the bravery of its cadets during the Civil War, and General George C. Marshall's alma mater, was subjected to a lawsuit in 1990 when the United States Justice Department responded to the complaint of a female high school student who wanted to attend VMI. The Justice Department argued that women were being denied equal protection of the state's laws in violation of the Fourteenth Amendment because they could not attend the publicly funded military academy. The case came before U.S. District Court Judge Jackson Kiser, who ruled in favor of VMI, concluding that the presence of women would fundamentally change the atmosphere at the school and likely require the abolition of the institute's famed adversative method of training (in which first-year students are labeled "rats," and treated as such by upperclassmen). The Justice Department appealed the decision to the Fourth Circuit Court of Appeals, which found VMI in violation of the Fourteenth Amendment's equal protection clause and offered the school three options: (1) admit women; (2) establish an equivalent all-female program; or (3) transform the state-supported institute into a private school. In 1993 the U.S. Supreme Court let stand the Fourth Circuit's decision.[17]

The Citadel, the only other state-supported military college with an all-male admission policy, found itself in a similar litigation in the early 1990s when Shannon Faulkner, an eighteen-year-old female, filed suit to enter that institution. She had removed all references to her gender on her application, and The Citadel had unwittingly admitted her. It retracted its offer after discovering that she was a female. Pending further litigation, Chief Justice Rehnquist ordered The Citadel to permit Faulkner to take classes with, but not become a member of, the corps of cadets. Faulkner enrolled for the fall 1994 term but dropped out after only a few days at the school, citing mental and physical stress.

In 1996 the Supreme Court ruled 7:1, via Justice Ginsburg, that the 157-year-old VMI's all-male status, which was heavily state-funded, violated the equal protection clause of the Fourteenth Amendment. Ginsburg's majority opinion asserted that "[p]arties who seek to defend gender-based government action must demonstrate an 'exceedingly persuasive justification' for that action." Although the Court did not place gender classification in the "suspect" category, it came close to doing so by splitting the difference between "strict" and "height-

17. *Virginia Military Institute v. United States,* 61 LW 3786.

Table 8.1. Representative Decisions by the U.S. Supreme Court in Recent Gender-Based and Other Discrimination Cases

Case	Year Decided	Issue and Disposition	Vote	Dissents
Reed v. Reed, 404 U.S. 71	1971	State of Idaho gave preference to males in intestate administration. Declared a violation of the equal protection clause of the Fourteenth Amendment, based on the Court's "rationality" test.	7:0	None
Frontiero v. Richardson, 411 U.S. 677	1973	Federal law that automatically qualified male service personnel for spousal benefits but that required female personnel to show proof of dependency. Declared unconstitutional infringement of due-process clause of the Fifth Amendment, since Court found no "compelling" state interest.	8:1	Rehnquist
Kahn v. Shevin, 416 U.S. 351	1974	Florida law granting widows but not widowers $500 property-tax exemption. Declared constitutional because a woman's loss of spouse imposed greater financial disability usually than a man's loss of spouse.	6:3	Douglas Brennan Marshall
Geduldig v. Aiello, 417 U.S. 484	1974	State of California disability insurance payments to private employees not covered by workmen's compensation, excluding normal pregnancies, among other disabilities. Upheld as a rational choice by state.	6:3	Douglas Brennan Marshall
Schlesinger v. Ballard, 419 U.S. 498	1975	Federal law on mandatory navy discharges: women guaranteed 13 years of service; men automatically discharged after failing twice to be promoted. Upheld as rational because women have less opportunity for promotion.	5:4	Douglas Brennan Marshall
Taylor v. Louisiana, 419 U.S. 522	1975	Louisiana statutory and constitutional provision excluded women from juries unless they manifest a desire to serve via a written request. Declared unconstitutional as violation of equal protection clause of the Fourteenth Amendment.	8:1	Rehnquist
Stanton v. Stanton, 421 U.S. 7	1975	Utah law that provides for lower age of majority for girls than for boys in connection with parental obligation to pay child support. Struck down as "irrational" legislative action.	8:1	Rehnquist
Weinberger v. Wiesenfeld, 420 U.S. 636	1975	U.S. Social Security Act provision for payment of death benefits to surviving spouse and minor children in case of husband's death, but only to the latter in case of wife's demise. Struck down as violative of Fifth Amendment's due process of law guarantees.	8:0	None

Case	Year	Description	Vote	Dissenters
General Electric Co. v. Gilbert, 429 U.S. 125	1976	Private employer's disability plan excluded pregnancies from coverage. Upheld as not invidiously discriminatory under due process of law clause of the Fifth Amendment. (Later overturned in corrective legislation by Congress.)	6:3	Brennan Marshall Stevens
Craig v. Boren, 429 U.S. 190	1976	Oklahoma statute prohibiting sale of 3.2 percent beer to males under 21 years of age but to females only under 18. Held to be invidiously discriminatory under equal protection clause of the Fourteenth Amendment, the Court here introducing the "heightened scrutiny" test.	7:2	Burger Rehnquist
Califano v. Webster, 430 U.S. 313	1977	Section of federal Social Security Act providing that wives may exclude three more of their lower earning years in computing average wage for retirement benefits than husbands may. Upheld as "benign," not illogical, and thus not constitutionally defective. Cf. *Califano v. Goldfarb,* 430 U.S. 199 (1977).	9:0	None
Vorchheimer v. School District of Philadelphia 430 U.S. 703	1977	Philadelphia's existence of some "all-boy" and some "all-girl" public schools is permissible, provided enrollment is voluntary and quality is equal.	4:4	Brennan Marshall Blackmun Stevens
Nashville Gas Co. v. Satty, 434 U.S. 136	1977	Distinguishing *Gilbert,* above, Court holds that losing all accumulated seniority when returning to work after pregnancy violates Title VII of Civil Rights Act of 1964.	9:0	None
City of Los Angeles Department of Water v. Manhart, 435 U.S. 702	1978	Municipal regulation that required female employees to pay 15 percent more into pension fund than male employees because women are expected statistically to live longer than men. Declared unconstitutional as violation of equal protection of the laws clause of Amendment Fourteen.	6:2	Burger Rehnquist
Orr v. Orr, 440 U.S. 268	1979	Alabama law providing that husbands but not wives are liable to pay post-divorce alimony. Struck down as violation of equal protection clause of Fourteenth Amendment.	6:3	Burger Powell Rehnquist
Califano v. Westcott, 443 U.S. 76	1979	Section of federal Social Security Act providing benefits to needy dependent children only because of father's unemployment, not because of mother's. Struck down as violation of the due process clause of the Fifth Amendment.	9:0	None
Wengler v. Druggists Mutual Insurance Co., 446 U.S. 142	1980	Section of Missouri's workmen's compensation law that requires a husband to prove actual dependence on his spouse's earnings but does not require wife to prove such dependence. Declared unconstitutional as violation of the equal protection clause of the Fourteenth Amendment.	8:1	Rehnquist

(continued)

Table 8.1. (continued)

Case	Year Decided	Issue and Disposition	Vote	Dissents
Michael M. v. Superior Court, 450 U.S. 464	1981	California statutory rape law punishing males, but not females, for sexual intercourse with an underage partner of the opposite sex upheld as not irrational because "only women may become pregnant." Law defines unlawful sexual intercourse as "an act of sexual intercourse accomplished with a female not the wife of the perpetrator where the female is under the age of 18."	5:4	Brennan White Marshall Stevens
Rostker v. Goldberg, 453 U.S. 57	1981	Draft Registration Act of 1980, confined to males. See text below for discussion.	6:3	Brennan White Marshall
McCarty v. McCarty, 453 U.S. 210	1981	Federal law to preserve regular and reserve commissioned officers' military pensions as the service member's "personal entitlement" not subject to being considered for anyone else's benefit in a property or divorce settlement. (Later overturned by corrective legislation by Congress.)	6:3	Brennan Stewart Rehnquist
Kirchberg v. Feenstra, 450 U.S. 455	1981	Louisiana law giving husband the unilateral right to dispose of property jointly owned by husband and wife declared unconstitutional as invidious discrimination by gender.	9:0	None
Mississippi University for Women v. Hogan, 458 U.S. 718	1982	Single-sex public institution of higher learning discriminates against males. See text below for discussion (including the 1996 VMI decision of *United States v. Virginia,* 518 U.S. 515).	5:4	Blackmun Powell Rehnquist Burger
Arizona v. Norris, 464 U.S. 808	1983	Title VII of Civil Rights Act of 1964, which outlaws employment discrimination on the basis of both race and sex, requires employees to be treated as individuals rather than as members of a group (here women's level of pensions).	5:4	Burger Blackmun Powell Rehnquist
Roberts v. U.S. Jaycees, 465 U.S. 555	1984	Rejecting freedom of association argument by the Jaycees, Court rules through Brennan that the "large and basically unselective" nature of the organization could not vitiate Minnesota's law forbidding discrimination in "public accommodations." (See text, above, for discussion.)	7:0	None
Hishon v. King & Spaulding, 467 U.S. 69	1984	The no-gender-discrimination mandate of Title VII of the Civil Rights Act of 1964 reaches the issue of promotion of lawyers to the status of partners in a law firm. Burger's opinion overturns two federal court holdings to the contrary, rejects the argument that "partners" are not "employees" under Title VII and should therefore not be covered by its terms. Also turned aside freedom-of-association claims.	9:0	None

Case	Year	Description	Vote	Dissents
Grove City College v. Bell, 465 U.S. 555	1984	Title IX of the Federal Education Act of 1972 subjects noncompliant institutions to federal fund cutoffs, since any aid to students constitutes aid to their colleges. However, the law's verbiage "any educational program or activity receiving federal financial assistance" means only the specific program of a college and not the entire institution. The holding was reaffirmed 6:3 in 1986 in *Department of Transportation v. Paralyzed Vets of America,* 477 U.S. 597. (But Congress took corrective action in 1988 over President Reagan's veto with the enactment of its "Civil Rights Restoration Act.")	6:3	Brennan Marshall Stevens
Meritor Savings Bank v. Vinson, 477 U.S. 57	1986	The Court here extended protection against sexual harassment, holding that lewd statements, sexual conduct, and certain other actions violated a woman's civil rights if the actions created "a hostile work environment" that made it difficult for her to perform her job.	9:0	None
California Savings & Loan Association v. Guerra, 479 U.S. 272	1987	Upheld a California law requiring employers to grant up to four months of unpaid leave to women "disabled" by pregnancy and childbirth, even if similar leaves are not granted for other disabilities. Dissenters saw a violation of the 1978 federal law prohibiting employers from treating pregnant employees differently from other employees who are "similar in their ability or inability to work."	6:3	White Rehnquist Powell
Johnson v. Transportation Agency of Santa Clara County, 480 U.S. 616	1987	Civil Rights Act of 1964 permits employers to promote a woman over a more qualified man. See text below for discussion.	6:3	Rehnquist White Scalia
Board of Directors of Rotary International v. Rotary Club of Duarte, 481 U.S. 537	1987	Decision similar to *Roberts,* above: states may outlaw gender discrimination by certain types of private clubs. See text, above, for discussion.	7:0	None
New York State Club Ass'n. v. City of New York, 487 U.S. 1	1988	Upheld New York City ordinance (against facial challenge) that prohibits discrimination based on race, creed, or sex by institutions, except benevolent orders or religious ones, with more than 400 members that provide regular meal service and require payment from nonmembers for "the furtherance of trade or business." (See above, this chapter.) Reconfirmed implicitly in a 1989 case (*Burning Tree Club v. Maryland,* 493 U.S. 816) and in 1991 in its refusal to review the New Jersey Supreme Court's order requiring the all-male Princeton Tiger Inn club to admit women (*Tiger Inn v. Frank,* 498 U.S. 1073).	9:0	None

(continued)

Table 8.1. *(continued)*

Case	Year Decided	Issue and Disposition	Vote	Dissents
Watson v. Fort Worth Bank and Trust, 487 U.S. 977	1988	In a further expansion of federal antidiscrimination law, the justices rendered it easier for women and minorities to prove discrimination in hiring or promotions by ruling that employers' "subjective" decisions need not prove intentional discrimination. Instead, they may use statistical evidence showing "underrepresentation" of women and minorities in the workplace. (But contrast *Wards Cove Packing Co. v. Atonio,* 490 U.S. 642 [1989], below, this chapter.)	8:0	None
Price Waterhouse v. Hopkins, 490 U.S. 228	1989	Significantly altering the burden of proof plantiffs must carry to prevail in many lawsuits based on alleged sex (and race and age) discrimination, the Court ruled that once a woman presents evidence that she was denied promotion because of illegal "sex stereotyping," it is up to the employer to prove by a "preponderance of evidence" that there were other legitimate reasons for denying the promotion. (But compare *Wards Cove Packing Co. v. Atonio,* 490 U.S. 642 [1989], this chapter.) On remand, U.S. District Court Judge Gerhard Gesell ruled that Price Waterhouse had not met its burden (737 F. Supp. 1203 [1990]).	6:3	Kennedy Rehnquist Scalia
International Union, United Auto Workers v. Johnson Controls, 499 U.S. 187	1991	Employers may not arbitrarily exclude all women of childbearing age from jobs in which exposure to toxic substances could harm a developing fetus— notwithstanding fears of possible lawsuits.	9:0	None
Franklin v. Gwinnett County Public, Schools, 503 U.S. 60	1992	Students who are victims of sexual harassment and other forms of sex discrimination have the right to win money damages from schools that receive federal funds.	9:0	None
St. Mary's Honor Center v. Hicks, 509 U.S. 502	1993	Employees endeavoring to prove illegal job discrimination under Title VII of the Civil Rights Act of 1964, as amended (relating to race, sex, religion, and national origin), must furnish "direct evidence" of discrimination (not merely, for example, that an employer is lying).	5:4	Souter White Blackmun Stevens
Harris v. Forklift Systems, 510 U.S. 17	1993	An allegedly sexually harassed employee need not prove that he or she was injured "psychologically" in order to win money damages. The Court generally defined unlawful harassment as creating a work environment that a reasonable person would find "hostile or abusive." In a footnote to her brief concurring opinion, Justice Ruth Bader Ginsburg reraised the question whether classifications based on gender are inherently suspect.	9:0	None

Case	Year		Vote	Dissenters
J.E.B. v. Alabama ex rel. T.B., 511 U.S. 127	1994	Neither prosecutors nor the defense may use peremptory challenges to disqualify potential jurors because of gender (sex).	6:3	Scalia Rehnquist Thomas
NOW v. Scheidler, 510 U.S. 249	1994	Utilization of the federal RICO statute's application does not require an "economic motive" to be applicable to regulations governing abortion clinic picketing.	9:0	None
United States v. Virginia, 518 U.S. 515	1996	The Equal Protection Clause of the Fourteenth Amendment does not permit the exclusion of women from the 157-year-old, all-male Virginia Military Institute, a heavily state-supported institution. "Either admit women or go private" was the "heightened scrutiny" (plus "exceedingly persuasive justification") standard of review mandate, penned by Justice Ginsburg.	7:1	Scalia
Oncale v. Sundowner Offshore Services, 523 U.S. 75	1998	A federal law against sexual harassment on the job covers misconduct even when the victim and the harasser are of the same sex (here male).	9:0	None
Faragher v. Boca Raton, 524 U.S. 742	1998	An employer may well be liable for sexual advances, harassment, or other sexual discrimination by a supervisor—even if unaware of specific offense(s).	7:2	Thomas Scalia
Gebser v. Lago Vista Independent School Dist., 524 U.S. 274	1998	Students may not be awarded money damages in a sexual harassment suit unless a district school official knows of the misconduct and does nothing about it.	5:4	Stevens Ginsburg Souter Breyer
Miller v. Albright, 523 U.S. 410	1998	Federal law may favor the mother over the father in bestowing natural derivative citizenship.	6:3	Ginsburg Breyer Souter
Davis v. Monroe Co. School Bd., 526 U.S. 574	1999	If public schools are "deliberately indifferent," they can be sued and forced to pay damages for failing to stop sexual harassment by students.	5:4	Kennedy Rehnquist Scalia Thomas
Kolstad v. American Dental Association, 67 LW 4522	1999	Job-bias victims (here a promotion dispute) can collect so-called punitive damages from employers without having to show that their employer's conduct was "egregious" (9:0). But (6:3) employers cannot be forced to pay such damages if a manager's discriminatory conduct runs counter to the employer's good-faith efforts to run a bias-free workplace.	9:0 6:3	None Stevens Souter Ginsburg

(continued)

Table 8.1. (continued)

Case	Year Decided	Issue and Disposition	Vote	Dissents
United States v. Morrison and *Brzonkala v. Morrison*, 529 U.S. 598	2000	The Federal Violence Against Women Act's subtitle C could not create a federal civil remedy, on top of existing state remedies, for violence (here alleged rape) motivated by gender-based animus. Rehnquist's majority opinion struck down the VAWA provision, which had been enacted under Congress's interstate commerce power, because it went beyond that power's parameter and interfered with the state's (here Virginia's) authority. "Gender-motivated crimes" are not the kind of economic activity covered by Congress's interstate commerce power. Moreover, Congress may not utilize the enforcement clause of the Fourteenth Amendment to regulate *private* actions and conduct, for the Amendment only reaches *state* action.	5:4	Souter Stevens Ginsburg Breyer
Boy Scouts of America v. Dale, 530 U.S. 640	2000	Based on the right of all Americans to "freedom of expressive association," Rehnquist ruled for the Court that the Boy Scouts have the right to bar gay men from becoming scout leaders and, by extension, bar gay boys from joining the scouting ranks.	5:4	Stevens Souter Ginsburg Breyer
PGA Tour v. Martin, 532 U.S. 731	2001	The 1990 Americans with Disabilities Act requires the PGA to waive its requirement that players *walk* the golf course during tournament play. The surprisingly expansive Stevens-authored opinion held that Title III of the ADA prohibits the PGA from denying Martin (who suffers from a debilitating circulatory disease in his legs) equal access to the tournaments, via a cart.	7:2	Scalia Thomas
Alabama v. Garrett, 531 U.S. 356	2001	Congress has no constitutional authority to subject *states* to lawsuits in *federal* court, on pain of violating the Eleventh Amendment, for damages allegedly sustained by employees on the job. The ADA does not reach such claims. (See also a related 5:4 2001 ruling, in *Alexander v. Sandoval*, 532 U.S. ___, here involving a Title VI claim under the Civil Rights Act of 1964.)	5:4	Stevens Souter Ginsburg Breyer
Clark Co. School Dist. v. Breeden, 532 U.S. ___	2001	Alleged victims of sexual harassment (here a single, smart-aleck verbal comment) may sue under Title VII of the 1964 Civil Rights Act *only* if the alleged harassment "is so severe or pervasive as to alter the conditions of the victim's employment and create an abusive working environment."	9:0	Per curiam

ened" scrutiny in equal protection analysis. The lone dissenter was Justice Scalia, who argued that the Court's ruling would jeopardize even private single-gender institutions. (Justice Thomas had recused himself because his son attended VMI.) The decision applied to The Citadel as well and disallowed a separate "leadership" program for women at Mary Baldwin College that had been established in cooperation with VMI.[18] The Citadel immediately made plans to admit women in the fall of 1996, and four females enrolled that term. Yet two refused to return for the spring 1997 semester, alleging that they had been harassed by their fellow cadets, some of whom doused them with flammable liquid, which ignited their clothing. VMI initially balked at the Court's ruling and considered going private. It relented, however, and began recruiting female applicants for the fall of 1997, but it vowed to maintain its tough adversative approach to educating young cadets. As soon as they became eligible, by virtue of their third-year status at the institute, women became part of the school's elite "cadre," which actually administers the adversative training of "rats," proving that women could not only take adversity but also "dish it out." And in May 2001 thirteen women, of the first thirty who had enrolled at VMI in 1997, graduated from the tradition-bound school. The male and female dropout rates over four years were nearly equal.[19]

Table 8.1 demonstrates that the Court has, in general, followed the test developed in *Craig v. Boren,* but it has not been unwilling to apply the *Reed* rationale when it has seemed appropriate. (The ultimate impact of the *V.M.I. Case*'s "exceedingly persuasive justification" standard is, as yet, unknown.) Consequently, as the plethora of successive decisions amply manifests, while the vast majority of holdings in the cascading number of cases on the gender discrimination front has favored claims of invidious gender discrimination, rulings *permitting* differences based on sex are not unknown. Among them have been the following: Florida (1974) may grant widows but not widowers a $500 tax exemption, because a woman's loss of a husband normally imposes a greater financial disability than a man's loss of a wife;[20] the U.S. Navy (1975) may guarantee female officers thirteen years of service, whereas men are automatically discharged after twice failing of promotion, because women have less opportunity for promotion;[21] Philadelphia (1977) may have "all-boy" and "all-girl" public schools, provided that enrollment is voluntary and the quality of instruction is equal;[22] the federal Social Security Act (1977) may permit wives to exclude three more of their lower-earning years in computing the average wage for

18. *United States v. Virginia,* 518 U.S. 515.

19. Josh White, "Loud and Clear at VMI: 'Yes, Ma'am!'" *Washington Post,* August 9, 1999, p. B1; Lisa Rein, "13 Women in VMI's First Coed Class Will Graduate Today," *Washington Post,* May 19, 2001, p. B1.

20. *Kahn v. Shevin,* 416 U.S. 351.

21. *Schlesinger v. Ballard,* 419 U.S. 498.

22. *Vorchheimer v. School District of Philadelphia,* 430 U.S. 703.

retirement benefits than may husbands, because of the "historical disparity in earning power";[23] a California law (1981) that punishes males but not females for statutory rape (under eighteen) is considered permissible and not irrational, because "only women may become pregnant."[24] But a glance at Table 8.1 will quickly indicate that, especially of late, few differences based on sex have been Court-sanctioned. One that was, and deserves special notice, is the Draft Registration Act of 1980.

Draft Registration: Rostker v. Goldberg.[25] The contentious enactment of the draft registration statute of 1980, which specifically *excluded* women, created natural controversy by friend and foe of sexual equality alike, all of which tended to blur lines between otherwise predictable supporters and opponents of legislative classification by gender. A major class-action suit was filed almost instantly in federal court by a group of *male* registrants, alleging invidious sex discrimination. *Either,* so their argument went, the exclusion of women constitutes a violation of their Fifth Amendment constitutional rights of due process of law ("equal protection" per se not being applicable because it is confined to *state* infractions under the Fourteenth Amendment) *or* it constitutes a violation of the rights of *males* because they are being "singled out." The Court's answer came in June 1981. Speaking through Justice Rehnquist, who applied the heightened scrutiny test developed in *Craig v. Boren*—although, in a dissenting role, he had rejected it there—it ruled (6:3) that the registration provisions excluding women do not violate the Fifth Amendment; that Congress acted well within its constitutional authority to raise and regulate armies and navies. Noting that Congress had already acted to bar women from combat roles, the majority insisted that the "customary deference" accorded Congress's judgments is "particularly appropriate" in national defense and military affairs. Dissenting, Justices Brennan, White, and Marshall contended that the *complete* exclusion of women was not a valid governmental objective and thus violated the due process of law guarantees of both sexes.

Brennan and Marshall were the only dissenters when the Court ruled (6:2) three years later that a much-debated law, which required male college students to register for the draft if they wish to obtain federal financial aid, was constitutional as "a plainly rational means to improve compliance with the registration requirements" (which had been flouted by a sizable number of potential registrants).[26] The application of the registration statute itself and prosecution thereunder was upheld (7:2) in early 1985, again with Justices Brennan and Marshall

---

23. *Califano v. Webster,* 430 U.S. 213.
24. *Michael M. v. Superior Court,* 450 U.S. 464.
25. 453 U.S. 57 (1981).
26. *Selective Service System v. Minnesota Public Interest Resource Group,* 468 U.S. 841 (1984).

in dissent, here on grounds of First Amendment freedom of expression as well as Fifth Amendment due process of law.[27]

The 1980s and 1990s witnessed a spate of decisions—but as yet with far from yardstick preciseness—to come to definitional terms in the contentious realm of on-the-job or job-related sexual harassment. Three holdings in mid-1998 and one in 1999 attempted to point the way more clearly (see Table 8.1). Perhaps the most notable of these was *Oncale v. Sundowner Offshore Service,*[28] where the Court, speaking unanimously through Justice Scalia, ruled that sexual harassment on the job emphatically covers misconduct even when the victim and the harasser are of the same sex, here male.

THE 1973 ABORTION DECISIONS AND THEIR OFFSPRING

If any Supreme Court ruling lies at the center of gravity of the success of the feminist movement, it is that tribunal's seminal holding in the now legendary *Abortion Cases* of *Roe v. Wade* and *Doe v. Bolton.*[29] Already analyzed briefly in connection with the developing law of privacy,[30] the two decisions did not, like the vast majority of the aforementioned or discussed gender discrimination cases, turn on claims of violation of the equal protection of the laws. Rather, the basic rights they created on that Opinion Day in 1973 were based upon the newly articulated (largely Justice Douglas–developed) right of privacy in the Ninth Amendment, coupled with the due process of law commands of the Fourteenth Amendment (and, by implication, of the Fifth Amendment on the federal level). When the two controversial decisions were handed down, abortion law was already in a state of flux and change throughout the several states of the nation. Liberalization of state abortion laws, as the Court's opinion, written by Justice Blackmun, recognized, had been well under way for some time. However, a well-organized, highly vocal "right-to-life" movement had begun to succeed in either delaying or even reversing that tide, and criminal abortion statutes remained on the books of many a state.

The *Roe* and *Doe* decisions, which instantly became and remain a veritable constitutional, legal, medical, sociological, anthropological, social, religious, moral, psychological, and—markedly—political storm center, personify women's civil rights strivings. Justice Blackmun's opinion for the 7:2 Court—which took two years to compose—frankly recognized "the sensitive and emotional nature of the abortion controversy, of the vigorous opposing views, even among physicians, and of the deep and seemingly absolute convictions that the

27. *Wayte v. United States,* 470 U.S. 598.
28. 523 U.S. 75.
29. 410 U.S. 113 and 410 U.S. 179, respectively.
30. See *supra* chapter 3.

subject inspires." Indeed, six of the nine justices were moved to pen opinions, four on the side of the majority (Blackmun, Burger, Stewart, and Douglas) and two in dissent (White and Rehnquist). Justice Blackmun's controlling opinion for the Court held that the right to personal privacy includes the abortion decision, but he acknowledged that this right is not unqualified and must be considered against important state regulatory interests. On the other hand, he made it clear that such a "fundamental right" as abortion may be limited by the state only in the face of a "compelling state interest" and that "legislative enactments must be narrowly drawn to express only the legitimate state interests at stake. . . ." He concluded that the Texas and Georgia abortion control statutes in front of the Court failed that basic test by "sweeping too broadly." Over Justice White's outcry that the decisions constituted "an exercise of raw judicial power," and that by Justice Rehnquist that there is no such thing as the right of "privacy" involved in the matter at issue, the lengthy Blackmun opinion, replete with references to medical science, biology, psychology, and history, ultimately neatly summarizes the pioneering constitutional holding as follows:

> (a) For the stage prior to approximately the end of the first trimester [of the pregnancy], the abortion decision and its effectuation must be left to the medical judgment of the pregnant woman's physician.
> (b) For the stage subsequent to approximately the end of the first trimester, the State, in promoting its interest in the health of the mother, may, if it chooses, regulate the abortion procedure in ways that are reasonably related to maternal health.
> (c) For the stage subsequent to viability the State, in promoting its interest in the potentiality of human life, may, if it chooses, regulate, and even proscribe, abortion except where it is necessary, in appropriate medical judgment, for the preservation of the life or health of the mother.[31]

That the creation of what opponents have called a "national abortion code created by judicial fiat rather than by legislative action" would spawn a torrent of attacks on a host of judicial, legislative, and executive fronts[32] is hardly astonishing. Yet, in essence, the basic right to abort remains constitutionally protected, notwithstanding a plethora of cases before the Court, eight new justices on it, and the passage of over three decades. Nevertheless, changes in the Court's personnel have resulted in the tribunal's increased willingness to accept legislative forays in the abortion realm.

That proved to be the case when Justice Powell's replacement, Anthony M. Kennedy, joined the other two Reagan appointees, Sandra Day O'Connor and Antonin Scalia, plus the two dissenters in *Roe* in July 1989 on the last day of the term. Without overruling that crucial decision, the Court nonetheless made clear

31. *Roe v. Wade,* 410 U.S. 113 at 164.
32. See *supra* chapter 3.

that it would henceforth be much more hospitable than heretofore to efforts by the states to enact provisions restrictive of abortions. By a 5:4 vote it thus upheld a series of the latter by Missouri in *Webster v. Reproductive Health Services,*[33] and the several opinions on the victorious side gave promise of possible further chipping away at the original *Roe* holding. The Court docketed three new abortion issue cases for 1989–90, but the immediate battleground would now lie at the state level in the political arena. It did, indeed, and a spate of state activities ensued, punctuated by the Court's anticipated rulings in 1990 on the three alluded-to cases. In two 5:4 opinions and one 6:3, the justices ruled (1) that a Minnesota law requiring pregnant teenagers to inform *both* parents before obtaining an abortion was unconstitutional, but (2) that such a law could pass constitutional muster if it gives minors the option to ask a judge to waive the notification requirement (known as "judicial bypass"), which Minnesota provided as an alternative; and (3) that Ohio's law regulating notification of *one* parent, while also allowing a judicial bypass, was constitutional.[34] A 1991 decision upholding (5:4) a ban against abortion advice by federally funded family planning clinics was hotly but unsuccessfully contested on First (freedom of speech) and Fifth Amendment (due process of law) grounds.[35] In 1999 the Court refused to review, and thus upheld, Virginia's parental notification statute, which requires unmarried women under eighteen, and not living on their own, to notify one parent at least twenty-four hours before having an abortion.[36]

The end of the Court's 1991–92 term in June then saw a landmark development on the abortion litigation front: defying predictions that its "Reagan-Bush majority" would overrule *Roe v. Wade,* the Court adopted a middle-ground approach that sanctions restrictions on abortion, such as the four of five enacted by Pennsylvania at issue in the case, unless they impose an "undue burden" on a woman's right to choose—while repeatedly reaffirming what the five-member majority called the "central holding" of *Roe,* namely, that a woman's choice of whether to terminate her pregnancy is based upon the prerogative of a constitutionally protected personal liberty.[37] However, the controlling opinion penned jointly (an unusual practice) by Justices O'Connor, Kennedy, and Souter—with Kennedy's vote representing a reversal of his *Webster* posture—abandoned *Roe*'s trimester criterion in favor of the "undue burden" test. The Court defined such a "burden" as one that "has the purpose or effect of placing a *substantial* obstacle

---

33. 492 U.S. 490.

34. *Hodgson v. Minnesota I* and *II* and *Ohio v. Akron Center of Reproductive Health,* 497 U.S. 417 and 497 U.S. 502, respectively. But a South Dakota law that lacked the judicial bypass option fell 6:3 in 1996 (*Janklow v. Planned Parenthood,* 64 LW 3724).

35. *Rust v. Sullivan,* 500 U.S. 173.

36. *Planned Parenthood v. Camblos,* 67 LW 350 (1999).

37. *Planned Parenthood of Pennsylvania v. Casey,* 505 U.S. 833 (1992). Also see *Ada v. Guam Society of Obstetricians and Gynecologists,* certiorari denied, 506 U.S. 1011 (1992).

in the path of a woman seeking an abortion of a nonviable fetus."[38] Applying the test in this case, the Court upheld, for example, the twenty-four-hour waiting period for women seeking abortions but rejected the spousal notification provision of the Pennsylvania statute. Heavily emphasizing perceived obligations of precedent, the controlling trio also appeared to abandon *Roe*'s central emphasis on the privacy component of the Ninth Amendment in favor of one based on the "liberty" component of the Fourteenth Amendment's due process of law clause. Justice Blackmun, although joining the governing trio to render the victorious majority, would have simply affirmed *Roe* and struck down all of Pennsylvania's enactments. His colleague Stevens, who also dissented, did so only in part: he voted to uphold two of the five Pennsylvania provisions. The four dissenters, in two opinions by Chief Justice Rehnquist and Justice Scalia, joined by Justices White (who, together with Rehnquist had been the two *Roe* dissenters almost twenty years earlier) and Thomas would have overturned *Roe*. "We believe that *Roe* was wrongly decided," wrote the chief justice, and that "it can and should be overturned consistently with our traditional approach to stare decisis in constitutional cases." And in his separate opinion, signed by all three of his colleagues in the minority, Justice Scalia flayed the Court's majority opinion as "a new mode of constitutional adjudication that relies not upon text and traditional practice to determine the law, but upon what the Court calls 'reasoned judgment' which turns out to be nothing but philosophical predilection and moral intuition." In 1997 the Court let stand, with an unsigned opinion, Montana's law forbidding physician assistants to carry out abortions. By a 6:3 vote, the justices ruled that restricting the performance of abortions to licensed physicians did not constitute an "undue burden" on women.[39] That the Court is not eager to revisit the abortion syndrome frequently was again demonstrated by its 6:3 sidestepping of the "late-term abortion" issue in 1998.[40] However, it bit the proverbial bullet two years later, ruling 5:4 that Nebraska's "late term" or "partial birth" prohibition constituted an "undue burden" on a woman's right to choose the procedure. The Court's liberal quartet (Stevens, Souter, Ginsburg, and Breyer) triumphed by virtue of Justice O'Connor's concurrence.[41]

Not all of the goals of the women's movement have been achieved, yet enormous strides have been taken toward the eradication of invidious gender discrimination. Although increased publicity about alleged sexual harassment indicates that much still remains to be done,[42] the improvements that have

38. Italics supplied.

39. *Mazurek v. Armstrong,* 520 U.S. 968.

40. *Voinovich v. Women's Medical Professional Corporation,* 66 LW 3619. Justices Scalia and Thomas and Chief Justice Rehnquist dissented from the denial of certiorari in the case.

41. *Stenberg v. Carhart,* 530 U.S. 914 (2000).

42. The 1991 televised Senate Judiciary Committee hearings investigating the sexual harassment charges by University of Oklahoma law professor Anita Hill against U.S.

characterized the past two decades are proof positive of genuine achievements on the egalitarian agenda. The absence of the ERA has not stifled or truncated the continuing commitment to the enhancement of women's rights, and a glance at the demonstrably significant gains achieved on a host of fronts—economic, social, legal, and political—underscores that fact. Testimony to the economic realm is the following set of statistics: as of mid-1996 there were 7,790,000 companies owned by women, up 78 percent from 4,480,000 in 1987. In 1980 their sales were $25 *billion;* by 1996 they had risen to $2.25 *trillion.* On the educational front, in 1960, only 19 percent of bachelor's degrees were awarded to women. One third of a century later, women received 55 percent of BAs and 54 percent of MAs. Such visible political triumphs as, for example, a vice-presidential candidate in 1984 (Geraldine Ferraro); appointments to the U.S. Supreme Court in 1981 and 1993 (Sandra Day O'Connor and Ruth Bader Ginsburg, respectively); 20 percent of the federal courts of appeals judgeships in 2002; in 1997 the first woman secretary of state (Madeleine K. Albright); 20 members of cabinets under Presidents Carter, Reagan, Bush I, Clinton, and Bush II as of 2001 (*all* states had women heading cabinet-level agencies by 1991); 35 percent of state leadership positions in 2001, including several governors and mayors of a number of our largest cities (e.g., Dallas, San Francisco, Chicago, Houston, Washington, D.C., and Pittsburgh); 72 (up from 27 in 1992) members of Congress (59 representatives and 13 senators in 2001); 25,000 elective posts overall, including some 1,900 state legislators (2001); 2,850 women jurists, 80 of these on the states' highest courts, 10 as chief justices (2001); numerous college and university presidencies (including the University of Chicago, Duke University, the University of Pennsylvania, and the University of Wisconsin); deanships of prestigious law schools (e.g., Columbia, Stanford, and Georgetown Universities)—all point to progress. The latter will unquestionably continue. And it is clear that in considerable measure the nation's commitment to "affirmative action" programs, however controversial and embattled they may be, has played a major role in the quest for equality in the universes of both gender and race.

Supreme Court Justice nominee Clarence Thomas shocked the nation and created a new awareness of such conduct. Although Hill's charges were never proved and Thomas was ultimately, albeit narrowly, confirmed by the Senate, the ensuing debates over proper relations between men and women in the workplace continued, fueled by the highly publicized investigation of the navy's Tailhook scandal and disclosures that Senator Bob Packwood (R.-Ore.) allegedly made unwanted advances toward women with whom he worked. In the spring of 1993 the U.S. Supreme Court granted certiorari to the first major sexual harassment case to come to the high tribunal since the Hill-Thomas hearings. In *Harris v. Forklift Systems,* 510 U.S. 17, the Court decided unanimously that a woman may win a sexual harassment case if she was subjected to conduct that would have offended a reasonable victim, that she does not need to prove "severe psychological injury" in order to recover damages.

A Note on the Americans with Disabilities Act (ADA) of 1990. Enacted under the leadership of Senators Ted Kennedy (D.-Mass.), Robert Dole (R.-Kans.), and Tom Harkin (D.-Iowa), the complicated but significant statute has occupied a growing share of the federal courts' dockets since it became the law of the land in 1990. During the first six years of its existence, 108,939 complaints were filed with the Equal Employment Opportunity Commission (EEOC), their gravamen being the presence of "impairment" of an individual's job performance, owing to sight, hearing, learning, locomotion, or emotional disability. In accordance with the law's provisions, a plaintiff claiming "impairment" must demonstrate that while its presence "substantially" limits a major life activity, an employer's "reasonable accommodation" of it would render the employee qualified to perform the job at issue. The impairments most frequently claimed in cases reaching the EEOC—and ultimately the courts—have been, in declining numbers of filings: back problems, emotional/psychiatric, neurological, extremities, heart, diabetes, substance abuse, hearing, blood disorders, vision, cancer, asthma.[43]

In reviewing the bevy of cases that have worked their way through the federal system to the Supreme Court of the United States, it would be accurate to conclude that, in general, the EEOC has been generous in finding for plaintiffs, whereas the highest tribunal in the land has narrowed or limited the scope of the ADA in rulings ranging from 9:0 to 6:3 against plaintiffs. Thus, in six recent cases between mid-1999 and mid-2002 the Court held as follows: 7:2, that United Airlines could require uncorrected vision of 20-100; 9:0, that a commercial truck driver would have to meet tough vision requirements; 7:2, that UPS's blood pressure standards were not unreasonable in the case of a mechanic; 6:3, that Georgia could not be compelled to reject the pleas of an individual with a borderline mental disorder and those of another, mildly retarded and diagnosed as schizophrenic, to be moved from a state mental hospital in Atlanta to a community-based care facility; 9:0, that an "impairment" must have a "substantial effect" on a person's daily life to qualify as a "disability" under the ADA; and 7:2 (5:2:2), that the ADA does not normally require companies to bend their seniority rules so disabled employees can have particular jobs.[44]

There is little doubt that claims under the statute will continue apace. Whether ameliorative action by Congress might be forthcoming in order to reinterpret the semantically contentious law is highly conjectural, at best.

---

43. See statistics supplied by the EEOC to the *Washington Post,* June 23, 1999, pp. A1 and A10.

44. Respectively, *Sutton v. United Airlines,* 527 U.S. 471 (1999); *Albertsons v. Kirkingsburg,* 529 U.S. 555 (1999); *Murphy v. United Parcel Service,* 527 U.S. 516 (1999); *Olmstead v. L.C.,* 527 U.S. 581 (1999); *Toyota v. Williams,* 534 U.S. 184 (2002); and *United States v. Barnett,* 535 U.S. ___ (2002).

THE WRENCH OF "AFFIRMATIVE ACTION"
AND "REVERSE DISCRIMINATION"

As the history of the post–World War II period, especially the post–*Brown I* and *II*[45] days, has demonstrated incontestably, the advances in the desegregation-integration and gender realms have been as widespread and evident as they have been gratifying. The nation, led by the judiciary, then joined by the executive and legislative branches, acknowledged the injustices of the past and proceeded, however gradually at first, to make amends.

Yet much remains to be done, in particular on the economic frontier. It is thus hardly surprising that the 1960s and, more insistently, the 1970s and 1980s would bring demands from blacks, as well as other minority groups and, of course, women that programs be established, both in and out of government, that would go well beyond "mere" equality of opportunity and provide compensatory treatment for the injustices of three centuries by commitments not only to remedial action but to outright preferment on a host of fronts, headed by employment and education. Known as "affirmative action"[46] to bring about increased employment opportunities, promotions, and admission to colleges and universities for minorities and women, the programs soon became controversial because of their use of *quotas,* particularly racial quotas, also called "goals" and/or "guidelines." In other words, the basic plea, along with the philosophy of the *proponents* of affirmative action, was (and is) that it is not enough to provide a full measure of absolute equality of opportunity, based upon *individual* merit. Given the ravages of the past, preferential treatment, so its proponents argue, must be accorded through affirmative action that, in effect, all but guarantees numerically targeted slots or posts based upon membership in racial (and gender) *groups.* The *opponents* of such a course of public and, to a lesser degree, private policy do not necessarily object to affirmative action per se — such as aggressive recruiting, remedial training (no matter what the expense), and perhaps even what Justice Powell in the *Bakke* case styled "plus" consideration of race along with other equitable factors in admissions to educational institutions. For while he stated that race or ethnicity could be a "plus" factor in consideration of a particular applicant, race or ethnicity should "not insulate the individual from comparison with all other candidates for the available seats."[47] Hence opponents do object to preferential policies that may be regarded as "reverse discrimination," generally

---

45. *Brown v. Board of Education of Topeka,* 347 U.S. 483 (1954) and 349 U.S. 294 (1955)—commonly referred to as *Brown I* and *Brown II.*

46. Although affirmative action's genesis is usually credited to LBJ's administration (1963–68), it was actually Richard Nixon who, as president in his first term (1969–73), approved the first federal initiative—the so-called Philadelphia Plan—requiring contractors to institute goals and timetables, and indeed quotas, to all intents and purposes, for minority hiring as a precondition for obtaining federal contracts.

47. *Regents of the University of California v. Bakke,* 438 U.S. 265 (1978) at 317.

comprehending the *numerus clausus* (rigid quotas set aside to benefit identifiable racial or other groups), as in the *Weber* case;[48] double standards in grading, rating, ranking, admissions, job placement, promotions, dismissals, and similar requirements on the employment, educational, and other pertinent thresholds of opportunity; and so-called set-aside laws that guarantee specified percentages of contracts to minority groups, as in the *Fullilove, Croson, Metro Broadcasting,* and *Adarand* cases.[49]

The Bakke Case. It was a foregone conclusion that, sooner or later, the reverse discrimination issue(s) would reach the Supreme Court—especially in view of what seems to be the proscriptive intent of the Fourteenth Amendment with respect to race; judicial precedents pointing to "color blindness"; and, perhaps most clearly, the ringing mandates of both the language and the intent of the seminal Civil Rights Act of 1964, in general, and Titles VI and VII, in particular.[50] As described earlier, the high tribunal was far from eager to come to grips with this explosive, emotion-charged, delicate, and vexatious issue, and it had managed to moot it in its nondecision *De Funis* decision of 1974.[51] But events would not be denied, and the nine justices confronted on its merits—more or less—the reverse discrimination aspect of affirmative action for the first time in the now historic *Bakke* case of 1978. Yet the long-in-coming ruling provided neither clear-cut "winners" nor clear-cut "losers"—and that may well be precisely what the justices intended. Still, disappointment by friends, foes, and neutrals was widespread, for very little was in fact settled finally by *Bakke.* The verbose opinions that were handed down were seriously divided—a stark contrast to the brief, unanimous decision in the seminal *Brown I* and *II* cases[52] a quarter of a century earlier. Still, the multiple, seven-opinion, 154-page judgments did spell out some basics, although the case neither settled, nor did it pretend to settle, the ongoing controversy at issue.

Essentially, and summarily, three identifiable groups of justices rendered at least three different opinions; the two controlling ones were fashioned by the swing vote of the key justice in the case, Lewis F. Powell Jr.—who considered it the most important opinion he penned during his fifteen years on the Court.[53] In

48. *United Steelworkers of America v. Weber,* 443 U.S. 193 (1979).

49. *Fullilove v. Klutznick,* 448 U.S. 448 (1980); *City of Richmond v. J. A. Croson Co.,* 488 U.S. 469 (1989); *Metro Broadcasting v. FCC,* 497 U.S. 547 (1990); and *Adarand Constructors v. Peña,* 515 U.S. 200 (1995).

50. See *supra* chapter 7 for the act's main titles and commentary.

51. See *supra* chapter 7.

52. See *supra* chapter 7.

53. In his *Behind Bakke: Affirmative Action and the Supreme Court* (New York: New York University Press, 1988), Bernard Schwartz credits the persuasive lobbying by Justice Brennan with the thrust of Powell's decisional structure, thereby ascertaining that race may indeed be taken into account for "remedial" and "compensatory" policy actions (see pp. 96–147).

one of these, joined by Justices Stevens, Stewart, Rehnquist, and Chief Justice Burger, Powell's 5:4 stewardship affirmed the California judiciary's decision ordering the University of California's School of Medicine at Davis to admit Allan Bakke, a white applicant who had twice been rejected by Davis, notwithstanding the university-acknowledged fact that he was more highly qualified than any of the admittees from the sixteen-member minority group. These students had entered the medical school under a special program that had set aside, on an *admitted* quota basis, sixteen of the hundred openings at the school for "minorities." Justice Powell held the university's action to be an unconstitutional violation of the equal protection of the laws clause of the Fourteenth Amendment, whereas the other four regarded *any* racial quota systems utilized by government-supported programs (such as higher education) to be an obvious violation of the explicit language of Title VI of the Civil Rights Act of 1964. The four dissenters, Justices Brennan, White, Marshall, and Blackmun, on the other hand, saw neither a constitutional nor a statutory infraction; they called for the permissive use of race as a justifiable "compensatory" action to redress past wrongs generally. (No racial discrimination against blacks or any other minorities had ever been charged against the University of California at Davis.) While refusing to join these four in so expansive a constitutional stance, Justice Powell nevertheless also held for them and himself (5:4) that the California courts had been wrong in ruling that race could *never* be a factor in admissions decisions (the state's judiciary had been *adjudging* such a practice to be *both* illegal *and* unconstitutional); that a state university had "a substantial interest" in a diverse student body "that legitimately may be served [here pointing to Harvard] by a properly devised admission program involving the competitive consideration of race and ethnic origin."[54]

What the Supreme Court did, then, in *Bakke* was (1) disallow (5:4) the kind of explicit, specific, rigid racial quota established by California; and (2) uphold (5:4) the use of "race" as a tool of affirmative action programs in the absence of Davis-like quota arrangements; but, at least for the time being, (3) reject (4:5) the interpretation by the Stevens, Stewart, Rehnquist, and Burger group that found the use of race in *any* programs benefiting from statutorily provided federal financial assistance to be illegal; and also (4) reject (4:5), at least by implication, the position of the Brennan, White, Marshall, and Blackmun group that any *benign* affirmative action use of race, far from being constitutionally or legally proscribed, was permitted. In a sense, then, the *Wall Street Journal* was justified in headlining the *Bakke* verdict as "The Decision Everyone Won"[55]—although, de minimis, that statement needs both considerable explication and qualification. In fine, the Court's long-awaited decision left intact the bulk of affirmative action programs that give special consideration to statutorily identified minority groups

54. *Bakke,* op. cit., at 321–24.
55. June 29, 1978, p. 1.

(and women), while running up a caveat flag on obvious, *rigid* racial (and, by implication, probably sexual and other) quotas. The controversial matter at issue in *Bakke*—confined, as it was, to higher education—hardly settled the overall reverse discrimination problem. In 1979 a string of cases winding their way through the judicial structure toward the highest court of the land were headed by a number of potentially seminal "quota cases" in education[56] and, particularly and naturally, in employment.

Weber. Among the cases in the "judicial mill" was the *Weber* case,[57] decided by the Supreme Court one year after *Bakke.* Together with the latter and the forthcoming 1980 *Fullilove* decision,[58] it would become one of the triad of reverse discrimination cases that, in effect, provided a green light, or at least a green-and-yellow one, for the widespread affirmative action programs pushed aggressively by the Carter administration—and ultimately cemented in the 1980s by the Court, despite strong opposition by the Reagan administration.

At issue in *Weber* was an allegedly "voluntary" and "temporary" affirmative action plan devised by the Kaiser Aluminum and Chemical Corporation and the United Steelworkers of America for Kaiser's Gramercy, Louisiana, plant, under which at least one-half of the available thirteen positions in an on-the-job training program had been reserved for blacks. Finding himself excluded solely because he was white, Brian Weber filed suit in federal district court, claiming a prima facie violation of Title VII of the Civil Rights Act of 1964, which categorically bans any racial discrimination in employment, no matter whether the individual's race be black, white, or any other color, and which specifically states that its provisions are not to be interpreted "to require any employer . . . to grant preferential treatment to any individual or to any group because of the race, color, religion, sex, or national origin of such individual or group on account of an imbalance which may exist. . . ." Moreover, the congressional history of the statute's enactment made it crystal clear that Congress meant precisely what it said, and that the Civil Rights Act's proponents had so assured the doubters during the exciting eighty-three days of floor debate in 1964.[59] Basing their deci-

56. By the margin of one vote the Court declined in 1979 to review the "Italian Bakke" case of an Italian-American New Yorker whose application under the University of Colorado Law School's special admissions program for blacks, Chicanos, and American Indians had been refused consideration because he did not belong to any of the eligible groups (*DiLeo v. Board of Regents,* 441 U.S. 927).

57. *United Steelworkers of America v. Weber,* 443 U.S. 193 (1979).

58. *Fullilove v. Klutznick,* 448 U.S. 448 (1980).

59. Thus, in an exchange between the Civil Rights Act's floor manager, Senator Hubert H. Humphrey (D.-Minn.), and a principal opponent, Senator Willis Rohertson (D.-Va.), Humphrey insisted: "If the Senator can find in Title VII . . . any language which provides that an employer will have to hire on the basis of percentage or quota related to color . . . I will start eating the pages, one after another, because it is not in there" (110 *Congressional Rec*ord 7420). Senator Edmund Muskie (D.-Maine) said that the provision

sions on *both* the language of Title VII and that of the congressional debates, enshrined in the *Congressional Record,* the two lower federal courts that had adjudicated the case[60] upheld Weber's contentions and ruled the affirmative action plan at issue to be illegal under Title VII.

But in an astonishing decision, handed down during the last week of its 1978–79 term, the Supreme Court reversed the courts below in a 5:2 holding, Justices Powell and Stevens abstaining (although it is fair to conjecture that, based upon their votes *up to that point,* they would have dissented). Writing for the majority, Justice Brennan (joined by Justices Marshall, Stewart, White, and, with reservations, Blackmun) frankly conceded that the rulings by the lower courts had *followed the letter* of the Civil Rights Act of 1964 but not its *spirit.*[61] He conjectured that Congress's primary concern had been with "the plight of the Negro in our economy," and that it would be "ironic indeed" if Title VII would be used to prohibit "all voluntary private, race-conscious efforts to abolish traditional patterns" of discrimination.[62]

Chief Justice Burger and Justice Rehnquist dissented vehemently, charging that the majority had engaged in the crassest kind of judicial activism, which amounted to blatant judicial legislation; that it had, in fact, "totally rewritten a crucial part" of the law. As a member of Congress, the chief justice admonished, he "would be inclined to vote for" the views expressed by the majority; but as a judge he had no business in writing legislation. "Congress," he explained with feeling, "expressly *prohibited* the discrimination against Brian Weber" that the five-member majority now approved.[63] And in what may well constitute one of the angriest dissenting opinions in recent times, Justice Rehnquist accused the Court majority of acting like Harry Houdini, the escape artist.[64] "Were Congress to act today specifically to prohibit the type of racial discrimination suffered by [Weber]," he noted, "it would be hard pressed to draft language better tailored to the task than that found in [sections 703(a) and (d)] of Title VII [of the Civil Rights Act of 1964]."[65] Congress sought to require racial equality in govern-

calls for "not equal pay, not 'racial balance.' Only equal opportunity" (ibid. at 12617). Senator Leverrett Saltonstall (R.-Mass.) avowed that 703(j) "provides no preferential treatment for any group of citizens. In fact, it specifically forbids it" (ibid. at 12691). Senator Joe Clark (D.-Pa.) noted: "The bill establishes no quotas. It leaves an employer free to select whomever he wishes to employ" (ibid. at 13080).

60. 415 F. Supp. 761 and 563 F.2d 216 (1977).

61. Alexander Hamilton viewed the notion of "spirit" quite differently in his *Federalist* No. 79: "[T]here is not a syllable [in the proposed Constitution] which directly empowers the national courts to construe the laws according to the spirit of the Constitution, or which gives them any greater latitude in this respect than may be claimed by the courts of every state" ([New York: New American Library Edition, 1962], p. 482).

62. *Weber,* op. cit., at 201.

63. Ibid. at 218; italics in original.

64. Ibid. at 222.

65. Ibid. at 226.

ment, Rehnquist contended, and "there is perhaps no device more destructive to the notion of equality than . . . the quota. Whether described as 'benign discrimination' or 'affirmative action,' the racial quota is nonetheless a creator of castes, a two-edged sword that must demean one in order to prefer the other." He concluded:

> With today's holding, the Court introduces . . . a tolerance for the very evil that the law was intended to eradicate, without offering even a clue as to what the limits on that tolerance may be. . . . The Court has sown the wind. Later courts will face the impossible task of reaping the whirlwind.[66]

Fullilove. Since the *Weber* majority held that, notwithstanding prohibitory statutory language, racial quotas were neither illegal nor unconstitutional if adopted by a private employer (and later extended to governmental employment, too)[67] on a "voluntary" and "temporary" basis, the Court's six-opinion reverse discrimination decision in *Fullilove v. Klutznick*[68] one year later did not come as a major surprise. For at issue in the latter case was the constitutionality of a 1977 congressional law that, in a floor amendment, adopted without prior hearings, had set aside 10 percent of a $4 billion public works program for "minority business enterprises." The latter were defined in the statute as companies in which blacks, Hispanic Americans, Oriental Americans, American Indians, Eskimos, or Aleuts controlled at least a 50 percent interest. It was noteworthy that the governing plurality opinion was written by the chief justice, who had so sternly dissented in *Weber.*[69] But speaking also for Justices White and Powell—with the latter additionally filing a separate concurring opinion[70]—and joined on far more expansively permissive grounds in another concurrence by Justice Marshall, who in turn was joined by Justices Brennan and Blackmun,[71] Chief Justice Burger found warrant for his ruling that the program did "not violate the equal protection component of the Due Process Clause of the Fifth Amendment"[72] in the power of Congress "to enforce by appropriate legislation" the equal protection guarantees of the Fourteenth Amendment.[73] Rejecting the contention by the nonminority business enterprises that Congress is obligated to act in a "color blind" fashion, and is in fact forbidden to employ racial quotas under the Constitution's mandates, he referred repeatedly to what he viewed as the temporary nature of the "narrowly tailored" program, one designed by the national legislature to rem-

66. Ibid. at 225.
67. *Bushey v. New York State Civil Service Commission,* 469 U.S. 1117 (1985).
68. 448 U.S. 448.
69. *United Steelworkers of America v. Weber,* 443 U.S. 193 (1979).
70. *Fullilove v. Klutznick,* op. cit., at 495–517.
71. Ibid. at 517–21.
72. Ibid. at 450, 473.
73. Ibid. at 476.

edy long-standing past wrongs.[74] (In fact, the policy became permanent and, in 1987 controversially added "women" to the "MBE" entitlees.)

There were three vocal dissenters, their leading opinion being written by Justice Stewart, who had joined the majority in *Weber*—he never explained his *Weber* vote—but had been on the other side in *Bakke*. This dissenting opinion was also signed by Justice Rehnquist, who consistently opposed racial quotas in all three cases. The other dissent was filed by Justice Stevens, who did not sit in *Weber* but whose views were in accord with Rehnquist's in *Bakke* as well as now in *Fullilove*. Bristling with anger, Stewart accused his colleagues on the other side of the decision of having rendered a "racist" decision,[75] an adjective he veritably spit out while reading his dissent in full from the bench on that 1980 July Opinion Day. Styling the "set-aside law" an "invidious discrimination by government"—and the Court's decision "wrong for the same reason *Plessy v. Ferguson* was wrong"—he pleaded that the Constitution permits no discrimination of any kind between the races; that the

> Fourteenth Amendment was adopted to ensure that every person must be treated equally by each State regardless of the color of his skin. . . . That it would honor no preference based on lineage. . . .[76]

He concluded:

> Today the Court derails this achievement and places its imprimatur on the creation once again by government of privileges based on birth.[77]

In his even more scathing dissenting opinion, which he read aloud from the bench on the day of the decision, Justice Stevens charged that the "minority set-aside law"—which had been written on the House floor through the efforts of the Black Caucus and had not been sent to committee—represents a "perverse form of reparation," a "slapdash" law that rewards some who may not need rewarding and hurts others who may not deserve hurting.[78] Suggesting that such a law could be used simply as a patronage tool by its authors, he warned that it might breed more resentment and prejudice than it corrects,[79] and he asked what percentage of "oriental blood or what degree of Spanish-speaking skill is required for membership in the preferred class."[80] Sarcastically, he said that now the government must devise its version of the Nazi laws that defined who was a Jew, musing that "our statute books will once again have to contain laws that reflect the odious

---

74. Ibid. at 482, 490.
75. Ibid. at 532.
76. Ibid. at 531.
77. Ibid. at 532.
78. Ibid. at 534, 539–40.
79. Ibid. at 545.
80. Ibid. at 552, note 30.

practice of delineating the qualities that make one person a Negro and make another white."[81] Eight years later Justice Stevens would concur in a 6:3 ruling that invalidated a Richmond, Virginia, law that channeled 30 percent of public work funds to minority-owned construction companies.[82] But just one year thereafter, he concurred separately with the majority's 5:4 upholding of minority preferential broadcasting practices by the FCC in *Metro Broadcasting;* and in 1995, he dissented from the Court's explicit rejection of a *Fullilove*-type racial preference program in *Adarand,*[83] as well as its overturning of *Metro Broadcasting.*[84]

Stotts. However, after having upheld several racial quota affirmative action arrangements in employment, the Supreme Court, to the pleasant surprise of some observers and the consternation of others, appeared to shift gears in a case reaching it from Memphis, Tennessee, in 1984.[85] A lower federal court had forced the layoff or demotion of senior white firefighters in that city in order to protect black hiring and promotion gains achieved under a court-approved affirmative action plan in 1980. The latter required that at least 50 percent of all new employees be black until two-fifths of the department was black. Responding to long-term pressure that generated the arrangement, Memphis increased the proportion of black firefighters from 4 percent in 1974 to 11.5 percent in 1980.

As a result of a 1981 budget crunch, however, the city announced that it would abide by a "last-hired-but-first-fired" seniority system negotiated with the union. It thus began to lay off those who had most recently been hired, a group that included many of the new black firefighters. A federal district court denied the city's right to reduce the proportion of blacks in the department, and as a result three whites lost their jobs to three blacks who had less seniority. Both the city of Memphis and the union appealed to the U.S. Supreme Court.

In a 6:3 opinion, written by Justice White—who had been on the "other" side in *Bakke, Weber,* and *Fullilove*—the Court held that Title VII of the Civil Rights Act of 1964 clearly "protects bona fide seniority systems," unless the plans are *intentionally discriminatory* or black workers can demonstrate that they were *individually* victimized by hiring discrimination.[86] Joined in dissent by Justices Brennan and Marshall, Justice Blackmun—perhaps loath to reach the merits of the case—contented himself by voting to throw out the controversy as being legally irrelevant to those involved because the layoff orders had since been rescinded.

---

81. Ibid. at 534.
82. *City of Richmond v. J. A. Croson Company,* 488 U.S. 469. See discussion *infra* this chapter.
83. *Adarand Constructors v. Peña,* 515 U.S. 200.
84. *Metro Broadcasting v. FCC,* 497 U.S. 547 (1990).
85. *Firefighters Local v. Stotts,* 467 U.S. 561 (1984).
86. Ibid.

Wygant. The Court continued to receive affirmative action/reverse discrimination cases, and two years after *Stotts* it handed down a decision in which it seemed to say both yes and no to racial preferences, while evidently promising to return to the fray in yet other cases then still on its 1985–86 docket. In the former, *Wygant v. Jackson Board of Education,*[87] the Court held unconstitutional as a violation of the equal protection of the laws clause of the Fourteenth Amendment a Michigan school board's plan for laying off teachers that gave preference to members of minority groups. Under that plan the school district had sought to protect minority hiring gains by laying off white teachers ahead of blacks who had *less* seniority. But the six-opinion 5:4 holding, written by Justice Powell, was so diverse in reasoning that it seemed to provide a bit of triumph for both foes *and* friends of affirmative action. The Reagan administration could take solace from the majority's view that the mere fact of discrimination in American life is not in and of itself a constitutionally sufficient reason for resorting to the type of affirmative action remedy propounded by the Jackson school board. For, as Justice Powell cautioned, giving preference to "minority role models" to overcome discrimination in society was not a sufficiently "compelling reason" to lay off nonminority employees. On the other hand, the supporters of affirmative action per se could and did find much satisfaction in Justice O'Connor's concurring opinion, which appeared to be *the* controlling one in terms of the practice's future.

The Court's junior justice professed to see a forging of "a degree of unanimity" in rejecting a central contention of the administration, namely, that affirmative action is appropriate only as a device to remedy discrimination *against specific individual victims.* But as Justice O'Connor saw the gravamen of the issue, "a carefully constructed affirmative-action program . . . need not be limited to the remedying of specific instances of identified discrimination," and the Court would be prepared to approve such a course. The Jackson school board, however, had not "narrowly tailored" its plan, as Justice Powell put it, and he suggested that, while such race-based *firing* schemes were too harsh on the innocent, the Court might well look more favorably upon some *hiring* plans—thus signaling a case-by-case approach. While rejecting the four dissenters' willingness to find constitutional authority even in such firing schemes, Powell acknowledged that "in order to remedy the effects of prior discrimination, it may be necessary to take race into account"—even if that meant that "innocent persons may be called upon to bear some of the burdens of the remedy." The last word obviously had not yet been spoken on the wrenching issue.

The 1986 Cleveland and New York Cases. Indeed, shortly after *Wygant* down came two highly significant holdings, which, despite their ten opinions and 135 pages of writing, emphatically rejected the key rationale that had been urged in

87. 476 U.S. 267 (1986).

opposition to racially explicit goals and quotas: namely, that the Civil Rights Act of 1964, especially its Section 706(g), offered relief *not* to large groups of people but *only* to specifically identifiable individuals who could prove that they were victims of racial bias, and that "hiring goals" and "timetables," viewed as *quotas,* constituted a constitutionally as well as statutorily proscribed form of reverse discrimination against whites. Led by the author of *Weber,* Justice Brennan, the Court here refused to accept that contention in two plurality opinions, with six of the nine justices—Brennan, Marshall, Blackmun, Powell, Stevens, and O'Connor—endorsing the use of affirmative action, including specific goals, to remedy past employment discrimination. The justices thus upheld, by a 6:3 vote—with Chief Justice Burger and Justices Rehnquist and White dissenting— a lower-court-approved voluntary settlement between the city of Cleveland, Ohio, and minority firefighters that called initially for promotion of one minority for every white.[88]

In the second case, involving New York sheet metal workers—with Justice O'Connor now joining the three *Cleveland* dissenters—the majority upheld (5:4) a federal court order requiring a local union to meet specific minority targets of 29.23 percent.[89] It is not astonishing that Justice O'Connor would agree with her three colleagues in dissent, Burger, White, and Rehnquist, who viewed that demonstrably specific figure as a racial quota pure and simple: "The legislative history, fairly read, indicates," she wrote, "that such racial quotas are impermissible as a means of enforcing Title VII [notably Section 706(g)] and that even racial preferences short of quotas should be used only where clearly necessary if these preferences would benefit nonvictims at the expense of innocent nonminority workers."[90] Justice White, dissenting separately, also found the New York plan to constitute an impermissibly strict quota,[91] and Justice Rehnquist, in a separate dissent joined by the chief justice, found it "simply incredible" that the Court "reads out of existence" the 706(g) limitation on courts below.[92]

Yet the solid pro–affirmative action wing of the Court—Justices Brennan, Marshall, and Blackmun, and, after 1985, albeit with some reservations, Justice Stevens, together with the considerably more tempered concurrences by Justice Powell and, in part, Justice O'Connor—unquestionably triumphed by arguably writing new law for a new day: "Our examination of the legislative history of Title VII convinces us," wrote Brennan in the New York case, "that, when examined in context, the statements relied upon by the petitioners and the solicitor general do not indicate that Congress intended to limit relief under Section 706(g) to that which benefits only actual victims of unlawful discrimination. [Its]

88. *Firefighters v. Cleveland,* 106 S. Ct. 3063 (1986).
89. *Sheet Metal Workers v. EEOC,* 106 S. Ct. 3019 (1986).
90. Ibid. at 3059.
91. Ibid. at 3061.
92. Quoting from his *Cleveland* dissent, op. cit., at 3087.

language plainly expressed Congress's intent to vest district courts with broad discretion to award 'appropriate' equitable relief to remedy unlawful discrimination. . . . The availability of race-conscious affirmative relief . . . as a remedy for a violation of Title VII also furthers the broad purposes underlying the statute."[93] Still, evidently taking note of the reservations of such key votes as those by Justices Powell and O'Connor, Brennan stipulated: "We do not mean to suggest that such relief is always proper. . . . We emphasize that a [lower] court's judgment should be guided by sound legal principles. In particular the court should exercise its discretion with an eye towards Congress's concern that race-conscious affirmative measures not be invoked simply to create a racially balanced work force."[94]

Notwithstanding that demurrer-cum-reservation, however, the Supreme Court's holding in the *Cleveland* and *New York* cases left little doubt that, at least for the then present status of affirmative action law: (1) racially based hiring and promotion programs may be applied to minority groups "generally," *not* being merely confined to benefit only individually identified victims of discrimination; (2) federal trial judges may set goals and timetables for employers to meet in order to remedy past discrimination; and (3) states and cities have broad discretion to agree to adopt affirmative action plans that go well beyond what courts may order. Nonetheless, a plethora of unanswered questions remained as a result of these July 1986 decisions, and the Court's 1986–87 docket listed several potentially significant cases on the issue for oral argument. Late February and late March 1987 brought two decisions that, absent a drastic change in both Supreme Court personnel *and* the latter's jurisprudential philosophy, might justifiably have been viewed as having gone the proverbial last mile toward settling the affirmative action/reverse discrimination syndrome—at least in the eyes of the judicial branch.

Paradise. In the earlier of the two cases, *United States v. Paradise,*[95] a deeply divided Court ruled for the first time that judges may order *strict racial promotion quotas* to overcome "long-term, open and pervasive discrimination." There was no majority opinion, but Justice Brennan—the latter-day key architect of the Court's rulings on the basic issues of affirmative action/reverse discrimination— upheld an Alabama federal district judge's orders in 1983 and 1984 requiring Alabama to promote one black state trooper for each white state trooper until the state could develop a promotion procedure acceptable to the judge. Brennan's plurality opinion was joined in full by his colleagues Marshall and Blackmun, with Stevens and Powell penning separate concurrences. Justice Powell's vote in favor of promotion quotas represented a clear departure from his contrary stance in

93. *Sheet Metal Workers,* op. cit., plurality opinion at 3035.
94. Ibid. at 3050.
95. 480 U.S. 149 (1987).

Bakke I nine years earlier,[96] a fact of which he seemed to take note by explaining that a rigid quota was proper in this instance because it was "short in duration" and the "effect of the order on innocent white workers is likely to be relatively diffuse." He pointed to evidence that the state "had engaged in persistent violation of constitutional rights and repeatedly failed to carry out court orders."[97]

Four justices dissented in two opinions: Justice White, in a brief solo dissent, argued that the Alabama judge had plainly exceeded his legal and constitutional authority in ordering the quota involved.[98] Justice O'Connor, in the leading dissent, in which she was joined by Chief Justice Rehnquist and their new colleague, Justice Antonin Scalia, insisted that the Alabama judge "unquestionably had the authority to fashion a remedy designed to end [the state's] egregious history of discrimination." But she contended that the judge was obligated to find a solution "that was narrowly tailored to accomplish this purpose"; that there was "no evidence in the record that such an extreme quota was necessary to eradicate the effects of [the state's] delay," or to compel the state to develop a nondiscriminatory hiring plan. She suggested that the judge should have considered other alternatives to spur action by the state, alternatives that "would have a lesser effect on the rights of [white] troopers," such as imposing fines on the state.[99] But five votes beat four—and the seminal holding, rendered largely possible by Justice Powell's crucial vote, meant in effect that strict racial quotas in both promotion and hiring would henceforth be upheld by the Supreme Court of the United States.

Johnson v. Transportation Agency, Santa Clara County. Four weeks after *Paradise,* the Court came down with an even more far-reaching decision. In what must be regarded as its most significant affirmative action/reverse discrimination decision since the *Bakke* holding in 1978, it ruled (6:3), in another Brennan-authored landmark opinion, that it was permissible to take *gender* and *race* into account in employment decisions.[100] Here, then, the highest judicial body in the land, absent any action by Congress, explicitly held that women as well as blacks and other (albeit undefined) minorities can receive preferential treatment—demonstrably a direct violation of the language and legislative history of Title VII of the Civil Rights Act of 1964. The ruling was the Court's first involving an affirmative action plan according job preferences to women. But not only did it reject a civil rights suit by white male Paul Johnson, who had worked for the agency for thirteen years and had scored two points higher than the successful applicant, Diane Joyce, on the qualifying test for the position of road dis-

---

96. See *supra* chapter 7.
97. *United States v. Paradise,* op. cit., at 4221.
98. Ibid. at 196.
99. Ibid.
100. *Johnson v. Transportation Agency, Santa Clara County,* 480 U.S. 616 (1987).

patcher—one no woman had ever held—the victorious Brennan opinion also marked the first time that the Court unambiguously held that *without any proof of past discrimination* against women or minorities by a particular employer, the latter may use racial and sexual preferences in hiring and promotions to bring the workforce into line with the local population or labor market. Building on his controversial *Weber* opinion of 1979,[101] Justice Brennan—who was joined in full by Justices Marshall, Blackmun, and, perhaps surprisingly, Powell, and in part by Justices Stevens and O'Connor (who both wrote separate concurrences)—insisted that the Santa Clara Transportation Agency's plan was "consistent with Title VII's purpose of eliminating the effects of employment discrimination." He concluded: "Given the obvious imbalance in the skilled craft division and given the agency's commitment to eliminating such imbalances . . . it was appropriate to consider as one fact the sex of Ms. Joyce in making its decision."[102]

Justice O'Connor, distinctly uncomfortable with her senior colleague's reasoning, yet agonizingly opting to vote in favor of the agency's action, criticized the majority for having gone too far in taking "an expansive and ill-defined approach to voluntary affirmative action . . . despite limitations imposed by the Constitution and by the provisions of Title VII."[103] But she resolved to go along "with the reality of the course that the majority of the Court has determined to follow . . . in light of our precedents."[104] Established precedents, as she viewed these, thus became decisive in casting her vote.

There were three dissenters, who wrote two opinions. The leading one was authored by Justice Scalia, joined in full by Chief Justice Rehnquist and in part by Justice White, who also wrote a separate dissent. Like his colleague, White called for the overruling of *Weber,* as now broadened by the *Johnson* holding, as a perversion of Congress's intent in Title VII.[105] White had been in the majority in *Weber,* but he now concluded that the Court had impermissibly overextended it. It was Justice Scalia's opinion, however, that manifested the fundamental disagreement between the two—or arguably three—camps then on the Court. In harsh, blistering, forceful language he contended that the *Johnson* decision now "effectively requires employers, public as well as private, to engage in intentional discrimination on the basis of race or sex." He charged that the decision will insulate employers who adopt affirmative action plans against reverse discrimination suits, and that, accordingly, it would be "economic folly" in many cases for employers not to engage in reverse discrimination.[106] He was particularly critical of that part of the *Johnson* holding permitting statistical imbalance to constitute criteria for justifying an affirmative action program, rather than re-

---

101. See *supra* chapter 7.
102. *Johnson v. Transportation Agency, Santa Clara County,* op. cit., at 4385.
103. Ibid. at 4388.
104. Ibid.
105. Ibid. at 4391.
106. Ibid. at 4396.

quiring that there be evidence of past discrimination. "This is an enormous expansion," he wrote, "undertaken without the slightest justification or analysis."[107] With deep feeling he concluded:

> A statute designed to establish a color-blind and gender-blind work place has thus been converted into a powerful engine of racism and sexism, not merely permitting intentional race- and sex-based discrimination but often making it, through operation of the legal system, practically compelled. . . .
>
> The only losers in the process are the Johnsons of the country, for whom Title VII has been not merely repealed [by the Court] but actually inverted. The irony is that these individuals—predominantly unknown, unaffluent, unorganized—suffer this injustice at the hands of a court fond of thinking itself the champion of the politically impotent. I dissent.[108]

Where, then, did we stand on the so deeply troubling issue as the Court began to address its 1988–89 term? It would have been far too sanguine—or foolhardy—to conclude that the broad sweep of the 1986–87 rulings, especially those in *Paradise* and *Johnson,* represented the last word. However, as a good many students of both issue and Court hazarded after these two early 1987 decisions, absent dramatic changes in Court personnel and Court Weltanschauung—and the utterly unlikely event of definitive legislative action by Congress—*Paradise* and *Johnson,* and particularly the latter, could have been regarded as having anchored the permissible parameters on the affirmative action/reverse discrimination front for the foreseeable future.[109] Thus, it seemed then quite clear that both public and private companies and agencies would have the option of adopting more or less voluntary programs to hire and promote *qualified* minorities and women to correct a "manifest imbalance" in their representation in various job categories, *even* when better-qualified other candidates are available, and *even* when there is *no* evidence of past discrimination. Race or gender might, as *Johnson* taught, accordingly be legally, and presumably constitutionally, weighed in the balance as a primary "plus"—to use Justice Powell's terminology in *Bakke II*—although not inevitably so. However, job layoffs and firings would fall into a different category, as *Stotts* and *Wygant* demonstrated. In the realm of inaction by employers, federal courts now possessed incontrovertible authority to impose involuntary affirmative action plans in the face of strong evidence of previous discrimination against women, blacks, and other minorities. Moreover, executive orders might—and indeed do—require evidence of minority employment for federal contractors. Finally, and notwithstanding Court demurrers and protestations to the contrary in erstwhile decisions, such as *Bakke I,* the justices seemed prepared to sanction rigid court-imposed numerical quotas for the em-

---

107. Ibid. at 4394.
108. Ibid. at 4396.
109. See, e.g., the excellent summary in *Time,* April 6, 1987, p. 20.

ployment of minorities, as the 1986 *Cleveland* firefighters and *New York* sheet metal workers and the 1987 Alabama *Paradise* state troopers cases manifested. Thus, some lines had indubitably been drawn. How certain their future would prove to be remained necessarily at least somewhat conjectural—as the next few years would demonstrate.

The June 1989 Quintet. Although they were in a good many ways intricate and technical, there is little doubt that the five decisions, handed down by a closely divided Supreme Court between June 5 and June 22, 1989, pointed to the difference one person can make on the body. Thus it was the replacement of Justice Lewis F. Powell Jr. by Anthony M. Kennedy, who took his seat in February 1988, that made possible a significant shift in rulings involving the affirmative action/reverse discrimination realm. Although Powell was by no means a no-questions-asked devotee on the issue of the Brennan-Marshall-Blackmun group, the author of *Bakke I* and *II* was more often than not a supporter of generous applications of affirmative action, with the notable exception of busing. But in each of the five cases adjudicated, and in *Croson,* Kennedy's vote was cast on "the other" side, amid predictable plaudits and chagrin by protagonists and antagonists of a slowdown or even reversal of affirmative action programs. Thus, the Court held:

> 5:4 that in attempts by employees to sue to try to show by use of statistical evidence that an employer's policies have resulted in discrimination against broad groups of workers, the burden of proof under Title VII of the Civil Rights Act of 1964 falls upon the employees. It is *they* who must prove that the policies they are challenging cannot be justified as necessary to the employer's business. A statistical disparity between the racial composition of the community and that of a firm's workforce is not sufficient to prove discrimination. In effect the decision overturned the 1971 *Griggs v. Duke Power Co.* opinion,[110] in which the then Court had placed the legal burden on employers to justify policies that had the statistical effect of screening out women or minorities *(Wards Cove Packing Co. v. Atonio).*[111]

> 5:4 that Court-approved affirmative action settlements (consent decrees) are open to *subsequent* legal challenges by disappointed white workers who took no part in the case leading to the original accord, but who then alleged reverse discrimination because of the accord's impact upon them. The ruling, which also applied to sex discrimination cases, was based on the mandates of the equal protection of the laws provisions of the Fourteenth Amendment *(Martin v. Wilks).*[112]

110. 401 U.S. 424.
111. 490 U.S. 642
112. 490 U.S. 755.

5:3 that filing of lawsuits challenging seniority systems that are alleged to be discriminatory must be brought within 300 days of their adoption, in accordance with requirements regarding filing of such suits in the Civil Rights Act of 1964 *(Lorance v. AT&T Technologies).*[113]

5:4 that the Civil Rights Act of 1866 cannot be used to bring damage suits against state or local governments for acts of racial discrimination; that the Civil Rights Act of 1871 provides the only means to bring damage suits against state and local governments for the type of discrimination banned by the 1866 law *(Jett v. Dallas Independent School District).*[114]

The Court unanimously *upheld* (9:0) the important pro–civil rights precedent it had established in the herewith reconsidered 1976 decision of *Runyon v. McCrary,*[115] in which it had given a very liberal interpretation of the Civil Rights Act of 1866, and reaffirmed the latter's application as a tool in combating discrimination in the private sector at the *initial hiring stage. However,* it now ruled (5:4) that the statute could *not* be similarly applied regarding claims of *on-the-job* discriminatory treatment because, in Justice Kennedy's opinion for the majority, Congress had not intended the 1866 law's key Section 1981 to reach such allegations; but that, of course, other antidiscrimination laws are applicable and usable *(Patterson v. McLean Credit Union).*[116]

1990–93. Yet just when it seemed that a reasonably secure Court majority had set its face relatively predictably against extension of affirmative action policies—as manifested by the preceding quintet of 1989 holdings—the last week of the Court's 1989–90 term saw a dramatic converse development. The vehicle turned out to be two cases arising out of a twofold policy established by the Federal Communications Commission during the Carter administration in 1977–78. It provided for (1) a program awarding an enhancement for minority ownership in comparative proceedings for new licenses and (2) a "minority distress sale" program, which permits a limited category of existing radio and television broadcast stations to be transferred *only* to minority-controlled firms. Two nonminority firm applicants for ownership were adversely affected by the two policies and brought suit, charging violation of the Constitution's equal protection of the laws principles—here applicable to the federal government via the due process of law provisions of the Fifth Amendment. The Supreme Court consolidated the two cases as *Metro Broadcasting, Inc. v. Federal Communications Commission,* and, in a 5:4 ruling, upheld the constitutionality of the two policies in question.[117] It

113. 490 U.S. 900.
114. 490 U.S. 701.
115. 427 U.S. 160.
116. 491 U.S. 164.
117. 497 U.S. 547 (1990). Five years later it would be overruled 5:4 in *Adarand Constructors v. Peña,* 515 U.S. 200 (1995).

was not surprising that the Court's opinion was authored by Justice Brennan, nor that he was joined by his faithful allies on the overall issue, namely, Justices Marshall and Blackmun. What did astonish a good many close observers of the Supreme Court's membership and its jurisprudence, however, was that Justice White joined the majority, without explaining his vote, and that Justice Stevens did likewise—although writing an equivocal concurring opinion.

As noted earlier, Stevens had delivered a stinging dissent in the 1980 parent preferential treatment case of *Fullilove v. Klutznick*.[118] Now, obviously squeamish about the change in his position, he penned a brief concurring opinion, in which he attempted to distinguish *Fullilove* and *Metro Broadcasting* by justifying the latter as entitled to "disparate treatment" because it was one of those "extremely rare situations in which racial and ethnic characteristics" are relevant.[119] Justice White's switch, as indicated, was accompanied by total silence. He had joined the Court's 6:3 declaration of unconstitutionality of the Richmond, Virginia, 30 percent set-aside law for minority construction business enterprises in the 1989 *Croson* holding[120]—as had Justice Stevens in his concurring opinion—but he offered no explanation.

There were four unhappy dissenters in *Metro Broadcasting*, who joined in two opinions. One was by *Croson*'s author, Justice O'Connor, who saw a gross violation of the white applicants' constitutional entitlement to equal protection of the laws. Decrying the allocation of "benefits and burdens among individuals based on the assumption that race or ethnicity determines how to act or think," she observed: "We are a nation not of black and white alone, but one teeming with divergent communities. . . . Upon that basis, we are governed by one Constitution, providing a single guarantee of equal protection, one that extends equally to all citizens."[121]

An even more impassioned dissent was composed by the then Court's junior member, Justice Anthony M. Kennedy, who saw not only a disturbing departure "from our precedents" but a "renewed toleration of racial classifications," concluding: "I regret that after a century of judicial opinions, we interpret the Constitution to do no more than move us from 'separate but equal' to 'unequal but benign.'"[122] Chief Justice Rehnquist and Justices Scalia and Kennedy joined Justice O'Connor's dissent; Justice Scalia also joined Justice Kennedy's. But the eighty-four-year-old master judicial tactician and craftsman, Justice William J. Brennan, had carried the day by capturing the two votes he needed. "We hold," he wrote, "that benign race conscious measures mandated by Congress—even if those measures are not 'remedial' in the sense of being designed to compensate

118. 448 U.S. 448 (1980) at 534.
119. 497 U.S. 547.
120. 488 U.S. 469.
121. 58 LW 5053 at 5067.
122. Ibid. at 5077.

victims of past governmental or societal discrimination—are constitutionally permissible."[123] And pending in the wings that summer of 1990 was a major piece of congressional legislation, titled the Civil Rights Act of 1990, designed to overturn sundry aspects and components of the Supreme Court's 1989 quintet of "anti"–affirmative action/reverse discrimination holdings. In November 1991, after an intensive, often bitter struggle on and off the floor of Congress, the Civil Rights Act of 1991 became law—and it did overturn, in whole or in part, the aforementioned quintet of cases statutorily. It represented a dramatic assertion of the invocability of institutional checks and balances. As a result the Court agreed in 1993 to decide whether the new statute should apply to lawsuits *pending* when it was passed.[124] "No," it held 8:1, in an opinion by Justice Stevens, with only the retiring Justice Blackmun in dissent.[125]

In two victories for white males who claimed they had suffered reverse discrimination, the Supreme Court let stand, by denying review, lower court rulings that (1) threw out a quota for promotion of black firefighters in Birmingham, Alabama, and (2) awarded a white engineer $425,000 in damages because he was passed over for a promotion.[126] Also, the long-simmering issue of race-specific scholarships gave promise of becoming ripe when the Supreme Court denied certiorari in a case involving the University of Maryland's Banneker program, under which the university provided forty annual *blacks-only* scholarships. An otherwise fully qualified Hispanic student was denied participation simply because he was not an African-American; he filed suit, lost in the U.S. District Court, but won in the U.S. Court of Appeals for the Fourth Circuit, which declared the policy unconstitutional.[127] The University of Maryland then appealed unsuccessfully to the U.S. Supreme Court, the high tribunal simply refusing to review the holding below, thus letting it stand.[128] And in 1996 the Fifth United States Court of Appeals declared unconstitutional the University of Texas School of Law's admissions program that gave special racial preferences to minorities.[129] The U.S. Supreme Court denied certiorari, thus upholding the lower tribunal's significant ruling. Subsequently, the Fifth Circuit reaffirmed its earlier ruling, and the U.S. Supreme Court again denied certiorari in June 2001. Later that year the University of Texas decided not to pursue any further appeals, thus effectively terminating a case that ipso facto ended—at least theoretically— the use of race as a

123. Ibid.

124. *Landgraf v. USI Film Products* and *Rivers v. Roadway Express,* 61 LW 3580, certiorari granted.

125. Ibid., 311 U.S. 244 and 511 U.S. 298.

126. *Arrington v. Wilks,* 63 LW 3753 (1995); and *Duquesne Light Co. v. Claus,* 63 LW 3754 (1995), respectively.

127. *Podberesky v. Kirwan,* 63 LW 2287 (1994).

128. *Kirwan v. Podberesky,* 63 LW 3832 (1995).

129. *Hopwood v. Texas,* 78 F.3d 932 (1996). But see *Farmer v. University of Nevada,* 66 LW 3316 (1998).

factor in admissions to public universities in Texas, Louisiana, and Mississippi (the three states in the Fifth Circuit's jurisdiction). An even more blatant use of race favorably in admission by the University of Georgia was struck down as being patently unconstitutional by a three-judge panel of the Eleventh Circuit Court of Appeals in late 2001. Contentious cases from the Universities of Michigan and Washington remained in the judicial pipeline in 2002. Black enrollment at the UT Law School dropped from thirty-one in the 1996 entering class to four in 1997.[130] Following the enactment of Proposition 209, the antidiscrimination measure initiated by the people of California in late 1996, the Supreme Court refused to hear a resulting case in 1997, with a subsequent drop in minority student enrollment.[131] However, California's minority admissions rebounded significantly in 1999, as did Texas's.[132]

The end of the Court's 1994–95 term had provided additional indications that broad-based affirmative action programs faced mounting constitutional challenges. The case of *Adarand Constructors v. Peña*[133] was a prime example, casting serious doubts on federal set-aside programs that give preferences based on race. Applying "strict scrutiny"—the most exacting standard of review—Justice O'Connor announced that in the future such a standard would be required for all federal, state, and local racial classifications. She declared that trying to accomplish diversity as an independent goal is too unrelated to any legitimate basis for employing racial classifications. Remanding the *Adarand* case to the Tenth Circuit Court of Appeals—and explicitly overruling *Metro Broadcasting,* which had applied intermediate scrutiny—the Court majority (also consisting of the chief justice and Justices Kennedy, Scalia, and Thomas) ruled that all such programs must be "narrowly tailored" to accomplish "a compelling governmental interest."

Justices Scalia and Thomas wanted to go further, concluding that *all* racial classifications by any governmental actor can *never* meet the "compelling governmental interest" test and would therefore violate the Constitution. Dissenting opinions were filed by Justices Stevens, Souter, and Ginsburg, with Justice Breyer joining the latter two. In the lead dissenting opinion, penned perhaps surprisingly by Justice Stevens, who had dissented in *Fullilove* and concurred in *Croson,* the senior associate justice contended that the Court's majority had refused to distinguish between federal (justifiable) and state (nonjustifiable) such

---

130. *Texas v. Hopwood,* 64 LW 3868 (1996). For enrollment statistics see Richard Cohen, "Not Just About Race," *Washington Post,* July 22, 1997, p. A15. The case was back in the lower courts in 2000.

131. *Coalition for Economic Equity v. Wilson,* 66 LW 3316.

132. "California Sees Minority Admissions Rebound," *New York Times,* April 4, 1999, p. 16 NE; and James Traub, "The Class of Prop. 209," *New York Times Magazine,* May 2, 1999, p. 44ff.

133. 515 U.S. 200 (1995). The Court seemed thus to make clear that affirmative action may henceforth be used only where there is a showing of identified, not general, societal discrimination.

programs; between "invidious" discrimination and efforts to foster equality; and that, furthermore, precedential considerations mandated adherence to the *Fullilove* decision—which, however, the Court in *Adarand* declared to be no longer controlling. It reconfirmed the principle of *Adarand,* per curiam, in 2000,[134] and again in 2001.[135] But that landmark civil rights case was back at the Supreme Court for a third visit in June 2001. Hearing the now well-known case on October 31, 2001, while sitting in the anthrax-scare-induced weeklong "exile" at the U.S. federal court building several blocks from its own edifice, the Court ultimately rendered a unanimous "DIG," per curiam, that is, the justices dismissed the case as having been granted "improvidently" on several procedural grounds.[136]

In 1997 the Supreme Court upheld the Fourth Circuit's ruling striking down Prince George County's (Maryland) cap on the number of whites and blacks who could be hired under an affirmative action program for its firefighters[137]—a logical confirmation of *Adarand.* So was the much publicized Third Circuit Court of Appeals ruling against the New Jersey School Board of Piscataway, which had utilized the sole criterion of race in retaining a black teacher while firing a similarly situated white teacher.[138] The board initially appealed to the U.S. Supreme Court, which scheduled the case for oral argument on January 14, 1998. However, sensing certain defeat and possibly dire consequences, civil rights organizations persuaded Piscataway to drop the appeal by agreeing to pay the white teacher (Taxman) an indemnity. The Court consequently dismissed the case on December 2, 1997.[139]

CODA

The numerous affirmative action/reverse discrimination rulings once again underscore not only the wrench of the quest for equal justice under law but also the omnipresent question of the judicial role—of how to draw that line between judicial restraint and judicial activism, between the judiciary's presumed role of

134. *Adarand Constructors v. Slater,* 68 LW 3451.

135. *Fulton County v. Webster,* certiorari denied, 64 LW 3628.

136. *Adarand Constructors v. Mineta,* 534 U.S. ___; and *Adarand Constructors v. Mineta,* 534 U.S. ___ .

137. *Prince George's County v. Alexander,* 65 LW 3691.

138. *Piscataway v. Taxman,* 91 F.3d (1997).

139. *Piscataway v. Taxman,* 66 LW 3393. See also the Court's denial of certiorari of a Fifth Circuit Court of Appeals striking of a Dallas program designed to benefit minority firefighters to the detriment of whites (*Dallas Fire Fighter Association v. Dallas,* 67 LW 3592 [1998]); the D.C. Court of Appeals declaration of unconstitutionality of the FCC's affirmative action program, which required stations to apply workforce proportional representation on behalf of minorities (*Lutheran Church–Missouri Synod v. FCC,* 141 F.3d 344 [1998]); and *Montgomery County Public Schools v. Eisenberg,* 68 LW 3593 (2000).

finding rather than making the law, and its other assumed role of being the country's "conscience."[140] As for the so divisive issue of affirmative action/reverse discrimination itself, the words of the late constitutional law and theory scholar Philip B. Kurland are worth keeping in mind. In his view the entire syndrome would almost certainly be with us for years to come, given what he regarded in the 1970s as the troublesome "fundamental shift of constitutional limitations from protection of individual rights to protection of class rights . . . to the measurement of equality of opportunity to equality of condition or result."[141] But, recently, a more conservative Supreme Court (albeit with a bare majority) has tried to shift the balance back toward individual rights, as demonstrated in *Adarand I*. The one-vote difference between majority and dissenting sides in many civil rights and liberties cases assures divisive Supreme Court appointment debates when they next occur—as inevitably they must.

To the Supreme Court of the United States we have thus turned again and again to help us in our unending need to draw lines. Despite the storms of controversy that have engulfed it, with some notable exceptions it has remained true to its assumed role as our national conscience and our institutional common sense. In the long run, if not always in the short, the Court has served us well in maintaining that blend of change and continuity that is so necessary to the stability of the governmental process of a democracy. It has seemed to adhere to the basic American value so beautifully phrased by Thomas Jefferson and inscribed around the ceiling of the rotunda of the Jefferson Memorial: "I have sworn upon the altar of God eternal hostility against every form of tyranny over the mind of man."

140. See Henry J. Abraham, *The Judicial Process,* 7th ed. (New York: Oxford University Press, 1998), chapters 7–9.
141. "The Private I . . . ," 10 *University of Chicago Record* 4 (July 19, 1976).

Appendix A: Statistical Data on Supreme Court Justices

Appointing President	President's Political Party	Dates of President's Service	Name of Justice	Dates of Birth and Death	Justice's Nominal Party Allegiance on Appointment	State from Which Justice Was Apptd.#	Dates of Service on Supreme Court
Washington	Federalist	1789–1797	1. Jay, John*	1745–1829	Federalist	N.Y.	1789–1795
"	"	"	2. Rutledge, John	1739–1800	"	S.C.	1789–1791
"	"	"	3. Cushing, William	1732–1810	"	Mass.	1789–1810
"	"	"	4. Wilson, James	1724–1798	"	Pa.	1789–1798
"	"	"	5. Blair, John	1732–1800	"	Va.	1789–1796
"	"	"	6. Iredell, James	1750–1799	"	N.C.	1790–1799
"	"	"	7. Johnson, Thomas	1732–1819	"	Md.	1791–1793
"	"	"	8. Paterson, Wm.	1745–1806	"	N.J.	1793–1806
"	"	"	9. Rutledge, John*	1739–1800	"	S.C.	1796‡
"	"	"	10. Chase, Samuel	1741–1811	"	Md.	1796–1811
"	"	"	11. Ellsworth, Oliver*	1745–1807	"	Conn.	1796–1800
Adams	"	1797–1801	12. Washington, Bushrod	1762–1829	"	Va.	1798–1829
"	"	"	13. Moore, Alfred	1755–1810	"	N.C.	1799–1804
"	"	"	14. Marshall, John*	1755–1835	"	Va.	1801–1835
Jefferson	Republican	1801–1809	15. Johnson, Wm.	1771–1834	Republican	S.C.	1804–1834
"	"	"	16. Livingston, H. Brockholst	1757–1823	"	N.Y.	1806–1823
"	"	"	17. Todd, Thomas	1765–1826	"	Ky.	1807–1826
Madison	"	1809–1817	18. Duval, Gabriel	1752–1844	"	Md.	1811–1835
"	"	"	19. Story, Joseph	1779–1845	"	Mass.	1811–1845
Monroe	"	1817–1825	20. Thompson, Smith	1768–1843	"	N.Y.	1823–1843
Adams	"	1825–1829	21. Trimble, Robert	1777–1828	"	Ky.	1826–1828
Jackson	Democrat	1829–1837	22. McLean, John	1785–1861	Democrat	Ohio	1829–1861
"	"	"	23. Baldwin, Henry	1780–1844	"	Pa.	1830–1844
"	"	"	24. Wayne, James M.	1790–1867	"	Ga.	1835–1867
"	"	"	25. Taney, Roger B.*	1777–1864	"	Md.	1836–1864
"	"	"	26. Barbour, Philip P.	1783–1841	"	Va.	1836–1841
"	"	"	27. Catron, John§	1778–1865	"	Tenn.	1837–1865
Van Buren	"	1837–1841	28. McKinley, John	1780–1852	"	Ala.	1837–1852
"	"	"	29. Daniel, Peter V.	1784–1860	"	Va.	1841–1860

President	Term	Party	Justice	Birth–Death	State	Party	Tenure
Tyler	1841–1845	Whig	30. Nelson, Samuel	1792–1873	N.Y.	"	1845–1872
Polk	1845–1849	Democrat	31. Woodbury, Levi	1789–1851	N.H.	"	1845–1851
"		"	32. Grier, Robert C.	1794–1874	Pa.	"	1846–1870
Fillmore	1850–1853	Whig	33. Curtis, Benjamin R.	1809–1874	Mass.	Whig	1851–1857
Pierce	1853–1857	Democrat	34. Campbell, John A.	1811–1889	Ala.	Democrat	1853–1861
Buchanan	1857–1861	"	35. Clifford, Nathan	1803–1881	Maine	"	1858–1881
Lincoln	1861–1865	Republican	36. Swane, Noah H.	1804–1884	Ohio	Republican	1862–1881
"		"	37. Miller, Samuel F.	1816–1890	Iowa	"	1862–1890
"		"	38. Davis, David	1815–1886	Ill.	"	1862–1877
"		"	39. Field, Stephen J.	1816–1899	Calif.	Democrat	1863–1897
"		"	40. Chase, Salmon P.*	1808–1873	Ohio	Republican	1864–1873
Grant	1869–1877	"	41. Strong, William	1808–1895	Pa.	"	1870–1880
"		"	42. Bradley, Joseph P.	1803–1892	N.J.	"	1870–1892
"		"	43. Hunt, Ward	1810–1886	N.Y.	"	1872–1882
"		"	44. Waite, Morrison R.	1816–1888	Ohio	"	1874–1888
Hayes	1877–1881	"	45. Harlan, John M.	1833–1911	Ky.	"	1877–1911
"		"	46. Woods, William B.	1824–1887	Ga.	"	1880–1887
Garfield	Mar.–Sept. 1881	"	47. Matthews, Stanley	1824–1889	Ohio	"	1881–1889
Arthur	1881–1885	"	48. Gray, Horace	1828–1902	Mass.	"	1881–1902
"		"	49. Blatchford, Samuel	1820–1893	N.Y.	"	1882–1893
Cleveland		Democrat	50. Lamar, Lucius Q. C.	1825–1893	Miss.	Democrat	1888–1893
"		"	51. Fuller, Melville*	1833–1910	Ill.	"	1888–1910
Harrison	1889–1893	Republican	52. Brewer, David J.	1837–1910	Kans.	Republican	1889–1910
"		"	53. Brown, Henry B.	1836–1913	Mich.	"	1890–1906
"		"	54. Shiras, George, Jr.	1832–1924	Pa.	"	1892–1903
"		"	55. Jackson, Howell E.	1832–1895	Tenn.	Democrat	1892–1895
Cleveland	1893–1897	Democrat	56. White, Edward D.	1854–1921	La.	"	1894–1910
"		"	57. Peckham, Rufus W.	1838–1909	N.Y.	"	1895–1909
McKinley	1897–1901	Republican	58. McKenna, Joseph	1843–1926	Calif.	Republican	1898–1925
Roosevelt	1901–1909	"	59. Holmes, Oliver W., Jr.	1841–1935	Mass.	"	1902–1932
"		"	60. Day, William R.	1849–1923	Ohio	"	1903–1922
"		"	61. Moody, William H.	1853–1917	Mass.	"	1906–1910
Taft	1909–1913	"	62. Lurton, Horace	1844–1914	Tenn.	Democrat	1909–1914
"		"	63. Hughes, Charles E.	1862–1948	N.Y.	Republican	1910–1916
"		"	64. White, Edward D.†*	1845–1921	La.	Democrat	1910–1921

(continued)

Appointing President	President's Political Party	Dates of President's Service	Name of Justice	Dates of Birth and Death	Justice's Nominal Party Allegiance on Appointment	State from Which Justice Was Apptd.#	Dates of Service on Supreme Court
"	"	"	65. Van Devanter, Willis	1859–1941	Republican	Wyo.	1910–1937
"	"	"	66. Lamar, Joseph R.	1857–1916	Democrat	Ga.	1910–1916
"	"	"	67. Pitney, Mahlon	1858–1924	Republican	N.J.	1912–1922
Wilson	Democrat	1913–1921	68. McReynolds, J. C.	1862–1946	Democrat	Tenn.	1914–1941
"	"	"	69. Brandeis, Louis D.	1856–1941	Republican**	Mass.	1916–1939
"	"	"	70. Clarke, John H.	1857–1945	Democrat	Ohio	1916–1922
Harding	Republican	1921–1923	71. Taft, William H.*	1857–1930	Republican	Conn.	1921–1930
"	"	"	72. Sutherland, George	1862–1942		Utah	1922–1938
"	"	"	73. Butler, Pierce	1866–1939	Democrat	Minn.	1922–1939
"	"	"	74. Sanford, Edward T.	1865–1930	Republican	Tenn.	1923–1930
Coolidge	"	1923–1929	75. Stone, Harlan F.	1872–1946		N.Y.	1925–1941
Hoover	"	1929–1933	76. Hughes, Charles E.*	1862–1948		N.Y.	1930–1941
"	"	"	77. Roberts, Owen J.	1875–1955		Pa.	1930–1945
"	"	"	78. Cardozo, Benjamin	1870–1938	Democrat	N.Y.	1932–1938
Roosevelt	Democrat	1933–1945	79. Black, Hugo L.	1886–1971		Ala.	1937–1971
"	"	"	80. Reed, Stanley F.	1884–1980		Ky.	1938–1957
"	"	"	81. Frankfurter, Felix	1882–1965	Independent	Mass.	1939–1962
"	"	"	82. Douglas, William	1898–1980	Democrat	Conn.	1939–1975
"	"	"	83. Murphy, Frank	1893–1949		Mich.	1940–1949
"	"	"	84. Byrnes, James F.	1879–1972		S.C.	1941–1942
"	"	"	85. Stone, Harlan F.†*	1872–1946	Republican	N.Y.	1941–1946
"	"	"	86. Jackson, Robert H.	1892–1954	Democrat	N.Y.	1941–1954
"	"	"	87. Rutledge, Wiley B.	1894–1949		Iowa	1943–1949
Truman	"	1945–1953	88. Burton, Harold H.	1888–1965	Republican	Ohio	1945–1958
"	"	"	89. Vinson, Fred M.*	1890–1953	Democrat	Ky.	1946–1953
"	"	"	90. Clark, Tom C.	1899–1977		Tex.	1949–1967
"	"	"	91. Minton, Sherman	1890–1965		Ind.	1949–1956
Eisenhower	Republican	1953–1961	92. Warren, Earl*	1891–1974	Republican	Calif.	1953–1969

President	Term	Party	Justice	Dates	Party	State#	Service
"	"	"	93. Harlan, John M., Jr.	1899–1971	"	N.Y.	1955–1971
"	"	"	94. Brennan, Wm. J., Jr.	1906–1997	Democrat	N.J.	1956–1990
"	"	"	95. Whittaker, Charles	1900–1973	Republican	Mo.	1957–1962
"	"	"	96. Stewart, Potter	1915–1985	"	Ohio	1958–1981
Kennedy	1961–1963	Democrat	97. White, Byron R.	1917–2002	Democrat	Colo.	1962–1993
"	"	"	98. Goldberg, Arthur	1908–1990	"	Ill.	1962–1965
Johnson	1963–1969	"	99. Fortas, Abe	1910–1982	"	Tenn.	1965–1969
"	"	"	100. Marshall, Thurgood	1910–1993	Republican	N.Y.	1967–1991
Nixon	1969–1974	Republican	101. Burger, Warren E.*	1907–1995	"	Va.	1969–1986
"	"	"	102. Blackmun, Harry A.	1910–1999	Democrat	Minn.	1970–1994
"	"	"	103. Powell, Lewis F., Jr.	1907–1998	Republican	Va.	1972–1987
"	"	"	104. Rehnquist, William H.	1924–	"	Ariz.	1972–1986
Ford	1974–1977	"	105. Stevens, John Paul	1920–	"	Ill.	1975–
Reagan	1981–1989	Republican	106. O'Connor, Sandra Day	1930–	Republican	Ariz.	1981–
"	"	"	107. Rehnquist, William H.†*	1924–	"	Ariz.	1986–
"	"	"	108. Scalia, Antonin	1936–	"	Va.	1986–
"	"	"	109. Kennedy, Anthony M.	1936–	"	Calif.	1988–
Bush	1989–1993	"	110. Souter, David H.	1939–	"	N.H.	1990–
"	"	"	111. Thomas, Clarence	1948–	Democrat	Va.	1991–
Clinton	1993–2001	Democrat	112. Ginsburg, Ruth Bader	1933–	"	D.C.	1993–
"	"	"	113. Breyer, Stephen G.	1938–	"	Mass.	1994–

*Chief justice.
‖Resigned without sitting.
‡Unconfirmed recess appointment, rejected by Senate, December 1797.
#Not necessarily, but often, state of birth.
§Catron was nominated by Jackson but he was not confirmed until Van Buren had assumed the presidency.
†Promoted from associate justice.
**Many—and with some justice—consider Brandeis a Democrat; however, he was in fact a registered Republican when nominated.

Appendix B: Civil Rights and Liberties in the Constitution

AMENDMENT I

Congress shall make no law respecting an establishment of religion, or prohibiting the free exercise thereof; or abridging the freedom or speech, or of the press, or the right of the people peaceably to assemble and to petition the Government for a redress of grievances.

AMENDMENT II

A well-regulated militia being necessary to the security of a free State, the right of the people to keep and bear arms, shall not be infringed.

AMENDMENT III

No soldier shall, in time of peace, be quartered in any house without the consent of the owner, nor in time of war but in a manner to be prescribed by law.

AMENDMENT IV

The right of the people to be secure in their persons, houses, papers, and effects, against unreasonable searches and seizures, shall not be violated, and no warrants shall issue but upon probable cause, supported by oath or affirmation, and particularly describing the place to be searched, and the persons or things to be seized.

AMENDMENT V

No person shall be held to answer for a capital, or otherwise infamous crime, unless on a presentment or indictment of a Grand Jury, except in cases arising in the land or naval forces, or in the militia, when in actual service in time of war or public danger; nor shall any person be subject for the same offense to be twice in jeopardy of life or limb; nor shall be compelled in any criminal case to be a witness against himself, nor be deprived of life, liberty or property, without due process of law; nor shall private property be taken for public use, without just compensation.

AMENDMENT VI

In all criminal prosecutions, the accused shall enjoy the right to a speedy and public trial, by an impartial jury of the State and district wherein the crime shall have been committed, which districts shall have been previously ascertained by law, and to be informed of the nature and cause of the accusation; to be confronted with the witnesses against him; to have compulsory process for obtaining witnesses in his favor, and to have the assistance of counsel for his defense.

AMENDMENT VII

In suits at common law, where the value in controversy shall exceed twenty dollars, the right of trial by jury shall be preserved, and no fact tried by a jury, shall be otherwise reexamined in any court of the United States, than according to the rules of the common law.

AMENDMENT VIII

Excessive bail shall not be required, nor excessive fines imposed, nor cruel and unusual punishments inflicted.

AMENDMENT IX

The enumeration in the Constitution of certain rights shall not be construed to deny or disparage others retained by the people.

AMENDMENT X

The powers not delegated to the United States by the Constitution, nor prohibited by it to the States, are reserved to the States respectively, or to the people.

OTHER AMENDMENTS

AMENDMENT XIII (Ratified in 1865)

Section 1. Neither slavery nor involuntary servitude, except as a punishment for crime whereof the party shall have been duly convicted, shall exist within the United States, or any place subject to their jurisdiction.

Section 2. Congress shall have power to enforce this article by appropriate legislation.

AMENDMENT XIV (Ratified in 1868)

Section 1. All persons born or naturalized in the United States, and subject to the jurisdiction thereof, are citizens of the United States and of the State wherein they reside. No State shall make or enforce any law which shall abridge the privileges or immunities of citizens of the United States; nor shall any State deprive any person of life, liberty, or property, without due process of law; nor deny to any person within its jurisdiction the equal protection of the laws. . . .

Section 5. The Congress shall have power to enforce by appropriate legislation the provisions of this article.

AMENDMENT XV (Ratified in 1870)

Section 1. The right of citizens of the United States to vote shall not be denied or abridged by the United States or by any State on account of race, color, or previous condition of servitude.

Section 2. The Congress shall have power to enforce this article by appropriate legislation.

AMENDMENT XIX (Ratified in 1920)
Section 1. The right of citizens of the United States to vote shall not be denied or abridged by the United States or by any State on account of sex.
Section 2. Congress shall have power to enforce this article by appropriate legislation.

AMENDMENT XXIV (Ratified in 1964)
Section 1. The right of citizens of the United States to vote in any primary or other election for President or Vice-President, for electors for President or Vice-President, or for Senator or Representative in Congress, shall not be denied or abridged by the United States or any State by reason of failure to pay any poll tax or other tax.
Section 2. The Congress shall have power to enforce this article by appropriate legislation.

AMENDMENT XXVI (Ratified in 1971)
Section 1. The right of citizens of the United States, who are 18 years of age or older, to vote shall not be denied or abridged by the United States or any State on account of age.
Section 2. The Congress shall have power to enforce this article by appropriate legislation.

PROVISIONS FROM THE ORIGINAL CONSTITUTION

Article I
Section 9. . . .
2. The privilege of the writ of habeas corpus shall not be suspended, unless when in cases of rebellion or invasion the public safety may require it.
3. No bill of attainder or ex post facto law shall be passed.
Section 10.
1. No State shall . . . pass any bill of attainder, ex post facto law, or law impairing the obligation of contracts. . . .

Article III
Section 2. . . .
1. Treason against the United States shall consist only in levying war against them, or in adhering to their enemies, giving them aid and comfort. No Person shall be convicted of treason unless on the testimony of two witnesses to the same overt act, or on confession in open court.

Article IV
Section 2.
1. The citizens of each state shall be entitled to all privileges and immunities of citizens in the several States.

Article VI
3. . . . no religious test shall ever be required as a qualification to any office or public trust under the United States.

General Index

Abortion, 481–84
  compelling state interest and, 482
  late-term, 484
  privacy rights and, 82, 84–85, 481, 482, 484
  protests at clinics, 191, 381
ACLU. *See* American Civil Liberties Union
ADA. *See* Americans with Disabilities Act
Advertising, 189–90, 214
Affirmative action, 487–507
  contract set-asides, 488, 492–94, 503, 505–6
  demands for, 372
  as discrimination remedy, 495, 496, 497, 499
  in higher education, 487, 504–5
  opposition to, 381
  quotas, 487, 489, 490, 492, 496, 497–98, 500–501, 504
  for women, 487, 498–99
African Americans
  citizenship, 36–37, 39, 374
  economic situations, 370–72
  elected officials, 368, 369–70, 374, 426n, 429
  judges, 368–69, 370
  middle class, 370–71
  population, 368
  problems, 371–73
  purpose of Fourteenth Amendment, 50
  registered voters, 368, 425–26, 427, 428–30
  slavery, 373, 374, 379
  See also Affirmative action; Civil rights movement; Race; Voting rights
AJC. *See* American Jewish Congress
Alien and Sedition Acts of 1798, 219–20
American Bar Association, 47, 207, 208
American Civil Liberties Union (ACLU), 445
American Communist Party, 223–24, 228, 229

American Jewish Congress (AJC), 363–64
Americans with Disabilities Act (ADA) of 1990, 486
Arrest warrants, 156, 160–61
Assembly, freedom of, 62
Assize of Clarendon, 87
Association, freedom of
  of government employees, 221–22
  national security and, 220
  privacy rights and, 82
  private clubs and, 454, 457, 458
  protection of, 463
  violations of, 230
Atheists, 312

Bail, 101–2
Bail Reform Acts, 101–2
Bavarian Motor Works (BMW), 24
Bill of Rights
  applied to national government alone, 34
  due process requirements, 130–31
  language of, 26–29
  penumbras, 82
  purpose, 25, 34
  ratification, 33, 34
  See also Incorporation of Bill of Rights; *individual amendments*
Birth control, 81–84
Blacks. *See* African Americans
Blue Laws. *See* Sunday-closing laws
BMW. *See* Bavarian Motor Works
Bob Jones University, 462
Border Patrol, 157
Boston School Committee, 406–7
Brandeis brief, 466

519

Name Index

Case Index